Sport and Exercise Psychology

A CANADIAN PERSPECTIVE THIRD EDITION

Sport and Exercise Psychology

A CANADIAN PERSPECTIVE THIRD EDITION

EDITED BY **PETER R.E. CROCKER**

UNIVERSITY OF BRITISH COLUMBIA

Toronto

Editorial Director: Claudine O'Donnell
Executive Acquisitions Editor: Lisa Rahn
Senior Marketing Manager: Kimberly Teska
Program Manager: Darryl Kamo
Project Manager: Richard Di Santo/Rohin Bansal
Developmental Editor: Rebecca Ryoji
Production Services: Cenveo® Publisher Services
Permissions Project Manager: Kathryn O'Handley
Photo Permissions Research: Nazveena Begum Syed
Text Permissions Research: James Fortney
Cover Designer: Alex Li
Interior Designer: Cenveo Publisher Services
Cover Image: Bikeriderlondon/Shutterstock

Credits and acknowledgments for material borrowed from other sources and reproduced, with permission, in this textbook appear on the appropriate page within the text.

4 18

Library and Archives Canada Cataloguing in Publication

Sport psychology
        Sports and exercise psychology : a Canadian perspective / edited by Peter R.E. Crocker, University of British Columbia. – Third edition.

First edition published under title Sport psychology.
Includes bibliographical references and index.
ISBN 978-0-13-357391-6 (pbk.)

        1. Sports—Psychological aspects—Textbooks. 2. Exercise—Psychological aspects—Textbooks. I. Crocker, Peter R. E. (Peter Ronald Earl) author, editor II. Title.

GV706.4.S67 2015   796.01'9   C2014-907952-4

ISBN: 978-0-13-357391-6

Peter R.E. Crocker

Dr. Peter Crocker is a professor in the School of Kinesiology at the University of British Columbia (UBC) and is an associate member in health psychology in the Department of Psychology. His research focuses on stress and adaptation, with a particular interest in understanding sport, exercise, and health-related behaviour. Ongoing research includes investigating perfectionism, stress, and coping in athletes, self-compassion in sport, the link between physical self-perceptions and health behaviour, and the role of self-conscious emotions in motivation in physical activity settings.

Dr. Crocker is a two time president of the Canadian Society of Psychomotor Learning and Sport Psychology (SCAPPS) and a former section head for sport and exercise psychology in the Canadian Psychological Association. He has also been recognized as a Fellow in the Association of Applied Sport Psychology and SCAPPS. Actively involved as a reviewer for several scholarly journals and granting agencies, he is a former editor of *The Sport Psychologist*, a former associate editor for the *Journal of Sport & Exercise Psychology*, as well as an editorial board member of *Sport, Exercise, and Performance Psychology*. Dr. Crocker has also served as a consultant for athletes in gymnastics, volleyball, basketball, baseball, and soccer. He presently volunteers as a performance psychology consultant with the UBC golf teams. Dr. Crocker played competitive basketball and soccer as a youth and was also a soccer coach for several University and Provincial-select soccer teams.

Dr. Crocker completed an undergraduate degree in psychology and a Masters degree in Kinesiology from Simon Fraser University. His PhD, under the supervision of Dr. Rikk Alderman at the University of Alberta, focused on sport psychology and skill learning. He has taught previously at Lakehead University (1986–1990) and the University of Saskatchewan (1990–1999). In his leisure time, he struggles with golf and Scrabble® on the internet. He lives in Vancouver, B.C. with his wife Linda and has two adult children, Julisa and Douglas.

About the Contributors

Dr. Kelly Arbour-Nicitopoulos is an assistant professor in the Faculty of Kinesiology and Physical Education at the University of Toronto and an adjunct scientist at the Bloorview Research Institute. She teaches courses in adapted physical activity, exercise psychology, knowledge translation, and research methodology. Her research focuses on promoting community-based physical activity and sport participation across the lifespan in populations suffering from mental illness and physical disability.

Dr. Joseph Baker is an associate professor in the School of Kinesiology and Health Science at York University. His research examines the development and maintenance of expert performance across the lifespan and the psychosocial factors influencing involvement in physical activity in older adults. Joe has also been the president of the Canadian Society for Psychomotor Learning and Sport Psychology (SCAPPS). In his leisure time, Joe is an avid runner and cyclist.

Dr. Mark R. Beauchamp, is an associate professor in the School of Kinesiology at the University of British Columbia. He is a Chartered Psychologist and Associate Fellow of the British Psychological Society (BPS). He teaches courses in sport and exercise psychology, with his research primarily focusing on group processes within health, exercise, and sport settings.

Dr. Gordon A. Bloom is an associate professor in the Department of Kinesiology and Physical Education at McGill University. His applied and translational research program incorporates health-related educational objectives with particular emphasis on coaching knowledge and behaviours and sport concussions. When not competing in sports himself, he can often be found coaching his children in ice hockey, soccer, or baseball. Additionally, Gordon is a founding member of the managing council of the Canadian Sport Psychology Association.

Dr. Jennifer Brunet is an assistant professor in the School of Human Kinetics at the University of Ottawa and holds an appointment as a affiliate investigator within the Cancer Therapeutic Program of the Ottawa Hospital Research Institute. Her research is focused on identifying and understanding determinants of physical activity in order to better inform interventions to address physical inactivity in Canada. In addition, she is working to develop and evaluate evidence-based interventions aimed at increasing physical activity levels.

Dr. Jean Côté is a professor and director of the School of Kinesiology and Health Studies at Queen's University. His research interests are in the areas of children in sport, athlete development, and coaching. Dr. Côté serves on the scientific committee of the International Council for Coaching Excellence (ICCE). He enjoys spending time with his family and playing ice hockey, tennis, and racquetball.

Dr. Kimberley A. Dawson is a professor in the Department of Kinesiology and Physical Education at Wilfrid Laurier University, specializing in psychological factors associated with participation in physical activity. She teaches courses in research design, sport psychology, behaviour modification, and children and sport. She is the mental skills consultant for the Canadian Sport Institute (Ontario Centre) and a member of the Canadian Sport Psychology Association. Her research interests focus on exercise adherence, sport performance, and injury rehabilitation factors, as well as using physical activity as a coping mechanism for dealing with chronic disease.

Dr. Kim D. Dorsch is a professor in the Faculty of Kinesiology and Health Studies at the University of Regina. Her current research interests include examining the sources of stress and practical applications of coping among officials. She is also the chair of the Coaching Association of Canada's research committee and is highly interested in identifying and combatting negative coaching behaviours. She also has roles as a mental training consultant and board member with the Saskatchewan Sport Science and Medicine Council, the Canadian Sport Centre – SK, and she facilitates courses for the Advanced Coaching Diploma.

Dr. Mark Eys is an associate professor and Canada Research Chair (Tier II) in the Departments of Kinesiology/Physical Education and Psychology at Wilfrid Laurier University. His research examines group dynamics in physical activity with a specific focus on role perceptions and cohesion in sport teams. He was named Canadian Interuniversity Sport Women's Soccer Coach of the Year in 2001 and continues to participate and coach in the sports of basketball and soccer.

Dr. Guy Faulkner is currently a professor in the Faculty of Kinesiology and Physical Education at the University of Toronto and an adjunct scientist at the Centre for Addiction and Mental Health (CAMH). His research has focused on two interrelated themes: the effectiveness of physical activity promotion interventions, and physical activity and mental health. He is the founding co-editor of the Elsevier journal *Mental Health and Physical Activity* and co-editor of the book *Exercise, Health and Mental Health*.

Dr. Jessica Fraser-Thomas is an associate professor in the School of Kinesiology and Health Science at York University. Her research focuses on children and youths' development through sport, with a particular interest in positive youth development, psychosocial influences, and withdrawal. Currently, she is working on projects exploring children's earliest introductions to organized sport, characteristics of sport programs that facilitate optimal youth development, and how youth sport models may inform Masters Athletes' development. Jessica is a former high performance athlete; she now parents five young sport participants and occasionally competes in triathlons.

Dr. Kimberley L. Gammage is an associate professor in the Department of Kinesiology at Brock University. Her research focuses on social-psychological factors related to exercise and health behaviours, with a focus on self-presentational concerns and body image. She is especially interested in how these factors may operate in group exercise settings. She is also interested in how psychological variables, such as self-efficacy, may mediate the effects of exercise on balance outcomes in older adults. She is also the director of the Brock SeniorFit Exercise Program.

Dr. Patrick Gaudreau is an associate professor in the School of Psychology at the University of Ottawa. His research interests are in the self-regulation of achievement-related behaviours, with research projects on coping, goal management, and motivation in sport, education, and exercise. The overarching goal of his research program is to uncover the role of self-regulatory processes in goal attainment and psychological adjustment of individuals in performance-related activities. In his spare time, he enjoys coaching baseball for the teams of Olivier and Antoine. He can also be found in the bushes searching for the golf balls of Peter Crocker!

Dr. Melanie Gregg is an associate professor in the Department of Kinesiology and Applied Health at the University of Winnipeg. Her research interests focus on athletes' motivational imagery ability and examining the effectiveness of psychological skill use by athletes with an intellectual disability. She also does applied work with athletes from a variety of sports and enjoys coaching track and field.

Dr. Craig Hall is a professor in the School of Kinesiology at Western University. His research primarily focuses on imagery use in sport, exercise, and athletic injury rehabilitation. He has also investigated other topics, including self-efficacy, self-talk, motivation, and observational learning. He is a co-author of *Psychological Interventions in Sport, Exercise & Injury Rehabilitation*. Family and squash take most of his non-academic time.

Dr. Sharleen Hoar is a performance psychology consultant with the Canadian Sport Institute, working with high performance athletes, coaches, and support staff within the sports of cross-country skiing, swimming, and triathlon. A former competitive figure skater, she is also an adjunct associate professor with the Department of Kinesiology and Physical Education at the University of Lethbridge and has published research on stress, coping, and emotional control in sport.

Dr. Sean Horton is an associate professor in the Department of Kinesiology at the University of Windsor. His research focus is on skill acquisition and expert performance throughout the lifespan, as well as how stereotypes of aging affect seniors' participation in exercise. In his spare time, Sean can usually be found on the squash court or on the golf course.

Dr. Kent C. Kowalski is a professor at the College of Kinesiology at the University of Saskatchewan. His general area of interest includes exploring the role of self-compassion in the lives of athletes, as well as coping with stress and emotion in sport and physical activity. He is also currently an assistant coach with the University of Saskatchewan Huskie Men's soccer program.

Dr. Todd M. Loughead is a professor in the Department of Kinesiology at the University of Windsor. His current research interests include group dynamics in sport with a personal interest in aggression. Specifically, his interests are the development of athlete leadership skills in all athletes, the importance of developing cohesion in sport, and the influence of peer-to-peer mentoring in sport and its impact on team functioning. As a coach in several sports, he understands the importance of reducing aggression to ensure not only player safety but continued enjoyment of sport. Dr. Loughead teaches courses in group dynamics, leadership, and applied sport psychology.

Dr. Meghan McDonough is an associate professor in the Department of Health and Kinesiology at Purdue University. Her research examines social relationships, self-perceptions, motivation, and emotion in physical activity. She has a particular focus on social processes in physical activity among clinical and marginalized populations, including breast cancer survivors and low-income youth.

Dr. Diane E. Mack is a professor in the Department of Kinesiology at Brock University. Research interests include the role of health-enhancing physical activity as a mechanism to promote well-being and the cognitive and behavioural manifestations of self-presentation on health behaviours.

Dr. Krista Munroe-Chandler is a professor in the Department of Kinesiology at the University of Windsor. Her research interests include imagery use in sport and exercise as well as youth-sport development and body image issues. She works with able-bodied athletes as well as athletes with a disability of all ages, levels, and sports, helping them achieve their personal performance goals.

Dr. David Paskevich is an associate professor in the Faculty of Kinesiology at the University of Calgary. His research interests centre upon the integration of the science-practitioner model, bringing the science of sport psychology into practical/applied settings, particularly in regard to the leadership, mental skills, and toughness required for 'performance consistency' and 'performance on demand' competitions. Dave has worked with Canadian athletes at a number of Olympic Games and has also consulted with professional and other high-performance athletes in a variety of sports including hockey, football, soccer, lacrosse, golf, rodeo, and volleyball.

Dr. Ryan E. Rhodes is a professor in the School of Exercise Science, Physical & Health Education at the University of Victoria, and director of the UVic Behavioural Medicine Laboratory. He has research expertise in physical activity and social cognition theories, personality theory, psychometric measurement, analysis, and design, with an applied focus on physical activity and early family development.

Dr. Jennifer Robertson-Wilson is an associate professor in the Department of Kinesiology and Physical Education at Wilfrid Laurier University. Her academic interests include health promotion and the psychology of physical activity. Her research applies a social ecological lens to understand individual, environment (social and physical), and policy influences on physical activity across a variety of settings, including schools. A secondary area of interest involves a focus on the built environment and physical activity and obesity.

Dr. Catherine Sabiston is an associate professor of exercise and health psychology in the Faculty of Kinesiology and Physical Education at the University of Toronto. Her research examines the interrelations among physical self-perceptions and body-related emotions, social influences, mental health, and physical activity motivation in diverse populations who tend to be at risk for low levels of physical activity, including breast cancer survivors, overweight and obese individuals, and adolescents.

Dr. David Scott is an associate professor of sport psychology in the Faculty of Kinesiology at the University of New Brunswick in Fredericton. He teaches and researches in the area of sport and exercise psychology, focusing primarily on performance enhancement, and physical activity and mental health. He has been a psychological consultant with a number of national teams in addition to working with teams in the National Hockey League.

Dr. Whitney A. Sedgwick is a registered psychologist and clinical coordinator at the University of British Columbia's Counselling Services. She has taught undergraduate and graduate sport psychology courses at three Canadian universities and has co-authored a mental training book for triathletes. Dr. Sedgwick has also been consulting with athletes at all levels for the past 17 years, including a year in Paris, France, where she worked with national team and Olympic athletes.

Dr. Kevin S. Spink is a professor in the College of Kinesiology at the University of Saskatchewan, specializing in group dynamics, specifically cohesion. He teaches courses involving the application of social psychology to exercise and sport behaviour. One focus of his research is the study of group dynamics and the application of group interventions to promote exercise and adherence behaviour. His other main interest is in examining the relationship between various social-psychological correlates/determinants and adherence to physical activity across the lifespan.

Dr. Katherine A. Tamminen is an assistant professor in the Faculty of Kinesiology and Physical Education at the University of Toronto. Her areas of research include stress, coping, and emotion in sport, psychosocial aspects of youth sport participation, and interpersonal processes and social psychology in sport.

Dr. Linda Trinh is a post-doctoral fellow in the Faculty of Kinesiology and Physical Education at the University of Toronto. Her research interests are focused on the area of cancer control and survivorship from a health and exercise psychology perspective, for which she develops and implements theory-based behaviour change interventions. She is currently examining the link between sedentary behaviour and health outcomes among cancer survivors.

Dr. Philip M. Wilson is an associate professor in the Department of Kinesiology at Brock University. His research interests focus on the interplay between measurement and theory for understanding motivational processes responsible for health behaviours. In his spare time, Dr. Wilson can be found enjoying active living with Diane while finding time to follow his two favourite football teams (Liverpool F.C. and England) and spoiling a good outdoor walk by 'trying' to play golf!

Brief Contents

Contents

12 Aging and Involvement in Sport and Physical Activity   318

13 Physical Activity and Mental Health   341

14 Body Image in Sport and Exercise   371

Preface

Most people are familiar with the term "sport psychology" from popular media, which frequently refer to elite athletes working with sport psychologists to enhance performance. However, this is only a small part of sport and exercise psychology. Involving the study of psychological factors in physical activity settings, this field includes diverse areas, such as the mental health benefits of physical activity, motivation, aging well, group dynamics, leadership, the benefits of youth sport, effective coaching, emotional- and self-regulation, and body image, just to name a few.

Research and practice has a significant impact on the lives of exercisers, athletes, coaches, health professionals, and scholars in the field. Today, many Canadian scholars are recognized as world leaders in this research and practice, and their important work influences the lives of many involved in physical activity in Canada.

Developed for an introductory undergraduate course in sport and exercise psychology taught at Canadian institutions, the Third Edition of *Sport and Exercise Psychology: A Canadian Perspective* presents an overview of the discipline while building a solid foundation in core concepts.

APPROACH AND PHILOSOPHY

Three unique features characterize this resource. First, Canadian scholars who are all active teachers of undergraduate sport and exercise psychology courses have written the chapters. Second, this resource illustrates important concepts by showcasing many Canadian examples. Third, the book not only highlights research by Canadian scholars, but also recognizes the contributions of distinguished academics around the world.

NEW TO THE THIRD EDITION

Based on feedback from peer reviewers, educators, and authors, we made several changes to the Third Edition:

- Added a new chapter on body image, an important though seldom addressed topic
- Incorporated a new chapter on leadership, highlighting the processes and impact of effective leadership in sport and exercise
- Removed the research perspectives chapter, as this topic is covered in other courses
- Shifted critical ideas related to research and evidence-based practice to the introductory chapter
- Updated all chapters to reflect the latest developments in theory, research, and practice
- Increased the number of case studies
- Incorporated a new, fresh colour design to improve the resource's visual appeal

ORGANIZATION

The 15 chapters of this book present the key topics covered in a typical introductory course. While educators may wish to vary the sequence of coverage, we recommend covering the first six foundational chapters in order. Depending on the needs of specific courses, some educators may wish to cover psychological interventions (Chapter 7) before covering the chapters on group processes, leadership, aging, exercise and mental health, body image, and physical activity interventions.

Chapter 1 provides an overview of the field. Topics include the diverse nature of sport and exercise psychology, differences in career orientations and educational training opportunities, a brief history of sport and exercise psychology in Canada and the world, ethics in sport and exercise psychology, and a basic primer in research methods and the importance of evidence-based practice. It concludes with predicted trends in the field.

Chapter 2 examines personality perspectives in sport and exercise. It covers conceptions of personality, ethics related to measuring personality, and the limitations of personality in explaining athletic behaviour and performance as well as exercise behaviour. The chapter also emphasizes contemporary topics in sport and exercise personality, including the five-factor model, competitiveness, sensation-seeking, passion, perfectionism, and mental toughness.

Chapter 3 focuses on models and principles of motivation and behavioural change in sport and exercise. It provides students with a brief review of behavioural, cognitive, and cognitive–behavioural principles. The number of theories and models of motivation applied to sport and exercise were reduced in accordance with reviewer feedback, but this chapter continues to cover the transtheoretical model, theory of planned behaviour, social cognitive theory, achievement goal theory, and self-determination theory. The chapter also discusses social approaches to motivation.

Chapter 4 discusses stress, emotion, and coping in sport and exercise. The chapter emphasizes types of cognitive evaluations, types of coping, individual and group (team) level coping, and the relationship between appraisal, stress, and diverse emotions, such as anger, happiness, anxiety, and fear. Major modifications include increased emphasis on emotional regulation, neurophysiological effects of stress, coping effectiveness and outcomes, and intervention strategies.

Chapter 5 concentrates on anxiety in sport and exercise. It defines types and dimensions of anxiety, personal sources of anxiety in sport and exercise settings, the specificity of anxiety to competitive and exercise settings, and how anxiety affects exercise and sport behaviour. Changes to this chapter include increased coverage of physiological arousal, the effects of the exercise environment on anxiety, and the phenomenon of choking in sport. It also explains how anxiety and arousal affect sport performance using three different models and theories, including inverted-U, zones of optimal functioning, and catastrophe theory.

Chapter 6 focuses on moral development and aggression in sport. Important additions to this chapter include bullying and hazing, as well as fan violence. It reviews various perspectives on how youth learn moral behaviour in sport and the role of the environmental and personality factors, such as motivational climate, team and sport norms, and motivational orientation. Discussing key theories useful for understanding why athletes (and spectators) behave aggressively, this chapter also explores how personal, situational, and group factors influence aggressive behaviour, while examining ways to reduce this type of conduct in sport.

Chapter 7 discusses how to enhance performance and well-being in sporting populations. Addressing specific intervention techniques for arousal, cognitive, and emotional self-regulation, this chapter features many applied examples and exercises. Specific topics include relaxation procedures, psyching strategies, attention control, self-talk, imagery, performance profiling, goal setting, and mindfulness.

Chapter 8, a new chapter, explores the factors associated with leadership in sport and exercise settings. The chapter covers the various ways to study leadership, including personality, situational, and interactional approaches. Highlighting key processes of effective leadership within sport and exercise, this chapter focuses on transactional and transformational leadership styles and their application to various physical activity settings. It concludes with a list of best practices.

Chapter 9 offers a comprehensive review of group cohesion in sport and exercise. Students will learn about group dynamics, group cohesion and its measurement, how and why cohesion affects behaviour in both sport and exercise settings, a conceptual model of cohesion, team-building concepts, the effects of hazing on cohesion, and important correlates of cohesion. The chapter also covers social loafing, self-handicapping, role clarity and acceptance, and leader behaviour.

Chapter 10 describes the health and developmental benefits of youth sport participation. The chapter explains the potential outcomes of youth sport participation, principles of positive youth development, and how youth sport programs and types of activities lead to positive sport experiences. The Third Edition includes greater emphasis on how coaches, parents, and peers can influence the development of a child's competence, confidence, connection, and character.

Chapter 11 discusses the complexity of coaching psychology. Describing the structure and process of coaching education in Canada, the chapter chronicles the steps to becoming an elite coach, the psychological factors involved in coaching, and the common characteristics and coaching principles of youth sport coaches. Additions to the chapter include a discussion of the 3 + 1 Cs model for studying the relationship between a coach and an athlete's emotions, behaviours, and cognitions.

Chapter 12 covers the psychological factors related to sport and exercise in the older person. We included this chapter to acknowledge that many "older" Canadians are, and should be, involved in physical activity. Highlighting a wide range of issues—including the factors influencing sport and exercise involvement in this group, and the impact of societal perceptions of aging on physical and cognitive performance—this chapter offers strategies for increasing sport and exercise involvement in older adult populations.

Chapter 13 explores the relationship between exercise and mental health. The chapter has been rewritten to distinguish between mental health and mental illness. Examining how and why physical activity might be an effective mental health promotion strategy, this chapter showcases evidence about how physical activity may perform a preventive function, a treatment function, a quality of life function, and a feel-good function for emotional well-being among healthy populations and those with existing mental or chronic illness. It also covers the different mechanisms that could explain the relationship between exercise and mental health, while providing a framework for understanding physical activity and mental health relationships.

Chapter 14, a new chapter on body image, details the multidimensional nature of body image and its link to motivated behaviour in sport and exercise. The chapter discusses key factors in the development of body image and the association between body image and mental health, emotions, stress, and cardiometabolic outcomes. Practical strategies are identified to help reduce negative body image and/or enhance positive body image in sport and exercise settings.

Chapter 15 outlines exercise interventions and builds upon concepts from previous chapters related to exercise psychology while highlighting the means by which to increase physical activity in all populations. It describes how specific theories can be used to understand and enhance physical activity interventions, nontheoretical approaches to exercise intervention, the key components to increase the success rate of exercise interventions, and how exercise can enhance the lives of nonclinical and clinical populations. The chapter includes many practical guidelines about interventions to increase physical activity.

PEDAGOGICAL FEATURES

We continue to employ the pedagogical features that facilitate learning and enhance understanding.

- **Learning Objectives.** A set of four to eight learning objectives provide a road map at the beginning of each chapter to help students read the material more effectively. The learning objectives also form the basis of the review questions found near the end of the chapter.

- **Vignette.** Each chapter begins with a scenario that raises issues and topics to be addressed in the chapter; many of the vignettes present actual real-world situations.

- **Common Myths.** Each chapter includes three to five common myths about the chapter's subject. We clarify and dispel each myth by presenting clear evidence to the contrary.

- **Key Terms in Margins.** Key terms are boldfaced where they are introduced in the text and appear in the margins with definitions, providing an effective way for students to engage with important terms and concepts.

- **Case Studies.** Case studies illustrate and exemplify key ideas and concepts.

- **Reflections Boxes.** Each chapter contains Reflections boxes that require students to consider how key concepts and ideas apply to their personal knowledge and experiences.

- **Canadian Examples.** Numerous Canadian examples support concepts, making the material more relevant to students studying at Canadian institutions.

- **Figures and Tables.** Diagrams, graphs, and tables illustrate and clarify important points.

- **Photos.** New and timely colour photos throughout the book feature athletes and participants in physical activity.

- **Weblinks.** References to many useful websites for sport and exercise psychology, advanced papers, scholarly organizations, and scholarly journals are included.

- **Chapter Summary.** A summary of the main points appears near the end of each chapter.

- **Review Questions.** A set of review questions requiring short answers help educators and students determine whether the learning objectives have been mastered.

- **Suggested Reading.** Each chapter concludes with a list of several readings for the interested student.
- **Glossary.** All the key terms are presented at the end of the text, organized by chapter, with full definitions.

INSTRUCTOR RESOURCES

To aid instructors in presenting lectures, fostering class discussion, and administering examinations, we prepared the ancillaries outlined below. They are downloadable from a password-protected section of Pearson Canada's online catalogue, catalogue.pearsoned.ca, from which you can navigate to your book's catalogue page. Contact your Pearson Canada sales representative for details and access.

- **Instructor's Manual.** The Instructor's Manual includes:
  - chapter overview
  - lecture outline
  - projects and assignments
  - case studies for class discussion
  - answers to review questions
  - discussion questions

- **PowerPoint® Slides.** Every chapter features a Microsoft PowerPoint® slide deck that highlights, illuminates, and builds on key concepts for your lecture or online delivery. Each deck can be tailored to suit individual requirements.
- **Computerized Test Bank.** Pearson's computerized test banks allow instructors to filter and select questions to create quizzes, tests, or homework. Instructors can revise questions or add their own, and they may be able to choose print or online options. These questions are also available in Microsoft Word format.
- **Image Library.** An Image Library provides access to many of the figures and tables in the textbook. Instructors can utilize these images for in-class presentations and lectures.

COURSESMART FOR INSTRUCTORS

CourseSmart goes beyond traditional expectations—providing instant, online access to the textbooks and course materials you need at a lower cost for students. And even as students save money, you can save time and hassle with a digital eTextbook that allows you to search for the most relevant content at the very moment you need it. Whether it's evaluating textbooks or creating lecture notes to help students with difficult concepts, CourseSmart can make life a little easier. See how when you visit www.coursesmart.com/instructors.

PEARSON CUSTOM LIBRARY

For enrollments of at least 25 students, you can create your own textbook by choosing the chapters that best suit your own course needs. To begin building your custom text, visit www.pearsoncustomlibrary.com. You may also work with a dedicated Pearson Custom Library editor to create your ideal text—publishing your own original content or mixing and matching Pearson content. Contact your local Pearson representative to get started.

PEERSCHOLAR

Firmly grounded in published research, peerScholar is a powerful online pedagogical tool that helps develop students' critical and creative thinking skills through creation, evaluation, and reflection. Working in stages, students begin by submitting written assignments. peerScholar then circulates their work for others to review, a process that can be anonymous or not, depending on instructors' preferences. Students immediately receive peer feedback and evaluations, reinforcing their learning and driving development of higher-order thinking skills. Students can then resubmit revised work, again depending on instructors' preferences.

Contact your Pearson representative to learn more about peerScholar and the research behind it.

Acknowledgments

We would like to acknowledge all the contributors to this textbook. These individuals represent many of the scholars in sport and exercise psychology in Canada, and they have all made a special contribution. We would also like to recognize those instructors who provided us with formal reviews of parts of the manuscript. Their observations, ideas, and comments greatly improved the quality of all chapters.

LIST OF REVIEWERS

- Theresa Bianco, Concordia University
- Basil Kavanagh, Memorial University of Newfoundland and Labrador
- Melanie Keats, Dalhousie University
- Larkin Lamarche, Brock University
- David Sangster, Champlain College – Lennoxville Campus
- Christopher Shields, Acadia University
- Kim A. Thompson, University of Ottawa
- Selina Tombs, Sheridan Institute
- Gary L. Worrell, University of New Brunswick

I would also like to thank all of the individuals involved at Pearson Education who supported the book through development and production: Lisa Rahn, executive editor; Darryl Kamo, program manager; Rebecca Ryoji, developmental editor; Richard Di Santo, project manager; Rohin Bansal, project manager; Kimberly Teska, senior marketing manager; and Laurel Sparrow, copy editor.

Peter R.E. Crocker

Chapter 1

Introducing Sport and Exercise Psychology

Peter R. E. Crocker   David Scott   Melanie Gregg

Chapter Objectives

After reading this chapter, you should be able to do the following:

1   Explain what sport and exercise psychology is and what sport and exercise psychology specialists do.
2   Explain the differences between educational and clinical/counselling orientations in sport and exercise psychology.
3   List the diverse educational training opportunities in sport and exercise psychology.
4   Identify the basic standards of conduct and service in sport and exercise psychology.
5   Identify key moments in the history of sport and exercise psychology in Canada and the world.
6   Identify key concepts in sport and exercise psychology research.
7   Explain basic differences in quantitative and qualitative methods in sport and exercise psychology.
8   Describe future trends in sport and exercise psychology.

Alex is a 16-year-old competitive soccer player hoping to make the transition to the provincial team. Unlike several of his teammates who specialized early in soccer, Alex played many different sports (hockey, tennis, and golf) until deciding in the last year to focus on soccer. Although a little behind his teammates in terms of technical skill, Alex is considered a mentally tough athlete who is highly motivated to become a better player at the highest levels.

Alex is struggling, however, to manage the stress of being both a top athlete and a student. He is concerned with teammates' pressure to bend the rules to ensure team success. His coach is also very demanding, and often tries to control Alex's behaviour both on and off the field. However, he feels the coach also helps by establishing clear group norms for acceptable behaviour. His parents are very supportive but they also stress the importance of education. The pressure to perform is leading Alex to experience increased anxiety and performance difficulties. Alex feels that he needs better psychological skills to meet all of his achievement goals.

Alex's mother faces different physical activity challenges in her life. Having recently turned 50, Christine would like to increase her activity levels to improve her health and fitness. She is worried about her long-term health profile, as both her parents died of heart attacks in their 60s. Christine was moderately active as a youth and young adult but the demands of career and child-raising derailed her exercise regimen. She remembers how regular exercise boosted her spirits and also enhanced her physical functioning.

Some of Christine's older friends tell her to "chill out" since women put on weight as they age, and exercise is for the young. Christine has identified several key barriers to exercise including lack of time and difficulty in getting to a gym, as well as anxiety about showing off her body in exercise settings. She has a very good friend, Dorothy, who would also like to become healthier. Both women have been thinking about exercising for the last few months but just cannot get started.

Alex and his mother decide that they could benefit from professional help. Through a registry established by the provincial Sport Medicine Council, Alex's parents are able to contact Dr. Coxen, a registered psychologist who specializes in sport. Dr. Coxen also uses the services of Dr. Lenny, a well known expert in exercise psychology and older adults. What can Dr. Coxen and Dr. Lenny do to help?

The above vignette illustrates common situations that capture many elements of sport and exercise psychology. Alex's experiences involve personality, motivation, stress and coping, anxiety and performance, aggression and moral reasoning, group cohesion, coaching and parental leadership, and issues surrounding early specialization in sport. Christine's story reflects issues involving motivation, aging, body image, mental health, and physical activity interventions.

The vignette also highlights the services of qualified sport and exercise psychology consultants. To help Alex and his mother, a sport and exercise psychology consultant must have expertise in a number of areas informed by strong research. These areas include knowledge of how psychological factors may influence performance and motivation; knowledge about exercise adoption and adherence in older adults; knowledge of the technical, physical, and psychological demands of competitive sport; knowledge of assessment to determine the psychological skills of the athlete; knowledge related to motivational factors in exercise; and intervention skills to design and implement an effective intervention for either Alex or his mother. Indeed, sport and exercise psychology consultants require knowledge and skills in many areas.

Are interventions related to performance enhancement or exercise adoption the only roles of sport and exercise psychology specialists in Canada? How does one become a sport and exercise psychology specialist? How does research help us understand the interrelationship between psychological factors and involvement in physical activity, and inform evidence-based practices of practitioners? In this chapter, we will discuss the various roles and training in sport and exercise psychology. As you will discover, sport and exercise psychology specialists work in a variety of settings, have a multiplicity of educational training opportunities, and possess varying competencies. There are also ethical standards that govern the application of sport and exercise psychology principles. Many of the practices and controversies in sport and exercise psychology were shaped by its history, a history unlike that of other fields in psychology. In this chapter, we will address many of these issues related to sport and exercise psychology. We will also provide a primer on basic research issues that can help students understand the role of research in providing insight into how personal and environmental factors influence participants' performance, thoughts, and emotions. But before we go any further, it is important to identify a few common myths about sport and exercise psychology. We will address these myths at the end of the chapter.

 COMMON MYTHS ABOUT SPORT AND EXERCISE PSYCHOLOGY

MYTH: Only athletes or exercisers with serious mental problems need a sport or exercise psychologist.

MYTH: All sport psychology specialists work with elite athletes to enhance their performance.

INTRODUCTION

Canada has a great sporting history, with numerous athletes reaching the peak of performance in world championships, Olympics, Paralympics, and professional championships. Today, millions of Canadians are involved in organized sport. Beyond sport, there is recognition that participation in regular physical activity across the lifespan is important for physical and mental health. Sport and exercise are important elements of Canadian life. Physical activity experiences might involve running a 10-km Fun Run in British Columbia, playing hockey on an outdoor rink in the Prairies, canoeing the waterways of the Yukon or Quebec, working out in an exercise class in Winnipeg, engaging in a specialized activity session for people with spinal cord injuries in Hamilton, kayaking with whales in Newfoundland–Labrador, or competing in a golf tournament on the Highlands Links on Cape Breton Island.

Understanding sport and exercise involves many subdisciplines in the sport sciences, including sport and exercise psychology. Reflect on your own experiences of participating in and watching sports or exercise. How do we make sense of athletes who are unable to concentrate or control anxiety in crucial situations, of acts of violence by parents at a children's sport event, and of athletes' feelings of joy or shame after events? What are the characteristics and behaviours of effective coaches? Why do some people seem to find it easy to be physically active, whereas others cannot even get started despite their best intentions? How do we answer even the seemingly simple question of why some people choose to participate in a specific physical activity? It is little wonder that people are interested in sport and exercise psychology.

Sport and exercise psychology is a legitimate scientific and applied discipline throughout the world and is an important component of the sport sciences in Canada. National accreditation standards identify sport and exercise psychology as a core discipline in undergraduate kinesiology and physical education programs (www.ccupeka.ca). We will provide you with a clearer understanding about sport and exercise psychology, especially in Canada.

THE NATURE OF SPORT AND EXERCISE PSYCHOLOGY

The term *sport and exercise psychology* means different things to various people in an array of situations. If you entered "definition of sport and exercise psychology" into an internet search engine, the results would reveal numerous definitions. Some definitions would emphasize sport science, some would emphasize performance enhancement, and still others would address psychological principles applied to physical activity settings. The reason for this inconsistency is that sport and exercise psychology has been shaped by theoretical and methodological influences of both kinesiology and psychology (Vealey, 2006). However, much of the research and practice in sport and exercise psychology is heavily dominated by theoretical perspectives that were developed in the general field of psychology.

In Canada, students can take sport and exercise psychology courses in most sport science programs (kinesiology, physical education, human kinetics). Most university professors in sport and exercise psychology also work in sport science programs. An increasing number of psychology programs are offering sport and exercise psychology courses at the undergraduate level. Sport and exercise psychology is recognized within both the Canadian Psychological Association (CPA) and the American Psychological Association (APA) Division 47. Sport and exercise psychology consultants have training in both sport sciences and psychology. Thus we believe that **sport and exercise psychology** is an interdisciplinary scientific and applied field that embraces the integration of sport science and psychological knowledge.

Sport and exercise psychology: An interdisciplinary scientific and applied field that embraces the integration of sport science and psychological knowledge.

SPORT AND EXERCISE PSYCHOLOGY: A MULTIDIMENSIONAL PERSPECTIVE

Students might ask what makes sport and exercise psychology unique as a field of study and practice from other areas of psychology. Not only does it integrate both sport science and psychological knowledge, but it integrates many areas of psychology (Anshel, 2012). Many traditional and emerging disciplines within psychology continue to have an impact on sport and exercise psychology. These include, but are not restricted to, cognitive psychology, clinical and counselling psychology, biological psychology, social psychology, developmental psychology, and health psychology. You will recognize the impact of many areas of psychology on sport and exercise psychology.

It should be recognized that all areas of psychology are influenced by developments in other academic disciplines, including computer science, sociology, medicine, education, family studies, and women's studies, to name a few. The search for knowledge regarding human challenges goes beyond arbitrarily defined academic boundaries. Think about a person trying to recover physical and social functioning following a stroke. Recovering, rediscovering, and redefining oneself will require integrating knowledge from many disciplines, including neurophysiology, exercise physiology and rehabilitation, exercise motivation, stress and emotion, social psychology, and counselling. Canadian researchers and practitioners are aware that many human health and wellness challenges require a transdisciplinary approach. Sport and exercise psychology specialists are well positioned to make a positive contribution to Canadian society.

Positive Psychology in Sport and Exercise

There is a common belief that sport and exercise psychology focuses on abnormal or problematic behaviour—that is, that the field is driven by a medical model to reduce or eliminate pathological mental behaviours. Indeed, much has been made of how sport and exercise can be employed as an effective intervention with respect to certain psychological problems and their possible solutions. There can be little doubt that this has had important and positive consequences with regard to the growth of sport and exercise as a vehicle for bringing about improvements in quality of life. However, the question of what makes life worth living remains more elusive. What role does sport and exercise play with regard to general satisfaction and happiness with life? For example, does supporting a particular team or playing a specific sport allow people to thrive? Can sport and exercise contribute to an individual's self-acceptance, personal growth, purpose in life, and positive social relationships? What kinds of sporting and/or physical activities do people who are contented, satisfied, and fulfilled with everyday life participate in?

Recent years have seen renewed interest in the field of **positive psychology**, an area of psychology concerned primarily with understanding the processes that enable people and groups to thrive. Seligman (2002) criticized psychology (and much of his own earlier work) for focusing too much on mental illness and repair and not enough on the human side of strength and personal growth. This is not to say that studying phenomena such as anxiety or fear is not worthwhile; however, much can be learned from the positive aspects of life. Kobau and colleagues (2011), for example, have proposed that positive psychology be thought of as focusing on the more favourable attributes or strengths that an individual may possess, and Seligman and Csikszentmihalyi (2000) have suggested that positive psychology can be thought of as an examination of the subjective experience: well-being, satisfaction, fulfillment, pleasure, and happiness.

So how does positive psychology relate to sport and exercise? Much of the research in sport and exercise psychology is directed toward enhancing performance, social and physical well-being, and positive emotion. For example, adopting a positive psychology approach may have many benefits in the world of performance enhancement. Often, skill development and performance improvement is a slow, frustrating, and sometimes deflating process. The adoption of a mindset that encourages satisfaction, pleasure, and

Positive psychology:
An area of psychology concerned primarily with understanding the processes that enable people and groups to thrive.

happiness often leads to resiliency and perseverance. Resiliency can be thought of as the process of positive adaptation in the context of adversity or risk (Masten & Reed, 2005), and positive psychology can strengthen psychological resilience through the development of skills based on avoiding thinking traps, staying calm and focused, and putting things in perspective (Lorig et al., 2000). The development of resiliency is important in the sport and exercise environment. It has been suggested by Ericsson and colleagues (1993) that it takes approximately 10,000 hours of deliberate practice to develop expert ability. This cannot be achieved without resiliency. Similarly, many of the benefits of exercise only occur over a sustained period of activity.

Positive psychology in sport and exercise can include emotional, cognitive, and behavioural intervention approaches (Park-Perin, 2013). Emotional methods can focus on positive emotional states such as joy, happiness, enjoyment, and satisfaction. Such states are important for motivation and well-being. Cognitive methods include examining how factors such as optimism influence moods, motivation, health, and performance (Park-Perin, 2013; Peterson & Seligman, 2004). Behavioural methods involve enhancing behavioural self-regulation strategies. One specific example is nurturing psychological strengths. Rather than trying to reduce weaknesses, this approach gets athletes to focus on their strengths to improve confidence and facilitate developing mental toughness (Gordon, 2012).

Many studies in sport and exercise psychology research are rooted in positive psychology. Research has focused on such topics as intrinsic motivation, confidence, enjoyment, satisfaction, positive psychological growth, team cohesion, effective leadership, mental well-being, goal-setting, self-compassion, challenge, and success. Even when exercise psychologists work with clinical conditions, such as spinal cord injuries, cancer, and cardiac rehabilitation, a major focus is related to enhancing well-being by increasing positive qualities like confidence, independence, social and physical functioning, and life satisfaction (Motl, 2013; Vallance et al., 2013).

Teaching is an important role for many sport and exercise psychology specialists.

John MacLeod

Careers in Sport and Exercise Psychology

Many students want to know what career options are available in sport and exercise psychology, and what are the best academic pathways to these careers. These career options can be classified into three major areas: teaching, research, and consulting. We will briefly discuss each of these roles below.

Teaching In Canada and the United States, most sport and exercise psychology specialists are employed in universities and colleges and have a primary responsibility for teaching undergraduate and graduate courses. Courses may range from introductory sport and exercise psychology to more specialized courses such as applied sport psychology, mental training, motivational counselling, developmental and lifespan sport and exercise psychology, and behavioural medicine. Some sport and exercise psychologists also provide educational services to community and sport organizations. These teaching situations may involve increasing the awareness of sport and exercise psychology, teaching basic principles of sport and exercise psychology, helping athletes to develop and use psychological skills to enhance performance, or working with clients to enhance exercise behaviour and well-being (Cox, 1998).

Research A primary responsibility of sport and exercise psychology specialists working in universities is to advance knowledge. Through specialized training, researchers are able to design, conduct, and evaluate many research questions. Researchers in the areas of personality, motivation, anxiety, stress and coping, group cohesion, aggression and moral behaviour, youth sport, aging and physical activity, leadership and coaching, body image, exercise and mental health, and physical activity and sport psychology interventions seek to describe, predict, explain, and sometimes change cognition, emotion, and behaviour in physical activity settings. Research findings are presented at conferences and in refereed journals and books (see Tables 1.1 and 1.2 for lists of professional organizations and

Table 1.1 Selected Sport and Exercise Psychology Professional Organizations	
Canadian Society for Psychomotor Learning and Sport Psychology/Société Canadienne d'Apprentissage Psychomoteur et de Psychologie du Sport (SCAPPS)	www.scapps.org
Canadian Sport Psychology Association (CSPA)	www.cspa-acps.ca
International Society of Sport Psychology (ISSP)	www.issponline.org
European Federation of Sport Psychology/Fédération Européenne de Psychologie des Sports et des Activités Corporelles (FEPSAC)	www.fepsac.com
Association for Applied Sport Psychology (AASP)	www.appliedsportpsych.org
American Psychological Association Division 47: Exercise and Sport Psychology	www.apa47.org
North American Society for the Psychology of Sport and Physical Activity (NASPSPA)	www.naspspa.org
Australian Psychological Society: College of Sport and Exercise Psychologists	www.groups.psychology.org.au/csep

Table 1.2 Representative Sport and Exercise Psychology Journals	
Journal of Sport & Exercise Psychology	www.humankinetics.com/JSEP
Journal of Applied Sport Psychology	www.tandfonline.com/toc/uasp20/.U40-5Jj0gUU
The Sport Psychologist	www.humankinetics.com/TSP
International Journal of Sport and Exercise Psychology	www.tandfonline.com/toc/rijs20/.U40-kJj0gUU
International Journal of Sport Psychology	www.ijsp-online.com
Psychology of Sport and Exercise	www.sciencedirect.com/science/journal/14690292
Journal of Sport Psychology in Action	http://www.appliedsportpsych.org/publications/journal-of-sport-psychology-in-action

journals, respectively). These presentations and publications allow scholars to engage in discussions and debates about the strengths and limitations of various theories, methods, and paradigms.

Consulting A third major role of the sport and exercise psychology specialist is to help individuals, teams, and organizations improve performance, change physical activity behaviour, manage sport and life demands, and enhance personal well-being. These specialists providing consulting services might be licensed sport psychologists, or might be individuals who have a strong knowledge of educational and psychological skills but are not formally licensed. The issues concerning who can provide sport and exercise psychology services and who can call themselves sport and exercise psychologists are discussed later in this chapter.

In Canada, many professional sport teams and national sport organizations employ sport psychology consultants. In the United States, many major universities have full-time consultants (Weinberg & Gould, 2011), but this is not the case in Canada. However, an increasing number of Canadian universities do use sport psychology consultants on a limited basis. There are also consultants working in the fitness industry, in rehabilitation settings, and progressively more in the business community (Anshel, 2012). In Canada, very few individuals make their living as full-time sport and exercise psychology consultants, however. Most sport and exercise psychology specialists combine sport consulting with university or college careers or psychological consulting in other areas.

Sport and exercise psychology consultants tend to play three general roles. Educational consultants typically teach people psychological skills to facilitate performance, increase exercise, and enhance well-being. Counselling consultants help people with developmental concerns, adjustment, and challenges (Petitpas, 1996). Clinical psychology consultants can assist clients in educational and counselling areas, but they also have special training in psychopathology. Of course, both counselling and clinical psychologists might also provide educational services in physical activity settings. We will discuss the specialized training required in the next section.

An increasing role of sport psychology specialists is as a consultant to athletes.

Sakala/Shutterstock

TRAINING TO BE A SPORT AND EXERCISE PSYCHOLOGY SPECIALIST

Since sport and exercise psychology is an interdisciplinary field, there are multiple career pathways. The training required to be a sport and exercise psychology specialist, however, is contentious and a source of constant debate. Silva (2002) noted that there was little controversy in the 1960s and 1970s since most sport and exercise psychology specialists were academically oriented. Now, an increasing number of students and academics are interested in applied sport and exercise psychology. However, working in applied settings requires a set of competencies different from that required in academic settings.

So what kind of training is required? Unfortunately, there is no easy answer! To a large extent, educational training depends on what career path a person chooses. There are multiple career tracks that combine teaching, research, performance enhancement, and the provision of clinical or counselling services. The APA provides some guidance on graduate training and career possibilities in exercise and sport psychology (http://www.apadivisions.org/division-47/index.aspx). For simplicity, we will briefly describe two general training orientations: (1) sport science education and (2) clinical and counselling sport and exercise psychology.

Sport Science Education

In Canada, most sport and exercise psychology specialists work in university and college settings and thus require strong teaching and research skills. Typically, they are extensively trained in the sport sciences and in research methods and take additional courses in psychology and/or counselling. Nevertheless, there are trends toward more interdisciplinary training that combines the sport sciences and psychology. Currently, a wide range of academic programs that provide varied learning experiences are available to students. Interested students can find relevant information in an Association for Applied Sport Psychology (AASP) directory of graduate programs in Canada, the United States, Australia, and Great Britain.

Clinical and Counselling Sport and Exercise Psychology

Clinical psychology and counselling psychology are closely associated fields. Clinical psychology training typically focuses on the assessment and rehabilitation of serious psychological dysfunctions. Counselling training tends to focus more on helping people with adjustment or development problems. However, there is significant overlap in the training of clinical and counselling psychologists (see Petitpas, 1996).

The training of clinical and counselling psychologists is well grounded in psychological theory, assessment, intervention, research methods, and ethics and often requires a supervised internship. Clinical and counselling psychologists who work as sport psychologists usually have completed graduate courses or supplementary training in the sport sciences. The specific training for clinical psychologists is linked to the registration (licensing) standards of individual provincial and territorial regulatory bodies. Students interested in the specific requirements and accredited academic programs can visit the Canadian Psychological Association website (www.cpa.ca) for appropriate links.

Licensing of Sport and Exercise Psychologists

Psychologist: A term that is defined and regulated by provincial and territorial boards in Canada.

Many individuals providing performance enhancement services to athletes are called sport psychologists by the media. However, is this appropriate? In Canada, provincial and territorial laws regulate the use of the term **psychologist**. These laws were enacted to protect people from being exploited, possibly by untrained individuals. In most cases, psychologists must complete specific types of educational training and pass examinations set by psychological licensing boards. The specific rules for the use of the title *psychologist* vary across provinces and territories.

Table 1.3 Membership Criteria for the Canadian Sport Psychology Association
The Canadian Sport Psychology Association lists consultants who fulfill the following basic criteria:
• A master's degree in sport psychology or a related field
• Successful completion of a variety of courses relevant to sport psychology consultation and foundational disciplines, such as human kinetics or kinesiology, psychology, and counselling
• Extensive sport psychology consulting experience
• Hands-on experience in sport
• Favourable supervisor and client evaluations

There are a number of professionals who are well trained in sport sciences, exercise motivation counselling, psychology, and performance enhancement techniques, but who are not licensed sport psychologists. In applied settings, people have used such designations as *mental skills* trainer, *sport and exercise psychology consultant*, and *sport science consultant*. Regardless of the title that practitioners adopt, they are responsible for meeting standards of conduct when providing sport and exercise psychology services. The CPA, the Canadian Sport Psychology Association (CSPA), and the AASP have been proactive in identifying the necessary standards and competencies required for providing sport and exercise psychology services to athletes (see Table 1.3). The next section discusses these standards and competencies.

STANDARDS OF CONDUCT AND PRACTITIONER COMPETENCIES IN SPORT AND EXERCISE PSYCHOLOGY

Many sport and exercise psychology specialists act as consultants for athletes, teams, and coaches in an effort to enhance performance. However, who should provide specific types of sport and exercise psychology services? How do consultants deal with conflicts of interest, demands from coaches for athletes' private information, challenges that exceed their professional competencies, or potential romantic interest in clients? The style in which each individual consultant works with an athlete or a team will probably differ considerably from one consultant to another. Nevertheless, a number of basic standards of conduct and service always apply when a sport and exercise psychology consultant interacts with clients.

Ethics is concerned with matters of right and wrong as they relate to human behaviour. With regard to the duties and responsibilities of a sport and exercise psychology consultant, ethics also refers to the nature, terms, and parameters of the relationship between the consultant and the client. Consultants provide a service, but they must be mindful that this service can be both beneficial and harmful to clients. Consultants have an ethical responsibility (at best) to assist athletes and (at worst) to do no harm. However, consultants often find themselves faced with situations in which the right course of action is far from clear (Moore, 2003). This is where ethical codes become invaluable because they provide guidelines for what to do, when to do it, and how to do it (see Case Study 1.1).

Ethics: Concerned with matters of right and wrong as they relate to human behaviour.

A number of professional organizations have drawn up codes of ethics, or guidelines, that govern the relationship between a practitioner and a client. Three of these codes of ethics are particularly relevant to the sport and exercise psychology consultant working in Canada:

1. Ethics Code: AASP Ethical Principles and Standards (www.appliedsportpsych.org/about/ethics/ethics-code)
2. CSPA Code of Ethics (www.cspa-acps.ca/ethics-1.html)
3. CPA Canadian Code of Ethics for Psychologists (www.cpa.ca/aboutcpa/committees/ethics/resources)

Professional ethics are typically covered in more detail in advanced sport and exercise psychology courses. We provide a brief overview of the CPA guidelines in Table 1.4. However, you should be aware that ethical standards are complex and are constantly being modified and refined (see Moore, 2003; Whelan, Meyers, & Elkin, 2002).

Sport and Exercise Psychology Competencies and Referral

Dr. Simser is a professor of sport and exercise psychology, has a PhD from a human kinetics program, and focuses her research on group dynamics in sport. Dr. Simser's work is guided by the CPA's code of ethics (see Table 1.4). As part of her service responsibilities to the community, she occasionally consults with teams and educates them about sport psychology (Principle 4).

Recently, Dr. Simser was contacted by the parents of Allison, a competitive gymnast. Allison is also Dr. Simser's niece. The parents requested that Dr. Simser meet with their daughter to help her overcome a newly developed fear of dismounting the balance beam. In response to Allison's request to quit gymnastics, her parents cut down her participation from 30 hours per week to 25 hours. The parents feel that if Allison could overcome her fear then she would want to continue participating in the sport. They also expressed concern that Allison has started to become focused on her appearance and worries about her weight; they have seen her measuring her waist on several occasions. The gymnastics club recently hired a

new coach and Allison's parents have heard rumours that he is demanding body fat measurements each month of all the competitive stream gymnasts. They believe that this new coach may be contributing to Allison's fears and worries. Allison's parents feel that this is a concern for the whole family and they should all be present during the consulting sessions.

Dr. Simser explained to the parents that she could not meet with Allison because she felt she could not be unbiased and that it would be a conflict of interest to consult with her niece (Principle 3). Dr. Simser also advised that, unless Allison freely consented to consulting with a sport psychology consultant and agreed that her parents could participate in the session, the CPA's code of ethics was being violated (Principle 1). Finally, because she is not a licensed psychologist, Dr. Simser feels she may not have the competency to help Allison with her concerns about her appearance and weight (Principle 2). Dr. Simser gave Allison's parents the contact information for a counselling psychologist experienced in consulting youth athletes.

SPORT AND EXERCISE PSYCHOLOGY IN CANADA AND THE UNITED STATES

The previous sections have highlighted how sport and exercise psychology is a multidisciplinary field that involves both psychology and the sport sciences, but how did it evolve into its present condition in Canada and the United States? The development of sport and exercise psychology in both countries has been closely intertwined. A brief history will allow the student to more clearly understand the present day issues, challenges, and status of sport and exercise psychology in Canada.

In the early 20th century, Canadian universities were few and enrolment was low. In sport and exercise psychology, there was little evidence of systematic research or teaching. The post–World War II expansion of universities in the United States had an important impact on sport and exercise psychology. Several universities established laboratories in motor learning and behaviour, seeking to determine how people learned motor skills and how practice and feedback influenced learning. Dr. Franklin Henry, a faculty member at the University of California, Berkeley, became a strong advocate of a scholarly and scientific approach to physical education studies. Notably, two graduates of Dr. Henry's laboratory became prominent pioneering sport psychology researchers in Canada: Dr. Rikk Alderman and Dr. Albert Carron. In North America, many sport psychology instructors were trained in motor behaviour in physical education departments.

Nurtured primarily by academics in the movement and sport sciences, sport psychology began to grow in both Canada and the United States during the 1960s and 1970s

The code comprises four general principles, listed below in order of priority.

Principle 1: Respect for the Dignity of Persons

This principle reinforces the moral rights of all people regardless of individual differences, including culture, religion, gender, marital status, sexual orientation, etc. Respect extends to upholding the individual's privacy, confidentiality, and freedom to consent for consulting services and as a research participant. These rights must be upheld at all times, particularly for vulnerable persons (e.g., children), except in circumstances when the physical safety of an individual is threatened if intervention does not occur.

Principle 2: Responsible Caring

This principle requires sport and exercise psychology consultants to weigh the costs and benefits of various methods and select those that will minimize harm and maximize benefits. The consultant must take responsibility and corrective action for any harmful effects that may have occurred as a result of their research, teaching, or practice. To avoid causing harm, sport and exercise psychologists work within their range of competence or engage in activities for which they have adequate supervision.

Principle 3: Integrity in Relationships

This principle is upheld through self-knowledge and critical analysis. Sport and exercise psychologists are expected to be accurate and honest, to be straightforward and open, to be as objective and unbiased as possible, and to avoid conflicts of interest.

Principle 4: Responsibility to Society

Sport and exercise psychologists benefit society through the development of knowledge and by practising freedom of inquiry and debate. However, respect and responsible caring for the athlete must be the first priority and must not be violated by attempts to benefit society.

Source: Copyright 2011, Canadian Psychological Association. Permission granted for use of material.

REFLECTIONS 1.1

A practitioner in Ontario is providing exercise psychology services to women enrolled in a fitness facility. The specialist is teaching a number of psychological strategies, such as goal setting, increasing confidence, and relaxation training. There have been some questions about the specialist's knowledge and practices, however. Although the person is a former elite athlete, there is no indication that the specialist has had formal training in the theory and use of psychology strategies in exercise settings. What principles might the specialist have violated, based on the CPA standards of conduct?

(Gould & Pick, 1995). This growth corresponded with the establishment of many new universities and junior colleges. The teaching of sport psychology courses became widespread, and graduate training programs began to appear in the major universities.

In Canada, Dr. Rikk Alderman at the University of Alberta developed the first PhD program. Along with Dr. Albert Carron, Alderman could be considered one of the modern parents of sport and exercise psychology in Canada. Under the guidance of

Dr. Alderman and Dr. Robert Wilberg (a motor behaviour specialist), the University of Alberta program produced several influential Canadian sport psychology researchers and practitioners in the 1970s. They include John Salmela (Université de Montréal, University of Ottawa), Terry Orlick (University of Ottawa), Cal Botterill (University of Winnipeg), Len Wankel (University of Alberta), Craig Hall (University of Western Ontario), and Peter Klavora (University of Toronto).

Two major scholarly professional organizations were established in the United States and Canada. First, the North American Society for the Psychology of Sport and Physical Activity (NASPSPA) was formed in 1967. It reflected the close ties between the training of specialists in motor learning and in sport psychology in the 1960s. Second, the Canadian Society for Psychomotor Learning and Sport Psychology/Société Canadienne d'Apprentissage Psychomoteur et de Psychologie du Sport (SCAPPS) was founded as a society in Banff, Alberta, in 1977. Its main objectives were on improving the quality of research and teaching in the psychology of sport, motor development, and motor learning and control. However, applied psychology was not emphasized. SCAPPS continues to have a strong influence on the research and academic development of sport and exercise psychology in Canada.

The late 1970s and the 1980s were periods of consolidation in sport psychology as it separated from its motor learning parentage. Many universities had specialists in sport psychology, more graduate programs were established, and quality research flourished. The practice of sport psychology also became more widespread, and sport psychology services

Clients are increasingly utilizing the skills of exercise psychology consultants in Canada.

Russell Sadur/Dorling Kindersley, Ltd

were increasingly sought by professional and Olympic sport organizations. The 1980s also witnessed the growth of exercise psychology in North America. In Canada, sport psychology practices were included in the National Coaching Certification Program (NCCP). Three prominent sport psychology journals were established: *The Journal of Sport Psychology* (1979), *The Sport Psychologist* (1986), and the *Journal of Applied Sport Psychology* (1989).

A key event was the formation of the Association for the Advancement of Applied Sport Psychology (AAASP) in 1986. This association has changed its name slightly, dropping "Advancement." The new Association for Applied Sport Psychology (AASP) is now the largest organization devoted to the promotion of applied sport (and exercise) psychology. AASP conferences highlight research and professional issues in sport, exercise, and health psychology, as well as provide continuing education workshops.

Since the 1990s there has been tremendous growth in sport and exercise psychology in North America. Within universities, the growth of sport and exercise psychology has been propelled and shaped by societal concerns about health and health care costs. Many programs currently place an emphasis on health and health promotion through physical activity. One impact of this health movement has been the diversification and expansion of exercise and health psychology. Research topics now increasingly focus on body image, self-esteem, physical and mental well-being, behavioural change, exercise adherence, eating disorders, and other health behaviours affected by physical activity. Many university programs currently offer undergraduate courses in sport psychology, exercise psychology, and exercise and health psychology. Major granting agencies in Canada and the United States are directing significant research funding to sport and exercise psychology researchers, especially if the work is linked to health.

Practitioners are also working with major organizations to provide better access to certified mental or psychological skills consultants. To this end, the CSPA (www.cspa-acps.ca/membership-requirements-1.html) and the AASP (www.appliedsportpsych.org/certified-consultants/become-a-certified-consultant) have developed a process to certify qualified consultants.

Sport and Exercise Psychology around the World

The discipline and profession of sport and exercise psychology has witnessed tremendous growth in many parts of the world over the last 25 years. Not surprisingly, sport and exercise psychology is the best developed in the wealthiest economic regions, such as North America, Europe, the United Kingdom, Australia, and Japan. Reviewing the worldwide developments in sport and exercise psychology is beyond the scope of this chapter. We will, however, provide a snapshot of prominent organizations and events.

The former Soviet Union boasted one of the first sport psychology programs in the world. Around 1919, the Institute for the Study of Sport and Physical Culture was established in Petrograd (later Leningrad, now St. Petersburg). The institute developed a systematic approach to the application of sport sciences. Psychologists worked with other sport scientists to develop and apply training and competition principles to maximize performance. This system was adopted by more than 130 sport institutes throughout the former Soviet Union and later in the Soviet-controlled Eastern bloc (Silva, 2002).

Two major events occurred in the 1960s that played significant roles in the establishment of sport psychology in Europe. First, the first World Congress of Sport Psychology was held in Rome in 1965. This led to the formation of the International Society of Sport Psychology (ISSP), which also sponsored the first scholarly sport psychology journal, the *International Journal of Sport Psychology*. Second, the European Federation of Sport Psychology/Fédération Européenne de Psychologie des Sports et des Activités Corporelles (FEPSAC) was founded in 1969. In 2014, FEPSAC had representation from more than 20 European sport and exercise psychology organizations. Both ISSP and FEPSAC have had a major impact on the advancement of sport and exercise psychology in Europe and throughout the world.

At the time of writing in 2015, there are many strong academic programs and professional organizations around the world. In Britain, sport and exercise psychology is now widespread in the university system. Coaches can learn about sport psychology applications through sports coach UK, and the British Association of Sport and Exercise Sciences (BASES) offers individual accreditation in sport psychology. In Australia, psychology departments cooperate with sport science programs to offer graduate training. Sport psychology is well accepted by the Australian sporting community and is fully integrated into the Australian Institute of Sport (www.ausport.gov.au/ais/sssm/psychology). In Asia, the leading countries are Japan, China, and Korea. Major sporting events there (such as the Olympics and Asian Games) have fuelled the practice of applied sport psychology and other sport sciences. Unfortunately, academic and professional development have been slow in many poorer areas of the world, such as Africa and Central America.

STUDYING SPORT AND EXERCISE PSYCHOLOGY: A BASIC PRIMER

Basic Concepts

A major challenge for undergraduate students is learning to understand the role of science processes in developing knowledge and informing effective practice. In the world of the 21st century, people are constantly exposed to many terms, ideas, opinions, viewpoints, models, and theories. For example, some hockey commentators argue that fighting in hockey is necessary to reduce built-up tension and prevent players from engaging in more dangerous stick-related violent behaviour. This idea raises the question of how statements or positions are supported by scientific evidence. How does one evaluate the strengths and weaknesses of various statements concerning sport and exercise psychology behaviour? And what is the role of scientific research in sport and exercise psychology? This section will provide a basic introduction to some key ideas about the scientific process in sport and exercise psychology. Since most kinesiology and psychology undergraduate programs provide research methods courses, we will not go into great detail. But understanding some key concepts is necessary to gain a better appreciation of theoretical ideas and evidence-based practice in sport and exercise psychology.

In everyday conversations about sport and exercise, one commonly hears terms like *aggression*, *stress*, *motivation*, and *anxiety*. People typically believe they have a good understanding of these terms, but how people use these terms in everyday conversation and how researchers define them may be quite different. This happens for a good reason: Terms that have been created for a scientific purpose—called **scientific constructs**—are defined specifically so that they can be distinguished from other related but distinct ideas. The difference between a scientific construct and common language use of a term often creates confusion for students, but scientific constructs are critical in developing knowledge in a field. For example, people will often use the term *aggression* to refer to behaviours in sport that include both legitimate goal-directed behaviour and illegal harm-related behaviour. From a scientific perspective, such lack of clarity in the use of a word would be problematic. How could you distinguish between the two types of behaviours if you used the same term?

Often in research, key variables are identified to describe, predict, or explain a phenomenon. A **variable** is simply a construct that can be assigned a specific value to be counted. A variable must be able to change over time, contexts, or people. Typically, a construct is operationally defined by a measure that captures specific behaviours and thoughts. For example, recall our scenario involving Christine's desire to exercise. She reported concerns about body anxiety in public settings. From a research perspective, it would be necessary to define this anxiety variable (social physique anxiety) and then to use a specific instrument (social physique anxiety scale) to measure the construct. A researcher could investigate whether scores on the instrument change over time (Does Christine's score change after three months of exercise?) or across people (Is Christine's score different from other exercise participants' scores?).

Of course, we are often interested in studying the relationships among several variables, or determining if changing one variable causes another variable to change. For example, do changes in exercise behaviour predict changes in social physique anxiety, as well as mental and physical well-being? We might find that as Christine exercises over a 12-week period, her social physique anxiety decreases and her mental and physical well-being improves. A researcher may note similar changes in many middle-aged women. Does this mean that there is a causal effect of exercise on these three variables? To examine causal relationships, we must identify differences between an **independent variable (IV)** and a **dependent variable (DV)**. The independent variable is supposed to change the dependent variable or variables. Ideally, researchers should manipulate the IV (exercise) to determine if the change is associated with a systematic change in the DV (social physique anxiety, mental and physical well-being).

Scientific constructs: Specifically defined terms that have been created for a scientific purpose.

Variable: A scientific construct that can be assigned a specific value to be counted.

Independent variable (IV): The manipulated variable (cause) that produces a change in the dependent variable.

Dependent variable (DV): A non-manipulated variable (outcome) that is expected to change as a result of manipulating the independent variable.

But determining if exercise causes changes in the three dependent variables can be tricky. Maybe there is another unknown and unmeasured variable that is causing changes in the DVs. Maybe there are multiple unknown variables. For example, if the exercise program starts at the beginning of spring, the change in weather might make people feel better. Determining causation requires three key factors. First, there must be a systematic statistical relationship between IV and DV. That is, as exercise levels change, the DVs change in a systematic (non-random) manner. Second, there must be a clear temporal order between the IV and DV. Thus, changes in exercise must precede changes in social physique anxiety and mental and physical well-being. Third, plausible reasonable explanations must be ruled out. Thus, factors that can systematically affect the DVs must be eliminated or controlled. In our example these variables could include motivation, diet, drug use, weather, or simply wanting to please the researcher. It is often difficult to control the effects of these extraneous variables.

Students will come across many models and theories that attempt to predict or explain phenomena in sport and exercise psychology. One of the most difficult topics is the difference between a model and a theory. Sometimes models are precursors to theories, and in other cases, models are developed based on a specific theory. For our purposes, models tend to be more restrictive in explanatory scope than theories.

Scientific models can be of various types, including scale models, analog models, and theoretical models (Giere, 1997). Kinesiology students are very familiar with scale models that are often used as teaching aids, such as models of muscles, cells, and DNA structure. These are not often used in sport and exercise psychology. Analog models are more common in social sciences in that phenomena are explained as being like some kind of system or structure that is better understood. For example, human information processing is often modelled as being like a computer structure with hardware and software components. The most common model in sport and exercise psychology is the theoretical model, composed of a number of scientific constructs whose interrelationships are clearly stipulated. Typically, such theoretical models are often based on research evidence and should correspond to the real world. A theoretical model commonly used to explain relationships among exercise variables is the Theory of Planned Behaviour.

Theories and theoretical models are very similar, except that theories classically are more general. A **theory** specifies relationships across a number of scientific constructs and attempts to explain phenomena across a number of different times, contexts, and people. Sometimes a theory will go far beyond the existing evidence. However, a good theory provides sound reasoning (logical consistency) about proposed relationships among constructs. The construction of theories is a major goal of science; however, we need to realize that theories can be wrong. An example of such a flawed theory is psychodynamic theory in relation to aggression in contact sports such as boxing.

A key element of both models and theories is that they should be testable. Good models and theories allow for **research hypotheses** to be generated and scientifically evaluated. A research hypothesis is often described as an educated guess about the nature of the relationships among scientific constructs given specific conditions. For example, we could hypothesize that moderate intensity exercise will improve mental and physical well-being in women. This hypothesis could be based on previous research evidence or it could be based on theoretical models that link moderate exercise to changes in brain chemistry that could alter mental and physical functioning. The construction of hypotheses allows researchers to

Sport and exercise psychologists often use theories to understand the relationships among scientific constructs such as emotion and performance.

Rich Lam/Getty Images Sport/Getty Images

devise experiments to evaluate models and theories. The resulting research evidence allows scientists to determine under what conditions a model or theory works or does not work. For example, we might find that moderate, but not intense, exercise produces enhanced mental well-being in untrained women. Building upon such scientific research allows for the confirmation, modification, or rejection of theories. One reason for the number of models and theories in various areas of sport and exercise psychology is that most have had only moderate success in explaining specific phenomena under various conditions.

Qualitative Approaches to Research

Prior to 1990, much of the published research in sport and exercise psychology typically employed research methodology and terminology associated with what has been termed *quantitative research*. **Quantitative inquiry** focuses on counting the amount of a particular variable or set of variables and sometimes has been referred to as empirical–analytic (Hathaway, 1995; Wilson & Bengoechea, 2011). Researchers in sport and exercise psychology, like other areas of social sciences, adopted the use of quantitative methodology from the natural sciences (e.g., physics, biology, and chemistry) because they believed such methods were the best way to advance understanding in the field. The use of quantitative methods is also based on a number of philosophical assumptions about the nature of reality (ontology) and the structure of knowledge (epistemology). Although a detailed discussion of these philosophical assumptions is far beyond the scope of this chapter, it is important to note that quantitative methods often assume that reality is objective and

Quantitative inquiry: Focuses on quantifying or counting the amount of a particular variable or set of variables.

governed by laws, and that knowledge is formed over time by objective reports from objective researchers (see Hathaway, 1995; Wilson & Bengoechea, 2011, for more detailed discussion). Students will see many examples of research using quantitative inquiry.

Over the last decade, there has been a surge in research using qualitative inquiry. Qualitative inquiry has roots in various disciplines such as anthropology, sociology, and clinical psychology as well as cultural and feminist studies (Denzin & Lincoln, 2005). Unlike quantitative methods, **qualitative inquiry** often assumes that reality is constructed by the person in a particular situation or context (Hathaway, 1995). Thus, understanding a person's lived experiences is often a central aim of qualitative methods. Wilson and Bengoechea (2011) noted that an appeal of qualitative methods in sport and exercise psychology is that they provide detailed information and a level of understanding not typically found in quantitative methods.

There are three primary ways to collect "data" using qualitative methods: in-depth interviews with participants; direct observations of participants' behaviour; and analysis of written documents such as diaries, letters, and written responses. The most common approach in sport and exercise psychology is the use of interviews (Anshel, 2012), which range from a single interview about a particular event to multiple interviews over a period of time such as a competitive sport season. These transcribed interviews are typically analyzed using inductive methods to identify important categories, themes, patterns, and relationships in the text. Researchers use what is usually called an **emic focus**, which aims to capture the participant's viewpoint in a particular setting. Students should be aware that there are many different types of qualitative research approaches in sport psychology, such as case studies, grounded theory, ethnography, phenomenology, and narrative analysis (see Wilson & Bengoechea, 2011). A detailed description of these various methods is beyond the scope of this chapter; however, the use of qualitative methods is making strong contributions to the study of sport and exercise psychology.

To help students more clearly understand some basic ideas behind qualitative methods, let us consider a study by McDonough and colleagues (2013) examining stress and coping in high performance adolescent swimmers. The researchers interviewed eight competitive swimmers before and after athlete-identified major swim meets across the course of a season. Interview questions focused on each athlete's perceived stressors and coping strategies associated with their most important event within a swim meet. The transcribed interviews were then analyzed in two steps. The first step was to use content analysis to identify the types of stressors and coping strategies for each swimmer. Researchers read each interview and coded the data according to specific rules. Higher order themes were developed to capture the meaning of the coded text. Examples of higher order themes for stressors included pressure to perform, potential to excel, poor prerace preparation, injury, fatigue, and interpersonal conflict with coaches. Themes for coping included such strategies as seeking social support, increasing effort, focusing on technique, acceptance, and avoidance. The second step was to create idiographic profiles of each athlete's stress appraisals and coping before and after each of the four meets. The researchers then formed profiles based on the way swimmers evaluated stressors and how they tried to manage the stressor. This analysis found some distinct profiles. One group of swimmers reported avoiding stressors and typically did not anticipate upcoming stressors. In this group, swimmers primarily used cognitive and behavioural avoidance and distraction to deal with stressors. Another group of swimmers typically saw stressors as a challenge and used multiple strategies to deal with the stressors. A third group of

Qualitative inquiry: Often assumes that reality is constructed by the person in a particular situation or context.

Emic focus: Captures the participant's viewpoint in a particular setting.

Charles Hamelin won several Olympic and World Championship medals but also suffered some disappointing races. Qualitative methods could help researchers understand his experiences in high performance sport competitions.

PCN/Corbis

swimmers reported low levels of stress as they saw swimming as fun. Athletes were also shown the researchers' interpretations of the interviews and generally agreed with these interpretations. A key aspect of this study was that the researchers focused on the lived experience of the swimmers, carefully considering the perceived reality of each swimmer's experiences across each of the swim meets. The detailed information from the interviews provided rich evidence of the complexity of stress and coping in adolescent swimmers.

Evidence-Based Practice

Recall the scenario from the beginning of the chapter where Alex and his mother Christine are facing multiple challenges in sport and exercise settings. What are the best ways to intervene to improve Alex's and Christine's experiences in their respective situations? A practitioner could select a number of intervention techniques and programs, but which ones are the best for Alex and Christine? This brings us to a fundamental issue in all areas of professional help-giving—*evidence-based practice*. The Canadian Psychological Association holds that evidence-based practice involves the use of the best available research evidence to inform clinical decision-making and service delivery in the context of specific client characteristics, cultural backgrounds, and treatment preferences. Practitioners should select intervention practices that maximize potential benefits and minimize harm to their clients.

Evidence-based practice is consistent with the ethical codes or standards of professional conduct covered earlier in this chapter. But how do we determine the best evidencebased practice? First, we must consider research studies from scholarly *peer-reviewed* journals that clearly specify the treatment process and outcomes. *Peer-reviewed* means that articles are evaluated for quality by other professionals in the field. It is important to consider the characteristics of the treatment population in the study. Sometimes, treatment effects can be specific to an age group, gender, cultural or ethnic group, as well as the initial condition of the treatment group. For example, an intervention may be effective for middle-aged Caucasian women who are moderately body anxious but not for other participants who have different age, gender, and ethnic characteristics or initial body anxiety symptomology. Clearly, understanding the research process is a key factor in providing evidence-based practice. Second, it is important to consider the ethical guideline related to the dignity of the person. Practitioners need to work in collaboration with their clients. Although practitioners may have knowledge about treatment effectiveness, clients bring their lived experiences that influence motivation and preferences for types of interventions. Effective intervention requires collaboration between the client and the practitioner. Third, practitioners need to consider their level of competence to deliver specific interventions. Students need to carefully consider the research evidence that supports various psychological models and the use of specific interventions.

PREDICTED TRENDS AND ISSUES IN CANADA

Sport and exercise psychology is an interdisciplinary field involving researchers, educators, and practitioners from both the sport sciences and psychology. Many social, economic, and political forces have shaped the present form of sport and exercise psychology in Canada. It has faced many challenges and growing pains but has made very impressive gains in the last two decades. So what does the future hold? We believe that a number of trends and issues will dominate the advancement of sport and exercise psychology over the next 20 years.

Increased Specialization and Diversification

Federal and provincial/territorial health initiatives and policies, combined with knowledge development, will drive increased specialization and diversification. Much of the growth in the field will be in exercise related to health, primarily because physical activity is an effective, and relatively inexpensive, way to maintain or improve health. Hot topics are likely to be exercise adherence, obesity, aging, well-being, and youth development. There will be continued expansion of sport and exercise psychology principles in clinical settings, such as the study and treatment of cancer, stroke, spinal cord injuries, and Parkinson's disease.

Increased Research and Teaching Opportunities

Most Canadian universities and colleges offer sport and exercise psychology courses. Because of continued specialization and diversification, the number and types of courses will continue to grow at both the undergraduate and graduate level. Research opportunities will increase as major funding agencies recognize the quality and applicability of sport and exercise psychology research. Although funding for sport-related research has improved in the last few years, the major focus for increased funding will be on health-related research.

Increased Demands for Training in Clinical and Counselling Psychology

Working in diverse sport and exercise settings will require a range of sport science and psychological competencies. Students will demand and require counselling training and possibly clinical psychology training. Unfortunately, Canadian (and US) universities have been slow to respond to this demand. Kinesiology and exercise science programs largely focus on research and teaching, and few psychology departments offer sport and exercise psychology programs. This leaves students with two choices. First, students in kinesiology programs can supplement their training by taking appropriate counselling courses in psychology or educational psychology programs. Second, students can do a graduate degree in clinical or counselling psychology. An advantage to this route is generalized training that is applicable to many domains. Unfortunately, most clinical and counselling programs lack a critical mass of faculty trained in applied sport and exercise psychology.

Ethics and Competencies

There will be increased pressure on practitioners to adhere to professional standards of conduct when working with clients. Regulatory bodies are likely to become more vigilant in monitoring the use of the title *sport psychologist* or *exercise psychologist* as well as the practices of sport and exercise psychology consultants. Consultants from both sport science education and clinical and counselling psychology backgrounds will need to acquire and demonstrate competencies to work with specific populations in sport and exercise.

Working in Performance Enhancement Teams

There will be an increased demand for applied sport psychology services by national and provincial sport organizations. Some of these services are being provided through the various Canadian Sport Centres. These centres provide sport science support to national team athletes or those athletes identified as potential national team members. Within this environment, sport psychology consultants are asked to be accountable for the effectiveness of their services: consultants must find some way to measure the effectiveness of their consulting. A second demand is for the consultants to work in collaboration with other sport science professionals, including biomechanists, nutritionists, and physiologists. Rather than working alone, sport psychology consultants must devise methods of integrating members of these performance enhancement teams in order to most effectively service the athletes.

Online Consulting and Service Provision

In attempts to service more athletes and exercisers, particularly those outside of urban centres, there is a growing trend toward online consultation and service provision. Although this is an effective method of transmitting knowledge to a greater number of clients, sport and exercise psychologists must be especially vigilant that what they want to communicate is being received correctly, that they adhere to an ethical code, that they are not misrepresenting their competencies, and, most importantly, that the privacy and confidentiality of the client are being upheld. The Canadian Psychological Association has developed ethical guidelines for online consulting (www.cpa.ca/aboutcpa/committees/ethics/psychserviceselectronically).

Consulting with Athletes and Exercisers with Disabilities

Government health initiatives are on the rise as activity levels of Canadians continue to decline and obesity rates increase. The lowest rates of physical activity participation continue to be among individuals with disabilities. There will be increased demand on sport and exercise psychologists to involve individuals with disabilities in sport and exercise programs in order to improve overall health. At the 2014 Special Olympics Canada Summer Games, many teams benefitted from the expertise of sport psychology specialists.

Knowledge Translation

There is a critical need to bridge the gap between research evidence and professional practice in sport and exercise psychology. Knowledge must be accessible, understandable, and useful for practitioners such as applied sport psychologists, physical educators, coaches, rehabilitation specialists, and fitness specialists. Traditional knowledge translation methods have been primarily of a top-down nature. These methods have included university courses, textbooks, coaching manuals, and workshops taught by specialists. However, these traditional methods are not always effective. Partnerships among researchers, educators, and practitioners are required—partnerships that exchange and apply ethically based sport and exercise psychology knowledge.

CHAPTER SUMMARY

Sport and exercise psychology is an interdisciplinary field that is recognized in Canada as a core discipline within kinesiology and physical education programs. Sport and exercise psychology specialists are involved in teaching, research, and consulting roles, although most specialists in Canada are employed in universities and colleges. Various educational pathways involve training in the sport sciences or in clinical or counselling psychology. Specific training is often dependent on career objectives, whether as an academic (in either sport sciences or psychology) or as a practitioner. Some scholarly organizations, such as CSPA, do provide a certification process for consultants. However, provincial and territorial bodies regulate the use of the term *psychologist* as well as the specific training and examinations required to become a registered psychologist. All sport and exercise psychology consultants are guided by standards of conduct set out by organizations such as the CPA, AASP, and CSPA. Although the term *psychologist* has a specific legal meaning, we will use the term *sport and exercise psychologist* to refer to specialists in the three areas of teaching, research, and consulting.

The state of sport and exercise psychology in Canada, including its strengths and controversies, has been shaped by its parentage. In North America, sport and exercise psychology has been nurtured primarily in the sport sciences. The major Canadian scholarly professional organization is SCAPPS, although many academics and practitioners also affiliate with NASPSPA and AASP. At the applied level, CSPA is likely to have a major impact over the next decade. At present, sport and exercise psychology is taught in most universities, and research is flourishing. There is increased diversification into health and clinical populations. Sport and exercise psychology also continues to flourish around the world, with major academic organizations in Europe, Australia, New Zealand, the United Kingdom, and Asia.

Sport and exercise psychology is strongly shaped by both qualitative and quantitative research. In Canada, this research is funded by several national and provincial granting agencies and is primarily conducted in university settings. Research allows for the development and testing of models and theories to promote the understanding of sport and exercise psychology in multiple settings. Evidence-based practice involves practitioners using the latest research evidence to inform clinical decision-making and service delivery in the context of specific client characteristics, cultural backgrounds, and treatment preferences.

 COMMON MYTHS ABOUT SPORT AND EXERCISE PSYCHOLOGY REVISITED

MYTH: Only athletes or exercisers with serious mental problems need a sport or exercise psychologist.

Any athlete or person wanting to become more physically active and enhance psychological well-being can benefit from the services of a qualified sport and exercise psychology specialist. First, specialists design the majority of interventions to prepare athletes to manage the demands of training and competition and to enhance their well-being. Athletes can learn to develop and apply effective psychological skills to manage stress, focus attention, and augment motivation. In addition, specialists can teach coaches and physical activity leaders how to develop more effective training environments. Second, there are many effective interventions that can help people adopt and maintain healthy levels of physical activity, often leading to enhanced physical and mental health.

MYTH: All sport psychology specialists work with elite athletes to enhance their performance.

This is a restrictive view of sport psychology. In Canada, the majority of sport psychology specialists work in universities and colleges, primarily as teachers and researchers. Others may work as independent consultants, in schools, in government, or in private clinical and counselling settings. Many of these professionals do provide services to athletes to facilitate performance and promote psychological growth and development. The athletes range from young to old, and the athletes perform at developmental to elite competitive levels. Furthermore, sport and exercise psychology specialists are increasingly working with people in other areas of physical activity, including physical fitness and rehabilitation.

The next 20 years should witness several major trends, including increased specialization, diversification, research, and teaching opportunities. There will be pressure to improve educational opportunities and training of specific competencies for applied sport and exercise psychology services. It is hoped that faculty in programs in psychology, educational psychology, and sport science will collaborate to enhance the future development of sport and exercise psychology. Lastly, there is a critical need to bridge the gap between research evidence and professional practice in sport and exercise psychology. This process will require effective partnerships among practitioners, educators, and researchers so that sport and exercise principles can be effectively applied across multiple physical activity settings to enhance performance, increase participation, and improve well-being.

Review Questions

1. What are the three major roles of a sport and exercise psychology specialist? Are different types of training needed for the three roles?

2. What is positive psychology, and how is it relevant to the study and practice of sport and exercise psychology?

3. What are the differences between a sport and exercise psychology specialist trained in sport sciences and one trained in clinical or counselling psychology?

4. Is a counselling psychologist able to work with athletes to provide performance enhancement strategies? What standards of conduct guide such decisions?

5. How would the principles of integrity in relationships and respect for the dignity of persons help guide your decision to reveal information about an athlete's psychological state to a coach who demands it?

6. What are the major Canadian scholarly organizations that promotes sport and exercise psychology research and practice?

7. What are some key differences between quantitative and qualitative inquiry?

8. What are the characteristics of evidence-based practice?

9. What is knowledge translation, and why is it important for the advancement of sport and exercise psychology?

Suggested Reading

Oliver, J. (2013). Ethical practice in sport psychology: Challenges in the real world. In S. J. Hanrahan & M. B. Andersen (Eds.), *Routledge handbook of applied sport psychology* (pp. 60–68). New York: Routledge.

Park-Perin, G. (2013). Positive psychology. In S. J. Hanrahan & M. B. Andersen (Eds.), *Routledge handbook of applied sport psychology* (pp. 141–149). New York: Routledge.

Wilson, P. M., & Bengoechea, E. G. (2011). Research perspectives in sport and exercise psychology. In P. R. E. Crocker (Ed.), *Sport and exercise psychology: A Canadian perspective* (pp. 26–52). Toronto, ON: Pearson.

References

Anshel, M. H. (2012). *Sport psychology: From theory to practice* (5th ed.). San Francisco: Benjamin Cummings.

Cox, R. H. (1998). *Sport psychology: Concepts and applications* (4th ed.). Boston: McGraw-Hill.

Denzin, N. K., & Lincoln, Y. S. (2005). *The Sage handbook of qualitative research* (3rd ed.). Thousand Oaks, CA: Sage Publications.

Ericsson, K. A., Krampe, R. T., and Tesch-Roemer, C. (1993). The role of deliberate practice in the acquisition of expert performance. *Psychological Review, 100,* 363–406.

Giere, R. N. (1997). *Understanding scientific reasoning* (4th ed.). New York: Holt, Rinehart & Winston.

Gordon, S. (2012). Strengths-based approaches to developing mental toughness: Team and individual. *International Coaching Psychology Review, 7,* 210–222.

Gould, D., & Pick, S. (1995). Sport psychology: The Griffith era, 1920–1940. *The Sport Psychologist, 9,* 391–405.

Hathaway, R. (1995). Assumption underlying quantitative and qualitative research: Implications for institutional research. *Research in Higher Education, 36,* 535–562.

Kobau, R., Seligman, M. E. P., Peterson, C., Diener, E., Zach, M., Chapman, D., & Thompson, W. (2011). Mental health promotion in public health: Perspectives and strategies from positive psychology. *American Journal of Public Health, 101,* 1–9.

Lorig, K., Holman, H., Sobel, D., Laurent, D., González, V., & Minor, M. (2000). *Living a healthy life with chronic conditions* (2nd ed.). Palo Alto, CA: Bull Publishing.

Masten, A. S., & Reed, M. J. (2005). Resilience in development. In C. R. Synder & S. J. Lopez (Eds.), *Handbook of positive psychology* (pp. 74–88). Oxford University Press: New York.

McDonough, M., Hadd, V., Crocker, P. R. E., Holt, N. L., Tamminen, K. A., & Schonert-Reichl, K. (2013). Stress and coping among adolescents across a competitive swim season. *The Sport Psychologist, 27,* 143–155.

Moore, Z. E. (2003). Ethical dilemmas in sport psychology: Discussion and recommendations for practice. *Professional Psychology: Research & Practice, 34,* 601–610.

Motl, R. W. (2013). Physical activity and quality of life in multiple sclerosis. In P. Ekkekakis (Ed.), *Routledge handbook of physical activity and mental health* (pp. 530–540). New York: Routledge.

Park-Perin, G. (2013). Positive psychology. In S. J. Hanrahan & M. B. Andersen (Eds.), *Routledge handbook of applied sport psychology* (pp. 141–149). New York: Routledge.

Peterson, C., & Seligman, M.E.P. (2004). Character strengths and virtues: A handbook and classification. New York: Oxford University Press.

Petitpas, A. J. (1996). Counseling interventions in applied sport psychology. In J. L. Van Raalte & B. W. Brewer (Eds.), *Exploring sport and exercise psychology* (pp. 189–204). Washington, DC: American Psychological Association.

Seligman, M. E. P. (2002). *Authentic happiness.* New York: Free Press.

Seligman, M. E. P., & Csikszentmihalyi, M. (2000). Positive psychology: An introduction. *American Psychologist, 55,* 5–14.

Silva, J. M. (2002). The evolution of sport psychology. In J. M. Silva & D. E. Stevens (Eds.), *Psychological foundation of sport.* Toronto, ON: Allyn and Bacon.

Vallance, J. S., Culos-Reed, N., MacKenzie, M., & Courneya, K. S. (2013). Physical activity and psychosocial concerns among cancer survivors. In P. Ekkekakis (Ed.), *Routledge handbook of physical activity and mental health* (pp. 518–529). New York: Routledge.

Vealey, R. S. (2006). Smock and jocks outside the box: The paradigmatic evolution of sport and exercise psychology. *Quest, 58,* 128–159.

Weinberg, R., & Gould, D. (2011). *Foundations of sport and exercise psychology* (5th ed.). Champaign, IL: Human Kinetics.

Whelan, J. P., Meyers, A. W., & Elkin, T. D. (2002). Ethics in sport and exercise psychology. In J. L. Van Raalte & B. W. Brewer (Eds.), Exploring sport and exercise psychology (2nd ed., pp. 503–524). Washington, DC: APA.

Wilson, P. M., & Bengoechea, E. G. (2011). Research perspectives in sport and exercise psychology. In P. R. E. Crocker (Ed.), *Sport and exercise psychology: A Canadian perspective* (pp. 26–52). Toronto, ON: Pearson Canada.

Chapter 2

Personality in Sport and Exercise

Peter R. E. Crocker   Whitney A. Sedgwick   Ryan E. Rhodes

Steve Nagy/Design Pics/Corbis

Chapter Objectives

After reading this chapter, you should be able to do the following:

1   Define personality and incorporate the concept of individual differences.

2   Describe traits and various perspectives on traits such as the Big Five.

3   Differentiate how personality might develop, involving humanistic and cognitive–behaviour perspectives.

4   Briefly explain personality measurement and related ethical issues.

5   Explain recent personality research findings in sport and exercise psychology.

6   Discuss the limitations of personality in explaining athletic and exercise behaviours and performance.

Ronda is an elite youth lacrosse player for the New Westminster Salmonbellies. She has been the top playmaker for the last two years; she also has a reputation for aggressive play. Her coach states, "Ronda has the right personality for sport. She is outgoing and highly competitive, works diligently, and is mentally tough." Opposing coaches also recognize her character. One coach noted that Ronda is very passionate about lacrosse. Ronda thinks, however, that she is still not good enough. She tells her best friends that she hates making mistakes and worries about letting her team and herself down. She states, "I have to get better. I just cannot seem to play as well as I think I should. I have trouble sleeping at night because I keep ruminating about errors I have made." Ronda is also a good student but does not seem to have the same drive to succeed or the same levels of self-criticism.

Ronda's mother, Carol, also worries about Ronda's mental well-being and fears that Ronda might be too much like her father, Jack, a former lacrosse great. He was known for being hyper-competitive in sport. Indeed, he seems to have transferred this characteristic to exercise. Jack works out for two hours, five times a week. He feels obsessed about exercise, sometimes missing family functions and even exercising when he is injured. Jack is also successful in business but seems more relaxed in social situations. Carol feels it would be hard to change Jack's exercise behaviour since she thinks it is just driven by his competitive personality.

In the above scenario, a number of different adjectives are used to describe the behaviours of Ronda and Jack. These descriptors might refer to such personality factors as competitiveness, extraversion, conscientiousness, perfectionism, passion, and mental toughness. Think about how you might describe a friend. We often describe people in terms of specific traits, with words like *shy, aggressive, submissive, sensitive, happy-go-lucky, funny, competitive,* and *social.* In many cases, such descriptors imply that we expect people to display these characteristics across time and situations. In the scenario, coaches and significant others attempt to understand and explain Ronda's sport behaviour and Jack's exercise behaviour by referring to the construct of personality. Ronda's coach goes even further by suggesting that there is a right type of personality for sport.

The above scenario raises a number of questions when we consider personality in sport, questions that also apply to exercise and physical activity. Is the uniqueness of a person consistent across situations, or can a person be different in different contexts, such as sport and exercise, work, and school? Can personality predict sport performance or exercise behaviour? Is there a distinct sport or exercise personality? Does personality interact with the environment to influence sport and/or exercise performance? For that matter, what is personality? In this chapter, we will address these and several other questions related to personality in sport and exercise.

 ## COMMON MYTHS ABOUT PERSONALITY IN SPORT AND EXERCISE

MYTH: A distinct elite athlete personality profile exists.

MYTH: People choose physical activities and remain in these activities based on their personality.

INTRODUCTION

Personality is a complex, integral part of human individuality. Although researchers find personality challenging to define, the average person freely uses descriptors to describe others' (and their own) personalities. In Canadian sport, spectators and the media might use *confident* to describe soccer player Christine Sinclair and *dedicated* to describe hockey player Sidney Crosby. Olympic gold medallist Alex Bilodeau has been described as humble. Not surprisingly, sport researchers have been interested in personality for many decades. Over the last 30 years, researchers have also been interested in the potential link between personality and regular exercise (Rhodes, 2006). Students should realize that there are many complex questions regarding personality in sport, and there are many disagreements among sport researchers and consultants about the importance of personality in sport (for more detailed discussions see Allen et al., 2013; Crust, 2007). In the 1970s and 1980s, there was a heated debate, termed *the credulous–skeptical argument*, about the ability to use personality to predict sport success. However, as with most arguments, extreme positions do not really capture the relevance of personality in sport research in the 21st century. Many psychological factors investigated in sport psychology today are related to personality. These include, among many others, self-esteem, trait anxiety, mental toughness, passion, optimism, competitiveness, ego and mastery goal orientation, perfectionism, sensation seeking, conscientiousness, and extraversion.

WHAT IS PERSONALITY?

Personality: The overall organization of psychological characteristics—thinking, feeling, and behaving—that differentiates us from others and leads us to act consistently across time and situations.

When we use the term *personality*, we are referring primarily to the consistency of social behaviour, thoughts, and emotions. A useful definition of **personality** is "the overall organization of psychological characteristics—thinking, feeling, and behaving—that differentiates us from others and leads us to act consistently across time and situations"

Sport researchers have long been interested in studying the personalities of sport performers.

(Lindsay, Paulhas, & Nairne, 2008, p. 472). This definition clearly emphasizes individual differences. Each person is thought to be unique. Reflect back to the vignette at the beginning of the chapter. Both Ronda and Jack seem to have unique ways of meeting the challenges presented by lacrosse and other achievement domains.

Another term often used in sport–personality research is **disposition**, defined as "broad, pervasive, encompassing ways of relating to particular types of people . . . or situations" (Lazarus & Folkman, 1984, p. 120). For example, to say that a teammate has a cheerful disposition would mean that this person is typically upbeat, regardless of whom he or she is talking with or the environment he or she is in. In sport research, *disposition* has often been applied to behaviours, thoughts, and emotions that are relatively stable, such as competitiveness, optimism, and motivational orientation.

Disposition: Broad, pervasive, encompassing ways of relating to particular types of people or situations.

REFLECTIONS 2.1

Carefully consider the definition of personality provided above. Think about Clara Hughes, a six-time Olympic medallist in cycling and speed skating. She has been described as intense and demanding in training, qualities that contributed to her success. Can you make inferences about an athlete's personality simply by watching him or her in specific situations? What types of information would you need to determine an athlete's personality?

PERSONALITY TRAITS

Think about the numerous behavioural expressions that can exist in sport and exercise settings. Work in the 1930s identified over 4000 adjectives that described observable behaviours that could be considered relatively permanent (Lindsay et al., 2008). How can we make sense of the enormous number of combinations such that we can come up with a science of personality? The most common way scientists do this is by using statistical methods to look at clusters of behaviours that are related or correlated. These clusters of behavioural (plus cognitive and emotional) expressions are called *traits*, the central element of personality (Lindsay et al., 2008). Most students have probably heard of personality traits. A **trait** is a relatively stable characteristic or quality that is a portion of one's personality. For example, perfectionism consists of a cluster of expressions that includes being organized, compulsive, socially precise, controlled, self-disciplined, and self-critical. Individuals can vary in these attributes; however, a person scoring high in perfectionism should demonstrate many of these expressions. Conversely, a person scoring low in perfectionism might be characterized as tolerant of disorder, flexible, impulsive, careless of social rules, and uncontrolled. Perfectionism will be discussed in more detail later in the chapter.

Trait: A relatively stable characteristic or quality that may represent a portion of one's personality; a quality used to explain an individual's behaviour across time and situations.

Contrary to traits, **psychological states** refer to momentary feelings and thoughts that change depending on the situation and time. Take the following example. In a 2013 NHL hockey game, the Buffalo Sabres' John Scott elbowed Louie Eriksson of the Boston Bruins in the head. Scott was suspended seven games by the NHL. Were Scott's actions representative of the trait of aggression, or were they the result of a temporary atypical state? This is a very difficult question. Opinions may differ, but the example highlights questions regarding athletic personality (not to mention the influence of game situations, role expectations for a hockey enforcer, and the nature of the sport).

Psychological states: Momentary feelings and thoughts that change depending on the situation and time.

A common assumption in many trait models of personality is that traits have a normal distribution throughout the population. This means that most people have moderate levels of a specific trait, with only a small percentage having extremely low or extremely high levels of the trait. What makes the prediction of behaviour difficult, however, is that personality is composed of several different traits that combine to influence specific behaviours.

Various trait models have been developed over time, with many having been applied in sport and exercise psychology research. Two example models are Cattell's (1946, 1995) trait personality model and Digman's five factor model (1990). Cattell's model proposes that there are 16 personality factors, called source traits, that capture personality. These factors are warmth, reasoning, dominance, liveliness, social boldness, rule consciousness, sensitivity, vigilance, abstractedness, privateness, apprehension, openness to change, self-reliance, perfectionism, tension, and emotional stability. Cattell's work was a primary source for many sport psychology studies in the 1960s and 1970s.

Digman (1990) suggests that all people can be described in terms of the prevalence of five global factors (nicknamed the "Big Five"): **openness to experience** (opposite of closed-mindedness, curious), **conscientiousness** (achievement–striving, self-discipline), **extraversion** (assertiveness, energetic approach to the world), **agreeableness** (compliance, positive approach toward others), and **neuroticism** (feelings of tension and nervousness). A useful acronym to remember these factors is OCEAN. This model has become a pre-eminent theory in personality psychology. A recent review by Allen and colleagues (2013) suggests that long-term success in sport might be influenced by personality. For example, conscientiousness was positively associated with gymnasts' quality of preparation, whereas emotional stability predicted effective coping during competition (Woodman et al., 2010). Interestingly, conscientiousness is also linked to health behaviours and mortality (Bogg & Roberts, 2004). Researchers in exercise psychology have been exploring the usefulness of the Big Five to help understand exercise behaviour (e.g., Courneya & Hellsten, 1998; Rhodes & Smith, 2006). For example, research in exercise psychology by Rhodes and colleagues (2002) suggests that personality variables may moderate motivational variables in the prediction of exercise behaviour. Individuals higher in extraversion and conscientiousness are more likely to meet their intentions to exercise.

HOW DOES PERSONALITY DEVELOP?

The study of personality has been shaped by various viewpoints, ranging from biological to sociocultural. An in-depth review of the various ways that personality can develop is more appropriately covered in an advanced personality course. However, we will provide a brief review of two different perspectives that capture approaches to studying the development of personality in sport and exercise psychology. These perspectives are humanistic and cognitive–behavioural.

Humanistic Psychology

Humanistic psychology focuses on personal responsibility, human growth, personal striving, and individual dignity. In this approach, each person's experiences, beliefs, values, and perceptions are emphasized in the present moment. One often sees the term *self-actualization* associated with humanistic approaches. Certainly in competitive athletics, athletes are trying to be the best they can be, to reach their potential; this is a quick way to summarize

Openness to experience: Trait including level of curiosity, the opposite of being closed-minded.

Conscientiousness: Trait comprising striving for achievement and self-discipline.

Extraversion: Trait involving level of assertiveness and energetic approach to the world.

Agreeableness: Trait involving general compliance and positive approach toward others.

Neuroticism: Trait comprising feelings of tension and nervousness.

Humanistic psychology: Psychological approach that focuses on personal responsibility, human growth, personal striving, and individual dignity.

self-actualization. Dr. Terry Orlick of the University of Ottawa has been a strong proponent of humanistic approaches to sport psychology consulting. He emphasizes that it is important to understand the needs and desires of athletes, to respect their perceptions and ideas, and to view their athletic participation in the bigger picture of personal growth (Orlick, 1989).

Carl Rogers (1959) was a humanist psychologist who contributed greatly to the field of personality study. Rogers believed that when there is a discrepancy between a person's self-perceptions and what is being experienced, this person might deny what is actually happening. Abraham Maslow (1943) was another of the founding humanist psychologists. He published a hierarchy of needs in a five-tiered triangular model (see Figure 2.1), which suggests that as our basic human needs (lower tiers of the pyramid) are met, we strive to meet higher needs. The base of the triangle represents physiological needs, such as food, water, sleep, and shelter. The second tier represents safety needs, provided in personal and social settings. If physiological and safety needs are met, then the individual moves to the third tier to satisfy social needs: feelings of belonging, connections to others, and the acts of giving and receiving love. The fourth tier of the pyramid is for esteem needs, which can be internal (e.g., self-respect and achievement) or external (e.g., recognition and status). Self-actualization, at the top of the pyramid, refers to the constant striving to make the most of one's special abilities. Olympic champions or individuals who have succeeded in spite of physical or mental disabilities, such as Terry Fox and Rick Hansen, could be considered self-actualized.

Self-actualization: An individual's attempt to be the best he or she can be or a desire to fulfill one's potential.

Cognitive–Behavioural Approach

Early learning theories suggested that behaviour was determined by interactions involving reward and punishment with the environment. The learning perspective suggests that all behaviour is learned through experience, and this perspective discarded notions of disposition, drives, or instincts. B. F. Skinner (1999) argued that behaviour followed by a reward would increase in probability of reoccurrence, whereas behaviour followed by punishment

Figure 2.1 Maslow's hierarchy of needs pyramid

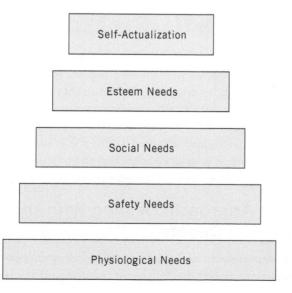

would decrease in probability of reoccurrence. Thus, behavioural patterns such as personality developed primarily because of the reinforcement and punishment of specific behaviour over time. This thinking influenced many sport psychologists during the 1960s and 1970s to develop explanations and interventions based on behavioural learning principles.

Over time, other psychologists argued that learning was very complex and involved such aspects as beliefs, expectancies, and goals. Over the last 40 years, social learning theorists, such as Albert Bandura (1977, 1997), have influenced thinking about how personality may develop. Bandura argued that people's behaviour is highly influenced by their **self-efficacy**, the belief in one's capabilities to achieve a goal or an outcome. Bandura also emphasized the importance of **social learning theory**, which suggests that people are active agents in shaping their behaviours, influenced by their inner drives and environments. Social learning theory involves **observational learning (modelling)**, which occurs through observing, retaining, and at times replicating others' behaviours. Bandura determined that individuals can learn simply by being reinforced or punished for behaviours, as well as by being exposed to, or observing, the behaviours of others. For example, watching the behaviours of an athlete can influence a person's future behaviour. Bandura's work demonstrated that people can and do learn from multiple sources, such as television, magazines, and social interactions. We know that individuals are more likely to adopt behaviour if the behaviour results in valued outcomes. If a person engages in exercise behaviour and the behaviour results in being perceived as more attractive, then an observer is likely to imitate that behaviour in a similar exercise setting.

Social learning theories focus on how situations and individuals reciprocally influence each other. If a situation has an influence on an individual (or vice versa), this influence could subsequently have a lasting effect on the individual's personality. Simply put, the strict learning behaviourists suggest that personality is the sum of all that you do, not of what you think or feel. However, social learning theorists believe that people are active agents in shaping their behaviour, with many factors determining a person's actions. It should not be surprising, then, that there are multiple applications of social learning theory in sport and exercise.

Self-efficacy: Belief in one's capacities to achieve a specific goal or outcome.

Social learning theory: Theory that suggests people are active agents in shaping their behaviours, influenced by their inner drives and environments.

Observational learning (modelling): Learning through observing others' behaviours.

REFLECTIONS 2.2

Bandura argued that, through observing role models, people learn that specific types of behaviour are acceptable. In many advertisements, men and women are presented as working hard to shape their bodies. These images are often associated with socially desirable outcomes such as being happy and being socially and sexually attractive. People may learn that this type of behaviour is expected and valued. Do you think that people can adopt exercise personalities by this process of modelling and imitation? Think of your own behaviour. Who are your role models, and are your sport or exercise behaviours similar to those of your role models?

Interactionist Approach: Dealing with the Person–Situation Debate

An ongoing controversy in the area of human behaviour is the person–situation debate. Some psychologists have argued that behaviour is highly influenced by relatively stable person forces (the person side of the debate), whereas others have argued for the central role of the environment (the situation side of the debate). One major issue in the debate concerns the cross-situational consistency of behaviour. Research in the 1960s suggested that personality was a weak predictor of behaviour in specific situations (Mischel, 1968). Thus, behavioural psychologists argued that "personality traits" were not very useful in understanding behaviour. However, research in the 1970s also indicated that situations were equally inept at predicting behaviour (Epstein, 1979). To make a long story short, the end result of this debate was to recognize that both personal and situational factors impact behaviour in a predictive fashion.

Thus, the interactionist perspective came into vogue in the 1970s in response to perceived limitations of the person-versus-environment approaches. According to Endler and Magnusson's (1976) interactionist approach, it is the situational interplay between the person and the environment that determines the specific behaviours of an individual. Most current research of personality in sport and exercise emphasizes an **interactionist approach**. This acknowledges that each person brings specific dispositions, experiences, and genetic variables to a physical activity situation. The majority of behaviour is best understood by considering the interaction of personality and the environment. This viewpoint has led some personality theorists to argue that personality is best understood in terms of the specific type of context in which a person is embedded (Vernoff, 1983), such as cultural, organizational, and interpersonal realms. This has led some sport and exercise psychology researchers to develop sport specific measures of traits and dispositions.

Instead of searching for stability of behaviour across all situations, interactionist researchers are trying to understand how various traits or dispositions affect behaviour

Interactionist approach: Interplay between a person and the environment that determines specific behaviours of the individual.

Athletes and exercisers can demonstrate different behaviours depending on their personality and the competitive context.

Walter Zerla/Cultura/Getty Images

depending on the sport or exercise context. In this view, we can consider the interplay among the stable characteristics of the person, the goals and motivations of the person, and the opportunities for and appropriateness of specific behaviours in a given context. The expression of personality is most evident during specific situations that are relevant and important to the person (Lindsay et al., 2008). Let's reconsider Ronda from the opening scenario. It is important for her to be successful in sport. She engages in high achievement striving but also is very self-critical. These psychological characteristics in sport are likely to influence her behaviour in many competitive sport situations. However, her specific behaviours will also be influenced by her goals or expectancies that become activated during specific game and training situations (importance of team success), along with the types of behaviours that are deemed appropriate in lacrosse. In many instances, sport and exercise psychology examines both personal and environmental factors with the aim of understanding specific types of behaviour.

| CASE STUDY 2.1 | Aggression in the World Cup: Personality, Environment, or Both |

In the 2014 World Cup, Uruguay forward Luis Suárez bit the shoulder of Italian defender Giorgio Chiellini. The incident occurred during a collision between the two players when the game was still tied, with advancement to the next round of the World Cup on the line. Amazingly, this was the third reported time Suárez had bitten an opponent during a stressful game. Suárez originally denied the biting but later apologized after he was banned for nine international matches and four months by the sport's governing body, the Fédération Internationale de Football Association (FIFA). Were Suárez's actions influenced by personality characteristics such as competitiveness and aggression? How did contextual factors contribute to his behaviour? How might interactional theorists explain his lack of emotional control and subsequent inappropriate behaviour? Do you think he will repeat this behaviour in future stressful competitions?

ETHICAL CONSIDERATIONS OF PERSONALITY MEASUREMENT

There are multiple tools to measure personality characteristics of athletes, but certain questions should be considered when using such tools. For example, under what conditions should a personality test be used? Should these tests be utilized to screen or select athletes? How should the test be selected and then administered? Some tests have been developed and validated for specific populations and contexts, and only qualified professionals should administer and assess scores from certain measurement tools. You would not want a layperson to give you a medical exam and diagnosis, so the same standard should hold for the use of psychological assessments. Students and athletes should also be very cautious about online sport personality tests offered for a fee. There are often a number of ethical problems with these tests.

Ethical principles are typically devised by a specific organization and used by members of that organization to shape professional judgment and behaviour. Integrity and the responsibility to protect the public's well-being are examples of ethical issues. With respect to psychological testing, individuals need to be informed of the nature of tests, how the results will be used, and who will have access to the results. Using tests or

Ethical principles: Guidelines that shape professional judgment and behaviour.

inventories for team selection is frowned upon since there is little evidence to support the validity of such use. Some professional teams have used psychological tests in team selection or to explore an athlete's personality. However, many professional organizations, such as the NFL Players Association, have forbidden the use of such tests with their members. Breaches in confidentiality and the potential financial cost of testing athletes are also considerations when using psychological tests with athletic populations. As well, the person administering the test must be qualified. This person must be competent, meaning that he or she has a broad range of experience administering, scoring, and interpreting the particular test. Licensed psychologists or individuals with specialized training in test administration are usually the best resources for psychological testing and interpretation. For students wanting more information, there are some good discussions of ethics in assessment and testing in sport and exercise psychology (see Etzel et al., 2004).

PERSONALITY RESEARCH IN SPORT AND EXERCISE

Personality research in sport and exercise has a long history. In sport, much of the research in the 1960s and 1970s was directed toward determining if sporting performance could be predicted by personality traits. Associated research also examined if athletes had different personalities than non-athletes, and whether personality could predict the types of sports (team versus individual sports) athletes selected. Overall, the research has indicated that there is little or weak evidence that personality can predict performance in a specific situation, athletes from non-athletes, or the type of sport people will select. Most studies that have found relationships between personality and sport or exercise participation have demonstrated small effects (see Allen et al., 2013; Rhodes, 2006; Vanden Auweele et al., 2001). That is, personality is only a small part of the story. However, the reviews have indicated that personality still has an important place in the study of sport and exercise, as personality interacts with other key psychological and environmental factors to impact various types of behaviours, cognitions, and emotions.

In the following section, we will provide some examples of personality constructs that are important in sport and exercise. We have selected representative research from specific areas to show how specific personality factors might affect sport and exercise behaviour. These research areas are risk taking and sensation seeking, competitiveness, perfectionism, passion, and mental toughness. This will be followed by a specific discussion on whether there is a specific personality associated with exercise.

Risk Taking and Sensation Seeking

Canadian Olympic divers Émilie Heymans and Alexandre Despatie at the 2012 Olympic Games in London might epitomize sensation-seeking athletes. To stand on a three-metre springboard and then execute a complicated routine with somersaults and twists and enter the water flawlessly is a challenging feat. Or, consider Lori-Ann Muenzer, Athens Olympic gold medallist in cycling, who, in that particular race, averaged 56 km/h on a bicycle with no brakes with her feet attached to the pedals. These athletes became experts in sports in which the thrill of height and speed is inherent.

The term **risk taking** involves narrowing the margin of safety, both physically and psychologically (Anshel, 2003). The elements of danger and possibility of bodily harm, injury, and physical loss are inherent in some sports, such as skydiving, race-car driving,

Risk taking: Narrowing of the margin of safety, both physically and psychologically.

Although males generally score higher in sensation seeking, there are many females who compete in high-risk physical activity.

Tyler Olson/Shutterstock

Sensation (stimulus) seeking: Seeking of varied, novel, complex, and intense sensations and experiences, and the willingness to take multiple risks for the sake of such experiences.

and downhill skiing. Do the athletes who participate in these sports have personalities different from those who remain rooted to the ground, participating in what might be considered safer sports? **Sensation (stimulus) seeking** has been defined as "the seeking of varied, novel, complex and intense sensations and experiences, and the willingness to take physical, social, legal and financial risks for the sake of such experiences" (Zuckerman, 1994, p. 27). Malone (1985) characterized stimulus seeking as a motivational factor for athletes not only to participate in sport but also to engage in risk-taking behaviours. Research suggests that stimulus seekers have higher physiological activation levels or chronic levels of high excitation, which are rewarded when they take risks in sport.

Malone (1985) conducted a review of the literature on risk taking in sport and concluded that the perception of danger creates excitement in athletes. Athletes also have a desire to conquer the situation. The personalities of high-risk athletes were examined by Kajtna and colleagues (2004), who compared high-risk athletes (e.g., skydivers, white water kayakers, and ski jumpers) to non-risk athletes (e.g., swimmers, Nordic skiers, and track athletes). Using an instrument associated with the Big Five personality model, they found that high-risk athletes scored highest in emotional stability, conscientiousness, and energy, while openness was highest in non-risk athletes (with no significant differences for agreeableness). Finally, Llewellyn and Sanchez (2008) studied individual differences and risk taking in rock climbers. They found that male climbers and individuals high in self-efficacy were more likely to take increased risks; however, they caution against assuming that all people take risks across domains due to elevated sensation seeking needs (i.e., there may be other reasons individuals take risks).

Other researchers have been interested in particular aspects of sensation seeking such as thrill and adventure seeking, experience seeking, boredom susceptibility, and disinhibition. With respect to gender and age, it would appear that sensation seeking declines with age and that males are more drawn to high-risk sports than are females

(Butkovic & Bratko, 2003). Nevertheless, many women excel in high-risk sport; examples are Canadian mountain bikers Catharine Pendrel and Emily Batty.

Competitiveness

We all know athletes who seem to possess that "killer instinct," those athletes who attack competition and even regular training workouts with high levels of intensity. These athletes want to succeed and are determined to do everything within their power to achieve this goal. Canadian athletes such as Carol Huynh have demonstrated such competitiveness and positive determination. Huynh was the Olympic gold medallist in women's wrestling in the 2008 Beijing Games. Canada's national team coach, Leigh Vierling, described Huynh as dangerous and praised her attacking skills and intensity.

Competitiveness is conceptualized as a desire to engage in and strive for success in sport achievement situations. Gill and Deeter (1988) argued that competitiveness is part of a multidimensional achievement orientation, which is composed of three dimensions: competitiveness (the desire to enter and strive for success in sport competition), win orientation (a focus on interpersonal standards and winning), and goal orientation (a focus on personal standards). These researchers compared non-athletes and athletes and found that athletes scored higher on all three dimensions and that males scored higher than females. Interestingly, Gill and Dzewaltowski (1988) found that high-level athletes enjoy performing successfully and place more emphasis on performance, or personal best goals, than on outcome, or winning goals.

Gould and colleagues (2002) studied competitiveness as a psychological characteristic of Olympic champions. They found competitiveness to be present in Olympic medal winners. Durand-Bush and Salmela (2002), sport researchers from the University of Ottawa, conducted interviews with Canadian World or Olympic medallists. Their research indicated that competitiveness was an important characteristic of these elite athletes. Not surprisingly, the research results across studies are varied with respect to gender differences and competitiveness.

Simply put, competitiveness involves how motivated one is toward achievement. Gender, sport level, and cultural differences have been studied in relation to competitiveness, with varying results. Again, individual differences should not be discounted because people can interpret the notion of competitiveness differently. There are various ways to describe the dispositions related to achieving goals and success in sport.

Competitiveness: Desire to engage in and strive for success.

Perfectionism

Jennifer Jones, 2014 Olympic curling champion, and Carey Price, Olympic gold medallist in ice hockey, are examples of two outstanding Canadian athletes who trained for numerous years to achieve sporting excellence. Success at this elite level would seem to require that athletes (1) set high personal standards for performance, (2) monitor progress toward these standards, (3) be highly organized, and (4) manage the pressure and expectations of significant others, such as parents, coaches, teammates, and partners. But what about athletes who incur psychological or physical costs while striving for high achievement? The danger is that setting unrealistic high standards could lead to stress and anxiety and could subsequently result in maladaptive behaviours. These concerns lead to an increased interest in the area of perfectionism in sport.

Searching the internet for the term *perfectionism* would result in a host of different terminology, including *healthy and unhealthy perfectionism, maladaptive and adaptive perfectionism, personal standard perfectionism, evaluative concerns perfectionism*, and *self-oriented, other-oriented*, and *socially prescribed perfectionism*. These differences occur because scientists have conceptualized perfectionism in various ways. Reading about perfectionism can also be confusing as the word is commonly used in the English language, and common language usage and scientific construct definitions are often not the same. Most scientists view perfectionism as a multidimensional personality disposition or trait that influences thought, emotions, and behaviour (see Gotwals et al., 2012). Perfectionism in sport is often characterized by very high performance standards combined with overly critical self-evaluations (Flett & Hewitt, 2005).

A major controversy in the sport literature is whether perfectionism is associated with positive or negative psychological adjustment. This debate often centres around the two main dimensions of perfectionism: personal standards perfectionism and evaluative concerns perfectionism. **Personal standards perfectionism** (PSP) refers to establishing high personal performance standards and self-oriented achievement striving. **Evaluative concerns perfectionism** (ECP) reflects aspects of the negative social evaluation, including excessive self-criticism, concerns over mistakes, and doubts about actions. Recent systematic reviews (Gotwals et al., 2012; Stoeber, 2011) suggested that ECP is typically associated with poor outcomes and other indicators of maladjustment such as negative emotions, dysfunctional thoughts, and burnout. PSP is more likely to be associated with adaptive functioning in sport, especially if ECP is low.

Sport researchers have studied if the combination of perfectionism dimensions has specific effects on athletes. For example, Dunn and colleagues (2002) from the University of Alberta have suggested that unhealthy perfectionism involves the combination of excessively high PSP (excessive, unrealistic standards of performance) and high ECP (high doubt, high self-criticism, fear of failure). Healthy perfectionism consists of high but realistic goal striving (PSP) but relatively low ECP.

Gaudreau and Thompson (2010) at the University of Ottawa proposed a 2 × 2 model of perfectionism that examines the main effects of ECP and PSP, but also the interactive effects of these dimensions. Thus, the model organizes perfectionism using four distinct subtypes of perfectionism:

1. pure personal standards perfectionism (pure PSP) is captured by low ECP and high PSP
2. mixed perfectionism is composed of both high ECP and high PSP
3. pure evaluative concerns perfectionism (pure ECP) is represented by high ECP and low PSP, and
4. non-perfectionism is captured by low ECP and low PSP.

Hill (2013) provided support for a 2 × 2 model predicting burnout in junior male soccer players. Findings showed that pure PSP was associated with lower levels of total burnout than non-perfectionism and mixed perfectionism. Pure ECP was associated with higher total burnout than non-perfectionism and mixed perfectionism. Crocker and colleagues (2014) examined stress during competitions in Canadian university athletes, and found that pure PSP was associated with higher perceptions of control and challenge, higher perceptions of athletic achievement, and higher positive affect compared to pure

The effects of perfectionism in sport can be complex.

Image100/Cardinal/Corbis

ECP. Pure ECP was also associated with higher perceptions of threat and higher levels of avoidance coping. Overall, the sport literature suggests that it is important to consider the dimensions of perfectionism when predicting athletes' psychological adjustment.

Passion

Many people feel passionate about sport and exercise, but there is evidence that not all types of passion are adaptive. Vallerand and colleagues (2003) developed a dualistic model of passion (DMP) that distinguishes between harmonious passion and obsessive passion. **Harmonious passion** (HP) involves engaging in activity as part of one's identity and for the pleasure of the activity. The activity becomes important, but is in balance (in harmony) with the rest of the person's life. For example, an athlete with HP may play a sport because it is an important part of their sense of identity, allows the attainment or pursuit of personally important outcomes, and is associated with enjoyment for its own sake (also called intrinsic regulation). **Obsessive passion** (OP), on the other hand, involves a more rigid and uncontrolled urge to engage in activities because of external control or feelings of guilt. Thus an athlete who demonstrates OP might be involved in sport to receive awards or enhance social status, or might feel compelled to engage to avoid feelings of guilt. OP can often conflict with other aspects of the person's life such as school, jobs, and interpersonal relationships (Vallerand et al., 2006).

Harmonious passion: Engaging in an activity as part of one's identity and for the pleasure of the activity.

Obsessive passion: Involves a more rigid and uncontrolled urge to engage in activities because of external control or feelings of guilt.

In a review, Vallerand (2010) reported that research has found HP to be associated with positive outcomes, and OP to be associated with negative outcomes. Positive outcomes include positive emotions, positive relationships, the ability to concentrate during an activity, and the experience of the psychological state of flow (the state of complete immersion in an activity for its own sake). OP has been associated with negative emotions, injury, rigid persistence in exercise, burnout, and aggression. There is evidence that HP and OP are also related to components of stress. In research examining how dancers cope with injury, Rip and colleagues (2006) found that OP was associated with dysfunctional coping such as ignoring pain and hiding an injury. Schellenberg, Gaudreau, and Crocker (2013) found that types of passion were related to specific coping strategies and subsequently to burnout and athletic goal attainment. Specifically, HP was positively related to task-oriented coping (such as increasing effort, problem-solving, and logical analysis), which was subsequently related to attaining athletic goals. OP, on the other hand, was positively related to disengagement and avoidance strategies which, in turn, were positively related to burnout and negatively associated with athletic goal attainment.

There is even evidence that sport fans' obsessive passion for sport can be associated with negative outcomes such as missing important events to attend a game, arguments over a team, difficulty concentrating on game day, relationship conflict, and hate emotions (Vallerand, Mageau, et al., 2008). In a study of Canadian hockey fans during the 2012–13 NHL lockout, Schellenberg, Bailis, and Crocker (2013) found that levels of obsessive passion were associated with perceptions of stressfulness and threat, avoidance of information about the lockout, and a number of emotional and disengagement coping strategies such as denial, disengagement, seeking social support, and substance use.

Although types of passion are important in considering specific positive and negative outcomes, research seems to suggest that both HP and OP are positively related to performance. Vallerand, Ntoumanis, and colleagues (2008) found that both HP and OP are positively related to practice and subsequent performance in high school basketball players. Li (2010) found that both HP and OP were positively associated with a subjective measure of sport performance. Overall, the literature suggests that although HP is typically associated with positive outcomes and OP with negative outcomes, both HP and OP are positively associated with performance. It is likely that research in the area of passion will be a hot topic in sport and exercise psychology.

Mental Toughness

One of the most popular terms used by coaches, athletes, and sport commentators to explain how elite performers successfully manage stressful high performance demands is *mental toughness*. Mental toughness has been identified as one of the most critical psychological characteristics for achieving excellence in elite sport (Connaughton, et al., 2011; Crust, 2007; Gucciardi & Gordon, 2011). But what is mental toughness? Jones and colleagues (2002) found that **mental toughness** has been described as a personality trait, an outward expression of an inner commitment, and a collection of psychological attributes and skills. Many researchers in the field of mental toughness believe mental toughness to be a multidimensional construct made up of a number of components that develop over time (Connaughton et al., 2011). Psychological characteristics associated with mental toughness include control, competitiveness, concentration, confidence, commitment, determination, desire, focus, emotional intelligence, resilience, persistence, and optimism (Andersen, 2011; Jones et al., 2002).

Mental toughness:
Personal characteristics that allow individuals to cope with stress and anxiety while remaining focused on competition demands.

Although mental toughness in sport has been popularized in the press through two key applied sport psychology books by Loehr (1986) and Goldberg (1998), knowledge development was hampered by a lack of a clear definition and systematic research until the early 2000s. One of the first models of mental toughness was developed by Clough and colleagues (2002), who identified challenge, control, commitment, and confidence as the critical components of the so-called 4C model. It was proposed that mentally tough people who encounter negative experiences (1) appraise the situation as a *challenge* to be overcome and as part of personal development and growth, (2) believe they have personal *control* over the experiences, (3) have *confidence* they can overcome these experiences, and (4) have a strong *commitment* to achieving personal goals.

In an attempt to better understand athletes' perspectives on mental toughness, Jones et al. (2002) had 10 international athletes (seven men and three women) identify the qualities and characteristics of mental toughness. Using qualitative research methods, they found many similarities with the results of previous research. Mental toughness was a skill that allowed athletes to cope with competition demands better than their opponents. Some athletes thought that this skill was innate, whereas others believed mental toughness could be developed over time with the right competitive experiences. Ten key characteristics in three broad categories were identified: (1) very strong self-confidence and motivation, (2) ability to manage the stress of competition and training, and (3) ability to maintain or regain focus in the face of distraction.

Based on their work, Jones and colleagues (2002) defined mental toughness as:

> Having the natural or developed psychological edge that enables you to: generally cope better than your opponents with the many demands (competition, training, lifestyle) that sport places on a performer. Specifically, be more consistent and better than your opponents in remaining determined, focused, confident, and in control under pressure (p. 209).

Connaughton and colleagues (2008) examined whether mental toughness requires maintenance. After interviewing seven elite performers (representing six sports), these researchers found that demonstrating mental toughness involves the motivational climate (i.e., enjoyment, mastery), various individuals (e.g., peers, coaches), experiences in and outside sport, psychological skills and strategies, and insatiable desire and internalized motives to succeed. These results suggest that athletes need to continue to practise psychological skills within a positively supportive network to enhance their desire and internal motivation.

Many sport psychologists believe that high-level performance requires athletes to be mentally tough.

Keith Christy/123RF

The key characteristics identified by Jones and colleagues are consistent with findings on athletic excellence in Canadian athletes. Orlick and Partington's (1988) early research with Canadian Olympians found that high levels of commitment and the ability to focus and refocus when confronted with distractions were two elements that distinguish more-successful athletes from less-successful athletes. Durand-Bush and Salmela's (2002) interviews with 10 world or Olympic champions revealed that competitiveness, self-confidence, and motivation were important personal characteristics of excellence. They also found that athletes reported the use of psychological skills to help manage stress and allow a strong competition and training focus.

Recent work on mental toughness is focusing on developing strong measurement tools that can capture the key components across various sporting contexts (Gucciardi et al., 2011). There are still many unanswered questions about mental toughness in sport. Currently, the research indicates that mental toughness involves a number of personal characteristics and psychological skills that allow athletes to cope with stress and anxiety while remaining focused on competition demands.

Personality Traits and Exercise: Is There an Exercise Personality?

Are some people more predisposed to exercise simply because of their personality? Think of how two people can be exposed to the same gym environment but walk away with a different perception of the experience. Alternatively, some people seem to be able to juggle and organize several daily tasks, including getting regular exercise, while others struggle. Might this be attributed to personality? Rhodes and Smith (2006) conducted a meta-analysis on 35 studies that examined the correlation between major personality traits and physical activity. Their results suggested that extraversion and conscientiousness had a positive association with exercise, while neuroticism had a negative relationship. These researchers point out, however, that the relationships were small, suggesting that personality has a relatively minor association with exercise and physical activity. Personality traits like openness to experience, agreeableness, and psychoticism did not have a relationship with exercise. There is also evidence that conscientiousness may affect the successful translation of good exercise intentions into behaviour. Researchers have shown that the intention–behaviour relationship is larger for more-conscientious individuals than their less-conscientious counterparts (Rhodes & Dickau, 2013). It has been suggested that the organization and self-discipline marked by those high in conscientiousness translate into these individuals planning and executing exercise behaviours compared to individuals who do not plan as conscientiously.

Industriousness–ambition: Trait comprising aspects of achievement–striving and self-discipline.

Type A personality: Blend of ambition, low patience, competitiveness, high organization, and hostility with agitated behaviour patterns.

As we mentioned earlier in this chapter, the super-traits featured in the five-factor model are very useful for understanding the basic building blocks of personality trait structure, but more specific underlying traits may better describe exercise behaviour. Rhodes and Pfaeffli (2012) reviewed the evidence for several of these more specific traits and their relationship with exercise. They focused on Type A personality, sociability, optimism, activity, and **industriousness–ambition**. While optimism and sociability did not show a consistent relationship with exercise, there was some evidence for Type A personality and considerable evidence for activity. **Type A personality** gained popularity from its association with coronary heart disease (Jenkins, 1976). It is described as a blend of competitiveness and hostility with agitated behaviour and continual movement patterns (Friedman, 1996). In terms of the five factor model, Type A is a blend of high extraversion, high neuroticism, high conscientiousness, and low agreeableness. Rhodes and Pfaeffli reviewed six studies that appraised the relationship between Type A and exercise, and five of the six studies showed some significant positive association between Type A and exercise in the small to medium effect size range. It would seem that exercise could be a natural behaviour to satisfy the hard driving, competitive, and constantly moving Type A individuals. This is interesting because some negative health behaviours, such as smoking and drinking, are also linked to Type A personality.

Extraversion's **activity** trait represents a disposition toward a fast lifestyle, being high energy, talking fast, and keeping busy, as opposed to a more easygoing disposition. People who are high in activity like to be on the move, so it seems conceivable that regular exercise could be a behaviour of choice given its energy demands. Rhodes and Pfaeffli's literature review identified six studies that applied the activity trait with physical activity. In all cases, the trait showed a medium to large effect-size correlation with behaviour. More compelling, the three direct tests that compared the predictive capacity of activity against the super-trait of extraversion showed the superiority of the activity trait. Overall, the results suggest that extraversion's activity trait is a reliable and strong predictor of exercise.

Activity: Trait involving a general tendency for a fast lifestyle, high energy, fast talking, and keeping busy.

The conscientiousness facet of industriousness–ambition has also received attention in four studies (Rhodes & Pfaeffli, 2012). The trait comprises aspects of achievement–striving and self-discipline, and a natural extension of this type of disposition could be regular exercise given its challenge, impact on health and appearance, and self-regulatory barriers to fit it into a daily schedule. Three of the four studies found a significant relationship between this trait and behaviour, suggesting it may be the critical link between conscientiousness and physical activity.

AntonioDiaz/Fotolia

Personality may predict why some people may prefer to exercise in groups.

TARGETING EXERCISE PROGRAMS BASED ON PERSONALITY

The view that personality traits are enduring and stable also suggests that traits are essentially unchangeable. How can the findings of personality research be used to promote exercise if you can't change personality? Rhodes (2006) suggests that this line of research may help to identify at-risk personalities—people who may struggle with adhering to a new exercise program. In turn, these people may need extra intervention in order to succeed. There is very limited research on exercise promotion and personality. Rhodes and Matheson (2008) examined whether a planning intervention among low conscientiousness individuals could help improve physical activity over a control group. The effects were null, but this may have been because of an ineffective intervention, as most participants reported that they did not even complete the planning worksheet. By contrast, Why and colleagues (2010) examined the effects of a walking intervention and found that messages were more effective in increasing walking behaviour among conscientious individuals than their less conscientious counterparts. The results here underscore that personality traits may need targeting to help less conscientious individuals.

Some other research has focused on whether preferences for exercise differ by personality. This line of reasoning suggests that different programs could be targeted to various personalities to create a good match (Rhodes, 2006). Courneya and Hellsten (1998) examined several exercise preferences and their relationship with traits from the five factor model. Of interest, extraverts preferred exercises with company, presumably because of the social element of the experience. Those who were open to experience preferred outdoor activities rather than exercising at home or in a fitness centre.

Personality has also shown different relationships with modes of physical activity. Howard and colleagues (1987) evaluated the relationship of extraversion to several different modes of activity. These researchers found that extraverts were more likely to engage in swimming, aerobic conditioning, dancing, and tennis. In contrast, introverts were more inclined to engage in gardening and home improvement, while no differences were identified for walking, jogging, golf, and cycling. Overall, the relationship between preferences for exercise and personality is interesting, but limited research has actually been performed to assess whether a personality match for exercise is actually effective in improving adherence.

CHAPTER SUMMARY

You were introduced to many ideas in this chapter. From these ideas and concepts, what is known about personality in sport and exercise? Most researchers would probably accept the following key points about personality in sport and exercise today.

Personality is a very complex subject, and numerous theories represent various conceptual approaches. There has been a shift from grand, or global, theories toward more specific key aspects of personality. Investigations and viewpoints are influenced by the particular conceptualizations of personality. Furthermore, researchers are investigating how specific personality factors interact with other psychological factors in specific physical activity contexts.

Measurement of personality requires careful ethical considerations. Personality tests should be administered and interpreted only by individuals with appropriate qualifications. Personality tests generally should not be used to select athletes for teams or positions within teams.

There is little evidence of a distinct athletic personality, or that personality can predict successful athletes. Athletes have varied personality profiles. Personality will interact with the competition environment to influence behaviour, cognitions, and emotions. Exercise is positively associated with extraversion and conscientiousness and negatively associated with neuroticism, but the links are weak.

Aspects of personality can be shaped by experience. This implies that sport can change personality. However, there is little systematic research examining how sport can impact personality traits. This may be due to two reasons. First, to determine the long-term impact of sport on personality would require extensive longitudinal research covering many years. Such research does not exist. Second, many youths enter intensive competitive sport in later adolescence, and bring many years of socialization that have already had a major influence on their personality development. These reasons also hold for how exercise might influence personality changes.

A number of personality characteristics have been shown to be related to thoughts, emotions, and behaviours in sport and exercise. Scientific constructs such as competitiveness, sensation seeking, passion, perfectionism, and mental toughness—along with the Big Five personality traits of openness to experience, conscientiousness, extraversion, agreeableness, and neuroticism—are being actively examined by sport and exercise psychology researchers. These personality characteristics, along with many others, often interact with other less stable psychological variables and environmental factors to influence motivation, stress, emotions, psychological well-being, and sport and exercise participation.

Personality can influence the behaviour of individual athletes and exercisers in various contexts. Predicting the strength of personality's influence on specific behaviours across people or even within a specific person across multiple events is often difficult because of contextual and unstable personal factors. Contextual factors include sociocultural norms, the culture and structure of a given physical activity, role-related behaviour, and the specific dynamics within a particular sport or exercise event. Unstable personal factors might be physiological states, emotional states, psychological strategies, and motivation.

COMMON MYTHS ABOUT PERSONALITY IN SPORT AND EXERCISE REVISITED

MYTH: A distinct elite athlete personality profile exists.
Despite multiple research studies, specific characteristics common to elite athletes remain elusive. There are many individual differences among elite athletes both within and across sports and genders. Some people believe that competitiveness and self-confidence are necessary qualities for elite athletes to rise to the highest levels of sport. This seemingly logical belief has been only partially supported in the literature. This means that some world champions and Olympic gold medallists do not rank themselves high on the self-confidence or competitiveness scales. Furthermore,

some relatively unsuccessful athletes rate themselves high in self-confidence and competitiveness.

> **MYTH:** People choose physical activities and remain in these activities based on their personality.
>
> There is little evidence that engagement in any particular activity is related to a particular personality profile. There is some evidence that individuals scoring high on sensation seeking might be more likely to engage in high-risk activities, but the strength of this relationship is weak. The research evidence suggests that both activity choice and activity maintenance are regulated by a number of complex factors. Personality is only a small piece of this puzzle.

Review Questions

1. How does the definition of personality differ from that of disposition?

2. Is there an exercise personality? How does conscientiousness influence exercise behaviours?

3. Compare and contrast the state perspective with the trait perspective of personality. Why do you think the trait perspective has had a greater impact on research in sport psychology?

4. What is the interactionist approach to personality in sport? Create an example considering one of your favourite athletes.

5. How might personality interact with exercise motivation?

6. What are the advantages of sport-specific tests of personality?

7. Can exercise programs be matched to meet different personalities?

8. Can a personality test tell you which athletes are going to be successful in a specific sport? Why or why not?

9. What are the differences between competitiveness and sensation seeking?

10. What are the differences between evaluative concerns perfectionism and personal standards perfectionism?

11. List the attributes of mental toughness. Try to identify an athlete who has demonstrated all or most of these attributes.

12. What are the differences between obsessive passion and harmonious passion?

Suggested Reading

Allen, M. S., Greenlees, I., & Jones, M. (2013). Personality in sport: a comprehensive review. *International Review of Sport and Exercise Psychology*, 6, 184–208.

Rhodes R. E., & Pfaeffli L. A. (2012). Personality and Physical Activity. In E. O. Acevedo (Ed.), *The Oxford handbook of exercise psychology* (pp. 195–223). New York: Oxford University Press.

Vanden Auweele, Y., De Cuyper, B., Van Mele, V., & Rzewnicki, R. (1993). Elite performance and personality: From description and prediction to diagnosis and intervention. In R. N. Singer, M. Murphey, & L. K. Tenant (Eds.), *Handbook of research in sport psychology* (pp. 257–289). New York: Macmillan.

References

Allen, M. S., Greenlees, I., & Jones, M. (2013). Personality in sport: A comprehensive review. *International Review of Sport and Exercise Psychology, 6*, 184–208.

Andersen, M. B. (2011). Who's mental, who's tough, and who's both? Mutton constructs dressed up like lamb. In D. F. Gucciardi & S. Gordon. (Eds.), *Mental toughness in sport: Developments in theory and research* (pp. 69–88). New York: Routledge.

Anshel, M. H. (2003). *Sport psychology: From theory to practice* (4th ed.). San Francisco: Benjamin Cummings.

Bandura, A. (1977). *Social learning theory.* New York: General Learning Press.

Bandura, A. (1997). *Self-efficacy: The exercise of control.* New York: W. H. Freeman.

Bogg, T., & Roberts, B. W. (2004). Conscientiousness and health-related behaviors: A meta-analysis of the leading behavioral contributors to mortality. *Psychological Bulletin, 130*, 887–919.

Butkovic, A., & Bratko, D. (2003). Generation and sex differences in sensation seeking: Results of the family study. *Perceptual and Motor Skills, 97*, 965–970.

Cattell, R. B. (1946). *Description and measurement of personality.* New York: Harcourt, Brace & World.

Cattell, R. B. (1995). Personality structure and the new fifth edition of the 16PF. *Educational & Psychological Measurement, 55*, 926–937.

Clough, P. J., Earle, K., & Sewell, D. (2002). Mental toughness: The concept and its measurement. In I. Cockerill (Ed.), *Solutions in sport psychology* (pp. 32–43). London: Thomson.

Connaughton, D., Thelwell, R., & Hanton, S. (2011). Mental toughness development: Issues, practical implications and future directions. In D. F. Gucciardi & S. Gordon (Eds.), *Mental toughness in sport: Developments in theory and research* (pp. 135–162). New York: Routledge.

Connaughton, D., Wadey, R., Hanton, S., & Jones, G. G. (2008). The development and maintenance of mental toughness: Perceptions of elite performers. *Journal of Sports Sciences, 26*, 83–95.

Courneya, K. S., & Hellsten, L. A. (1998). Personality correlates of exercise behavior, motives, barriers and preferences: An application of the five-factor model. *Personality and Individual Differences, 24*, 625–633.

Crocker, P. R. E., Gaudreau, P., Mosewich, A. M., & Kljajicb, K. (2014). Perfectionism and the stress process in intercollegiate athletes: Examining the 2 × 2 model of perfectionism in sport competition. *International Journal of Sport Psychology: Special issue on perfectionism in sport 45*, 61–84.

Crust, L. (2007). Mental toughness in sport: A review. *International Journal of Sport and Exercise Psychology, 5*, 270–290.

Digman, J. M. (1990). Personality structure: Emergence of the five-factor model. *Annual Review of Psychology, 41*, 417–440.

Dunn, J. G. H., Causgrove, J., Dunn, J., & Syrotuik, D. G. (2002). Relationship between multidimensional perfectionism and goal orientations in sport. *Journal of Sport & Exercise Psychology, 24*, 376–395.

Durand-Bush, N., & Salmela, J. H. (2002). The development and maintenance of expert athletic performance: Perceptions of World & Olympic Champions. *Journal of Applied Sport Psychology, 14*, 154–171.

Endler, N. S., & Magnusson, D. (1976). Toward an interactional psychology of personality. *Psychological Bulletin, 83*, 956–974.

Epstein, S. (1979). The stability of behaviour: On predicting most of the people much of the time. *Journal of Personality and Social Psychology, 37*, 1097–1126.

Etzel, E., Watson, J. C., II, & Zizzi, S. (2004). A Web-based survey of AAASP members' ethical beliefs and behaviours in the new Millennium. *Journal of Applied Sport Psychology, 16*, 236–250.

Flett, G. L., & Hewitt, P. L. (2005). Perfectionism and maladjustment: An overview of theoretical, definitional, and treatment issues. In G. L. Flett & P. L. Hewitt (Eds.), *Perfectionism: Theory, research, and treatment* (pp. 5–31). Washington, DC: American Psychological Association.

Friedman, M. (1996). *Type A behavior: Its diagnosis and treatment*. New York, Plenum Press.

Gaudreau, P., & Thompson, A. (2010). Testing a 2 × 2 model of dispositional perfectionism. *Personality and Individual Differences, 48*, 532–537.

Gill, D. L., & Deeter, T. E. (1988). Development of the sport orientation questionnaire. *Research Quarterly for Exercise and Sport, 59*, 191–202.

Gill, D. L., & Dzewaltowski, D. A. (1988). Competitive orientations among intercollegiate athletes: Is winning the only thing? *The Sport Psychologist, 2*, 212–221.

Goldberg, A. S. (1998). *Sports slump busting: 10 steps to mental toughness and peak performance*. Champaign, IL: Human Kinetics.

Gotwals, J. K., Stoeber, J., Dunn, J. G. H., & Stoll, O. (2012). Are perfectionistic strivings in sport adaptive? A systematic review of confirmatory, contradictory, and mixed evidence. *Canadian Psychology/Psychologie canadienne, 53*, 263–279.

Gould, D., Dieffenbach, K., & Moffett, A. (2002). Personal characteristics and their development in Olympic champions. *Journal of Applied Sport Psychology, 14*, 172–204.

Gucciardi, D. F., & Gordon, S. (2011). *Mental toughness in sport: Developments in theory and research*. New York: Routledge.

Gucciardi, D. F., Mallett, C. J., Hanrahan, S. J., & Gordon, S. (2011). Measuring mental toughness in sport: Current status and future directions. In D. F. Gucciardi & S. Gordon (Eds.), *Mental toughness in sport: Developments in theory and research* (pp. 108–132). New York: Routledge.

Hill, A. P. (2013). Perfectionism and burnout in junior soccer players: A test of the 2 × 2 model of dispositional perfectionism. *Journal of Sport & Exercise Psychology, 35*, 18–29.

Howard, J. H., Cunningham, D. A., & Rechnitzer, P. A. (1987). Personality and fitness decline in middle-aged men. *International Journal of Sport Psychology, 18*, 100–111.

Jenkins, C. D. (1976). Recent evidence supporting psychological and social risk factors for coronary heart disease. *New England Journal of Medicine, 294*, 1033–1038.

Jones, G., Hanton, S., & Connaughton, D. (2002). What is this thing called mental toughness? An investigation of elite sports performers. *Journal of Applied Sport Psychology, 14*, 205–218.

Kajtna, T., Tuscaronak, M., Baricacute, R., & Burnik, S. (2004). Personality in high-risk sports athletes. *Kinesiology, 36*, 24–35.

Lazarus, R. S., & Folkman, S. (1984). *Stress, appraisal and coping*. New York: Springer.

Li, C-H. (2010). Predicting subjective vitality and performance in sports: The role of passion and achievement goals. *Perceptual and Motor Skills, 110*, 1029–1047.

Lindsay, D. S., Paulhus, D. L., & Nairne, J. (2008). *Psychology: The adaptive mind* (3rd Canadian ed.). Toronto, ON: Nelson.

Llewellyn, D. J., & Sanchez, X. (2008). Individual differences and risk taking in rock climbing. *Psychology of Sport and Exercise, 9*, 413–428.

Loehr, J. E. (1986). *Mental toughness training for sports: Achieving athletic excellence*. Lexington, MA: Stephen Green Press.

Malone, C. (1985). Risk-taking in sport. In L. K. Bunker, R. J. Rotella, & A. S. Reilly (Eds.), *Sport psychology: Psychological considerations in maximizing sport performance* (pp. 264–281). Ithaca, NY: Mouvement.

Maslow, A. H. (1943). A theory of human motivation. *Psychological Review, 50*, 370–396.

Mischel, W. (1968). *Personality and assessment*. New York: Wiley.

Orlick, T. (1989). Reflections on sport psychology consulting with individual and team sport athletes at summer and winter Olympic Games. *The Sport Psychologist, 3*, 358–365.

Orlick, T., & Partington, J. (1988). Mental links to excellence. *The Sport Psychologist, 2*, 105–130.

Rhodes, R. E. (2006). The built-in environment: The role of personality with physical activity. *Exercise and Sport Sciences Reviews, 34*, 83–88.

Rhodes, R. E., Courneya, K. E., & Hayduk, L. A. (2002). Does personality moderate the theory of planned behavior in the exercise domain? *Journal of Sport & Exercise Psychology, 24*, 120–132.

Rhodes R. E., & Dickau, L. (2013). Moderators of the intention–behavior relationship in physical activity: A systematic review. *British Journal of Sports Medicine, 47*, 215–225.

Rhodes, R. E., & Matheson, D. H. (2008). Does personality moderate the effect of implementation intentions on physical activity? *Annals of Behavioral Medicine, 35*, S209.

Rhodes R. E., & Pfaeffli L. A. (2012). Personality and physical activity. In E. O. Acevedo (Ed.), *The Oxford handbook of exercise psychology* (pp. 195–223). New York: Oxford University Press.

Rhodes, R. E., & Smith, N. E. I. (2006). Personality correlates of physical activity: A review and meta-analysis. *British Journal of Sports Medicine, 40*, 958–965.

Rip, B., Fortin, S., & Vallerand, R. J. (2006). The relationship between passion and injury in dance students. *Journal of Dance Medicine & Science, 10*, 14–20.

Rogers, C. R. (1959). A theory of therapy, personality and interpersonal relationships as developed in the client-centered framework. In S. Koch (Ed.), *Psychology: A study of a science: Vol. III. Formulations of the person and the social context* (pp. 184–256). New York: McGraw-Hill.

Schellenberg, B., Gaudreau, P., & Crocker, P. R. E. (2013). Passion and coping: Relationships with changes in burnout and goal attainment in collegiate volleyball players. *Journal of Sport & Exercise Psychology, 35*, 270–280.

Schellenberg, B. J., Bailis, D. S., & Crocker, P. R. E. (2013). Passionate hockey fans: Appraisals of, coping with, and attention paid to the 2012–2013 National Hockey League lockout. *Psychology of Sport and Exercise, 14*, 842–846.

Skinner, B. F. (1999). *The behavior of organisms: An experimental analysis.* New York: D. Appleton Century. (Original work published 1938).

Stoeber, J. (2011). The dual nature of perfectionism in sports: Relationships with emotion, motivation, and performance. *International Review of Sport and Exercise Psychology, 4*, 128–145.

Vallerand, R. J. (2010). On passion for life activities: The dualistic model of passion. In M. P. Zanna (Ed.), *Advances in experimental social psychology* (pp. 97–193). New York, NY: Academic Press.

Vallerand, R. J., Blanchard, C. M., Mageau, G. A., Koestner, R., Ratelle, C., Léonard, M., & Gagné, M. (2003). Les passions de l'âme: On obsessive and harmonious passion. *Journal of Personality and Social Psychology, 85*, 756–767.

Vallerand, R. J., Mageau, G. A., Elliot, A. J., Dumais, A., Demers, M., & Rousseau, F. (2008). Passion and performance attainment in sport. *Psychology of Sport and Exercise, 9*, 373–392.

Vallerand, R. J., Ntoumanis, N., Philippe, F. L., Lavigne, G. L., Carbonneau, N., Bonneville, A., & Maliha, G. (2008). On passion and sports fans: A look at football. *Journal of Sport Sciences, 26*, 1279–1293.

Vallerand, R. J., Rousseau, F. L., Grouzet, F. M. E., Dumais, A., Grenier, S., & Blanchard, C. M. (2006). Passion in sport: A look at determinants and affective experiences. *Journal of Sport and Exercise Psychology, 28*, 454–478.

Vanden Auweele, Y., Nys, K., Rzewnicki, R., & Van Mele, V. (2001). Personality and the athlete. In R. N. Singer, H. A. Hausenblas, & C. M. Janelle (Eds.), *Handbook of sport psychology* (2nd ed., pp. 239–268). New York: Wiley.

Vernoff, J. (1983). Contextual determinants of personality. *Personality and Social Psychology Bulletin, 9*, 331–343.

Why, Y. P., Huang, R. Z., & Sandhu, P. K. (2010). Affective messages increase leisure walking only among conscientious individuals. *Personality and Individual Differences, 48*, 752–756.

Woodman, T., Zourbanos, N., Hardy, L., Beattie, S., & McQuillan, A. (2010). Do performance strategies moderate the relationship between personality and training behaviors? An exploratory study. *Journal of Applied Sport Psychology, 22*, 183–197.

Zuckerman, M. (1994). *Behavioral expressions and biosocial bases of sensation seeking.* New York: Cambridge University Press.

Chapter 3

Motivation and Behavioural Change

Diane E. Mack   Catherine M. Sabiston   Meghan H. McDonough   Philip M. Wilson
David M. Paskevich

Mark Tilly/123RF

Chapter Objectives

After reading this chapter, you should be able to do the following:

1   Define motivation and apply the definition to your own physical activity behaviour.

2   Describe the different approaches to understanding motivation as applied to behavioural change.

3   Apply select theories and models of motivation to your sport or exercise behaviour.

4   Understand how various social influences, including family and peers, affect motivation for physical activity.

Competing at the Olympics is often the pinnacle of an athlete's career, the culmination of hours of relentless training and sacrifice for an opportunity that comes every four years. Considering this, would you voluntarily give up your chance to compete on the Olympic stage so that a teammate could take your place? Canadian long-track speed skater Gilmore Junio did! Junio qualified to represent his country in the 2014 Winter Olympic Games in the 500 metre and 1000 metre events. His teammate and three-time Olympian Denny Morrison did not qualify in his specialty—the 1000 metres. A disappointing performance at the Canadian trials left Morrison named as a reserve. However, with the Olympic 1000 metre race looming, Junio withdrew, effectively gifting his spot to Morrison. Junio wasn't injured! The Canadian coaching staff had raised withdrawal as a possibility to Junio, but the decision was his to make. How did Morrison repay Junio? He skated to a second place finish, earning a silver medal for Morrison and pride for the Canadian long-track speed skating team and country. What about Junio's Olympic experience? He placed out of the medals in the 500 metre event. However, his incredible gesture did not go unnoticed by the Olympic community or the Canadian public. In May 2014, months after the Olympic experience, Junio was awarded a commemorative, crowd-funded medal following a social media campaign in recognition of a gesture that few would likely make.

Most of us reading this story will never know the Olympic experience as competitors. Yet, certain themes may be applicable to our own physical activity history. What have you endured to achieve your physical activity goals? Were you ever asked to sacrifice your personal goals for those of your team? Did your personal motives differ from those of others around you? Did your motives for continuing to train or compete change as a consequence? With reflection, you may develop an understanding of how motivational processes are key to understanding initiation, maintenance, and termination of all forms of physical activity behaviour.

COMMON MYTHS ABOUT MOTIVATION AND BEHAVIOURAL CHANGE

MYTH: Motivation is a trait. You are either a motivated individual or you are not.

MYTH: A single motivational concept such as competence is enough to explain behaviour.

MYTH: Enjoyment is the best motive to help us understand physical activity behaviour.

INTRODUCTION

What motivates you? You have likely considered this question on more than one occasion. Although various definitions can be found in the literature, in general, **motivation** involves the internal processes, such as your needs, thoughts, and emotions, that give your behaviour energy and direction (Reeve, 2009). Energy can help us understand the strength, intensity, and persistence of motivated behaviour. How fiercely do you strive to achieve something you want? How forcefully will you persist to attain it when in a rut or after experiencing failure? This is the essence of energy! Direction gives motivated

Motivation: The internal processes, such as your needs, thoughts, and emotions, that give your behaviour energy and direction.

Table 3.1 Questions to Help Understand Motivation

General Question	Sport and Exercise Examples
Why did you start engaging in sport/exercise?	Who influenced your decision not only to participate in sport, but to choose the sport you competed in? Was it a parent? Was the choice of sport determined in part because you had siblings who were also participating in that sport?
Why did (or do) you persist in sport/exercise?	Was it simply because you enjoyed it? Did you experience personal and competitive success? Did the expectations of others influence your decision to continue?
Why is your behaviour directed toward certain sport/exercise goals rather than others?	Goals impose priorities on our behaviour. How have your goals for your sport/exercise participation changed over time? Do your goals include any of the following: Fun? Personal success? Competitive success? Lean and fit body? Having the identity of an athlete?
Why did your sport/exercise behaviour change?	Are you still a competitive athlete? Do you still compete at a level similar to what you did a few years ago? Or, has your sport participation transformed into behaviour more consistent with regular exercise?
Why does your sport/exercise behaviour vary in intensity?	Were you always fired up to train? Or, were there times when training was tedious or frustrating? How did various external sources (e.g., coaches, family, exercise buddy) influence the intensity of your motivation?
In the short or long term, why did your sport/exercise behaviour stop?	What may have influenced your decision to stop being physically active? Was it loss of interest, injury, no accessibility to facilities, or a change in lifestyle (e.g., parenthood)?

Source: Adapted from Reeve, J. M. (2009). *Understanding motivation and emotion* (5th ed.). Hoboken, NJ: Wiley & Sons.

behaviour purpose and directs us to the achievement (or avoidance) of a specific goal. In simple terms, motivation is the reason why you do the things you do (Reeve, 2009). To help you fully understand what motivates you, consider addressing each of the questions in Table 3.1. You will see how intricate and daunting understanding motivation can be.

With thoughtful consideration of these questions, you will gain an understanding of the complexity of (and ongoing fascination with) the topic of motivation among scholars, athletes, coaches, and those interested in health promotion. The examples provided should make it obvious that personal, cognitive, and environmental factors coexist to influence physical activity behaviour.

APPROACHES TO UNDERSTANDING MOTIVATION FOR BEHAVIOURAL CHANGE

How would you describe yourself? As a person who is highly motivated? As someone who internalizes criticism? As one who is strongly influenced by rewards? Or, does your motivation vary depending on the situation you are in? Relatively stable traits or dispositions can influence behaviour, but what is the influence of the environment? Or how one evaluates the environment? Three approaches are described briefly below to help understand motivation as it applies to behavioural change.

Behavioural Approaches

The **behavioural approach** to understanding motivation focuses on conditioning, or learning from the environment. Founders of behaviourism, including Watson and Skinner, believed that learning from the environment—not personality or free will—determined people's actions. Basic features of behavioural approaches to understanding motivation include operant conditioning, vicarious conditioning, and operant strategies.

In operant conditioning, the athlete/exerciser associates behaviours with consequences that are learned through reinforcement (i.e., any factor that is associated with and increases the frequency of a behaviour) or punishment (i.e., any factor that decreases the probability of a behaviour reoccurring). Positive reinforcement involves any factor (usually a reward) that increases behaviour. Negative reinforcement involves the removal of any factor (usually something aversive like criticism) that increases behaviour. Punishment is any factor that decreases the behaviour.

Vicarious conditioning results from observing others. If, through watching our friends be physically active, we observe changes in their energy and appearance, we may be more likely to engage in physical activity. This of course assumes that the changes we observe in others are valued by us. Children may model the post-scoring celebrations of athletes like Christine Sinclair of Canada's women's soccer team because they respect and admire those athletes.

Operant strategies, such as self-monitoring, are effective for developing and maintaining skills. Self-monitoring involves actually recording your own behaviour in specific situations. A person who wants to increase their exercise behaviour would do well to record the kind of exercise engaged in, frequency, duration, and intensity to increase individual awareness of their habits.

Behavioural approach: An approach to understanding motivated behaviour that focuses on conditioning, or learning from the environment.

Cognitive Approaches

Aaron Beck, the founder of the **cognitive approach**, emphasized the role of thought patterns and cognitive habits as determinants of behaviour. In contrast to the behavioural approach, in the cognitive approach the individual is viewed as an active participant such that it is his or her interpretation of the external environment (as opposed to the external environment itself) that exerts a powerful influence on behaviour. A basic premise is the belief that automatic thought processes (e.g., saying "I messed up again" following a disappointing performance), cognitive errors (e.g., personalization of negative events, all-or-none thinking), and core beliefs (e.g., low self-esteem) can be altered with continued persistence. Alteration of thought patterns is based on recognition and identification of one's systematic thought biases, automatic thoughts, and basic beliefs. Once thought processes have been recognized, they can be challenged and changed to more accurately reflect reality. The cognitive approach teaches people to use rational thought, logic, and empiricism to reform thought patterns. The emphasis on cognition and cognitive evaluation is a key feature of many of the motivational models covered in this chapter.

Cognitive approach: An approach to understanding motivated behaviour that emphasizes the role of thought patterns and cognitive habits.

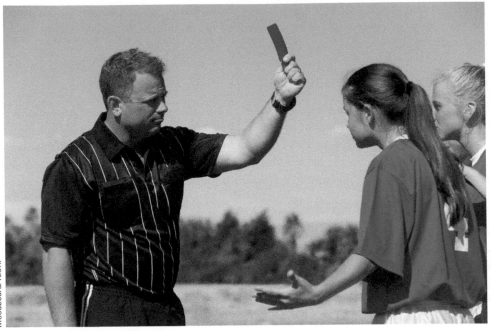

This soccer player was ejected from the game for on-the-field behaviour.

Cognitive–Behavioural Approaches

University of Waterloo professor Donald Meichenbaum is credited with being the founder of **cognitive–behavioural approaches** to changing behaviour. Cognitive–behavioural approaches to understanding motivated behaviour are based on two central tenets: (1) our cognitions influence our emotions and behavior; and (2) our behaviour can affect our thought patterns and emotions. Cognitive–behavioural approaches, including self-monitoring, goal setting, feedback, and decision making, have been found to be effective for increasing self-reported exercise behaviour (Brawley et al., 2000).

Cognitive–behavioural approaches: Approaches to understanding motivated behaviour that outline the reciprocal influence between cognitions and behaviour.

MODELS OF MOTIVATION AND BEHAVIOURAL CHANGE

Campaigns to get people more physically active, such as ParticipACTION (www.participaction.com) and MoveU (http://www.participaction.com/programs-events/programs/moveu/), are based on an understanding of the factors that shape the behavioural decisions people make about their health. The primary application of motivational models has been either to predict physical activity or to describe the thoughts and feelings of people who have engaged in a particular pattern of behaviour (e.g., fluctuations in physical activity). More recently, researchers have used motivational models of behavioural change to develop interventions designed to get people more physically active (e.g., VERB, www.cdc.gov/YouthCampaign; Wheeling Walks, www.wheelingwalks.org) or to help children have a more positive experience in sport (e.g., the PAPA project, www.projectpapa.org). In the next section, we outline various approaches that are thought to motivate people to engage in physical activity and the research supporting these approaches. Implications of this knowledge for the design and implementation of initiatives to promote physical activity behaviour are briefly discussed.

Transtheoretical Model

The transtheoretical model, or TM (Prochaska & DiClemente, 1986), has emerged as a framework to understand how individuals initiate and adopt regular physical activity. The TM proposes that individuals move through a temporal sequence of five stages: (1) **precontemplation** (individuals do not consider exercising in the next six months), (2) **contemplation** (individuals seriously consider beginning exercise in the next six months), (3) **preparation** (individuals have taken small steps toward becoming more physically active), (4) **action** (individuals have begun exercising in the past six months), and (5) **maintenance** (individuals exercise and have done so for more than six months). Stage progress is not necessarily linear, and people can enter the process at any stage and may relapse (or regress) to a previous stage, particularly for behaviours that are difficult to change, such as physical activity.

One simplistic way of understanding the TM is through the intention–behaviour continuum. The first two stages of change (precontemplation and contemplation) are defined by an individual's intent to engage in physical activity (Marcus et al., 1994). In these stages, individuals are not thinking about being physically active at any time in the near future. But to label them as unmotivated may be unfair! Individuals could be in the precontemplation or contemplation stage because they lack knowledge, or perhaps have tried to be physically active in the past but failed to keep it up. Preparation is the stage that combines intentional and behavioural criteria (Prochaska & Marcus, 1994). Individuals in this stage have typically taken some action to get them ready to be active. They could have consulted a physician about physical activity or looked online to find exercise or sport facilities convenient to their home or work. The action and maintenance stages are defined exclusively by behavioural criteria, that is, the length of time performing the behaviour at the appropriate level. For physical activity, this might mean meeting Canada's physical activity guidelines. For more detailed information on the TM, consult www.uri.edu/research/cprc/transtheoretical.htm.

Factors Influencing Stage Progression The TM identifies different factors that influence individuals' decisions to become more physically active at each stage (Prochaska & DiClemente, 1986). The first factor is **self-efficacy**, or the belief in one's capabilities to organize and execute the course of action required to produce specific outcomes. Self-efficacy is lower in earlier stages but increases with stage progression (Plotnikoff et al., 2001). Based on expectancy theory, **decisional balance** is a multi-dimensional set of values linked with advantages and disadvantages of behavioural change. As a general rule, the disadvantages of physical activity outweigh the benefits for those who are inactive, whereas the opposite is true for those who are engaging in physical activity (Prochaska & Velicer, 1997). Finally, **processes of change** reflect strategies that individuals use to progress through the stages (Marcus & Simkin, 1994) and are divided into two dimensions that serve as targets for intervention programs. The first dimension, experiential or cognitive processes, includes strategies used to help an individual modify thought patterns. Typically used in the pre-activity stages, experiential processes include seeking information, reconsidering the consequences of inactivity, expressing feelings about inactivity, and evaluating the consequences of engaging in physical activity for others (e.g., spouse, children). The second dimension, behavioural processes, includes increased social support for behavioural engagement, the use of

Precontemplation: A stage of change in which individuals do not consider exercising in the next six months.

Contemplation: A stage of change in which individuals are considering exercising in the next six months.

Preparation: A stage of change in which individuals have taken small steps toward becoming more physically active.

Action: A stage of change in which individuals have begun exercising in the past six months.

Maintenance: A stage of change in which individuals exercise and have done so for more than six months.

Self-efficacy: Beliefs in one's capabilities to organize and execute the course of action required to produce given attainments.

Decisional balance: Advantages and disadvantages of behavioural change.

Processes of change: Strategies that individuals use to progress through the stages of change.

rewards and reinforcement, and the use of appropriate cues for maintaining behaviour (e.g., running shoes placed by the front door). The use of behavioural processes is greatest in the action and maintenance stages.

Research on the Transtheoretical Model in Exercise Psychology

Demographic and health-related variables have been examined for their association with a particular stage of physical activity. Using population health data from the United States, Garber and colleagues (2008) noted that 58% of people reported being in the maintenance stage. Being female, being of non-Caucasian ethnicity, and having completed a lower level of education were generally associated with lower stages of change. Age, marital status, and current smoking status were not associated with stage of change. In a meta-analytic review of the application of the TM to exercise behaviour, Marshall and Biddle (2001) found that as stage increased, so did reported physical activity.

Canadian researchers have also examined the TM to determine its use in physical activity settings. Here is a sample of this research:

- Gorczynski and colleagues (2010) found that individuals living with mental illness reported greater self-efficacy and perceived benefits to engaging in physical activity if they were in the action or maintenance stage as opposed to other stages of change.

- Health care practitioners, including physiotherapists (Harman et al., 2014) and nurse practitioners (Farrell & Keeping-Burke, 2014), have reported using techniques consistent with TM to help individuals move through the stages of change and become more physically active.

- Plotnikoff and colleagues (2007) found that female employees who received physical activity information targeted for their individual stage of change increased their physical activity compared to those who did not receive stage-matched information.

Applications of the Transtheoretical Model The TM holds considerable appeal at an individual and population health level since it includes guidelines on what information to provide at each stage of behaviour. Indeed, one of the basic principles of stage-matched interventions is to attract the attention of individuals by exposing them to messages that are specific to their motivation to act (see Table 3.2).

REFLECTIONS 3.1

Heather is a healthy 30-year-old woman who recently gave birth to her first child. Before getting married and becoming a mom, Heather regularly participated in sport. However, that was over two years ago. She has recently recognized the need to get active again, not only for her health, but also to be a good role model to her child moving forward. It is clear that Heather has just entered into the contemplation stage of change in the TM. As someone who has knowledge of motivation and the processes of change outlined in the TM and in Table 3.2, what specific strategies would you recommend for Heather? With stage progression, what are the strategies that you would recommend for Heather in the preparation stage?

Table 3.2 Transtheoretical Model: Key Concepts and Physical Activity Examples

Stage	Potential Change Strategies	Examples
Precontemplation	Increase awareness of need for change; personalize information about risks and benefits	Health communication activities Health risk appraisals/health screening Increase perceived susceptibility and perceived severity
Contemplation	Motivate; encourage making specific plans	Incentives Encouragement from significant others Supportive policies (e.g., reduced gym membership fees for those who enroll)
Preparation	Assist with goal development and progression to achieve targeted behaviour	Guidelines to change behaviour Individual and environmental support approach for behaviour change
Action	Assist with feedback, problem solving, social support, and reinforcement	Continued social and environmental support Incentives for reaching behavioural goals Self-efficacy awareness
Maintenance	Assist with coping, reminders, finding alternatives, and avoiding slips/relapses	Relapse-prevention techniques Continued social, environmental, and policy support

Source: Adapted from Table 3, p. 15, in National Cancer Institute, *Theories at a glance: A guide for health promotion practice*, 2nd ed., NIH publication no. 05-3896, September 2005. http://www.healthcentral.com/prostate/pdfs/theory-at-a-glance-a-guide-for-health-promotion-practice

Theory of Planned Behaviour

The **theory of planned behaviour** (TPB) (Ajzen, 1985) is a widely adopted theory that highlights personal and social factors as influences of behaviour. The TPB stipulates that the most proximal determinant of behaviour is **intention**, that is, a person's motivational readiness to perform a behaviour (see Figure 3.1). More simply put, if an overweight man has no intention of exercising three times a week, he is not likely to do so. The intention–behaviour relationship demonstrates temporal fluctuation, with weaker relationships occurring with distal (e.g., Do you intend to exercise in the next three months?) versus proximal measures (e.g., Do you intend to exercise in the next week?) (Symons Downs & Hausenblas, 2005). While not often used in sport research, the TPB is a popular theory in accounting for exercise and leisure time physical activity behaviour.

As a means of understanding the forces influencing behavioural intention, three main antecedents are identified with each reflected in a set of underlying beliefs. The first antecedent, **attitude**, reflects the positive or negative evaluation of engaging in a

Theory of planned behaviour: Personal and social factors influencing intention to engage in a behaviour.

Intention: A person's readiness to perform a behaviour.

Attitude: Positive or negative evaluations of engaging in a behaviour.

Figure 3.1 Theory of planned behaviour

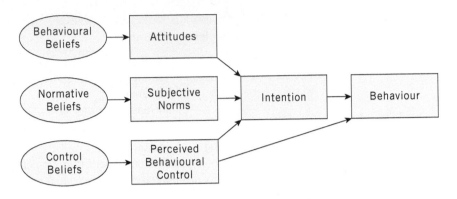

Source: Adapted from "Organizational Behavior and Human Decision Processes" (1991) by Ajzen, Icek. *The Theory of Planned Behavior,* 179–211, Figure 1, p. 182.

Behavioural beliefs: Consideration of the consequences of engaging in a behaviour and evaluation of these consequences.

behaviour. **Behavioural beliefs** linked with attitudes toward physical activity will lead to certain affective (e.g., enjoyable/unenjoyable, fun/not fun) and instrumental (e.g., beneficial/harmful, useful/useless) consequences. In other words, when considering a person's attitude toward physical activity, examining both behavioural belief components is important. Common behavioural beliefs include that exercise enhances fitness and health, improves physical appearance, is fun, and promotes social interactions (Hagger et al., 2001).

Subjective norms: Perceived social pressures to perform a behaviour from personal and/or environmental sources.

The second antecedent of behavioural intention is **subjective norms** reflective of perceived social pressures to perform a behaviour. These pressures may stem from personal (e.g., family, physicians) or environmental (e.g., media) sources. **Normative beliefs** reflect perceptions of significant others, including family, friends, and medical professionals, and the value that they place on physical activity behaviour. To help understand the influence of others on physical activity, it is important to note not only whether those in one's social network like friends and family are active (descriptive norms), but whether one believes that others think it important for them to be active (injunctive norms).

Normative beliefs: Perceptions of the values and importance that significant others place on behavioural engagement.

The third antecedent of behavioural intention, **perceived behavioural control,** reflects the degree to which behaviour is impeded by personal and environmental barriers such as capacity or cost. Perceived behavioural control is thought to indirectly affect behaviour through behavioural intention, as well as being a direct influence on how physically active a person is. **Control beliefs** are perceived barriers (e.g., resources) and facilitators (e.g., opportunities) of engaging in a behaviour. Common control beliefs for exercise include lack of time, lack of energy, age, and weather (Godin et al., 1991). Self-efficacy is also included as a control belief. To fully understand the role of control beliefs, health promoters should look to whether a person believes he or she has the capacity to engage in the behaviour, but also consider the extent to which there is personal control over engagement.

Perceived behavioural control: The extent to which behaviour is volitional.

Control beliefs: Perceived barriers and facilitators of engaging in a behaviour.

Research on the Theory of Planned Behaviour in Sport and Exercise Psychology Reviews of the TPB literature support the relationships described in the model framework. More specifically, attitude and perceived behavioural control

Yes, You Can!

"Yes, you can!" is the official tagline of Team Hoyt. You might ask, "Who is Team Hoyt?" Team Hoyt has two members: Rick Hoyt is a 52-year-old quadriplegic with cerebral palsy; Dick Hoyt is his 72-year-old father. Since birth, Rick has only been able to voluntarily move his head and knees. He is only able to communicate with the assistance of a computer and a voice synthesizer.

Team Hoyt started in 1977 when Rick was 15 and asked his father if they could run a five-mile road race together to benefit a local athlete paralyzed in an accident. At the time, his father was not a runner. And of course, Rick used a wheelchair and was dependent on others to push him. But together they lined up at the start line of the five-mile road race, with Rick in his wheelchair and his father behind him, ready to push him the entire distance. They crossed the finish line, the first of many finish lines, as it turned out. In fact, since that time Team Hoyt has completed over 1000 endurance events, including over 60 marathons, six Ironman triathlons, and a 3375-mile cross-country bike and run, all with the father pushing (or pulling) his son in modified racing equipment. In 2013, a statue of the Hoyts was unveiled near the start line of the Boston Marathon in honour of their achievements. April 21, 2014, is the final running of the Boston Marathon for Team Hoyt.

Why would Dick and Rick Hoyt endure this for almost 40 years? What is their motivation? What has kept Dick Hoyt training even after a heart attack in 2003 and numerous knee surgeries? When Rick and Dick Hoyt crossed the finish line following that first five-mile benefit, Rick communicated "Dad, when I'm running, it feels like I'm not handicapped." And so began their journey.

The question of what truly motivates the Hoyts could only really be answered by them. But perhaps you can show your understanding of the theory of planned behaviour by applying it to the remarkable story of Team Hoyt!

Rick Friedman/Corbis Sports/Corbis

Team Hoyt breaks the tape at the 2006 Boston Marathon.

are correlates of exercise intentions (Hagger et al., 2002). Subjective norms have generally shown weaker (but still meaningful) associations with exercise intentions (Hausenblas et al., 1997). Finally, Godin and Kok (1996) reported that the intention to engage in physical activity explained just over one-third of the individual differences in exercise behaviour.

Given the strong support for the TPB, it is not surprising that researchers in Canada have turned to this theory to develop research studies and explore intervention techniques. Here are just a few examples:

- There is considerable evidence of the ability of the TPB to predict physical activity behaviour in diverse clinical populations, including colorectal, prostate, and breast cancer survivors (Forbes et al., 2014), individuals with spinal cord injuries (Arbour-Nicitopoulos et al., 2010), and individuals showing symptoms of peripheral artery disease (Galea & Bray, 2006).

- In an effort to get colon cancer survivors engaging in physical activity, Jeffrey Vallance and colleagues have developed a physical activity guidebook based on TPB constructs (Vallance et al., 2010). The guidebook contains information for increasing knowledge of the benefits of physical activity (attitudes) and support for physical activity from important others, such as oncologists and family (subjective norms). Finally, various resources linked to increasing physical activity, such as goal setting and diaries (perceived behavioural control), are outlined.

Applications of the Theory of Planned Behaviour Given the influence of intention on behaviour, intervention strategies need to focus on enhancing an individual's intention to exercise. For those wanting to change their exercise behaviour, attitude toward physical activity may be increased by increasing the knowledge of the benefits of exercise and the importance of those benefits. Education can occur at multiple levels, including government health messages, public service announcements, news stories and other media outlets, research findings, and tips posted in fitness facilities. To address changing an individual's intentions to exercise, interventions need to target subjective norms. This can be done by helping individuals identify exercise environments where everyone is physically active or by eliciting the support of others who are physically active.

Finally, target the individual's perceived behavioural control through a range of strategies, such as highlighting coping skills for dealing with barriers. For example, to address the commonly cited barrier of "no time," an individual could do a greater number of shorter bouts of exercise (e.g., 10 minutes three times a day) to fit their schedule as opposed to one long bout (e.g., 30 minutes once a day).

Social Cognitive Theory

Social cognitive theory:
The personal, behavioural, and environmental factors that affect and determine behaviour.

Reciprocal determinism:
Three sets of influences—person, environment, and behaviour—all interact to influence one another.

Social cognitive theory (SCT) (Bandura, 1997) is a widely used theory describing the factors that affect and determine behaviour. SCT is rooted in the belief that individuals are proactively engaged in their own development, with motivation viewed as the product of a dynamic interplay of personal (i.e., expectations, values, beliefs, attitudes), behavioural (i.e., effort, persistence, and choice in sport and exercise), and environmental (i.e., social pressures, motivational climate, physical space, and opportunities) influences (see Figure 3.2). According to Bandura (1986), a central tenet is **reciprocal determinism**, such that these three influences operate to continuously interact with each other.

Figure 3.2 Social cognitive theory

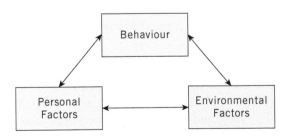

Source: Adapted from *Self-efficacy: The exercise of control* by Bandura, A. New York: W.H. Freeman, 1997, Figure 1.1, p. 6.

How athletes interpret their behaviour informs and alters their environment and the personal factors they possess. Collectively, this in turn informs and alters subsequent behaviours. With the acknowledgement that person, behaviour, and environmental factors influence each other, SCT allows for a complex examination of motivation and many possible avenues for intervention (see Case Study 3.2).

With the idea of reciprocal determinism the over-arching principle guiding SCT, Bandura (1997) identifies many personal, environmental, and behavioural constructs that

---

CASE STUDY 3.2 | **The Saga of Roberto Luongo: Reciprocal Determinism in Action**

Roberto Luongo had been one of the faces of the NHLs Vancouver Canucks since 2006. A two-time Olympic gold medallist and the league's most valuable player in 2007, he enjoyed a playing career linked with incredible highs. But inconsistencies also plagued his time with the Vancouver Canucks, inconsistencies that saw him splitting goaltender duties with Cory Schneider. After signing a long-term contract in 2009 (for 12 years and $64 million), team officials spent months trying to broker a deal that would relieve Vancouver of his contract and see Luongo start fresh with a new team. With a trade out of Vancouver not forthcoming, Luongo even explored the possibility of voiding his contract. Confident that he was leaving the Canuck organization, Luongo put his home on the market and prepared to be traded. But instead, it was Schneider who was traded to the New Jersey Devils, leaving Luongo as the starting goaltender in Vancouver for the 2013–14 season. But his time with the Canuck organization was not to last: one day before the trade deadline, Luongo was traded to the Florida Panthers organization.

Can you apply Roberto Luongo's story to the idea of reciprocal determinism? Let us use self-efficacy as our personal factor. Self-efficacy has been linked to effort, persistence, choice, and behaviour (Bandura, 1997). Luongo's efficacy beliefs likely influenced the effort he put forth on and off the ice (personal-to-behaviour). However, it is also likely that his performance at key moments including playoff games influenced his self-efficacy (behaviour-to-personal). The link between personal and environmental factors in SCT may be linked to changes in club personnel, including general managers, coaching staff, and teammates. His personal self-efficacy may have been influenced by coaching turnover (personal-to-environ-

ment). Similarly, as Luongo adapted to the new demands placed by the coaching staff, his self-efficacy may have increased (environment-to-personal). Finally, as Luongo went from being the clear starting goaltender to sharing duties with Cory Schneider, his behaviour during practice and performance on-ice may have been altered (environment-to-behaviour). With Schneider's subsequent trade and the realization that Luongo would be reinstated as the starting goaltender, his behaviour may have changed to reflect the perceived confidence placed in him from team management and coaching staff (behaviour-to-environment).

Roberto Luongo formerly played hockey for the Vancouver Canucks.

Andy Martin Jr / Alamy

can help us understand motivated behaviour. These constructs embedded within SCT are summarized below:

Observational learning:
Behaviour is learned and acquired by watching the actions and outcomes of others' behaviours.

- **Observational learning:** Individuals learn and acquire behaviour by watching the actions and outcomes of others in their social environment. Observational learning (for example, video analysis) allows the athlete to learn without actually having to do. This may result in enhanced learning while also saving the wear and tear on the body that physically performing the task would demand.

Goals: Ambitions that direct people's behaviour.

- **Goals:** Behaviour is directed by the goals that individuals have. Goals are what people are trying to attain either in the short or long term. Short-term goals, such as intending to exercise for 150 minutes per week, help motivate and guide a person's effort. Long-term goals (e.g., running a mile in six minutes) allow an exerciser to compare current performance to goal attainment.

Outcome expectations:
Behaviour is a function of its expected positive and negative consequences.

- **Outcome expectations:** Behaviour is a function of the expected positive and negative consequences associated with a particular behaviour. An athlete who trains hard will expect to do well in an upcoming competition and/or feel better about herself as a consequence of the increased effort. Outcome expectations serve as a motivational force. The athlete will train hard overtime if she believes it will produce the desired outcomes.

Outcome expectancies:
Expectations that a valuable outcome will follow a given behaviour.

- **Outcome expectancies:** An outcome that is valuable for the individual will follow a given behaviour. When deciding to participate in sport, an individual would consider what might be gained or lost as a consequence. A gain from sport participation might be increasing one's social network. However, sport participation may also be linked with fatigue and missing opportunities to do other interesting things.

Self-regulation: Behaviour is self-directed and is initiated, monitored, and evaluated by the individual in a way that is consistent with accomplishing personal goals.

- **Self-regulation:** Behaviour is self-directed and is initiated, monitored, and evaluated by the individual in a way that is consistent with accomplishing his or her goals. Once a goal is set, an exerciser may regulate her behaviour through self-monitoring (e.g., running log) and make decisions as to whether to adjust her goals based on progress. Once a goal is attained, that same exerciser is likely to reflect on her experience and learn what factors contributed to success and what the impediments were.

Behavioural capacity:
Behaviour is dependent on the individual's knowledge and skills.

- **Behavioural capacity:** Behaviour is dependent on the individual's knowledge and skills for performing that behaviour. The provision of tools such as a pedometer, Canada's Physical Activity Guide, or a child monitoring area in a fitness centre are examples of strategies that can be used to help an exerciser initiate or maintain behaviour.

Self-efficacy: Beliefs in one's capabilities to organize and execute the course of action required to produce given attainments.

- **Self-efficacy:** People need to believe in their capabilities to organize and execute the course of action required to produce given attainments. As we have seen self-efficacy identified both in the TM and TPB, a longer look at this important psychological construct is warranted.

Social Cognitive Theory: A Focus on Self-Efficacy

At the very core of SCT are self-efficacy beliefs, which serve as the foundation for human motivation, well-being, and personal accomplishment. Self-efficacy is a situation-specific form of self-confidence that focuses on the extent to which an individual feels he will be successful in producing a specific outcome given his skills and the situation. For example, self-efficacy

Table 3.3 Sources of Self-Efficacy

Source	Definition	Example
Mastery experience	Past performance success and failures for similar behaviours	A woman who signs up for a marathon training program at Runner's World may derive her self-efficacy beliefs from her previous experiences with walking or jogging.
Vicarious experience	Modelled behaviours associated with development of and change in self-efficacy, including imagery, use and target similarity	A trauma patient at Sunnybrook Health Sciences Centre in Toronto could watch a fellow patient successfully complete a series of exercises in a strength training program.
Social persuasion	Verbal and non-verbal feedback from significant, knowledgeable others	Personal strategies, such as self-talk, may be used to provide persuasion. Feedback from coaches, friends, fitness trainers, and/or medical professionals also serves as a good source.
Physiological and affective states	Physical and emotional cues associated with performance and behaviour	Physical signs and feelings, such as pain or fatigue, may lead an exerciser to doubt her capability to successfully run on the treadmill for 45 minutes. Personal coping strategies (e.g., rhythmic breathing, relaxation, or meditation) may be used to help decrease physiological and affective states.

Source: Adapted from Chapter 3, pp. 79–113, from Bandura, A. (1997). *Self-efficacy: The exercise of control.* New York: W.H. Freeman.

would explain how confident a Canadian athlete is that she will win a gold medal at the upcoming summer Olympic Games in Brazil (specific outcome) given her training and preparation (skills) and the pressure to perform in front of a crowd (the situation). Bandura recognized four main personal and environmental ways to change an individual's self-efficacy beliefs: **mastery experience, vicarious experience, social persuasion,** and **physiological and affective states** (see Table 3.3).

Research Linking Social Cognitive Theory Constructs and Sport and Exercise Behaviour Research in sport and exercise psychology has rarely included all SCT dimensions when examining their influence on behaviour. For those that have examined multiple (but not all) SCT constructs, the included variables have accounted for between 40% and 55% of physical activity behaviour (McAuley et al., 2003). Reviews have supported the unique role of outcome expectancies (Williams et al., 2005), goal setting (Shilts et al., 2004), and self-efficacy in sport and exercise settings (Moritz et al., 2000; Standage & Duda, 2004).

Mastery experience: Past performance success and failure for similar behaviours influence self-efficacy.

Vicarious experience: Modelled behaviours are associated with the development and change in self-efficacy.

Social persuasion: Verbal and nonverbal feedback from significant knowledgeable others.

Physiological and affective states: Physical and emotional cues associated with performance and behaviour.

Canadian researchers have contributed to the sport and exercise literature specific to SCT across diverse study populations. A sample of this research is offered below:

- Plotnikoff and colleagues (2008) demonstrated that SCT variables of self-efficacy, outcome expectations, impediments, and social support predicted over 50% of the individual differences in physical activity behaviour goals across a six-month period in a population-based sample of Canadian diabetics.

- Self-efficacy is linked to behavioural outcomes, such as sport performance (Beauchamp et al., 2002) and exercise adherence (Rodgers & Brawley, 1993). Relational efficacy (the extent to which an individual believes another person, such as a coach or teacher, thinks the individual is capable) has also been associated with physical activity in adolescents and youth (Bourne et al., 2013; Saville et al., 2014).

- Self-regulatory strategies, such as self-monitoring, goal setting, and social support, predicted physical activity in individuals living with a spinal cord injury (Martin Ginis et al., 2011) and walking behaviour in those waiting for total joint replacement surgery (Fiala et al., 2013).

Application of Social Cognitive Theory The reciprocal nature of the determinants in SCT makes it possible for coaches or health promotion specialists to intervene at personal, environmental, or behavioural levels. For example, using SCT as a guiding framework, coaches can work to improve athletes' emotional states and correct faulty self-beliefs (personal factors), improve athletic skills and self-regulatory practices (behaviour), and alter the sporting environment (e.g., more skill-focused training environment as opposed to outcome-focused) that may undermine achievement (environmental factors).

SCT is also used in the health sector. Many health messages and mission statements from Canadian organizations and agencies are founded on SCT-based evidence. For example, the Public Health Agency of Canada's Healthy Living Unit has the following goals:

- To encourage and assist all Canadians to be physically active by increasing their awareness and understanding about the benefits of physical activity and the range of opportunities to be physically active in daily life

- To influence positive social and physical environments and opportunities that facilitate the integration of physical activity into daily life, and that are accessible to, and equitable for, all Canadians

- To establish partnerships with government and non-governmental agencies across levels and sectors, and encourage and support collaborative action and increased capacity to foster physical activity in Canada

In line with these goals, Canadian Physical Activity Guidelines to Healthy Active Living (http://www.csep.ca/english/view.asp?x=804) highlights the benefits of physical activity and informs Canadians of the amount of physical activity they should strive to do and how to get started.[1]

Self-Determination Theory

Self-determination theory: A global theory of human motivation and development.

Self-determination theory (SDT) (Deci & Ryan, 2002) is a global theory of human motivation and development that has evolved from the pioneering work of psychologists

---

[1] Based on Public Health Agency of Canada.

Figure 3.3 Schematic overview of SDT

Source: Adapted from Chapter 1 in Deci, E. L., & Ryan, R. M. (2002). *Handbook of self-determination research.* Rochester, NY: University of Rochester Press.

Edward L. Deci and Richard M. Ryan (http://www.selfdeterminationtheory.org/). The main focus of the SDT framework is the extent to which behaviours such as sport and exercise participation are undertaken volitionally, as opposed to being controlled by some external agent (e.g., coach, physician) or contingency (e.g., rewards, deadlines). SDT asserts that people are naturally endowed with innate tendencies for personal growth and development that flourish when social environments provide optimal conditions. SDT comprises five "mini theories" that collectively inform our understanding of motivated behaviour, cognition, and affective experiences in various life domains (see Figure 3.3).

Much of the early work in SDT focused on *cognitive evaluation theory* (CET), which specifies how various conditions shape (or thwart) the development of intrinsic motivation (Deci & Ryan, 2002). CET identifies the importance of competence and autonomy to intrinsic motivation. Sport and exercise contexts include such aspects as social pressure, negative reinforcement, punishment, and deadlines that undermine intrinsic motivation. Therefore, consideration of the principles of CET may help coaches to understand how certain reward structures (e.g., negative reinforcement) may undermine intrinsic motivation.

Given that not all behaviour is intrinsically motivated (such as exercising for health as opposed to enjoyment, or choosing to eat low instead of high fat foods because you value your health), *organismic integration theory* (OIT) describes the extent to which behaviour is motivated for different extrinsic reasons that represent varying degrees of internalization. Within the SDT framework, extrinsic motives can range from being highly autonomous (also called "self-determined") to being more controlling in nature.

Causality orientations theory (COT) uses personality-level constructs to describe individual differences in the degree to which people are autonomous as opposed to controlled. A person who is more autonomous will orient himself into an environment that holds interest or value to him. A person who is more inclined to a control-orientation behaves as she thinks she should in her environment.

Basic psychological needs theory (BPNT) is the fourth subcomponent of the SDT framework and is concerned with the nature and function of psychological needs for

Amotivation: The absence of motivation.

Intrinsic regulation: Activity is undertaken because it is enjoyable, interesting, stimulating, or self-rewarding.

External regulation: Activities are performed to fulfill an external demand, achieve a reward, or avoid punishment.

Introjected regulation: Activity is engaged in to avoid negative emotions.

Identified regulation: Physical activity participation is linked to important and valued goals.

Integrated regulation: Physical activity participation is consistent with a person's identity.

What might be his motivation?

competence, autonomy, and relatedness in relation to motivation, well-being, and behaviour change. These psychological needs are discussed in more detail later in this section.

Goal contents theory (GCT) was created to answer the question of *what* people strive to attain. Intrinsic goals, such as affiliation, personal growth, and health/fitness, are linked with psychological need satisfaction, enhanced effort, and well-being. Conversely, the pursuit of extrinsic goals, such as appearance, wealth, or social status, thwarts psychological need satisfaction and lowers well-being. We are not so naïve as to suggest that people have no extrinsic goals! However, their negative effects occur when goals such as appearance take precedence over intrinsic goals such as health (Vansteenkiste et al., 2008). Unique to GCT is the suggestion that the beneficial effects of pursuing intrinsic goals occur regardless of attainment (Vansteenkiste et al., 2008). This is in stark contrast to many other theories (e.g., social cognitive theory) that link the benefits of goals to their achievement.

Self-Determination Theory: A Focus on Organismic Integration Theory for Understanding Motivation

OIT deals with the special nature of motivation in contexts such as sport and exercise and the manner in which motivation is developed (or internalized) by athletes and exercisers. Deci and Ryan (2002) propose within the framework of OIT that motivation is best understood as a multidimensional concept that ranges along a continuum of self-determination (see Table 3.4). At one end of the continuum is **amotivation**, or the absence of motivation, which occurs when individuals perceive no connection between their actions and the outcomes to be derived from the activity. At the other end of the motivational continuum is intrinsic regulation. **Intrinsic regulation** is concerned with athletes and exercisers engaging in activity because it is enjoyable, interesting, stimulating, or autotelic (self-rewarding). With intrinsic motivation for an activity comes curiosity, exploration, and the desire to master optimal challenges.

Four different forms of extrinsic motivation (see Table 3.4) are proposed to exist along SDT's motivational continuum (Deci & Ryan, 2002). **External regulation** is the least self-determined form of extrinsic motivation and is concerned with exercising or playing sport to fulfill some external contingency or demand, such as appeasing another person (e.g., trainer, coach) or winning a trophy. The next form of extrinsic motivation is **introjected regulation**. People who engage in exercise or play sport for introjected reasons are attempting to avoid negative emotions (e.g., guilt, shame) or maintain a fragile sense of self-worth. **Identified regulation** occurs when participation in sport or exercise is linked to personally important and valued goals that stem from participation. For example, an athlete might train hard because he realizes how important practice is to improved performance even if he does not like training, or an exerciser may engage in weight training because she realizes that it is an important part of being healthy, which she values. The final extrinsic motive in SDT's motivational continuum is **integrated regulation**, which is concerned with participating in sport or exercise because these activities are symbolic of the person's identity. Extrinsic motives differ from one another on the basis of the degree of self-determination accompanying their development and regulation, with more self-determined motives linked to behavioural persistence and more positive cognitive and affective feelings.

Application of Self-Determination Theory to Behavioural Change

According to Deci and Ryan (2002), all humans have three basic psychological needs that, when authentically fulfilled, facilitate the internalization of behavioural regulation

Table 3.4 Self-Determination Theory's Motivational Continuum

Level of Self-Determination	Behavioural Regulation	Sample Statement
Lower	Amotivation	I don't see why I should have to exercise. I participate in my sport, but I question why I am putting myself through this.
Non-self-determined or controlled	External regulation	I exercise because other people say I should. I participate in my sport because people push me to play.
	Introjected regulation	I feel guilty when I don't exercise. I participate in my sport because I would feel guilty if I quit.
	Identified regulation	It is important to me to exercise regularly. I participate in my sport because the benefits of sport are important to me.
Self-determined or autonomous	Integrated regulation	I consider exercise a fundamental part of who I am. I participate in my sport because it is a part of who I am.
Higher	Intrinsic regulation	I enjoy my exercise sessions. I participate in my sport because I enjoy it.

Source: Adapted from Lonsdale, C., Hodge, K., & Rose, E. A. (2008). The Behavioral Regulation in Sport Questionnaire (BRSQ): Instrument development and initial validity evidence. *Journal of Sport & Exercise Psychology, 30*, 323–355; Markland, D., & Tobin, V. (2004). A modification to the Behavioural Regulation in Exercise Questionnaire to include an assessment of amotivation. *Journal of Sport & Exercise Psychology, 26*, 191–196; Wilson, P. M., et al. (2006). The Psychological Need Satisfaction in Exercise Scale. *Journal of Sport & Exercise Psychology, 28*, 231–251.

via more self-determined than controlled motives. In other words, psychological need satisfaction is integral to facilitating more autonomous as opposed to controlled motives that sustain behaviour. But the satisfaction of psychological needs has also been deemed essential to behaviour change. So, let us take a closer look at BPNT and these "essential nutriments" (Ryan, 1995, p. 410).

Psychological needs are thought of as the qualities of experience universally required by individuals to thrive. **Competence** is concerned with feeling effective and capable when undertaking challenging tasks. **Autonomy** is concerned with feeling ownership over behaviour such that one's actions stem from a sense of perceived choice and internal control. A sense of autonomy can be achieved internally through making personal choices or through external sources (e.g., doctors, coaches) assuming the rationale for the request is fully explained and consequently accepted as their own. The third need, **relatedness**, is concerned with feeling meaningful authentic connections with others in environments such as sport and exercise. According to the SDT model of behaviour change (see Figure 3.4), psychological need satisfaction is essential to facilitating psychological and physical health.

For an individual to initiate and maintain any behaviour change, the person must experience competence to make the change, value the behaviours and endorse their importance, and feel respected and cared for by those around them as they engage in the activity. Closer inspection of Figure 3.4 also demonstrates the importance of

Competence: Feeling effective and capable when undertaking challenging tasks.

Autonomy: The feeling that one has choice and is in control of one's behaviour.

Relatedness: Feeling meaningful connections with others in environments such as exercise.

Figure 3.4 Self-determination theory model of behaviour change

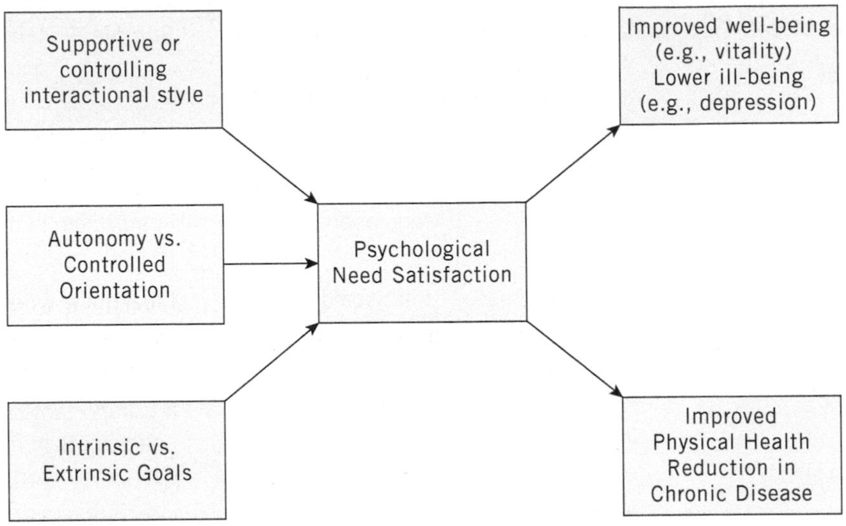

Source: Adapted from Ryan, R. M., Patrick, H., Deci, E. L., & Williams, G. C. (2008). Facilitating health behaviour change and its maintenance. Interventions based on Self-Determination Theory. *The European Health Psychologist, 10*, 2–5; taken from p. 4, Figure 1.

understanding personality-level constructs (i.e., COT) and what a person is trying to achieve (i.e., GCT) when trying to promote psychological need satisfaction. However, there is another feature that is particularly salient. Applications of SDT attempting to initiate and sustain behavioural change in either sport or exercise can focus on the interactional style used by the coach or fitness professional to work with athletes or exercise clients (see Table 3.5). Deci and Ryan contend that a supportive interactional style is characterized by the use of autonomy support, structure, and involvement. This is in direct contrast to a controlling interpersonal style that is typified by telling others what to do and pressuring people to perform in restrictive ways. **Autonomy support** refers to the provision of choices and options and the reduction of pressure, while **structure** concerns the provision of appropriate feedback and the clarification of expectations to be derived from behaviour. **Involvement** refers to the extent to which individuals (such as athletes or exercisers) feel others are genuinely invested in their health and well-being.

Autonomy support: An interpersonal style associated with the provision of choices and options.

Structure: An interpersonal style associated with the provision of feedback and the clarification of expectations.

Involvement: An interpersonal style whereby individuals feel others are invested in their health and well-being.

REFLECTIONS 3.2

Think about your own experiences in a particular sport or exercise context. What types of regulations were driving specific motivated behaviour? Was all your motivated behaviour driven by highly self-determined or even intrinsic motivation? What types of behaviour were regulated more by external regulation? Introjected regulation?

Table 3.5 Developing Supportive Interactional Styles

Supportive Style	Description	Physical Activity Example
Autonomy support	Avoid pressurizing language. Provide a variety of options that athletes/fitness clients can select from.	"Attack the ball this way!" "Here are three exercises that all work the quadriceps muscle group in a comparable fashion. Try them and select one or two that you like the most for your workout."
Structure	Interact with athletes/exercisers with empathy, especially when overcoming barriers. Promote realistic self-referenced standards that provide a path for future individually tailored development.	"I understand how difficult this must be for you at the moment." "If you are able to read your opponent's line of vision and the manner in which he opens his body up on approaching the penalty shot, you might have a better chance of guessing the correct direction to dive."
Involvement	Encourage small group activities that foster a sense of involvement, which are expressed with empathy and authentic concern for the individuals' development.	"I know you are having difficulty striking the ball with your left foot. Using a different foot is never easy at the best of times. Remember the basic mechanics of staying on top of the ball and planting your non-kicking foot. With time and practice, you will be able to clip that ball down the line with either foot. Remember that working on all aspects of our game makes us better players and a stronger team. Don't expect to get this right away."

Research Linking Self-Determination Theory and Sport and Exercise Behaviour Physical activity research has supported Deci and Ryan's arguments given the observations that greater endorsement of self-determined motives is associated with increased effort in physical education classes and intention to be physically active (Standage et al., 2003), exercise intensity (Edmunds et al., 2006), and training outcomes such as burnout in elite rugby athletes (Creswell & Eklund, 2005). According to BPNT (Deci & Ryan, 2002), the fulfillment of each psychological need is most likely to be associated with greater internalization and more self-determined than controlled motivation. This supposition has been supported in various physical activity contexts, including physical education (Standage et al., 2003), exercise (Wilson et al., 2003), and sport (Sarrazin et al., 2002).

Examples of Canadian research examining different components of the SDT framework are summarized below:

■ Identifying with the importance (i.e., identified regulation) and enjoying participating (intrinsic regulation) have consistently been shown to be the strongest predictors of physical activity (Sweet et al., in press; Wilson et al., 2012) in comparison to other motivational regulations in OIT.

■ Changes in more intrinsic goals for physical activity over a six-month period were associated with increased autonomous motives, increased psychological need satisfaction, and increased well-being in a sample of community based exercisers (Gunnell et al., 2014).

■ Autonomy-supportive coaching behaviours were associated with increased psychological need fulfillment of autonomy and relatedness in a sample of Canadian Paralympic athletes (Banack et al., 2011).

Achievement Goal Theory

Inherent within many models of motivational change is the understanding of the role of competence or ability. Competence, whether defined as a psychological need, self-efficacy, or perceived behavioural control, is a central motive for behavioural change. Nicholls (1989) proposed that competence could be described as **achievement goal orientation**, which is a theory of motivation using two disposition-oriented dimensions based on how people define success and failure. **Task goal orientation** involves reference to one's own past performance or knowledge as the origin of competence feelings. For those demonstrating a task goal orientation, sport is perceived as providing opportunities for personal growth and mastery, the belief that success emanates from hard work, learning, and collaboration (Duda & Nicholls, 1992). Conversely, an **ego goal orientation** (sometimes called a performance orientation) is based on comparisons with others and has been associated with the belief that sport provides opportunities for gaining social status and wealth and that success emanates from outperforming others.

Whether a person is in a state of ego involvement or task involvement depends not only on dispositional goal orientation but also on developmental and situational factors (Roberts, 2001). First, young children are unable to distinguish between effort and ability, often equating the two. With cognitive maturity, children by the age of 12 or 13 years are able to differentiate between effort and ability. Second, the perceived motivational climate can change the person's psychological achievement goal state. Motivational climate refers to athletes' perceptions of state achievement goals promoted by coaches (and significant others such as parents). Coaches and instructors can structure the teaching setting to emphasize various state achievement goals (Ames, 1992). Environments that stress interpersonal competition, winning, and social comparison tend to evoke ego involvement. On the other hand, an emphasis on mastery learning, effort, individual improvement, and cooperation tends to evoke task involvement (Roberts, 2001).

Research on the Achievement Goal Theory in Sport and Exercise Psychology Considerable research has examined the correlates of achievement goal orientations in sport and physical education settings and, to a lesser extent, structured exercise contexts. In an attempt to synthesize this research, Biddle and colleagues (2003) conducted a review of existing literature. A pattern was identified that demonstrated some general differences, as well as some similarities, between those individuals with more of a task orientation as opposed to an ego orientation (see Table 3.6).

It may be naïve to think that any individual could be classified as being either just task oriented or just ego oriented as opposed to considering both goal orientations in combination. This approach has been termed *goal profiling*, which reflects the relative tendencies of task and ego involvement in combination with socialization. Goal profiling results in individuals being classified into one of four high–low combinations

---

Achievement goal orientation: A theory of motivation that focuses on differences in how individuals evaluate competence and define success and failure.

Task goal orientation: Focuses on past performance or knowledge as the origin of perceptions of competence.

Ego goal orientation: Performance evaluations are based on comparisons with others as the determinant of competence.

Table 3.6 Characteristics Associated with Task and Ego Orientation

Task Goal Orientation	Ego Goal Orientation
Greater belief that effort results in success	Greater belief that ability results in success
Greater endorsement that sport and physical education is associated with mastery experiences, cooperation, fitness/health, and self-esteem	Greater endorsement that sport is associated with the procurement of social status
Linked to adaptive achievement strategies (e.g., persistence in practice)	No clear relationship with adaptive achievement strategies
Associated with perceptions of competence	Associated with perceptions of competence
Associated with greater positive affect but no relationship with negative affect	No relationship with positive and negative affect
Positively related to sportsmanlike behaviours (e.g., fair play)	Positively related to unsportsmanlike behaviours (e.g., intentional injury)
Effort, intention to continue	Lower effort and less intent to continue

Source: Adapted from Biddle, S., Wang, J., Kavussanu, M., & Spray, C. (2003). Correlates of achievement goal orientations in physical activity: A systematic review of research. *European Journal of Sport Science, 3*, 1–20, pp. 12–13.

(i.e., high-task/high-ego, high-task/low-ego, etc.). Research generally demonstrates that moderate-to-high task orientation in combination with similar levels of ego orientation can be beneficial (Hodge & Petlichkoff, 2000). Consequently, having a high ego orientation is not detrimental when combined with a moderate-to-high task orientation.

Researchers have attempted to expand the ideas in achievement goal theory by examining the role of approach goals and avoidance goals (Elliot & Church, 1997; Roberts, 2001). **Avoidance goals** involve actively moving away from situations, often to avoid failing or demonstrating incompetence. **Approach goals**, in contrast, involve active engagement with the environment. The trichotomous model of achievement motivation involves examining three conditions. The first condition is performance-approach, which is concerned with making good impressions by demonstrating high ability relative to others. The second condition is performance-avoidance, which centres on avoiding making poor impressions, primarily through avoiding situations in which one would perform worse relative to others. Mastery is the third condition, and is the same as described above. Elliot and Conroy (2005) have suggested that a 2 × 2 (ego goal/mastery goal × approach/avoidance) achievement motivation framework could advance understanding in sport and exercise. Three of the four factors are the same in the trichotomous model. In addition, mastery avoidance is characterized by the fear that one may be unable to master a sporting or exercise task or make the best of the situation.

Canadian researchers have examined goal orientations in combination with both individual and situational characteristics:

- Dunn and colleagues (2002) demonstrated that ego orientation was associated with "maladaptive" perfectionism (e.g., concerns over mistakes and parental criticism)

Avoidance goals: An individual is focused on avoiding a negative outcome (e.g., failure).

Approach goals: An individual is focused on approaching a positive outcome (e.g., success).

Table 3.7 Recommendations for Creating a Mastery Motivational Climate

Thoughtfully select tasks that foster and maximize task involvement.

Distribute authority to shift the locus of responsibility to the learner.

Reinforce task-involved behaviours.

Emphasize individual and cooperative goals over competitive goals.

Reinforce personal performance evaluations based on effort and personal improvement.

Use time-management skills to consider the influence of instruction and physical practice on motivation.

Source: Adapted from Ames, C. (1992). Classrooms: Goals, structures, and student motivation. *Journal of Educational Psychology, 84*, (3): 261–271. Copyright © 1992 by the American Psychological Association.

in a sample of high-school football players. Endorsement of a task orientation was associated with a more "adaptive" style of perfectionism (e.g., set high standards for performance but allow for mistakes).

■ The dispositional tendency to adopt task-involved goals was positively related (1) to the perception of a situational emphasis on personal improvement and learning, and (2) to perceived competence in a sample of children with movement difficulties (Causgrove Dunn, 2000). Environments that emphasized performance were associated with ego orientation.

Achievement Goal Theory in Practice The consistent beneficial outcomes associated with a high task orientation (alone or in combination with high ego orientation) have varied instructional implications for physical education teachers and coaches that emphasize an environment conducive to mastery performance. Ames (1992) has outlined six practical recommendations (see Table 3.7). However, relatively little research has evaluated these recommendation in physical activity settings. The research that has been done (e.g., Harwood & Swain, 2002) has shown that environments promoting a task learning style resulted in increased self-regulatory behaviour and more positive cognitions.

MOVING BEYOND INDIVIDUAL APPROACHES TO SOCIAL APPROACHES TO MOTIVATION

Several motivational theories reviewed thus far have highlighted the important role that influential social factors can have on an individual's behaviour. In general, these motivational theories suggest that other people can influence behaviour through modelling, social norms, and providing support for the behaviour. However, the focus has been largely on individual cognitive factors (e.g., perceptions of competence) in physical activity contexts. Features of sport or exercise contexts, including interpersonal relationships, also play an important role in motivation (King et al., 2002) and deserve attention in this chapter. There is considerable evidence that people need frequent, positive contact with

Those around us can have a significant impact on our physical activity!

spotmatik/Shutterstock

others within stable, mutual relationships (Baumeister & Leary, 1995) and that nurturing such relationships could enhance motivation and consequent behavioural factors.

Research Linking Social Influences to Motivational Outcomes and Behaviour

Evidence is mounting that social relationships with significant others, such as coaches, parents, peers, and siblings, play an important role in motivational processes for youth. Coaches who are more autonomy-supportive and less controlling of their athletes, who create a mastery/task motivational climate, and who provide positive performance–contingent feedback promote more adaptive forms of motivation on their teams (Duda, 2001). Peer relationship characteristics, such as being accepted and supported by the peer group, friendship quality, and having physically active peers, predict physical activity behaviour among youth (Smith & McDonough, 2008). Furthermore, there is evidence to suggest that the combination of different aspects of peer relationships and the combined effects of social relationships with parents and peers may have an impact on youth-sport and physical activity motivation (Smith et al., 2006; Ullrich-French & Smith, 2006). Social support for exercise has also been shown to be a contributor to motivation for exercise in research with older adults (Resnick et al., 2002).

Canadian researchers have considered social influence variables on motivation and physical activity participation as part of their program of research:

- Balneaves and colleagues (2014) reported the importance of supportive others for physical activity in a sample of breast cancer survivors. In particular, being active with other breast cancer survivors and having fitness leaders who were supportive and knowledgeable about cancer were key to their involvement.

- Hancock and colleagues (2013) proposed that social agents including coaches, parents, and other athletes influence the phenomenon known as the relative age effect in sport. The relative age effect has been deemed a competitive advantage for athletes. However, these researchers suggest that relative age effects can be explained in part by consideration of these social influences.

- Wilson and Bengoechea (2010) demonstrated that young adults who felt more connected and a greater sense of belongingness to others in their physical activity environment were more likely to report higher levels of well-being than those who did not feel as connected to others.

Social Influence in Practice

Of particular interest to practitioners, we still need to learn more about how to effectively promote and support positive social relationships in sport and exercise that foster adaptive motivation. From a practical perspective, it is key to note that social interactions and relationships matter for the motivation of many participants. Coaches can work to provide positive, contingent, instructional feedback and build more supportive relationships with their athletes. Parents can give their kids the resources to be active, discuss their child's sport experiences with them in a positive, supportive way, and participate in activity themselves. And all those involved can provide the time and feedback to help nurture positive relationships among participants. Parents can promote sport and activity motivation by acting as role models (i.e., participating in activity themselves), helping their children interpret their sport and activity experiences in an adaptive way, and providing physical activity opportunities to their children (Fredricks & Eccles, 2004).

CHAPTER SUMMARY

Few topics are so intricate yet universally applicable as the study of motivation. Motivation was simply described as the reasons why we do the things we do; however, this chapter has outlined the complexity of understanding motivational processes. The main factors that influence our motivation are personal, cognitive (i.e., what we think), and environmental factors. All of these can be targeted through behaviour change strategies outlined in this chapter. The main objective of this chapter was to highlight various theories and models that individuals interested in sport and exercise psychology have devised to understand how motivational processes influence physical activity behaviour. As seen with these theories, understanding motivation as applied to behavioural change is a complex interplay of personal and environmental considerations. For those interested in facilitating behavioural change, various practical strategies were identified. While many approaches to understanding motivation were outlined in this chapter, it is not fully inclusive of all the ways that motivation in physical activity contexts has been studied (e.g., social–ecological models and environmental approaches to understanding physical activity behaviour have gained prominence in the literature in recent years).

COMMON MYTHS ABOUT MOTIVATION AND BEHAVIOURAL CHANGE REVISITED

MYTH: Motivation is a trait. You either are a motivated individual or you are not.

The belief that motivation is a trait stems from the person-centred approach. Certainly, personal characteristics do influence our motivation, but it is naïve to think that there is nothing else that can influence motivated behaviour. In this chapter, you have been introduced to how changing environmental influences, the support of important others, and intervention strategies can be targeted to influence motivational processes.

MYTH: A single motivational concept such as competence is enough to explain behaviour.

Of course, people are motivated to do things in which they feel they are competent. While understanding how competent an individual feels is important for understanding the motivation–behaviour relationship, it should not be considered to the exclusion of other variables. In this chapter, you were introduced to the role of attitudes, social influences, and perceptions of autonomy as important constructs to consider when understanding how to motivate behaviour.

MYTH: Enjoyment is the best motive to help us understand physical activity behaviour.

Engaging in sport and exercise for enjoyment (or intrinsic reasons) is one, but not the only, factor of continued involvement. There are many other reasons why people persist. For example, physical activity has been linked to various health outcomes. Understanding the role of self-determined motives (e.g., valuing the outcome or identity maintenance) may help those interested in health promotion better work with their clients.

Review Questions

1. You have been hired by your university to develop a plan to improve the health of staff and faculty through physical activity. Select a theory that was discussed in this chapter and design an intervention that links theoretical concepts with the target behaviour, namely increased and sustained physical activity participation.

2. Weight loss shows on television have become more common in recent years. Shows like *The Biggest Loser*, *Extreme Weight Loss*, and *Heavy* use health professionals to support individuals' weight loss efforts. Conduct a content analysis of at least one of these televised episodes. Document how the trainers try to motivate those who are attempting to lose weight. Identify the central terms used in the text when discussing motivation.

3. The Centers for Disease Control and Prevention in the United States has developed a communication campaign to encourage people with arthritis to be physically active. The campaign is called "Physical Activity. The Arthritis Pain Reliever." Go to the following link and review the brochure: ftp://ftp.cdc.gov/pub/Publications/arthritis/brochure1_nat_4c. pdf. Can you determine what (if any) motivational approach to behavioural change informed the development of this brochure?

4. Which of the theories of motivation are consistent with the cognitive–behavioural approach to understanding behaviour?

5. Understanding the role of others (e.g., social approaches) in motivation in sport and exercise is valuable. Which theories discussed in this chapter include consideration of the influence of others?

Suggested Reading

Gilson, T. A., & Feltz, D. L. (2012). Self-efficacy and motivation in physical activity and sport: Mediating processes and outcomes. In G. Roberts and D. Treasure (Eds.), *Advances in motivation in sport and exercise* (3rd ed.; pp. 271–298). Champaign, IL: Human Kinetics.

Hagger, M., & Chatzisarantis, N. (2007). *Intrinsic motivation and self-determination in exercise and sport*. Champaign, IL: Human Kinetics.

Williams, D. M., & Marcus, B. H. (2012). Theoretical approaches to exercise promotion. In E. O. Acevedo (Ed.), *The Oxford handbook of exercise psychology* (pp. 241–251). Oxford: Oxford University Press.

References

Ajzen, I. (1985). From intention to actions: A theory of planned behavior. In J. Kuhl, & J. Beckman (Eds.), *Action control: From cognition to behavior* (pp. 11–39). Heidelberg, Germany: Springer.

Ames, C. (1992). Classrooms: goals, structures, and student motivation. *Journal of Educational Psychology, 84*, 261–271.

Arbour-Nicitopoulos, K. P., Martin Ginis, K. A., Wilson, P. M., & SHAPE-SCI Research Group. (2010). Examining the individual and perceived neighbourhood associations of leisure-time physical activity in persons with spinal cord injury. *Annals of Behavioral Medicine, 39*, 192–197. doi: 10.1007/s12160-009-9149-9.

Balneaves, L. G., Van Patten, C., Truant, T. L. O., Kelly, M. T., Neil, S. E., & Campbell, K. L. (2014). Breast cancer survivors' perspectives on a weight loss and physical activity lifestyle intervention. Support Cancer Care. doi 10.1007/s00520-014-2185-4.

Banack, H. R., Sabiston, C. M., & Bloom, G. A. (2011). Coach autonomy support, basic need satisfaction and intrinsic motivation in Paralympic athletes. *Research Quarterly for Exercise & Sport, 82*, 722–730.

Bandura, A. (1986). *Social foundations of thought and action: A Social Cognitive Theory*. Englewood Cliffs, NJ: Prentice Hall.

Bandura, A. (1997). *Self-efficacy: The exercise of control*. New York: W. H. Freeman.

Baumeister, R. F., & Leary, M. R. (1995). The need to belong: Desire for interpersonal attachments as a fundamental human motivation. *Psychological Bulletin, 117*, 497–529.

Beauchamp, M. R., Bray, S. R., & Albinson, J. G. (2002). Pre-competition imagery, self-efficacy and performance in collegiate golfers. *Journal of Sports Sciences, 20*, 697–705.

Biddle, S., Wang, J., Kavussanu, M., & Spray, C. (2003). Correlates of achievement goal orientations in physical activity: A systematic review of research. *European Journal of Sport Science, 3*, 1–20.

Bourne, J., Liu, Y., Shields, C., Jackson, B., Zumbo, B., & Beauchamp M. (2013). The relationship between transformational teaching and adolescent physical activity: The mediating roles of personal and relational efficacy beliefs. *Journal of Health Psychology*, doi: 10.1177/1359105313500096.

Brawley, L. R., Rejeski, W. J., & Lutes, L. (2000). A group-mediated cognitive behavioral intervention for increasing adherence to physical activity in older adults. *Journal of Applied Behavior Research, 5*, 47–65.

Causgrove Dunn, J. (2000). Goal orientations, perceptions of the motivational climate, and perceived competence of children with movement difficulties. *Adapted Physical Activity Quarterly, 17*, 1–19.

Creswell, S. L., & Eklund, R. C. (2005). Motivation and burnout among top amateur rugby players. *Medicine & Science in Sports & Exercise, 37*, 469–477.

Deci, E. L., & Ryan, R. M. (2002). *Handbook of self-determination research*. Rochester, NY: University of Rochester Press.

Duda, J. L. (2001). Achievement goal research in sport: Pushing the boundaries and clarifying some misunderstandings. In G. C. Roberts (Ed.), *Advances in motivation in sport and exercise* (pp. 129–182). Champaign, IL: Human Kinetics.

Duda, J. L., & Nicholls, J. (1992). Dimensions of achievement motivation in schoolwork and sport. *Journal of Educational Psychology, 84*, 290–299.

Dunn, J., Causgrove Dunn, J., & Sytotuik, D. (2002). Relationship between multidimensional perfectionism and goal orientations in sport. *Journal of Sport & Exercise Psychology, 24*, 376–395.

Edmunds, J., Ntoumanis, N., & Duda, J. L. (2006). A test of self-determination theory in exercise domain. *Journal of Applied Social Psychology, 36*, 2240–2265.

Elliot, A. J., & Church, M. A. (1997). A hierarchical model of approach and avoidance achievement motivation. *Journal of Personality and Social Psychology, 72*, 218–232.

Elliot, A. J., & Conroy, D. E. (2005). Beyond the dichotomous model of achievement goals in sport and exercise psychology. *Sport and Exercise Reviews, 1*, 17–25.

Farrell, T. C., & Keeping-Burke, L. (2014). The primary prevention of cardiovascular disease: Nurse practitioners using behaviour modification strategies. *Canadian Journal of Cardiovascular Nursing, 24*, 8–15.

Fiala, B., Rhodes, R. E., Blanchard, C., & Anderson, J. (2013). Using social–cognitive constructs to predict preoperative exercise before total joint replacement. *Rehabilitation Psychology, 58*, 137–147. doi: 10.1037/a0032196.

Forbes, C., Blanchard, C., Mummery, K. W., & Courneya, K. (2014). A comparison of physical activity correlates across breast, prostate and colorectal cancer survivors in Nova Scotia, Canada. *Supportive Care in Cancer, 22*, 891–903.

Fredricks, J. A., & Eccles, J. S. (2004). Parental influences on youth involvement in sports. In M. R. Weiss (Ed.), *Developmental sport and exercise psychology: A lifespan perspective* (pp. 145–164). Morgantown, WV: Fitness Information Technology.

Galea, M. N., & Bray, S. R. (2006). Predicting walking intentions and exercise in individuals with intermittent claudication: An application of the theory of planned behavior. *Rehabilitation Psychology, 51*, 299–305.

Garber, C. E., Allsworth, J. E., Marcus, B. H., Hesser, J., & Lapane, K. L. (2008). Correlates of the stages of change for physical activity in a population survey. *American Journal of Public Health, 98*, 897–904.

Godin, G., & Kok, G. (1996). The theory of planned behavior: A review of its applications to health-related behaviors. *American Journal of Health Promotion, 11*, 87–98.

Godin, G., Valois, P., Jobin, J., & Ross, A. (1991). Prediction of intention to exercise of individuals who have suffered from coronary heart disease. *Journal of Clinical Psychology, 47*, 762–772.

Gorczynski, P., Faulkner, G., Greening, S., & Cohen, T. (2010). Exploring the construct validity of the transtheoretical model to structure physical activity interventions for individuals with serious mental illness. *Psychiatric Rehabilitation Journal, 34*, 61–64. doi: 10.2975/34.1.2010.61.64.

Gunnell, K. E., Crocker, P. R. E., Mack, D. E., Wilson, P. M., & Zumbo, B. D. (2014). Goal contents, motivation, psychological need satisfaction, well-being and physical activity: A test of self-determination theory over six months. *Psychology of Sport and Exercise, 15*, 19–29.

Hagger, M. S., Chatzisarantis, N. L. D., & Biddle, S. J. H. (2001). The influence of self-efficacy and past behaviour on the physical activity intentions of young people. *Journal of Sport Sciences, 19*, 711–725.

Hagger, M. S., Chatzisarantis, N. L. D., & Biddle, S. J. H. (2002). A meta-analytic review of the theories of reasoned action and planned behavior in physical activity: Predictive validity and the contribution of additional variables. *Journal of Sport & Exercise Psychology, 24,* 3–32.

Hancock, D. J., Adler, A. L., & Côté, J. (2013). A proposed theoretical model to explain related age effects in sport. *European Journal of Sport Science, 13,* 630–637.

Harman, K., Macrae, M., Vallis, M., & Bassett, R. (2014). Working with people to make changes: A behavioural change approach used in chronic low back pain rehabilitation. *Physiotherapy Canada, 66,* 82–90. doi: 10.3138/ptc.2012-56BC.

Harwood, C. G., & Swain, A. B. (2002). The development and activation of achievement goals in tennis: II. *The Sport Psychologist, 16,*111–138.

Hausenblas, H. A., Carron, A. V., & Mack, D. E. (1997). The theory of reasoned action and planned behavior in exercise behavior: A meta-analysis. *Journal of Sport & Exercise Psychology, 19,* 36–51.

Hodge, K., & Petlichkoff, L. M. (2000). Goal "profiles" in sport: A cluster analysis. *Journal of Sport & Exercise Psychology, 22,* 256–272.

King, A. C., Stokols, D., Talen, E., & Brassington, G. S. (2002). Theoretical approaches to the promotion of physical activity: Forging a transdisciplinary paradigm. *American Journal of Preventive Medicine, 23,* 15–25.

Lonsdale, C., Hodge, K., & Rose, E. A. (2008). The Behavioral Regulation in Sport Questionnaire (BRSQ): Instrument development and initial validity evidence. *Journal of Sport & Exercise Psychology, 30,* 323–355.

Marcus, B. H., Eaton, C. A., Rossi, J. S., & Harlow, L. L. (1994). Self-efficacy, decision making, and stages of change: An integrative model of physical exercise. *Journal of Applied Social Psychology, 24,* 489–508.

Marcus, B. H., & Simkin, L. R. (1994). The transtheoretical model: Application to exercise. In R. K. Dishman (Ed.), *Advances in exercise adherence* (pp. 1400–1444). Champaign IL: Human Kinetics.

Markland, D., & Tobin, V. (2004). A modification to the Behavioural Regulation in Exercise Questionnaire to include an assessment of amotivation. *Journal of Sport & Exercise Psychology, 26,* 191–196.

Marshall, S. J., & Biddle, S. J. H. (2001). The transtheoretical model of behavior change: A meta-analysis of applications to physical activity and exercise. *Annals of Behavioral Medicine, 234,* 229–246.

Martin Ginis, K. A., Latimer, A. E., Arbour-Nicitpoloulos, K. P., Bassett, R. L., Wolfe, D. L., & Hanna, S. E. (2011). Determinants of physical activity among people with spinal cord injury. A test of social cognitive theory. *Annals of Behavioral Medicine, 41,* 127–33. doi: 10.1007/s12160-011-9278-9.

McAuley, E., Jerome, G. J., Elavsky, S., Marquez, D. X., & Ramsey, S. N. (2003). Predicting long-term maintenance of physical activity in older adults. *Preventive Medicine, 37,* 110–118.

Moritz, S. E., Feltz, D. L., Fahrbach, K. R., & Mack, D. E. (2000). The relation of self-efficacy measures to sport performance: A meta-analytic review. *Research Quarterly for Exercise & Sport, 71,* 280–300.

Nicholls, J. G. (1989). *The competitive ethos and democratic education.* Cambridge, MA: Harvard University Press.

Plotnikoff, R. C., Brunet, S., Courneya, K. S., Spence, J. C., Birkett, N. J., Marcus, B., & Whiteley, J. (2007). The efficacy of stage-matched and standard public health materials for promoting physical activity in the workplace: The Physical Activity Workplace Study (PAWS). *American Journal of Health Promotion, 21,* 501–509.

Plotnikoff, R. C., Hotz, S. B., Birkett, N. J., & Courneya, K. S. (2001). Exercise and the Transtheoretical Model: A longitudinal test of a population sample. *Preventive Medicine, 33,* 441–452.

Plotnikoff, R. C., Lippke, S., Courneya, K. S., Birkett, N., & Sigal, R. J. (2008). Physical activity and social cognitive theory: A test in a population sample of adults with Type 1 or Type 2 diabetes. *Applied Psychology: An International Review, 57*, 628–643.

Prochaska, J. O., & DiClemente, C. C. (1986). Towards a comprehensive model of change. In W. R. Miller & N. Heather (Eds.), *Treating addictive behaviours: Processes of change*. New York: Plenum Press.

Prochaska, J. O., & Marcus, B. H. (1994). The transtheoretical model: Applications to exercise. In R. K. Dishman (Ed.), *Advances in exercise adherence* (pp. 161–180). Champaign, IL: Human Kinetics.

Prochaska, J. O., & Velicer, W. F. (1997). The transtheoretical model of health behavior change. *American Journal of Health Promotion, 12*, 11–12.

Reeve, J. M. (2009). *Understanding motivation and emotion* (5th ed.). Hoboken, NJ: Wiley & Sons.

Resnick, B., Orwig, D., Magaziner, J., & Wynne, C. (2002). The effect of social support on exercise behavior in older adults. *Clinical Nursing Research, 11*, 52–70.

Roberts, G. C. (2001). Understanding the dynamics of motivation in physical activity: The influence of achievement goals on motivational processes. In G. C. Roberts (Ed.), *Advances in motivation in sport and exercise* (pp. 1–50). Champaign, IL: Human Kinetics.

Rodgers, W. M., & Brawley, L. R. (1993). Using both self-efficacy theory and the theory of planned behavior to discriminate adherers and dropouts from structured programs. *Journal of Applied Sport Psychology, 5*, 195–206.

Ryan, R. M. (1995). Psychological needs and the facilitation of integrative processes. *Journal of Personality, 63*, 397–427.

Ryan, R. M., Patrick, H., Deci, E. L., & Williams, G. C. (2008). Facilitating health behaviour change and its maintenance: Interventions based on Self-Determination Theory. *The European Psychologist, 10*, 2–5.

Sarrazin, P., Vallerand, R. J., Guillet, E., Pelletier, L. G., & Cury, F. (2002). Motivation and dropout in female handballers: A 21-month prospective study. *European Journal of Social Psychology, 32*, 395–418.

Saville, P. D., Bray, S. R., Martin Ginis, K. A., Cairney, J., Marinoff-Shupe, D., & Pettit, A. (2014). Sources of self-efficacy and coach/instructor behaviors underlying relation inferred self-efficacy (RISE) in recreational youth sport. *Journal of Sport & Exercise Psychology, 36*, 146–56. doi: 10.1123/jsep.2013-0144.

Shilts, M. K., Horowitz, M., & Townsend, M. (2004). Goal setting as a strategy for dietary and physical activity behavior change: A review. *American Journal of Health Promotion, 19*, 81–93.

Smith, A. L., & McDonough, M. H. (2008). Peers. In A. L. Smith, & S. J. H. Biddle (Eds.), *Youth physical activity and sedentary behavior: Challenges and solutions* (pp. 295–320). Champaign, IL: Human Kinetics.

Smith, A. L., Ullrich-French, S., Walker, E., & Hurley, K. S. (2006). Peer relationship profiles and motivation in youth sport. *Journal of Sport & Exercise Psychology, 28*, 362–382.

Standage, M., & Duda, J. L. (2004). Motivation processes among older adults in sport and exercise settings. In M. R. Weiss (Ed.), *Developmental sport and exercise psychology: A lifespan perspective* (pp. 357–381). Morgantown, WV: Fitness Information Technology.

Standage, M., Duda, J. L., & Ntoumanis, N. (2003). A model of contextual motivation in physical education: Using constructs and tenets from self-determination and goal perspective theories to predict leisure-time exercise intentions. *Journal of Educational Psychology, 95*, 97–110.

Sweet, S. N., Fortier, M. S., & Blanchard, C. M. (in press). Investigating motivational regulations and physical activity over 25 weeks. *Journal of Physical Activity & Health*.

Symons Downs, D., & Hausenblas, H. A. (2005). The theories of reasoned action and planned behavior applied to exercise: A meta-analytic update. *Journal of Physical Activity & Health, 2*, 76–97.

Ullrich-French, S., & Smith, A. L. (2006). Perceptions of relationships with parents and peers in youth sport: Independent and combined prediction of motivational outcomes. *Psychology of Sport & Exercise, 7*, 193–214.

Vallance, J., Lesniak, S. L., Belanger, L. J., & Courneya, K. S. (2010). Development and assessment of a physical activity guidebook for the Colon Health and Life-Long Exercise Change (CHALLENGE) Trial. *Journal of Physical Activity & Health, 7*, 794–801.

Vansteenkiste, M., Timmermans, T., Lens, W., Soenens, B., & Van den Broeck, A. (2008). Does extrinsic goal framing enhance extrinsic goal oriented individuals' learning and performance? An experimental test of the match-perspective vs. self-determination theory. *Journal of Educational Psychology, 100*, 387–397.

Williams, D. M., Anderson, E. S., & Winett, R. A. (2005). A review of the outcome expectancy construct in physical activity research. *Annals of Behavioral Medicine, 29*, 70–79.

Wilson, P. M., & Bengoechea, E. G. (2010). The relatedness to others in physical activity scale: Evidence for structural and criterion validity. *Journal of Applied Biobehavioral Research, 15*, 61–87.

Wilson, P. M, Rodgers, W. M, Blanchard, C. M., & Gessell, J. (2003). The relationship between psychological needs, self-determined motivation, exercise attitudes, and physical fitness. *Journal of Applied Social Psychology, 33*, 2373–2392.

Wilson, P. M., Rogers, W. T., Rodgers, W. M., & Wild, T. C. (2006). The psychological needs satisfaction in exercise scale. *Journal of Sport & Exercise Psychology, 28*, 231–251.

Wilson, P. M., Sabiston, C. M., Mack, D. E., & Blanchard, C. M. (2012). On the nature and function of scoring protocols used in exercise motivation research: An empirical study of the behavioral regulation in exercise questionnaire. *Psychology of Sport and Exercise, 13*, 614–622.

Chapter 4

Stress, Emotion, and Coping in Sport and Exercise

Katherine A. Tamminen   Kent C. Kowalski   Patrick Gaudreau

Wavebreakmedia/Shutterstock

Chapter Objectives

After reading this chapter, you should be able to do the following:

1   Define stress and coping.

2   Describe the relationship between stress and emotions and illustrate the role of cognitive appraisal and coping in the stress process.

3   Describe typical sources of stress in sport and exercise.

4   Describe neurophysiological effects of stress and emotions.

5   Describe interventions to promote coping in sport and exercise.

Jessica, a 20-year-old undergraduate student in Kinesiology, finds that competing as a swimmer has become a stressful experience. She grew up swimming competitively in club teams and has competed provincially and nationally, but now that she is swimming with the university team, she is experiencing more and more stress associated with her sport.

Jessica finds many things about her sport to be stressful which never seemed to bother her in the past. She used to be able to handle the intense training schedule, but now she is having trouble getting up early to go to practice, sitting through classes, and swimming again in the evenings several days of the week. She barely passed her midterm exams and she is concerned that she may not pass all her classes this term. She has started to feel tired all the time, she is becoming more and more irritated with her friends and teammates, and she has gotten sick with a cold several times this year. After having shoulder surgery last year to deal with her chronic tendonitis, she has mostly recovered to her previous training levels, but Jessica gained some weight while she was recovering. She has been thinking to herself lately, "I look fatter in my swimsuits than I used to" and "I wish I looked as good in my suit as the other girls on the team." She has started to hate walking out on the pool deck before her races because she thinks everyone will be watching her and judging her, especially people who come to competitions from her old swim club and who will know she's gained weight. She finds it increasingly harder to focus on her pre-race plan because she is thinking about her appearance and her race times have started to suffer as a result. She is starting to worry about her chances of qualifying for the CIS Championships in February.

Jessica has tried a number of strategies to try to deal with her stress. She has tried to manage her time better, but she finds that she has had to cut out the time she spends socializing with her friends in order to be able to sleep, study, and train. She had been working three shifts a week at her job, but she asked her boss to be cut back to one shift a week. Unfortunately, this means that she has less money to spend, and she is already in debt because of the cost of rent, books, tuition, gas, and food. She tried to talk casually about her stress with some of her teammates, but she has trouble talking to them about her feelings and being overwhelmed. Even though they all joke about how much stress they all have, she feels pressured to keep up with her teammates and not complain. Her other friends don't really understand the kinds of pressures she is feeling, and their advice to "spend less time training" and "just sleep more" is not very helpful, especially since she feels the need to train more in order to lose weight and improve her race times.

What does it mean when someone says that he or she is stressed? And what role does coping play in the experience of stress? Jessica's story provides us with some insight into the complexity of stress and the coping process. There are many facets to a person's life that are often competing with one another and making the management of stress extremely challenging. Such is the case with Jessica and her attempts to manage her stress in a way that does not create other academic or financial stress and does not jeopardize her spot on the team. In addition, seldom are situations easily resolved. Often they play out over a long period of time and significantly strain people's personal resources as they attempt to cope.

In this chapter, the concepts of stress, emotion, and coping in sport and exercise will be explored, with special emphasis on Canadian perspectives and examples. Although definitions of stress and coping have changed over time, one constant theme is that these two concepts are intimately linked.

> ## COMMON MYTHS ABOUT STRESS, EMOTION, AND COPING IN SPORT AND EXERCISE
>
> **MYTH:** Elite sport is inherently stressful.
>
> **MYTH:** Exercise always reduces stress.
>
> **MYTH:** Dropping out of sport or stopping exercise is an ineffective coping strategy.

INTRODUCTION

Any conversation about stress, emotion, and coping in sport and exercise needs to begin by addressing the basic question: What is stress? Is competing in mixed martial arts stressful? Is it stressful to have to work out in a gym where you think everyone else is better than you? Is it stressful as a student to find the time to read a chapter about stress in sport and exercise in order to prepare for an academic class? The answer to these questions is a resounding "It depends." As we will discuss, situations are not inherently stressful. Instead, people play an active role in how they interpret the situations they face, and it is often very difficult to predict when stress will occur.

THE CONCEPT OF STRESS

The term *stress* is frequently used in day-to-day conversations, but it has proven very challenging to define. Carpenter (1992) described how the concept of stress most often has one of two meanings. First, stress can represent what is often referred to as the **stress response**, which consists of our physiological, cognitive, affective, and behavioural reactions when we are faced with heavy demands. A few minutes before attempting a difficult alpine ski trail, it is not rare that athletes and even amateur skiers will experience increased blood pressure, heart rate, and perspiration. This stress response serves a very adaptive function for human beings, and athletes are more able to get pumped up or get the adrenaline flowing to achieve peak performance when there is sympathetic nervous system arousal (Aldwin, 2000).

A second approach to defining stress is to consider it as a process that links situational demands with an individual's reactions to the outcomes of that experience. This second definition is consistent with cognitive-based models of stress that emphasize the dynamic interrelationships between the environment and people's thoughts and behaviours in that environment. This approach suggests that what is stressful for one person might not be stressful for another, or even for that same person at another time (Aldwin, 2000). Hence, **stress** can be defined as an experience that is produced through a person–situation relationship that is perceived as taxing or exceeding the person's resources.

Stressors, on the other hand, are the external events, forces, and situations that have the potential to be interpreted as stressful. Examples of potential stressors include playing in

Stress response: Physiological, cognitive, affective, and behavioural reactions when we are faced with heavy demands.

Stress: An experience that is produced through a person–situation relationship that is perceived as taxing or exceeding the person's resources.

Stressors: External events, forces, and situations that have the potential to be interpreted as stressful.

Each athlete interprets stressors in a personal way. The things that may be stressful for one athlete may not be stressful for others

a championship match, getting injured, being yelled at by a coach or personal trainer, losing national team funding, or facing increased fitness club fees. The implication is that each athlete or exerciser might interpret situations and stressors in unique ways. For example, in the opening vignette, walking out on the pool deck in her swimsuit was a stressful experience for Jessica, however for another athlete it might not be seen as stressful at all.

STRESS, EMOTIONS, AND APPRAISAL

The concept of stress is closely tied to the concept of emotion (Lazarus, 1999). Richard Lazarus was a prominent researcher in the area of stress, emotion, and coping, and he suggested that the concepts of stress and emotion are indeed similar; however, he also said that we can learn more about what an individual is experiencing, what a situation means to an individual, and how the individual is likely to respond by looking at the specific emotion that is experienced rather than by looking at the more general concept of stress. As Lazarus (2000) stated, "each discrete emotion is said to tell a different story about a person's adaptational struggle" (p. 232). For example, when we say we are stressed about something, we could be referring to feelings of guilt, anxiety, or fear. The concept of stress is much simpler than the concept of emotion and, as a result, tells us much less information about the person's experience and what is happening in the situation.

Lazarus (1991) identified 15 core emotions in his cognitive–motivational–relational theory (CMRT), including both positive and negative emotions. His list of emotions includes anger, anxiety, fright, guilt, shame, sadness, envy, jealousy, happiness, pride, relief, hope, love, gratitude, and compassion. To date, sport and exercise psychology research has been dominated by studies on anxiety, with some research attention paid to other discrete negative and positive emotions, especially in sports performance research. Lazarus's CMRT is useful to us because each of the emotions he identified has a core relational theme that describes the essence of the relationship between a person and their environment. For example, the core relational theme for anxiety is that the person is facing an uncertain, existential threat; suggesting that when someone is experiencing anxiety, they are not sure of what will happen, when it will happen, or even what can be done about it (Lazarus, 2000). If we look at competitive anxiety in sport, much of the stress that is experienced is simply the result of not knowing what the outcome will be (e.g., "Will I perform well today?"). We can also see an example of this in the vignette, where much of Jessica's anxiety stems from being unsure of what others think of her.

However, both stress and emotions depend a lot on what is at stake for the individual and his or her perceived resources to cope with the situation (Lazarus, 1999). Clearly, knowing about a specific emotion does tell us more about what is going on in someone's life than just knowing that they are stressed. In the past, research on stress has been centred primarily on athletes' appraisals of negative emotions. However, it is becoming increasingly clear that positive emotions also play a very important role in the stress process (Folkman, 2008).

From the definitions of stress and emotion, we can see that someone's interpretation of a situation, or their cognitive appraisal, is a key concept. Lazarus (1999) suggested that there are two components of the appraisal process: primary and secondary appraisals. **Primary appraisal** is an evaluation of what is at stake for a person in a situation. Whether or not something is at stake depends on whether the occurrence is relevant to that person's goals and whether the situation is interpreted as having the potential to be beneficial or harmful. Alternatively, **secondary appraisal** is an evaluation of what can be done in the situation, which depends on an individual's available resources, level of perceived control, and expectations regarding what is likely to occur in the future. While these evaluations about stressors are called primary and secondary appraisals, they are thought to be equally important and to occur very rapidly and at the same time.

The cognitive appraisal process (primary and secondary appraisals) can result in various kinds of psychological experiences, including feelings of harm/loss, threat, and challenge. **Harm/loss appraisal** refers to an evaluation of a situation in which psychological damage has already been done and the loss is irrevocable. For example, a university athlete might experience stress over not being able to play Canadian interuniversity sport as a result of using up her five years of eligibility. Her personal identity might be strongly tied to being a member of the university team, and once that identity was taken away she could really struggle in her search for a new identity. A **threat appraisal** refers to the anticipation of harm that might occur or is likely to occur. An example would be a weightlifter who is fearful of maximum weight testing because of the potential for injury or the embarrassment of lifting a maximum weight that is lighter than it is for everyone else. **Challenge appraisal**, on the other hand, stems from the interpretation that although there are obstacles in the way, they can be overcome. For example, University of Victoria field hockey player Ali Lee said before the championship game, "My body is so tired, I've got bruises and scratches and everything. But your mind can carry you a lot further than your body can. We have a great rivalry with UBC and U of A, so doesn't matter who, I just want to win this the right way and earn this" (Lowther, 2008). Although the outcome of the game was unknown to her at that time, it is clear that she was looking forward to the opportunities that the final game presented. Recent progress has been made in delineating the conditions typically associated with threat and challenge appraisals. According to the theory of challenge and threat states in athletes (Jones et al., 2009), challenge appraisals are likely to be experi-

Primary appraisal: An evaluation of what is at stake for a person in a situation.

Secondary appraisal: An evaluation of what can be done in the situation, which depends on an individual's available resources, level of perceived control, and expectations regarding what is likely to occur in the future.

Harm/loss appraisal: An evaluation of a situation in which psychological damage has already been done and the loss is irrevocable.

Threat appraisal: An appraisal of a situation where an individual anticipates harm might occur or is likely to occur.

Challenge appraisal: An appraisal that although there are obstacles in the way, they can be overcome.

enced when someone has a high level of self-efficacy, perceived control, and an approach achievement goal orientation. Identifying the antecedents of different cognitive appraisals appears like a promising theoretical development to help sport psychologists in creating the conditions to foster challenge rather than threat states in competitive athletes.

TYPES OF STRESSORS IN SPORT CONTEXTS

Three distinctions have been made in the literature in an attempt to categorize types of sport stressors, including chronic versus acute stressors, expected versus unexpected stressors, and competitive versus non-competitive stressors. The first distinction is between chronic and acute stressors. **Chronic stressors** occur over a long period of time, such as in the case of ongoing harassment, relationship issues, and chronic pain; **acute stressors** occur within a shorter period of time, and their onset is much more sudden. Anshel and his colleagues have identified a number of acute stressors that athletes might face, such as making a physical or mental error, being criticized or reprimanded by a coach, sustaining pain or injury, receiving a bad call by an official, and being distracted by a crowd, to name a few (Anshel et al., 2001). If acute stressors are not managed effectively, they can lead to long-term chronic stress and burnout.

The second distinction is between expected and unexpected stressors (Dugdale et al., 2002). **Expected stressors** are those that an athlete plans or prepares for, whereas **unexpected stressors** are not anticipated. Dugdale and colleagues asked athletes representing New Zealand at the 1998 Commonwealth Games to identify the most stressful experience they had prior to or during the Games. They found that more than two-thirds of athletes who reported stress said that the source of stress was unexpected. Examples given by the athletes

Chronic stressors: Stressors that occur over a long period of time.

Acute stressors: Stressors that occur within a short period of time, and their onset is much more sudden.

Expected stressors: Stressors that an athlete plans or prepares for.

Unexpected stressors: Stressors that are not anticipated and cannot be prepared for.

Joannie Rochette cries after her short program skate at the 2010 Vancouver Olympics. Her mother died suddenly two days before the competition; Joannie won a bronze medal.

Hannibal Hanschke/epa/Corbis Wire/Corbis

included things like transportation delays, poor food, and bad refereeing decisions. One of the study's most interesting findings was that the athletes perceived the unexpected stressors to be more threatening than the expected ones, suggesting that athletes might experience more or less stress depending on the type of stressor they face. Surely the extreme distress that Canadian figure skater Joannie Rochette experienced after the sudden death of her mother two days before the 2010 Olympics was due to the unexpectedness of her mother's heart attack: "That's just not something I could have planned" (Olympic News Service, 2014).

The third distinction is between competitive and non-competitive stressors (Dugdale et al., 2002). **Competitive stressors** would be those that are experienced prior to, during, or immediately following competition; they include making mistakes in competition, injury, poor officiating, and expectations from others. **Non-competitive stressors** would be those that are related to sport but not directly part of an actual competitive performance; they include having to deal with the media, travel, rehabilitation, and team meetings. For example, Noblet and Gifford (2002) interviewed professional Australian Football League players who reported competitive stressors like poor technique, constant pressure to perform, and high performance expectations, as well as a wide variety of non-competitive stressors, including job insecurity, long training sessions, lack of feedback, constant public scrutiny, and difficulty balancing sport with other commitments.

Some non-competitive stressors can be classified as different types of **organizational stressors**, which are "environmental demands (i.e., stimuli) associated primarily and directly with the organization within which an individual is operating" (Fletcher et al., 2006, p. 329). Fletcher and colleagues (2012) identified five categories of organizational stressors reported by professional and non-professional athletes, including: (1) factors intrinsic to the sport (e.g., the training and competition load, travel and accommodation arrangements, risk of injury), (2) roles in the sport organization (e.g., being team captain, responsibilities associated with being an athlete in a particular team or organization), (3) sport relationships and interpersonal demands (e.g., lack of support, poor leadership, abrasive personalities), (4) athletic career and performance development issues (e.g., income and funding stressors, concerns about position on the team, meeting career goals), and (5) the organizational structure and climate of the sport (e.g., cultural and political environment of the sport organization, coaching/management style, media problems).

Competitive stressors: Stressors that are experienced prior to, during, or immediately following competition.

Non-competitive stressors: Stressors that are related to sport but are not directly part of an actual competitive performance.

Organizational stressors: Environmental demands associated primarily and directly with the organization within which an individual is operating.

REFLECTIONS 4.1

Think back to your own experiences in sport. What different types of acute/chronic, expected/unexpected, and competitive/non-competitive stressors have you witnessed as an athlete, a spectator, or a coach?

Canadian researchers studied sources of stress for members of a women's national soccer team during preparations for the 1999 women's soccer World Cup finals (Holt & Hogg, 2002). They found four main categories of stressors: coaches' communication, demands of international soccer, competitive stressors, and distractions. Examples of coaches' communication stressors included a negative, punitive coach–player interaction during training and negative, excessive feedback during the games. Demands of international soccer that they identified revolved primarily around the need to adjust to the technical and tactical demands of a fast-paced international game. A number of competitive stressors were identified by the players, including having pre-game anxiety, having high expectations of going to the Olympics, making mistakes, coming off the bench, fearing being cut from the team, and getting evaluations of their performance. The two primary distractions that the athletes mentioned were the fatigue from practising twice a day during camp and opponent aggression. As Holt and Hogg identified, one of the unique aspects of their study was finding that many of the stressors were related to the social interactions that are part of a team environment.

As you can see, different stressors in sport can be classified according to the types of stressors described earlier. These different ways of sorting or classifying stressors represent different attempts by researchers to try to understand the wide variety of stressors that athletes may experience in their sports.

NEUROPHYSIOLOGICAL EFFECTS OF STRESS AND EMOTIONS

When emotions are triggered, a number of physiological processes are activated automatically to prepare the individual for action (Ekman & Cordaro, 2011). These processes include increased or decreased breathing and rate of respiration, heart rate and cardiovascular activity, body temperature, and skin conductance (sweat gland activity and the moisture level of the skin). Emotions and the body's stress response are characterized by an endocrine response in which hormones such as cortisol and epinephrine (also known as adrenaline) are released throughout the body. Different emotions are associated with specific cognitive activity in the brain—for example, positive emotions appear to be associated with greater cognitive activity in the left prefrontal cortical areas of the brain, whereas negative emotions are associated with greater activity in the right prefrontal cortical areas of the brain (Harmon-Jones et al., 2010). Some emotions also seem to have distinctive facial expressions—happiness and joy are typically characterized by raised eyebrows, widening the eyes, and smiling, while anger is typically characterized by furrowed eyebrows, frowning, and lips pressed firmly. While some emotions appear to have distinctive patterns of physiological responses, sometimes the same pattern of physiological activation is associated with different emotions; for example, emotions such as anxiety, fear, anger, happiness and joy are all associated with increases in heart rate, respiratory rate, and skin conductance (Kreibig, 2010).

Cognitive appraisals of threat and challenge appear to have their own differentiated cardiovascular pattern (Blascovich & Tomaka, 1996). Episodes of threat and challenge both signify that something is at stake. Therefore, both are accompanied by increased heart rate, stroke volume, and global cardiac output. Yet, threat and challenge appraisals are experienced differently at both the phenomenological and cardiovascular levels. Episodes of challenge appear to produce more increases in ventricular contractility while simultaneously generating a decline in vascular resistance. These cardiovascular processes enable more blood to circulate in a more efficient manner. Threat appraisals also increase cardiac output (heart rate, stroke volume) but do not result in decreases in vascular resistance. The increased stroke volume during threat appraisals faces serious roadblocks and the relative absence of reduction in vascular resistance could explain why perceived stress is often associated with increased blood pressure. Cardiovascular indicators of challenge states measured while athletes are talking about their sport have been used to predict sport performance of competitive athletes. The results of a study conducted with 34 baseball and softball players have shown that pre-season cardiovascular challenge states predicted significantly better offensive baseball/softball performance during the season (Blascovich et al., 2004).

The relationships among emotions, physiological processes, and performance are complex. While the physiological processes enacted in the body can contribute to attentional narrowing and muscle tension, athletes can often learn to regulate their emotions and still perform successfully despite feeling anxious, scared, or joyful. Some athletes also report that they perceive negative emotions, such as anger, to be facilitative for performance. For example, a study by Robazza and Bortoli (2007) asked rugby players whether they thought anger was facilitative or debilitative for sport performance. The athletes generally reported that they felt they could control their angry feelings and consequently perceived anger to be advantageous for performance. This study is supported by evidence that anger was associated with gross muscular peak performance during a laboratory task (Woodman et al., 2009) and may be beneficial for activities that involve gross-motor movements such as lifting, jumping, or striking (Parfitt et al., 1995).

COPING

When people are faced with stress and emotion, how they attempt to manage their experiences can take many forms. First, if athletes or exercisers believe that they can effectively manage a situation, they will be less likely to experience stress and negative emotions. Second, how people attempt to cope with stress can affect both the level and the type of stress and emotion experienced. Essentially, if stress and emotions are experienced when an important objective is harmed/lost, threatened, or challenged, then coping is the way in which the person attempts to deal with that psychological stress and emotion (Lazarus, 1999).

Thus, an important question to start with is, "What is coping?" A formal definition was provided by Lazarus (1991), who described **coping** as "cognitive and behavioural efforts to manage specific external or internal demands (and conflicts between them) that are appraised as taxing or exceeding the resources of the person" (p. 112). Thus, coping efforts include both *thoughts and actions*. For example, if Jessica from the opening vignette tries to convince herself that nobody is judging her body in her swimsuit, it is as much an effort to cope as is increasing her training to lose weight. However, it is important also to point out that coping has to be an effortful process to manage stress. If athletes engage in behaviours that are routine but that still help them to avoid problems, such as going to practice every day, those behaviours are not coping per se. Instead, routine behaviours are probably more appropriately viewed as **management skills** that help prevent stress from happening in the first place, although these management skills themselves might have developed initially as ways of coping (Aldwin, 2000). For example, a soccer player might have initially begun wearing shin pads to cope with the frustration of being kicked; however, once that behaviour (wearing shin pads) becomes relatively automatic, it is better considered a management skill rather than actual coping. Most importantly, efforts to manage stress are *constantly changing* and are extremely complex. People's coping will depend, in part, on available coping resources and expectations. Their coping efforts then

Coping: Cognitive and behavioural efforts to manage specific external or internal demands (and conflicts between them) that are appraised as taxing or exceeding the resources of the person.

Management skills: Behaviours that are routine but that still help the individual to avoid problems and help prevent stress from happening in the first place.

must shift as the effectiveness of particular strategies becomes evident and as the situation itself changes over time. Sometimes the changing dynamics of a situation can require all the effort that one can muster, such as Simon Whitfield's inspirational finishing sprint in the triathlon at the 2008 Beijing Olympics. Following his silver medal performance, he reported to CBC, "I kind of fought my way on there, and I thought there's no time like the present. I tried to make it a battle of pure willpower. I gave it everything I had" (Canada's Whitfield, 2008).

Coping Strategies: Micro- and Macro-Analytic Approaches

A micro-analytic approach to coping involves organizing the specific coping strategies that people engage in to cope with stress—essentially trying to describe what athletes actually do to cope with stress. An example of a micro-analytic approach to coping is provided by Crocker and Graham (1995). They assessed the coping strategies of competitive athletes who had used the strategies in a recent athletic situation—either a practice or a game—in which there was a performance difficulty or pressure to perform. The strategies Crocker and Graham assessed were active coping, seeking social support for instrumental or emotional reasons, planning, denial, humour, behavioural disengagement, venting of emotion, and suppression of competing activities. These categories group together different ways that athletes deal with stress in sport. The micro-analytic approach provides a rich description of the diversified coping repertoire of athletes and exercisers. A limitation with this approach is that it tells us little about *why* athletes are using those particular strategies or what goals they are trying to accomplish via their coping efforts.

A macro-analytic approach to coping considers the goals or functions of the strategies used by athletes or exercisers. A macro-analytic approach attempts to classify various coping strategies (e.g., seeking support, planning, increasing effort, avoidance) based on their *function*, essentially to understand why athletes use particular coping strategies to deal with stress.

An important macro-level distinction often made in the literature is between problem-focused coping and emotion-focused coping. **Problem-focused coping** refers to efforts that help people change the actual situation in some way, such as seeking information to improve performance, changing tactics to beat an opponent, confronting a teammate to resolve a conflict, or adopting new equipment to gain a competitive advantage. For example, a few years ago many Canadian speed skaters began using clap skates (skates with a spring-loaded hinge under the heel) in order to deal more effectively with the stress of increasing performance demands in world-class speed skating. Catriona Le May Doan, a Canadian speed skater who won a number of Olympic medals and broke many world records, had to adjust to clap skates during her career and had a great deal of success with them. **Emotion-focused coping**, on the other hand, is an attempt to change the way a situation is attended to or interpreted—to deal with the emotions that arise during the situation. An example of emotion-focused coping would be an exerciser who tries to convince himself that no one in the gym actually cares about the exercises he is doing or how he is doing them. Finally, a third distinct type of coping often included in the literature is **avoidance coping**, in which athletes attempt to remove themselves from the stressful situation. A common example of avoidance coping in sport would be

Problem-focused coping: Coping efforts that help people change the actual situation.

Emotion-focused coping: Coping efforts to change the way a situation is attended to or interpreted, to deal with the emotions that arise during the situation.

Avoidance coping: Coping efforts in which athletes attempt to remove themselves from the stressful situation.

an athlete abandoning the pursuit of an important personal goal, or avoiding a situation that creates feelings of anxiety.

Often the same coping strategy may serve different functions. For example, seeking support to deal with poor performance may serve an emotion-focused function (e.g., if the athlete is seeking support to deal with his anger or frustration), but it may also serve a problem-focused function (e.g., if the athlete is seeking information from a coach or teammate about how to improve his performance).

AN INTEGRATIVE APPROACH

Some researchers have attempted to integrate micro- and macro-analytic approaches. For example, Gaudreau and Blondin (2002) developed a framework for coping that consists of 10 coping strategies regrouped under three broader dimensions of coping (see Figure 4.1).

Figure 4.1 Coping Inventory for Competitive Sport framework for classifying coping strategies

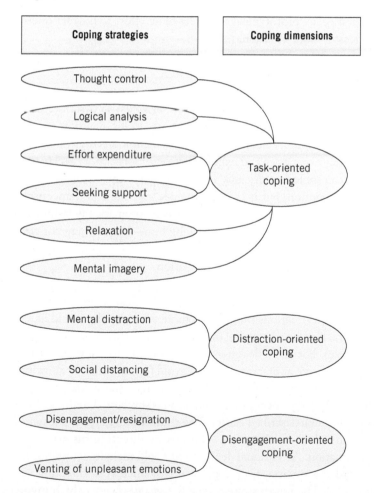

Source: Based on Gaudreau, P., & Blondin, J. P. (2002). Development of a questionnaire for the assessment of coping strategies employed by athletes in competitive sport settings. *Psychology of Sport and Exercise, 3*, 1–34.

The Coping Inventory for Competitive Sport can be used with francophone and anglophone athletes—a nice feature given the bilingual nature of the Canadian sport population. **Task-oriented coping** aims at dealing directly with the source of stress and its resulting thoughts and emotions. It is often difficult to know why athletes use relaxation, mental imagery, thought control, logical analysis, increased effort, and seeking support because these strategies can be used to directly manage the stressful situation and/or the psychological experience generated by these situations. As such, task-oriented coping captures both problem-focused coping and active forms of emotion-focused coping strategies known to facilitate task engagement.

Disengagement-oriented coping and **distraction-oriented coping** are two forms of avoidance coping. In disengagement coping, the athletes are using strategies to disengage themselves from the process of trying to make progress on a personal goal. It is not rare to see athletes cursing, swearing, letting themselves feel hopeless, and hoping that the stressor will end immediately. These avoidance strategies, however, need to be distinguished from distraction coping in which athletes momentarily focus on internal and external stimuli that are unrelated to the stressful situation. Thinking about leisure or friends and creating distance between oneself and the situation by keeping other people at a distance are prototypical examples of an effort to distract oneself during the course of a stressful sport situation.

EMOTION REGULATION

James Gross proposed a *process model of emotion regulation* to describe the way in which people regulate their emotions. According to Gross (1998), **emotion regulation** refers to "the processes by which individuals influence which emotions they have, when they have them, and how they experience and express these emotions" (p. 275). He stated that emotion regulation can include conscious and effortful attempts to manage the experience and expression of emotion, but it can also include automatic and unconscious responses to an emotion. Take the example of a hockey player automatically lashing out in anger at an opponent who was repeatedly cross-checking him—Lazarus may not consider lashing out in anger to be a volitional coping strategy, but Gross would consider this response a type of automatic, unconscious emotion regulation.

Gross's (1998) model consists of five types of emotion regulation strategies. The first strategy type is *situation selection*, in which an individual takes actions to increase the likelihood of being in situations that will promote emotions she would like to experience (or to decrease the likelihood of being in situations that will promote emotions she would prefer not to have). For example, after showing up late to a few practices, a basketball player might try to arrive at practices early to avoid feeling guilty for showing up late. The second strategy type is *situation modification*, in which an individual tries to influence the situation directly. This type of emotion regulation is similar to Lazarus's (1999) concept of problem-focused coping described earlier. The third strategy type is *attentional deployment*, in which an individual regulates his emotions by directing his attention toward (or away from) a situation. Attentional deployment could include rumination (i.e., directing attention toward the situation), or cognitive avoidance (i.e., directing attention away from the situation). The fourth strategy type is *cognitive change*, which involves changing the emotional significance of the event by changing how one thinks about the event.

Task-oriented coping: Coping strategies aimed at dealing directly with the source of stress and its resulting thoughts and emotions.

Disengagement-oriented coping: Coping strategies to disengage from the process of trying to make progress on a personal goal.

Distraction-oriented coping: Coping strategies to focus on internal and external stimuli that are unrelated to the stressful situation.

Emotion regulation: The processes by which individuals influence which emotions they have, when they have them, and how they experience and express these emotions.

For example, if an athlete does not secure an automatic spot in the play-offs and has to compete in another match for the remaining spot, she might use cognitive reappraisal to change her disappointment to optimism about the situation: "I didn't get an automatic spot in the play-offs, but now I have the opportunity to play another match and get more practice against my competitors, which will only help to refine my skills and keep me sharp." The final strategy type is *response modulation*, which refers to an individual's physiological, experiential, or behavioural responses to try to regulate emotions. One common form of response modulation occurs when individuals try to regulate their emotions by hiding or suppressing them—for example, if an athlete is angry with the referee's calls, she may hide her anger and avoid yelling at the referee because that could result in further penalties. Taken together, these five types of emotion regulation strategies capture a broad array of strategies that can be used before, during, and after an individual experiences an emotion.

EFFECTIVENESS AND OUTCOMES OF COPING

When trying to understand coping in sport and exercise, it is important to make a distinction between the concept of coping strategies and the outcomes of the coping process. Coping is an effort to deal with stress; however, an outcome of coping is the result (either good or bad) of those coping efforts. In this section, we discuss the concept of coping effectiveness and we consider several different types of achievement, emotional, and physical outcomes of coping.

Perceived Coping Effectiveness
Are some coping strategies more effective than others? This is an important question to help sport psychologists in choosing which coping strategies they should try to teach their athletes. Perceived **coping effectiveness** is based on how athletes believe a particular coping strategy has been effective at reducing or managing stress, or effective at managing worries/concerns. Overall, athletes seem to think that task-oriented coping strategies are more effective compared to disengagement-oriented strategies (e.g., Kaiseler et al., 2009). These findings are consistent with the research of Skinner and colleagues (2003), who proposed that a distinction can be made between "good news" and "bad news" coping. **Good news coping** attempts are organized, flexible, and constructive, whereas **bad news coping** attempts are rigid, disorganized, and destructive responses to unmanageable levels of stress. People who use ways of coping such as helplessness, constant opposition to others, and social withdrawal might be at risk for long-term maladaptive consequences, such as low self-confidence, increased depression, and reduced social functioning. Although it is informative to ask athletes directly whether they think their coping was effective, this approach does not investigate whether coping can actually predict outcomes that are important in the life of an athlete.

Achievement Outcomes
Much of the focus of coping research in sport sciences has been specifically on athletes in competitive sports (Nicholls, 2010), in part because enhancing the performance of athletes and teams is a key component of sport psychology. In one study, judo competitors from France completed a measure of coping strategies a few minutes before the start of a competition serving as a qualifier for a national championship (Filaire et al., 2001). Results indicated that losers used more avoidance-oriented coping, self-blame, and seeking social support, whereas winners used more positive

Coping effectiveness: A decision about whether or not a coping strategy helped to deal with the problem and/or to deal with any distress associated with the problem.

Good news coping: Coping attempts that are organized, flexible, and constructive.

Bad news coping: Coping attempts that are rigid, disorganized, and destructive.

reappraisal. In another study, greater use of mental skills, such as relaxation, imagery, emotional control, and self-talk, was related to higher levels of self-perception of quality of performance in a sample of NCAA Division I collegiate athletes (Frey et al., 2003). Athletes perceiving themselves as successful were using these coping skills during both practice sessions and competition.

Coping might play a more important role in the successful pursuit of personal goals. Across a series of studies, problem-focused strategies were associated with higher perceived goal attainment, whereas avoidance-oriented strategies were associated with lower levels of goal attainment (Gaudreau & Antl, 2008; Gaudreau & Blondin, 2002). For example, athletes who use strategies like planning, increased effort, relaxation, thought control, and mental imagery to deal with the demands of sport are more likely to make progress in the pursuit of their goals. The positive role of distraction-oriented coping was also evident in a study with Canadian amateur elite golfers participating in a provincial championship (Gaudreau & Blondin, 2004). Specifically, momentarily focusing on things unrelated to the competition during the golf round was associated with greater likelihood of goal attainment, but only for athletes who were also using task-oriented coping to a large extent. Making it to the "big leagues" is a significant life goal of several competitive athletes. In a longitudinal study, Van Yperen (2009) compared male soccer players who successfully made it into professional soccer and those who did not reach this level. Problem-focused coping and seeking social support during adolescence significantly predicted the likelihood of making it into professional soccer during adulthood. These results were obtained even when controlling for the initial performance and goal commitment of the players during adolescence.

Athletes who are using more task-oriented coping are more likely to attain better achievement outcomes than other competitors. Sport psychologists typically try to improve the performance of individual athletes and coping is thought to be a key process to help athletes learn, improve, and reach their own maximum potential. Gaudreau and colleagues (2012) have shown that golfers were able to perform better than their own average during golf rounds during which they used more task-oriented coping compared to their own habitual coping tendency. Coping can also change from one point to the other during a competitive match. Therefore, it might assist the athletes in creating the needed conditions to enter and stay in "the zone" to generate some positive performance momentum. Accordingly, Doron and Gaudreau (2014) have recently shown that using task-oriented coping between points of a fencing match increases the likelihood of winning points in succession (i.e., winning streaks) while diminishing the probabilities of losing points in succession (i.e., losing streaks).

Overall, coping appears to play a key role of sport performance, goal attainment, and the likelihood of making it to the highest levels of sport competition. Furthermore, coping can also explain why the performance of athletes fluctuates from one day to another as well as from one moment to another during the course of a competitive match.

Emotional Outcomes *Emotional well-being.* The most common outcomes in sport coping research are emotional states. Generally, problem-focused coping strategies are positively related to positive emotional states and even to general feelings of life satisfaction. Emotion-focused strategies, such as seeking social support for emotional reasons, and avoidance-oriented strategies, are more related to negative emotional states. The link between emotional states and coping was found in a study by Amiot and colleagues (2004), who examined affective states a few days before a competition and a few days after the competition in Canadian athletes. The goal of the study was to determine whether the affective states of athletes would change after the competition, compared to before the competition, as a result of their use of coping strategies. Using task-oriented coping during a competition resulted in increased positive affect, whereas disengagement-oriented coping was associated with increased negative affect. Another study with Canadian athletes examined whether coping in sport competition can create positive changes in the general life satisfaction of athletes (Gaudreau & Antl, 2008). Athletes using task-oriented coping were more satisfied about their life after a competition (as compared to their initial level of life satisfaction), thus implying that the mere effort of actively pursuing one's goal can lead to a substantial change in emotional well-being not only in their sport but also in their life in general. It does seem like coping with the stress of a competition can have spillover effects in the life of an athlete outside of the sport domain.

Burnout. Athletic burnout is a syndrome composed of three characteristics: physical exhaustion, devaluation of one's sport, and reduced sense of accomplishment (Raedeke & Smith, 2001). These symptoms can result, in part, from chronic stress and the inability to effectively manage excessive demands in training and competition, and they are thought to develop gradually over time. Early signs of athlete burnout include poor performance, exhaustion, mood disturbance, decreased motivation, and frustration over lack of accomplishment or lack of ability. In addition to high training demands, other causes of burnout are thought to be school and work demands, stressful social relationships, lack of recovery time, early sport success (Gustafsson, Kenttä, & Hassmén, 2011), having limited control over one's sport career and limited involvement in activities outside of sport (Coakley, 1992), and feelings of entrapment—athletes continuing participation in sport because they "have to," not because they want to (Raedeke, 1997).

Burnout is thought to be a particularly important issue in some sports, such as swimming, where athletes train at high volumes and intensities throughout the year.

Eric Raptosh Photography/Getty Images

Coping is significantly linked with athletic burnout. Raedeke and Smith (2004) reported that general coping skills, such as taking quiet time each day and effective management of time, were associated with lower levels of physical exhaustion, sport devaluation, and reduced sense of accomplishment. In a study of competitive athletes from various sports, Hill and colleagues (2010) have also found that problem-focused coping and avoidance coping were respectively associated with lower and higher levels of athletic burnout. More recently, Schellenberg and colleagues (2013) examined the role of coping in understanding changes in athletic burnout across the course of a competitive season in Canadian college and university level volleyball players. Task-oriented coping was associated with significant decreases in athletic burnout across the season, whereas avoidance coping aggravated the symptoms of athletic burnout during the season.

Physical Outcomes *Injury.* Just as stress is a contributor to burnout among athletic populations, it can also contribute to injuries in sport. How can stress lead to injuries? Anxiety can contribute to athletes' muscle tension, changes in information processing, and increased susceptibility to distraction. In a study of high school soccer players, Rogers and Landers (2005) found support for the idea that attentional narrowing is a mechanism through which stress leads to injuries in sport. They also found that injured athletes reported significantly more negative life events than non-injured athletes, and athletes with greater ability to cope with stress were less likely to be injured. These studies support the idea that athletes with higher levels of stress and low coping ability may be at risk of being injured. Coping can also protect athletes. Smith and colleagues (1990) indicated that the harmful effect of negative life events on subsequent injuries can be reduced for athletes possessing good coping skills and a rich social support network.

Stress can lead to injuries, which affect individual athletes and their teammates.

Stephen Coburn/Shutterstock

Since high stress and low coping ability are related to athletic injuries, researchers and sport psychologists have been interested in trying to reduce injuries through coping interventions. For example, athletes at risk of sustaining an injury were given a brief cognitive intervention to improve their coping strategies, and they had significantly fewer injuries for the following five months compared to a control group of athletes who did not receive the coping intervention (Johnson et al., 2005). Other programs which improve athletes' self-confidence and stress management have also been shown to prevent injuries and reduce athletes' number of days lost to injury (Maddison & Prapavessis, 2007; Perna et al., 2003).

Researchers have also focused on improving athletes' ability to cope with injuries once they have occurred. Coping with the stress of injury is complex, and injuries can be difficult experiences, causing anxiety about whether returning to play will be possible and fear of re-injury. Many athletes report using different coping strategies at different times, depending on the stage of their recovery: Johnston and Carroll (2000) found that injured athletes used more coping strategies at the beginning of their injury and rehabilitation program, and the use of coping strategies decreased as rehabilitation progressed. It is likely that both problem-focused and emotion-focused coping strategies are important for athletes to facilitate the rehabilitation process.

Not surprisingly, coping has been recognized as an important factor by sport trainers and athletic therapists for effective injury rehabilitation (Ford & Gordon, 1998), and there is evidence that coping can contribute to a more rapid return to competition and a lower chance of repeat injuries (Udry, 1997). While it is difficult to say which specific strategies lead to better recovery outcomes, a study of injured athletes from the United Kingdom found that athletes' use of active coping, planning, and seeking instrumental social support increased the likelihood of attending rehabilitation sessions over a three-week period (Hagger et al., 2005). Seeking support appears to be a particularly important coping strategy for dealing with injury, especially for highly competitive athletes. Johnston and Carroll (2000) found that athletes who reported high levels of involvement in their sport (e.g., eight hours or more per week) used more support-seeking as a coping strategy to deal with injury compared to athletes who had low levels of involvement in their sport (e.g., athletes who participated less than one hour per week).

CASE STUDY 4.1 — The Case of the Injured Basketball Player

You are a coach of an under-19 women's basketball team, and your best athlete, Amy, suffers a significant knee injury. She is a top-ranked player who was going to be captain of the provincial team this summer and play university basketball in the fall. She comes to you and says that she is having a very difficult time dealing with her injury. She has been told by her doctor and physiotherapist that she will not be able to participate in any team basketball drills for at least three months and that, at best, her knee will be at 80% for university tryouts in the fall. Amy describes her rehabilitation to date as "slow, frustrating, and boring." You can also tell that she has lost confidence in her ability to play at an elite level. What are the key issues in this case study that you need to be aware of as a coach? What would you say to Amy in your next conversation with her? What resources would you recommend to her that could help her more effectively manage the stress of her injury?

Factors Influencing Coping

After reading the preceding section, you have probably come to the conclusion that certain coping strategies are associated with positive sport outcomes, reducing burnout and withdrawal, preventing injuries, and promoting adherence to rehabilitation. However, as mentioned earlier, the effectiveness of particular coping strategies depends on the person and the situation they are facing. In this section, we will discuss several factors that influence the ways in which athletes cope with stressors and emotions in sport.

Gender Do male and female athletes cope with stressors differently? Unfortunately, gender differences in coping in sport are not well understood, with recent reviews suggesting that differences are often small and inconsistent across studies (Crocker, et al., in press; Kaiseler & Polman, 2010). It is often difficult to study gender differences because males and females may be facing different types of stressors, plus the organizational and cultural expectations for different genders may constrain the types of coping options for athletes.

Tamres and colleagues (2002) proposed that there are different views to explain potential gender differences in coping. Role constraint theory states that differences in stress are primarily the result of the different roles men and women play in society, as opposed to any inherent gender differences. Beach volleyball provides a good example, because the women might have to develop coping strategies to manage **self-presentation** concerns that the men do not, simply because of the expectations of what they wear in competition. On the other hand, the gender socialization hypothesis predicts that males and females learn to use different coping strategies to manage the same types of situations (Hoar et al., 2006). Through sex-role stereotyping and role expectations, females more than males are generally encouraged to express their emotions and turn to others for emotional support. While male and female athletes may cope using some different strategies in specific situations, it appears that the type of stressor and the athlete's appraisal of the stressor may be just as important in predicting athletes' coping strategies. An alternative hypothesis, the dispositional hypothesis, suggests that gender differences will be present even when males and females are presented with the same stressor and have similar cognitive appraisals. However, this hypothesis doesn't really tell us why.

Culture Culture should impact the stress, coping, and emotion process because culture strongly influences what events are important and the meaning of sporting success and failure (Crocker et al., in press). Culture will also constrain what coping options are considered appropriate. Limited attention has been devoted to direct comparisons of coping across groups of athletes from different countries and cultures. Nonetheless, research on sport coping has been conducted with athletes from different areas of the world, thus providing some indirect evidence about cross-cultural coping differences. For example, a number of studies have shown the particular importance of prayer as a coping strategy for Korean athletes (Park, 2000; Yoo, 2001). There may also be differences among cultures. For example, Hoedaya and Anshel (2003) found differences in stress intensity and ways of coping in Indonesian and Australian athletes. For example, Indonesian athletes perceived a bad call by a referee to be less stressful then Australian athletes. Indonesian athletes used more denial, restraint, and active coping during the game.

Self-presentation: The process by which individuals attempt to control the impressions others form of them (also referred to as impression management).

There have been surprisingly few studies to see if Canadians have a particular way of coping with stress in sport, as well as a limited number of coping studies within more well-defined cultures in Canada. However, we have to be careful since there are many different cultures within Canada.

Individual Factors *Age, development, and expertise.* Level of expertise has also been shown to influence the use of coping strategies, with more proficient athletes using more task-oriented coping (Gaudreau & Blondin, 2002). For instance, in a study with a large sample of athletes from the United Kingdom, international and national athletes were more likely to use problem-solving, planning, increased effort, and relaxation than their counterparts competing at the county, university, and club level (Nicholls et al., 2007).

Personality. Personality represents the tendency of an individual to act and to feel in a relatively stable manner. Personality has long been recognized as an important factor in how athletes typically react under stressful situations. For the sake of brevity, we will cover just a few areas that show links between personality and coping.

Optimism, which is the tendency to believe that good things will happen in the future, has been studied in the context of performance slumps. Grove and Heard (1997) showed that both trait self-confidence and optimism were positively associated with usage of problem-focused coping and with lesser use of emotion-focused coping. Similar results were more recently found in a large sample of British athletes from various sports (Nicholls et al., 2008). The importance of optimism is not limited to coping. In a study of Canadian competitive golfers, Gaudreau and Blondin (2004) found that optimistic athletes were more likely to attain their performance goals and to experience subjective well-being following a competition. In their study, task-oriented coping was an important factor because optimistic athletes were using strategies such as increased effort, mental imagery, and relaxation which, in turn, positively related to goal attainment and positive affect.

Similar results were obtained in studying dispositional perfectionism of athletes (Gotwals et al., 2012). Athletes pursuing perfectionistic standards to please significant others have been found to experience lower levels of well-being (Flett & Hewitt, 2005). In a study of Canadian athletes from various sports, socially prescribed perfectionism was associated with the use of disengagement-oriented coping, which was related to lower levels of life-satisfaction (Gaudreau & Antl, 2008). Similar findings have been found in the relations among perfectionism, coping, and athletic burnout (Hill et al., 2010). However, some athletes pursue perfectionistic goals without feeling pressured by their significant others. These self-oriented, perfectionistic athletes use task-oriented coping during the course of competition, which facilitates both goal attainment and increased life-satisfaction. Overall, more research is needed to understand which combination(s) of personality traits appear to improve coping and coping effectiveness.

Cognitive appraisals of emotion. Cognitive appraisal in the experience of stress and subsequent coping efforts is important. For now, it suffices to reiterate that perceiving a situation as a challenge is likely to facilitate the usage of task-oriented coping, whereas athletes are more likely to use avoidance coping when they appraise a situation as a threat. Yet, other cognitive factors are worth considering in the prediction of coping. Trait anxiety represents a general tendency to feel anxious, worried, and preoccupied in the competitive sport arena. Research has indicated that trait-anxious athletes are more likely to use disengagement-oriented forms of coping such as self-blame, denial, wishful thinking, and behavioural disengagement (Giacobbi & Weinberg, 2000). However, perceiving anxiety as facilitative before a sport competition has recently been associated with greater usage of problem-focused coping and lesser usage of disengagement-oriented coping during competition among a small sample of swimmers with international competitive experience (Hatzigeorgiadis & Chroni, 2007).

Social Environmental Factors Social environmental factors such as coaching and teammate interactions also influence athletes' emotions, coping, and emotion regulation. In terms of teammate influences on emotions and coping, there is evidence that emotions can be contagious within teams—athletes' positive, happy moods have been associated with the moods of their teammates during competitions (Totterdell, 2000), and soccer players' celebratory behaviours after a successful penalty kick (e.g., smiling, arms extended in the air, hands in fists) have been associated with their team's eventual success (Moll et al., 2010). Likewise, athletes' negative emotions can affect their teammates as well—researchers have used the term "a cancer on the team" to describe the spreading of destructive, negative emotions throughout a team (Cope et al., 2010).

Given that emotions and emotional expressions can affect those around us, it is important for athletes to regulate their emotions effectively in team settings. Athletes may try to hide their negative emotions from teammates to avoid upsetting the rest of the team. Tamminen and Crocker (2014) found that high-performance curlers who trained and competed closely together were aware of the effect their emotional displays could have on their teammates and they reported regulating their own emotions for the benefit of the team's performance. The athletes also reported using specific strategies to try to regulate their teammates' emotions during practices and competitions—for example, providing teammates with positive/technical feedback after missing a shot, or using humour and making jokes to lighten the mood on the team. Similarly, athletes undergoing long-term injury rehabilitation have reported that they attempted to control or suppress their negative emotions in public and around their teammates, as they did not feel comfortable disclosing their negative emotions to others (Mankad et al., 2009).

Coaches can also directly or indirectly influence athletes' emotions and coping before and during competitions. Coaches' pre-game and intermission speeches are reported to influence athletes' emotions before competitions (Breakey et al., 2009), and coaches' behaviours are associated with athletes' coping during competitions. For example, Nicolas and colleagues (2011) found that athletes who perceived their coaches to use unsupportive coaching behaviours reported using greater disengagement-oriented coping to deal with stressors during competition. Conversely, athletes who perceived that their coaches used supportive behaviours, such as "providing advice on how to stay focused" and "showing understanding for the athlete as a person," reported increased task-oriented coping to deal with stressors, which was reported to lead to greater sport achievement. Similar findings were found regarding the motivational climate created by coaches (e.g., Kristiansen et al., 2008). Coaches with a focus on learning and task mastery appear to be creating the needed social conditions to facilitate the usage of task-oriented coping. In contrast, a focus on performance, bottom-line outcomes, and social comparison instilled by the coaches is likely to favour the usage of avoidance-oriented coping among their athletes.

Athletes' negative emotions can spread throughout a team. Think of a time when one person's emotions affected other people around them—what was it like? How did you respond? How do athletes improve or worsen each other's emotions on a team? What role can leaders and coaches play to deal with negative emotions on a team?

Monkey Business/Fotolia

Coping and Emotion Regulation Interventions

Studies such as the ones described throughout this chapter are generally conducted to facilitate the development of sport psychology interventions that are based on sound, empirically proven principles. Intervention studies are needed to help researchers identify weaknesses in their theoretical models.

Stress reduction. A recent review of the literature has highlighted the numerous and diversified attempts to help athletes to become better at managing stress (Rumbold et al., 2012). Twenty-two of the 23 studies that used a randomized controlled trial research design have shown that stress management interventions can be effective to reduce stress of participants. However, only 50% of the studies examining stress and performance outcomes have shown that stress management interventions can be effective to simultaneously improve performance and stress-related outcomes.

Self-compassion. An approach that seems particularly promising in helping athletes and exercisers manage emotionally challenging situations is the development of self-compassion. Neff (2003) described **self-compassion** as the desire to be moved by one's own suffering, as well as a desire to alleviate that suffering. The development of

Self-compassion: The desire to be moved by one's own suffering, as well as a desire to alleviate that suffering. It involves three components: self-kindness, common humanity, and mindfulness.

self-compassion is particularly beneficial for coping in circumstances involving negative evaluations and difficult emotional experiences, and, in contrast with self-esteem, is not dependent upon positive self-evaluations or evaluations by others. Self-compassion involves three components (Neff, 2003): (1) self-kindness (treating oneself with warmth and non-judgmental understanding); (2) common humanity (one's own experiences are viewed as part of the larger human experience); and (3) mindfulness (identifying with one's painful feelings and not avoiding or repressing them).

Self-compassion is an important area in sport and exercise psychology. Several recent studies have collectively formed the following conclusions. First, self-compassion is clearly relevant to the lives of young women athletes and exercisers, and it appears to be important beyond self-esteem. Second, there are aspects of self-compassion in different domains (e.g., "body self-compassion"). Third, prominent potential ways through which self-compassion might impact psychological flourishing seem to be increased positivity and perseverance and decreased passivity. Fourth, self-compassion interventions are effective in decreasing self-criticism, rumination, and concern over mistakes for highly self-critical women athletes (see Ferguson et al., 2014; Magnus et al., 2010; Mosewich et al., 2011; Mosewich et al., 2013; Sutherland et al., 2014).

However, one concern raised by athletes is that being *too* self-compassionate might lead to complacency (Ferguson et al., 2014). The research evidence to date does not support this concern, and in fact shows that self-compassionate people are actually *more* motivated to work on changing personal weaknesses (Breines & Chen, 2012). Athletes need to accept self-compassion as an alternative to self-criticism, particularly when coping with the emotional pain associated with failure.

Expressive writing. Another strategy that might be useful for helping cope with stress in sport and exercise is expressive writing. Expressive writing is often part of a therapeutic process and is typically associated with improvements in both physical and mental health (Pennebaker, 1997). Thus, it is likely no surprise that self-compassion interventions, which focus on the development of healthy conceptualizations of the self, also often employ writing tasks focused on each component of self-compassion (i.e., self-kindness, common humanity, mindfulness). The basic premise of expressive writing is that disclosure itself is an important part of healing when experiencing emotional pain.

Hudson and Day (2012) studied athletes' experiences of expressive writing about competitive sport stressors by having them write about a significant stressor across six 20-minute writing sessions over a two- to three-week period. They showed that expressive writing about a stressful event, particularly writing from a number of different perspectives, is effective in increasing the experience of positive emotions and hopes of successful performance in the future. One of the biggest benefits of expressive writing was that the process led to a re-evaluation of the stressful situation and a change in perspective. However, some of the athletes in their study experienced temporary negative emotions as part of the writing process, as well as initial fears related to reliving the event through expressive writing. Recent evidence from the non-sport literature suggests that expressive writing might be best suited to people who are already comfortable expressing emotion, but that expressive writing might actually create increases in anxiety for those who do not typically express emotions (Niles et al., 2014).

Two notes of concern are warranted when implementing intervention programs. First, planning interventions have the potential to be deleterious when used by clients

Coping and emotion regulation strategies help individuals to deal with stressful experiences. What coping and emotion regulation skills do you possess that help you to deal with stress? What do you need to work on in order to improve your ability to cope with stress in sport and exercise?

Peter Bernik/Shutterstock

with high levels of socially prescribed perfectionism since they already have a tendency to strive toward their goals in an unduly rigid and inflexible manner (Powers et al., 2005). Second, planning interventions are more optimal when clients do not feel pressured to adhere to the planning strategy (Koestner et al., 2006). Providing meaningful choices and encouraging the clients to formulate a personalized plan that fits their lifestyle can go a long way in maximizing the usefulness of these coping interventions.

CHAPTER SUMMARY

If we reflect on the opening vignette, we can see the complexity of stress and coping. Swimming is obviously important to Jessica and, as a result, she is dealing with a number of stress sources, ranging from time management and financial concerns to concerns about being evaluated by others. Her ways of coping are numerous, including time management, spending less time socializing and working, and trying to seek support from her teammates. Maybe most importantly, the vignette clearly demonstrates that coping with stress is a process that plays out over time, often with no simple resolution.

Cognitive appraisal is a key component of the stress experience. How people interpret the situations they face in sport and exercise is now generally considered as important as the situations themselves. People are not passive agents who must succumb to the demands placed upon them. Instead, they interpret situations in relation to their goals and their perceived coping options. Various psychological, physical, social, environmental, and career demands are often reported as threatening, as challenging, or as a harm/loss. These general sources of stress include acute and chronic stressors, expected and unexpected stressors, competitive and non-competitive stressors, as well as organizational stressors.

Coping is a dynamic process. It is a response to stress that includes a wide variety of cognitive and behavioural efforts. These efforts can range from accepting the situation, to making a plan of action, to leaving the situation altogether. Often, multiple coping efforts are made in any given situation as someone tries to figure out the most effective way to manage the demands. These coping efforts themselves then reshape the situation and possibly the person's cognitive appraisal of the situation, making new coping attempts necessary (if stress remains). Emotion regulation is a slightly different way of thinking about the ways in which people deal with stress, and it refers to the emotions and reactions that people have in a particular situation, as well as voluntary and involuntary efforts to regulate their emotions.

Coping strategies are inherently neither effective nor ineffective. Whether or not a coping strategy is effective depends on the fit between the coping efforts and the stress that is experienced. Although there is some evidence to suggest that, in general, problem-focused coping efforts are most effective in the long term, ultimately the effectiveness of coping needs to be considered in relation to a person's goals and well-being, which sometimes contradict each other. Much more work is needed in establishing predictors of coping in sport and exercise. The challenge is that all situations seem to be unique at some level because not only do the characteristics of situations change, but so do individuals' appraisals of those situations. Researchers have only begun to look at consistencies across situations that might help establish whether strong predictors of coping can be established.

Despite the many unknowns regarding stress and coping in sport and exercise, coping intervention programs seem to be effective in helping people manage stress. Coping interventions seem to have a great deal of potential for helping people develop a set of resources that allow them to more effectively meet the demands of sport and exercise. Ultimately, however, an interest in stress and coping in sport and exercise stems from a desire not only to help people meet the demands of sport and exercise in a healthy way but also to promote a lifetime of enjoyable physical activity involvement.

COMMON MYTHS ABOUT STRESS, EMOTION, AND COPING IN SPORT AND EXERCISE REVISITED

MYTH: Elite sport is inherently stressful.

How athletes interpret specific situations is the key factor that will determine whether or not they experience stress (and what level of stress). Even situations that one might think should be stressful might not cause stress, depending on a particular athlete's goals and interpretation of what is happening. Two track-and-field event favourites in the 2008 Olympic Summer Games were Russian pole vaulter Yelena Isinbayeva and Portuguese long jumper Naide Gomes. Heading into the Olympics, Isinbayeva was the only woman to clear 5 m in pole vault, and Gomes was the only woman among those competing with a season-best long jump heading into the Olympics beyond 7 m. Isinbayeva went on to win the Olympic gold medal and set a new world record; she said of the spotlight, "I love it so much. I feel like an actress" (Butcher, 2008). Alternatively, Gomes reported to CBC, "I lacked confidence and felt a lot of pressure" (Canada's Charles, 2008). Gomes failed to qualify for the long jump final.

MYTH: Exercise always reduces stress.

While in a lot of cases exercise is indeed a good way to cope with stress, for some people, as the chapter vignette suggests, exercise is the primary source of stress. Many times the exercise setting is abound with potential triggers—such as mirrors, crowded gyms, and revealing attire—that can lead to self-presentation concerns. Or, for others, exercise simply is not a very enjoyable experience, and it can be a cause of stress. In many cases, we need to work with people to develop coping strategies to deal with their exercise participation, in addition to encouraging them to use exercise as a coping strategy to deal with other life stresses.

MYTH: Dropping out of sport or stopping exercise is an ineffective coping strategy.

Although in many cases dropping out of sport or stopping exercise may not be the best or preferable option to manage stress, in some cases these actions might be the most effective coping strategy. Coping strategies are not inherently good or bad. Effective coping depends on the matches among the situation, the person's goals and values, and the strategies that are used.

Review Questions

1. What does it mean to describe stress as a "process"?
2. What roles do cognitive appraisal and coping play in the experience of stress?
3. How are the concepts of stress and emotion related?
4. Discuss why it is important to distinguish between *coping* and *outcomes of coping*.
5. Compare and contrast micro- and macro-analytic dimensions of coping.
6. What predictors of coping in sport were discussed in the chapter? What relationship do they have to coping?
7. Discuss challenges to understanding stress and coping in sport and exercise.

Additional readings

Crocker, P. R. E., Tamminen, K. A., & Gaudreau, P. (in press). Conceptual advances in stress and coping in sport. In S. Hanton & S. Mellalieu (Eds.), *Contemporary advances in sport psychology: A review.* New York: Routledge.

Nicholls. A. R. (2010). *Coping in sport: Theory, methods, and related constructs.* New York: Nova Science.

References

Aldwin, C. M. (2000). *Stress, coping, and development: An integrative perspective.* New York: Guildford.

Amiot, C. E., Gaudreau, P., & Blanchard, C. M. (2004). Self-determination, coping, and goal attainment in sport. *Journal of Sport & Exercise Psychology, 26,* 386–411.

Anshel, M. H., Jamieson, J., & Raviv, S. (2001). Coping with acute stress among male and female Israeli athletes. *International Journal of Sport Psychology, 32,* 271–289.

Blascovich, J., & Tomaka, J. (1996). The biopsychosocial model of arousal regulation. In M. P. Zanna (Ed.), *Advances in experimental social psychology* (vol. 28, pp. 1–51). New York: Academic Press.

Blascovich, J., Seery, M. D., Mugridge, C. A., Norris, R. K., & Weisbuch, M. (2004). Predicting athletic performance from cardiovascular indexes of challenge and threat. *Journal of Experimental Social Psychology, 40,* 683–688.

Breakey, C., Jones, M. I., Cunningham, C. T., & Holt, N. L. (2009). Female athletes' perceptions of a coach's speeches. *Journal of Sport Science and Coaching, 4,* 489–504.

Breines, J. G., & Chen, S. (2012). Self-compassion increases self-improvement motivation. *Personality and Social Psychology Bulletin, 38,* 1133–1143. doi:10.1177/0146167212445599.

Butcher, P. (2008, August 19). Isinbayeva puts on a show. IAAF. Retrieved August 19, 2008, from www.iaaf.org.

Canada's Charles leaps into long jump final. (2008, August 19). CBC Sports. Retrieved August 19, 2008, from www.cbc.ca.

Canada's Whitfield takes silver in triathalon. (2008, August 19). CBC Sports. Retrieved August 19, 2008, from www.cbc.ca.

Carpenter, B. N. (1992). Issues and advances in coping research. In B. N. Carpenter (Ed.), *Personal coping: Theory, research, and application* (pp. 1–13). Westport, CT: Praeger.

Coakley, J. (1992). Burnout among adolescent athletes: A personal failure or social problem? *Sociology of Sport Journal, 9,* 271–285.

Cope, C. J., Eys, M. A., Schinke, R. J., & Bosselut, G. (2010). Coaches' perspectives of a negative informal role: The 'cancer' within sport teams. *Journal of Applied Sport Psychology, 22,* 420–436. doi:10.1080/10413200.2010.495327.

Crocker, P. R. E., & Graham, T. R. (1995). Coping by competitive athletes with performance stress: Gender differences and relationships with affect. *The Sport Psychologist, 9,* 325–338.

Crocker, P. R. E., Tamminen, K. A., & Gaudreau, P. (in press). Conceptual advances in stress and coping in sport. In S. Hanton & S. Mellalieu (Eds.), *Contemporary advances in sport psychology: A review.* New York: Routledge.

Doron, J., & Gaudreau, P. (2014). A point-by-point analysis of performance in a fencing match: Psychological processes associated with winning and losing streaks. *Journal of Sport & Exercise Psychology, 36,* 3–13.

Dugdale, J. R., Eklund, R. C., & Gordon, S. (2002). Expected and unexpected stressors in major international competition: Appraisal, coping, and performance. *The Sport Psychologist, 16,* 20–33.

Ekman, P., & Cordaro, D. (2011). What is meant by calling emotions basic. *Emotion Review, 3,* 364–371.

Ferguson, L. J., Kowalski, K. C., Mack, D. E., & Sabiston, C. M. (2014). Exploring self-compassion and eudaimonic well-being in young women athletes. *Journal of Sport & Exercise Psychology, 36,* 203–216.

Filaire, E., Maso, F., Sagnol, M., Ferrand, C., & Lac, G. (2001). Anxiety, hormonal responses and coping during a judo competition. *Aggressive Behavior, 27,* 55–63.

Fletcher, D., Hanton, S., & Mellalieu, S. D. (2006). An organizational stress review: Conceptual and theoretical issues in competitive sport. In: S. Hanton & S. Mellalieu (Eds.), *Literature reviews in sport psychology* (pp. 321–373). Hauppauge, NY: Nova Science.

Fletcher, D., Hanton, S., Mellalieu, S. D., & Neil, R. (2012) A conceptual framework of organizational stressors in sport performers. *Scandinavian Journal of Medicine & Science in Sports, 22,* 545–557.

Flett, G. L., & Hewitt, P. L. (2005). The perils of perfectionism in sports and exercise. *Current Directions in Psychological Science, 14,* 14–18.

Folkman, S. (2008). The case for positive emotions in the stress process. *Anxiety, Stress, and Coping, 21,* 3–14.

Ford, I. W., & Gordon, S. (1998). Perspective of sport trainers and athletic therapists on the psychological content of their practice and training. *Journal of Sport Rehabilitation, 7,* 79–94.

Frey, M., Laguna, P. L., & Ravizza, K. (2003). Collegiate athletes' mental skill use and perceptions of success: An exploration of the practice and competition settings. *Journal of Applied Sport Psychology, 15,* 115–128.

Gaudreau, P., & Antl, S. (2008). Athletes' broad dimensions of dispositional perfectionism: Examining changes in life-satisfaction and the mediating role of sport-related motivation and coping. *Journal of Sport & Exercise Psychology, 30,* 356–382.

Gaudreau, P., & Blondin, J. P. (2002). Development of a questionnaire for the assessment of coping strategies employed by athletes in competitive sport settings. *Psychology of Sport and Exercise, 3*, 1–34.

Gaudreau, P., & Blondin, J. P. (2004). Different athletes cope differently: A cluster analysis of coping. *Personality and Individual Differences, 36*, 1865–1877.

Gaudreau, P., Nicholls, A., & Levy, A. R. (2012). The ups and downs of coping and sport achievement: An episodic process analysis of within-person associations. *Journal of Sport & Exercise Psychology, 32*, 298–311.

Giacobbi, P. R., Jr., & Weinberg, R. S. (2000). An examination of coping in sports: Individual trait anxiety differences and situational consistency. *The Sport Psychologist, 14*, 42–62.

Gotwals, J. K., Stoeber, J., Dunn, J., & Stoll, O. (2012). Are perfectionistic strivings in sport adaptive? A systematic review of confirmatory, contradictory, and mixed evidence. *Canadian Psychology, 53*, 263–279. doi: 10.1037/a0030288.

Gross, J. (1998). The emerging field of emotion regulation: An integrative review. *Review of General Psychology, 2*, 271–299.

Grove, J., & Heard, P. N. (1997). Optimism and sport confidence as correlates of slump-related coping among athletes. *The Sport Psychologist, 11*, 400–410.

Gustafsson, H., Kenttä, G., & Hassmén, P. (2011). Athlete burnout: An integrated model and future research directions. *International Review of Sport and Exercise Psychology, 4*, 3–14.

Hagger, M. S., Chatzisarantis, N. L. D., Griffin, M., & Thatcher, J. (2005). Injury representations, coping, emotions, and functional outcomes in athletes with sports-related injuries: A test of self-regulation theory. *Journal of Applied Social Psychology, 35*, 2345–2374.

Harmon-Jones, E., Gable, P. A., & Peterson, C. K. (2010). The role of asymmetric frontal cortical activity in emotion-related phenomena: A review and update. *Biological Psychology, 84*, 451–462.

Hatzigeorgiadis, A., & Chroni, S. (2007). Pre-competition anxiety and in-competition coping in experienced male swimmers. *International Journal of Sports Science & Coaching, 2*, 181–189.

Hill, A. P., Hall, H. K., & Appleton, P. R. (2010). Perfectionism and athlete burnout in junior elite athletes: The mediating role of coping tendencies. *Anxiety, Stress, and Coping, 23*, 415–430. doi: 10.1080/10615800903330966.

Hoar, S. D., Kowalski, K. C., Gaudreau, P., & Crocker, P. R. E. (2006). A review of coping in sport. In S. Hanton & S. Mellalieu (Eds.), *Literature reviews in sport psychology* (pp. 47–90). New York: Nova Science.

Hoedaya, D. & Anshel, M. H. (2003). Sources of stress and coping strategies among Australian and Indonesian athletes. *Australian Journal of Psychology, 55*, 159–165.

Holt, N. L., & Hogg, J. M. (2002). Perceptions of stress and coping during preparations for the 1999 women's soccer World Cup finals. *The Sport Psychologist, 16*, 251–271.

Hudson, J., & Day, M. C. (2012). Athletes' experiences of expressive writing about sports stressors. *Psychology of Sport and Exercise, 13*, 798–806.

Johnson, U., Ekengren, J., & Andersen, M. B. (2005). Injury prevention in Sweden: Helping soccer players at risk. *Journal of Sport & Exercise Psychology, 27*, 32–38.

Johnston, L. H., & Carroll, D. (2000). The psychological impact of injury: Effects of prior sport and exercise involvement. *British Journal of Sports Medicine, 34*, 436–439.

Jones, M., Meijen, C., McCarthy, P. J., & Sheffield, D. (2009). A theory of challenge and threat states in athletes. *International Review of Sport and Exercise Psychology, 2*, 161–180, doi: 10.1080/17509840902829331.

Kaiseler, M., & Polman, R. C. J. (2010). Gender and coping in sport: Do male and female athletes cope differently? In A. R. Nicholls (Ed.), *Coping in sport: Theory, methods, and related constructs* (pp. 79–93). New York: Nova Science Publishers.

Kaiseler, M., Polman, R., & Nicholls, A. (2009). Mental toughness, stress, stress appraisal, coping and coping effectiveness in sport. *Personality and Individual Differences, 47*, 728–733. doi: 10.1016/j.paid.2009.06.012.

Koestner, R., Horberg, E. J., Gaudreau, P., Powers, T. A., Di Dio, L., Bryan, C., et al. (2006). Bolstering implementation plans for long haul: The benefits of simultaneously boosting self-concordance and self-efficacy. *Personality and Social Psychology Bulletin, 32,* 1547–1558.

Kreibig, S. (2010). Autonomic nervous system activity in emotion: A review. *Biological Psychology, 84,* 394–421.

Kristiansen, E., Roberts, G. C., & Abrahamsen, F. E. (2008). Achievement involvement and stress coping in elite wrestling. *Scandinavian Journal of Medicine & Science in Sports, 18,* 526–538. doi: 10.1111/j.1600-0838.2007.00646.x.

Lazarus, R. S. (1991). *Emotion and adaptation.* New York: Oxford University Press.

Lazarus, R. S. (1999). *Stress and emotion: A new synthesis.* New York: Springer.

Lazarus, R. S. (2000). How emotions influence performance in competitive sports. *The Sport Psychologist, 14,* 229–252.

Lowther, N. (2008, November 1). GAME 9 CIS championship: Vikes clinch berth in final, Birds have to wait. CIS. Retrieved May 2, 2009, from www.cisport.ca/e/championships/w_fieldhockey/2008.

Maddison, R., & Prapavessis, H. (2007). Preventing sport injuries: A case for psychology intervention. In D. Pargman (Ed.), *Psychological bases of sport injuries* (pp. 25–38) Morgantown, WV: Fitness Information Technology.

Magnus, C. M. R., Kowalski, K. C., & McHugh, T. L. F. (2010). The role of self-compassion in women's self-determined motives to exercise and exercise-related outcomes. *Self and Identity, 9,* 363–382. doi:10.1080/15298860903135073.

Mankad, A., Gordon, S., & Wallman, K. (2009). Perceptions of emotional climate among injured athletes. *Journal of Clinical Sports Psychology, 3,* 1–14.

Moll, T., Jordet, G., & Pepping, G. (2010). Emotional contagion in soccer penalty shootouts: Celebration of individual success is associated with ultimate team success. *Journal of Sport Sciences, 28,* 983–992.

Mosewich, A. D., Crocker, P. R. E., Kowalski, K. C., & DeLongis, A. (2013). Applying self-compassion in sport: An intervention with women athletes. *Journal of Sport & Exercise Psychology, 35,* 514–524.

Mosewich, A. D., Kowalski, K. C., Sabiston, C. M., Sedgwick, W. A., & Tracy, J. L. (2011). Self-compassion: A potential resource for young women athletes. *Journal of Sport & Exercise Psychology, 33,* 103–123.

Neff, K. (2003). Self-compassion: An alternative conceptualization of a healthy attitude toward oneself. *Self and Identity, 2,* 85–101. doi:10.1080/15298860309032.

Nicholls. A. R. (2010). *Coping in sport: Theory, methods, and related constructs.* New York: Nova Science.

Nicholls, A. R., Polman, R. C. J., Levy, A. R., & Backhouse, S. H. (2008). Mental toughness, optimism, pessimism, and coping among athletes. *Personality & Individual Differences, 44,* 1182–1192.

Nicholls, A. R., Polman, R., Levy, A. R., Taylor, J., & Cobley, S. (2007). Stressors, coping, and coping effectiveness: Gender, type of sport, and skill differences. *Journal of Sports Sciences, 25,* 1521–1530.

Nicolas, M., Gaudreau, P., & Franche, V. (2011). Perception of coaching behaviors, coping, and achievement in a sport competition. *Journal of Sport & Exercise Psychology, 33,* 460–468.

Niles, A. N., Byrne Haltom, K. E., Mulvenna, C. M., Lieberman, M. D., & Stanton, A. L. (2014). Randomized controlled trial of expressive writing for psychological and physical health: The moderating role of emotional expressivity. *Anxiety, Stress, and Coping, 27,* 1–17.

Noblet, A. J., & Gifford, S. M. (2002). The sources of stress experienced by professional Australian footballers. *Journal of Applied Sport Psychology, 14,* 1–13.

Olympic News Service. (2014, February 18). Joannie Rochette says 2010 Olympics were 'a blur' after death of her mother. Retrieved July 14, 2014, from www.canada.com.

Parfitt, G., Hardy, L., & Pates, J. (1995). Somatic anxiety and physiological arousal: Their effects upon a high anaerobic, low memory demand task. *International Journal of Sport Psychology, 26,* 196–213.

Park, J. K. (2000). Coping strategies used by Korean national athletes. *The Sport Psychologist, 14,* 63–80.

Pennebaker, J. W. (1997). Writing about emotional experiences as a therapeutic process. *Psychological Science, 8,* 162–166.

Perna, F. M., Antoni, M. H., Baum, A., Gordon, P., & Schneiderman, N. (2003). Cognitive behavioral stress management effects on injury and illness among competitive athletes: A randomized clinical trial. *Annals of Behavioral Medicine, 25,* 66–73.

Powers, T. A., Koestner, R., & Topciu, R. A. (2005). Implementation intentions, perfectionism and goal progress: Perhaps the road to hell is paved with good intentions. *Personality and Social Psychology Bulletin, 31,* 902–912.

Raedeke, T. D. (1997). Is athlete burnout more than just stress? A sport commitment perspective. *Journal of Sport & Exercise Psychology, 19,* 396–417.

Raedeke, T. D., & Smith, A. L. (2001). Development and preliminary validation of an Athlete Burnout Measure. *Journal of Sport & Exercise Psychology, 23,* 281–306.

Raedeke, T. D., & Smith, A. L. (2004). Coping resources and athlete burnout: An examination of stress mediated and moderation hypotheses. *Journal of Sport & Exercise Psychology, 26,* 525–541.

Robazza, C., & Bortoli, L. (2007). Perceived impact of anger and anxiety on sporting performance in rugby players. *Psychology of Sport and Exercise, 8,* 875–896. doi:10.1016/j.psychsport.2006.07.005

Rogers, T. M., & Landers, D. M. (2005). Mediating effects of peripheral vision in the life event stress/athletic injury relationship. *Journal of Sport & Exercise Psychology, 27,* 271–288.

Rumbold, J., Fletcher, D., & Daniels, K. (2012). A systematic review of stress management interventions with sport performers. *Sport, Exercise, and Performance Psychology, 1,* 173–193.

Schellenberg, B., Gaudreau, P., & Crocker, P. R. E., (2013). Passion and coping: Relationships with changes in burnout and goal attainment in collegiate volleyball players. *Journal of Sport & Exercise Psychology, 35,* 270–280.

Skinner, E. A., Edge, K., Altman, J., & Sherwood, H. (2003). Searching for the structure of coping: A review and critique of category systems for classifying ways of coping. *Psychological Bulletin, 129,* 216–269.

Smith, R. E., Smoll, F. L., & Ptacek, J. (1990). Conjunctive moderator variables in vulnerability and resiliency research: Life stress, social support and coping skills, and adolescent sport injuries. *Journal of Personality and Social Psychology, 58,* 360–370.

Sutherland, L. M., Kowalski, K. C., Ferguson, L. J., Sabiston, C. M., Sedgwick, W. A., & Crocker, P. R. E. (2014). Narratives of young women athletes' experiences of emotional pain and self-compassion. *Qualitative Research in Sport, Exercise and Health, 6,* 499–516.

Tamminen, K., & Crocker, P. (2014). Simplicity does not always lead to enlightenment: A critical commentary on "Adaptation processes affecting performance in elite sport." *Journal of Clinical Sport Psychology, 7,* 75–91. doi: 10.1123/jcsp.2014-0013

Tamres, L. K., Janicki, D., & Helgeson, V. S. (2002). Sex differences in coping behavior: A meta-analytic review and an examination of relative coping. *Personality and Social Psychology Review, 6,* 2–30.

Totterdell, P. (2000). Catching moods and hitting runs: Mood linkage and subjective performance in professional sport teams. *Journal of Applied Psychology, 85,* 848–859.

Udry, E. (1997). Coping and social support among injured athletes following surgery. *Journal of Sport & Exercise Psychology, 19,* 71–90.

Van Yperen, N. W. (2009). Why some make it and others do not: Identifying psychological factors that predict career success in professional adult soccer. *The Sport Psychologist, 23,* 317–329.

Woodman, T., Davis, P. A., Hardy, L., Callow, N., Glasscock, I., & Yuill-Proctor, J. (2009). Emotions and sport performance: An exploration of happiness, hope, and anger. *Journal of Sport & Exercise Psychology, 31,* 169–188.

Yoo, J. (2001). Coping profile of Korean competitive athletes. *International Journal of Sport Psychology, 32,* 290–303.

Chapter 5
Anxiety in Sport and Exercise

Kimberley L. Gammage   Sharleen D. Hoar

Robert Michael/AGE Fotostock

Chapter Objectives

After reading this chapter, you should be able to do the following:

1   Define and differentiate among different anxiety-related concepts, such as arousal, trait anxiety, state anxiety, cognitive anxiety, somatic anxiety, social anxiety, social physique anxiety, and competitive anxiety.

2   List and describe the dimensions of an anxiety response, such as intensity, frequency of cognitive intrusions, and directional interpretation of anxiety.

3   List and describe personal and environmental sources of anxiety in sport and exercise settings.

4   Describe how anxiety affects exercise behaviour.

5   Identify and describe the key theories that explain the performance–anxiety relationship in sport, and the cognitive and physiological mechanisms by which anxiety affects performance.

6   Define choking and identify the key explanations of this phenomenon.

Ethan and Jason are best friends and teammates on their high school basketball team. They are both starters and this is their senior year—so they have worked hard all season to help the team succeed. They are on the bus, riding back from the provincial championships, talking about their experience in the game.

Ethan is extremely excited and can barely stay in his seat. "That was the greatest time in my life. Think about it—the game was on the line and it was up to me to sink those last two free throws to win the game. That's what I've been dreaming about my whole life. The gym was so noisy and the crowd was going crazy. I felt everyone's eyes on me, and the pressure of all my teammates counting on me. My heart was pounding in my chest and I could feel the butterflies in my stomach. I thought to myself 'This is it, my last game as a high school player.' Of course, there's always a little bit of worry—what if you miss? But you know what? I love all those feelings. When I experience all those sensations, I know that it just means that I am prepared and that all my training is going to pay off. Standing on the line, I just knew I would make those shots. I go through my routine, and it's like everything is automatic—I don't think about a thing. I just wait to hear the swoosh of the ball as it goes through the net."

Jason can't believe what he is hearing. He says, "I am so glad that it was you standing on the free throw line at the end of the game, and not me. I hate feeling all that pressure, knowing everyone is watching me and counting on me. When my heart starts racing and the butterflies come out, all I can think about is that I'm going to let everyone down, and I'm not ready for any of this. I feel way too tense in my shoulders. And when that happens, it's like my heart starts pounding even harder, and I can't breathe. My thoughts turn to the mechanics of the shot—breaking down every little step in the process. Then, my shot is too choppy, and it usually hits hard against the hoop—and misses. Then all I can think about is how I will let everyone down."

Anxiety is commonly experienced as part of physical activity. It is frequently described by exercisers, athletes, trainers, coaches, sports writers, and sport and exercise psychology researchers in different ways. For example, Mike Weir explains that what he felt in the final round of the 2003 Masters Tournament was "gut wrenching" (Jarrett, 2003, p. 40). Other terms that are commonly used to refer to this psychological state include *nervous, emotional basket case, stressed, self-conscious, pumped*, and *psyched*. Feelings of anxiety can result from hundreds of different events that occur prior to, during, and after participation in physical activity. In the opening vignette, Ethan and Jason both felt pressure because of the perceived importance of the game, their teammates' expectations, and the crowd. Many exercisers can also fall victim to feelings of anxiety. There are, however, instances when performers thrive in their anxious states to produce personal-best performances. Canadian rower Adam Kreek, a 2008 Olympic gold medallist, keeps a blog leading up to his race at the 2008 Beijing Olympic Games. He commented on his race day that he could feel himself getting fired up, using an analogy of a mini-nuclear reactor. He also sensed that his teammates felt the same (Kreek, 2008). In this chapter, the following questions will be addressed: What is anxiety? What causes anxiety in sport and exercise settings? What effect does anxiety have on exercise and athletic performance?

INTRODUCTION

Athletes, coaches, exercisers, exercise trainers, and sport and exercise psychology researchers have been interested in understanding anxiety for many years (Ekkakakis & Petruzzello, 2000; Smith et al., 1998). It is often thought that the difference between successful performances (e.g., a personal best, a winning performance, or adherence to an exercise class) and those performances that are evaluated to be failures lies in the performers' ability to manage their nervousness or anxiety. Because it has been assumed that elevated levels of anxiety are always debilitating for sport and exercise performance, sport and exercise psychology researchers have sought to better understand the causes and consequences of this psychological state.

REFLECTIONS 5.1

Hero Images/Fancy/Corbis

Think about when you felt nervous or under pressure prior to an important competitive event or exercise session. What caused you to feel nervous? How did the anxiety affect your performance in that setting?

Anxiety is experienced in a variety of physical activity settings, including sport and exercise.

DEFINITIONS AND BASIC CONCEPTS OF ANXIETY

Today, sport and exercise psychology researchers emphasize the importance of developing precise definitions for emotion-related terminology, including *anxiety* (Ekkakakis & Petruzzello, 2000). In this section, we define what is meant by *anxiety* in the physical activity literature.

Arousal: Physiological and psychological activation that varies on a continuum from deep sleep to peak activation (or frenzy).

Anxiety Is Not Arousal

Arousal is a blend of physiological and psychological activation of an individual's autonomic nervous system. It varies in intensity on a continuum ranging from deep sleep to peak activation or frenzy (Gould et al., 2002). At the high end of the continuum, high-arousal athletes commonly exhibit both physiological and psychological symptoms. For example, a highly aroused athlete is likely to have a racing heart, shallow breathing, and sweaty palms, as well as tunnel vision and possibly confusion. Arousal is neither a pleasant nor an unpleasant experience. Increases in arousal states can occur from positive and exciting events as well as from negative and potentially threatening events. There is also no ideal level of arousal. For some tasks, like putting in golf, low levels of arousal are generally best, while for other tasks, like tackling in football, higher levels may be better. Early sport psychology research examining the influence of anxiety on sport performance viewed anxiety as a unidimensional construct equivalent to that of arousal (Cerin et al., 2000). More recently, anxiety has been observed to be considerably more complex in nature than arousal.

Anxiety Is an Emotion and Is Multidimensional in Nature

Anxiety is most commonly understood as a negative emotion. Anxiety is proposed to have the following characteristics: (1) it is elicited following an appraisal (i.e., evaluation) of a specific situation or event, (2) it is universally observed across people of all cultures, (3) it has a distinct physiology, (4) it is observed through a discrete facial expression, and (5) it is associated with a unique set of behaviours that are called action tendencies (Lazarus, 2000).

> **Anxiety:** A negative emotion that is elicited following an appraisal of a situation or event.

Sport and exercise psychology researchers have investigated anxiety from a multidimensional perspective (Martens et al., 1990). Anxiety might be experienced by physical activity performers in different ways. Some performers report feeling nauseated or having heavy legs, while others report images of disaster. For example, Canadian Olympic diver Blythe Hartley joked about how viewers at home would be able to identify her: "I'm pretty much a nervous wreck the whole competition. . . . I don't look happy, but that's what works for me" (Gatehouse, 2004, p. 28).

Within this multidimensional framework, anxiety is composed of a mental and a physical component. The mental component is called **cognitive anxiety**, and it reflects the athlete's concerns or worries and the reduced ability to focus or concentrate (Krane, 1994). The physical component, called **somatic anxiety**, refers to people's perceptions of their body states, such as clammy hands or a racing heart. It is important to note that it is really our *perceptions* of the physical symptoms of arousal, rather than the symptoms themselves, that define somatic anxiety, and differentiate it from physiological arousal (Martens et al., 1990). Thus, somatic anxiety is only experienced to the degree that the athlete becomes aware of arousal symptoms. In the opening vignette, both Ethan and Jason described experiencing cognitive anxiety (e.g., the worry and the pressure) and the somatic anxiety (e.g., pounding heart, butterflies in the stomach, tense muscles). Although cognitive and somatic anxiety are conceptualized to be independent and distinct, cognitive and somatic anxiety responses are moderately interrelated and levels of both anxiety responses are experienced in most competitive events.

> **Cognitive anxiety:** Mental component of anxiety referring to worries and concerns.

> **Somatic anxiety:** Physical component of anxiety referring to perceptions of body states, such as a racing heart or butterflies in the stomach.

Anxiety Is Context Specific

Social anxiety is a specific type of anxiety that occurs during social situations. For instance, speaking in front of a large group of people, competing in a stadium full of fans,

> **Social anxiety:** A specific sub-type of anxiety that occurs when people believe they will receive a negative evaluation from others.

Anxiety is experienced in different ways, such as feelings of worry, a racing heartbeat, or shaky hands.

Cadalpe/Image Source/Corbis

and working out at the local gym are all situations in which anxiety may arise due to interactions with other people. Specifically, social anxiety occurs when people experience, or think that they will experience, evaluations from other people that may lead them to form negative impressions (Leary, 1992). Athletes may feel anxious that their coach or teammates are evaluating their performance during games; exercisers may feel anxious if they think others will be judging their appearance. Some researchers have suggested that **competitive anxiety** is a form of social anxiety (Leary, 1992). In this form of anxiety, athletes may be concerned about their body, their performance, their fitness level, or their skills being evaluated by spectators, teammates, coaches, family, or friends. In the exercise context, **social physique anxiety** is most commonly studied. Social physique anxiety is the tendency to experience anxiety as a result of perceiving that others may evaluate one's physique in social settings (Hart et al., 1989).

It Is Important to Consider Both Trait and State Anxiety

Anxiety is both a part of our personality and a response that fluctuates from situation to situation. **State anxiety** is associated with worries and apprehension that change from moment to moment (Speilberger, 1966). For example, an exerciser may experience mild symptoms of anxiety when entering the locker room, with symptoms increasing in intensity in the moments waiting in the exercise studio for her instructor to begin the aerobics class. During the warm-up, the anxiety symptoms may subside and she may feel more comfortable in the setting and be distracted by the aerobic routine. In contrast, **trait anxiety** is a relatively stable part of an individual's personality, predisposing the individual to perceive a variety of situations as physically or psychologically threatening.

Competitive anxiety: A sub-type of social anxiety that occurs in competitive sport situations, and results from worry about their body, performance, or skills being evaluated negatively by others.

Social physique anxiety: A specific sub-type of social anxiety that occurs when people are worried about receiving a negative evaluation about their body from others.

State anxiety: Anxiety that is experienced at a particular moment in time, and can change from moment to moment.

Trait anxiety: A general predisposition to perceive a variety of situations as threatening.

Anxiety Involves a Transaction between the Person and the Environment

Anxiety and stress are considered to be ongoing processes, rather than single events. They are influenced by the demands placed on the athlete or exerciser by the environment (e.g., how good is the competition, how many other exercisers are in the class) and the evaluation by the athlete or exerciser of the available resources (e.g., previous experience, level of fitness). If there is a mismatch, such that the demands are thought to outweigh the resources, anxiety may result. That is, when an athlete or exerciser does not believe that he or she has the resources needed for the demands of the task, anxiety will result (Neil et al., 2011). For example, if a tennis player faces a competitor she has never beaten in the past (high task demand), and she has not been playing well lately because she has been sick (low resources), she will likely experience a high level of anxiety prior to the match.

DIMENSIONS OF THE ANXIETY RESPONSE

What does it mean to state that one exerciser or sport participant has more anxiety than another? *More* could be referring to the intensity of the anxiety symptoms, the number (or frequency) of anxiety-related thoughts or physical symptoms, as well as the directional interpretations of anxiety symptoms for sport performance or exercise behaviour (Mellalieu et al., 2006).

Intensity of Symptoms

Most of the sport and exercise research investigating anxiety has exclusively examined the intensity of symptoms (Mellalieu et al., 2006). This dimension of anxiety involves the amount or level of symptoms experienced by physical activity and sport participants.

Frequency of Cognitive Intrusions

The frequency of cognitive intrusions or symptoms refers to the amount of time (expressed as a percentage) that thoughts and feelings about the competition occupy an individual's mind (Mellalieu et al., 2006). This dimension of anxiety is deemed to be important for understanding the temporal nature of the anxiety response. Even though it is thought to be important, few sport and exercise psychology researchers have investigated anxiety from this perspective.

Directional Interpretation of Symptoms

Most sport and exercise psychology researchers agree that negative emotions do not always negatively affect performance (Uphill, 2008). Sometimes anxiety is perceived to have a positive influence on sport and exercise behaviours. Think about how two elite Canadian athletes describe the implications of their anxiety symptoms for future athletic performances. Blythe Hartley (Olympic diver) stated that the feelings of being a "nervous wreck" are positively interpreted as being in a state of readiness for competition. Alternatively, Steve Podborski (Olympic ski racer) referred to a specific intensity of "nervousness" that, if reached, resulted in poor performance. The third dimension of an anxiety response, the directional interpretation of symptoms, refers to the extent to which the intensity of the cognitive and somatic anxiety symptoms is labelled as either facilitative (i.e., positive) or debilitative (i.e., negative) to sport or physical activity performance (Jones & Swain, 1992). In the opening vignette, Ethan and Jason interpreted the same symptoms very differently—for Ethan, they meant he was excited and ready. For Jason, they meant he was scared. A variety of factors—such as personality traits, psychological skills, skill level, experience, and sport type—can also influence whether anxiety is experienced as facilitative or debilitative (see Hanton et al., 2008, for review).

SOURCES OF ANXIETY

Anxiety responses are experienced by virtually all physical activity participants at different times. Over the years, many environmental and personal sources of anxiety have been identified. A complete review of this work is beyond the scope of this chapter. (Interested readers are directed to Mellalieu et al., 2006.) Instead, we highlight select personal sources of anxiety and then draw attention to certain aspects of the sport and exercise environment that interact with personal sources to elicit participants' anxiety.

Personal Sources of Anxiety

Sport and exercise psychology researchers have identified several important personal sources of anxiety. In this section, we discuss the research findings on five of the most-studied personal sources of anxiety, including (1) experience and skill level, (2) gender, (3) trait anxiety, (4) self-confidence and self-presentational beliefs, and (5) self-regulation strategies.

Experience and Skill Level The relationship between skill level or experience and competitive anxiety has been equivocal. It general, it appears that athletes of different skills or abilities do not differ in the intensity of anxiety symptoms prior to competition. Rather, more skilled athletes view anxiety symptoms to be facilitative or helpful for performance. By contrast, less skilled athletes view anxiety symptoms to be debilitative or harmful for sport performance (Hanton & Jones, 1997; Jones & Swain, 1995).

Competitive experience may be a more sensitive indicator related to differences in athletes' experience of anxiety. The results from studies that use "competitive experience" as an operation of expertise reveal that more-experienced performers report lower intensities of pre-competitive anxiety and evaluate anxiety to be more facilitative for sport performance compared to the less-experienced performers.

Gender The sport research on gender differences in anxiety has been inconsistent. Early research provided some evidence that female athletes report higher intensities of trait and state anxiety symptoms prior to competition in comparison with male athletes (Krane & Williams, 1994). Some research, however, has failed to find differences between male and female competitive anxiety responses (e.g., Hammermeister & Burton, 2004). In exercise and other physical activity settings, females consistently experience higher levels of social physique anxiety compared to males (Crocker et al., 2006). However, different factors are related to social physique anxiety for males and females in physical activity settings (Hausenblas & Fallon, 2002).

Trait Anxiety A number of personality traits, or dispositions, are known to influence an individual's level of competitive state anxiety and social physique anxiety. These characteristics include competitiveness, extraversion, hardiness, neuroticism, optimism/pessimism, perfectionism, self-consciousness, and self-esteem. Of the personality traits that have been investigated, trait anxiety (i.e., **competitive trait anxiety**, or the tendency to experience anxiety during competitive situations, as well as social physique anxiety) has received the most attention from sport and exercise psychology researchers. Interestingly, low trait anxious and high trait anxious athletes interpret state anxiety symptoms in a similar manner; the difference appears to be in the intensity of the anxiety symptoms.

Competitive trait anxiety: The tendency for athletes to experience anxiety during competitive sport situations.

Self-Confidence and Self-Presentational Beliefs An individual's personal beliefs about being capable of achieving sport success as well as being able to present his or her body and skills in a favourable manner are critical sources of anxiety for sport and exercise participants. Research with sport competitors reveals that confidence in oneself and one's team is associated with less pre-competitive anxiety (Bray et al., 2000; Eys et al., 2003). Further, self-confident athletes are also more likely to view state anxiety symptoms as facilitative for performance despite the intensity of anxiety symptoms felt (Hanton et al., 2008). Perhaps an elevation in anxiety symptoms is viewed to be evidence that the athlete is ready to compete. Take the example of an Olympic swimmer: "I mean, you have to get nervous to swim well. . . . If you're not bothered by it, you are not going to swim well. . . . I think that the nerves bring out the best in you, and I soon realized that I wanted to feel this way" (Hanton & Jones, 1999, p. 9).

Another set of beliefs that are related to anxiety are self-presentational concerns. **Self-presentation** is the process by which people attempt to monitor and control the impressions that other people hold of them (Leary, 1992). Athletes who are concerned about what others (such as competitors, teammates, coaches, and family) think of their skill level, fitness, or ability to handle pressure are more likely to experience elevations in competitive trait and state anxiety intensity (McGowan et al., 2008).

Self-presentation: The process by which people attempt to monitor and control the impressions that other people form of them.

Self-presentation beliefs are also a source of anxiety for many exercisers, especially as they relate to physical appearance. For example, as women become more dissatisfied with their bodies, they experience more social physique anxiety. Studies also reveal that as people exercise more to control their weight and appearance, social physique anxiety is also increased (Sabiston et al., 2005).

Another self-presentational belief that is important in exercise settings is **self-presentational efficacy**, which is the confidence in one's ability to present images of being an exerciser. Exercisers who believe that others will see them as fit, coordinated, and attractive report lower levels of social anxiety and social physique anxiety than those who do not believe they will successfully portray those same images (Gammage et al., 2004). Thus, different forms of self-confidence beliefs are important sources of anxiety.

Self-presentational efficacy: Confidence in one's ability to successfully present a desired image to others.

Self-Regulation Strategies How a physical activity participant manages anxiety symptoms has been identified as another important source of anxiety. In sport, a variety of coping skills, such as relaxation, self-talk and cognitive restructuring, and imagery, can be used to adjust physiological arousal and the degree of worry or concern that is experienced. In addition, coping skills to manage anxiety responses prior to and during competitive performances can distinguish between more and less successful athletes (Orlick & Partington, 1988). The use of coping skills can also reduce pre-competitive cognitive and somatic anxiety responses (Haney, 2004).

A series of recent studies to identify the ways in which male and female adolescents manage social physique anxiety revealed that adolescents coped by engaging in exercise behaviour (Kowalski et al., 2006). In fact, physical activity as a coping strategy was reported by approximately 12% of the adolescents (Kowalski et al., 2006). This result should not be surprising since exercise is recommended by physicians as an important strategy for managing anxiety.

Another self-regulation strategy that has received attention by sport researchers is the use of **self-handicapping**. Self-handicapping is defined as "any action or choice of performance setting that enhances the opportunity to externalize (or excuse) failure and internalize (reasonably accept credit for) success" (Berglas & Jones, 1978, p. 406). Athletes who use self-handicapping strategies are likely to diminish efforts during competition, select unattainable goals to achieve, exaggerate the pain associated with an injury, or complain illegitimately about the fairness of the referee in order to confuse whether performance failure is due to athletic ability or due to external problems that the athlete had to manage (Coudevylle et al., 2008; Prapavessis et al., 2003). These athletes also have higher intensity levels of trait and state anxiety. Interestingly, the anxiety symptoms are more likely to be viewed as facilitative for performance (Coudevylle et al., 2008).

In sum, physical activity participants' anxiety responses are related to a number of sources that are specific to the person, although we have highlighted only those personal sources that have received the most attention by sport and exercise researchers. Most of the

Self-handicapping: Behaviours that are used in performance settings such as sport or exercise, in order to excuse any failures that may occur in advance.

| CASE STUDY 5.1 | Identifying Personal Sources of Competitive Anxiety for an Elite Athlete |

Consider Kyle Shewfelt's comments in his blog entry prior to the 2008 Olympic Games in Beijing. What personal sources are likely to be contributing to Kyle's anxiety?

"This morning when I woke up I was a little panicked. The thought that I am actually leaving for Beijing and the Olympic Games felt very real and it freaked me out. . . .

Am I ready? Will I be able to deliver the performance I need to? Will I be able to withstand the Olympic pressure? Have I worked hard enough? Have I done enough routines? Do I need more time? Will my legs hold up? Is my difficulty high enough? What if I don't win again? What if I mess up during the qualification? What if I can't get my second vault? What if I forget how to do gymnastics . . . ?

Feeling the crunch

I am feeling the crunch. The expectation I have of myself and the pressure of the Olympic Games are beginning to build. . . . It's almost as if every moment that I am not in the gym and proving to myself that I can do gymnastics, I am doubting my ability. I am only getting relief and confirmation when I am physically there and going through the motions.

I find myself worrying about the thoughts that are going to go through my head when it's time to compete. I want to be focused and prepared and not wishing that I could escape the moment and run away and hide.

When the sharks attack

I am so scared that my physical, emotional and mental selves are not going to align at the moment I need them to. What if I completely destroy my performance? What if I stand there waiting to compete and I don't trust the work I have done? What if I let the sharks attack and I am left with severed limbs and a devastating experience?

I think these thoughts are normal . . ." (Shewfelt, 2008).

Source: Used with permission of Kyle Shewfelt.

research has examined anxiety responses in light of the intensity of symptoms experienced. Some research has examined select personal sources that affect athletes' interpretation of anxiety symptoms as facilitative or debilitative for sport performance. It can be generally concluded that elevations in the intensity of anxiety responses in athletes and exercisers are associated with (1) novice expertise, (2) being female, (3) high trait anxiety, (4) low self-confidence (and low self-efficacy) in individual and team competencies, (5) negative or poor self-presentational beliefs, (6) poor self-regulatory skills, and (7) the use of self-handicapping strategies.

Environment-Based Sources of Anxiety

Sport and exercise psychology research also reveals that individuals' anxiety responses are related not only to personal sources. The environment also uniquely contributes to anxiety in physical activity participants. In sport, athletes' anxiety is related to the temporal period within competitive events. In the exercise context, exercisers' anxiety responses are related to specific aspects of the exercise setting, including the physical environment and the other people that are present.

Temporal Patterning in the Sport Environment The intensity of an athlete's anxiety response changes during the lead-up to a competitive event as well as over the course of the event (see Figure 5.1). Generally, somatic anxiety remains at a low intensity until several hours prior to competition, after which there is a sharp rise until the onset of performance. During and after competition, the intensity level of somatic anxiety decreases. Cognitive anxiety demonstrates a different pattern. Unless there is a change in the athlete's evaluation of the potential for success prior to competition, no changes in

Figure 5.1 Hypothesized temporal patterning of cognitive anxiety and somatic anxiety before and after a sport performance

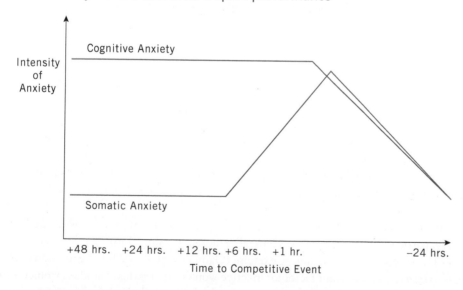

Source: Stress and performance in sport by Jones, J. Graham; Hardy, Lew. Reproduced with permission of JOHN WILEY & SONS, INCORPORATED in the format Republish in a book via Copyright Clearance Center.

Anxiety changes over the different phases of a competition. The ability to control anxiety prior to, during, and after competition is critical for competitive success.

Hero Images/Corbis

the intensity level of cognitive anxiety are expected to occur prior to competition. After the onset of competition, there is a steady decline in the intensity of cognitive anxiety.

Temporal patterning of competitive anxiety has also been studied according to the frequency of cognitive intrusions/symptoms as well as the directional interpretation of anxiety symptoms. Swain and Jones (1993) found that while the intensity of cognitive anxiety remained stable, the frequency of cognitive intrusions increased as competition neared. Conclusions drawn from the research examining changes in directional interpretation across the competitive temporal phases suggest that directional perceptions of cognitive anxiety become less facilitative as the competition draws nearer (Cerin et al., 2000; Rich et al., 2007).

Exercise: The Physical Environment Specific factors in the exercise environment may also be sources of anxiety. Studies have suggested that the presence of mirrors during exercise may increase the levels of state anxiety and social anxiety experienced (Focht & Hausenblas, 2004). This may be particularly true in women who are already high in trait social physique anxiety, for those who do not regularly exercise, or for exercisers performing very simple tasks (e.g., riding a stationary bike), as the mirrors may be used to focus on physical appearance. However, for regular exercisers or for more complex tasks, mirrors might be useful in providing performance information because they provide an opportunity to watch one's performance rather than appearance (Raedeke et al., 2007). In these conditions, mirrors may not increase anxiety.

The type of clothing worn in the exercise environment is also associated with anxiety, particularly social anxiety. Generally, more revealing clothing is associated with higher levels of social anxiety during exercise (Gammage et al., 2004). Again, however, it seems to be a more important factor for inactive women. In a series of studies, women who engaged in little physical activity and who were high in social physique anxiety preferred less-revealing attire, while those lower in social physique anxiety preferred more-revealing clothing. However, in participants who were already active, this difference disappeared (Crawford & Eklund, 1994; Eklund & Crawford, 1994).

Other People in the Exercise Environment Simply exercising in the presence of others can increase anxiety in women. For instance, Focht and Hausenblas (2004) found that women who were higher in social physique anxiety and who exercised when other people were present experienced greater state anxiety during exercise than those who exercised in a lab setting by themselves. Specific characteristics of other exercisers may also lead to greater anxiety, such as when other participants are highly interactive, positive, and enthusiastic during an exercise class ("enriched" participants; Martin & Fox, 2001). Why would a friendlier environment be associated with more anxiety? The authors suggested that the exercisers wanted the other class participants to like them and cared more about what others thought about them, which may have increased their social anxiety. In addition, because the exercisers were interacting with other participants more, they may also have believed that others were watching their performance and were perhaps evaluating it more closely. Another factor that seems to lead to anxiety in women, but not in men, is the gender of the other exercise participants. Specifically, women who imagined exercising in mixed-gender rather than all-female settings reported higher levels of social physique anxiety.

Finally, characteristics of the exercise leader may affect the anxiety experienced during exercise. However, unlike studies that have shown that highly interactive and enthusiastic participants may lead to increases in anxiety, an enriched leadership style is associated with less social anxiety, perhaps because participants feel less intimidated and are less worried about being judged negatively by the instructor. The appearance of the exercise leader may also affect anxiety. For instance, one study examined the impact that the clothing worn by the instructor in an exercise video had on women's anxiety. Women who thought they had less attractive bodies than the instructor experienced greater social physique anxiety than those who thought they were just as or more attractive than the instructor, regardless of what the instructor actually looked like (Martin Ginis et al., 2008).

The exercise environment may increase anxiety.

Starush/Fotolia

ANXIETY INFLUENCES ON EXERCISE BEHAVIOUR AND SPORT PERFORMANCE

What effect does anxiety have on exercisers and sport participants? One obvious consequence of anxiety is its potential effect on exercise behaviour and sport performance. Exercisers who experience excessive levels of anxiety are likely to feel uncomfortable in the exercise environment, to experience less enjoyment, and not to engage in exercise behaviour in the future. Similarly, athletes who consistently experience high levels of worry and apprehension prior to sport competition also tend to have lowered levels of enjoyment with sport, increased susceptibility to athletic injury, enhanced feelings of burnout, and increased dropout rates (Smith et al., 1998). Although these outcomes are important to understand, most of the scientific study of anxiety consequences has focused on exercise adherence and athletic performance. Thus, we will focus on the research investigating the relationship between anxiety and these physical activity behaviours.

The Influence of Anxiety on Exercise Behaviours

Most anxiety research has attempted to determine how various forms of anxiety may influence exercise-related behaviours and cognitions. This research has examined the relationship between social anxiety and exercise primarily through a self-presentational framework. Self-presentation occurs when people try to control how others see them (Leary, 1992). For example, if you want people to see you as fit, you could tell them that you exercise, you could wear exercise clothing, or you could actually exercise. Leary suggested that at very high levels, social anxiety may prevent people from exercising altogether. This idea makes some sense. If people experience anxiety when exercising—or even when thinking about exercising—they may do everything they can to avoid it. Therefore, it is important to understand how anxiety can affect exercise-related behaviours and cognitions. Much of this research has examined the influence of social physique anxiety.

Individuals high in social physique anxiety may exercise more as a way to improve their bodies and therefore receive positive evaluations from others. However, individuals high in social physique anxiety might also avoid exercise, to avoid situations in which others could evaluate their bodies. So, which hypothesis is correct? Researchers have found support for both! Some research has found that those higher in social physique anxiety actually exercise more (Frederick & Morrison, 1996), other research indicates that they exercise less (Culos-Reed et al., 2002), and still other research has found no relationship between the two (Crocker et al., 2006).

Because of the mixed findings, researchers have attempted to examine other variables that may influence this relationship. For example, Angove and colleagues (2003) investigated the exercise behaviours of older women who were and were not confident in their ability to be seen positively in an exercise setting (i.e., low self-presentational efficacy). The results revealed that social physique anxiety led to lower levels of physical activity only in women with low levels of self-presentational efficacy. Similar findings have been shown in adolescent girls (Cumming & Thøgersen-Ntoumani, 2011). Interestingly, however, recent work by Canadian researchers has shown that in college men and women, only self-presentational efficacy (and not social physique anxiety) predicted exercise behaviour (Gammage et al., 2014).

One exercise-related health risk behaviour that may be related to self-presentational concerns is excessive exercise. For instance, Martin and Leary (2001) found that men often over-lifted at the gym in order to be seen as brave and attractive by others. In contrast, Hausenblas and Fallon (2002) found that social physique anxiety was not significantly related to symptoms of exercise dependence when the body mass index, gender, and exercise behaviour of the individual were taken into consideration.

Anxiety–Sport Performance Relationship Models

Much of the research on anxiety and physical activity has occurred in the sport performance field. Early explanations about the influence of competitive anxiety on sport performance, such as the drive theory and inverted-U theory (see Woodman & Hardy, 2001), were based on anxiety being equivalent to arousal. Since 1990, sport research has largely ignored these explanations in favour of more complex theories that examine anxiety from a multidimensional perspective. Two theories have recently gained support in sport psychology research: zones of optimal functioning (Hanin, 1980), and cusp catastrophe theory (Fazey & Hardy, 1988; Hardy, 1990).

Drive Theory and Inverted-U Hypothesis Two of the earliest theories used to understand the arousal–performance relationship are Hull's (1951) drive theory and the inverted-U hypothesis (Yerkes & Dodson, 1908). Drive theory suggests that performance is a function of two factors: habit strength and arousal, or drive. The more well-learned a task (the higher the habit strength), and the greater the arousal (higher drive), the better the performance. Thus, according to this theory, higher levels of arousal lead to better performance (see Figure 5.2). Unfortunately, as tasks (such as competitive sport) become more complex, this theory has generally not been supported.

A second theory of arousal that has been investigated in the sport literature is the inverted-U hypothesis. This theory suggests that performance improves as arousal increases, but only up to a certain point. After that point, increases in arousal will lead

Figure 5.2 Drive theory: As physiological arousal increases, performance improves

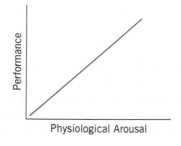

Figure 5.3 Inverted U-hypothesis: As physiological arousal increases, performance improves but only up to a certain point, after which performance will decline

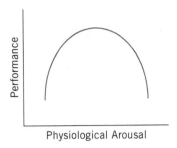

to poorer performance (see Figure 5.3). The optimal level of arousal differs from skill to skill. For example, in the biathlon (in which athletes cross country ski as quickly as possible to targets where they must shoot the targets accurately), the cross country skiing likely requires a higher level of arousal for optimal performance compared to the shooting. Further, the optimal level of arousal will also differ from person to person.

While these theories intuitively make sense, they do have some limitations. First, they are unidimensional and address only physiological arousal, rather than anxiety, which as previously described is multidimensional. Specifically, they do not address the cognitive component of anxiety. They also describe the arousal–performance relationship, but do not explain how arousal affects performance. More recent theories addressing anxiety attempt to account for these more complex relationships.

Zones of Optimal Functioning Theory In his work with Russian athletes, Yuri Hanin (1980) noted that athletes demonstrated considerable variability in the level of pre-competitive state anxiety that was associated with optimal athletic performance. Some athletes performed best with high levels of state anxiety, while others achieved superior performances with moderate or low levels of state anxiety. These observations led Hanin to contend that best performances are more likely to occur with optimal levels of state anxiety (Figure 5.4). Further, Hanin argued that optimal state anxiety is a bandwidth, or zone, of state anxiety intensity scores (not a single value) that is specific to the individual athlete and is not dependent on motor skill requirements of the sport or the athlete's skill level (Raglin & Hanin, 2000).

The key principle of the zones of optimal functioning (ZOF) hypothesis is that an athlete who is within his or her identified optimal competitive state anxiety zone will be more likely to have a best athletic performance. If the athlete has anxiety that is outside of his or her optimal zone (either too low or too high), performance is likely to be impaired (Robazza, 2006). The ZOF hypothesis has been tested in a number of investigations with athletes from a wide variety of countries. The research reveals that, in general, athletes who are within personally identified optimal zones of competitive state anxiety are more likely to have best performances compared with athletes who are outside the determined optimal zone (Jokela & Hanin, 1999). Hanin has expanded the theory to investigate multiple emotional states on sport performance (see Robazza, 2006). This theory has been important for understanding (1) how the relationship between anxiety and performance differs between athletes, and (2) that anxiety is not always detrimental to sport performance.

Figure 5.4 Individual zones of optimal functioning model, depicting the bandwidth of optimal performance for athletes with three different zones

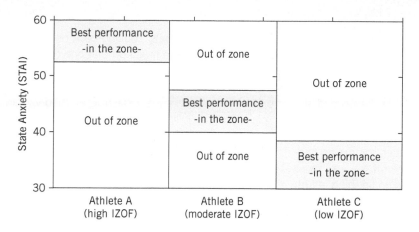

Source: Hanin, Yuri L. (2003). Performance related emotional states in sport: A qualitative analysis. *Forum Qualitative Sozialforschung/Forum: Qualitative Social Research, 4* (1), Art. 5, http://www.qualitative-research.net/index.php/fqs/article/view/747/1618.

Practically speaking, this theory suggests that the optimal intensity zone of competitive state anxiety required for optimal performance from members of a sport team is likely to differ among the players. For example, some hockey players may play their best even if there are large fluctuations in the intensity of anxiety symptoms (i.e., a wide zone of competitive state anxiety), whereas others may play best when the intensity of state anxiety stays constant (i.e., a narrow zone of competitive state anxiety). Moreover, some of the team members may require a low to moderate intensity band of competitive state anxiety, while others display personal best performances when experiencing moderate to high levels of competitive anxiety. The point is that each hockey player's optimal intensity band of competitive state anxiety is individual and is dependent on the player, not the type of sport or sport skills that the athlete is to perform.

The main limitation to the ZOF hypothesis is that it does not account for why there are differences in optimal zones from one person to the next. Also, in most instances, the optimal zones are identified by retrospective recall—that is, people are asked to remember their best or worst performances, and their levels of anxiety before and during those performances. Thus, it is possible that errors in memory or other biases may influence how people identify their optimal zones.

Cusp Catastrophe Theory The cusp catastrophe theory attempts to describe the combined, or interactive, influences of the multiple components of competitive anxiety and physiological arousal on athletic performance, rather than looking at them separately (Fazey & Hardy, 1988; Hardy, 1990). Catastrophe theory is a three-dimensional model that includes the interaction of physiological arousal (rather than somatic anxiety), cognitive anxiety, and performance. Few sport psychology researchers have applied this model to understand the relationship between anxiety and sport performance, and it has been criticized for being overly complex (e.g., Gill, 1994). But why would one expect anxiety and performance relationships to be simple? Canadian downhill ski racer Steve Podborski describes how his competitive anxiety affected his athletic performance: "I discovered that

Canadian Olympic athlete Mellisa Hollingsworth won a bronze medal in women's skeleton in the 2006 Turino games. Going into the Vancouver Olympics in 2010, she was hoping to build on that success. She was ranked number one in the World Cup rankings that season and she was certainly a medal favourite. Going into the last of her four runs, she was sitting in second place. Her start in the skeleton was her personal best—but then something happened on the way down. She bounced off the wall twice partway down the track and she ended up finishing in fifth place, out of the medals. Looking back on that race, she said, "I just focused so much on that one corner. If you're too strong on your sled, too aggressive, that's when mistakes happen" (Hollingsworth, 2012).

Thinking about cusp catastrophe theory, can you explain Mellisa Hollingsworth's performance in the final run at the Vancouver Olympics? Think about the interaction between physiological arousal, cognitive anxiety, and performance during that final run.

after a certain point of nervousness, I would start to deteriorate pretty rapidly. There was a real drop-off point in my ability to perform if I got too nervous . . . so it was just being able to find that little narrow comfort zone" (Orlick & Partington, 1986, p. 162).

The advantage to using the cusp catastrophe theory is that it recognizes that anxiety has a complex relationship with athletic performance (see Case Study 5.2). Further, unlike some other theories, catastrophe theory predicts that under certain circumstances, elevations in the intensity of anxiety are not always detrimental for performance—in fact, they might be facilitative. Essentially, this model makes five predictions (Woodman & Hardy, 2005).

1. When cognitive state anxiety is low, the relationship between physiological arousal and performance is uniform or an inverted-U shape (as shown by the back face of Figure 5.5).

Figure 5.5 Cusp catastrophe theory describing the interactions of cognitive state anxiety, physiological arousal, and sport performance

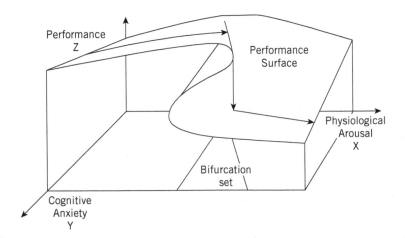

Source: Stress and performance in sport by Jones, J. Graham; Hardy, Lew. Reproduced with permission of JOHN WILEY & SONS, INCORPORATED in the format Republish in a book via Copyright Clearance Center.

Carefully consider the tenets of the different competitive-anxiety performance models. Can we explain Perdita Felicien's performance in her final race at the 2004 Olympic Games in Athens? She was ranked number one in the world in the 110 m hurdles. At the Olympic Games, she performed well in her heats and easily qualified for the finals. However, what happened in the final race was what she described as "my worst nightmare come true" ("This is," 2004, p. 2). A few metres into the race, she missed a hurdle, hitting the barrier instead. Losing her balance, she fell into another competitor and fell to the ground. She could not complete her race and was disqualified.

How might each of the models presented in this chapter describe Felicien's competitive anxiety in relation to her performance?

2. When physiological arousal is low, elevations in cognitive state anxiety are associated with enhanced performance relative to baseline (as shown by the left side of Figure 5.5).

3. When physiological arousal is high, elevations in cognitive state anxiety are associated with declines in performance (as shown by the right side of Figure 5.5).

4. When cognitive state anxiety is high (as shown by the front face of Figure 5.5), increases in physiological arousal can be positive for performance, but only up to a certain point. Thus, high cognitive state anxiety and moderately low levels of physiological arousal should produce more successful performances (compared with those produced under conditions of low cognitive anxiety). This proposition implies that a high level of cognitive anxiety is not always detrimental to sport performance. For athletes who are able to sustain moderately low levels of physiological arousal, an increase in worry and concern can function to enhance athletic performance.

5. When physiological arousal is moderately high and cognitive state anxiety is high, it is predicted that a dramatic performance drop (similar to that described by Steve Podborski), called a *catastrophe*, will occur. Thus, cognitive anxiety determines the effect of physiological arousal on performance. A performance catastrophe is not proposed to occur when cognitive state anxiety is low. To improve performance after the catastrophe, it is not enough to just return to pre-competitive anxiety levels—a decrease in physiological arousal is required.

Studies investigating the proposed relationships of the catastrophe model have produced results that support these predictions across a range of sports (e.g., Edwards & Hardy, 1996; Woodman & Hardy, 2005).

UNDERLYING MECHANISMS OF THE ANXIETY–PERFORMANCE RELATIONSHIP

Despite important advancements in documenting anxiety and performance relationships, sport psychology researchers still do not completely know why this relationship forms at all. That is, the question "Why does competitive anxiety affect athletic performance?" still remains unanswered. To explore this question, it is important to consider the critical components of sport skill execution. Optimal performance of any motor skill requires at least the following: (1) the cognitive processing of relevant amounts and types of information from the environment, and (2) the appropriate levels and coordination of muscle activation. Consider wheelchair athlete Chantal Petitclerc, Canada's 2008 Athlete of the Year, who completed her Paralympic career by winning five gold medals at the Beijing Games. In a 1500 m race, she must focus her attention on numerous external stimuli, such as the condition of the track, the position of other racers, her placement on the track (straightaway or curve), and the actual stage of the race. Throughout the race, she must also generate the correct action plans for producing specific forces and translate these plans into movement programs to produce the appropriate movements. If there are problems in either the action plans or the movement programs, she will not have effective actions. Sport researchers believe that competitive anxiety and arousal processes affect sport performance through interfering with the attentional processes (i.e., processing of external and internal stimuli) and/or the neuromuscular control systems (Jones & Uphill, 2004).

Attentional Mechanisms

Results from studies have demonstrated that competitive anxiety affects the amount and the type of information that is attended to (i.e., task relevant versus task irrelevant) and the type of cognitive processing (i.e., conscious control versus automatic) that occurs during competitive sport performances.

The first attentional focus problem associated with elevations in competitive anxiety is called the attentional focus and selectivity hypothesis, which states that an elevation in competitive state anxiety reduces the ability to attend to and process large amounts of information (Easterbrook, 1959). Likened to travelling down a tunnel, an increase in competitive state anxiety is associated with the narrowing of attentional focus, meaning the athlete is not paying attention to all the cues in the environment (Naylor et al., 2002). This narrowing of attention may have two effects on performance. If unimportant distracting cues are blocked out for the athlete, performance may be improved by increases in competitive anxiety. But, if important task-relevant cues are missed, then performance may be diminished by elevated competitive anxiety.

The second attentional focus problem associated with elevated competitive anxiety is the type of information that is processed. Highly anxious athletes attend to threatening task-irrelevant information to a greater extent than low anxious athletes. In general, the results from this line of research show that the information attended to by highly anxious athletes is governed by the subjective importance of the cues (i.e., threat) rather than the location of the cues in the visual field (Jones & Uphill, 2004). The implication of these findings for sport performers is that attention that is selectively focused to task-irrelevant cues when the athlete is anxious is detrimental for sport performance, because it may lead to missing the important task-relevant cues.

The third attentional focus problem that occurs in the presence of competitive anxiety is the shifting to a conscious, controlled processing system (Liao & Masters, 2002; Maxwell et al., 2006). This phenomenon is likened to "a paralysis by analysis" (Moran, 2004). It is proposed that during high-pressure sport situations, heightened anxiety is associated with increases in a performer's self-conscious awareness about the performance, which becomes disruptive for expert performance of motor skills. This can be illustrated in an example of a university basketball player's free-throw shots at the end of regulation time with the score tied. In this situation, the basketball player is likely to experience elevations in anxiety (i.e., due to the increased importance of making a successful shot) that are associated with increased attention paid to the mechanics of the shot. Although increasing attention to the shot mechanics may seem like the right thing to do in order to increase the likelihood of success, research demonstrates that it has a paradoxical effect (Masters, 1992). Heightened conscious control of a previously automatic skilled behaviour disrupts the coordinated fluidity that is associated with a well-learned skill, and often leads to inferior performance. This is exactly what Jason described, in the opening vignette. For Ethan, however, he remained "on automatic."

Physiological Mechanisms

The relationship between competitive anxiety and athletic performance can also be explained through anxiety-related changes to the functional patterns of muscle activation (Parfitt et al., 1990). Traditionally, it has been proposed that increased physiological arousal disrupts the performance of motor skills that require manual dexterity and fine motor control. Elevated physiological arousal can increase anaerobic power, which, in turn, may enhance the performance of simple tasks such as jumping (Parfitt & Pates, 1999). Jones and Uphill (2004) state that caution is warranted in suggesting that arousal elevations associated with competitive anxiety states have a unitary response on sport performance. Arousal is likely to impact an athlete's physical functioning in a number of ways. Notebook and his colleagues provide empirical evidence that high levels of arousal can decrease performance on fine motor tasks through increasing muscular tension, which can impact motor control (Notebook et al., 2001). High arousal has also been associated with difficulties in coordination of movement among soldiers required to do stepping tasks and weightlifters performing a snatch lift (Collins et al., 2001). The implication of this research is that elevations in anxiety result in less fluid movement patterns and lowered sport performance. It was suggested that the elevated anxiety state of the sport performer may predispose the athlete to injury.

Anxiety may affect performance through changes to attention or through physiological changes to the body.

CHOKING IN SPORT

Choking is defined as experiencing an acute, significant decrement in performance under situations of high pressure or anxiety (Baumeister, 1984; Hill et al., 2009). According to Clark and colleagues (2005), when an athlete chokes, he or she is able to engage in decision making and create a plan of action, but is not able to actually execute that plan due to psychological factors.

Why does choking occur? We can look at several potential explanations. According to cusp catastrophe theory (see above), high levels of cognitive anxiety and physiological

Choking: An acute, significant decrement in performance that occurs in situations of high pressure or anxiety.

REFLECTIONS 5.3

Have you ever choked while playing a sport? Think about that performance. What happened leading up to the event that could account for your performance? Was it due to high levels of anxiety and arousal? Were there attentional errors? Or did you experience increased self-focus?

arousal should create a situation where choking may occur (which may be considered a catastrophe). However, while this combination leads to choking in some athletes, it does not always lead to choking (Vickers & Williams, 2007).

Other researchers believe that changes to attention underlie choking. For example, distraction theories suggest that worry about performance leads to inefficient information processing, making it difficult to effectively process the information needed to perform well. When anxiety is very high, or the task demands are very high, athletes' abilities to process necessary information are overburdened, performance declines, and choking may be the result.

Other researchers believe an increase in self-focus may lead to choking (Leary, 1992). This line of thinking suggests competitive anxiety may lead to greater self-consciousness (that is, thinking about yourself and your performance), which leads even high-level athletes to begin to break down their skills into specific, individual parts—just as a novice athlete would do. This breakdown leads to slowed information processing along with more performance errors—resulting in choking (Masters & Maxwell, 2008).

Obviously, not every athlete chokes, even in the most high pressure situations. Some athletes actually exhibit their best performances when everything is on the line (think about Ethan in the opening vignette). So what factors influence choking? Hill and colleagues (2010) outlined several factors that seem to predispose athletes to choking under pressure. For example, athletes doing more **reinvesting** (consciously controlling their movements, even for very well learned, automatic tasks), those with high levels of trait anxiety, and athletes with low self-confidence are more likely to choke. The specific skill also has an impact—complex tasks are more likely to lead to choking than simpler ones. Environmental factors—in particular the presence of an audience who can evaluate performance—can also increase the likelihood of choking. Skill level may also be important. Interestingly, novice athletes tend to choke due to attentional problems, while experts tend to choke more due to self-focus. But, no one is immune to choking.

Reinvesting: Consciously controlling physical movements, even for well-learned tasks, rather than performing them automatically.

| CASE STUDY 5.4 | Choking in Sport |

Spencer O'Brien, competing in the 2014 Sochi Olympic games, was expected to medal in the women's inaugural slopestyle snowboard event. She was the world champion, she had had a great practice, and she felt inspired by the bronze medal won the previous day by Canadian Mark McMorris in the men's event. Unfortunately, on day two of the competition, O'Brien lost her balance on her first run, which she had to cut short before finishing. On the second—and final—run, still in the running for a medal, she slipped again, not finishing the run and ending up in last place.

Is this an example of choking in sport? What individual and environmental factors may have contributed to this situation?

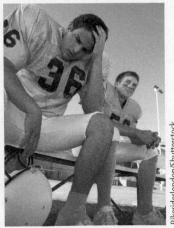

Bikeriderlondon/Shutterstock

Choking occurs when there is an acute, significant decline in performance in situations of high pressure or anxiety.

Physical activity is associated with anxiety. What does more than 40 years of research reveal to us about anxiety-related emotions in sport and exercise? The following key points are conclusions that are generally accepted by sport and exercise psychology researchers about the effects of anxiety in sport and physical activity.

Anxiety is a complex, multidimensional psychological construct. It is important to distinguish between cognitive and somatic anxiety in order to understand what causes competitive anxiety to occur and what effects competitive anxiety has on physical activity performance and other important outcomes.

Several dimensions of the anxiety response can be examined. Most of the research within sport and exercise psychology has investigated anxiety responses according to the intensity of anxiety symptoms. However, it is acknowledged that anxiety can be observed in forms other than intensity. Specifically, sport psychology researchers also examine anxiety responses according to the frequency of anxiety-related thoughts and the directional interpretation of anxiety for performance.

There are multiple personal and environmental sources of anxiety in sport and exercise settings. Also, it is recognized that different performers in similar environments may vary in their anxiety response. This is attributed to the interaction of the environment with personal factors.

Anxiety can lead to negative outcomes in sport and exercise. High levels of competitive anxiety may lead to poor athletic performance. Recent advances in sport psychology researchers' understanding of this relationship reveal that arousal theories, zones of optimal functioning, and cusp catastrophe theory are appropriate to explain the competitive anxiety–performance relationship. Competitive anxiety is not necessarily debilitating for all athletes. Exercise psychology research has produced evidence that some social physique anxiety increases exercise behaviour in some people, while it decreases exercise behaviour in others.

Changes to cognitive processes and neuromuscular control systems explain why competitive anxiety affects athletic performance. Competitive anxiety affects how athletes process the information they receive from internal and external environments. Research also demonstrates that anxiety-related emotion affects the tension and coordination of muscle action. Both mechanisms are directly related to sport performance.

Choking refers to experiencing a significant decline in performance in situations of high pressure. Slowed information processing, changes to attention, and increased self-focus may all account for choking.

COMMON MYTHS ABOUT ANXIETY IN SPORT AND EXERCISE REVISITED

MYTH: Anxiety symptoms are generally the same for all sport and exercise participants.

The reality is that the exact anxiety response to a sport or exercise event is specific to the individual. Sport and exercise psychology researchers state that anxiety symptoms can differ with respect to the kind of symptom (e.g., "gut wrenching," concerns about past failed performance), intensity of anxiety (e.g., high or low), frequency of symptoms, and duration of the felt anxiety (Jones, 1995). The individual anxiety response displayed by physical activity participants is important to understanding how anxiety affects performance.

MYTH: Anxiety is only relevant for athletes—since exercise is non-competitive, it doesn't lead to feelings of anxiety.
Anxiety is an important emotion that is also experienced by exercisers. One of the most studied types of anxiety in exercise settings is social physique anxiety—anxiety that results when people are concerned that others will evaluate their body. But, the relationship is complex. For some exercisers, anxiety may result in increased exercise as they try to improve their appearance. In some instances, it may even lead to excessive exercise behaviour. For others, however, anxiety may lead them to avoid exercise altogether.

MYTH: Pre-competitive anxiety always negatively affects sport performance.
Traditional research efforts assumed that elevated levels of pre-competitive anxiety were always detrimental to athletic performance. However, for many athletes this assumption is false! There are many examples in which Canadian athletes have excelled in elite competition despite their feelings of pre-competitive nervousness. If you reflect on your own competitive sport performances, it is likely that you can recall a time when you enjoyed the benefits of competitive anxiety. Today, most sport psychology researchers agree that pre-competitive anxiety can have both positive (e.g., facilitative) and negative (e.g., debilitative) consequences for sport performance.

Review Questions

1. Compare and contrast the following concepts of anxiety: arousal, social anxiety, competitive anxiety, trait anxiety, social physique anxiety, state anxiety, cognitive anxiety, and somatic anxiety.

2. Summarize five personal sources contributing to a performer's anxiety response.

3. Describe how the temporal phase of competition affects cognitive and somatic anxiety responses of athletes. How would the expertise or gender of an athlete affect the anxiety response exhibited prior to and during a competition?

4. Discuss four attributes of the exercise environment that are related to exercisers' anxiety response. Which personal sources of anxiety affect the anxiety response of exercisers in different exercise environments?

5. Discuss the major differences in how the following theories explain how competitive anxiety affects sport performance: drive theory, inverted-U hypothesis, zones of optimal functioning, and cusp catastrophe theory.

6. Describe two mechanisms that are likely responsible for the relationship between competitive anxiety and sport performance.

7. Define choking. What explanations are there for why some athletes may choke in high pressure situations?

Suggested Reading

Hanton, S., Wadey, R., & Mellalieu, S. D. (2008). Advanced psychological strategies and anxiety responses in sport. *The Sport Psychologist, 22,* 472–490.

Lox, C. L., Martin Ginis, K. A., & Petruzzello, S. J. (2014). Anxiety and exercise. The psychology of exercise: *Integrating theory and practice* (3rd ed., pp. 257–282). Scottsdale, AZ: Holcomb Hathway.

Wagstaff, C. R. D., Neil, R., Mellalieu, S. D., & Hanton, S. (2011). Key movements in directional research in competitive anxiety. In J. Thatcher, M. M. Jones, & D. Lavallee (Eds.). *Coping and emotion in sport* (pp. 143–166). Abingdon, UK: Routledge.

References

Angove, J., Martin Ginis, K. A., & Sinden, A. R. (2003). Physical activity and social physique anxiety in older women: The moderating effects of self-presentation efficacy. *Journal of Applied Biobehavioral Research, 8,* 116–127.

Baumeister, R. F. (1984). Choking under pressure. Self-consciousness and paradoxical effects of incentives on skillful performance. *Journal of Personality and Social Psychology, 46,* 610–620.

Berglas, S., & Jones, E. E. (1978). Drug choice as a self-handicapping strategy in response to non-contingent success. *Journal of Personality and Social Psychology, 36,* 405–417.

Bray, S. R., Martin, K. A., & Widmeyer, W. N. (2000). The relationship between evaluative concerns and sport competition state anxiety among youth skiers. *Journal of Sport Sciences, 18,* 353–361.

Cerin, E., Szabo, A., Hunt, N., & Williams, C. (2000). Temporal patterning of competitive emotions: A critical review. *Journal of Sports Sciences, 18,* 605–626.

Clark, T. P., Tofler, I. R., & Lardon, M. T. (2005). The sport psychologist and golf. *Clinics in Sports Medicine, 24,* 959–971.

Collins, D., Jones, B., Fairweather, M., Doolan, S., & Priestley, N. (2001). Examining anxiety associated changes in movement patterns. *International Journal of Sport Psychology, 31,* 223–242.

Coudevylle, G. R., Martin Ginis, K. A., Famose, J. P., & Gernigon, C. (2008). Effects of self-handicapping strategies on anxiety before athletic competition. *The Sport Psychologist, 22,* 304–315.

Crawford, S., & Eklund, R. C. (1994). Social physique anxiety, reasons for exercise, and attitudes toward exercise settings. *Journal of Sport and Exercise Psychology, 16,* 70–82.

Crocker, P. R. E., Sabiston, C., Kowalski, K., McDonough, M., & Kowalski, N. (2006). Longitudinal assessment of the relationship between physical self-concept and health-related behavior and emotion in adolescent girls. *Journal of Applied Sport Psychology, 18,* 185–200.

Culos-Reed, S. N., Brawley, L. R., Martin, K. A., & Leary, M. R. (2002). Self-presentation concerns and health behaviors among cosmetic treatment patients. *Journal of Applied Social Psychology, 32,* 560–569.

Cumming, J., & Thøgersen-Ntoumani, C. (2011). Self-presentational cognitions for exercise in female adolescents. *Journal of Applied Social Psychology, 41,* 429–444.

Easterbrook, J. A. (1959). The effect of emotion on cue utilization and the organization of behavior. *Psychological Review, 66,* 183–201.

Edwards, T. C., & Hardy, L. (1996). The interactive effects of intensity and direction of cognitive and somatic anxiety and self-confidence upon performance. *Journal of Sport & Exercise Psychology 18,* 296–312.

Ekkakakis, P., & Petruzzello, S. J. (2000). Analysis of the affect measurement conundrum in exercise psychology. I. Fundamental issues. *Psychology of Sport & Exercise, 1,* 71–88.

Eklund, R. C., & Crawford, S. (1994). Active women, social physique anxiety, and exercise. *Journal of Sport and Exercise Psychology, 16,* 431–448.

Eys, M. A., Hardy, J., Carron, A. V., & Beauchamp, M. R. (2003). The relationship between task cohesion and competitive state anxiety. *Journal of Sport & Exercise Psychology, 25,* 66–76.

Fazey, J. A., & Hardy, L. (1988). *The inverted-U hypothesis: A catastrophe for sport psychology?* (British Association of Sports Sciences Monograph, 1). Leeds, UK: White Line Press.

Focht, B. C., & Hausenblas, H. A. (2004). Baseline anxiety and perceptions of evaluative threat influence state anxiety during exercise in women with high social physique anxiety. *Journal of Applied Sport Psychology, 16,* 361–368.

Frederick, C. J., & Morrison, C. S. (1996). Social physique anxiety: Personality constructs, motivations, exercise attitudes, and behaviors. *Perceptual and Motor Skills, 82,* 963–972.

Gammage, K. L., Lamarche, L., & Drouin, B. (2014). Self-presentational efficacy: Does it moderate the relationship between social physique anxiety and physical activity in university students? *International Journal of Sport and Exercise Psychology.* doi: 10.1080/1612197X.2014.932824.

Gammage, K. L., Martin Ginis, K. A., & Hall, C. R. (2004). Self-presentational efficacy expectancy: Its influence on anxiety in an exercise context. *Journal of Sport and Exercise Psychology, 26,* 179–190.

Gatehouse, J. (2004, August 16). Athens' 04. *Maclean's, 117,* 26–35.

Gill, D. L. (1994). A sport and exercise psychology perspective on stress. *Quest, 46,* 20–27.

Gould, D., Greenleaf, C., & Krane, V. (2002). Arousal–anxiety and sport behavior. In T. Horn (Ed.), *Advances in sport psychology* (2nd ed., pp. 207–241). Champaign, IL: Human Kinetics.

Hammermeister, J., & Burton, D. (2004). Gender differences in coping with endurance sport stress: Are men from Mars and women from Venus? *Journal of Sport Behavior, 27,* 148–164.

Haney, C. J. (2004). Stress-management interventions for female athletes: Relaxation and cognitive restructuring. *International Journal of Sport Psychology, 35,* 109–118.

Hanin, Y. (1980). A study of anxiety in sports. In W. F. Straub (Ed.), *Sport psychology: An analysis of athlete behaviour* (pp. 236–249). Ithaca, NY: Mouvement.

Hanin, Y. L. (2003). Performance related emotional states in sport: A qualitative analysis. *Forum Qualitative Sozialforschung/Forum: Qualitative Social Research, 4*(1), Art. 5, http://www.qualitative-research.net/index.php/fqs/article/view/747/1618.

Hanton, S., & Jones, G. (1997). Antecedents of intensity and direction dimensions of competitive anxiety as a function of skill. *Psychological Reports, 81,* 1139–1147.

Hanton, S., & Jones, G. (1999). The effects of a multimodal intervention program on performers. II: Training the butterflies to fly in formation. *The Sport Psychologist, 13,* 22–41.

Hanton, S., Neil, R., & Mellalieu, S. D. (2008). Recent developments in competitive anxiety direction and competition stress research. *International Review of Sport and Exercise Psychology, 1,* 45–57.

Hardy, L. (1990). A catastrophe model of performance in sport. In J. G. Jones, & L. Hardy (Eds.), *Stress and performance in sport* (pp. 81–106). New York: Wiley.

Hart, E. H., Leary, M. R., & Rejeski, W. J. (1989). The measurement of social physique anxiety. *Journal of Sport & Exercise Psychology, 11,* 94–104.

Hausenblas, H. A., & Fallon, E. A. (2002). Relationship among body image, exercise behavior, and exercise dependence symptoms. *International Journal of Eating Disorders, 32,* 179–185.

Hill, D. M., Hanton, S., Fleming, S., & Matthews, N. (2009). A re-examination of choking in sport. *European Journal of Sport Science, 9,* 203–212.

Hill, D. M., Hanton, S., Matthews, N., & Fleming, S. (2010). Choking in sport: A review. *International Review of Sport and Exercise Psychology, 3,* 24–39.

Hollingsworth, M. (2012). melissahollingsworth.com, February 3, 2012.

Hull, C. L. (1951). *Essentials of behavior.* New Haven, CT: Yale University Press.

Jarrett, R. (2003, April 21). New man of the moment. *Sports Illustrated, 98,* 38–44.

Jokela, M., & Hanin, Y. L. (1999). Does the Individual Zones of Optimal Functioning model discriminate between successful and less successful athletes? A meta-analysis. *Journal of Sports Sciences, 17,* 873–887.

Jones, G. (1995). More than just a game: Research developments and issues in competitive anxiety in sport. *British Journal of Psychology, 86,* 449–478.

Jones, G., & Swain, A. B. J. (1992). Intensity and direction: dimensions of competitive state anxiety and relationships with competitiveness. *Perceptual and Motor Skills, 74,* 467–472.

Jones, G., & Swain, A. B. J. (1995). Predispositions to experience debilitative and facilitative anxiety in elite and nonelite performers. *The Sport Psychologist, 9*, 201–211.

Jones, M. V., & Uphill, M. (2004). Emotion in sport: Antecedents and performance consequences. In D. Lavallee, J. Thatcher, & M. V. Jones (Eds.), *Coping and emotion in sport* (pp. 9–28). Hauppauge, NY: Nova Science Publishers.

Kowalski, K. C., Mack, D. E., Crocker, P. R. E., Niefer, C. B., & Fleming T. L. (2006). Coping with social physique anxiety in adolescence. *Journal of Adolescent Health, 39*, 275.e9–275.e16.

Krane, V. (1994). The mental readiness form as a measure of competitive state anxiety. *The Sport Psychologist, 8*, 189–202.

Krane, V., & Williams, J. M. (1994). Cognitive anxiety, somatic anxiety, and confidence in track and field athletes: The impact of gender, competitive level, and task characteristics. *International Journal of Sport Psychology, 25*, 203–217.

Kreek, A. (2008, August 11). Race day. CBC. Beijing: The Olympic Games 2008. Columns, Blogs and Diaries. Message posted to http://www.cbc.ca/olympics/blog/athletes/adam_kreek/race_drama.html.

Lazarus, R. S. (2000). Cognitive–motivational–relational theory of emotion. In Y. L. Hanin (Ed.), *Emotions in sport* (pp. 39–63). Champaign, IL: Human Kinetics.

Leary, M. R. (1992). Self-presentational processes in exercise and sport. *Journal of Sport & Exercise Psychology, 14*, 339–351.

Liao, C., & Masters, R. S. W. (2002). Self-focused attention and performance failure under psychological stress. *Journal of Sport and Exercise Psychology, 24*, 289–305.

Martens, R., Vealey, R. S., & Burton, D. (Eds.). (1990). *Competitive anxiety in sport*. Champaign, IL: Human Kinetics.

Martin, K. A., & Fox, L. D. (2001). (References and further reading may be available for this article. To view references and further reading you must purchase this article.) Group and leadership effects on social anxiety experienced during an exercise class. *Journal of Applied Social Psychology, 31*, 1000–1016.

Martin, K. A., & Leary, M. R. (2001). Self-presentational determinants of health risk behavior among college freshmen. *Psychology and Health, 15*, 1–11.

Martin Ginis, K. A., Prapavessis, H., & Haase, A. (2008). The effects of physique-salient and physique non-salient exercise videos on women's body image, self-presentational concerns, and exercise motivation. *Body Image, 5*, 164–172.

Masters, R. S. W. (1992). Knowledge, knerves, and know-how: The role of explicit versus implicit knowledge in the breakdown of a complex motor skill under pressure. *British Journal of Psychology, 83*, 343–358.

Masters, R. S. W., & Maxwell, J. (2008). The theory of reinvestment. *International Review of Sport and Exercise Psychology, 1*, 160–184.

Maxwell, J. P., Masters, R. S. W., & Poolton, J. M. (2006). Performance breakdown in sport: The roles of reinvestment and verbal knowledge. *Research Quarterly for Exercise and Sport, 77*, 271–276.

McGowan, E., Prapavessis, H., & Wesch, N. (2008). Self-presentational concerns and competitive anxiety. *Journal of Sport & Exercise Psychology, 30*, 383–400.

Mellalieu, S. D., Hanton, S., & Fletcher, D. (2006). A competitive anxiety review: Recent directions in sport psychology research. In S. Hanton, & S. D. Mellalieu (Eds.), *Literature reviews in sport psychology* (pp. 1–45). New York: Nova Science Publishers.

Moran, A. (2004). *Sport and exercise psychology: A critical introduction*. London, UK: Routledge.

Naylor, S., Burton, D., & Crocker, P. R. E. (2002). Competitive anxiety and sport performance. In J. M. Silva III, & D. E. Stevens (Eds.), *Psychological foundations of sport* (pp. 132–154). Boston: Allyn & Bacon.

Neil, R., Hanton, S., Mellalieu, S. D., & Fletcher, D. (2011). Competition stress and emotions in sport performers: The role of further appraisals. *Psychology of Sport & Exercise, 12*, 460–470.

Notebook, J. T., Fleshner, M., & Enoka, R. M. (2001). Activation of the arousal response can impair performance on a simple motor task. *Journal of Applied Physiology, 91*, 821–831.

Orlick, T., & Partington, J. (1986). *Inner views of winning: Psyched.* Ottawa, ON: Coaching Association of Canada.

Orlick, T., & Partington, J. (1988). Mental links to excellence. *The Sport Psychologist, 2*, 105–130.

Parfitt, G., Jones, J. G., & Hardy, L. (1990). Multidimensional anxiety and performance. In J. G. Jones & L. Hardy (Eds.), *Stress and performance in sport* (pp. 43–80). New York: Wiley.

Parfitt, G., & Pates, J. (1999). The effects of cognitive and somatic anxiety and self-confidence on components of performance during competition. *Journal of Sports Sciences, 17*, 351–356.

Prapavessis, H., Grove, J. R., Maddison, R., & Zillmann, N. (2003). Self-handicapping tendencies, coping, and anxiety responses among athletes. *Psychology of Sport and Exercise, 4*, 357–375.

Raedeke, T. D., Focht, B., & Scales, D. (2007). Social environmental factors and psychological responses to acute exercise for socially physique anxious females. *Psychology of Exercise and Sport, 8*, 463–476.

Raglin, J. S., & Hanin, Y. L. (2000). Competitive anxiety. In Y. Hanin (Ed.), *Emotions in sport* (pp. 93–112). Champaign, IL: Human Kinetics.

Rich, N., Mellalieu, S. D., Hanton, S., & Mitchell, I. (2007). Temporal patterning of precompetitive state anxiety symptoms in female netballers. *Journal of Sport & Exercise Psychology, 29*, S193.

Robazza, C. (2006). Emotion in sport: An IZOF perspective. In S. Hanton & S. D. Mellalieu (Eds.), *Literature reviews in sport psychology* (pp. 127–158). New York: Nova Science Publishers.

Sabiston, C. M., Crocker, P. R. E., & Monroe-Chandler, K. J. (2005). Examining current-ideal discrepancy scores and exercise motivations as predictors of social physique anxiety in exercising females. *Journal of Sport Behavior, 28*, 68–85.

Shewfelt, K. (2008, July 15). It's starting to get scary. CBC. Beijing: The Olympic Games 2008. Columns, Blogs and Diaries. Message posted to http://www.cbc.ca/olympics/blog/athletes/kyle_shewfelt/its_starting_to_get_scary.html#more.

Smith, R. E., Smoll, F. L., & Wiechman, S. A. (1998). Measurement of trait anxiety in sport. In J. Duda (Ed.), *Advancement in sport and exercise psychology measurement* (pp. 105–127). Morgantown, WV: Fitness Information Technology.

Speilberger, C. D. (1966). Theory and research on anxiety. In C. D. Speilberger (Ed.), *Anxiety and behaviour* (pp. 3–22). New York: Academic.

Swain, A. B. J., & Jones, G. (1993). Intensity and frequency dimensions of competitive state anxiety. *Journal of Sports Sciences, 11*, 533–542.

"This is my worst nightmare come true": Felicien. (2004, August 25). CBC. Retrieved January 31, 2005, from http://www.cbc.ca/olympics/story/2004/08/24/perdita040824.html.

Uphill, M. (2008). Anxiety and sport: Should we be worried or excited? In A. M. Lane (Ed.), *Sport and exercise psychology: Topics in applied psychology* (pp. 35–52). Hachette Livre, UK: Hodder Education.

Vickers, J., & Williams, M. (2007). Performing under pressure: The effects of physiological arousal, cognitive anxiety, and gaze control in biathlon. *Journal of Motor Behavior, 39*, 381–394.

Woodman, T., & Hardy, L. (2001). Stress and anxiety. In R. Singer, H. A. Hausenblas, & C. M. Janelle (Eds.), *Handbook of research on sport psychology* (pp. 290–318). New York: Wiley.

Woodman, T., & Hardy, L. (2005). Tenebaum and Becker's critique: Much ado about nothing. *Journal of Sport & Exercise Psychology, 27*, 382–392.

Yerkes, R. M., & Dodson, J. D. (1908). The relationship of strength of stimulus to rapidity of habit formation. *Journal of Comparative Neurology and Psychology, 18*, 459–482.

Chapter 6
Aggression and Moral Behaviour in Sport

Todd M. Loughead   Kim D. Dorsch

Image Source/Corbis

Chapter Objectives

After reading this chapter, you should be able to do the following:

1   Explain how moral behaviour develops and what its impact is in sport.
2   Discuss the factors that influence the development of moral behaviours.
3   Define *aggression* and differentiate it from other terms, such as *assertion* and *violence*.
4   Discuss key theories useful for understanding why people behave aggressively.
5   Outline how some of the personal, situational, and group factors influence aggressive behaviour.
6   Understand the consequences of aggressive behaviour on athletes and spectators.
7   Discuss ways to reduce aggressive behaviour in sport.

On March 8, 2004, the Colorado Avalanche of the NHL played the Vancouver Canucks. Late in the third period, Todd Bertuzzi of Vancouver followed Steve Moore of Colorado around the ice, attempting to engage the latter in a fight. Moore ignored the advances made by Bertuzzi. Finally, Bertuzzi grabbed Moore's jersey from behind and punched Moore on the side of his head. As Moore fell to the ice, Bertuzzi and other players from both teams landed on top of Moore. Once the players were removed from the pile, Moore remained lying on the ice for several minutes until he was removed with the help of a stretcher. As a result of this brutal incident, Moore suffered three fractured vertebrae in his neck, a severe concussion, vertebral ligament damage, nerve damage, and facial cuts. To date, Moore has not appeared in another professional hockey game. For his actions, Bertuzzi was suspended indefinitely by the NHL. He was later reinstated after sitting out 20 games. On June 24, 2004, the criminal justice branch of the British Columbia Ministry of the Attorney General announced that Bertuzzi was formally charged with assault causing bodily harm. On December 22, 2004, Bertuzzi pleaded guilty to the assault charge after arranging a plea bargain with prosecutors. He was given a conditional discharge and one year's probation. During sentencing, Bertuzzi said in a pre-recorded video statement that was played in court, "I made a terrible mistake that I wish I could take back. I crossed the line that professional hockey players, like anyone else, should never cross" (Girard, 2004, p. A01). In another video statement released to the media, Bertuzzi said that "What happened that night in March is not who I am. One thing I want to do for the game is to let everyone know how important it is to respect the limits of what can be tolerated. Those of us who play the game at all levels—professional and amateur—never do anything intended to cause each other serious bodily harm. When we do that, it's not hockey" (Girard, 2004, p. A01).

The incident described above is one of many that have occurred in ice hockey. But acts of aggression have also tarnished sports other than hockey. In baseball, we often see bench-clearing brawls, brush-back pitches, or deliberate "beanings" of hitters. In basketball, elbows are thrown and a coach assaults his players. Specifically, Mike Rice, Jr., of Rutgers University routinely abused his players during practices. Basketball players also get into altercations with fans. Arguably the most notorious incident happened when Ron Artest, then of the Indiana Pacers, attacked a fan who reportedly threw a beverage on him during a game against the Detroit Pistons. In soccer, Luis Suárez of Uruguay was banned for four months after biting Italian defender Giorgio Chiellini during 2014's FIFA World Cup in Brazil. Aggressive behaviours occur so often in sport that Russell (1993) suggested that "outside of wartime, sports is perhaps the only setting in which acts of interpersonal aggression are not only tolerated but enthusiastically applauded by large segments of society" (p. 191).

There are also aggressive behaviours committed by fans toward athletes. In February 2012, in a soccer match between al-Masry and Al Ahli from Egypt's top soccer league, an Al Ahli fan descended onto the pitch carrying an iron bar after his club lost the match in an attempt to attack al-Masry players. The al-Masry fans reacted by rushing onto the field and attacked the Al Ahli players and rival supporters. Live television coverage showed fans running onto the field and chasing Al Ahli players.

A small group of police officers tried to protect the players but they were eventually overwhelmed by the fans on the field. In total, more than 70 people died and at least 1000 were injured. Sepp Blatter, president of FIFA, soccer's world governing body, expressed shock at this tragedy by saying, "This is a black day for football [soccer]. Such a catastrophic situation is unimaginable and should not happen" (The Telegraph, 2012, para. 5).

 COMMON MYTHS ABOUT AGGRESSION AND MORAL BEHAVIOUR IN SPORT

MYTH: Aggression in sport is a good characteristic. It is something to be encouraged in players.

MYTH: Aggression is only a physical behaviour.

MYTH: Athletes are born with certain moral behaviours.

INTRODUCTION

It is because of incidents such as those described at the beginning of the chapter that we need to become aware of aggression and moral behaviour in sport. We need to know what aggression is, why it occurs, what factors (such as morality) may cause people to behave aggressively, and, perhaps most importantly, what we can do to try to change these behaviours. In this chapter, we will address these issues with respect to aggression and moral behaviour in sport.

It is common for people to say that sport builds character and helps develop moral values. This notion is based on the belief that sport provides opportunity for its participants to learn how to cooperate with teammates, develop self-control, and play fair (Shields & Bredemeier, 1995). A great example of this occurred when Central Washington University played against Western Oregon University in intercollegiate softball. In the second inning of the game, Western Oregon player Sara Tucholsky hit her first-ever collegiate home run. Overjoyed by the occasion, Tucholsky missed first base, and when she turned back to touch it, her knee gave out and she suffered a torn anterior cruciate ligament, rendering her unable to touch the remaining bases and turning her first home run into a single. However, two opposing players from Central Washington University asked if they could carry the injured player around the bases. In a remarkable display of sportspersonship, Mallory Holtman and Liz Wallace lifted Tucholsky and carried her from base to base, allowing her to touch each base with her foot.

DEVELOPMENT OF MORAL CHARACTER

How can we explain the actions of Mallory Holtman and Liz Wallace? While there are diverging perspectives about how an athlete's character develops, two distinct perspectives are the most widely accepted: structural–developmental and social learning.

Structural–Developmental Perspective

Moral development: The process in which an individual develops the capacity to reason morally.

Structural–developmental theorists view **moral development** as the change in reasoning patterns that are related to a person's cognitive growth and development. Lawrence Kohlberg (1984) suggested that in contrast to Piaget's (1932) theory of cognitive development, moral reasoning develops and progresses well into adulthood. Based on his testing through interviews using hypothetical moral dilemma scenarios, Kohlberg arrived at six developmental stages of moral judgment, grouped into three levels. The first level was labelled as pre-conventional morality, in which children abide by rules in fear of punishment (stage 1) or in hopes of receiving rewards (stage 2). The second level is conventional morality, whereby individuals will conform to avoid disapproval of others (stage 3) and will uphold laws and social rules (stage 4). The final level, post-conventional morality, is established as individuals' moral reasoning is no longer confined by the strict boundaries of rules. That is, actions are guided by principles commonly agreed on as being essential (stage 5), and these actions are self-selected and guided by ethical principles (stage 6). According to Kohlberg, the majority of people, including athletes, will never progress beyond the second level, and less than 10% of individuals display stage 6 moral reasoning.

So the question becomes, can sport be used to develop character? When Canadian researchers Martin Camiré and Pierre Trudel (2010) interviewed 20 high school athletes and asked them about character development, many of the athletes reported not learning much about moral development through sport. This research tells us that moral development doesn't happen simply because a person participates in sport; instead, character development can occur in sport when it is targeted. For instance, programs, such as the First Tee golf life skills program (Weiss, 2006) and Sports United to Promote Education and Recreation life skills program (Papacharisis et al., 2005), have shown that young athletes feel better about solving problems and physically perform better, and that these life skills transfer outside of sport, compared to control groups.

Social Learning Perspective

Moral behaviour: The carrying out of an action that is deemed right or wrong.

The social learning perspective maintains that **moral behaviour**—the carrying out of an action that is deemed right or wrong—is learned through the processes of reinforcement and modelling. This perspective would then suggest that participation in sport teaches and/or reinforces sportspersonship behaviours. In fact, some people argue that athletes tend to be more unsportspersonlike than their non-athlete counterparts, and that sports involving physical contact (e.g., hockey, football) negatively impact an athlete's moral reasoning (Bloom & Smith, 1996). On the one hand, Beller and Stoll (1995) found that non-athletes in high school had higher moral reasoning scores than did athletes in high school. On the other hand, Stanger and colleagues (2012) conducted an experiment with undergraduate sport science students to examine the effects of empathy on aggression. Participants were randomly assigned to either a high-empathy group (i.e., asked to take the perspective of another individual) or a low-empathy group (i.e., asked to be objective and detached from another person's feelings). The results showed that the high-empathy group experienced stronger negative emotional reactions to aggressive acts than the low-empathy group. These findings suggest that empathy can be used to reduce aggressive behaviour.

How can we explain the differences in the research findings? The following section will examine some of the factors that influence our moral behaviours.

FACTORS INFLUENCING MORAL BEHAVIOUR

Sport Environment

The sport environment is an important context in which moral behaviours can be developed by providing opportunities for moral practice and development. Sport enables individuals to learn rules and appropriate conduct of fair play. Sport can be where moral behaviours flourish by the promotion of cooperation, team loyalty, fair play, respect for opponents, and perseverance when faced with adversity.

Coaching impacts an athlete's moral development. A coach can prohibit acts that disrespect or violate rules and encourage conduct that demonstrates respect and fair play. Athletes who learn morally appropriate behaviours from their coaches are more likely to transfer these positive behaviours outside the sporting environment. However, coaches who display a lack of proper leadership, by emphasizing winning or encouraging immoral actions, can promote an environment that is more conducive to unsportspersonlike and aggressive behaviours.

Shields and colleagues (2007) surveyed nearly 700 athletes, ranging in age from 9 to 15 years, from a variety of team sports (e.g., basketball, hockey, soccer). Perceptions of the coach were related to whether an athlete would behave in an appropriate manner. That is, if an athlete believed that his or her coach supported or reinforced unsportspersonlike behaviours, then the athlete was more likely to adopt poor sportspersonship behaviours (i.e., cheating, hurting an opponent, arguing with a sport official, verbalizing mean or hurtful things to an opponent, or acting like a poor sport).

Motivational Climate

Another factor influencing moral behaviour is motivational climate. Motivational climate can be categorized into two types: mastery motivational climate and performance motivational climate. Mastery motivational climate is when the coach encourages cooperation and learning from past mistakes; performance motivational climate is when the coach emphasizes winning and stresses competition among teammates.

Kavussanu and colleagues (2006) examined the motivational climate of adolescent male soccer players in relation to their prosocial and antisocial behaviours. **Prosocial behaviour** is intended to assist or benefit another individual or team. The example in the introduction of the two softball players assisting their opponent around the bases would be considered a prosocial behaviour. An **antisocial behaviour** is intended to harm or disadvantage another individual or team. This could include pretending to be injured, trying to injure, or hitting an opponent, such as in the Bertuzzi–Moore incident. The results showed that antisocial behaviours were carried out at a higher frequency and with a wider range of expression than prosocial behaviours. In addition, prosocial behaviours decreased as the players got older. Furthermore, as athletes got older, their motivational climate

Prosocial behaviour: A behaviour that is intended to assist or benefit another individual or team.

Antisocial behaviour: A behaviour that is intended to harm or disadvantage another individual or team.

Donald, a head hockey coach for the university varsity team, is entering his second year with the team. For the first time in the university's history, the team is ranked in the top 10 in the nation. Coach Donald feels that this team has a legitimate chance of winning a national championship. Unfortunately, all is not as wonderful as it seems. The team's captain (who is also its leading scorer) and the team's starting goalie were involved in an on-ice brawl against a conference opponent.

The league's president has decided that both players will receive a five-game suspension in terms of disciplinary action. These suspensions could influence whether the team makes the playoffs. Coach Donald calls you, the team's sport psychology consultant, and asks you whether he should appeal the suspensions and what impact this would have on the team.

changed from mastery based to more performance based. It would appear that developing a motivational atmosphere based on learning and improvement rather than on winning may lead to a decrease in antisocial behaviours and promote prosocial behaviours.

Team Norms

Team norms: Standards for the behaviour that is expected of members of the group.

Team norms can be defined as standards or expectations that influence team members' behaviour. Not surprisingly, the expectations of teammates, coaches, and parents are a prominent element in influencing an athlete's moral behaviour. Stuart and Ebbeck (1995) compared young (grades 4 and 5) and older (grades 7 and 8) athletes in relation to the social approval of significant others (teammates, coaches, and parents) when faced with a moral dilemma. That is, the athletes were asked about their perceptions of each significant other's approval of a moral dilemma, such as, "Does your dad [mom, coach, teammate] think it is okay for you to argue with an official over a bad call?" The findings showed that for both younger and older athletes, perceived social approval from a significant other was related to moral behaviour. However, when examining who had the biggest influence on athletes, the results indicated that mothers had the largest effect on younger athletes, while teammates had the largest effect on older athletes.

Using a sample of youth soccer players, Chow and colleagues (2009) examined the factors influencing a player's tendency to aggress against an opponent. Players were given a hypothetical soccer situation where tripping an opponent would probably injure but would prevent a shot on an open goal. The results showed that players who believed a high number of teammates would trip the opponent (i.e., there is a team norm to aggress) were more likely to aggress than players who thought a lower number of players on their team would trip the opponent.

Goal Orientation

According to Nicholls' (1989) achievement goal theory, two major goal orientations are assumed to function within the context of sport, namely, task orientation and ego orientation. Athletes who are task oriented tend to use self-referenced criteria and feel successful

Acts of aggression are very common in ice hockey.

Mathieu Belanger/REUTERS

when they have mastered the task. The ego-oriented athlete, on the other hand, tends to use other-referenced criteria and defines success by outperforming others. These two goal orientations appear to be important for understanding moral behaviour in sport. Given that an ego-oriented athlete perceives success as a function of outdoing others, he or she is more likely to break the rules and behave in an unsportspersonlike manner when winning is a concern. In contrast, a task-oriented athlete is more likely to want to play by the rules of the sport since competence is judged against self-referenced criteria.

Kavussanu and Roberts (2001) had athletes respond to moral dilemmas describing unsportspersonlike behaviours that could occur during competition. Athletes high in ego orientation had lower levels of moral judgment and thus were more likely to describe the behaviours as appropriate and more likely to engage in these behaviours. Stephens (2004) studied floor hockey athletes and found that lower task orientation was a predictor of the likelihood to aggress. These two studies help to highlight that both ego and task orientations have important implications for moral behaviour in sport. In summary, it would appear that there is a need to teach athletes to focus on the process rather than the outcome. That is, we need to focus less on winning-at-all-costs and emphasize the importance of mastering the task.

Aggression

The development of moral behaviours can have a big impact on whether athletes will behave in a sportspersonlike or unsportspersonlike manner. One of the most obvious unsportspersonlike behaviours in sport is aggression. In sport settings in particular, we often hear about a baseball player aggressively running the bases or a volleyball player aggressively digging the ball. From a sport psychology perspective, however, this is not the correct use of the term. Silva (1980) suggested that **aggression** is any overt verbal or physical act that is intended to injure another living organism either psychologically or physically. A **violent behaviour** is an extreme act of physical aggression that bears "no

Aggression: Any overt verbal or physical act that is intended to injure another living organism either psychologically or physically.

Violent behaviour: An extreme act of physical aggression that bears no direct relationship to the competitive goals of sport, and relates to incidents of uncontrolled aggression outside the rules of sport.

direct relationship to the competitive goals of sport, and relates to incidents of uncontrolled aggression outside the rules of sport" (Terry & Jackson, 1985, p. 27). Keep in mind that because the aggressive action is directed at another living organism, there is always an aggressor and a victim in any aggressive or violent act.

Using Silva's (1980) definition, the term *aggressive* is not appropriate for the description of the baseball and volleyball players' behaviours provided above. Sport psychologists prefer to describe those behaviours as *assertive*. The difference between an aggressive and an assertive action is that the latter behaviour does not include the intent to harm another living being. **Assertive behaviour** includes those actions that are forceful, vigorous, and legitimate, but the individual performing these behaviours does not intend to injure an opponent (e.g., a hard tackle in football). Therefore, when a coach or parent tells an athlete or child to play more aggressively, in most situations what they are encouraging is behaviour that is more assertive.

Consequently, defining aggressive behaviour involves four key points:

1. It is a behaviour (i.e., an act), not an emotion or a feeling or a personality trait.

2. It can be verbal or physical.

3. It is intended to cause physical or psychological harm.

4. It is directed toward another living organism.

Let's go back to the case study presented at the beginning of this chapter. Todd Bertuzzi "sucker-punched" Steve Moore on the side of the head. Based on the definition of aggression provided above, this behaviour would be considered aggressive because the intent to harm was present.

Sport psychologists make one further distinction in defining acts of aggression based on the reason why the individual behaved in such a way—that is, what they wanted to accomplish. As a result, two kinds of aggression have been identified in the sport psychology literature: instrumental aggression and hostile or reactive aggression. In both types of aggression, the intent is to harm. However, there is a distinction in terms of the goals being sought. **Instrumental aggression** serves as the means to a particular goal—such as winning, money, or prestige—in which intended injury to the opponent is involved. This type of injury is impersonal and designed to limit the effectiveness of the opponent. A hockey example for instrumental aggression would be when a player bodychecks his or her opponent, who is driving hard to the net trying to score a goal. The player who delivered the bodycheck has the intention of intimidating, or psychologically harming, the opponent so that next time, the opponent will think twice before driving to the net. This type of aggression is instrumental in helping the team achieve its goal of winning the game. On the other hand, the primary objective of **hostile aggression** is to injure another person deliberately. The intent is to make the victim suffer, either physically, psychologically, or both. For instance, the Todd Bertuzzi sucker-punch on Steve Moore was a clear attempt to intentionally and deliberately injure—the goal was to cause suffering.

Each sport has its own written and unwritten rules. It is through socialization and experience gained through participation in the sport that participants become knowledgeable regarding the normative standards (i.e., unwritten rules) of that sport. Therefore, acts that may be aggressive in one sport are not necessarily considered aggressive in another sport. Fighting in ice hockey is a prime example of this. Many people involved within ice hockey (e.g., players and coaches) do not believe that fights are an aggressive action.

Assertive behaviour: Actions that are forceful, vigorous, and legitimate, performed by an individual who does not intend to harm another living being.

Instrumental aggression: Aggressive acts serving as a means to a particular goal—such as winning, money, or prestige—in which injury to the opponent is involved. This type of injury is impersonal and designed to limit the effectiveness of the opponent.

Hostile aggression: Aggressive acts undertaken for the purpose of harming or injuring the victim.

Chris Faytok/Star Ledger/Corbis Sports/Corbis

These individuals believe that fighting is not an attempt to injure, but an attempt to control some of the more potentially harmful behaviours, like stick work, kicking, or kneeing. Hockey tough guys like John Scott have stated that "when fighting's out of the game then everyone's going to be taken off on stretchers because of hits from behind and high-sticks and dirty checks. It'll be a little different story" (Whyno, 2013). Should this same act occur in another sport, such as volleyball or basketball, where the unwritten rules do not sanction fighting, the perception of the act as non-aggressive would definitely change.

Another factor that tends to influence a person's perception of whether or not an act is aggressive is the outcome of the act (i.e., did someone get hurt?). However, if you refer back to the definition of aggression, the key point is the intent to harm another living being. This description does not mean that the actor has to succeed in harming an opponent, only that he or she intended to harm the other individual. If an act was committed with the intent of psychologically intimidating an opponent but does not succeed, it is still an aggressive behaviour? The answer is yes.

REFLECTIONS 6.1

If you were in charge of handing out suspensions for a sport governing body, on what evidence would you base the length of time of the suspension?

Bullying and Hazing in Sport

Typically when we talk about who is involved in acts of aggressive behaviour, we simply look at the aggressor and the victim; we don't often look at the relationship between the two. Most of the research examining aggressive behaviours in sport assumes these two individuals are on opposing teams. But what happens when aggressive behaviours occur between members of the same team? Think, for example of Jonathan Martin—a 1.96 m, 142 kg, 24-year-old member of the Miami Dolphins. One day, midway through the National Football League season, Martin walked out of practice, leaving behind a professional career that he loved, and checked himself into a hospital requesting psychological treatment. His reason was persistent name calling, racial slurs, sexual comments about himself and his sister, monetary "fines," and ridicule by teammates Richie Incognito, John Jerry, and Mike Pouncey (Wells et al., 2014). These intentionally harmful behaviours are categorized as **bullying** and are differentiated from other aggressive behaviours by the relationship between the aggressor and the victim. Bullying is based on an imbalance of power between peers (i.e., teammates) where the one who is more powerful (e.g., has more seniority, as was the case with Incognito, Jerry, and Pouncey) repeatedly attacks the less powerful with an intention to harm (Stirling et al., 2011). While the form of bullying described above was primarily verbal, it can also be physical (using physical actions to gain power and control), social/emotional (excluding others, spreading rumours), sexual (vulgar gestures, uninvited touching, crude comments), prejudicial (based on race, religion, or sexual orientation), or electronic (using the internet or other technology to threaten, post images, send hurtful emails or texts) (Shannon, 2013). With the popularity of social media that now allows direct, immediate, and extremely public communication, electronic bullying (or cyberbullying) is a very serious issue within sport (Kavanagh & Jones, 2014).

Bullying behaviours also tend to increase when the team norms do not prohibit this behaviour (Duffy & Nesdale, 2009). **Hazing** is another behaviour among team members that is strongly influenced by team norms (Waldron & Kowalski, 2009). Members engage in dangerous activities with the belief that participation in such acts will strengthen team bonds (Keating et al., 2005) or, for rookies, will show their dedication and commitment to the team (Kirby & Wintrup, 2002). What is not well understood by athletes is that hazing activities cross the line from the more acceptable initiation, tradition, or rite of passage activities in which teams engage for positive team building purposes. Hazing activities are considered acts of aggression as they are:

> Any potentially humiliating, degrading, abusive, or dangerous activity expected of a junior-ranking athlete by a more senior teammate, which does not contribute to either athlete's positive development, but is required to be accepted as part of a team, regardless of the junior-ranking athlete's willingness to participate (Crow & Macintosh, 2009, p. 449).

Senior members of the team use intimidation and peer pressure to humiliate, dominate, and often physically abuse junior team members in their attempt to preserve the power structure of the team (Waldron & Kowalski, 2009). In other words, veterans use intimidating behaviours directed at rookies to maintain their dominant position on the team, to appear more important than the rookies, or to degrade the rookies so they don't have the confidence to challenge the veterans for their spot on the team.

Bullying: Imbalance of power between peers where the one who is more powerful repeatedly attacks the less powerful with the intention to harm.

Hazing: Any potentially humiliating, degrading, abusive, or dangerous activity expected of an individual to belong to a group, regardless of their willingness to participate.

THEORIES OF AGGRESSION

Why do some athletes act aggressively? Are people born to be aggressive, or are they products of their environment? In order to explain what causes athletes to be aggressive, scientists have advanced several theories and explanations. These theories and explanations can be classified into five groups: psychodynamics, frustration–aggression theory, physiological explanations, social learning theory, and moral disengagement.

Psychodynamics

This theory, developed near the beginning of the last century, holds that humans are born with certain psychic drives (i.e., instincts) that will cause them to act in certain ways. For example, Freud (1925) believed that aggressive behaviour was an innate, natural response that evolved primarily through a struggle for survival. Aggression builds up naturally and must be released. Freud believed that numerous socially approved methods existed for releasing this pent-up aggression. Sport is one such socially acceptable activity that could curtail the negative results of aggression. This releasing process was termed **catharsis**, a word derived from the Greek term *katharsis*, which means to purge or cleanse the body. According to this theory, hitting an opponent in sport serves as a catharsis or release of built-up aggression.

> **Catharsis:** To purge or cleanse the self of aggressive feelings; typically, venting of aggressive tendencies through socially acceptable means.

Psychodynamic theory has far more detractors than supporters. Bandura (1973) noted that a large body of research, involving either direct or vicarious aggressive experiences, has demonstrated that aggression will actually be maintained rather than reduced. Further, the probability of subsequent aggression will increase rather than diminish! These findings are also apparent in a sport setting, where research has found no draining of aggressive tendencies through participation in physical activities. In fact, many sport researchers have argued that exposure to violence in sports serves as a reinforcer, not as a catharsis. Thus, many scientists have rejected this theory for understanding aggression in sport.

Frustration–Aggression Theory

Dollard and colleagues (1939) proposed the frustration–aggression theory, which viewed aggression as a natural response to frustration. Originally, it was hypothesized that all aggression was due to frustration and that frustration always leads to aggression. For instance, a rugby player who has been tackled high and hard might become frustrated and punch his opponent in retaliation. Although this theory has intuitive appeal because it seems reasonable that most aggression occurs when individuals are frustrated, the frustration–aggression theory has some definite shortcomings. For example, individuals are able to deal with their frustrations in non-aggressive ways. Consequently, Berkowitz (1989) proposed a revised frustration–aggression theory, recognizing that aggression can have causes other than frustration and that frustration can lead to behaviours other than aggression, such as withdrawal from sport. Berkowitz (1990) suggested that when an individual is frustrated, an emotional reaction of anger is produced that does not lead automatically to aggression but rather to a readiness to be aggressive. Some scientists have been reluctant to accept this theory since it implies an instinctual mechanism that accounts for the frustration–anger link.

Physiological Explanations

Proponents who believe that aggression is physiological in nature use two supportive mechanisms: brain pathology and blood chemistry. Insofar as brain pathology is concerned, research has shown that aggressive behaviour is often characteristic of people with brain tumours. In these people, aggressive behaviours can be elicited by stimulating various parts of the brain. As for blood chemistry, aggression has been linked primarily to the hormone testosterone. Although researchers have found a link between testosterone and aggressive behaviour in animal species, the relationship is less consistent in humans. That is, testosterone may cause individuals to be aggressive, but it is difficult to explain why people who possess high levels of this hormone are aggressive in some situations and not in others. As well, it is hard to explain why people who possess little testosterone, such as females, can act aggressively.

Although physiological explanations have been used to explain aggression in animal species, rarely has physiology been forwarded as a cause of aggression in sport. One exception concerns the use of steroids by athletes, most notably athletes in power and strength sports such as weightlifting, football, baseball, and track and field. The links between steroid use and feelings of aggressiveness, and between steroid use and aggressive behaviour, have been frequently documented among athletes (e.g., Sjoqvist et al., 2008). For instance, studies have shown that athletes who take steroids have higher levels of aggression toward objects, of verbal aggression, and of aggressiveness while training. It should be pointed out that when the athletes stopped using steroids, these characteristics disappeared.

Social Learning Theory

The most supported explanation of why aggression occurs is social learning theory. The leading advocate for this theory, relative to aggression, is Albert Bandura. According to social learning theory, a person is neither driven by inner forces nor controlled solely by environmental influences. Instead, Bandura (1973) believes that people are aggressive because they have learned that aggression pays. In other words, the use of aggressive behaviours can lead to success.

Bandura (1973) theorized that two forms of social interaction lead to the development of aggressive behaviours. The first form of interaction involves modelling. In its simplest form, modelling suggests that people can acquire aggressive behaviours from observing aggressive models and can retain these aggressive tendencies over time. For example, youth hockey players learn to be aggressive by watching their role models from professional leagues, like the NHL.

The second form of interaction involves learning or acquiring new responses because of reinforcement. When an action is performed and then positively reinforced (i.e., rewarded), the behaviour is strengthened. The behaviour will be discontinued if it is not rewarded or is punished. For example, research has suggested that parents, teammates, and coaches are the most influential providers of social reinforcement, especially for young athletes (Smith, 1979). Smith surveyed minor hockey players and found that those who engaged in fighting believed that their parents, teammates, and coaches approved of this behaviour. Specifically, Smith found that 31% of players said that their father would approve of fighting, and 21% said that their mother would approve. Similarly, hockey players said that 64% of their teammates and 26% of their coaches approved of fighting.

Approval is not the only possible reinforcer of aggression. The belief that aggression is related to success also can influence aggressive behaviours. Research has shown that players who perceived their coach to have a win-at-all-costs attitude expressed higher levels of aggression and were more willing to use illegal, aggressive tactics to win.

In short, social learning theory is a strong force in contemporary research, linking aggression to the environment and the individual. It is a model that contains provisions for direct learning and for vicarious learning. Furthermore, Bandura's (1973) theory contains a cognitive dimension that had previously been missing from other theories regarding aggression. Finally, since aggression allegedly does not originate internally and its environmental determinants are alterable, social learning theory holds a more optimistic view of reducing aggression in humans.

The social learning theory suggests that, since aggressive behaviour is learned, it can be unlearned.

Moral Disengagement

It should be noted that the moral disengagement view is an extension of social learning theory that has been developed specifically to address moral behaviour. Bandura (1999) attempted to explain how people who are engaged in a deviant behaviour, such as aggression, justify their choices. According to moral disengagement, individuals tend to refrain from engaging in behaviour that violates their own moral standards. That is to say, if hockey players believe fighting is an unacceptable behaviour, they may not engage in that behaviour since it violates their moral beliefs. However, these standards or beliefs do not necessarily function as fixed internal controls of aggression. That is, athletes do not always behave the way they should. Going back to our fighting example, players may engage in this behaviour even if it is against their own values.

In fact, there are eight methods by which individuals attempt to disengage themselves from the behaviour. Bandura refers to these as the mechanisms of moral disengagement.

1. *Moral justification* occurs when an individual reconsiders aggression as being a negative behaviour and makes it acceptable by portraying this behaviour as facilitating a social or moral purpose. For instance, a hockey player could argue that he or she fought an opponent to protect a teammate.

2. *Euphemistic labelling* involves changing the language to make the aggressive behaviour seem less harmful. For example, those involved in hockey often justify the existence of fighting by claiming that fighting allows players to "let off some steam."

3. *Advantageous comparison* is another way of making aggression seem acceptable. This involves comparing an aggressive behaviour with something that is more reprehensible. You will often hear athletes say, "We didn't do bad stuff, and if we did, it wasn't as bad as what the other team did."

4. *Displacement of responsibility* occurs when athletes shift the blame for their aggressive behaviours to other individuals. For instance, a baseball pitcher could say that the coach wanted her to go and throw a brush-back pitch at the hitter. By shifting the responsibility to the coach, athletes can employ these types of tactics when they wouldn't normally contemplate using them.

5. *Diffusion of responsibility* involves team members making a group decision to use aggressive behaviours. By making the decision to act aggressively as a team, no single athlete feels personally responsible.

6. *Distortion of consequences* is achieved when an athlete minimizes the harm caused by his or her actions. For instance, let us say a football player tackles his opponent and the opponent hits his head on the turf and suffers a concussion. The football player who delivered the hit may say that it was not that bad and that the concussion resulted from contact with the field and not from the hit itself.

7. *Dehumanization* involves cognitively relieving people of their human qualities. In sport, athletes are often portrayed as "goons," "animals," and "beasts." When athletes describe their opponents as such, they no longer view them as people but as subhuman objects.

8. *Attribution of blame* occurs when athletes see themselves as the victim and not the aggressor. This sort of behaviour occurs when athletes retaliate against their opponent and use this type of excuse as a way of justifying their behaviour.

CASE STUDY 6.2 The Hockey Enforcer: Should It Stay or Should It Go?

On the opening night of the 2013–14 NHL season, Colton Orr of the Toronto Maple Leafs engaged with the Montreal Canadiens' George Parros in a fight. During their altercation, Parros fell forward and hit his head face-first directly on the ice. Parros suffered a concussion and had to be removed from the ice on a stretcher. Both players were doing the job they are paid to do—police the game, fight when a change of momentum is needed, give their team a spark, or defend a teammate. Nonetheless, this incident has reignited the debate about the need for fighting in hockey. Some argue that fighting should be removed from hockey and have called for meaningful suspensions for those who fight. Others argue that fighting, enforcers like Colton Orr and George Parros, and the "aggressive" nature of hockey are an integral part of hockey and that their removal would drastically change the game. Using a moral disengagement perspective, where do you stand on this issue?

Minas Panagiotakis/Icon SMI/Corbis Wire/Corbis

Table 6.1 Theories Regarding Aggressive Behaviour

Theory	Major Tenet
Psychodynamic theory	Humans are born with the instinct for aggression.
Frustration-aggression theory	A blocked goal causes the individual to become frustrated, and frustration produces aggression.
Revised frustration–aggression theory	A blocked goal causes emotional reactions (e.g., anger), which lead to a readiness to behave aggressively; appropriate environmental cues cause this readiness to develop into aggression.
Physiological theories	Aggressive behaviour occurs because individuals have either a brain pathology or excess testosterone.
Moral disengagement	Aggressive behaviour occurs through individuals changing their morality under certain conditions.
Social learning theory	Individuals use aggression because they have learned that aggression pays.

Summary of Theories of Aggression

Several major theoretical frameworks have been utilized in the study of aggressive behaviour. These theoretical frameworks have attempted to explain or predict an individual's aggressive behaviour. We often hear people trying to explain aggression by saying such things as "boys will be boys" or "they are just blowing off steam." The belief in the basic tenets of psychodynamic theory and the frustration–aggression theory has had an impact on the sporting sphere. People will often justify aggression as natural and necessary. These justifications occur even though research indicates that these theories are not effective means of explaining aggressive behaviour. Bandura's attempt to explain aggression from a moral disengagement viewpoint is still in its infancy, but this perspective gives us another useful avenue to use in our quest for understanding. Up to this point, social learning theory provides the most plausible and empirically supported foundation for describing, understanding, predicting, and ultimately controlling aggressive behaviour in sport (see Table 6.1).

REFLECTIONS 6.2

Think back to a time when you behaved aggressively, saw someone behaving aggressively, or were a victim of another's aggressive action. Using the theories just discussed, try to explain why you or the other individual behaved in this manner.

FACTORS INFLUENCING AGGRESSION

Being frustrated or wanting reinforcement may partially explain why athletes behave aggressively. There are, however, other personal, situational, and group factors that help us to understand when aggression is more likely to occur. In this section, we will discuss some of these factors.

Personal Factors Influencing Aggression

Gender Historically, the majority of research examining aggression in sport has primarily examined male athletes. However, one study that compared male and female handball and soccer athletes found that male players committed more instrumental and hostile aggressive acts (Coulomb-Cabagno & Rascle, 2005). Nonetheless, more interest has been shown in understanding the aggressive behaviours in sport by women. Canadian researchers Todd Loughead, Gordon Bloom, and their colleagues (Bloom & Vanier, 2004; Shapcott et al., 2007; Vanier et al., 2005) conducted a series of studies specifically examining aggression in women's hockey. They discovered that the majority of aggressive behaviour in women's hockey occurs to (a) protect the goalie or themselves, (b) gain a competitive advantage (e.g., to obtain the puck, or stop their opponent from scoring), (c) get the opponent to retaliate and draw a penalty, (d) impede their opponents' progress using aggressive behaviours taught to them by the coach, (e) intimidate their opponent, and (f) simply hit their opponent. They also found that these women tended to rely more on psychological aggression than on physical aggression, verbally taunting and provoking their opponents into taking retaliatory penalties. Interestingly, most female players indicated that they never intended to injure anyone physically.

Age No conclusive statement can be made regarding the relationship between age and aggressive behaviour mainly due to the fact that not many studies have looked at age as the specific variable of interest. One study by Loughead and Leith (2001) compared aggressive behaviours of Atom (i.e., aged 10–11 years), Pee-Wee (i.e., aged 12–13 years), and Bantam (i.e., aged 14–15 years) hockey players. The results indicated that Atom players were more approving of instrumental aggression than their older Pee-Wee and Bantam counterparts. However, Pee-Wee and Bantam players were more approving of hostile aggression than were Atom players. Visek and Watson (2005) examined the perceived legitimacy of aggression in male ice hockey players at the youth, high-school, varsity, and professional levels. The results showed that as players aged (from youth to professional), they endorsed the use of both instrumental and hostile aggression to a greater extent.

There are contrary findings to the argument that there is a positive relationship between age and aggressive behaviour. Several studies have examined the desire to behave aggressively among male Pee-Wee ice hockey players (Dorsch, 1992), high-school ice hockey players (Sanszole, 1995), and university ice hockey players (Brice, 1990). As can be seen in Figure 6.1, desire to physically and psychologically injure opposing players peaks during the middle years. Consequently, we cannot definitively state the direction of the relationship between age and aggressive behaviour until more research examines this variable.

Physical Size One might think that bigger players are more likely to use their size to their advantage; however, one could also imagine that larger athletes may be aware of their size and not want to engage in activities that may injure an opponent. In one study looking at Pee-Wee hockey players, Dorsch (1992) found that both height and weight positively correlated to the number of aggressive penalties. This size–aggression relationship was supported by Lemieux and colleagues (2002), who compared the aggressive behaviour of athletes involved in contact sports (e.g., football and rugby), athletes involved in non-contact sports (e.g., track, baseball, golf, and volleyball), and individuals not involved in any sports. They found that regardless of whether an individual was an

Figure 6.1 Age and aggressive behaviour

At different levels of competition, the desire of male ice hockey players to injure an opponent physically and psychologically at least once per period

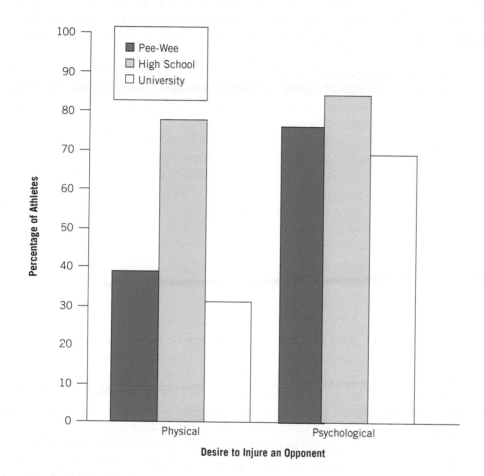

Source: Data from Brice, J. G. (1990). *Frustration in ice hockey: Extent, antecedents and consequences.* Unpublished master's thesis, University of Waterloo, Waterloo, ON, Canada; Dorsch, K. D. (1992). *The extent and antecedents of aggression in PeeWee hockey.* Unpublished manuscript, University of Waterloo, Waterloo, ON, Canada; Sanszole, M. (1995). *The extent, antecedents and response to sport frustration by high school students.* Unpublished manuscript, University of Waterloo, Waterloo, ON, Canada.

athlete or not, the bigger the person, the more he reported being involved in a fight in a non-sport setting.

Retaliation Motives Brice's (1990) study of university ice hockey players and Sanszole's (1995) study involving a variety of male and female athletes found that many athletes expressed wanting to harm an opponent physically because the opponent had attempted to injure them or a teammate. Although these researchers did not directly examine the link between these retaliation motives and the athletes' aggressive behaviour, Harrell (1980) did find the strongest predictor of high-school basketball players' aggressive behaviour to be the aggression of their opponent. In another study of basketball and ice hockey players, Kirker and colleagues (2000) found that the most severe aggressive acts were preceded by aggressive acts, often committed by the opponent. These retaliatory acts often led to further acts of aggression.

Annoyances Widmeyer and colleagues. (2002) suggested that some athletes might become aggressive because they are annoyed. Annoyances in sport could take the form of inconsistent calls by an official, mannerisms of opponents, or taunting by opposing players, coaches, or fans.

Brice (1990) found that officiating inconsistencies were one of the most annoying and most prevalent sources of anger for ice hockey athletes. These annoyances often led to verbally aggressive actions directed toward the officials. In soccer, 24.3% of referees stated that players had physically threatened them, while 63.6% said players had verbally abused them (Folkesson et al., 2002). Even in squash, officials state that verbal abuse occurs, on average, once every 5 to 10 matches (Dorsch et al., 2000). In Canadian ice hockey, 82.6% of officials reported verbal abuse by coaches, while 14.4% of them reported being threatened with physical abuse (Dorsch et al., 2012). Interestingly, the officials in this study had a mean age of 15 years with about 2.5 years of experience, were officiating the lowest levels of youth hockey, and were aggressed upon by adult coaches.

Although officials are usually the victims of verbal aggressive actions, sometimes the aggression becomes physical. In soccer, Folkesson and colleagues (2002) found that 12.1% of referees had suffered some form of physical aggression from players. In baseball and softball, Rainey (1994) discovered that 11% of umpires reported some form of assault, usually pushing, shoving, grabbing, hitting, or punching.

Self-presentation: The way individuals present themselves (i.e., behave, dress) in social situations.

Self-Presentation Sport psychologists often refer to **self-presentation** as the way individuals present themselves (i.e., behave, dress) in social situations. Some sport psychologists believe that some athletes may behave aggressively in order to convey or maintain an image of toughness to opponents and observers, particularly within contact sports, such as football, basketball, and ice hockey (Widmeyer et al., 2002). In support of this notion, Wann and Porcher (1998) found that intercollegiate ice hockey and football players whose names were printed on the backs of their jerseys were more aggressive. They surmised that because the players were now identifiable to others, they needed to portray a certain image. Similarly, McGuire (1990) found that professional ice hockey players who did not wear facemasks were more aggressive than those who did. A possible explanation for this finding is that because the players' identities are more apparent without the facial protection, the need to present themselves in a manner consistent with the norms of the game becomes more pressing.

Deindividuation: The process occurring when an individual feels less identifiable by others.

The contrasting viewpoint would suggest that aggressive impulses are increased when the individual feels less identifiable, a process known as **deindividuation**. Rehm et al. (1987) found that handball teams whose members wore the same jersey and consequently appeared similar to each other (i.e., exhibited high anonymity) committed more aggressive acts than the team in which each individual wore his own shirt. This finding supports the assumption that higher levels of anonymity contribute to actions that are more aggressive. However, few other studies have systematically examined deindividuation in sport.

Passion/Athletic Identity Canadian researcher Robert Vallerand and his colleagues (Vallerand, 2008; Vallerand & Miquelon, 2007) have examined the role passion plays in various activities. They define passion as "a strong inclination toward an activity that one likes, finds important, and invests with a significant amount of time and energy"

(Donahue et al., 2009, p. 526). They suggest that engagement in these activities ultimately becomes internalized into a person's identity and intrinsically motivating. They have identified two types of passion: harmonious and obsessive (Vallerand, 2008). Harmonious passion for an activity typically results in more positive experiences; whereas an obsessive passion may lead to uncontrollable urges to engage in an activity. Donahue and colleagues (2009) found that basketball athletes who were obsessively passionate about their sport were more likely to report aggressive behaviours than those with a harmonious passion, particularly when their athletic identity was challenged. Visek and colleagues (2010) also found that athletes with a high athletic identity in both the United States and Hong Kong reported more aggressiveness. Consequently, loving one's sport can positively impact one's experiences, however, when that passion is intimately tied to one's identity as an athlete, it may become maladaptive.

Situational Factors Influencing Aggression

Frequency of Competition It is not a stretch to think that the number of times competitors meet may have an impact on the amount of aggressive behaviour demonstrated in the matches. Indeed, Widmeyer and McGuire (1997) did find that aggressive behaviours occurred more often in intradivisional professional ice hockey games (i.e., teams competing in the same division) than in interdivisional games (i.e., teams competing in different divisions). For instance, in the NHL, teams competing within their division (e.g., Montreal Canadiens and Toronto Maple Leafs) had higher incidences of aggression than did teams competing outside their divisions (e.g., Montreal Canadiens and Edmonton Oilers). Even sport fans state that they are more willing to commit anonymous acts of aggression toward current or anticipated rival teams (Havard et al., 2013).

Home Advantage An archival study by McGuire and colleagues (1992) examined whether home teams in ice hockey exhibited more aggressive behaviours than visiting teams and whether or not this type of behaviour had an impact on the outcome of the game. They found that there was indeed a home advantage, with the home teams winning 58.5% of decided games. Furthermore, home teams received more aggressive penalties in games they won, while visiting teams incurred more aggressive penalties in games they lost. Using an observational methodology, Jones and colleagues (2005) found no difference in the frequency of aggression between the home and visiting teams in professional rugby. However, the authors found that the visiting team engaged in more aggressive behaviours when they lost compared to when they won.

Point Differentials Losing is often thought to be a frustrating situation. If this assumption is true, then according to the frustration–aggression theory, individuals should behave in an aggressive manner when they are losing. In general, when researchers examined the influence of losing during a game and took into account the score when an aggressive act occurred, these situations were not related to aggressive behaviours (McGuire, 1990). Despite the fact that there does not seem to be a relationship between aggressive behaviour and losing situations in general, there does seem to be some support for the occurrence of aggressive behaviours and various specific losing situations. For example, several studies in ice hockey have found that teams losing late in the game tend to be more aggressive (Kirker et al., 2000; Wankel, 1973). Other researchers have found that teams losing by a large margin tend to display more aggressive actions (Harrel, 1980; McGuire, 1990).

Group Factors Influencing Aggression

Individual's Role Individuals who occupy a specific role on a team are generally expected to behave in a manner consistent with the behaviours expected of that role. Within sports like ice hockey, we often see players designated as the "enforcer" or "policeman." The players who fill these roles are expected—and may even be recruited—to behave in an aggressive manner. As Marty McSorley, former Boston Bruins enforcer, stated, "The job of a tough guy is to inspire team-mates and to ensure the team's skilled players are not intimidated" (South Coast Today, 2000).

Team Norms As discussed earlier, team norms are the standards for the behaviour that is expected of members of the group. Typically referred to as the unwritten rules of the game, team norms provide the player with the information necessary to know what is or is not acceptable behaviour. Studies have consistently shown that the coach is one of the most influential significant others in terms of modelling team norms (Steinfeldt et al., 2012). Players' moral decisions about whether or not to aggress or bully are largely based on their perceptions of the coach's norms for cheating, aggression, and bullying.

Collective efficacy for aggression: A team's perception of their ability to use aggressive behaviour as a tactic or strategy.

Collective Efficacy for Aggression As teams develop an acceptance of aggressive behaviour and subsequent expectation that it is needed for success, they develop a perception of their ability to use aggression as a tactic or strategy within the game. This perception of their ability to use aggression as a strategy (i.e., **collective efficacy for aggression**) is similar to the sense of collective competence they feel for their offensive or defensive skills. A study of Canadian university and junior ice hockey teams by Dorsch (1997) found that collective efficacy for strategic aggression did predict future team aggressive behaviours. Furthermore, these perceptions were more similar among team members than between teams, suggesting that it is a group perception.

Group Cohesion Dorsch and colleagues (1996) examined perceptions of team cohesion and aggressive behaviour among Canadian junior ice hockey teams. They found that as the teams became more united in pursuit of their goals and objectives (i.e., more cohesive), they exhibited more aggressive behaviours. In a study of youth minor hockey, Bessette and Loughead (2007) found further support to suggest that both task and social cohesion predicted team norms regarding the use of physical aggression. Together these studies lead to the suggestion that group cohesion may in fact be a group factor that influences aggressive behaviour.

REFLECTIONS 6.3

As a sport psychology consultant, you have been asked by a youth hockey league to help reduce aggression levels. Which factors—personal, situational, or both—would you target, and why?

CONSEQUENCES OF AGGRESSIVE BEHAVIOUR

All aggressive acts have both an aggressor and a victim. Furthermore, most of these acts in a sport setting also have at least one observer. Consequently, within an aggressive interaction there can be consequences to the aggressor, victim, and observer. The most obvious of these consequences to the individuals involved in the altercation is injury. While many studies have examined the incidence of injury in sports, few have related the cause of the injury to the aggressive behaviour. In an attempt to address this limitation, Katorji and Cahoon (1992) reported that trainers and players in Canadian Junior B hockey said that approximately 59% of injuries occurred because of an opponent's aggressive act. They also found that, of the injuries that occurred to the aggressor, approximately 27% occurred when the actor was attempting to harm his opponent.

Falling back on the definition of an aggressive behaviour, intimidation or psychological harm is another possible consequence of an aggressive altercation. Even though it is very difficult to measure the amount of psychological harm that occurs within a sporting event, we can sometimes infer from a player's behaviour that the aggressor's intent has succeeded. For example, if we see the football receiver hesitate or alter his pattern to avoid the safety, or if we see that an ice hockey forward is afraid to go into the corners to get the puck, we assume that these players have been intimidated. The difficulty is that the athlete may have been intimidated by an assertive behaviour and not by an aggressive behaviour.

Regardless of whether one is attacked or is the attacker, another possible consequence of the altercation is an elevated arousal level. Anger or other emotions are often associated with involvement in an aggressive incident. Coupled closely with these emotions is an alteration in the individual's arousal level. In support of this suggestion, NHL referee Brad Watson indicated that players often fight to fire their team up (Tuchman, 2000).

Finally, penalization is the most common consequence that can occur to the aggressor and the team. In most sports, penalization is designed to discourage aggressive behaviour by reducing the individual's or team's chances of success.

Fan Violence

Aggression by spectators has been a concern for many years, particularly in soccer outside of North America. Spectator aggression includes behaviours that intend to injure another person (e.g., fans, players, referees) or destroy property. Earlier in the chapter, we heard of the incident from Egyptian soccer. What caused these fans to rush the field and behave so aggressively and violently? **Fan identification** may be one reason and refers to the extent to which fans feel psychologically connected to a team. One sports journalist stated, "The two loudest cheers you ever hear in a hockey game are when the home team scores a goal and when there is a fight" (Tuchman, 2000, p. 17).

The relationship between fan identification and spectator aggression can be explained by social identity theory, which states that a person's sense of who they are is based on their group membership. Belonging to a group (e.g., fans of a sport team) is an important source of pride and self-esteem. In sport, this theory would suggest that fans who highly identify with a team are more likely to experience a strong sense of group solidarity. Consequently, this strong identification by fans is related to positive attitudes

Fan identification: Extent to which fans feel psychologically connected to a team.

toward spectator aggression because it offers them an opportunity for identity reparation following their team's losses.

In order to see how sport team identification was related to a willingness to consider acts of aggression, Wann and colleagues (2003) asked participants to consider various acts of aggression toward players and coaches of a rival team. Specifically, participants were asked, if they could remain completely anonymous and there was no possibility of arrest, how likely were they to trip a star rival player and coach, and break a leg of a star rival player and coach? The results showed that 37% would trip a player, 36% would trip a coach, and 13% would break either a player or coach's leg. Clearly, the findings show that a fan's level of team identification is a key variable in whether a spectator will engage in a deviant manner.

We may believe that the majority of the aggressive acts that occur between fans and athletes happen at the professional level; however, a particularly disturbing incident occurred on January 4, 2014, between the father of a teen hockey player in Buffalo and the child's coach. The father physically attacked the coach after his son was pulled from a game during a high school tournament. The father pushed the coach and hit him several times. The coach was taken by ambulance to the hospital. The father was charged with third-degree assault.

REDUCING AGGRESSION IN SPORT

Before we can even attempt to reduce aggressive behaviours in sport, we have to understand why they occur. Up to this point, you should have a clear understanding why people behave aggressively and know some of the factors influencing an athlete's intent to harm another individual. We are suggesting five broad methods that may be useful in helping individuals participating in, or even observing, sports to curb their aggressive behaviours. These methods are not necessarily directed specifically at the athletes. Interventions targeted toward other individuals involved in the sporting system (e.g., coaches, parents, officials, and the media) may also prove to be beneficial in accomplishing successful behavioural change.

Punishment and Encouragement

Social learning theory suggests to us that people learn that aggression pays. Therefore, teaching individuals that aggression does not pay would be paramount for behavioural change. In order to make this shift, the individuals who strongly influence the athletes' learning process (i.e., coaches and parents) need to ensure that the penalty or punishment athletes receive for an act of aggression is more meaningful to them than any reinforcement they may receive. To this end, coaches and parents must emphasize the value of fair play, and encourage and reward such behaviours as great moves, strong effort, unselfish play, teamwork, and courage. Outside the field of play, it is beneficial for parents to focus on developing their child's ability using a task goal orientation instead of an ego goal orientation. Finally, parents and coaches need to provide young athletes with positive role models, ones who demonstrate non-aggressive, yet effective, assertive behaviours. In an attempt to ensure that positive behaviours are modelled in the sport environment, several youth sport organizations require coaches and parents to complete online certification such as Respect in Sport (respectinsport.com).

Educational Interventions

One way we can help those involved in sport understand that aggression does not pay is through educational interventions. These workshops teach athletes, parents, coaches, officials, media personnel, and authority figures the meaning of aggression, why it occurs, the cost of aggressive acts, and how to control aggression.

Another aspect of educational programs is the teaching of psychological skills. Such programs need not focus only on technical skills but also on teaching athletes to expect frustration, annoyance, and attack. Inherent in any sporting situation is an opponent's attempt to stop the athlete's ultimate goal of winning. The athlete has to be able to deal with these situations in an effective, yet non-aggressive, manner. Another feature of any educational program is the necessity to focus on the consequences of anabolic steroid use. Athletes, parents, and coaches need to become more familiar with the extremely negative impacts that the use of these drugs has on the future health of the user, including aggressive behaviour.

Behavioural Modification Practices

In the International Society of Sport Psychology's position on aggression and violence in sport, Tenenbaum et al. (1996) state, "The tightening of rules, imposing of harsher penalties and changing of reinforcement patterns are only part of the answer to inhibiting aggression in sport. Ultimately, the athlete must assume responsibility for his/her behaviour" (p. 234). Part of assisting the athlete to assume this responsibility could involve the athlete's participation in programs designed to help reduce the desire to behave aggressively. As part of daily training, working on self-awareness and developing strategies and coping skills would be beneficial.

Tenenbaum and colleagues (1996) also recognized that "like players, officials are placed under great stress during games" (p. 233). Consequently, they suggest that officials take measures to improve their psychological skills, for example, their ability to concentrate, to control unnecessary arousal, and to cope with pressure. Ultimately, the development of these skills will enable officials to become more competent and consistent in enforcing the rules of sport. According to Tenenbaum et al., the subsequent decline in the incidence of errors will help decrease athletes', coaches', and fans' levels of frustration, while also promoting fair play and minimizing aggressive behaviour.

Changes to the Sporting Environment

Even though we did not mention the use of alcohol previously, it is readily accepted that the ingestion of alcohol lowers an individual's inhibitions and consequently makes that individual more likely to act aggressively. Therefore, banning, or at the very least limiting, the sale of alcoholic beverages at sporting events may be useful. Cox (2002) suggests that "athletic events should be promoted and encouraged as family affairs" (p. 316). Sporting events should be an enjoyable experience, where parents and their children can learn about fair play.

Aggressive Behaviour in the Media

Previously, we acknowledged the fact that fans like aggression in the sports they observe. Bryant and Zillman (1983) suggest that the media exploits this desire by (1) sensationalizing and replaying acts of aggression repeatedly, (2) focusing on and glorifying aggression in feature stories, and (3) promoting previous aggressive behaviours between competitors to encourage future attendance. Instead of making aggressive behaviours the highlights, promoting a campaign to decrease aggressive behaviours in sport would be more beneficial. The assertive (not aggressive) plays and players should be glorified and those players held up as role models in order to promote these acceptable behaviours.

CHAPTER SUMMARY

The information we discussed in this chapter deals with the reasons that an individual may behave in an aggressive manner, including the role of moral behaviour in influencing aggression. In order for us to truly understand and attempt to control aggressive behaviour in sport, we must include other scientific disciplines (e.g., sociology, anthropology) in this quest. However, from a psychological viewpoint, we know the following points regarding aggressive and moral behaviour in sport.

Aggressive behaviour is *not* something we want to encourage or reinforce in athletes because the definition of aggression includes the intent to harm another physically or psychologically. We want to teach and encourage athletes to play assertively (i.e., with legitimate force and energy).

The notion that sport builds character has been and will continue to be a popular viewpoint, and terms, such as *sportspersonship*, *character building*, and *moral development*, will be pervasive in school textbooks and in the mainstream media. The study of moral behaviour within the context of sport is in its infancy. Nonetheless, this chapter introduced two classic paradigms in which moral behaviours have been studied—structural–developmental and social learning—and some of the factors that influence how we behave.

Many factors influence aggressive behaviour. Although many theories have helped us understand why people behave aggressively, the theory that provides the most promise for helping us control this behaviour in sport suggests that people behave aggressively because they have learned that aggression pays. Even though the social learning theory gives us a foundation from which to work, we need to be aware of many other personal, situational, and group factors that influence aggressive behaviour.

Reducing aggressive behaviour in sport involves everyone. Controlling aggression is not just an individual athlete's task. Many other actions or interventions could be implemented by, or even targeted at, other sport participants. Coaches, parents, officials, and the media are key stakeholders in the process of behaviour change.

 ### COMMON MYTHS ABOUT AGGRESSION AND MORAL BEHAVIOUR IN SPORT REVISITED

MYTH: Aggression in sport is a good characteristic. It is something to be encouraged in players.

Most coaches, when asked what kind of player they want on their team, would include *aggressive* in their description of the ideal player. However, from a sport psychology perspective, aggression is not a good thing. An aggressive act is one in which the player intentionally tries to hurt his or her opponent. The behaviours that coaches and parents should try to encourage in their athletes and children are correctly labelled *assertive* behaviours.

MYTH: Aggression is only a physical behaviour.

A classic scene in the movie *Slapshot* exemplifies this myth. An opponent was trying to get the Chiefs' goalie off of his game, so he skated by the goalie and said something insulting about a member of the goalie's family. The Chiefs' goalie then skated after the opposing player, trying to slash him with his stick. A verbal insult like trash talking can be considered an aggressive act since it is an intentional attempt to psychologically hurt (i.e., distract or intimidate) a person.

MYTH: Athletes are born with certain moral behaviours.

Similar to other behaviours in sport, moral behaviours are influenced by our environment. Coaches, parents, and teammates play a key role in how athletes will behave during competition.

Review Questions

1. Discuss the differences among aggression, assertion, and violence.

2. What are the two classic perspectives for examining the development of moral behaviour in sport?

3. Discuss the four factors that influence the development of moral behaviours in sport and provide a sport example of each.

4. Explain the difference between instrumental and hostile aggression.

5. Hockey Canada hires you as a consultant to offer workshops to players, coaches, and officials regarding the appropriateness of aggression in hockey. What will you tell them during the workshops?

6. As the sport psychology consultant for a Major Junior A team, you notice that one of the players frequently takes retaliation-type penalties after being bodychecked by an opposing player. How will you help the player understand why he behaves this way, and help him change his behaviour?

7. Describe four group factors that influence aggression in sport.

Suggested Reading

Gee, C. J., & Potwarka, L. R. (2014). Controlling anger and aggression. In A. Papaioannou & D. Hackfort (Eds.), *Routledge companion to sport and exercise psychology: Global perspectives and fundamental concepts* (pp. 650–667). London: Routledge.

Shields, D. L., & Bredemier, B. L. (2007). Can sports build character? In D. Smith & M. Bar-Eli (Eds.), *Essential readings in sport and exercise psychology* (pp. 423–432). Champaign, IL: Human Kinetics.

References

Bandura, A. (1973). *Aggression: A social learning analysis*. Englewood Cliffs, NJ: Prentice-Hall.

Bandura, A. (1999). Moral disengagement in the perpetration of inhumanities. *Personality and Social Psychology Review, 3*, 193–209.

Beller, J. M., & Stoll, S. K. (1995). Moral reasoning of high school student athletes and general students: An empirical study versus personal testimony. *Pediatric Exercise Science, 7*, 352–363.

Berkowitz, L. (1989). Frustration–aggression hypothesis: Examination and reformulation. *Psychological Bulletin, 106*, 59–73.

Berkowitz, L. (1990). On the formation and regulation of anger and aggression. A cognitive–neoassociationistic analysis. *American Psychologist, 45*, 494–503.

Bessette, N., & Loughead, T. M. (2007, November). *The examination of cohesion and norms for aggression on perceived belonging in youth minor hockey.* Paper presented to the Canadian Society for Psychomotor Learning and Sport Psychology Conference, Windsor, ON.

Bloom, G. A., & Smith, M. D. (1996). Hockey violence: A test of cultural spillover theory. *Sociology of Sport Journal, 13*, 65–77.

Bloom, G. A., & Vanier, J. L. (2004). Coaches' perceptions of aggression in elite women's ice hockey. In D. J. Pearsall & A. B. Ashare (Eds.), *Safety in ice hockey: Fourth Volume* (pp. 12–25). Philadelphia: American Society for Testing and Materials.

Brice, J. G. (1990). *Frustration in ice hockey: Extent, antecedents and consequences.* Unpublished master's thesis, University of Waterloo, Waterloo, Ontario, Canada.

Bryant, J., & Zillman, D. (1983). Sports violence and the media. In J. Goldstein (Ed.), *Sport violence* (pp. 195–211). New York: Springer Verlag.

Camiré, M., & Trudel, P. (2010). High school athletes' perspectives on character development through sport participation. *Physical Education and Sport Pedagogy, 15*, 193–207.

Chow, G. M., Murray, K. E., & Feltz, D. L. (2009). Individual, team, and coach predictors of players' likelihood to aggress in youth soccer. *Journal of Sport & Exercise Psychology, 31*, 425–443.

Coulomb-Cabagno, G., & Rascle, O. (2005). Team sports players' observed aggression as a function of gender, competitive level, and sport type. *Journal of Applied Social Psychology, 36*, 1980–2000.

Cox, R. H. (2002). *Sport psychology: Concepts and applications* (5th ed.). New York: McGraw Hill.

Crow, R. B., & Macintosh, E. W. (2009). Conceptualizing a meaningful definition of hazing in sport. *European Sport Management Quarterly, 9*, 433–451.

Dollard, J. C., Doob, L., Miller, N., Mowrer, O. H., & Sears, R. R. (1939). *Frustration and aggression.* New Haven, CT: Yale University Press.

Donahue, E. G., Rip, B., & Vallerand, R. J. (2009). When winning is everything: On passion, identity, and aggression. *Psychology of Sport and Exercise, 10*, 526–534.

Dorsch, K. D. (1992). *The extent and antecedents of aggression in PeeWee hockey.* Unpublished manuscript, University of Waterloo, Waterloo, Ontario, Canada.

Dorsch, K. D. (1997). *Examining aggressive behaviour from a group perspective.* Unpublished doctoral dissertation, University of Waterloo, Waterloo, Ontario, Canada.

Dorsch, K. D., McAuliffe, J., & Paskevich, D. M. (2000, April). Perceived stress, burnout, coping styles, and intentions to terminate among Canadian squash officials. *The Squash Official, 6–7.*

Dorsch, K. D., Riemer, H. A., Lawrence, D., Schinke, R. J., & Paskevich, D. M. (2012). The relationship between the extent and intensity of stressful experiences of Canadian minor hockey officials.

Dorsch, K. D., Widmeyer, W. N., Paskevich, D. M., & Brawley, L. R. (1996). Exploring relationships among collective efficacy, norms for aggression, cohesion, and aggressive behaviour in Junior hockey. *Journal of Applied Sport Psychology, 8*, 55.

Duffy, A. L., & Nesdale, D. (2009). Peer groups, social identity, and children's bullying behavior. *Social Development, 18*, 121–139.

Folkesson, P., Nyberg, C., Archer, T., & Norlander, T. (2002). Soccer referees' experience of threat and aggression: Effects of age, experience, and life orientation on outcome of coping strategy. *Aggressive Behavior, 28*, 317–327.

Freud, S. (1925). *Collected papers.* London, UK: Hogarth Press.

Girard, D. (2004, December 23). Canucks superstar; Gets discharge for brutal attack on Colorado's Moore. *Toronto Star*, p. A01.

Harrell, W. A. (1980). Aggression by high school basketball players: An observational study of the effects of opponents' aggression and frustration inducing factors. *International Journal of Sport Psychology, 11*, 290–298.

Havard, C. T., Wann, D. L., & Ryan, T. D. (2013). Investigating the impact of conference realignment on rivalry in intercollegiate athletics. *Sport Marketing Quarterly, 22*, 224–234.

Jones, M. V., Bray, S. R., & Olivier, S. (2005). Game location and aggression in rugby league. *Journal of Sports Sciences, 23*, 387–393.

Katorji, J. K., & Cahoon, M. A. (1992). *The relationship between aggression and injury in Junior B hockey.* Unpublished manuscript, University of Waterloo, Waterloo, ON, Canada.

Kavanagh, E. J., & Jones, I. (2014). Virtual maltreatment in sport. In D. Rhind & C. Brackenridge (Eds.) *Researching and enhancing athlete welfare. Proceedings of the second international symposium of the Brunel International Research Network for Athlete Welfare (BIRNAW) 2013* (pp. 34–43). London: Brunel University Press.

Kavussanu, M., & Roberts, G. C. (2001). Moral functioning in sport: An achievement goal perspective. *Journal of Sport & Exercise Psychology, 23*, 37–54.

Kavussanu, M., Seal, A. R., & Phillips, D. R. (2006). Observed prosocial and antisocial behaviors in male soccer teams: Age differences across adolescence and the role of motivational variables. *Journal of Applied Sport Psychology, 18*, 326–344.

Keating, C. F., Pomerantz, J., Pommer, S. D., Ritt, S. J. H., Miller, L. M., & McCormick, J. (2005). Going to college and unpacking hazing: A functional approach to decrypting initiation practices among undergraduates. *Group Dynamics: Theory, Research, and Practice, 9*, 104–126.

Kirby, S. L., & Wintrup, G. (2002). Running the gauntlet: An examination of initiation/hazing and sexual abuse in sport. In C. Brackenridge & K. Fasting (Eds.), *Sexual harassment and abuse in sport: International research and policy perspectives* (pp. 65–90). London: Whiting and Birch.

Kirker, B., Tenenbaum, G., & Mattson, J. (2000). An investigation of the dynamics of aggression: Direct observations in ice hockey and basketball. *Research Quarterly for Exercise and Sport, 71*, 373–386.

Kohlberg, L. (1984). *Essays on moral development: Vol. 1. The philosophy of moral development.* San Francisco: Harper & Row.

Lemieux, P., McKelvie, S. J., & Stout, D. (2002, December). Self-reported hostile aggression in contact athletes, no contact athletes and non-athletes. *Athletic Insight: The Online Journal of Sport Psychology, 4.* Retrieved December 29, 2004, from www.athleticinsight.com/Vol4Iss3/SelfReportedAggression.htm.

Loughead, T. M., & Leith, L. M. (2001). Hockey coaches' and players' perceptions of aggression and the aggressive behavior of players. *Journal of Sport Behavior, 24*, 394–407.

McGuire, E. J. (1990). *Antecedents of aggressive behaviour in professional ice hockey.* Unpublished doctoral dissertation, University of Waterloo, Waterloo, ON, Canada.

McGuire, E. J., Courneya, K. S., Widmeyer, W. N., & Carron, A. V. (1992). Aggression as a potential mediator of the home advantage in professional ice hockey. *Journal of Sport and Exercise Psychology, 14*, 148–158.

Nicholls, J. G. (1989). *The competitive ethos and democratic education.* Cambridge, MA: Harvard University Press.

Papacharisis, V., Goudas, M., Danish, S. J., & Thedorakis, Y. (2005). The effectiveness of teaching life skills program in a sport context. *Journal of Applied Sport Psychology, 17*, 247–254.

Piaget, J. (1932). *The moral judgement of the child.* New York: Harcourt & Brace.

Rainey, D. W. (1994). Assaults on umpires: A statewide survey. *Journal of Sport Behavior, 17*, 148–155.

Rehm, J., Steinleitner, M., & Lilli, W. (1987). Wearing uniforms and aggression – A field experiment. *European Journal of Social Psychology, 17*, 357–360.

Russell, G. W. (1993). *The social psychology of sport*. New York: Springer Verlag.

Sanszole, M. (1995). *The extent, antecedents and response to sport frustration by high school students*. Unpublished manuscript, University of Waterloo, Waterloo, ON, Canada.

Shannon, C. S. (2013). Bullying in recreation and sport settings: Exploring risk factors, prevention efforts, and intervention strategies. *Journal of Park and Recreation Administration, 31*, 15–33.

Shapcott, K. M., Bloom, G. A., & Loughead, T. M. (2007). Factors influencing aggressive and assertive intentions of women ice hockey players. *International Journal of Sport Psychology, 38*, 145–162.

Shields, D. L., & Bredemeier, B. J. (1995). *Character development and physical activity*. Champaign, IL: Human Kinetics.

Shields, D. L., LaVoi, N. M., Bredemeier, B. L., & Power, F. C. (2007). Predictors of poor sportspersonship in youth sports: Personal attitudes and social influences. *Journal of Sport & Exercise Psychology, 29*, 747–762.

Silva, J. M. (1980). Understanding aggressive behavior and its effects upon athletic performance. In W. F. Straub (Ed.), *Sport psychology: An analysis of athlete behavior*. Ithaca, NY: Mouvement Publications.

Sjoqvist, F., Garle, M., & Rane, A. (2008). Use of doping agents, particularly anabolic steroids, in sports and society. *The Lancet, 371*, 1872–1882.

Smith, M. D. (1979). Social determinants of violence in hockey. *Canadian Journal of Applied Sport Sciences, 4*, 76–82.

South Coast Today, Associated Press, McSorley says he didn't mean to hurt Brashear, September 28, 2000. http://www.southcoasttoday.com/apps/pbcs.dll/article?AID=/20000928/NEWS/309289921&cid=sitesearch.

Stanger, N., Kavussnu, M., & Ring, C. (2012). Put yourself in their boots: Effects of empathy on emotion and aggression. *Journal of Sport & Exercise Psychology, 34*, 208–222.

Steinfeldt, J. A., Vaughan, E. L., LaFollette, J. R., & Steinfeldt, M. C. (2012). Bullying among adolescent football players: Role of masculinity and moral atmosphere. *Psychology of Men and Masculinity, 13*, 340–353.

Stephens, D. E. (2004, Winter). Moral atmosphere and aggression in collegiate intramural sport. *International Sports Journal*, 65–75.

Stirling, A. E., Bridges, E. J., Cruz, E. L., & Mountjoy, M. L. (2011). Canadian academy of sport and exercise medicine position paper: Abuse, harassment, and bullying in sport. *Clinical Journal of Sport Medicine, 21*, 385–391.

Stuart, M. E., & Ebbeck, V. (1995). The influence of perceived social approval on moral development in youth sport. *Pediatric Exercise Science, 7*, 270–280.

Terry, P. C., & Jackson, J. J. (1985). The determinants and control of violence in sport. *Quest, 37*, 27–37.

The Telegraph (2012, February 2). Egypt football riots: FIFA president Sepp Blatter left saddened by 'black day for football'. *The Telegraph*. Retrieved from http://www.telegraph.co.uk.

Tenenbaum, G., Stewart, E., Singer, R., & Duda, J. (1996). Aggression and violence in sport: An ISSP position stand. *International Journal of Sport Psychology, 27*, 229–236.

Tuchman, G. (2000, September 26). Hockey player goes on trial for on-ice assault. CNN. Retrieved January 3, 2005, from http://archives.cnn.com/2000/LAW/criminal/09/25/mcsorley.trial.02/.

Vallerand, R. J. (2008). On the psychology of passion: In search of what makes people's lives most worth living. *Canadian Psychology, 49*, 1–13.

Vallerand, R. J., & Miquelon, P. (2007). Passion for sport in athletes. In S. Jowett & D. Lavallee (Eds.), *Social psychology in sport* (pp. 249–263). Champaign, IL: Human Kinetics.

Vanier, J., Bloom, G. A., & Loughead, T. M. (2005). Personal experiences, rules, procedures, and aspects of aggression in competitive women's ice hockey. *Avante, 11,* 66–82.

Visek, A., & Watson, J. (2005). Ice hockey players' legitimacy of aggression and professionalization of attitudes. *The Sport Psychologist, 19,* 178–192.

Visek, A. J., Watson, J. C., Hurst, J. R., Maxwell, J. P., & Harris, B. S. (2010). Athletic identity and aggressiveness: A cross-cultural analysis of the athletic identity maintenance model. *International Journal of Sport and Exercise Psychology, 8,* 99–116.

Waldron, J. J., & Kowalski, C. L. (2009). Crossing the line: Rites of passage, team aspects, and ambiguity of hazing. *Research Quarterly for Exercise and Sport, 80,* 291–302.

Wankel, L. M. (1973, October). An examination of illegal aggression in intercollegiate hockey. In *Proceedings: Fourth Canadian psycho-motor learning and sport psychology symposium* (pp. 531–544). Waterloo, ON: University of Waterloo.

Wann, D. L., Haynes, G., McLean, B., & Pullen, P. (2003). Sport team identification and willingness to consider anonymous acts of hostile aggression. *Aggressive Behavior, 29,* 406–413.

Wann, D. L. & Porcher, B. J. (1998). The relationship between players' names on uniforms and athletic aggression. *International Sports Journal, 2,* 28–35.

Weiss, M. R. (2006). *The First Tee 2005 research summary: Longitudinal effects of the First Tee Life Skills Educational Program on positive youth development.* St. Augustine, FL: The First Tee.

Wells, T. V., Karp, B. S., Birenboim, B., & Brown, D. W. (2014). Report to the National Football League concerning issues of workplace conduct at the Miami Dolphins. Miami, FL: Paul, Weiss, Rifkind, Wharton, & Garrison, LLP.

Whyno, S. (2013, November 7). Current and former NHL players bristle at debate over abolishing fighting. *The Globe and Mail.* Retrieved from http://www.theglobeandmail.com.

Widmeyer, W. N., Bray, S. R., Dorsch, K. D., & McGuire, E. J. (2002). Explanations for the occurrence of aggression: Theories and research. In J. M. Silva, & D. E. Stevens (Eds.), *Psychological foundations of sport* (pp. 352–379). Boston: Allyn & Bacon.

Widmeyer, W. N., & McGuire, E. J. (1997). Frequency of competition and aggression in professional ice hockey. *International Journal of Sport Psychology, 26,* 57–60.

Chapter 7

Sport Psychology Interventions

Krista Munroe-Chandler   Craig Hall

Chapter Objectives

After reading this chapter, you should be able to do the following:

1   Define and describe each of the five psychological skills most often used in a psychological skills training program.

2   Explain why these psychological skills work.

3   Describe the measurement and implementation of the skills.

4   Describe the components of a psychological skills training program.

Tyler is an 18-year-old high-school basketball player. He is consistent with his free throws and has been working for the past season on his three-pointers. He and his coach, Dave, have decided that for him to become a starter he needs to work not only on his physical skills but also on his mental skills. Tyler does not have a specific problem (e.g., extreme nervousness before games); however, both he and Dave recognize the importance of enhancing mental skills. To help him improve his mental skills, they have asked for the help of an applied sport psychology consultant. The consultant meets with them, and together they develop a psychological skills training program.

The applied sport psychology consultant first conducted performance profiling. Based on the results, the consultant determined that Tyler needed to relax prior to games as he was making unnecessary errors in the first five minutes of the game. He also needed to improve his focus during practice, since he was spending time watching other players rather than focusing on what he needed to do. Finally, he needed to enhance his confidence at the three-point line and inside the key.

To accomplish these objectives, Tyler introduced calming words into his pregame routine. He developed and followed a practice plan that outlined in detail what he had to accomplish during a practice. In addition, he started to regularly do imagery and developed and used a set of confidence-building self-statements at the three-point line and in the key. This initial intervention proved very effective, and Tyler continues to work with the applied sport psychology consultant on improving the mental side of his game.

Athletes approach applied sport psychology consultants for two general reasons: (1) to seek help with specific problems, such as performance anxiety and lack of self-confidence, and (2) to work to improve the mental side of sport, such as imagery and attention control. In the above scenario, Tyler decided to work with a sport psychology consultant for the second reason. Rather than dealing with a specific problem, the consultant was faced with generating a psychological skills training program for Tyler. The challenge for the consultant was to determine what techniques should be incorporated into the psychological skills training program (or intervention) and what emphasis should be placed on each. In this chapter we will address these and other issues.

🔍 COMMON MYTHS ABOUT SPORT PSYCHOLOGY INTERVENTIONS

MYTH: Psychological skills training is a Band-Aid solution.

MYTH: Only elite athletes can benefit from psychological skills training.

MYTH: Athletes need a sport psychology consultant only when they are performing poorly.

INTRODUCTION

For decades, sport psychology consultants have been studying and developing psychological skills interventions to help athletes enhance their performance and psychological well-being. A **psychological skills training** program, or intervention, entails the structured

Psychological skill training: A program or intervention that entails a structured and consistent practice of psychological skills and generally has three distinct phases (education, acquisition, and practice).

Joe Patronite/Getty Images

Athletes approach a sport psychology consultant to seek help with specific problems and to work to improve the mental side of sport.

and consistent practice of psychological skills and generally has three distinct phases: (1) education, (2) acquisition, and (3) practice. In the education phase, athletes recognize the importance of mental skills in sport and how the skills affect performance. There are various approaches to accomplishing this; however, one of the simplest ways is to ask athletes about the importance of mental skills in sport. Although most athletes realize the importance of the mental side of sport, very few actually spend time developing these skills in comparison with the time spent on physical skills.

Athletes often have some understanding of a psychological skill, but they do not fully comprehend its complexity and its optimal use. Therefore, in the acquisition phase, the focus is placed on helping athletes acquire the various psychological skills and learn how to employ them most effectively. In the practice phase, the goals are to have the athletes automate the various psychological skills through overlearning and to implement these skills in practice and competition.

PSYCHOLOGICAL SKILLS IN TRAINING PROGRAMS

The psychological skills that have been researched most extensively and incorporated into psychological skills training programs are goal setting, imagery, self-talk, arousal regulation, and attention control. Each of these five skills will be discussed in turn. We will define each skill and discuss why it works, how it can be measured, and how it can be integrated into a psychological skills training program. Another important psychological skill is coping with emotions. Measurement tools are discussed in some detail since without proper assessment there cannot be a successful psychological skills training program.

GOAL SETTING

Goal setting is the most commonly used performance enhancement strategy in sport psychology. Leading sport psychology consultants working with athletes of various ages and levels reported the frequent use of goal setting (Burton & Weiss, 2008); however, most athletes rate their goals as being only moderately effective in enhancing sport performance (Burton et al., 2001).

Goal: A target or objective that people strive to attain.

Performance goals: Goals that focus on improvement and attainment of personal performance standards.

Process goals: Goals that focus on specific behaviours in which athletes must engage throughout a performance.

Outcome goals: Goals that focus on social comparison and competitive results.

Types of Goals

A **goal** is a target or objective that people strive to attain. There are three types of goals that athletes can set. **Performance goals** focus on improving and attaining personal performance standards, such as learning an out-turn draw in curling or running a faster time. **Process goals** focus on specific behaviours that an athlete must engage in throughout a performance, such as snapping the wrist when stroking a squash ball or pulling the arms in tight while executing a spin in figure skating. In contrast to the first two types of goals, **outcome goals** focus on social comparison and competitive results, such as winning a race or outscoring an opponent. Thus, outcome goals are dependent on the ability and performance of one's opponents. **Goal setting**, therefore, is the practice of establishing desirable objectives for one's actions. While research suggests incorporating all three types of goals when developing a goal-setting program (Filby et al., 1999), emphasis should be placed on setting process and performance goals because athletes should strive to set goals that are personally controllable (Burton & Weiss, 2008).

Effectiveness of Goal Setting

Research suggests that goal setting works in various ways. According to Locke and Latham (1985), goals direct attention, mobilize effort, foster persistence, and promote the development of new learning strategies. Research has consistently demonstrated the positive effects of goal setting. In addition to goals influencing athletes' performance by enhancing their self-confidence and their sense of satisfaction (Moran, 2004), realistic goals help an athlete manage stress and remain optimistic when faced with adversity (Burton & Weiss, 2008). Many sport and exercise studies have shown moderate to strong effects on behaviour. For example, Wanlin and colleagues (1997) conducted a multiple baseline design in which youth speed skaters received training in goal setting. Over the course of the intervention, the skaters made improvements in their skating as a result of their goal setting. Senécal et al. (2008) examined the effects of a season-long team goal-setting intervention on cohesion. Eight teams were randomly assigned to the team goal-setting group or control group. The team goal-setting group held higher perceptions of cohesion than the control group, indicating that team goal setting was an effective team-building tool for enhancing levels of cohesion.

Initially, Locke (1991) indicated that only hard goals (e.g., achieved by less than 10% who attempt them) would result in high performance. However, in their meta-analysis, Kyllo and Landers (1995) found that moderately difficult goals result in the best performances. This latter finding has been supported by other researchers in the sport domain (Liu et al., 2012). As previously mentioned, most athletes rate goals as being only moderately effective (Burton et al., 2001) even though goal setting is one of the most extensively employed interventions in sport psychology. This is likely due to the fact that athletes are not certain about how to set goals effectively, and as a result they do not think that goal setting works. Additionally, a number of barriers, such as lack of time and everyday distractions, hinder the practice of goal setting among athletes (Weinberg, 2002). Later in this chapter, we shall examine some ways of setting effective goals.

Assessing Goals

Performance profiling is a flexible assessment tool that allows for the identification of athletes' performance-related strengths and weaknesses. It is often used as a first step in developing an intervention program. In addition to its utility as a general assessment

BluIz60/Shutterstock

There are three types of goals that athletes can set: performance (learning to execute a corner kick), process (focusing on foot placement to make an accurate pass to the winger), and outcome (to score a goal).

Goal setting: The practice of establishing desirable objectives for one's actions.

Performance profiling: A flexible assessment tool that allows for the identification of athletes' performance related strengths and weaknesses.

Table 7.1 Completed Performance Profile of a Major Junior Hockey Player

Performance Characteristic	Ideal Rating	Current Ability	Discrepancy Score
Confidence	10	8	2
Speed	10	9	1
Offensive contribution	10	7	3*
Mental toughness	10	8	2
Consistent effort	10	8	2
Communication	10	7.5	2.5

*Priority performance characteristic to be corrected.

procedure, it can be used as an aid to goal setting (Butler & Hardy, 1992; Jones, 1993). There are five steps in performance profiling:

1. Identify key performance characteristics of an elite athlete in your sport. Think of the best person in your sport and identify the characteristics of that athlete. These can include physical, technical, tactical, and mental characteristics.

2. Identify the ideal rating for each of your characteristics. On a scale from 1 to 10, with 1 being "not at all important" and 10 being "extremely important," indicate your ideal scores. This rating is also your target.

3. Rate your current ability for each characteristic on a scale of 1 to 10, with 1 being "not at all like me" and 10 being "completely like me." Be as honest as possible.

4. Find your discrepancy score by subtracting your current rating from your ideal rating. The higher the discrepancy score, the weaker you perceive your ability for that characteristic.

5. Prioritize your targets. After identifying your performance weaknesses (highest discrepancy scores), pick out the two or three that are most in need of correction.

Having identified performance characteristics most in need of urgent attention, you can now implement strategies (set goals) to improve these characteristics. Take the example of the hockey player (see Table 7.1) who, through performance profiling, has identified his offensive contribution as a weakness in need of immediate attention. Accordingly, he sets two goals: (1) to increase his opportunity for assists, he will work on improving stick-to-stick passing, and (2) to increase his scoring opportunity, he will improve the accuracy of his wrist shot over the course of four weeks. How to set effective goals, such as those established by the hockey player, is discussed next.

Recommendations for Goal Setting

The acronym SMART has been recommended to help athletes remember five important guidelines for effective goal setting. Goals should be specific, measurable, adjustable, realistic, and timely (see Table 7.2).

There are other important goal-setting guidelines that athletes should follow (see Table 7.3). First, athletes should set goals for both practice and competition. Often,

Table 7.2 Goal Setting Using SMART Guidelines

Specific	*Is the goal specific?*	Yes ☐ No ☐	
	Set a goal that is specific (e.g., "increase speed by 10%") rather than vague (e.g., "to improve").		
Measurable	*Is the goal measurable?*	Yes ☐ No ☐	
	Be sure you can measure the goal in order to assess progress.		
Adjustable	*Is the goal adjustable?*	Yes ☐ No ☐	
	Don't be afraid to adjust the goals if necessary (e.g., due to less playing time or an injury).		
Realistic	*Is the goal realistic?*	Yes ☐ No ☐	
	Goals should be moderately difficult. If goals are too easy, they are of little value. If they are too difficult, they may lead to a decrease in confidence.		
Timely	*Is the goal timely?*	Yes ☐ No ☐	
	You need to identify a point in time at which the goal is to be achieved, thereby increasing motivation.		

Source: Adapted from Holmes, P. S., & Collins, D. J. (2001). The PETTLER approach to motor imagery: A functional equivalence model for sport psychologists. *Journal of Applied Sport Psychology, 13*, 60-83. © 2001 by Taylor and Francis, Philadelphia. 73–89.

athletes focus only on competition goals; however, setting practice goals is important when one considers the time spent in practice compared with the time spent in competition. In the opening vignette, Tyler developed a practice plan and therefore has set goals for what he wants to accomplish in practice. NHL star Sidney Crosby sets daily practice goals: "I push myself to raise my game every day. I focus on improving little things like my passing technique" (Edger, 2010, para. 2–3). Second, it is important to record the goals and make them public. In doing so, athletes become more likely to attempt to achieve their goals, given that people around them are aware of their objectives and can be helpful in motivating them to accomplish them. Third, goals should be stated positively rather than negatively: "I want to run the best 100 m time possible" rather than "I don't want to come in last in the 100 m." Fourth, for teams to maximize potential, Dawson and colleagues (2002) suggested four types of goals to be considered: (1) individual athlete's goals for self, (2) individual athlete's goal for the team, (3) the team's overall goal, and (4) the team's goal for individual members. Finally, the progress toward goal achievement should be reviewed on a regular basis. Conducting this regular review allows the athlete to identify if the goals are appropriate.

Table 7.3 Goal-Setting Guidelines

Set SMART goals.

Set goals for practice and competition.

Make goals public.

State goals positively rather than negatively.

Consider the four types of team goals.

Review goals regularly.

An example of an intervention using SMART goals is the Wanlin et al. (1997) study previously mentioned. All skaters in this study receiving the goal-setting intervention were first shown a video of the instructions to be followed throughout the duration of the study. Athletes were asked to develop a mission, set long-term goals, set subgoals and practice goals, and employ self-talk and visualization to help them achieve the goals. Moreover, athletes were asked to keep a logbook in which their daily practice goals were reported and measured. Athletes were told that the goals must be flexible as well as challenging. The skaters made improvements in their skating performance over the course of the goal-setting intervention.

REFLECTIONS 7.1

Consider a goal that you have set (personal, athletic, or academic). Does it follow the SMART guidelines? If so, congratulations; if not, revise your goal so that it does follow the SMART guidelines. If you are having difficulties, use Table 7.2 as an example. Now, set another goal using the SMART guidelines.

Common Goal-Setting Problems

There are some common problems in implementing a goal-setting program (see Table 7.4). One of the most common mistakes made by athletes in implementing a program is setting too many goals. Athletes end up setting so many goals that they cannot properly monitor them, so they find the evaluation to be overwhelming and lose interest. Those who are just beginning a goal-setting program should work on achieving a small number of goals. Performance profiling will assist the athlete in determining those few goals in need of immediate attention.

Another common problem occurs when athletes do not willingly participate in the goal-setting program. Some individuals will not be excited about goal setting and may even have a negative attitude toward it. Forcing athletes to set goals is not very effective because individual commitment is required. One solution for recognizing individual differences is to expose all athletes to goal setting and work more with those who show the most interest.

Underestimating the time it takes to implement a goal-setting program is another common problem. Often, a coach will implement a program with athletes early in the season. As the season progresses, however, less and less time is spent on goal setting, and toward the end of the season the goal-setting program is completely forgotten. This is

Table 7.4 Common Goal-Setting Problems

Setting too many goals

Failing to recognize individual differences in goal-setting interest

Underestimating the time required to set goals

Failing to provide follow-up and evaluation

problematic, given that many researchers have noted the importance of setting goals over an entire season. Coaches and athletes need to recognize the time required to undertake a goal-setting program. It is better to devote 15 minutes a week throughout the season to goal setting than to attempt to devote 15 minutes a day and not be able to follow through on it.

Finally, failing to provide follow-up is one of the major problems with goal-setting programs. Evaluation of goals is imperative, and the continued use of performance profiling throughout the season is one effective way to achieve this. Without follow-up and evaluation, goal setting is simply a waste of time and effort.

Conclusions about Goal Setting

It is almost impossible to conceive of a psychological skills training program that does not include goal setting. For athletes to enhance their performance, weaknesses must be identified and corrected. In overcoming weaknesses, it is almost inevitable that goals will be set (see Case Study 7.1). What becomes important is ensuring that athletes set SMART goals that are supported and evaluated. Although goal setting is a complex process that requires hard work and discipline, it can be extremely effective in helping athletes achieve excellence in sport (Burton et al., 2001). Thus, it is highly recommended that athletes of all competitive levels engage in goal setting. Not only is it a skill that has proven effective in sport, but coaches have been known to promote goal setting as an example of a life skill for youth, thus contributing to positive youth development (Camiré et al., 2011).

CASE STUDY 7.1	Correcting Weaknesses through Goal Setting

Dr. Carter meets with Janice, a competitive figure skater. In their first session, Dr. Carter has Janice complete a performance profile in order to assess her strengths and weaknesses in skating. From the results, it is evident that Janice currently rates herself a 6/10 on her lutz jump (the lowest performance characteristic). When Dr. Carter asks her what goals she would like to set with respect to lutz, her answer is simply, "to improve."

Based on the SMART goal-setting guidelines, Dr. Carter knows that this goal is too vague. In order to be more specific, Dr. Carter asks Janice how she can improve her lutz jump. They determine that increasing the amount of practice on that specific jump by 20 minutes a week for the next six weeks will help her increase her landing of the jump by 20%. This goal will be evaluated at week 3 to determine if Janice is on track and if any adjustments are necessary.

IMAGERY

When asked what mental strategies he uses, Canadian Mike Weir stated:

> The only thing I'm trying to do is visualize what I'm trying to do, depending on the wind and where the pin is (Schuchmann, 2004, para 37).

Researchers and athletes alike have long been interested in imagery and its effect on sport performance. Some have gone so far as to hail it as the "central pillar of applied sport psychology" (Perry & Morris, 1995, p. 339). In addition, coaches view imagery as one of the most important psychological skills to teach their athletes (Rodgers et al., 1991).

The Nature of Imagery

In the above quotation, Mike Weir refers to visualization. Visualization suggests that only one sense is being used, that of sight. It has been documented, however, that athletes try to incorporate as many senses as possible, including, sight, sound, smell, touch, and kinesthetic sense. The latter sense is particularly important for athletes since it involves the feel or sensation of bodily movements. The more polysensory the image, the more real it becomes, and the more effective it will be on sport performance. Given the multidimensional nature of imagery, White and Hardy (1998) have defined **imagery** as follows:

> [Imagery is] an experience that mimics real experience. We can be aware of "seeing" an image, feeling movements as an image, or experiencing an image of smell, tastes, or sounds without actually experiencing the real thing. Sometimes people find that it helps to close their eyes. It differs from dreams in that we are awake and conscious when we form an image (p. 389).

Analytic Model of Imagery

Most of the recent imagery research has stemmed from Paivio's (1985) analytic model, which suggests that imagery has cognitive and motivational functions that operate on either a specific or a general level. Thus, **cognitive general imagery** includes images of strategies, game plans, or routines (e.g., imaging a floor routine in gymnastics); **cognitive specific imagery** includes images of specific sport skills (e.g., imaging a free throw in basketball). **Motivational general imagery** includes images relating to physiological arousal levels and affect (e.g., imaging feeling calm and relaxed in front of a crowd); **motivational specific imagery** includes images related to an individual's goals (e.g., imaging receiving a gold medal). Subsequent to Paivio's assertions, Hall et al. (1998) divided the motivational general function into a **motivational general–arousal** function, encompassing imagery associated with arousal and stress, and a **motivational general–mastery** function, representing imagery associated with being mentally tough, in control, and self-confident (see Table 7.5).

Imagery: An experience that mimics real experience. It differs from dreams in that we are awake and conscious when we form an image.

Cognitive general imagery: Images of strategies, game plans, or routines.

Cognitive specific imagery: Images of specific sport skills.

Motivational general imagery: Images relating to physiological arousal levels and emotions.

Motivational specific imagery: Images related to an individual's goals.

Motivational general–arousal: Imagery associated with arousal and stress.

Motivational general–mastery: Imagery associated with the notion of being mentally tough, in control, and self-confident.

Table 7.5 The Five Functions of Imagery

Level	Motivational Function	Cognitive Function
General	Mastery	Strategies
	Arousal	
Specific	Goals	Skills

Source: Adapted from Hall, C. R., Mack, D., Paivio, A., & Hausenblas, H. A. (1998). Imagery use by athletes: Development of the Sport Imagery Questionnaire. *International Journal of Sport Psychology, 29,* 73–89.

Figure 7.1 Applied model of imagery use in sport

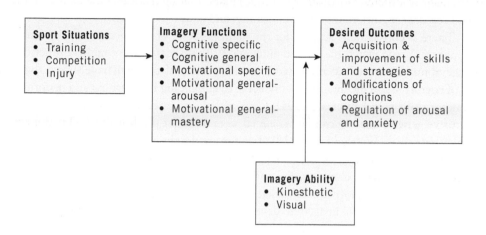

Source: Adapted, with permission, from Martin, K.A., Moritz, S.E., & Hall, C.R. (1997). Imagery use in sport: A literature review and applied model. *The Sport Psychologist, 13,* 245-268.

Based on the five functions, Martin and colleagues (1999) developed an applied model for depicting how imagery works in sport (see Figure 7.1). Although the model shows that athletes use imagery in three different situations, athletes report using imagery most in competition and, more specifically, just prior to competition (Munroe et al., 2000). According to the model, the desired sport outcome should be matched to the correct function of imagery. For example, if an athlete wanted to reduce anxiety prior to a competition, the type of imagery used should be motivational general–arousal. Athletes of all ages have been found to use all five functions of imagery; however, they report using motivational general–mastery the most (Munroe-Chandler et al., 2007).

Sportlibrary/Fotolia

When you use imagery, try to make it polysensory: see the wall, feel the water, smell the chlorine, hear the crowd cheer, taste the sweat on your lips.

Although far less research has been conducted on imagery use by injured athletes than healthy athletes, Driediger et al. (2006) found that such athletes use imagery for four main reasons: cognition, motivation, healing, and pain management.

There is considerable support for the main proposal of the model that the function of imagery should match the desired outcome. With respect to the cognitive functions of imagery, numerous studies conducted in a wide variety of contexts have shown that the use of cognitive specific imagery is conducive to enhancing the learning and performance of motor skills (Driskell et al., 1994). Case studies and anecdotal evidence suggest that cognitive general imagery can be beneficial when used for the learning and performance of play strategies (Westlund et al., 2012). For example, the performance benefits of using cognitive general imagery have been reported for rehearsing football plays, wrestling strategies, soccer strategies, climbing, and entire canoe slalom races.

With respect to motivational imagery, Munroe et al. (2000) reported that athletes use motivational specific imagery to develop goals, and Callow and Hardy (2001) argued that a benefit to using motivational specific imagery would be an increase in athletes' motivation to attain their goals. With respect to motivational general–mastery imagery, O and colleagues (2014), investigated the effect of a motivational general-mastery imagery intervention on the self-efficacy of youth squash players. A single-subject multiple-baseline design was employed spanning 13–18 weeks. Results indicated improvements in self-efficacy for three of the five athletes. These results provide support for the function–outcome relationship proposed in the applied model of imagery use in sport.

A recent study investigated the relationship between mental toughness with imagery in a sample of varsity athletes (Mattie & Munroe-Chandler, 2012). Motivational general–mastery imagery use significantly predicted mental toughness, thus, providing support for imagery use as a potential strategy for developing or enhancing mental toughness in athletes.

Lastly, research examining motivational general–arousal imagery has indicated that it can be used by athletes to regulate arousal and anxiety. More specifically, images of the emotions and arousal associated with competitive performance (e.g., anger, anxiety, excitement, fear, pressure, feeling psyched up) are related to increased levels of state anxiety (Strachan & Munroe-Chandler, 2006). In contrast, images of performing in a relaxed and calm state are related to decreased levels of state anxiety (Ryska, 1998).

While most of the motivational imagery research has been conducted with adult athletes, research has investigated the relationship between imagery use and confidence in young athletes (Munroe-Chandler et al., 2008; O et al., 2014). Munroe-Chandler and colleagues found that motivational general–mastery imagery was a significant predictor of self-confidence and self-efficacy in both recreational and competitive youth soccer athletes. This finding suggests that if a youth athlete, regardless of competitive level, wants to increase confidence or self-efficacy through the use of imagery, the motivational general–mastery function should be emphasized. Thinking back to the opening vignette, Tyler wanted to enhance his confidence at the three-point line and inside the key. As such, he should employ motivational general–mastery imagery as a strategy to increase his levels of confidence.

Imagery Assessment Tools

Two types of imagery assessment tools have typically been used in sport psychology. One tool measures imagery ability, and the other assesses the frequency of imagery use. One

Table 7.6 Sport Imagery Questionnaire Sample Items

I imagine my skills improving. (cognitive specific)

I imagine alternative strategies in case my event/game plan fails. (cognitive general)

I imagine winning a medal. (motivational specific)

I imagine appearing self-confident in front of my opponents. (motivational general–mastery)

I get psyched up when imagining performing. (motivational general–arousal)

of the most important factors influencing imagery effectiveness is imagery ability. Some athletes are better imagers than others, even though most athletes report using imagery. In addition, Rodgers et al. (1991) in their intervention study with figure skaters found that the imagery ability of the skaters improved with imagery practice. This and recent work by Cooley et al. (2013) suggests that imagery is not only an ability, but also a skill that can be improved through regular practice.

Instruments have been developed to measure imagery ability, such as the Vividness of Movement Imagery Questionnaire-2 (VMIQ-2; Roberts et al., 2008) and the Movement Imagery Questionnaire-Revised (MIQ-R; Hall & Martin, 1997). The MIQ-R is an eight-item questionnaire that assesses an individual's visual and kinesthetic imagery ability. Participants are asked first to physically perform four different movements, then visually or kinesthetically image the four movements. Each movement involves an arm, leg, or whole-body movement. Participants then rate how well they felt they were able to visually or kinesthetically image the movement, and imagery scores are calculated separately for both subscales.

In comparison, other instruments have been designed to assess imagery use. The Sport Imagery Questionnaire (SIQ; Hall et al., 1998) is a self-report measure that asks athletes to rate how frequently they use the five functions of imagery as described in Table 7.5. See Table 7.6 for a list of sample items from the SIQ. A number of studies have employed the SIQ to examine and provide support for the applied model of imagery proposed by Martin et al. (1999).

Recommendations for Using Imagery

Holmes and Collins (2001) have provided some guidelines in their PETTLEP model that are useful when conducting imagery interventions (see Table 7.7).

For imagery use to be effective, it must be incorporated into a daily routine. Bull and colleagues (1996) suggest brief sessions (five minutes) once or twice a day for athletes who are beginning imagery. As athletes become more comfortable with, and better at, using imagery, they should systematically increase the amount of imagery employed. In fact, recent research notes that more imagery leads to greater athletic success (Cooley et al., 2013). Imagery requires deliberate practice and, just as for physical practice, more is better (Cumming & Hall, 2002). Because imagery is a skill and improves with practice, athletes will become better imagers over the course of an imagery intervention. The better imagers they become, the more effective their imagery will be.

Here are other recommendations for using imagery:

- Images should be positive rather than negative (Hall, 2001).
- Athletes should be in a good mood when using imagery (Gregg et al., 2007).

Table 7.7 The PETTLEP Model of Imagery

P	Physical	The physical nature of the imagery is dependent upon the task. You must determine whether relaxation or increased arousal is helpful prior to imaging.
E	Environment	The image should be as real or as close to the actual environment as possible. If you are unfamiliar with the competition venue, perhaps video footage or pictures will enhance your image.
T	Task	Depending on the task, your imagery perspective may vary. Skills that rely heavily on form have been found to benefit most from an external imagery perspective.
T	Timing	The temporal characteristics or timing of the image should be equal to that of your physical performance (e.g., if a skating routine takes three minutes to physically execute, so too should the imagery).
L	Learning	The content of the image should change based on the learning of the skill. For example, the content of your image when you are first learning a camel spin should be different from when you have mastered the skill.
E	Emotion	Images will be more effective if you attach meaning or emotion to them. If imaging winning a gold medal, feel the excitement and the joy that is part of it.
P	Perspective	Consider both perspectives, internal and external, when imaging.

Source: Based on Holmes, P. S., & Collins, D. J. (2001). The PETTLEP approach to motor imagery: A functional equivalence model for sport psychologists. *Journal of Applied Sport Psychology, 13*, 60–83.

- Athletes need to be encouraged to use imagery during those times when imagery use is typically less frequent, such as in the off-season and early competitive season (Munroe et al., 1998).
- Less-skilled athletes need to be encouraged to use imagery (Hall, 2001).
- Athletes of all ages can benefit from imagery interventions (Munroe-Chandler et al., 2007).
- Slow motion imagery is best employed when the goal is to enhance the learning, development, review, or refinement of skills and strategies (O & Hall, 2012).

Conclusions about Imagery

Imagery is an integral part of many psychological skills training programs because of its wide-range applicability and the fact that imagery can be implemented virtually anywhere and anytime. Coaches, athletes, and sport psychology consultants have all recognized imagery as an effective intervention for influencing a number of factors, as evidenced in Martin et al.'s (1999) applied model. Moreover, every athlete (novice to elite, healthy or injured) can benefit from the use of imagery, providing the imagery is built into a daily routine and fits the needs of the athlete.

SELF-TALK

One of the skills most highly promoted by applied sport psychology consultants and frequently included in psychological skills intervention training programs is self-talk. In the opening vignette, Tyler has developed a set of positive self-statements as a means of increasing his confidence on the basketball court. Although many different definitions have been forwarded, Hardy (2006) proposed a strong definition of self-talk following his extensive research on athletes' self-talk at Western University. He argued that **self-talk** should be defined as verbalizations or statements that are addressed to the self, are multidimensional in nature and somewhat dynamic, have interpretive elements associated with the content of the self-statements employed, and serve at least two functions, instructional and motivational.

Functions of Self-Talk

Self-talk serves two basic functions in sport: instructional and motivational. **Instructional self-talk** is used by athletes for skill development, skill execution, strategy development, and general performance improvement (Hardy, Gammage, & Hall, 2001). For example, Landin and Hebert (1999) investigated the effectiveness of instructional self-talk by having varsity tennis players use the cue words *split* and *turn* in order to improve their volleying technique at the net. These two cue words were constructed to represent the two phases of the volleying: splitting the legs shoulder-width apart for a balanced position, and then turning the shoulders in order to reduce excessive racquet-head movement. Improvements in the players' volleying performance were observed, indicating that sport performance can be improved by self-talk.

According to Hardy, Hall, and Alexander (2001), athletes employ **motivational self-talk** for three purposes: (1) for mastery (e.g., building self-confidence, staying focused, being mentally ready, coping in difficult circumstances); (2) for arousal (e.g., psyching up, relaxing); and (3) for drive (e.g., increasing effort, increasing drive, reaching their potential). Research has shown motivational self-talk to have a beneficial impact on endurance performance in a cycle ergometer (Hamilton et al., 2007) and the distance of a softball throwing task (Chang et al., 2014). One of the most consistent findings in sport psychology research is the direct relationship between positive thinking and successful performance. Undoubtedly, positive thinking entails considerable positive self-talk. Applied sport psychology books often stress that athletes need to change "I can't" to "I can" and "It's difficult for me" to "It's a challenge for me" if they want to be more successful.

Recent studies examining the two functions of self-talk have led to the "task-matching hypothesis," which suggests that instructional and motivational self-talk are associated with specific tasks requiring fine and gross skills, respectively (Hatzigeorgiadis et al., 2011). Based on this hypothesis, instructional self-talk should be more beneficial for fine motor tasks (e.g., dart throwing), while motivational self-talk would be more beneficial for gross motor tasks (e.g., shot put). Despite the novelty of this hypothesis, it is important to note that it has received limited support in experimental and meta-analytic studies.

Assessment of Self-talk

Various approaches and measures have been employed by researchers to assess athletes' use of self-talk. The Self-Talk Grid (Hardy, Hall, & Alexander, 2001) measures two dimensions of self-talk: valence (positive versus negative) and directional interpretation (motivating versus demotivating). Athletes simultaneously report on both dimensions by placing a checkmark on a 9 × 9 grid: they indicate the valence of their self-talk, from

Self-talk: Verbalizations or statements that are addressed to the self, are multidimensional in nature and dynamic, have interpretive elements associated with the content of the self-statements employed, and serve at least two functions, instructional and motivational.

Instructional self-talk: The overt or covert speech that individuals use for skill development, skill execution, strategy development, and general performance improvement.

Motivational self-talk: The overt or covert speech that individuals use for mastery, arousal control, and drive.

Table 7.8 Example Items of the Self-Talk Use Questionnaire

Section on the STUQ	Example
When	How often do you use self-talk in relation to your sport before a practice?
What	In your opinion,
	generally what percentage of your self-talk is positive in nature? ——— %
	generally what percentage of your self-talk is neutral in nature? ——— %
	generally what percentage of your self-talk is negative in nature? ——— %
	(Percentages given should total to 100%.)
Why	How often do you say things to yourself in practice to refine an already learned skill?
How	How often do you combine self-talk with mental imagery when using self-talk to help learn/fine-tune a skill?

"extremely positive" to "extremely negative," as well as how they interpret their self-statements, from "extremely motivating" to "extremely demotivating." A weakness of the Self-Talk Grid is that it does not provide a detailed account of athletes' self-talk. Self-talk is multidimensional, and the Self-Talk Grid assesses only two of the six dimensions of self-talk, valence and directional interpretation.

A more comprehensive questionnaire for assessing athletes' self-talk was developed by Hardy and colleagues (2005). The Self-Talk Use Questionnaire (STUQ) is a 59-item, self-report instrument that assesses the frequency of athletes' use of self-talk. The STUQ has four sections: section 1 examines *when* athletes use self-talk; section 2, *what* athletes say to themselves; section 3, *why* athletes talk to themselves in both practice and competition; and section 4, *how* athletes use self-talk (see Table 7.8). The instrument appears to be both reliable and valid. To date, most of the self-talk measures have focused on the frequency of self-talk. Researchers recently proposed that more attention should be focused on the quality of athletes' self-talk (Burton et al., 2013). For example, although no one would dispute that positive self-talk statements are more helpful than negative self-talk statements, the process of effective counterarguments is an important aspect of an athletes' coping skills, particularly when faced with adversity or failure.

REFLECTIONS 7.2

You have just received a poor score on your tumbling routine. What could you say to yourself in order to build confidence and stay positive?

Recommendations for Using Self-talk

Hardy (2006) identified six self-talk dimensions that should be used as a guide when developing a self-talk intervention for athletes. The first dimension, valence, refers to

Self-talk can facilitate skilled performance.

self-talk being positive or negative. Most of the self-talk research has compared positive versus negative self-talk and has consistently shown that positive self-talk is better (Tod et al., 2011). For example, Dagrou and colleagues (1992) found that a positive self-talk group significantly outperformed a negative self-talk and control group on a dart-throwing task. It is recommended that interventions focus on the use of positive self-talk.

The second dimension is concerned with how athletes' self-statements are verbalized, whether overtly or covertly. To date, there has been no direct comparison between the effectiveness of overt and covert self-talk in the sport domain. Nevertheless, it is known that both coping statements and goals are more effective if they are publicly known. It is recommended, therefore, that some of the self-talk in an intervention be overt.

The third dimension involves the self-determination of the statements used by athletes. Statements can be conceptualized as assigned or freely chosen. Research, such as the tennis study conducted by Landin and Hebert (1999), demonstrates that assigned self-talk can be very effective. However, Hardy (2006) has argued that self-talk freely chosen by the athlete might have a greater motivational influence. Although several studies have examined the effectiveness of freely chosen self-statements, the design (no assigned statement group) did not allow for comparisons. Only one study has compared the effectiveness of assigned versus freely chosen self-talk in sport. Weinberg et al. (2012) found no differences in the mile run times of athletes in the assigned self-talk group when compared to the freely chosen self-talk group. Given this one study is inconsistent with Hardy's earlier contention, it is recommended that the coach, the sport psychology practitioner, and the athlete collaborate in the development of the athlete's self-talk statements.

The fourth and fifth dimensions of self-talk are closely related and entail the motivational interpretation of self-talk. The fourth dimension, directional interpretation, is concerned with whether athletes view their self-talk as motivating or demotivating. The fifth dimension is intensity and is concerned with the extent to which athletes interpret

Table 7.9 The Six Dimensions of Self-Talk

1. Valence—positive or negative
2. Verbalization—overt or covert
3. Self-determination—assigned or freely chosen
4. Directional interpretation—motivating or demotivating
5. Directional intensity—not at all or very much so
6. Frequency—often or never

their self-talk to be motivating—not at all or very much so. Different from the directional interpretation dimension, intensity is achieved regardless of whether athletes view self-talk as motivating or demotivating. In their review of the research literature, Tod et al. (2011) concluded that motivational self-talk generally has a positive influence on performance. Accordingly, for interventions, we recommend that athletes use self-talk that they perceive as very motivating.

The final dimension of self-talk is frequency (i.e., how often athletes employ self-talk). Research has found that successful athletes use more self-talk than unsuccessful athletes. For example, Mahoney and Avener (1977) found that male gymnasts who qualified for the US Olympic team reported a greater use of self-talk in competition and practice than those gymnasts who did not qualify for the Olympics. In addition, Hardy and colleagues (2009) found that the frequency with which athletes employ self-talk increases across phases of the season (e.g., off season to early competitive season to late season competitive), suggesting there is a dynamic aspect to self-talk. Based on such findings, it is recommended that athletes be encouraged to use self-talk frequently (see Table 7.9).

Landin (1994) provided some additional guidelines for the use of verbal cues in sport. Verbal cues should be brief, phonetically simple, logically associated with the particular elements of the respective task, and compatible with the rhythm and timing of the task.

CASE STUDY 7.2

Tips for Using Self-Talk: An Application

Jennifer is a varsity basketball player who has doubted her abilities as a starter. Her coach is aware of this because some of Jennifer's negative self-talk has been overt. The coach has suggested that Jennifer see a sport psychology consultant in the kinesiology department. Dr. Singh meets with Jennifer and provides her with some tips on how to use self-talk more effectively.

Dr. Singh recommends that her self-talk be brief, positive, motivating, easy to remember, and phonetically simple. Dr. Singh suggests that Jennifer use her self-talk in both practices and competitions as frequently as possible. Jennifer takes Dr. Singh's advice and over the next month implements these recommendations. The coach notices a considerable improvement in Jennifer's play and attitude and congratulates Jennifer on her improvements.

Conclusions about Self-talk

It is important that athletes practise positive self-talk. We encourage athletes to analyze the content of their self-talk and be on the lookout for negatively framed statements. When negative statements enter the mind, they should immediately be replaced with positive statements or a counterargument. Furthermore, athletes need to ensure that their self-talk incorporates both instructional and motivational statements. Athletes who invest in improving their self-talk will find their efforts well rewarded.

AROUSAL REGULATION

The relationship between arousal and anxiety is complex. Given that athletes may require different levels of arousal for peak performance, it is important that athletes learn to identify which mental and emotional states are necessary for success. For Tyler (the basketball player from the opening vignette), it was determined that he needed to relax prior to games as he was making unnecessary errors in the first five minutes of the game. The following quotations from Canadian Olympic ice dancing champions Tessa Virtue and Scott Moir represent the diversity in arousal levels needed for peak performance. Scott Moir said, "The important thing for me is remembering that everyone is nervous. For some reason, that's a really comforting thought. Rarely do I regret being nervous because as long as I'm nervous, I'm focused, and that's the main thing" (MacDonald, 2013, para. 3–4). Tessa Moir stated "I get really nervous and with that comes doubt. I can get very quiet and internalize things" (MacDonald, 2013, para. 5).

Once athletes can identify their optimal level of arousal, they can learn to program these responses voluntarily. Because the theories and research pertaining to the arousal–performance relationship are covered elsewhere in the text, this section will focus on techniques to reduce and increase levels of arousal.

Coaches and athletes would concur that performance fluctuations in sport are often the result of being overaroused or underaroused. In a recent study with a sample of mixed martial arts (MMA) fighters (Jensen et al., 2013), it was suggested that a fighter's ability to regulate arousal may be as important as technical fighting skills and tactical decision making for success. Given the relationship between arousal and performance, it is not surprising that athletes use techniques to regulate their arousal level.

Techniques to Reduce Arousal

Many performance problems arise because of overarousal. In order to avoid any detrimental effects on performance, learning to relax is vital. Below we discuss various techniques that have been shown to reduce arousal level effectively.

Breathing If done properly, breathing is a simple technique used to relax. Diaphragmatic breathing, as opposed to quick shallow breathing, increases the amount of oxygen being delivered through the body and facilitates the removal of waste. When athletes feel overaroused prior to a competition, their breathing rate usually increases and breathing becomes very shallow. By learning to breathe better, athletes can achieve deep relaxation or momentary relaxation. Scott Moir, a Canadian ice dancing champion, has noted the importance of breathing as a way to relax prior to competition: "I'm just always thinking about my breathing, and slowing it down, focusing on my thoughts" (MacDonald, 2013, para. 3).

In order to avoid any detrimental effects on performance, learning to relax is vital; proper diaphragmatic breathing is a simple relaxation technique.

Progressive relaxation: The systematic tensing and relaxing of specific muscles in a predetermined order.

Meditation: A relaxation technique that allows for deep relaxation of the mind which, in turn, relaxes the body.

Breathing Exercise Take a deep breath (dig down into the belly) and imagine your lungs are divided into three levels. Begin by filling the lower level of the lungs with air. You will notice the diaphragm moving down slightly and forcing the abdomen out. Next, fill the middle level of the lungs by expanding the chest cavity and raising the ribcage. Finally, fill the upper level of the lungs. Notice a slight rise in the chest and shoulders. Hold the breath for several seconds; then exhale slowly. Repeat this exercise until you feel comfortable with this breathing technique. To help enhance this technique, you may want to consider rhythmic breathing, in which you inhale for a count of four and exhale for a count of eight (a 1:2 ratio). This helps to slow the breathing and allows you to focus on the exhalation.

Progressive Relaxation Jacobson (1938) first introduced this technique as a means to relax. Progressive relaxation was based on the notion that tension and relaxation are mutually exclusive. This means that one cannot be relaxed and tense at the same time. Although the initial training program devised by Jacobson was lengthy and required a substantial amount of training, abbreviated exercises that are just as effective have evolved (Carlson & Hoyle, 1993). Once the technique has been mastered, athletes can achieve a relaxed state in a matter of minutes, thereby making it useful just prior to competition or during breaks in competition.

Progressive relaxation involves systematically tensing and relaxing specific muscles in a predetermined order: left arm, right arm, left leg, right leg, abdomen, back, chest, shoulders, neck, and face muscles. The tensing (or contraction phase) teaches awareness and sensitivity, while the letting go (or relaxing phase) teaches awareness of the absence of tension. Bernstein and Carlson (1993) propose that once the athlete can achieve the abbreviated version (which normally takes several weeks of practice), an even shorter version can be attained. This includes tensing the entire body, holding for 5–10 seconds, and then releasing the tension to achieve a relaxed state.

Progressive Relaxation In the following abbreviated version of progressive relaxation, tense each group of muscles and hold for 5–10 seconds, and then relax for 30–40 seconds.

1. Make tight fists with both hands, tighten the biceps and the forearms. Hold the tension, and then relax.
2. Tighten the muscles of both thighs; at the same time, curl your toes and tighten the calves. Hold. Relax.
3. Take a deep breath, hold it, and raise the shoulders while making the stomach hard and tightening the buttocks. Hold. Relax.
4. Tense all the facial muscles while also tensing the neck. Hold. Relax.

Meditation Meditation allows for deep relaxation of the mind, which, in turn, relaxes the body. Meditation has been found to facilitate athletic performance (Schaffer, 1992);

however, the positive effects seem most prominent in activities involving gross motor movements, such as running. Meditation involves the uncritical focus of attention on a single thought, sound, or object (usually called the mental device).

Meditation Exercise Before you begin, find a quiet place where you can get comfortable and where distractions are minimal. Choose a mental device (mantra), such as the word "calm" or "warm." Adopt a passive attitude in which thoughts and images enter the mind but are not attended to. Close your eyes, and relax all your muscles, beginning at your feet and progressing up to your face. Focus on your breathing. With each exhalation, repeat your mantra. Breathe easily and naturally. Continue this for 10–20 minutes. Once finished, remain seated with your eyes closed. After a few minutes, you may open your eyes. Practise the technique once or twice daily. Remember to remain passive by just letting the relaxation happen.

Autogenic Training **Autogenic training** focuses on feelings associated with limbs and muscles of the body. More specifically, the training consists of three components: (1) warmth and heaviness of the limbs, (2) visualizing relaxing scenes at the same time as imagining the first component, and (3) specific relaxing themes in self-statements. Just as progressive relaxation takes time and training to master, so does autogenic training. Several months of regular training are needed to become skilled at this technique.

Autogenic training:
Training that focuses on feelings associated with limbs and muscles of the body.

Autogenic Training Exercise Autogenic training consists of six sequential stages. As described in progressive relaxation, allow the feelings to happen without interference. Allow yourself to learn each stage before progressing to the next. Repeat the suggestion in each stage six times followed by the word "quiet" once (see Table 7.10). Once you have learned all the stages, the entire sequence can be practised.

Biofeedback With biofeedback, athletes are trained to use feedback from their own body signals (muscle tension, body temperature, heart rate, blood volume, and respiration) to improve performance (Schwartz & Andrasik, 2003). Given arousal is heightened for many athletes prior to and during competition, biofeedback is one way in which to help the athletes learn to control their levels of arousal.

Table 7.10 Autogenic Training Exercise

Stage	Sensation	Suggestion
1	Heaviness in the extremities	"My right (left) arm is heavy."
2	Warmth in the extremities	"My right (left) arm is very warm."
3	Regulation of cardiac activity	"My heartbeat is regular and strong."
4	Regulation of breathing	"My breathing rate is slow, calm, and relaxed: it soothes me."
5	Abdominal warmth	"My solar plexus is warm." (Place hand on upper abdominal area while saying this phrase.)
6	Cooling of the forehead	"My forehead is cool."

Techniques to Increase Arousal

Although the techniques mentioned thus far have dealt with relaxation, there are times when athletes need to psych themselves up and become energized. Some studies have found that high levels of arousal prior to competition could be beneficial (e.g., MMA). While relaxation training is used to lower arousal to optimal levels, **psyching up strategies** are used to increase arousal levels. When underaroused, athletes cannot perform effectively: Their reactions will be slowed down and their coordination reduced. Many attempts by athletes to energize themselves or their teams have been done at the wrong time, thereby causing overarousal (Cox, 2002). Athletes and coaches must first identify the signs and symptoms of low energy, and then decide which of the following techniques is best suited to their needs. Below we discuss various techniques that have been shown to increase arousal level effectively.

Psyching up strategies: Strategies used to increase arousal levels.

Pep Talks The pep talk is one of the most widely used and recognized energizing strategies. It is important, however, that the pep talk be meaningful and be applied at the correct time. If your player or team is already energized prior to a competition, you may want to think twice before giving the "win one for the gipper" speech.

Bulletin Boards Catchy phrases or quotes displayed in a location that is visually prominent (e.g., locker room door, above athlete's stall) are an easy way to increase arousal (activation). Athletes seeing these on a daily basis will remember them and use them as reinforcement when needed.

Pre-Competitive Workouts A pre-competitive workout can enhance activation. It is not uncommon for athletes to feel fatigued on the day of competition. Therefore, a light workout several hours prior to competition can combat this fatigue.

Verbal Cues Using energizing words such as *explode*, *quick*, or *go* can help a player or team to become activated quickly. There are situations where athletes do not have enough time to generate energy with a pre-competitive workout. In instances such as these, energizing words can be employed.

Breathing Although breathing is a technique that can be used to relax, it can also be used as an energizer. By increasing the rhythm of breathing and imagining activation and energy with each inhalation, an athlete can increase arousal.

Imagery Energizing images work in much the same way as energizing verbal cues. Be sure to formulate an image that is personally energizing. For instance, 2004 Olympic gymnastics floor champion Kyle Shewfelt stated, "The night before, I was trying to sleep, but I was going through my routine in my head. I wasn't too nervous, but I was trying to make it perfect. . . . [On competition day], I think I went through it about 5000 more times" (Senior men, 2004, para. 3). As a result, he was full of energy when arriving at the competition venue.

Music Many athletes use music to get psyched up. For many, music is part of their pre-competitive routine to help them achieve their optimal arousal level. When the NBA decided that athletes could no longer wear headphones and listen to music in the warm-up, Vince Carter, formerly of the NBA Toronto Raptors, noted that his pre-competitive routine would suffer as a result of this decision (Carter told, 2004).

Conclusions about Arousal Levels

Athletes' ability to know their optimal level of arousal and effectively regulate arousal is one of the most important techniques in ensuring athletic success. This is evident in the quote from Canadian golfer Graham DeLaet: "For me, I play my best golf when I'm at a certain intensity level and I just have to remember at all times when I'm out there not to get too high or too low because I play my best golf when I'm kind of right in the middle" (Hutchinson, 2013, para. 22). Pineschi (as cited in Pineschi & Di Pietro, 2013) suggested that for athletes to adequately regulate their arousal (relax or psych up), "three stages of mental training are required: (a) learning stage, in which athletes learn different techniques and identify those best suited to their needs; (b) training stage, in which athletes repeat, adjust, make automatic and integrate the selected techniques into their training and competition routine; and (c) application stage, in which athletes use the techniques they have learned and practiced in the stressful context of competitions" (p. 187). Athletes need to know how and when to relax or become energized in both training and competition. Using the techniques and exercises outlined above will aid athletes in achieving optimal arousal levels.

> ### REFLECTIONS 7.3
>
> This chapter has focused on specific psychological strategies around stress, anxiety, and coping. How would you develop a coping skills program for an athlete who reports experiencing high, debilitating levels of cognitive anxiety during critical parts of a competition? Think carefully about what information you would need and the potential psychological or mental skills a trained and competent helper could teach the athlete.

ATTENTION CONTROL

Attention is fundamental to skilled motor performance (Abernethy, 2001). Players often attribute performing poorly to a loss of concentration or becoming distracted. Even a very temporary loss of focus can mar performance and be the difference between winning and losing. For example, missing a short, easy putt in golf as a result of simply not exerting enough concentration has cost numerous professionals tournament wins. Given the importance of attention to successful sport performance, it comes as little surprise that many psychological skills training programs include attention control training.

Research has shown **attention** as a multidimensional construct having at least two components. First, it is considered to be a limited resource. This refers to the known limitations people have in performing two or more tasks at the same time. Our basketball player from the opening vignette, Tyler, must dribble the ball and at the same time monitor the position of teammates and opponents. Second, attention involves the selective processing of specific information while ignoring other information. Alternatively, it can be considered as focusing on relevant cues while disregarding irrelevant ones. For example, a goalie in hockey must determine from where a shot is being taken while disregarding the jostling players in front of the net.

Attention: A multidimensional construct having at least two components (limited resources and selectivity).

Research has shown that performing multiple tasks, such as dribbling a basketball while looking to make a pass, gets better with training (Abernethy, 2001). In addition, performers become better with practice at selecting pertinent information or cues (e.g., the goalie determining from where the shot is taken) and are less likely to be distracted by irrelevant ones.

Choking

Choking in sport occurs when there is a significant decline in performance under high pressure conditions (Hill et al., 2009). Most researchers agree that choking is maladaptive and is the result of misguided attention control combined with elevated anxiety. Although many questions remain, an increasing number of studies have examined the mechanisms of choking. Some researchers argue that choking can be explained by attentional theories. That is, choking is a result of an athlete simultaneously attempting to process anxiety-related cognitions (e.g., worries and self-doubt) and information required to execute their skill. This dual processing of task-relevant and task-irrelevant information may cause choking (Wilson, 2008). Although some research has identified possible intervention strategies to prevent choking (e.g., performance routines and process/attentional cues, see below for further explanation), further intervention studies are needed.

Casarsa/Vetta/Getty Images

Choking in sport is often due to poor attentional control.

Temporal occlusion: The process of examining the amount of time people take to select the information they need in order to respond.

Event occlusion: The process of examining which characteristics of the performance people use to make a correct response.

Assessing Selective Attention

There are multiple means of assessing selective attention. One approach to assessing the selection of relevant information is the use of visual occlusion techniques. **Temporal occlusion** examines the amount of time people take to select the information they need in order to respond. Researchers show people a videotape of a skill. At various points during the action, the videotape is stopped and the observers are required to make a response.

Event occlusion examines which characteristics of the performance people use to make a correct response. In this case, parts of the video are masked so that the observers cannot see selected parts of the action. The logic of this approach is that if people make poorer decisions when they cannot see a specific cue (e.g., the hitting arm of a badminton player making a shot), then that cue is important for successful performance.

Another approach to assessing selective attention is the use of self-report measures. One instrument for the assessment of concentration skills measures the degree to which athletes experience cognitive interference from distracting thoughts during competition (Hatzigeorgiadis & Biddle, 2000). Other measures typically address how well people are able to focus their attention. Attentional focus is sometimes considered in terms of width (i.e., a broad or narrow focus) and direction (i.e., an external or internal focus) (Test of Attentional and Interpersonal Style, TAIS; Nideffer, 1976). Taking a doubles tennis player as an example, the player would need a narrow external focus when volleying a ball at the net, but a broad internal focus when analyzing how to move at the net (e.g., to poach or not on a partner's upcoming serve). Attentional focus has also been considered using two other broad categories, namely, association and dissociation. **Association** is defined as turning focus inward and toward bodily sensation (e.g., breathing, muscle soreness), while **dissociation** is focusing outward and away from the body (e.g., a favourite song, a relaxing setting). Research has shown that elite marathon runners utilized an associative strategy during races and a dissociative strategy during training runs (Morgan & Pollock, 1977). To explain these findings, Tenenbaum (2001) has put forth an effort-related model in which he contends that during exercise of high intensity and long duration, dissociative strategies are not effective or utilized because attention is compelled to remain internal and narrow. Recent research with rowers supports this model (Tenenbaum & Connolly, 2008). It was found that attention shifted from dissociation to association as workload increased on a rowing ergometer task. From an applied perspective, athletes working at a low or moderate workload can voluntarily shift between associative and dissociative modes and thus can choose the one they find most beneficial.

Association: Turning focus inward and toward bodily sensation (e.g., breathing, muscle soreness).

Dissociation: Focusing outward and away from the body (e.g., a favourite song, a relaxing setting).

Using Attention-Control Strategies

There are different techniques for controlling attention (see Table 7.11). The most commonly used technique for learning to control attention is **attention simulation training**, in which athletes replicate the kinds of attention-demanding situations they find themselves in during competition. Players should practise simultaneously working on two tasks that typically must be performed together to produce optimal performance. Players should also practise focusing on relevant cues and disregarding irrelevant ones. The practice, however, is only likely to be effective if it is sport specific. In other words, the training situations must allow the performer to practise the specific attention-sharing and cue-selection strategies required in the sport skill. A defender in soccer should practise dribbling the ball while looking to pass to one of the forwards, and a goalkeeper should practise stopping shots with other players in front of the net.

Attention simulation training: Training in which athletes replicate the kinds of attention-demanding situations they find themselves in during competition.

Other attention-control strategies include performance routines, attentional cues, and imagery (Bull et al., 1996). **Performance routines** are a set sequence of thoughts and actions that are done before the performance of key skills. For example, professional golfer Mike Weir has a famous "waggle," which is part of a distinct pre-shot routine. What

Performance routines: A set sequence of thoughts and actions before the performance of key skills.

Table 7.11 Summary of Attention-Control Strategies

Simulation training

Performance routines

Attentional cues

Imagery

began as a physical move to counteract his hockey actions has become part of his pre-shot routine (Wilson, 2003). It is now identical from one swing to the next. In order for performance routines to be effective in competition, they must be carefully planned and then extensively practised in training.

Two types of routines are used by athletes. Pre-event routines are the fixed thoughts and actions athletes undertake in the time leading up to competition (e.g., the night before or the morning of a competition). Pre-performance routines are the fixed thoughts and actions athletes undertake immediately before executing a skill (e.g., bouncing the ball three times before taking a foul shot). These routines work because they encourage athletes to focus on task-relevant information. They also remind athletes to remain in the present rather than dwell on past events or possible future outcomes. Finally, performance routines prevent the athlete from attending too much to skill technique instead of letting skills happen automatically.

Attentional cues are words and actions that direct the athlete's attention. These cues help athletes to focus their concentration on the task at hand and to refocus their concentration if lost. Three types of concentration cues are verbal, visual, and physical. A verbal cue is typically a single word, which is repeated at the appropriate moment. Some examples of verbal cues are *smooth*, *high*, *speed*, *ready*, and *power*. A visual cue entails focusing keenly on something in the athlete's surroundings. For example, looking at the strings of a squash racquet, staring at the logo on the shaft of a field hockey stick, and fixating on the button in curling are all visual cues an athlete may use. A physical cue involves doing an action, such as taking a deep breath, banging the stick on the ice, or slapping the thigh. Some athletes use a single cue, while others prefer to use a combination. Just like performance routines, attentional cues need to be practised regularly and employed consistently before implementing them in competition.

Imagery as a means of controlling attention can be used in two ways. First, it can be used to prepare for various scenarios to ensure that athletes will not be distracted by unexpected events. For example, a skater could imagine how to react if the music stops during the middle of her program. Second, imagery can be used as a means of "parking" errors in order to prevent dwelling on mistakes. For example, a volleyball player may image placing errors in the garbage can at the side of the court, or a soccer player may image placing errors in the tree at the end of the pitch. Just as with the other techniques discussed above, parking errors requires considerable practice. In doing so, the athlete creates a link between parking the image and focusing attention on relevant performance cues.

Attentional cues: Words and actions that direct the athlete's attention.

Conclusions about Attention Control

It is difficult to conceive of anything more important in sport than paying attention to the task at hand. Attention-control strategies are often perceived as inherent in elite athletes; however, the old adage "practice makes perfect" is apt when it comes to developing effective strategies. An athlete's control over attentional focus is learned through practice just like any other difficult physical skill. Using the techniques discussed above, athletes can improve their attention control and perform successfully during the critical moments in their sport.

COMPLEMENTARY INTERVENTIONS TO IMPROVE SPORT PERFORMANCE

Mindfulness

Mindfulness, which emphasizes both awareness and acceptance of internal and external states, offers an alternative to those traditional mental control techniques (e.g., thought stopping) frequently used by athletes and sport psychology consultants. For example, an athlete who is having self-doubt about her performance on the diving board may be instructed to stop that thought and replace it with a successful self-statement about executing the dive perfectly. Some researchers have suggested that one's attempt to control or replace a negative thought may paradoxically increase the frequency and importance of those very thoughts. Mindfulness involves non-judgmental, present moment and task relevant awareness. The strategy, originally developed in the Buddhist meditative tradition, has received support in the sport domain (Gardner & Moore, 2012) as it has been associated with flow and increased attention. Simply put, in practising mindfulness awareness, an athlete's thoughts would be noted as passing states that require no action. This would allow the individual to respond to the situation more objectively than reflexively. This type of thought acceptance differs from traditional PST in which an athlete's thought (e.g., apprehension) would be replaced with a positive self-statement. Given the relative newness of mindfulness training in sport, much remains to be learned. As such, further research is needed to examine the possible impact mindfulness has on athletic performance.

CHAPTER SUMMARY

A variety of psychological intervention strategies to enhance sport performance have been discussed in this chapter. These strategies involve the following five key psychological skills. Athletes should set SMART goals that are supported and evaluated. Imagery should be part of every psychological skills training program because of its wide application and the fact that it can be implemented virtually anywhere and anytime. Athletes should analyze the content of their self-talk and modify negatively framed statements. Athletes need to know how and when to relax or become energized during both training and competition. Athletes should improve their attention control so that they can perform successfully during the critical moments in their sport.

The benefits of these strategies have been supported by research as well as by anecdotal reports from athletes, coaches, and applied sport psychology consultants. It is important to remember that these psychological strategies can be learned, practised, and applied in a variety of settings, such as during training, competition, and injury rehabilitation. These strategies will be beneficial, however, only if athletes are committed to putting the time and effort into mastering them. Consider the results for Tyler, the basketball player, in the opening vignette.

In addition to this chapter providing guidelines for athletes interested in using mental skills to improve performance, practitioners (sport psychology consultants) can also use the information when conducting interventions with athletes. However, we recommend that a strong working relationship be built with the athlete prior to implementing such skills. This will ensure that the athlete, trusting in the consultant, is comfortable using the skills. Building trust with an athlete will also allow the practitioner to customize the intervention, thus catering to the specific needs to the athlete.

It is important to remember that an intervention has to be tailored to the specific outcome desired. It is athlete- or team-specific and, therefore, will change depending on the needs of each athlete or team. Ask: What are the goals of the intervention? What are the needs of the athlete? and What are the demands of the sport? It is not a "best practices" application that works in every situation; it is athlete- and team-centred.

COMMON MYTHS ABOUT SPORT PSYCHOLOGY INTERVENTIONS REVISITED

MYTH: Psychological skills training is a Band-Aid solution.
Some athletes and coaches believe that the effective use of self-talk or imagery can be learned in one or two sessions to quickly fix a problem such as lack of confidence. Just as physical skills take time and effort to develop, so too do psychological skills. There are no quick fixes to problems, and dedicating time to psychological skills training over an extended period will enhance athletes' performance and help them reach their full potential.

MYTH: Only elite athletes can benefit from psychological skills training.
Successful performance at any level of sport involves technical, tactical, physical, and mental components. Although elite athletes can benefit from highly developed psychological skills, even young athletes will experience the gains garnered from improved psychological skills. Therefore, psychological skills training can be implemented at any stage of an athlete's career, but ideally it should be initiated at the grassroots level in order to ensure the most effective development of the mental side of sport.

MYTH: Athletes need a sport psychology consultant only when they are performing poorly.
Most successful athletes realize that achieving peak performance requires a detailed plan that includes understanding physiology and nutrition, implementing cutting-edge technology, and employing psychological skills training. It is harder to fix a problem once it has started than to keep a problem from occurring.

Review Questions

1. What are the five psychological skills discussed in this chapter?
2. Why are the five psychological skills effective?
3. Describe the SMART guidelines for goal setting.
4. What are the guidelines for using imagery?
5. What are the six self-talk dimensions?

6. What are the techniques that effectively reduce arousal level?

7. What are the techniques that effectively increase arousal level?

8. Describe each of the four attentional control strategies and provide an example of each.

Suggested Reading

Abernethy, B. (2001). Attention. In R. N. Singer, H. A. Hausenblas, & C. M. Janelle (Eds.), *Handbook of sport psychology* (2nd ed., pp. 53–85). New York: Wiley.

Cooley, S. J., Williams, S. E., Burns, V. E., & Cummings, J. (2013). Methodological variations in guided imagery interventions using movement imagery scripts in sport: A systematic review. *Journal of Imagery Research in Sport and Physical Activity, 8,* 1–22. doi:10.1515/jirspa-2012-0005

Tod, D., Hardy, J., & Oliver, E. (2011). Effects of self-talk: A systematic review. *Journal of Sport and Exercise Psychology, 33,* 666–687.

References

Abernethy, B. (2001). Attention. In R. N. Singer, H. A., Hausenblas, & C. M. Janelle (Eds.), *Handbook of sport psychology* (2nd ed., pp. 53–85). New York: Wiley.

Bernstein, D. A., & Carlson, C. R. (1993). Progressive relaxation: Abbreviated methods. In P. M. Lehrer, & R. L. Woolfolk (Eds.), *Principles and practices of stress management* (2nd ed., pp. 58–87). New York: Guilford Press.

Bull, S. J., Albinson, J. G., & Shambrook, J. (1996). *The mental game plan: Getting psyched for sport.* Brighton, UK: Sports Dynamic.

Burton, D., Gillham, A., Weinberg, R., Yukelson, D., & Weigand, D. (2013). Goal setting styles: Examining the role of personality factors on the goal practices of prospective Olympic athletes. *Journal of Sport Behavior, 36,* 23–44.

Burton, D., Naylor, S., & Holliday, B. (2001). Goal setting in sport: Investigating the goal effectiveness paradigm. In R. N. Singer, H. A. Hausenblas, & C. M. Janelle (Eds.), *Handbook of sport psychology* (2nd ed., pp. 497–528). New York: Wiley.

Burton, D., & Weiss, C. L. (2008). The fundamental goal concept: The path to process and performance success. In T. Horn (Ed.), *Advances in sport psychology* (3rd ed., pp. 339–375). Champaign, IL: Human Kinetics.

Butler, R. J., & Hardy, L. (1992). The performance profile: Theory and application. *The Sport Psychologist, 6,* 253–264.

Callow, N., & Hardy, L. (2001). Types of imagery associated with sport confidence in netball players of varying skill levels. *Journal of Applied Sport Psychology, 13,* 1–17.

Camiré, M., Forneris, T., Trudel, P., & Bernard, D. (2011). Strategies for helping coaches facilitate Positive Youth Development through sport. *Journal of Sport Psychology in Action, 2,* 92–99. doi: 10.1080/21520704.2011.584246.

Carlson, C. R., & Hoyle, R. H. (1993). Efficacy of abbreviated progressive muscle relaxation training: A quantitative review of behavioral medicine research. *Journal of Consulting and Clinical Psychology, 61,* 1059–1067.

Carter told to tune out. (2004, November 17). *The Windsor Star,* p. E2.

Chang, Y. K., Ho, L. A., Lu, F. J. H., Ou, C. C., Song, T. F., & Gill, D. (2014). Self-talk and softball performance: The role of self-talk nature, motor task characteristics, and self-efficacy in novice softball players. *Psychology of Sport and Exercise, 15,* 139–145. doi.org/10.1016/j.psychsport.2013.10.004.

Cooley, S. J., Williams, S. E., Burns, V. E., & Cummings, J. (2013). Methodological variations in guided imagery interventions using movement imagery scripts in sport: A systematic review. *Journal of Imagery Research in Sport and Physical Activity, 8,* 1–22. doi:10.1515/jirspa-2012-0005.

Cox, R. H. (2002). *Sport psychology: Concepts and applications* (5th ed.). New York: McGraw-Hill.

Cumming, J., & Hall, C. (2002). Deliberate imagery practice: The development of imagery skills in competitive athletes. *Journal of Sport Sciences, 20,* 137–145.

Dagrou, E., Gauvin, L., & Halliwell, W. (1992). Effets du langage positif, négatif, et neuter sur la performance motrice [Effects of positive, negative, and neutral self-talk on motor performance]. *Canadian Journal of Sports Sciences, 17,* 145–147.

Dawson, K. A., Bray, S. R., & Widmeyer, W. N. (2002). Goal setting by intercollegiate sport teams and athletes. *Avante, 8,* 14–23.

Driediger, M., Hall, C., & Callow, N. (2006). Imagery use by injured athletes: A qualitative analysis. *Journal of Sport Sciences, 24,* 261–271.

Driskell, J. E., Copper, C., & Moran, A. (1994). Does mental practice enhance performance? *Journal of Applied Psychology, 79,* 481–492.

Edger, M. (2010, September 29). Sidney Crosby's secret to success. *Sport Psychology Today.* http://www.sportpsychologytoday.com/sports-psychology-articles/sidney-crosby-secret-to-success/.

Filby, W., Maynard, I., & Graydon, J. (1999). The effect of multiple-goal strategies on performance outcomes in training and competition. *Journal of Applied Sport Psychology, 11,* 230–246.

Gardner, F. L., & Moore, Z. E. (2012). Mindfulness and acceptance models in sport psychology: A decade of basic and applied scientific advancements. *Canadian Psychology, 53,* 309–318.

Gregg, M., Hall, C., & Hanton, S. (2007). Perceived effectiveness of mental imagery. *Journal of Sport Behavior, 30,* 398–414.

Hall, C. R. (2001). Imagery in sport and exercise. In R. N. Singer, H. A. Hausenblas, & C. M. Janelle (Eds.), *Handbook of sport psychology* (2nd ed., pp. 529–549). New York: Wiley.

Hall, C. R., Mack, D., Paivio, A., & Hausenblas, H. A. (1998). Imagery use by athletes: Development of the sport imagery questionnaire. *International Journal of Sport Psychology, 29,* 73–89.

Hall, C. R., & Martin, K. A. (1997). Measuring movement imagery abilities: A revision of the movement imagery questionnaire. *Journal of Mental Imagery, 21,* 143–154.

Hamilton, R., Scott, D., & MacDougall, M. P. (2007). Assessing the effectiveness of self-talk interventions on endurance performance. *Journal of Applied Sport Psychology, 19,* 226–239.

Hardy, J. (2006). Speaking clearly: A critical review of the self-talk literature. *Psychology of Sport and Exercise, 7,* 81–97.

Hardy, J., Gammage, K., & Hall, C. R. (2001). A description of athlete self-talk. *The Sport Psychologist, 15,* 306–318.

Hardy, J., Hall, C. R., & Alexander, M. R. (2001). Exploring self-talk and affective states in sport. *Journal of Sport Sciences, 19,* 469–475.

Hardy, J., Hall, C. R., & Hardy, L. (2005). Quantifying athlete self-talk. *Journal of Sport Sciences, 23,* 905–917.

Hardy, J., Oliver, E., & Tod, D. (2009). A framework for the study and application of self-talk within sport. In S. D. Mellalieu & S. Hanton (Eds.), *Advances in applied sport psychology: A review* (pp. 37–74). Abingdon, Oxon: Routledge.

Hatzigeorgiadis, A., & Biddle, S. J. H. (2000). Assessing cognitive interference in sport: Development of the thought occurrence questionnaire for sport. *Anxiety, Stress and Coping, 13,* 65–86.

Hatzigeorgiadis, A., Gelanis, E., Zourbanos, N., & Theodorakis, Y. (2011). Self-talk and competitive sport performance. *Journal of Applied Sport Psychology, 26,* 82–95. doi: 10.1080/10413200.2013.790095

Hill, D. M., Hanton, S., Fleming, S., & Matthews, N. (2009). A re-examination of choking under pressure. *European Journal of Sports Science, 9,* 203–212. http://dx.doi.org/10.1080/17461390902818278.

Holmes, P. S., & Collins, D. J. (2001). The PETTLEP approach to motor imagery: A functional equivalence model for sport psychologists. *Journal of Applied Sport Psychology, 13,* 60–83.

Hutchinson, I. (2013, September 29). Delaet confident, but says controlling emotion is his Presidents Cup focus. *Golf News Now.* http://www.golfnewsnow.ca/blog/delaet-confident-but-says-controlling-emotions-is-his-presidents-cup-focus/.

Jacobson, E. (1938). *Progressive relaxation.* Chicago, IL: University of Chicago Press.

Jensen, P., Roman, J., Shaft, B., & Wrisberg, C. (2013). In the cage: MMA fighters' experience of competition. *The Sport Psychologist, 27,* 1–12.

Jones, G. (1993). The role of performance profiling in cognitive behavioral interventions in sport. *The Sport Psychologist, 7,* 160–172.

Kyllo, L. B., & Landers, D. M. (1995). Goal-setting in sport and exercise: A research synthesis to resolve the controversy. *Journal of Sport and Exercise Psychology, 17,* 117–137.

Landin, D. (1994). The role of verbal cues in skill learning. *Quest, 46,* 299–313.

Landin, D., & Hebert, E. P. (1999). The influence of self-talk on the performance of skilled female tennis players. *Journal of Applied Sport Psychology, 11,* 263–282.

Liu, W., Zhou, C., Ji, L., & Watson, J. C. (2012). The effect of goal setting difficulty on serving success in table tennis and the mediating mechanism of self-regulation. *Journal of Human Kinetics, 33,* 173–185.

Locke, E. A. (1991). Goal theory vs. control theory: Contrasting approaches to understanding work motivation. *Motivation & Emotion, 15,* 9–28.

Locke, E. A., & Latham, G. P. (1985). The application of goal setting to sports. *Journal of Sport Psychology, 7,* 205–222.

MacDonald, G. (2013, November 3). Olympians Tessa Virtue and Scott Moir on how they're preparing for Sochi. *The Globe and Mail.* http://www.theglobeandmail.com/life/healthand-fitness/fitness/tessa-virtue-and-scott-moir-explain-their-training-regimen-for-sochi/article 15214213/.

Mahoney, M. J., & Avener, M. (1977). Psychology of the elite athlete: An exploratory study. *Cognitive Therapy and Research, 6,* 225–342.

Martin, K. A., Moritz, S. E., & Hall, C. R. (1999). Imagery use in sport: A literature review and applied model. *The Sport Psychologist, 13,* 245–268.

Mattie, P., & Munroe-Chandler, K. J. (2012). Examining the relationship between mental toughness and imagery use. *Journal of Applied Sport Psychology, 24,* 144–156.

Moran, A. P. (2004). *Sport and exercise psychology.* New York: Taylor & Francis Group.

Morgan, W. P., & Pollock, M. L. (1977). Psychological characterization of the elite distance runner. *Annals of the New York Academy of Sciences, 301,* 382–403.

Munroe, K. J., Giacobbi, P. R., Hall, C., & Weinberg, R. (2000). The four Ws of imagery use: Where, when, why, and what. *The Sport Psychologist, 14,* 119–137.

Munroe, K. J., Hall, C. R., Simms, S., & Weinberg, R. (1998). The influence of type of sport and time of season on athletes' use of imagery. *The Sport Psychologist, 12,* 440–449.

Munroe-Chandler, K. J., Hall, C., & Fishburne, G. (2008). Playing with confidence: The relationship between imagery use and self-confidence in youth soccer players. *Journal of Sport Sciences, 26,* 1539–1546.

Munroe-Chandler, K. J., Hall, C., Fishburne, G., & Strachan, L. (2007). Where, when and why athletes use imagery: An examination of developmental differences. *Research Quarterly for Sport and Exercise, 78,* 103–116.

Nideffer, R. M. (1976). The test of attentional and interpersonal style. *Journal of Personality and Social Psychology, 34,* 394–404.

O, J., & Hall, C. R. (2012). A qualitative analysis of athletes' voluntary image speed use. *The Journal of Imagery Research in Sport and Physical Activity, 8(1),* 1–12.

O, J., Munroe-Chandler, K. J., Hall, C. R., & Hall, N. D. (2014). Using imagery to improve the self-efficacy of youth squash players. *Journal of Applied Sport Psychology, 26,* 66–81. doi: 10.1080/10413200.2013.778914.

Paivio, A. (1985). Cognitive and motivational functions of imagery in human performance. Canadian *Journal of Applied Sport Science, 10,* 22S–28S.

Perry, C., & Morris, T. (1995). Mental imagery in sport. In T. Morris & J. Summers (Eds.), *Sport psychology: Theory, applications and issues* (pp. 339–385). Brisbane, Australia: Wiley.

Pineschi, G., & Di Pietro, A. (2013). Anxiety management through psychophysiological techniques: Relaxation and psyching up in sport. *Journal of Sport Psychology in Action, 4,* 181–190.

Roberts, R., Callow, N., Hardy, L., Markland, D., & Bringer, J. (2008). Movement imagery ability: Development and assessment of a revised version of the Vividness of Movement Imagery Questionnaire. *Journal of Sport & Exercise Psychology, 30,* 200–221.

Rodgers, W. M., Hall, C. R., & Buckolz, E. (1991). The effect of an imagery training program on imagery ability, imagery use, and figure skating performance. *Journal of Applied Sport Psychology, 3,* 109–125.

Ryska, T. A. (1998). Cognitive–behavioral strategies and precompetitive anxiety among recreational athletes. *Psychological Record, 48,* 697–708.

Schaffer, W. (1992). *Stress management for wellness* (2nd ed.). New York: Harcourt Brace Jovanovich.

Schuchmann, J. (2004). The player's championship. ASAP Sports. Retrieved from http://www.asapsports.com/show_interview.php?id=12947.

Schwartz, M. S., & Andrasik, F. E. (2003). *Biofeedback: A practitioner's guide* (3rd ed.). New York: Guilford Press.

Senécal, J., Loughead, T., & Bloom, G. (2008). A season-long team-building intervention: Examining the effect of team goal setting on cohesion. *Journal of Sport & Exercise Psychology, 30,* 186–199.

Senior men: Kyle Shewfelt. (n.d.). Gymn.ca. Retrieved December 23, 2004, from http://gymn.ca/athletes/interviews/shewfelt_04.shtml.

Strachan, L., & Munroe-Chandler, K. J. (2006). Using imagery to predict self confidence and anxiety in young elite athletes. *Journal of Imagery Research in Sport and Physical Activity, 1,* Article 3.

Tenenbaum, G. (2001). A social–cognitive perspective of perceived exertion and exertion tolerance. In R. N. Singer, H. Hausenblas, & C. Janelle (Eds.), *Handbook of sport psychology* (pp. 810–820). New York: Wiley.

Tenenbaum, G., & Connolly, C. T. (2008). Attention allocation under varied workload and effort perception in rowers. *Psychology of Sport and Exercise, 9,* 704–717.

Tod, D., Hardy, J., & Oliver, E. (2011). Effects of self-talk: A systematic review. *Journal of Sport and Exercise Psychology, 33,* 666–687.

Wanlin, C. M., Hrycaiko, D. W., Martin, G. L., & Mahon, M. (1997). The effects of a goal-setting package on the performance of speed skaters. *Journal of Applied Sport Psychology, 9,* 212–228.

Weinberg, R. S. (2002). Goal setting in sport and exercise: Research to practice. In J. Van Raalte, & B. Brewer (Eds.), *Exploring sport and exercise psychology* (2nd ed., pp. 25–48). New York: American Psychological Association.

Weinberg, R. S., Miller, A., & Horn, T. (2012). The influence of a self-talk intervention on collegiate cross-country runners. *International Journal of Sport and Exercise Psychology, 10,* 123–134. doi:10.1080/1612197X.2012.645135.

Westlund, N., Pope, P., & Tobin, D. (2012). Cognitive general imagery: The forgotten imagery function? *Journal of Imagery Research in Sport and Physical Activity, 7,* Article 1. doi: 10.1515/1932-0191.1075.

White, A., & Hardy, L. (1998). An in-depth analysis of the uses of imagery by high level slalom canoeists and artistic gymnasts. *The Sport Psychologist, 12,* 387–403.

Wilson, M. (2003). A master champion. *GolfMag.* Retrieved December 23, 2004, from www.thegolfermag.com/the_golfer/archive/style03/story_style03_swingseq.htm.

Wilson, M. (2008). From processing efficiency to attentional control: A mechanistic account of the anxiety-performance relationship. *International Review of Sport and Exercise Psychology, 1,* 184–202. http://dx.doi.org/10.1080/17509840802400787.

Chapter 8

Leadership in Sport and Exercise

Mark R. Beauchamp   Mark A. Eys

Bruce Bennett/Getty Images Sport/Getty Images

Chapter Objectives

After reading this chapter, you should be able to do the following:

1   Consider both personal and situational factors associated with effective leadership in sport and exercise settings.

2   Explain the difference between transactional and transformational approaches to leadership in physical activity settings.

3   Describe critical characteristics of effective leadership, and consider how these relate to diverse physical activity settings (e.g., sport, physical education, and exercise).

4   Outline the key properties of effective peer-leadership in sport.

5   Explain some of the key components of leadership training and development in physical activity settings.

As one of the most successful ice hockey coaches of all time, Mike Babcock guided the Detroit Red Wings to win the Stanley Cup (2008) and also coached Team Canada to success in winning the men's gold medal at both the 2010 (Vancouver) and 2014 (Sochi) Winter Olympics. What is consistently evident through accounts from former and current players alike is the level of trust and respect he garners from his players and coaching staff, his attention to detail, and the extent to which he is able to foster complete commitment to the team concept (and processes). In preparation for the 2014 Winter Olympics during the preceding summer, Babcock was reported to be keen to illustrate the different systems and structures that he planned to use with the 46 Team Canada players in attendance at a familiarization camp. The excessive costs of insuring all the players meant that some of these systems couldn't be practised on the ice. Thus, with considerable enthusiasm, he illustrated these systems on a ball hockey surface with players wearing T-shirts, shorts, and running shoes. As one of the players, defenceman Shea Weber, remarked after the team won Olympic gold, "It started in the summer when we went there and we played ball hockey. Everyone laughed at us. We went over team systems. ... I think there might be a lot of teams that are going to try ball hockey now" (Brough, 2014). Beyond his creative thinking, other players on this team remarked about his ability to foster buy-in to a team system, whereby players ostensibly identified as "superstars" adhered to a philosophy that the whole was greater than the sum of its individual parts. As the Canadian assistant captain, Jonathan Toews, commented, "As soon as we didn't have possession [of the puck], we were working so hard to get it back. We had some skilled, skilled forwards and d-men, but everyone was committed to playing a defensive game, and we created offense off it" (Brough, 2014).

While it should certainly be recognized that the Canadian team that won the 2014 Olympic gold medal possessed a number of extremely talented players, it is noteworthy how many of the players emphasized the facilitative role of Babcock's coaching behaviours:

■ ***Attention to detail and enthusiasm.*** *Canadian team captain Sidney Crosby commented prior to the Olympics that "It's the energy he brings to the rink, the preparation that he brings. He's had a lot of success for a lot of different reasons, but the things that stand out to me are the energy and the preparation. Every detail matters to him" (Rosen, 2013).*

■ ***Ability to maintain optimism and a positive attitude in the face of adversity.*** *Babcock remarked during the middle of the Sochi tournament, "Is it going to go your way every time? No. But you choose your attitude and how you perform and how you dig in." After a difficult close encounter with Latvia during a quarterfinal match of the tournament, he emphasized, "The adversity that we faced tonight was a real positive thing" (Whyno, 2014).*

■ ***Ability to communicate with his players.*** *Toews noted that "A big part of playing well is being loose and confident. He [Babcock] wants that and I don't think he ever overreacts to any situation. He's always pretty calm on the bench. If you do something wrong, he lets you know right away, and he's very detailed and to the point" (Brough, 2014).*

■ ***Ongoing pursuit of excellence and high expectations for his players.*** *Canadian forward Patrick Sharp highlighted, "He wants the best out of his players.*

He pushes us every day. Even today in practice, [the] day in between the semis and gold, our idea was to get better out there and Babs was harping at us to improve every drill" (Whyno, 2014).

When one looks at exemplars of effective leadership in sport, such as Mike Babcock, invariably a number of questions arise as to what makes for successful leadership. For example, are his successes due to some inherent set of personality characteristics? Are his accomplishments due in part to his educational background, having completed a university degree (in physical education at McGill University)? Although he was regarded as an accomplished university-level player, he never played professionally in the National Hockey League. He coached at the university level (at the University of Lethbridge) and elite youth level (coaching Canada to gold at the 1997 World Junior Championships), so did these formative coaching experiences perhaps shape how he coaches at the professional and international levels?

Similar questions can be posed with regard to any exemplars of successful leadership in sport and exercise settings. That is, to what extent are personal or situational factors implicated in the development of exemplary leadership in sport and exercise settings, and to what extent can such exceptional leadership characteristics or behaviours be developed?

COMMON MYTHS ABOUT LEADERSHIP IN SPORT AND EXERCISE

MYTH: Great leaders (including coaches and team captains) are born, not made.

MYTH: Effective leadership is an intangible quality that cannot really be assessed.

MYTH: Leadership is a top-down process concerned with exerting control, authority, and power over others.

INTRODUCTION

Leadership is concerned with the behavioural processes through which one person influences another person, or a group of others, toward attaining a specific set of objectives or goals (Northouse, 2001). As such, it is perhaps unsurprising that leadership has been the focus of considerable interest to scholars, educators, and practitioners within the field of sport and exercise psychology. Perhaps the most widely studied social agent responsible for leadership within this field is the sport coach. At the grass-roots level, sport coaches are responsible for the development of motor skill competencies and social skills, and for enabling young children and adolescents to accumulate sufficient levels of health-enhancing physical activity. At the other end of the spectrum, coaching is "big business," with coaches being responsible not only for the performance of world-class athletes, but also for the profitability of large organizations. On sport teams, leadership is not the restricted preserve of coaches, and indeed it is widely recognized that athlete leaders play a major role in supporting effective group functioning. Leader behaviours also contribute to exercise adoption and promotion, via exercise class instructors, health promotion specialists (e.g., exercise counsellors), and personal trainers. In educational settings, leadership also plays a major role in enabling physical education teachers to encourage lifelong engagement in active lifestyles among children and adolescents alike.

In this chapter, we will provide an overview of some of the most widely used models (and theoretical frameworks) that have been used to understand leadership, as applied to different social agents (e.g., coaches, athlete leaders, exercise instructors, school physical education teachers) in various physical activity settings, as well as research that sheds light on what effective leadership looks like in these different contexts. We also highlight some practical considerations for developing effective leadership.

APPROACHES TO UNDERSTANDING LEADERSHIP

Over the years, a diverse array of perspectives have been presented to explain what makes for effective leadership. Some have taken a personality approach to understanding leadership, while others have recognized that situational or contextual factors are particularly salient, and may in fact interact with a range of personal factors (of both leaders and followers) in determining leadership effectiveness. In the following sections, we consider some of these diverse perspectives as they have been applied within sport and exercise psychology.

Personality and Leadership

Can effective leadership be explained by an underlying set of personality traits, or a personality profile? This compelling question has been of interest to researchers and practitioners alike for many years within the field of sport and exercise psychology, and received considerable attention in the early 20th century, especially in understanding the sources of effective leadership within workplace settings. Soon after the end of the Second World War, a highly influential review paper concluded that personality factors were less important than previously thought in the explanation of effective leadership, and that situational factors are likely to play a much greater role (Stogdill, 1948).

As the field of sport and exercise psychology began to emerge as a distinct discipline within the 1960s and 1970s, the link between personality and leadership gained traction, with some researchers even considering leadership to be a component of personality (Ogilvie, 1968; Tutko et al., 1969). A prominent example of this is the Athletic Motivation Inventory (AMI) (Tutko et al., 1969), which assessed personality traits such as drive, leadership, and responsibility. The authors of the AMI claimed that measures derived from the inventory were able to predict indices of athletic success, and marketed this instrument to be used within professional sport (e.g., for identifying promising prospects within selection drafts). However, subsequent research has raised many concerns about the AMI and its ability to predict athletic behaviour.

Although a personality centred view of sport leadership was popular in the 1960s and 1970s, especially in the press, research interest in personality traits associated with leadership in sports began to dwindle, mirroring what was happening at the time within the broader field of psychology. This was likely due, in large part, to the inconsistent nature of the findings. But this does not mean that personality has no impact on leadership. Over the past two decades, driven by the widespread recognition of the five factor model (FFM) of personality (Digman, 1990), there has been a resurgence of research linking personality to both the emergence of leadership and leadership effectiveness. The five personality traits in the model are extraversion, neuroticism, conscientiousness, agreeableness, and openness to experience.

Using a powerful research technique called **meta-analysis** that incorporated the results of many studies from both workplace and sport settings, Judge and colleagues (2002) found that the personality traits embedded within the FFM were associated with both leader emergence (people emerging or being appointed to leadership positions) and leader effectiveness. Specifically, higher extraversion, conscientiousness, and openness to experience, and lower neuroticism were found to be related to both leader emergence and leader effectiveness, with extraversion demonstrating the strongest relationship with both outcome measures. It should be noted, however, that only four studies included within the meta-analysis were conducted with athletes and coaches, and so any conclusions regarding the associations between personality and leadership in sport should be tempered. Nevertheless, assessing whether such a relationship consistently exists between these personality traits and leadership (emergence and effectiveness) in sport would seem a worthwhile research endeavour. For instance, is it the case that people with higher levels of extraversion are more likely to emerge into leadership roles (i.e., sport coaches and team captains) due to the fact that they are simply more outspoken when compared to their more introverted counterparts? Think of well-known Canadian leaders in sport (e.g., Steve Yzerman, ice hockey; Steve Nash, basketball; Christine Sinclair, soccer; Mark Tewksbury, swimming) and consider their personalities; what facets of these personalities might be well suited to leadership in sport?

While much of the research linking personality traits to leadership effectiveness has focused on the traits of leaders, some research has sought to examine the similarity between the personality traits of followers and leaders. In a recent study by Jackson and colleagues (2011), when athletes and coaches were found to be similar to each other with regard to the traits of extraversion and openness to experience, this was associated with improved relationship quality (e.g., greater commitment to each other). In contrast,

Meta-analysis: A powerful statistical technique that involves combining the results of multiple studies to examine the overall effect of a variable (or intervention) in relation to an outcome of interest to the researcher.

Good coaching makes a difference.

KidStock/Blend Images/Getty Images

when coaches and athletes were found to display dissimilar levels of these two personality traits, this was related to lower commitment and relatedness among both coaches and athletes toward one another. When taken together, the evidence to date suggests that (a) personality traits may play a role in shaping leadership emergence and effectiveness, and (b) the degree of similarity of personality traits between coaches and athletes may enable the respective coach–athlete relationship to either flourish or flounder.

Situational and Contingency Models of Leadership

As interest in personality-based explanations of leadership diminished following the Second World War, situation-based models of leadership became more popular. Some models focused on how leadership *styles* interact with various situational constraints to influence follower outcomes (e.g., Fiedler et al., 1952), whereas other models centred on how specific leadership *behaviours* interact with situational constraints to affect those same outcomes (e.g., House, 1971, 1996; Chelladurai, 1990). The difference between these two approaches is that in the former case leadership styles represent stable and enduring characteristics of the leader (personality traits), whereas in the latter case the focus is on the various actions and behaviours used by the coach that might well fluctuate over time. In this section, we describe research in sport psychology that has utilized these different approaches.

One of the earliest and most prominent situational models of leadership was Fiedler's (1952, 1967) **contingency model**, which suggested the effectiveness of specific leadership styles depends (is *contingent*) upon how much control the leader has over that situation (i.e., situational control), otherwise referred to as *situational favourableness*. Fiedler differentiated between two broad types of leadership style: task-oriented leadership and relationship-oriented leadership. **Task-oriented leadership** involves the pursuit of goal and performance attainment. **Relationship-oriented leadership** is concerned with maximizing the quality of relationships among those being led.

A task-oriented leader was expected by Fiedler to be more suitable when leaders have high situational control. Within this framework, high levels of situational control or favourableness were said to exist when (a) the quality of the relationships between the leader and followers is good, (b) the tasks and goals being pursued are clearly structured, and (c) the leader possesses clear authority and power. In sport settings, high levels of situational control might feature quality relationships in which: coaches and athletes are supportive and respectful of one another; athletes' training tasks are clearly laid out and athletes understand their *process*, *performance*, and *outcome* goals; and all parties have a clear sense of who is responsible for various decision-making considerations related to personnel selection and strategy. In professional soccer, for example, it has become common in recent years for managers to work alongside a director of football. In some clubs, decisions about signing and selecting players are made by the manager, whereas in other instances these decisions are primarily made by the director of football. Such arrangements have been questioned by a number of high profile managers, with Arsene Wenger (Arsenal Football Club) indicating that he could never see himself working under a director of football, commenting that, "A director of football buys the players. When they don't work, you (the manager) are guilty for them not playing well. If it works, the director of football has bought well . . . I am not against having people to help me buy

Contingency model: A model of leadership that suggests that the effectiveness of specific leadership styles depends (is contingent) upon how much control the leader has over that situation (i.e., situational control).

Task-oriented leadership: A leadership style that involves the pursuit of goal and performance attainment.

Relationship-oriented leadership: A leadership style concerned with maximizing the quality of relationships among those being led.

and sell. I cannot do it all—I am not Superman, but the final decision has to belong to the manager to decide who comes in and who goes out" (van Wijk, 2013).

In contrast, when the quality of relations between leader and members is less strong, the tasks and goals being pursued are less well-structured (or more ambiguous), and the leader lacks authority, the leader is said to possess low situational control. Fiedler suggested that, in such instances of low situational control, a task-oriented leader is needed to "right the sinking ship." That is, if a team was performing poorly, Fiedler would recommend a leader who would focus on the task-related demands to get the team to succeed, and place less emphasis on supporting social relationships. When faced with moderate levels of situational control, Fiedler thought that a relationship-focused style was best.

Interestingly, although Fiedler's contingency model would go on to be used extensively within workplace settings, the basis of this model was actually grounded in his early work with high school basketball teams (Fiedler et al., 1952). Support for Fiedler's model in sport settings has been mixed. In a longitudinal study involving 80 male intramural basketball teams over a nine-week season, Konar–Goldband and colleagues (1979) found that ratings of the leaders' behaviours interacted with measures of prior group atmosphere, as an indication of situational favourableness, to predict team performance. Konar–Golband et al. suggested that the findings provided some support for Fiedler's contingency model. In a study by Bird (1977), situational favourableness was considered in relation to the various winning percentages of teams from Division I and Division II U.S. university volleyball teams. In this study, greater success was considered to reflect greater situational favourableness, and less success was considered to reflect lower levels of situational favourableness. In Division II, athletes on teams with greater win percentages (i.e., high situational favourableness) perceived their coaches to be more task-oriented; athletes on unsuccessful teams (i.e., low situational favourableness) perceived their coaches to be more relationship-focused. However, the reverse effect was found for Division I teams, where athletes on winning teams perceived their coaches to be more relationship-oriented, and athletes on losing teams perceived their coaches to be more task-oriented. In sum, the (inconsistent) findings in the study by Bird, when taken together, did not yield support for the core tenets of Fiedler's contingency model.

While Fiedler's framework focused on the congruence between various *leadership styles* and the nature of the situation, other models emphasized that leadership effectiveness depends on the match between the situation and leader *specific behaviours*. Within his **path–goal theory**, House (1971, 1996) suggested that four dimensions of leadership behaviour have the potential to result in improvements in motivation, performance, and well-being among those being led. Those leadership behaviours included directive path–goal clarifying behaviour, supportive behaviour, participative leader behaviour, and achievement-oriented behaviour.

Directive path–goal clarifying behaviour involves those actions taken by the leader to ensure that athletes are clear about their roles and responsibilities, and the actions required to perform those responsibilities effectively. In sport, for example, clarification of roles has been found to be related to improvements in players' role-related efficacy beliefs and ratings of role performance effectiveness (e.g., Beauchamp et al., 2002).

Supportive behaviour has consistently been found to result in adaptive responses among athletes. Recent research from the sport domain has emphasized the utility of

Path–goal theory: A model of leadership which suggests that effective leadership is dependent on the match between the situation and the behaviours utilized by a leader in that situation.

different types of support that include emotional, esteem, informational, and tangible support (Holt & Hoar, 2006; Tamminen & Gaudreau, 2014).

Participative leader behaviour involves leaders consulting with others and gaining input from them. In athletic situations, this might involve coaches taking into account the opinions and suggestions of athletes when deciding on game strategies or a particular training regimen.

Finally, *achievement-oriented behaviour* takes place when leaders hold high expectations for those being led and demonstrate confidence that those being led can meet the leader's expectations. In essence, and as House (1996) remarked, achievement-oriented behaviour involves the pursuit of performance excellence.

According to House, the extent to which these leadership behaviours translate into being effective or not is dependent on various situational constraints, such as the nature of the task and/or role demands, as well as the various personal attributes of those being led. For example, behaviours designed to clarify what is expected of team members (task/goal clarification) might well be particularly effective when those team members have a high need for clarity, but be less influential for those team members who have a greater tolerance for ambiguity (Bray, Beauchamp, et al., 2005). In a similar regard, achievement-oriented behaviour might be very motivational for followers who are moderately or highly achievement motivated, but might be less effective for those who have low levels of achievement motivation (House, 1996).

House's path–goal framework provided the foundational basis for Chelladurai's **multidimensional model of leadership (MML)**, which became the most widely utilized framework for understanding leadership in sport settings (Chelladurai 1990, 2007; Chelladurai & Saleh, 1978). The MML framework is shown in Figure 8.1. Within the MML, effective leadership is considered to occur when athletes (a) are satisfied with their

Multidimensional model of leadership (MML): A complex model of leadership that was specifically designed to examine leadership behaviours in the context of sport, and their effects in relation to athlete satisfaction and team performance.

Figure 8.1 Multidimensional model of leadership

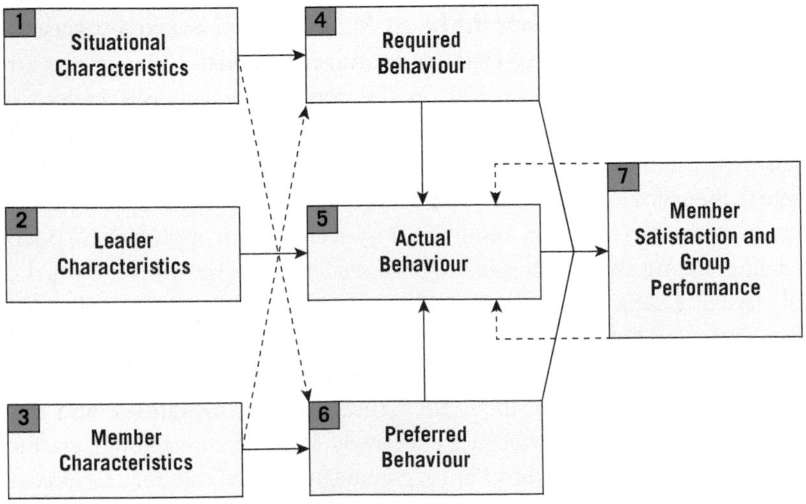

Source: "Leadership in Sports," by P. Chelladurai. In G. Tenenbaum & R. C. Eklund (Eds). *Handbook of sport psychology* (3rd. ed). John Wiley and Sons, NY, 2007, p. 117, Figure 5.2a.

experience with the coach, team, and sporting environment, and (b) maximize their potential to perform to the best of their abilities (see box 7). The outcomes of athlete satisfaction and team performance are dependent on the alignment of the actual behaviours utilized by the leader (see box 5), the behaviours required of the leader–coach within the situation or context (see box 4), and the leadership preferences of the athletes (see box 6).

Based on the MML framework, their governing organization or association influences leaders, through a range of situational influences, to use *required* behaviours (see box 1). These situational characteristics include the level at which the athletes are performing (e.g., elite versus recreational), the nature of the sport in question (e.g., individual versus team), as well as various cultural considerations. Required behaviours are also determined to some extent by the characteristics of the athletes being coached (see box 3). Member characteristics include factors such as athletes' age, gender, and developmental level. An example of required behaviours within this framework might include an elite swimming coach who is required by the organization in which she coaches to focus her efforts on training and instruction, but leave any involvement related to resolving athletes' personal issues to the organization's sport psychologist.

In addition to such required leadership behaviours, athletes will often have their own preferences for the way in which they would like to be coached (i.e., preferred leadership behaviours). These athlete preferences (see box 6) are largely influenced by the athletes' own personal characteristics (see box 3). Athletes' preferences are also shaped by situational cues such as those described above (e.g., recreational versus elite levels). Some athletes, for example, might have a particular preference to be coached by a very autocratic leader who makes all the decisions. Conversely, other athletes might prefer to be more heavily involved in all decision-making processes related to their training and performances.

Actual leader behaviours (see box 5) are the behaviours that coaches typically make use of, and are primarily formed by the coach's own personal characteristics (see box 2), which include factors such as diverse personal experiences, training, and coaching philosophy. However, as alluded to above, a coach's actual behaviours will also be influenced by both the requirements placed on the coach (see box 4) and the athletes' various preferences (see box 6). As a final consideration within the model, the outcomes attained by the athletes in terms of athlete satisfaction and performance (see box 7) act to inform a feedback loop that shapes the coach's actual behaviours (see box 5) over time. That is, if athletes are performing well and are satisfied, this will act to reinforce those behaviours used by the coach. However, if the athletes in question are not performing to their potential or are dissatisfied, this might act to bring about a different approach to coaching.

In order to test this model, Chelladurai and Saleh (1980) developed a **Leadership Scale for Sports (LSS)** that included assessment of five leadership behaviours/dimensions. These included training and instruction, positive feedback, social support, autocratic behaviours, and democratic behaviours. The LSS has since been revised by a separate set of researchers (Zhang et al., 1997) and utilized in subsequent research projects (e.g., Sullivan et al., 2012), although the original LSS remains a popular tool to assess leadership behaviours in sport. Overall, research conceptually based on the MML has provided mixed findings. In a study by Amorose and Horn (2000) involving university-level coaches and their athletes, when coaches were reported to make greater use of training and instruction, display more democratic behaviour and less autocratic behaviour, and

Leadership scale for sports (LSS): A scale designed to assess five leadership behaviours/dimensions.

provide greater positive feedback, their athletes tended to report higher levels of intrinsic motivation. In another study by Weiss and Friedrichs (1986) involving 251 NCAA basketball players, greater use of rewarding behaviour, social support, and democratic style were positively related to athlete satisfaction, while in terms of the prediction of team performance (win/loss percentage) social support was the strongest predictor, with higher levels of social support being *negatively* related to team performance. In short, while the relations between leadership behaviour and athlete satisfaction in this study were consistent with tenets of the MML, the relations between those leadership behaviours and athlete performance were not. Beyond these direct effects linking leadership behaviours to athlete outcomes, as highlighted above, an important consideration within this model corresponds to the congruency hypothesis (i.e., suggested importance of similarity between required, preferred, and actual leader behaviours). Unfortunately, very little research has tested this proposition to date, and it has not found much support for this contention (Riemer & Toon, 2001). When taken together, it should be noted that the MML is a very complex model, and while support has been derived for some aspects of the model, others remain to be tested comprehensively.

In spite of the widespread use of the LSS during the 1980s and 1990s, one of its limitations corresponds to the rather restricted range of behaviours operationalized within this questionnaire. For example, as noted by Beauchamp and colleagues (2005), on the dimension of training and instruction, a coach could spend considerable time providing training to athletes, but if the *quality* of that training was poor, one would not expect such interactions to benefit the athletes. Furthermore, although the remaining behaviours assessed within the LSS provide an important basis for understanding the effects of various leadership behaviours, the LSS also omits an important range of behaviours found to be salient in supporting athlete achievement, personal development, and performance. As we will see in the following section, recent research from both organizational and sport psychology suggests that, for leaders (e.g., coaches, team captains) to maximize adaptive functioning and performance among their followers (e.g., athletes), an additional range of leadership behaviours need to be considered that are not operationalized within the LSS.

TRANSACTIONAL AND TRANSFORMATIONAL LEADERSHIP

Organizational psychologist Bernard Bass developed a **full range model of leadership** that sought to explain the effects of exceptional as well as less than exceptional leadership behaviours on the cognitions, emotional states, and behaviours/actions of their followers (Bass, 1985, 1998, 1997; Bass & Riggio, 2006) (Figure 8.2). Within this framework, the least effective type of leadership, according to Bass, corresponds to **laissez-faire leadership**, which involves indifference, absence, or a hesitancy to make any substantive decisions. In essence, laissez-faire leadership is really non-leadership. In the sport context, this might involve a coach being disengaged, uninterested, and uninvolved in the athletes' training, development, and performances. The major distinction within Bass's model, however, corresponds to the differentiation between transactional leadership and transformational leadership. Broadly conceived, **transactional leadership** involves a series of exchanges or transactions between the leader and the person being led (e.g., employee, athlete) whereby the leader looks to make use of rewards and recognition

Full range model of leadership: A leadership model that includes a spectrum of leadership behaviours ranging from ineffective to highly effective.

Laissez-faire leadership: A style of leadership that is characterized by indifference, absence, and a hesitancy to make any substantive decisions.

Transactional leadership: A leadership style that is characterized by exchanges between the leader and the person being led whereby the leader looks to make use of rewards and recognition as well as compliance-maximizing behaviours to get that other person to accede to the leader's requests.

Figure 8.2 A schematic of leadership effectiveness based on Bass and Riggio's (2006) full range leadership model

Leadership Dimensions	Non-Leadership	Transactional Leadership			Transformational Leadership			
	Laissez Faire	Passive Management by Exception	Active Management by Exception	Contingent Reward	Intellectual Stimulation	Individualized Consideration	Inspirational Motivation	Idealized Influence
Key Behaviours	Absence, indifference, and hesitancy to make decisions.	Waiting for mistakes to arise and then provide corrective direction and punitive action.	Active monitoring of task execution and providing corrective direction.	Providing rewards and recognition that is contingent on the successful execution of tasks and role responsibilities	Engaging the reationality of others. Encouraging others to look at old problems in novel ways.	Recognizing and being sensitive to others' needs. Displaying empathy, care, and concern for others.	Displaying optimism and enthusiasm. High expectations. Articulating a compelling vision	Role modelling Engendering trust and respect of those being led. Articulation of personally held values.
Degree of Effectiveness	Ineffective				Effective			

In the meta-analysis by Judge and Piccolo (2004), correlations for 'leadership effectiveness' in relation to each leadership dimension were: −.54 for Laissez Faire, −.19 for Passive Management by Exception, .21 for Active Management by Exception, .55 for Contingent Reward, and .61 for Transformational Leadership.

Source: Based on Bass, B. M., and Avolio, B. J. (1994). Improving organizational effectiveness through transformational leadership (p. 5). Thousand Oaks, CA: Sage Publications.

as well as compliance-maximizing behaviours to get followers to accede to the leader's requests/orders. In contrast, **transformational leadership** occurs when leaders go beyond their own self-interests and inspire others to pursue a given course of action because the followers want to for their own reasons (self-determined motivation is fostered), and they understand why this pursuit is important (they internalize the leaders' own values and take these as their own) (Bass & Riggio, 2006).

Transactional leadership includes both *management by exception* and *contingent reward* components. Management by exception includes both an active and a passive dimension. With active management by exception, leaders monitor their followers to ensure that tasks and goals have been completed as requested and take corrective action as and when necessary. In exercise settings, this might involve an instructor actively monitoring the effective execution by members of a class routine, and proactively providing technical instruction that might allow those participants to perform that routine more smoothly. With the passive form of management by exception, leaders wait for serious problems to arise and, when they do, they weigh in with punitive action. An example of passive management by exception in sport would be a youth ice-hockey coach who sees that a child is struggling (i.e., unable to perform a specific skill effectively, such as skating backwards) and rather than intervening and assisting the child to develop the requisite skill, waits until the child's impairment undermines the team's ability to function, and then responds with providing fewer opportunities for the player to perform that role (i.e., reduced playing time).

The other form of transactional leadership articulated by Bass is contingent reward—providing rewards and recognition that are contingent on the successful completion of tasks and goals as specified by the leader. For example, in sport, if a coach specifies a

Transformational leadership: A leadership style that involves going beyond one's own self-interests with the purpose of empowering, inspiring, and giving those being led the confidence to achieve a higher level of functioning.

certain role to be undertaken by an athlete, and the athlete performs that role effectively, the coach might be inclined to provide the player with praise as well as further opportunities for the player to play a central role within the team (e.g., opportunities to fulfill a starter versus non-starter position). This behavioural dimension directly aligns with Chelladurai and Saleh's (1980) 'positive feedback' component within the LSS. The provision of positive feedback to athletes by coaches has been widely recognized as an important foundation to support athlete development (Escarti & Guzman, 1999).

CASE STUDY 8.1 | **Positive Feedback**

Joanne is a basketball coach with 15 years of coaching experience at the university level. She currently coaches a team of players who show much potential and who are very competitive about starting status and playing time. Joanne holds the view that, in order to keep her athletes motivated, on their toes, and driven to succeed, she needs to maintain arm's-length relationships with them. This means that after practices and games, Joanne does not let the athletes know whether they have personally trained and/or performed well, for fear that such communication will make them become complacent. As the season progresses, a couple of senior (veteran) players on the team start to become particularly frustrated with the coach's lack of feedback as well as their diminished playing opportunities during games. While both athletes featured prominently in the team during the previous season, their playing minutes have declined in the current season and they don't know why, as Joanne has not communicated her reasons to the players.

As Ken Blanchard and Spencer Johnson (2003), authors of *The One-Minute Manager*, note, one of the keys to developing people is to catch them doing things right and praise them accordingly. In both Chelladurai's (1990) and Bass and Riggio's (2006) models of leadership, the provision of positive feedback and contingent reward play an important role in supporting athlete development. In light of the potential benefits of providing such feedback and praise, think about how Joanne could and/or should communicate with her athletes to get the best out of them.

Bass argued that such contingent reward and corrective behaviours (i.e., active management by exception) are necessary in many instances. Indeed, active management by exception demonstrates small but positive correlations with follower performance and satisfaction (Judge & Piccolo, 2004), whereas passive management by exception is associated with negative follower outcomes (e.g., reductions in performance). However, such rewards and corrective behaviours are insufficient to get followers to maximize their potential. According to transformational leadership theory, for athletes to exceed minimally accepted standards and excel, leaders need to supplement the use of active management by exception and contingent reward with a range of transformational behaviours. Bass referred to this as an *augmentation effect*, whereby leaders need to augment the use of "stick and carrot" (transactional) behaviours with transformational leadership. In the context of sport, this would mean coaches supplementing the use of good observation and corrective instruction (active management by exception) plus rewards and recognition (contingent reward) with the use of transformational leadership behaviours (described below).

Transformational leadership occurs when leaders go beyond their own self-interests to empower, inspire, and encourage others to maximize their potential (Bass & Riggio, 2006). Transformational leadership takes place through the exhibition of four key behavioural dimensions: idealized influence, inspirational motivation, intellectual stimulation, and individualized consideration (Bass & Riggio, 2006).

- *Idealized influence* happens when leaders act as role models, through the demonstration of personally held ideals (values and beliefs). This involves sticking to one's principles, and not just talking the talk but also walking the walk!

- *Inspirational motivation* involves providing a compelling vision of the future, working to display optimism and enthusiasm with regard to what others can accomplish, and setting high expectations for others.

- *Intellectual stimulation* takes place when leaders foster independent thinking among others, by getting them to think for themselves, question assumptions, and approach various challenges from novel perspectives.

- *Individualized consideration* occurs when those in positions of leadership give particular attention to, and support, the psychological and physical needs of others by acting with genuine care, compassion, and empathy.

In examining these four dimensions of transformational leadership, it is important to note that these are conceptualized not as fixed aspects of one's personality (personality traits), but as *behaviours* that can be used by any leader in interactions with others.

In the vignette about Canadian hockey coach Mike Babcock, a number of athletes on his team repeatedly referred to displays of transformational leadership and its effects on them, personally, and on the team as a whole. For example, they referred to his *optimism* when faced with adversity (inspirational motivation), his philosophy for players to *choose to have a positive attitude* in their interactions with each other (idealized influence), his *vision* to get the whole team to *buy into the team system/concept* (inspirational motivation), his ability to get *players to think differently* about the various team systems using a novel approach to coaching (intellectual stimulation), as well as his attempts to *relate to and communicate with* every athlete on the team (individualized consideration).

Across business, sports, and education, these four dimensions of transformational leadership are strongly related to each other (e.g., Beauchamp et al., 2010; Bycio et al., 1995; Carless, 1998). Barling and colleagues (2010) suggested that when leaders are transformational and use any one of these behaviours, it is likely that they will also tend to use one or more of the other three behaviours. It should be quite evident from reading the descriptions of Babcock's coaching behaviours that most people have the potential to display these actions. They have no mystical properties, but are very tangible behaviours that most people can use in their interactions with others. We return to this topic later in the discussion of transformational leadership training.

A growing body of evidence has accumulated in recent years in support of the utility of this model within sport and exercise settings. In a study involving Canadian university athletes and their coaches, athletes' ratings of their coaches' transformational leadership behaviours were related to elevated levels of athlete intrinsic motivation, which in turn were related to higher coach ratings of the athletes' performance levels (Charbonneau et al., 2001). The research indicated that coaches have the capacity not only to influence their athletes' motivation to engage in sport, but also to affect how they subsequently perform.

The augmentation effect of transformational leadership has been supported by research in martial arts. Displays of transformational leadership were able to supplement the effects of transactional leadership in explaining coaching effectiveness (Rowold, 2006). Indeed, this suggests that while behaviours such as providing corrective instruction and feedback are important facets of coaching, in order for athletes to get the most out of themselves and their sporting experience these transactional behaviours should be supplemented with the different dimensions of transactional leadership.

Transformational leadership as displayed by coaches has an important and beneficial role in relation to the development of prosocial sportspersonship behaviours among their athletes. A study with Canadian youth ice-hockey players found that when coaches displayed transformational leadership, their athletes were less likely to display illicit aggressive behaviours (Tucker et al., 2010). Tucker and colleagues reasoned that this is because transformational leaders "do the right thing" and model prosocial behaviours, they set high expectations for performance and non-aggressive behaviours, they challenge followers to think differently (i.e., concerning the morality of aggressive behaviour in sport), and are considerate of the personal needs of others. This study also provided evidence that transformational leaders indirectly affect athletes' aggressive behaviour by creating a prosocial climate within the team as a whole that discourages illicit aggression.

How do these behaviours develop? That is, are they shaped by heritable factors? Perhaps early childhood influences (such as parenting styles) play a role? Alternatively, can these behaviours be shaped later in life through training and intervention? The research seems to indicate that many factors influence the development of transformational behaviours. Work from the field of behavioural genetics, using data involving identical and non-identical twins, suggests that both leadership behaviours and leadership occupancy (i.e., whether people occupy leadership roles) can be explained to some extent by heritable/genetic factors (Chaturvedi et al., 2011; De Neve et al., 2013). These findings suggest that *both* genetics and environmental factors likely play a substantive role in the prediction of transformational leadership.

There is also evidence that parents have an influence on transformational leadership behaviour in athletes. Zacharatos and her colleagues (2000) examined the relationship between the transformational leadership behaviours displayed by Canadian youth athletes and the leadership behaviours provided by their parents. Parents' demonstration of transformational leadership was found to be positively related to their adolescent child's transformational leadership behaviours in sport. This research suggests that leadership can be understood within a social learning framework (Bandura, 1986), whereby adolescents can acquire and learn to make use of transformational leadership as a result of the manner in which their parents interact with them.

REFLECTIONS 8.1

Transformational leadership by parents (i.e., transformational parenting) has been found to be related to:

- Greater confidence among adolescents to maintain a healthy diet and active lifestyle (Morton et al., 2011)

- A healthier diet and improved involvement in physical activity during leisure time among adolescents (Morton, Wilson, Perlmutter, & Beauchamp, 2012)
- Improved ratings of quality of life among adolescents (Morton et al., 2011).

Think back to your childhood and adolescent years. What types of leadership behaviours did your parents display? Did they influence your own involvement in sport and physical activity? If so, how? To what extent did your parents' behaviours align with the four dimensions of transformational leadership?

In support of a social learning perspective, transformational leadership can also be developed through training and intervention. Most work in this area has been conducted within organizational settings (Avolio et al., 2009); however, evidence from the field of education suggests that transformational leadership behaviours can be developed through professional development training (Beauchamp et al., 2011). Furthermore, these transformational behaviours, when developed through intervention, have been found to result in improvements in a range of outcomes for both the leader (i.e., displaying greater effectiveness) and followers in terms of greater self-confidence, motivation, and achievement (Beauchamp et al., 2011; Barling et al., 1996; Hardy et al., 2010). At the end of this chapter, we provide a synopsis of how transformational leadership can be developed among leaders in sport and exercise settings.

TRANSFORMATIONAL TEACHING IN PHYSICAL EDUCATION

Transformational leadership behaviours can be used by school physical education teachers to shape engagement in physical education, as well as physical activity more generally (see Table 8.1). Morton and colleagues (2010) interviewed a number of Canadian adolescents and found that when teachers made use of transformational leadership behaviours (i.e., *transformational teaching*), this was associated with improved beliefs and attitudes toward physical education, greater motivation toward physical education and physical activity, and greater enjoyment of physical education and satisfaction with the teacher, as well as improved behavioural engagement within class and involvement in leisure time physical activity.

Displays of transformational teaching can have a major impact on the satisfaction of students' psychological needs (Wilson et al., 2012) and self-efficacy beliefs (Bourne et al., in press). When physical education teachers make use of these transformational leadership behaviours, students also tend to display greater

Matthew Lewis-IDI/ICC/Getty Images

Teachers can support the healthy growth and development of children and adolescents.

Table 8.1 Transformational Teaching Behaviours in Physical Education

	Examples*	Interpretation
Idealized Influence	*"People respect Mr. E. so I know a lot of students that do [extracurricular] basketball because they like him and like how he teaches."*	By engendering the student's *trust and respect*, the teacher was reported to have a positive effect on the student's extra-curricular sport participation.
	"Mr R. kept telling the students that PE is not about how athletic you are—it's about how you participate and what you give to the community; I think that's true."	By speaking with the students about his *ideals*—taking part in physical activity and contributing the community—the teacher had an effect on the student's own ideals and values.
	"I dislike it when teachers don't practise what they preach . . . no-one liked PE."	The student highlighted the potential negative effects that can arise when teachers fail to act as *role models*.
Inspirational Motivation	*"When they're good teachers and they keep encouraging, you feel better about yourself and because you get better it makes you want to try stuff outside of school."*	When PE teachers *encourage* students about what can be achieved, students are more likely to engage in leisure time physical activities.
	"The teacher has to believe you can do it, so you can believe yourself, believe that you can do things."	By holding *high expectations* about what students can accomplish, teachers make students more likely to believe in themselves.
Intellectual Stimulation	*"[My teacher] talks to us and gives choices to his students, offers choices for the student, and I think that makes students like PE more."*	By fostering *autonomy and independent inquiry*, teachers make students more likely to enjoy physical education.
	"Mr. O is distinctive in that he likes to encourage students to find their own way where other teachers talk and talk and I find that really frustrating."	Encouraging students to *think for themselves* makes them more likely to respond positively.
	"If they just tell a student that running is good for them, it's not really a big influence. They don't explain why we need to run, they just say we do and tell us where we have to run."	If PE teachers fail to *intellectually engage* with students, students may fail to see the benefits of physical education.
Individualized Consideration	*"Miss G did influence my positive attitude towards PE because she was my first PE teacher in high school and really gave me her support [following an injury] and at the end of the year she gave me a little card that said 'thanks for your participation and good luck in future years'."*	By taking the time to display *empathy and understanding*, teachers can have a major effect on students' attitudes.
	"Instead of calling, you!, you!, you!, if you call [students'] names you feel that you are more a part of the class, you can feel more respected."	Taking the time to refer to students by name shows students that the *teacher cares*.
	"If you're really struggling with something he offers to meet up with you after school and he goes over it, so we get a lot better."	By displaying genuine *care and concern* for students' individual needs, teachers can foster student improvement.

*The examples of transformational teaching behaviours displayed by school physical education teachers are taken from Morton, K. L., Keith, S. E., & Beauchamp, M. R. (2010). Transformational teaching and physical activity: A new paradigm for adolescent health promotion? *Journal of Health Psychology, 15*, 248–257.

enjoyment of those classes, expend greater effort in class, and also engage in greater amounts of physical activity during their leisure time (Beauchamp et al., 2014). This research suggests that teachers matter and have the capacity to shape adolescent engagement in physical activity, and not just in terms of their within-class behaviours, but also outside of the school confines. Transformational leadership inspires others to exceed minimally expected standards; students elected to be active in their leisure time when they were not mandated by their teachers to do so!

ATHLETE LEADERSHIP IN SPORT

Leadership provided by peers has the potential to greatly influence group functioning as well as individual perceptions and behaviours. An **athlete leader** has been defined as a team member, acting in a formal or informal capacity, who guides and influences other team members toward a common objective (Loughead et al., 2006). A vivid example of athlete leadership in action was provided in the Canadian women's ice hockey program leading up to the team's gold medal performance at the 2014 Winter Olympics. Prior to the tournament, one of the most dominant women's ice hockey players, Hayley Wickenheiser, represented Canada as team captain. However, as evidence of the depth of quality leaders in the team, another longstanding player, Caroline Ouellette, was nominated as captain for 2014 while Wickenheiser was assigned an assistant/alternate leadership role. Clearly, the emergence of multiple leaders within a sport team has the potential to provide the group with rich sources of mentorship and direction or, conversely, cause division among group members. Ouellette's interactive perspective on athlete leadership offers some insight:

> A good leader gives herself the space to guide and sustain her teammates, but also to receive the energy and the know-how of the players by her side. I like to believe that "leadership" is defined by the actions that every player is ready to undertake in order to make the difference. That's the beauty of team sports (Ouellette, 2014).

The above definition, example, and quote highlight several issues regarding athlete leadership that researchers have considered within a sport context:

- What are the functions and behaviours of athlete leaders?
- Who typically emerges as an athlete leader?
- Is there a prescription for how many athletes should be leaders within a sport team?

Athlete Leaders' Functions and Behaviours

Athlete leaders can be thought to serve three general functions within the team (Loughead et al., 2006). First, they are involved in activities that are designed to help the team accomplish its *task objectives*. For example, these activities may include mentoring new members on team tactics or acting as a communication conduit between coaches and other players. Second, athlete leaders also address the *social needs* of the team through the promotion of interpersonal harmony and the organization of team activities outside of the sport context. While task and social functions relate to the internal team environment, some athlete leaders are also responsible for a third set of activities that deal with

Athlete leader: A team member, acting in a formal or informal capacity, who guides and influences other team members toward a common objective.

external functions, which may include representing the group at club meetings or within the community.

Athlete leaders employ specific behaviours to address their broader functions, and these behaviours have been examined in light of previously discussed models of leadership that include the MML (Chelladurai, 2007) as well as Bass and Riggio's full range model (2006). For example, Loughead and Hardy (2005) were interested in understanding whether athlete leader and coach behaviours were employed differentially in teams. They found that athletes perceived their peer leaders to engage in more social support, positive feedback, and democratic behaviours than their coaches, while the coaches were perceived to use greater training/instruction and autocratic behaviours. In essence, the two sources of leadership were acting in complementary ways.

With a focus on transformational leadership, Callow and colleagues (2009) reported that captains of Ultimate Frisbee teams were perceived to demonstrate a moderate to high frequency of behaviours related to individual consideration, inspirational motivation, intellectual stimulation, and fostering acceptance of team goals. Importantly, there were several positive links between transformational leadership behaviours and perceptions of both task and social cohesion. Smith and colleagues (2013) found that transformational leadership improved intrateam communication, resulting in higher levels of group cohesion. Overall, the research indicates that athlete leaders are responsible for addressing task, social, and external functions of the group and utilize a wide variety of leadership behaviours to get the team members to interact effectively with each other.

Who Are Athlete Leaders?

Although all team members could have the opportunity to provide leadership at varying times throughout group development, a typical prototype athlete leader is a higher skilled, veteran, well liked, intrinsically motivated, and centrally located individual (see Loughead et al., 2014). Furthermore, athlete leaders are not identified solely through formal roles (e.g., captains, assistant captains), although this is the most visible mechanism for peer leadership. Athletes have also indicated the positive impact that emergent informal leaders make within the team as a whole and also through more intimate mentoring functions (Cope et al., 2011). An example of an informal leader would be a senior/veteran player to whom new players might turn for advice and guidance, even though the senior player in question might not have been formally appointed as a captain or assistant captain on that team.

How Many Athlete Leaders Are Optimal?

In all likelihood, the answer to this question is, "It depends." For example, it may depend on the structural interdependencies within the group (Evans et al., 2012), which might dictate the task and social leadership needs. For example, an intercollegiate football team is a highly segmented group with a large number of players contributing separately to offence, defence, and special teams (that are further subdivided by specific positional responsibilities). In contrast to a smaller, compact group like a basketball team, football teams require more individuals to act in leadership roles. Overall, from an athlete's point of view, greater access to peer leadership seems to be desirable. Crozier and colleagues

(2013) reported that athletes viewed the optimal leader proportions in their teams to be roughly one-fifth for formal occupancy and two-thirds for informal occupancy. However, other studies suggest that a smaller, well-defined group of leaders may be beneficial for intrateam communication and cohesion (Hardy et al., 2008). The degree to which there is a relative *balance* of leaders addressing task, social, and external functions is tied to athlete satisfaction (Eys et al., 2007).

REFLECTIONS 8.2

A common practice across sports is to designate formal athlete leaders within the team (i.e., captains, co-captains, assistant captains). Consider the information contained within the above section, including the functions and behaviours of athlete leaders, as well as your own experiences. Can you think of contexts where the formal designation of athlete leaders may be unnecessary or detrimental to individual members and the team? At what stage in development are children and youth able to handle leadership positions in a larger group? What are the appropriate selection practices for these roles?

FOLLOWERSHIP ALSO MATTERS

Although leadership research in sport and exercise has focused mainly on the behaviours displayed by the leader (e.g., coach, captain) with the athletes and exercisers under their charge, there has been a growing call to consider **followership**. That is, to what extent is effective leadership dependent on the personal characteristics and behaviours of those being led? There are many examples in sport of coaches who have had a certain degree of success with one athlete (or team) being unable to extract the best out of another athlete (or team). In many instances, the nature of the coach's style remains the same but the personal characteristics of the different athletes mean that the coach's style is more effective for one athlete than another.

Followership: The way in which followers interact with and respond to a leader.

In one study that nicely illustrates this in the sport domain, Arthur and colleagues (2010) found that specific types of (transformational) leadership would likely be blunted or lessened among athletes who display high levels of a particular personality trait. Narcissism is a trait in which people exaggerate their talents and accomplishments and have an inflated sense of their own self-importance. The researchers examined how athletes who scored high on the trait of narcissism might respond differently to a coach's displays of transformational leadership than athletes who displayed low levels of this trait. In this study, Arthur and colleagues found that when coaches emphasized the importance of teamwork and group goals, athletes who scored low in narcissism put forth greater effort; however, among athletes who scored high in narcissism, those leadership behaviours tended to be less effective. The authors concluded that narcissists are more likely to withhold effort when group goals are promoted (rather than individual ones) as they are more concerned with self-promotion, rather than contributing to the collective good of the team. These findings suggest that one needs to consider follower (athlete, exerciser, student) characteristics alongside leadership characteristics when looking to understand what effects various leader behaviours might have (or not) on those being led.

EXERCISE LEADERSHIP

Exercise leaders can have a major impact on participants' physical and mental well-being. Research has indicated that leaders' behaviours can be enhanced to increase class attendance and satisfaction. Turner and colleagues (1997) compared the effects of instructors using either a highly enriched instructional style or a bland instructional style. In the enriched condition, leaders sought to use participants' names, give frequent individual attention, provide positive and encouraging feedback, and recognize participants' efforts. These behaviours are similar to the individualized consideration and positive feedback dimensions found in the models of Bass and Riggio (2006) as well as Chelladurai (2007) described above. This study revealed that participants in the enriched condition reported greater increases in revitalization and self-efficacy than those in the bland condition, which together suggests that the behaviours of instructors play a substantive role in how exercisers feel about themselves during their classes. Bray, Millen, and colleagues (2005) found that an enriched leadership style was positively related to greater enjoyment among Canadian exercise class participants. The evidence suggests that the way in which exercise instructors interact with class members has the potential to substantively affect their enjoyment of and engagement in those classes.

Another important leader within exercise settings is the personal trainer. Although there has been a distinct absence of research on the leadership behaviours displayed by personal trainers, the rapid growth and development of the personal training industry over the past couple of decades would suggest that personal trainers have the potential to support the physical fitness of people across the age spectrum within a highly personalized social setting. It remains to be empirically investigated which behaviours of personal trainers are most likely to support their clients' long-term involvement in active lifestyles. However, drawing from the extant literature on transformational leadership as well as research involving exercise class instructors described above, it would appear important to foster interactions that are characterized by:

- attention to clients' personal and psychological needs (individualized consideration)
- encouragement, enthusiasm, and optimism (inspirational motivation)
- behaviours that engender trust and respect (idealized influence)
- appropriate role modelling with regard to leading an active lifestyle (idealized influence), and
- an enriched (versus bland) exercise program and environment.

DEVELOPING EFFECTIVE LEADERSHIP: BEST PRACTICES

Since leadership can be developed through training, how can this be done effectively in sport and exercise settings? In this section, we draw from the accumulated evidence on leadership training, in particular with regard to transformational leadership, and provide a series of practical examples. Kelloway and Barling (2000) presented a conceptual framework for guiding transformational leadership interventions. They provide a multi-phase model in which leadership training should (a) illustrate what transformational behaviours look like in practice (through education, demonstration, and role modelling), (b) provide

How instructors interact with class members can affect exercisers' enjoyment of and engagement in those classes.

andresimaging/Getty Image

opportunities for leaders to carry out transformational leadership behaviours in practice, and (c) give feedback on the performance of those behaviours. Such an approach guides leader trainees to "learn by doing" (Freese et al., 2003). Based on the leadership development literature, leaders in sport and physical activity settings could be encouraged to:

■ Articulate a compelling vision of how they want their athletes, exercise class members, students, or clients to operate. On a sports team, this vision might relate to how a coach wants the team to play, train, and interact with one another away from the field of play. Where possible, team members should be involved in this process, as well as in decision-making activities. This increases athlete autonomy and also acceptance of the team concept. In a physical education setting, teachers could convey a persuasive plan for what students can accomplish toward achieving a healthy lifestyle within a given timeframe.

■ Be responsive to others' individual differences and needs. A "one-size-fits-all" approach might be rather limiting in getting the best out of those athletes, students, or class members. Provide specific feedback in a timely manner that will help the individual in question maximize potential.

■ Support athletes, students, and exercisers to see challenges as opportunities, and approach those challenges from multiple perspectives. Encouraging athletes to think for themselves, and look at old problems in new ways, will not only enable the development of more well-rounded athletes, but can also be very empowering for those athletes. Students, exercise class members, and clients (e.g., within rehab settings) who are encouraged to think about their own personal health and wellness from multiple perspectives, and to take personal responsibility for understanding their own personal health, are more likely to be motivated to be physically active.

- Discuss their personal values and beliefs (i.e., leader philosophy) with those being led, and articulate the standards to which they hold their athletes, students, exercisers, and clients (and themselves) to account. Leaders should consistently model the behaviours they wish to see among those being led. In essence, this involves leading by example and practising what they preach.
- Demonstrate enthusiasm and optimism about what athletes, students, exercisers, and clients can achieve. If leaders hold high (but realistic) expectations of others, those being led will likely rise to those expectations. Conversely, if leaders hold low expectations of others, those being led will likely meet (but not exceed) those low expectations.

CHAPTER SUMMARY

Leadership issues are pervasive within sport and exercise contexts. Whether one considers the interactions between coaches and athletes, captains and teammates, exercise instructors and clients, or physical educators and students, the ability to effectively integrate and motivate individuals to achieve their goals (and, in many cases, those of the group) is both challenging and rewarding. The opening vignette of this chapter highlighted the behaviours of a very successful professional hockey coach (Mike Babcock), but also raised questions about our understanding of leadership that have interested researchers and practitioners for decades.

In striving to understand leadership, researchers have put forward numerous definitions and theories that focus on leaders' personality, situational characteristics, and the interaction of these factors. At its core, leadership is concerned with the behavioural processes through which one person influences another person, or a group of others, toward attaining a specific set of objectives (Northouse, 2001). Furthermore, the interaction between personality characteristics (e.g., extraversion) and contextual factors (e.g., competitive level, type of sport) likely dictates the emergence and effectiveness of leadership within sport and exercise.

Nevertheless, effective (and ineffective) leadership practices should be considered across a full range of possible behaviours. In this chapter, we provided a particular focus on Bass and Riggio's (2006) full range model of leadership that includes laissez-faire leadership, passive management by exception, active management by exception, and contingent reward behaviours, as well as the four dimensions of transformational leadership. From a practical perspective, leaders within sport and physical activity settings are encouraged to move beyond transactional practices and engage their followers with a transformational approach, including behaviours that promote intellectual stimulation, individualized consideration, inspirational motivation, and idealized influence.

Leadership is not solely reserved for coaches, exercise instructors, and teachers, however. It is also important to consider the role of formal leadership provided by group members (e.g., captains) as well as informal leadership that might emerge among other individuals within a given team. Indeed, the evidence to date suggests that peers provide important sources of leadership regarding task, social, and external functions that play an essential role in complementing leadership behaviours provided by coaches, instructors, and teachers.

Often lost in the discussion of leadership behaviours are the roles, responsibilities, and characteristics of the follower. While researchers in sport and exercise have yet to extensively investigate the concept of followership, there is evidence to suggest that follower characteristics (e.g., narcissism) can interact with leadership characteristics in a manner that will influence the effectiveness of certain leadership behaviours. Clearly, leadership is irrelevant in the absence of followers, and attention should be paid to what constitutes the ideal follower in sport and exercise, as well as how to ensure that group members understand and value that role.

Finally, it is possible to *develop* leadership behaviours that are effective in sport and exercise contexts. The examples provided at the end of this chapter encourage leaders to articulate a compelling vision of how they want group members to behave, to be responsive to individual differences and the needs of their followers, to support athletes, exercisers, and students in viewing challenges as opportunities, to communicate and model their leadership philosophy (i.e., practise what they preach), and to convey enthusiasm and optimism about what it is possible to achieve. Overall, leaders are important social agents in sport and exercise contexts who have a responsibility to ensure the well-being of their followers, and help them achieve their goals with respect to sport performance, exercise enjoyment and adherence, and the development of a lifelong commitment to physical activity.

COMMON MYTHS ABOUT LEADERSHIP IN SPORT AND EXERCISE REVISITED

MYTH: Great leaders (including coaches and team captains) are born, not made. The extent to which leaders are born or made is often seen in binary terms (one or the other), with many believing that great leaders are born with those capabilities. The accumulated research evidence to date suggests that *both* nature and nurture play a role. Specifically, there is some evidence to indicate that the occupation of leadership roles and the display of effective (transformational) leadership have some heritable basis. However, there is also consistent evidence from across diverse domains of human achievement suggesting that leadership can be shaped by both early (childhood) experiences and also through training and mentorship later in life.

MYTH: Effective leadership is an intangible quality that cannot really be assessed. Contrary to the belief that leadership represents some mythical and intangible quality, there is evidence to suggest that some of the key dimensions of effective leadership are well known and can be reliably assessed. Across achievement domains, including sport, displays of transformational leadership have consistently been found to predict improved emotional responses, adaptive cognitions, and performance. These behavioural approaches appear to be substantively more effective than transactional approaches. As highlighted earlier in the chapter, simply providing extensive training and instruction (in terms of hours spent training) is no substitute for providing quality instruction. Furthermore, measures exist which have been found to display sound psychometric properties that assess these components of effective leadership in physical activity settings.

MYTH: Leadership is a top-down process concerned with exerting control, authority, and power over others.

Effective leadership appears to emerge when leaders empower, rather than exert power over, others. Research conducted within the framework of self-determination theory (Deci & Ryan, 1991) provides clear indication that leadership behaviours that foster autonomy, rather than control, are far more likely to result in adaptive outcomes (including motivation) among athletes (Hagger & Chatzisarantis, 2007). Research in sport settings suggests that transformational leadership behaviours tend to result in improved self-determined motivation, which has downstream effects on athlete performance (Charbonneau et al, 2001).

Review Questions

1. To what extent do you think personality plays a role in determining leadership emergence, occupancy, or performance?

2. Outline the five leadership behaviours assessed by the Leadership Scale for Sports (LSS).

3. Briefly describe the different types of leadership outlined in the full range model of leadership.

4. What are the differences between transactional and transformational leadership?

5. List the three general functions of athlete leaders.

Suggested Readings

Beauchamp, M. R., & Morton, K. L. (2011). Transformational teaching and physical activity engagement among adolescents. *Exercise and Sport Sciences Reviews*, *39*(3), 133–139.

Chelladurai, P. (1990). Leadership in sports: A review. *International Journal of Sport Psychology*, *21*, 328–354.

Loughead, T. M., & Hardy, J. (2005). An examination of coach and peer leader behaviors in sport. *Psychology of Sport and Exercise*, *6*, 303–312.

References

Amorose, A. J., & Horn, T. S. (2000). Intrinsic motivation: Relationships with collegiate athletes' gender, scholarship status, and perceptions of their coaches' behavior. *Journal of Sport & Exercise Psychology*, *22*(1), 63–84.

Arthur, C. A., Woodman, T., Ong, C. W., Hardy, L., & Ntoumanis, N. (2011). The role of athlete narcissism in moderating the relationship between coaches' transformational leader behaviours and athlete motivation. *Journal of Sport & Exercise Psychology*, *33*, 3–19.

Avolio, B. J., Reichard, R. J., Hannah, S. T., Walumbwa, F. O., & Chan, A. (2009). A meta-analytic review of leadership impact research: Experimental and quasi-experimental studies. *Leadership Quarterly*, *20*, 764–784.

Bandura, A. (1986). *Social foundations of thought and actions: A social cognitive theory*. Englewood Cliffs, NJ: Prentice–Hall.

Barling, J., Christie, A., & Hoption, C. (2010). Leadership. In S. Zedeck, (Ed.). *Handbook of industrial and organizational psychology*. Washington, DC: APA.

Barling, J., Weber, T., & Kelloway, E. K. (1996). Effects of transformational leadership training on attitudinal and financial outcomes: A field experiment. *Journal of Applied Psychology, 81,* 827-832.

Bass, B. M. (1985). *Leadership and performance beyond expectations*. New York: Free Press.

Bass, B. M. (1997). Does the transactional–transformational leadership paradigm transcend organizational and national boundaries? *American Psychologist, 52,* 130–39.

Bass, B. M. (1998). *Transformational leadership: Industry, military, and educational impact*. Mahwah, NJ: Erlbaum.

Bass, B. M., & Avolio, B. J. (1994). *Improving organizational effectiveness through transformational leadership*. Thousand Oaks, CA: Sage Publications.

Bass, B. M., & Riggio, R. E. (2006). *Transformational leadership* (2nd ed.). New Jersey: Lawrence Erlbaum Associated, Inc.

Beauchamp, M. R., Barling, J., Li, Z., Morton, K. L., Keith, S. E., & Zumbo, B. D. (2010). Development and psychometric properties of the transformational teaching questionnaire. *Journal of Health Psychology, 15*(8), 1123–1134.

Beauchamp, M. R., Barling, J., & Morton, K. L. (2011). Transformational teaching and adolescent self-determined motivation, self-efficacy, and intentions to engage in leisure time physically activity: A randomized controlled pilot trial. *Applied Psychology: Health and Well-Being, 3,* 127–150.

Beauchamp, M. R., Bray, S. R., Eys, M. A., & Carron, A. V. (2002). Role ambiguity, role efficacy, and role performance: Multidimensional and mediational relationships within interdependent sport teams. *Group Dynamics: Theory, Research, and Practice, 6*(3), 229–242.

Beauchamp, M. R., Bray, S. R., Eys, M. A., & Carron, A. V. (2005). Leadership behaviors and multidimensional role ambiguity in team sports. *Small Group Research, 36*(1), 5–20.

Beauchamp, M. R., Liu, Y., Morton, K. L., Martin, L. J., Wilson, A. H., Wilson, A. J., Sylvester, B. D., Zumbo, B. D., & Barling, J. (2014). Transformational teaching and adolescent physical activity: Multilevel and mediational effects. *International Journal of Behavioral Medicine, 23* (3), 537–546.

Bird, A. M. (1977). Team structure and success as related to cohesiveness and leadership. *Journal of Social Psychology, 103,* 217–223.

Blanchard, K., & Johnson, S. (1982). *The one-minute manager*. New York. Morrow.

Bourne, J., Liu, Y., Jackson, B., Shields, C. A., Zumbo, B. D., & Beauchamp, M. R. (in press). The relationship between transformational teaching and adolescent physical activity: The mediating roles of personal and relational efficacy beliefs. *Journal of Health Psychology*.

Bray, S. R., Beauchamp, M. R., Eys, M. A., & Carron, A. V. (2005). Does need for role clarity moderate the relationship between role ambiguity and athlete satisfaction? *Journal of Applied Sport Psychology, 17*(4), 306–318.

Bray, S. R., Millen, J. A., Eidsness, J., & Leuzinger, C. (2005). The effects of leadership style and exercise programme choreography on enjoyment and intentions to exercise. *Psychology of Sport and Exercise, 6,* 415–425.

Brough, J. (2014, February 3) In praise of Mike Babcock, who doesn't want you to be confused. *NBC Sports*. Retrieved (March 12, 2014) from http://prohockeytalk.nbcsports.com/2014/02/23/in-praise-of-mike-babcock-who-doesnt-want-you-to-be-confused/.

Bycio, P., Hackett, R. D., & Allen, J. S. (1995). Further assessments of Bass's (1985) conceptualization of transactional and transformational leadership. *Journal of Applied Psychology, 80,* 468–478.

Callow, N., Smith, M. J., Hardy, L., Arthur, C. A., & Hardy, J. (2009). Measurement of transformational leadership and its relationship with team cohesion and performance level. *Journal of Applied Sport Psychology, 21,* 395–412.

Carless, S. A. (1998). Assessing the discriminant validity of transformational leadership behaviour as measured by the MLQ. *Journal of Occupational and Organizational Psychology, 71*, 353–358.

Charbonneau, D., Barling, J., & Kelloway, E. K. (2001). Transformational leadership and sports performance: The mediating role of intrinsic motivation. *Journal of Applied Social Psychology, 31*, 1521–1534.

Chaturvedi, S., Arvey, R. D., Zhang, Z., & Christoforou, P. T. (2011). Genetic underpinnings of transformational leadership: The mediating role of dispositional hope. *Journal of Leadership & Organizational Studies, 18* (4), 469–479.

Chelladurai, P. (1990). Leadership in sports: A review. *International Journal of Sport Psychology, 21*, 328–354.

Chelladurai, P. (2007). Leadership in sports. In G. Tenenbaum & R. C. Eklund (Eds.). *Handbook of sport psychology* (3rd ed., pp. 113–135). New York: John Wiley & Sons, Inc.

Chelladurai, P., & Saleh, P. (1980). Dimensions of leader behavior in sports: Development of a leadership scale. *Journal of Sport Psychology, 2*, 34–45.

Chelladurai, P., & Saleh, S. D. (1978). Preferred leadership in sports. *Canadian Journal of Applied Sport Sciences, 3*, 85–92.

Cope, C. J., Eys, M. A., Beauchamp, M. R., Schinke, R. J., & Bosselut, G. (2011). Informal roles on sport teams. *International Journal of Sport and Exercise Psychology, 9*, 19–30.

Crozier, A. J., Loughead, T. M., & Munroe–Chandler, K. J. (2013). Examining the benefits of athlete leaders in sport. *Journal of Sport Behavior, 36*, 346–364.

Deci, E. L., & Ryan, R. M. (1991). A motivational approach to self: Integration in personality. In R. A. Dienstbier (Ed.), *Nebraska symposium on motivation: Perspectives on motivation* (Vol. 38, pp. 237–288). Lincoln: University of Nebraska.

De Neve, J., Mikhaylov, S., Dawes, S. T., Christakis, N. A., & Fowler, J. H. (2013). Born to lead? A twin design and genetic association study of leadership role occupancy. *Leadership Quarterly, 24*(1), 45–60.

Digman, J. M. (1990). Personality structure: Emergence of the five factor model. In M. R. Rosenweig & L. W. Porter (Eds.), *Annual Review of Psychology* (Vol. 41, pp. 417–440). Palo Alto, CA: Annual Reviews.

Escarti, A., & Guzman, J. F. (1999). Effects of feedback on self-efficacy, performance, and choice on an athletic task. *Journal of Applied Sport Psychology, 11*, 83–96.

Evans, M. B., Eys, M. A., & Bruner, M. W. (2012). See the 'we' in 'me' sports: The need to consider individual sport team environments. *Canadian Psychology, 53*, 301–308.

Eys, M. A., Loughead, T. M., & Hardy, J. (2007). Athlete leadership dispersion and satisfaction in interactive sport teams. *Psychology of Sport and Exercise, 8*, 281–296.

Fiedler, F. E., Hartman, W., & Rudin, S. A. (1952). *The relationship of interpersonal perception to effectiveness in basketball teams* (Technical Report No. 3). Champaign–Urbana, IL Contract n6ori-07135 between University of Illinois and Office of Naval Research. http://www.archive .org/stream/relationshipofin03fied#page/n7/mode/2up.

Fiedler, F. E. (1967). *A theory of leadership effectiveness*. New York: McGraw Hill.

Freese, M., Beimel, S., & Schoenborn, S. (2003). Action training for charismatic leadership: Two evaluations of studies of a commercial training module on inspirational communication of a vision. *Personnel Psychology, 56*, 671–697.

Hagger, M., & Chatzisarantis, N. L. (2007). *Intrinsic motivation and self-determination in exercise and sport*. Champaign, IL Human Kinetics.

Hardy, J., Eys, M. A., & Loughead, T. M. (2008). Does communication mediate the athlete leadership to cohesion relationship? *International Journal of Sport Psychology, 39*, 329–345.

Hardy, L., Arthur, C. A., Jones, G., Shariff, A., Munnoch, K., Isaacs, I., & Allsopp, A. J. (2010). The relationship between transformational leadership behaviours, psychological, and training outcomes in elite military recruits. *Leadership Quarterly, 21*, 20–32.

Holt, N. L., & Hoar, S. (2006). The multidimensional construct of social support. In S. Hanton, & S. D. Mellalieu (Eds.), *Literature reviews in sport psychology* (pp. 119–226). New York: Nova Science.

House, R. J. (1971). A path–goal theory of leadership effectiveness. *Administrative Science Quarterly, 16*, 321–338.

House, R. J. (1996). Path–goal theory of leadership: Lessons, legacy, and reformulated theory. *Leadership Quarterly, 7*(3), 323–352.

Jackson, B., Dimmock, J. A., Gucciardi, D. F., & Grove, J. R. (2011). Personality traits and relationship perceptions in coach–athlete dyads: Do opposites really attract? *Psychology of Sport and Exercise, 12*, 222–230.

Judge, T. A., Bono, J. E., Illies, R., & Gerhardt, M. W. (2002). Personality and leadership: A qualitative and quantitative review. *Journal of Applied Psychology, 87*, 765–780.

Judge, T. A., & Piccolo, R. F. (2004). Transformational and transactional leadership: A meta-analytic test of their relative validity. *Journal of Applied Psychology, 89*, 755–768.

Kelloway, E. K., & Barling, J. (2000). What we have learned about developing transformational leaders. *Leadership and Organization Development Journal, 21*, 355–362.

Konar–Goldband, E., Rice, R. W., & Monkarsh, W. (1979). Time-phased interrelationships of group atmosphere, group performance, and leader style. *Journal of Applied Psychology, 64*(4), 401–409.

Loughead, T. M., & Hardy, J. (2005). An examination of coach and peer leader behaviors in sport. *Psychology of Sport and Exercise, 6*, 303–312.

Loughead, T. M., Hardy, J., & Eys, M. A. (2006). The nature of athlete leadership. *Journal of Sport Behavior, 29*, 145–158.

Loughead, T. M., Mawn, L., Hardy, J., & Munroe–Chandler, K. J. (2014). Athlete leadership: Theory, research, and practice. In A. Papaioannou & D. Hackfort (Eds.), *Routledge companion to sport and exercise psychology: Global perspectives and fundamental concepts*. Oxford: Taylor & Francis.

Morton, K. L., Barling, J., Rhodes, R. E., Masse, L. C., Zumbo, B., & Beauchamp, M. R. (2011). The application of transformational leadership theory to parenting: Questionnaire development and implications for adolescent self-regulatory efficacy and life satisfaction. *Journal of Sport & Exercise Psychology, 33*, 688–709.

Morton, K. L., Keith, S. E., & Beauchamp, M. R. (2010). Transformational teaching and physical activity: A new paradigm for adolescent health promotion? *Journal of Health Psychology, 15*, 248–257.

Morton, K. L., Wilson, A. H., Perlmutter, L., & Beauchamp, M. R. (2012). Family leadership styles and adolescent dietary and physical activity behaviors: A cross-sectional study. *International Journal of Behavioral Nutritional and Physical Activity, 9*:48.

Northouse, P. G. (2001). *Leadership: Theory and practice* (2nd ed.). Thousand Oaks, CA: Sage.

Ogilvie, B. C. (1968). Psychological consistencies within the personality of high level competitors. *Journal of the American Medical Association, 205*, 156–162.

Ouellette, C. (2014, January 23). Ouellette feels lucky to be chosen as captain. *Canadian Broadcasting Corporation*. Retrieved (March 12, 2014) from http://www.cbc.ca.

Riemer, H. A., & Toon, K. (2001). Leadership and satisfaction in tennis: Examination of congruence, gender, and ability. *Research Quarterly for Exercise and Sport, 72*, 243–256.

Rosen, D. (2013, December 31). Babcock's leadership key to Canada's repeat hopes. Retrieved (March 12, 2014) from http://www.nhl.com/ice/news.htm?id=689207.

Rowold, J. (2006). Transformational and transactional leadership in martial arts. *Journal of Applied Sport Psychology, 18*, 312–325.

Smith, M. J., Arthur, C. A., Hardy, J., Callow, N., & Williams, D. (2013). Transformational leadership and task cohesion in sport: The mediating role of intrateam communication. *Psychology of Sport and Exercise, 14*(2), 249–257.

Sullivan, P., Paquette, K. J., Holt, N. L., & Bloom, G. A. (2012). The relation of coaching context and coach education to coaching efficacy and perceived leadership behaviors in youth sport. *The Sport Psychologist, 26,* 122–134.

Stogdill, R. M. (1948). Personal factors associated with leadership: A survey of the literature. *Journal of Psychology, 25,* 35–71.

Tamminen, K. A., & Gaudreau, P. (2014). Coping, social support, and emotion regulation in teams. In M. R. Beauchamp & M. A. Eys (Eds.), *Group dynamics in exercise and sport psychology* (2nd ed., pp. 222–239). New York: Routledge.

Tucker, S., Turner, N. A., Barling, J., & McEvoy, M. (2010). Transformational leadership and children's aggression in team settings: A short-term longitudinal study. *Leadership Quarterly, 21,* 389–399.

Turner, E. E., Rejeski, W. J., & Brawley, L. R. (1997). Psychological benefits of physical activity are influenced by the social environment. *Journal of Sport & Exercise Psychology, 34,* 119–130.

Tutko, T. A., Lyon, L. P., & Ogilvie, B. C. (1969). *Athletic Motivation Inventory.* San Jose, CA: Institute for the Study of Athletic Motivation.

van Wijk, J. (2013, September 1). I don't need a director of football—Wenger. *Independent.* Retrieved (April 2, 2014) from http://www.independent.ie/sport/soccer/i-dont-need-a-director-of-football-wenger-29542682.html.

Weiss, M. R., & Friedrichs, W. D. (1986). The influence of leader behaviors, coach attributes, and institutional variables on performance and satisfaction of collegiate basketball teams. *Journal of Sport Psychology, 8,* 332–346.

Whyno, S. (2014, February 23). Babcock shows Team Canada the way to gold. *The Star.* Retrieved (March 12, 2014) from http://www.thestar.com/sports/sochi2014/hockey/2014/02/23/babcock_shows_team_canada_the_way_to_gold.html#.

Wilson, A. J., Liu, Y., Keith, S. E., Wilson, A. H., Kermer, L., Zumbo, B. D., & Beauchamp, M. R. (2012). Transformational teaching, and child psychological needs satisfaction, motivation and engagement in elementary school physical education. *Sport, Exercise, & Performance Psychology, 1*(4), 215–230.

Zacharatos, A., Barling, J., & Kelloway, E. K. (2000). Development and effects of transformational leadership in adolescents. *The Leadership Quarterly, 11,* 211–226.

Zhang, J., Jensen, B. E., & Mann, B. L. (1997). Modification and revision of the Leadership Scale for Sport. *Journal of Sport Behavior, 20,* 105–112.

Chapter 9

Group Cohesion in Sport and Exercise

Kevin S. Spink

Jamie McDonald/FIFA/Getty Images

Chapter Objectives

After reading this chapter, you should be able to do the following:

1. Explain why the study of groups is important.
2. Provide a definition of group dynamics.
3. Identify group processes associated with group effectiveness.
4. Provide a definition of group cohesion.
5. Explain how to measure group cohesion.
6. Describe the conceptual model of group cohesion.
7. Explain the important correlates of group cohesion.

You have been selected as the next executive director of the group that will select the players for the women's soccer team that will attempt to qualify for the 2016 Olympic Games in Rio de Janeiro. You have big shoes to fill as the last team qualified, and then played extremely well in the London Olympics to earn the bronze medal. As this was the first soccer medal that Canada had won at the Olympic level, expectations are very high for the performance of the next Olympic team.

Before starting to make your decisions, you choose to consult with those who are closest to the pulse of elite women's soccer in Canada. After several meetings, it is clear that there are two different philosophies that could be used to select the team. One approach is simply to select the best athletes available. In that way, the players with the most talent and speed will represent Canada. It seems like a good recipe for success. After all, many of the other participating countries have longer and richer histories with soccer, and as a result, a deeper pool of strong players for selection, so selecting a team with the best skilled players at each of the positions makes the best sense. You also have heard the adage that there is no substitute for skill, and that the best players are likely the ones who will be able to adapt quickest to the new style required to play in an Olympic-level competition.

The other approach suggests that talent and speed are not enough, and that successful teams are those with strong team chemistry. Those advocating this philosophy do not dispute the fact that skill will be required to compete successfully against the other countries. However, their main argument for the importance of selecting players who will be cohesive revolves around the idea that soccer is a team game, so the group must factor highly into the selection procedure. Proponents of following this path suggest that players who have better chemistry will be better at communicating with each other, so it will be easier for them to make instant adjustments that will lead to successful outcomes than it would be for players who do not share any meaningful chemistry. Also, it was pointed out to you that, to be successful in a team sport, you need to be willing to contribute to the team's overall goal at the expense of your own personal agenda, and players with chemistry typically are more willing to make sacrifices for the team because it is easier for them to "leave their egos at the door."

In thinking about these two different approaches, you start to feel a little anxious. Possibly sacrificing talent for those who might fit in better is truly a scary thought, as you will be the one in the public eye if the team does not perform to expectations. Also, you will be the one who has to answer the inevitable question as to why you left more skilled players sitting at home.

As you can see in the vignette, both approaches to selecting the side appear to have points that are valid. What would you do? After reading this chapter about groups and how they function, you should be in a better position to make an informed decision as to which type of players you would select for the team.

 ## COMMON MYTHS ABOUT GROUP COHESION IN SPORT AND EXERCISE

MYTH: Team harmony is required for cohesion to develop.

MYTH: "There is no 'I' in TEAM."

MYTH: High cohesion is always a good thing.

The task in this chapter is to give an explanation of the group cohesion construct. However, before group cohesion is presented, the importance of groups, in general and in sport, will be discussed.

INTRODUCTION

You do not have to think very long to recognize that a lot of sport participation occurs in group settings. Sport groups come in the obvious guises of hockey, football, soccer, basketball, volleyball, or baseball teams. Although typically classified as individual sports, track and field, swimming, triathlon, and wrestling involve participation in teams. Group participation also occurs in many exercise activities, including aerobic, spin, or aqua fitness classes. Participation in group activities permeates most aspects of our non-sport lives as well, be it involvement in a drama club, debating group, band, choir, or local Mensa group.

STUDYING GROUPS AND GROUP DYNAMICS

Given that groups form a large part of our lives, it may not be surprising that a field of study has emerged that focuses on the behaviour of groups. The field is called *group dynamics*, and it is viewed as a major branch of social psychology. According to Cartwright and Zander (1968), **group dynamics** focuses on gaining knowledge about the nature of groups and their development and on understanding the interrelationships between groups and individuals, other groups, and larger institutions.

Implicit in the above description is the idea that a group is different from a mere collection of individuals. It has been known for many years that group composition, for instance, is an important variable in group settings. The term **assembly effect** refers to variations in group behaviour that are a function of the particular combinations of individuals in the group. Rosenberg and colleagues (1955) found that individuals contributed differently to a group's outcome depending on the particular other individuals with whom they were grouped.

This difference (between a group and a collection of individuals) is recognized in the academic community, and its significance is not lost on the sporting community. Michael Jordan, a retired basketball player, wrote, "Me, I'd rather have five guys with less talent who are willing to come together as a team than five guys who consider themselves stars and aren't willing to sacrifice" (Jordan, 1994, p. 24).

PROCESSES ASSOCIATED WITH GROUP EFFECTIVENESS

As the preceding quotes illustrate, there appears to be a strong connection between team effectiveness and group behaviour in the sport setting. Research supports this as there are a number of group processes associated with how effective a group becomes, including communication, decision-making, and cohesion.

Group dynamics: The study of the nature of groups and their development, and the interrelationships of groups with individuals, other groups, and larger institutions.

Assembly effect: Variations in group behaviour that are a result of the particular combinations of individuals in the group.

Communication

One of the key group processes involved with team effectiveness is how a group communicates. This is obviously important in the sport context. For example, the failure of a linebacker and a defensive lineman to communicate on a stunt may be the difference between a quarterback sack and a big play for the offence. A positive relationship between communication and group cohesion also has been demonstrated within exercise groups (Harden et al., 2014). As outlined in subsequent sections of this chapter, cohesion has been related to a number of variables important to both the individual and the group. This suggests that examining group communication as a means of enhancing team cohesion would be worthwhile.

To enhance communication in sport teams, Carron and Eys (2012) have suggested a number of strategies, such as providing opportunities to socialize to increase comfort levels among players, arranging the dressing room so that players are close enough to talk to each other easily, encouraging players to modify any dissenting ideas, and promoting cooperation and reducing rivalry by focusing on group goals and de-emphasizing personal goals and objectives.

This latter point is particularly important given that team members will typically set goals for both themselves and the team (Zander, 1971), which is a finding that emerged when Canadian varsity athletes were questioned about the goals they set (Dawson et al., 2002). When team and personal goals are set, it has been suggested that team goals will be more effective when the sport requires a high degree of coordination and cooperation (Locke & Latham, 1984).

Decision-Making

Another group process associated with team effectiveness involves how decisions are made. Common wisdom suggests that a decision made by the group should be better than one made by individuals, because it is generally believed that the group possesses more resources to inform a decision than any one individual member (i.e., two heads are better than one). However, this assumes that the group process is effective at getting all members to share their thoughts honestly and then is able to integrate the information meaningfully. Research has found that groups who use the **majority rule**, which is based on the simple principle of equal participation and equal power, tend to make more successful decisions (Hastie & Kameda, 2005). Unfortunately, the use of the majority rule does not always occur since members sometimes provide thoughts that reflect conformity rather than true personal beliefs. In this instance, groups are likely to make poorer decisions because of *groupthink* (Janis, 2007). **Groupthink** occurs when concurrence-seeking becomes so dominant in a cohesive group that it tends to overshadow realistic appraisals of alternative courses of action. A team should be very aware of the process it uses to solicit information because this can contribute greatly to the effectiveness of the decision being made.

Cohesion

Another key factor in understanding why teams become effective concerns the forces that bind members to their groups. The binding property that has been identified as

Majority rule: A rule of decision-making in groups based on the principles of equal participation and equal power for all members.

Groupthink: A mode of thinking that people engage in when the members of a cohesive group so strongly desire a unanimous decision that this overrides their motivation to realistically evaluate other possible options.

fundamental to understanding groups is cohesion. In fact, cohesion has been described as the most important small group variable (Lott & Lott, 1965). This suggestion makes sense when one considers that most researchers who use the term *cohesion* agree that it refers to the degree to which members are motivated to stay in the group (Shaw, 1976).

The recognition that cohesion is the glue that keeps the group together may be enough justification to examine the construct; however, there are other important reasons. One of the most important reasons is that the study of cohesion has revealed that enhanced levels of cohesion are associated with key outcomes for both the individual and the team in the sport setting. Consider the recognition of the importance of cohesion for team outcomes by one of the best individual basketball players of all time, Michael Jordan:

> Naturally, there are going to be ups and downs, particularly if you are trying to achieve at a high level. But when we stepped between the lines, we knew what we were capable of doing. When a pressure situation presented itself, we were plugged into one another as a cohesive unit. That's why we were able to beat more talented teams (Jordan, 1994, p. 23).

The Nature of Group Cohesion There is some general understanding that cohesion is the glue that binds members in a group. However, in terms of specific scientific definitions, many ideas have been expressed. Over the years, cohesion has been defined in various ways, including attraction to the group, level of motivation evidenced by group members, and coordination of group members (Shaw, 1976). One of the seminal definitions of cohesion stated that it is "the resultant of all forces acting on members to remain in the group" (Festinger, 1950, p. 274). In outlining his ideas, Festinger suggested that there are many reasons why individuals would want to remain in a group, including attractions to other members of the group, the specific activities of the group, and the prestige of the group. Although this important definition highlighted the multidimensional nature of cohesion, numerous studies that followed assumed that cohesion was unidimensional, with interpersonal attraction being the most common definition used in the early days of cohesion research (Lott & Lott, 1965). With so many definitions, it may not be a surprise that after reviewing 50 years of empirical research on cohesion, Mudrack (1989) concluded that the construct of cohesion was difficult to define precisely or consistently.

Although Mudrack noted the confusion in defining cohesion, he did identify one definition as being important. It was one forwarded by Canadian sport psychology researcher Bert Carron, who defined cohesion as a "dynamic process which is reflected in the tendency for a group to stick together and remain united in the pursuit of its goals and objectives" (Carron, 1982, p. 124). Since this definition was formulated, Carron and two of his Canadian colleagues, Larry Brawley and Neil Widmeyer, refined and revised the definition of cohesion to state that it is, "the dynamic process which is reflected in the tendency for a group to stick together and remain united in the pursuit of its instrumental objectives and/or for the satisfaction of member affective needs" (Carron et al., 1998, p. 213). This is currently the most accepted definition of group cohesion in sport.

Shariff Che'Lah/Fotolia

Examine the definition of cohesion outlined by Carron and colleagues (1998). Does their definition differ from what you think cohesion is? In what ways is it similar or different?

Carron and Eys (2012) noted that this definition captures the four key characteristics of cohesion: it is dynamic, multidimensional, instrumental, and affective.

Cohesion Is Dynamic One of the important characteristics of cohesion is that it is dynamic, not static: reasons for cohesion can change over time. For instance, from a sport perspective, team members may be drawn to a team in its early stages because it is very task oriented but stay with the group because they have all become good friends. An examination of the development of cohesion within exercise groups revealed that cohesion developed differently, with social cohesion changing over time, but task cohesion remaining relatively stable (Dunlop et al., 2013).

Cohesion Is Multidimensional This definition also reflects the fact that the factors that hold the group together can be varied and numerous, thus highlighting its multidimensional nature. Further, these factors may vary between groups. For instance, there could be two highly cohesive intramural hockey teams that are being held together for very different reasons. On the first team, the members remain in the group because the team is highly united around winning the intramural championship (i.e., task reasons). On the other team, the members stay together not because they will win games, let alone the championship, but because they are very socially compatible (i.e., social reasons).

Cohesion Is Instrumental Another important characteristic captured in the definition is the instrumental nature of cohesion. This characteristic reflects the most basic of facts, namely, that all groups form for a reason. Whether it be a professional football team staying together to pursue the Grey Cup or the "beer" league hockey team staying together to maintain lifelong friendships, all groups form for a purpose. As such, it is important to keep this instrumental basis of cohesion in mind when trying to define the construct.

Cohesion Is Affective Affective relationships are important in understanding cohesion. Outside of the instrumental reasons for members remaining in a group, sometimes groups stay together because there are strong emotional ties among the individuals in the group. For instance, a curling team may stay together because the members make each other laugh and feel comfortable. Likewise, members of a football team may form a tight bond because they have all gone through a gruelling initiation process in which those who could not take it quit, and those who made it through developed a greater respect for one another. A good example of this was portrayed in the sport movie

Remember the Titans, in which a new coach, in order to make a racially diverse football team very cohesive, unites the players by exposing them to a series of very demanding tasks (e.g., early morning runs).

MEASURING GROUP COHESION

Numerous general measures have been used to assess cohesion in the adult sport setting. These measures have assessed variables such as social and leadership choices (Lenk, 1969), as well as used **sociograms** that capture the task and social relationships within a team (Marcos et al., 2010). Graphic representations of the patterns of intermember relationships are depicted through **sociometry**, which is a research technique developed to graphically and mathematically summarize patterns of intermember relations. As a simple example, players on a team could be asked, "Who on the team would you like to play with during a game?" Players would identify appropriate teammates, and then all the relationships identified by the players would be graphed (sociogram). It would be expected that highly cohesive teams would show a large proportion of mutual selections, with few individuals not being selected.

Sociograms: Diagrams of the relationships among group members.

Sociometry: Research technique that graphs and mathematically summarizes patterns of intermember relationships.

In addition to these all-purpose measures, sport-specific questionnaires have been developed to assess cohesion, including the Sport Cohesiveness Questionnaire (Martens et al., 1972) and the Group Environment Questionnaire (GEQ) developed by the Canadian trio of Carron, Widmeyer, and Brawley (1985). The GEQ has been, by far, the most extensively used of the sport-specific cohesion instruments developed to date. Although there could be a number of reasons for the extensive use and longevity of the GEQ in the sport setting, its major strength likely stems from the fact that it is based on an accepted definition of cohesion (Carron, 1982) as well as an accepted conceptual framework of cohesion by Carron et al. (1985).

Conceptual Model of Group Cohesion

The conceptual model of cohesion developed by Carron et al. (1985) portrays cohesion as a multidimensional construct that includes individual and group aspects. The individual aspect refers to the beliefs each member holds about the personal benefits of group membership; the group aspect refers to the beliefs each member holds about the group as a collective. These two aspects each divide into task and social cohesion. Task cohesion refers to the players' willingness to work collectively to achieve the team's objectives, and social cohesion refers to the orientation toward developing and maintaining social relationships within the group. It is from this two-dimensional (group/individual, task/social) conceptual model formulated by Carron et al. (1985) that the GEQ was developed to assess cohesion in the sport setting. The GEQ instrument contains 18 questions that are divided into four subscales, which reflect the two dimensions in the conceptual model (see Figure 9.1):

1. individual attractions to the group–task ("I am happy with my team's level of desire to win")

2. individual attractions to the group–social ("For me, this team is one of the most important social groups to which I belong")

Figure 9.1 Conceptual model of group cohesion

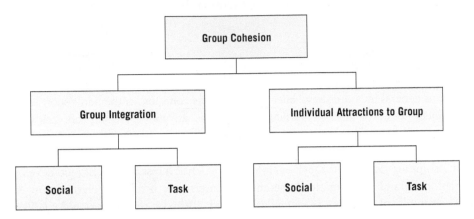

Source: Reprinted, by permission, from Carron, A. V., Widmeyer, W. N., & Brawley, L. R. (1985). The development of an instrument to assess cohesion in sport teams: The Group Environment Questionnaire. *Journal of Sport Psychology, 7*(3): 244-266.

3. group integration–task ("Our team is united in trying to achieve its performance goals")

4. group integration–social ("Our team would like to spend time together in the off-season")

These four related facets act together to create an integrated perception of cohesion. Although developed for the sport setting, this conceptualization of cohesion has broad acceptance in settings outside of sport (Cota et al., 1995).

The GEQ has been used extensively in the sport setting and has generally received good psychometric support across a wide range of teams and situations (see Carron et al., 1998; Whitton & Fletcher, 2014). Although the instrument is psychometrically sound, further adjustments, including positively rewording the negative items in the scale, have served to refine the GEQ (Eys et al., 2007). In addition, it has been modified for use in an exercise setting (Carron & Spink, 1992; Carron et al., 1988, Study 1). Using the conceptual model of cohesion (see Figure 9.1), instruments also have been developed that assess cohesion in older adult exercise groups (Estabrooks & Carron, 2000), youth (13–17 years) sport groups (Eys et al., 2009), and children's (9–12 years) sport groups (Martin et al., 2012). The development of the latter two measures reflects an increasing interest by researchers in examining cohesion in younger populations (Martin et al., 2014).

Correlates of Group Cohesion

Now that we have some sense of what cohesion is and how to go about measuring it, let us turn our attention to factors that have been associated with cohesion. A framework outlined by Carron and Eys (2012) illustrates the factors that correlate with group cohesion (see Figure 9.2). The use of the term *correlate*, which simply refers to a factor associated with another factor, is intentional, given that most research in group cohesion is of a correlational, rather than a cause-and-effect, nature. In fact, it is likely that many of

Figure 9.2 A general framework for examining the correlates of cohesion in sport and exercise groups

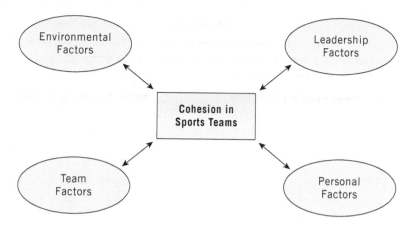

Source: *Group Dynamics in Sport*, 4th ed., (p. 274), by A. V. Carron and M. A. Eys, 2012, Morgantown, WV: Fitness Information Technology. Reprinted with permission from FiT Publishing.

the relationships between cohesion and these correlates are bidirectional. For instance, it is just as likely that cohesion will influence satisfaction as it is that satisfaction will influence cohesion (Spink et al., 2005). Similarly, it is equally likely that cohesion will influence intention to return to a group as intention to return will influence cohesion (Spink, 1995).

In Figure 9.2, four categories of correlates are illustrated: environmental, leadership, personal, and team factors. In this chapter, selected studies will illustrate different factors in each category. Two caveats are worth noting. First, the four categories outlined in Figure 9.2 are not intended to be independent; that is, factors within different categories may be related. Second, the placement of factors within the categories was not intended to be absolute but was based on what was perceived to be a good fit. The factors and studies selected to illustrate the categories were chosen to give the reader a sense of what has been examined over the years, and were not intended to be inclusive of all the research that has been conducted to study cohesion. Also, it is worth mentioning that the majority of the studies that will be reported involve sports. This should not be taken as a sign that cohesion is not important in exercise settings, but rather as a reflection of what appears in the literature. Relevant exercise studies are reported when they are available.

Environmental Correlates of Group Cohesion

Group Size Researchers have had a long-standing interest in the association between group size and cohesion. For the most part, an inverse relationship has emerged between cohesion and group size, both generally and specifically within sport and exercise. In terms of examining groups generally, the results of a meta-analysis across a wide range of groups led Mullen and Copper (1994) to conclude that the smaller the group, the greater the level of cohesion. This inverse relationship has been documented in both sport (Widmeyer et al., 1990) and exercise settings (Carron & Spink, 1995), with increases in group size being associated with decreases in task cohesion.

Specific Activity Setting Another environmental factor that has been associated with cohesion is the specific setting, or context, in which the activity occurs. As noted previously, cohesion is perceived to be multidimensional and, as such, it might be expected that the factors that hold the group together might change across situations. Given that individuals likely come to different situations with different expectations, one might wonder whether a specific setting (context) would affect the perceptions of cohesiveness that develop. Research in the sport setting suggests that this may be the case. For example, Granito and Rainey (1988) found that high-school football players endorsed task cohesion significantly more than university football players.

The effects of context on cohesion also appear to play out in the exercise setting. In one Canadian study, the type of exercise context (i.e., university versus private fitness club) changed the relationship between cohesion and adherence to an exercise program (Carron & Spink, 1995). Specifically, in the university context, those attending regularly reported perceiving greater levels of task cohesion in the class than did eventual dropouts. On the other hand, regular attendees in the private club context held greater perceptions of social cohesion than did eventual dropouts. The finding that task-cohesion factors were more salient to adherence in the university context, while social-cohesion factors were more related to adherence in the private club context, lends credibility to the suggestion that the specific context within the general setting may affect the type of cohesion that emerges.

Tono Balaguer/AGE Fotostock

What might be different between the private club and university exercise settings that would explain why social-cohesion factors were more salient in the former and task-cohesion factors were more important in the latter?

Leadership Correlates of Group Cohesion In sport, it might be expected that the development of cohesiveness would be associated with the behaviour of the coach. Research in the sport setting has provided abundant empirical support for the proposed association between coaching factors and cohesion across many different sports, including basketball (Pease & Kozub, 1994), football (Westre & Weiss, 1991), softball/baseball (Gardner et al., 1996), soccer (Murray, 2006), and ringette (Spink, 1998).

Leader's Behaviour In the leadership literature, examining the relationships among specific leader behaviour patterns and criteria such as member satisfaction and performance have been very important in determining leadership effectiveness. A similar tactic has been taken when examining the association between leadership and cohesion. Leadership behaviours have been assessed primarily through the Leadership Scale for

Sports (LSS) developed by Chelladurai and Saleh (1980). The LSS contains five leadership subscales, with three reflecting behaviours (training and instruction, social support, and positive feedback) and the remaining two reflecting decision style (autocratic style and democratic style). The behaviour subscales will be discussed in this section, and the decision style subscales will be included in the next section.

According to Chelladurai and Saleh (1980), **training and instruction** are captured in behaviours by the coach geared to improving the team members' performance by emphasizing and facilitating hard training; providing instruction in skills, techniques, and tactics; clarifying the relationship among team members; and structuring and coordinating the activities of the team members. **Social support**, on the other hand, involves leader behaviours characterized by a concern for the welfare of the individual athletes, the fostering of a positive group atmosphere, and warm relationships with team members. Finally, behaviours by the coach that reinforce an athlete by recognizing and rewarding strong performance are categorized as **positive feedback**. In several sport studies, it has been demonstrated that coaches who were perceived to engage in training and instruction, social support, and positive feedback behaviours had teams that were both more socially (Murray, 2006) and more task cohesive (Jowett & Chaundy, 2004).

Leader's Decision Style Another leader variable that has received attention in the cohesion literature is the leader's decision style. **Decision style** refers to the degree to which a leader allows participation by subordinates in decision-making. Much of the research examining leaders' decision style in the sport setting has used the LSS. As noted above, the LSS includes two decision-style subscales (Chelladurai & Saleh, 1980). The **autocratic style** signifies behaviour by the leader that involves independent decision-making and stresses personal authority on the part of the leader. This translates into the leader making decisions alone. The **democratic style** signifies behaviour by the leader that allows greater participation by the athletes in decisions relating to team goals, practice methods, and game tactics and strategies. In this approach, the final decision is made jointly, with the leader having no more and no less input into the final decision than any of the team members.

There appears to be some consensus in the cohesion literature that the more democratic the leader style, the greater the tendency for cohesion to develop. This relationship has been found across several sports (Gardner et al., 1996; Jowett & Chaundy, 2004). Also, evidence exists revealing that both task and social cohesion within a team are lower when coaches act independently when making decisions for the team (i.e., autocratic style, Gardner et al., 1996).

Although the focus in sport leadership typically involves the coach, emerging research now examines athlete leader behaviour (e.g., team captains and players who emerge as leaders from within the team). Similar to coaches, results indicate that the perception of athlete leaders engaging in the behaviours of training and instruction and social support was associated with higher levels of both task and social cohesion, while lower levels of task and social cohesion were associated with athlete leaders who engaged in autocratic behaviour (Vincer & Loughead, 2010). Based on the studies outlined above, it appears that the cohesion of a team is associated with specific leadership behaviours and styles. Cohesion within a team tends to be associated with athlete leaders and coaches who allow athletes' input into team decisions, exhibit positive feedback, and provide solid instruction and training.

Training and instruction: Behaviours by the coach that are geared to improving team members' performance.

Social support: Leader behaviours that are characterized by a concern for the welfare of the individual athletes, the fostering of a positive group atmosphere, and warm relationships with team members.

Positive feedback: Behaviours by a coach that reinforce an athlete by recognizing and rewarding strong performance.

Decision style: The degree to which a leader allows participation by subordinates in decision-making.

Autocratic style: A decision style that involves independent decision-making and stresses personal authority on the part of the leader.

Democratic style: A decision style that allows participation by team members in joint decision-making with the leader.

Before leaving leadership behaviours, it is worth noting that while the five subscales of the LSS typically have been used in the sport setting to understand leadership behaviour, another emerging approach comes in the form of **transformational leadership**. Building relationships with subordinates through personal, emotional, and inspirational exchanges form the foundation of this approach (Bass, 1985), and these types of leader–subordinate exchanges have been associated with group cohesiveness. Specifically, it has been reported that leaders in sport who engage in the behaviours of individual consideration (recognizing the needs of different players), fostering acceptance of group goals and teamwork, and promoting high performance expectations had teams reporting higher levels of task cohesion. Leadership behaviours and transformational leadership were discussed in more detail in Chapter 8.

Team-Building Activities In the research reported on leadership previously, the focus was on studies that examined simple associations between cohesion and leadership variables. In this section, the focus will be on research in which attempts were made to use the leader to create cohesion through the implementation of team-building protocols. Before we present the research, a few terms require clarification. First, what is meant by *team building*? Although defined in many ways, **team building** typically refers to programs that use group dynamics principles to increase cohesiveness, which then enables the group to function more effectively (Spink, 2014).

It is important to note that, in the research presented here, the intervention created was filtered through the coach or exercise leader. This is an indirect form of team building because the intervention was done through a third party; it contrasts with more direct forms of team building in which the intervention is presented directly to the team members (cf. Spink, 2014). In direct approaches, the intervention specialist works directly with the team members to provide them with greater insight and greater independence. It is assumed that, through the contact and education, team members will become more intrinsically motivated to team build as a result of their enhanced competence and self-determination (Carron et al., 1998). Although examples of direct interventions are interesting and can be effective forms of team building, they will not be included here since the focus in this section of the chapter is on the relationship between leadership and cohesion. Thus, only those studies in which the coach or exercise leader is the sole delivery agent of the intervention (i.e., indirect team building) will be presented.

Four-Stage Team-Building Model Canadian researchers have created and implemented a four-stage team-building model (introduction, conceptual, practical, and interventions) using the coach or exercise leader as the agent of delivery (Bruner & Spink, 2010, 2011; Carron & Spink, 1993; Prapavessis et al., 1996). The first three stages of the team-building model occur in a workshop conducted by the team-building specialist with coaches or exercise leaders. The final stage involves the coaches or leaders going back to their team or group and implementing the team-building strategies that were formulated during the workshop.

1. Introduction In the first stage, coaches or leaders are presented with a brief overview of the benefits of cohesion to their specific setting. For instance, coaches hear about the relationship between perceptions of cohesiveness and improved team outcomes as identified in the literature (Carron et al., 2002). On the other hand, if exercise leaders are

Transformational leadership: A method of leadership where the leader builds relationships with followers through inspirational exchanges that serve to increase the motivation, confidence, and satisfaction of followers beyond normal expectations.

Team building: Programs promoting an increased sense of unity and cohesiveness within a team.

Figure 9.3 Conceptual framework used as a basis for the implementation of a team-building program in exercise classes

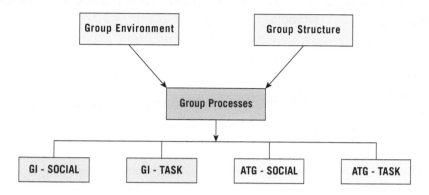

Source: Based on Carron, A. V., & Spink, K. S. (1993). Team building in an exercise setting. *The Sport Psychologist, 7*, 8–18.

being addressed, they hear about the benefits associated with cohesion in specific exercise settings. For instance, if the leaders run exercise classes for older adults, they hear about the positive relationships that have been established between elderly exercisers who perceive their group as more cohesive and better exercise class attendance (Estabrooks & Carron, 1999; Watson et al., 2004).

2. Conceptual The second stage provides a frame of reference for the participants. This is accomplished by introducing a conceptual model. In the conceptual model, cohesion within the group is viewed as an output (or product) of conditions that arise from three different categories of group characteristics. Two categories are inputs: the environment of the group and the structure of the group; and one category is a throughput: group processes. Furthermore, within each of the three categories, specific factors are identified that have previously emerged as being associated with enhanced group cohesiveness. The conceptual model that is used in the Carron and Spink (1993) team-building program in the exercise setting is presented in Figure 9.3.

As noted in Figure 9.3, distinctiveness has been identified in the group environment category as one factor to be manipulated to enhance cohesion in the exercise setting. When this is presented to the exercise leaders, they are told that when something in the group's environment is somehow made distinctive, members develop a stronger sense of "we," more readily distinguish themselves from nonmembers of the group, and ultimately develop stronger perceptions of cohesiveness (Carron & Spink, 1993). This procedure of presenting the leader with a research-based rationale justifying the inclusion of each factor is repeated for all factors outlined in Figure 9.3.

Although a similar conceptual model is used in the sport setting, the specific factors that are highlighted are different from those in the exercise setting, which is consistent with Brawley and Paskevich's (1997) suggestion that team-building factors may differ across situations because the importance of fundamental group processes

Table 9.1 Principles Underlying the Team-Building Program in a Sport Setting

Category	Principle
Team Structure	
Role clarity and acceptance	When group members clearly understand their role in the group, cohesiveness is enhanced. When group members are satisfied and accept their roles in the group, cohesiveness is enhanced.
Leadership	Task and social cohesiveness in the group are influenced by the behaviour of the team leaders. A participative style of coaching leadership contributes to enhanced cohesiveness.
Conformity to standards	Conformity to group social and task norms contributes to enhanced cohesiveness. Group norms are highly resistant to change.
Team Environment	
Togetherness	When group members are repetitively put in close physical proximity, feelings of cohesiveness increase.
Distinctiveness	The presence of group distinctiveness contributes to group cohesiveness.
Team Processes	
Sacrifices	When high-status members make sacrifices for the group, cohesiveness is enhanced.
Goals and objectives	Group goals are more strongly associated with team success than individual goals. Member participation in goal setting contributes to enhanced cohesiveness.
Cooperation	Cooperative behaviour is superior to individualistic behaviour for individual and group performance. Cooperative behaviour is superior to competitive behaviour for individuals and group performance. Cooperative behaviour contributes to enhanced cohesiveness.

Source: From Prapavessis, H., Carron, A. V., & Spink, K. S. (1996). Team building in sport. *International Journal of Sport Psychology, 27*, p. 275. Used with permission from Edizioni Luigi Pozzi.

changes across groups. As one example, under the group (or team) environment category in the sport setting (see Table 9.1), togetherness and distinctiveness are both factors to be manipulated, whereas under the same category in the exercise setting, only distinctiveness appears.

3. Practical The practical stage is the third part of the workshop. The main purpose of this stage is to have the coaches and exercise leaders become active agents in developing practical strategies that they will use in their own group settings (Carron & Spink, 1993). This is done by having them use the conceptual framework to brainstorm as many specific techniques, procedures, or protocols as possible to be used for team building in their own groups. In the case of exercise groups, the leaders are asked to use distinctiveness, norms, positions, sacrifice, and communication/interaction as frames of reference for generating their techniques. Some representative examples of the specific strategies suggested by the leaders to enhance group cohesiveness in exercise classes are presented in Table 9.2. From the lists of practical suggestions generated, each coach or leader is free to take the suggestions that he or she feels would work best.

4. Interventions In the intervention stage, the coaches and exercise leaders take the team-building protocols that they have developed at the workshop and introduce them into their groups. The duration of the team-building interventions varies across situations (Carron & Spink, 1993). Examples from research in both exercise and sport settings will now be presented to illustrate how the specific interventions are undertaken.

The initial studies into team building using the Carron and Spink (1993) model were conducted in the exercise setting. The purpose was simple—to determine if cohesion in

Table 9.2 Examples of Specific Strategies Suggested by Leaders to Enhance Group Cohesiveness in Exercise Classes

Category	Examples of Specific Strategies
Group Environment	
Distinctiveness	Have a group name. Make up a group T-shirt. Hand out neon headbands and/or shoelaces.
Group Structure	
Individual positions	Have signs to label parts of the group. Use specific positions for low-, medium-, and high-impact exercisers. Let them pick their own spot and encourage them to remain in it throughout the year.
Group norms	Encourage members to become fitness friends. Establish a goal to lose weight together. Promote a smart work ethic as a group characteristic.
Group Processes	
Sacrifices	Ask two or three people for a goal for the day. Ask regulars to help new people (as fitness friends). Ask people who aren't concerned with weight loss to make a sacrifice for the group on some days (more aerobics), and ask people who are concerned with weight loss to make a sacrifice on other days (more mat work).
Interaction and communication	Use partner work and have them introduce themselves to the person on the right and left. Work in groups of five and take turns showing a move. Use more partner activities.

Source: Reprinted, with permission, from Carron, A.V., & Spink, K.S. (1993). Team building in an exercise setting. *The Sport Psychologist, 7*(1):8-18.

exercise classes could be enhanced through a psychological intervention program focusing on team-building concepts and delivered by the exercise leaders. The results revealed that the team-building intervention significantly enhanced the members' cohesion in exercise classes for young adults (Carron & Spink, 1993) and older adults (Watson et al., 2004), as well as youth (Bruner & Spink, 2010).

The Carron and Spink team-building model (1993) also has been used in the sporting realm (Prapavessis et al., 1996). Unfortunately, the results revealed that the team-building intervention was not successful in enhancing levels of cohesion in soccer teams. One reason put forward to explain this result was the idea that sport teams are more complex than exercise groups, and, as such, the team-building intervention may require a different focus.

The fact that team building may be more difficult to implement in the sport setting is echoed in the results of a study examining expert Canadian ice hockey and basketball coaches. This study found that cohesion was perceived to be a complex construct that unfolded over the course of the season (Schinke et al., 1997). Interestingly, the results from studies that examine team building over longer time periods provide different results. Examination of a season-long implementation of a team-building intervention with basketball teams revealed that those in the team-building condition reported higher perceptions of cohesion at the end of the season than those not exposed to the intervention (Senecal et al., 2008). Further positive evidence in the sport setting, albeit more indirect, comes from a Canadian ice hockey study, which found that coaches who had introduced a team-building intervention to their Pee-Wee teams reported that their players bonded during the activities as well as improved their ability to work together as a team (Newin et al., 2008). The results from these latter two studies suggest that team building might be an effective method for enhancing cohesion in a sport team setting over the course of a season.

While the effects of team building are typically perceived to be positive, there is one aspect that may not be so attractive, and that comes in the form of hazing. **Hazing** refers to any activity that a person is expected to do when joining a group that serves to humiliate, degrade, abuse, or endanger that person (Johnson, 2011) (e.g., having rookies wear odd clothing in public places as a type of team initiation). It is often publicly accepted that team-building behaviours such as hazing serve to build cohesion within a team. However, there appears to be a fine line here between which types of hazing build cohesion and which cross the line to demean another's value as a human being. There have been a number of high profile sport cases in Canada in recent years where program cancellations were implemented as a result of hazing involving degrading practices. Two examples at Canadian universities include McGill University cancelling the remainder of its football season in 2005 because of a hazing incident that occurred during an initiation event (Wherry, 2005), and Dalhousie University suspending most of the players on its women's hockey team, thus forcing the forfeit of the team's remaining games in 2013, for a hazing incident that occurred at a house party (Ellwand, 2013). Hazing was also discussed in Chapter 6.

It has been suggested hazing activities that serve to demean, degrade, and embarrass new members to a team are not consistent with developing cohesion within a team and should be eliminated from any team initiation activities (Chin & Johnson, 2011). This suggestion is consistent with the results from a sport study, where it was revealed

Hazing: Using harassment, abuse, or humiliation as a way of initiating new members to a group.

that athletes who reported doing or seeing more hazing-type activities also reported that their teams were less cohesive. This indicates that hazing was associated with less, not more, cohesion (Van Raalte at al., 2007). Hazing should be replaced with positive team-building activities that help to unify the group such as having all players dress for team functions, attend a team skit night, or do community service as a team (Johnson, 2011).

Personal Correlates of Group Cohesion In this third category of correlates of group cohesion, selected personal correlates that have been associated with cohesion will be presented. By personal correlates, we mean those factors that are characteristic of the team members.

Individual Adherence One relationship that has been extensively examined in the exercise setting is the one between perceptions of group cohesiveness and individual adherence. In a series of studies, a greater sense of group cohesiveness (primarily task) was associated with improved adherence behaviour across both structured exercise settings (e.g., classes you sign up for such as a spin class, Fraser & Spink, 2002; Spink & Carron, 1992, 1993; Watson et al., 2004) and unstructured exercise settings (e.g., no sign-up required, such as going for a run with a fellow student or co-worker, Spink et al., 2014). Research in the area of team building has also shown adherence effects wherein those in the classes exposed to the team-building intervention exhibited better adherence than those not in the team-building groups in youth (Bruner & Spink, 2011), and both younger (Spink & Carron, 1993) and older adults (Watson et al., 2004).

To summarize, research findings have revealed that cohesion is related to a wide range of adherence measures. Also, relationships between cohesion and adherence have been found in youth and adults. Finally, research has demonstrated that cohesion can be enhanced in exercise classes through team-building interventions delivered by the exercise leader.

It may not be surprising to learn that cohesion has also been associated with adherence in the sport setting. In an examination of athletes from a number of sports, it has been found that individuals who maintained their involvement with their team as well as exhibited better adherence (i.e., were never late or absent) perceived more task and social cohesiveness than those individuals who dropped out or were frequently absent or late (Carron et al., 1988).

Intention to Return In the previously mentioned studies examining dropout behaviour (Carron et al., 1988; Spink & Carron, 1994), each used a short-term measure of adherence—withdrawal from the current group. What happens when the group disbands? In two Canadian studies (Spink, 1995, 1998), both recreational and elite female ringette players indicated that they would return to play with their team the next season if they perceived that their team was high in social cohesiveness, regardless of where their team ended up in the final league standings. This result has been extended to ice hockey (Spink et al., 2010), where it was found that elite male players who reported higher perceptions of task cohesion at the end of one season actually returned to play for the same team in the following season, regardless of the team's success. Taken together, the results of these three studies suggest that previous research indicating a relationship between cohesion and in-group adherence may be extended to the longer-term measure of intention to participate further with the team, in both male and female team sport settings.

Studies have revealed that, for females, social cohesion tends to be associated with wanting to return to the team for another season; while for males, task cohesion is associated with actual return. How might you explain these cohesion differences?

Individual Effort It has been suggested that individual adherence can manifest itself in other behaviours, such as apathy and reduced work output, which could be construed as a form of effort (Steers & Rhodes, 1978). In one study, Prapavessis and Carron (1997a) examined the relationship between cohesion and work output (i.e., effort) using participants from a variety of sports. They found that work output (measured by percentage of maximum oxygen consumption) was greater for athletes who held higher perceptions of the task cohesiveness of their team. It also was found that soccer players (Bray & Whaley, 2001) who perceived their team to be high in task cohesion were the players who reported working the hardest over the season. These two studies provide evidence that perceptions of a team's cohesiveness are associated with an individual's actual or perceived level of effort in a team-sport setting.

Social loafing: The reduction in individual effort when individuals work collectively compared to when they work alone.

Social Loafing An interesting twist on the cohesion–effort relationship is found in the **social loafing** literature. Social loafing is defined as the reduction in individual effort when individuals work collectively compared with when they work alone (Latane et al., 1979). A meta-analysis by Karau and Williams (1993) revealed that individuals tend to loaf when in groups, and that the effect occurs consistently across many populations and with many different tasks. Although social loafing appears to be a pervasive force when individuals work in groups, increases in group cohesion appear to reduce or eliminate social loafing in the sport setting. In one study examining soccer players, higher levels of team cohesiveness were associated with lower levels of perceived social loafing within the team (Hoigaard et al., 2006).

Individual Sacrifice Another interesting personal variable that has been related to cohesion is the sacrifice that individuals are willing to make for the group. From an intuitive perspective, it might be expected that individuals would want to remain in a group where team members make sacrifices for the group. Holt and Sparkes (2001) examined the factors that members of a collegiate soccer team identified as contributing to team cohesion over the course of an eight-month season. One key theme that they identified as contributing to team cohesion was personal sacrifice by team members.

Prapavessis and Carron (1997b) provided more support for the relationship between cohesion and sacrifice in their investigation of high-level cricket teams in New Zealand. They had team members describe the extent to which they and their teammates regularly made individual sacrifices for their teams, and then the researchers related this to members' perceptions of team cohesiveness. Sacrifices were assessed along two dimensions. The first dimension reflected the distinction between internal sacrifices (e.g., playing another position) and external sacrifices (e.g., lowering work commitments to allow for more team practices). The second dimension captured the distinction between an individual social sacrifice (e.g., "I give up my social life for the team") and teammate social sacrifice (e.g., "My teammates give up their social lives").

The results supported the conclusion that reports of individual sacrifice and teammate sacrifice contributed to team task and social cohesion. Internal sacrifices made by individuals and teammates had the most powerful effect on cohesion. One can only imagine the level of cohesion that existed on the 2008 Canadian Olympic triathlon team, given the sacrifice made by Colin Jenkins for teammate Simon Whitfield. Jenkins appeared to sacrifice his final placing in the Olympics by riding and swimming very hard to allow teammate Whitfield to draft behind him and remain with the lead pack coming into the final run stage of the triathlon, which was Whitfield's strength. After racing hard for the first two legs, Jenkins had nothing left in the tank and finished last overall. However, due in part to the sacrifices of his teammate, Whitfield was able to finish with the Olympic silver medal.

Self-Handicapping What the individual brings to the group can also affect cohesiveness. One such factor is the tendency to self-handicap. If you have ever remarked to a teammate before a big game that you may not play well because you were up all night with a cold, you may have been using a **self-handicapping** strategy. According to Jones and Berglas (1978), self-handicapping involves using strategies that protect one's self-esteem by providing excuses for forthcoming events (see Chapter 5). This is done by providing explanations wherein potential failure can be attributed to external factors (e.g., "I was up all night") rather than to internal factors (e.g., "I'm not prepared").

Self-handicapping: Using strategies that protect one's self-esteem by providing excuses for forthcoming events.

The relationship between team cohesiveness and self-handicapping has been examined in the sport setting. In one study examining male athletes from a number of different sports, a negative relationship was found between the self-handicapping trait and perceptions of task cohesion (Carron et al., 1994). One possibility to explain this relationship might be that the self-handicapper's perception of low task cohesion might be ego protective. If the team fails, the athlete can fall back on the thought, "I'm okay, but I'm not so sure about the team." The athlete externalizes the failure by blaming the team.

Team Correlates of Group Cohesion In team correlates, the final category of correlates of group cohesion, the focus is on those factors that are associated with the team as a unit. Without doubt, the team factor that has been most associated with cohesion over the years is team outcome (team success). The assumption is that when team cohesion is strong, the group is motivated to perform well and is better able to coordinate activities that will lead to a positive team outcome (Cartwright, 1968).

Team Success Given the insight provided by researchers (Cartwright, 1968) and the claims by coaches and athletes (see earlier quotes by Brad Gushue and Michael Jordan) about the proposed association between team cohesion and team success, it may come as a surprise that the research findings in this area have been mixed. There are studies showing that greater levels of team cohesion lead to success in intercollegiate ice hockey (Ball & Carron, 1976), studies showing that lesser levels of team cohesion lead to success in international rowing teams (Lenk, 1969), and studies showing no relationship between cohesion and team success in intramural basketball teams (Melnick & Chemers, 1974).

Based on the results of a meta-analysis, Mullen and Copper (1994) concluded that a small but significant positive relationship exists between cohesion and performance across many groups and tasks. Three other specific suggestions from their analysis were the following. First, the cohesion–performance relationship was strongest when cohesion was measured as task commitment (similar to task cohesion) rather than as social cohesion. Second, the cohesion–performance relationship was stronger in real groups (naturally occurring) than in artificial (ad hoc formed for experiment) groups. Third, within real groups, the link was strongest in sport teams.

Canadian researchers Carron et al. (2002) conducted a more focused meta-analysis wherein they examined the cohesion–performance relationship using only studies conducted with sport teams. Based on their analysis of 46 sport studies, they concluded that there was a moderate to large relationship between cohesion and performance. This is consistent with Mullen and Copper's (1994) suggestion that the cohesion–performance relationship is strongest in real groups, especially sport teams. In a third meta-analysis, Beal and colleagues (2003) also found that task and social cohesion related to performance across multiple group settings. They also reported that the relationship between cohesion and performance was stronger when performance was defined as behaviour (i.e., actions relevant to achieving the outcome) as opposed to outcome (i.e., results of behaviours).

Despite the mixed results from past research, the results from these three meta-analyses provide some strong evidence that cohesion and performance are related. Although this relationship appears to be established, one question still remains: Which is stronger, cohesion leading to performance or performance leading to cohesion?

This is an important question because it captures the essence of that age-old belief of coaches and athletes alike—that having more cohesiveness will lead to more wins. Unfortunately, at the present time, the research does not support this belief. From the results of Mullen and Copper's (1994) meta-analysis, it was concluded that there was more support for success leading to cohesion than for cohesion leading to success. The results from the Carron et al. (2002) meta-analysis using only sport teams found no difference. However, the results from a qualitative analysis of English soccer teams found that players believed that strong team cohesion had a positive influence on performance (Pain & Harwood, 2007). Despite these mixed results, the fact still remains that there is some evidence that task and social cohesion are associated with better performance.

Collective Efficacy for Cohesion Performance (team success) is the team correlate that has received the most attention in the research literature; however, there are other proposed correlates of team cohesion. One such correlate is **collective efficacy**. The term was coined by Bandura (1977) to capture the idea that groups often have collective expectations for success. There has been speculation that different properties of a group, such as cohesion, have great potential to contribute to a team's sense of efficacy (Spink, 1990a), and this has been borne out in the sport literature. In one Canadian study examining the relationship between cohesion and collective efficacy in volleyball teams, it was found that teams high in collective efficacy rated task and social cohesion higher than teams lower in collective efficacy (Spink, 1990b). Of interest, this relationship was found only for elite teams, not for recreational teams. In another study, which also examined

Collective efficacy: A group's shared perception of the group's capabilities to succeed at a given task.

volleyball teams in Canada, task cohesion measures differentiated between athletes who were low or high in their perception of their team's overall collective efficacy (Paskevich et al., 1999).

Psychological Momentum The "Big Mo" is another team factor that appears to be related to team cohesion. **Psychological momentum** refers to a perception on the part of team members that the team is progressing toward its goal. This definition was adapted from one posited for individual behaviour by Vallerand and colleagues (1988). The idea that cohesion and psychological momentum might be linked is not new. In one of the first works to discuss the effect of psychological momentum in sport events, Adler (1981) suggested that perceptions of psychological momentum and cohesion are linked. He went further by suggesting that coaches in team sports should attempt to develop a perception of cohesion in order to create a team climate favourable to momentum.

> Psychological momentum: A perception on the part of team members that the team is progressing toward its goal.

In the only test of this possible relationship in the sport setting, the relationship between perceptions of task cohesion and psychological momentum in high school volleyball teams was examined (Eisler & Spink, 1998). Results revealed that members of highly cohesive teams rated their team as possessing more psychological momentum than did the members of teams perceived as less cohesive. This finding supports Adler's (1981) contention that the development of cohesion creates a climate favourable to the perception of psychological momentum.

Athlete's Starting Status Another team factor linked to cohesion is the impact of an athlete's starting status. In one of the first studies to examine this relationship, Granito and Rainey (1988) found that players at both the high school and college levels who were selected to start games scored higher on measures of task cohesion than players who were not selected to start. In an extension of this result, an examination was undertaken of the perceived cohesion levels of starters and non-starters on less successful and more successful Canadian volleyball teams (Spink, 1992). Results revealed that starters perceived more task cohesion on their team than did non-starters, which supports the Granito and Rainey (1988) result. However, this occurred only on teams that were less successful. On teams that were more successful, there were no differences in the levels of perceived cohesion between the starters and non-starters. From the results of this study, it appears that team success might serve to ameliorate the possible negative impact of not starting and help to maintain task cohesion.

Group Cohesion as a Mediator

Mediators are mechanisms that account for the effect of one variable on another variable. Examples have appeared in the literature that illustrate that cohesion does, in fact, act as a mediator in a number of important relationships.

> Mediators: Mechanisms that account for the effect of one variable on another variable.

We have already come across one important example of cohesion acting as a mediator, and that involved team-building research. As you will recall, in the Carron and Spink (1993) team-building model, it was stated that team building impacts adherence through the mechanism of cohesion. In another study in the sport setting, social cohesion was examined as a mediator between leadership behaviour and intention to return to sport (Spink, 1998). Using female ringette players, it was found that specific forms of leadership behaviour (i.e., training and instruction) predicted who intended to return to the sport the next season, but the effect was minimized when social cohesion was added

In the 2014 Sochi Winter Olympics, the Canadian men's team won the gold medal in convincing fashion. They beat Team Sweden in the gold-medal game 3–0. In six tournament games, the team had three shootouts and allowed only three goals against while scoring seventeen, with six coming in one game. Also, two Canadians were selected to the all-star team, defenceman Drew Doughty and goaltender Carey Price. These are interesting outcomes given that before the tournament began, some pundits were suggesting that although the Canadian team was strong offensively, it might have some issues defensively as the blue liners weren't as strong as the forwards and there was no clear choice for a starting goaltender. Yet, most would agree that Canada won the gold medal based on the strength of its team defence and goaltending.

Was this simply another example of the old sport adage that "defence wins championships," or was there something else at play here? Consider the following quote from alternate captain, Jonathan Toews, following the victory, "I think everyone knows the talent and ability this team has and huge credit goes to our commitment to playing the team game" (Brophy, 2014).

Although the word *cohesion* was not mentioned, it was likely implied as cohesion has been defined as the tendency for a group to stick together and remain united in the pursuit of its instrumental objectives. In the case of Team Canada, that was the united pursuit of the "team" game, as noted in the quote. And, in the united pursuit of that valued objective, it is likely that many of the correlates associated with a cohesive team outlined in this chapter such as increased effort, the ability to make sacrifices for

the team, and a strong belief in the collective efficacy of the team all contributed in some way to the gold-medal winning performance.

Bruce Bennett/Getty Images Sport/Getty Images

to the prediction. The fact that the relationship between leadership and intention to return disappeared when social cohesion was entered suggests that social cohesion was the mechanism through which leadership behaviour was affecting intention to return (see Figure 9.4).

Two studies by Canadian researchers in the exercise setting provide further support for cohesion as an important mediator. The first study revealed that task cohesion mediated the relationship between an exercise leader's behaviours (i.e., availability, motivation, and enthusiasm) and both attendance and perceived exertion in older adult exercisers (Loughead et al., 2001). This suggests that exercise leaders need to engage in availability, motivation, and enthusiasm to increase the group's task cohesion, which, in turn, will improve the attendance and perceived exertion of older exercisers.

Figure 9.4 Proposed mediation model

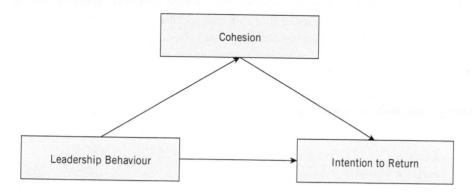

The second study examined whether cohesion in youth sport would mediate the relationship between athlete leadership and satisfaction (Paradis & Loughead, 2012). Results revealed that both task and social cohesion mediated the relationship between athlete leadership behaviours as assessed by the LSS and task athlete and social athlete satisfaction outcomes, respectively. The results from these three studies suggest that cohesion can be an important mechanism explaining other common relationships in the sport and exercise settings.

CHAPTER SUMMARY

After reading this chapter, it should be quite clear that a team is much more than the sum of its individual members, and that several group processes are associated with the effectiveness of a team. It also should be clear why team cohesion is often portrayed as the key group element that is associated with many factors that are of consequence to the group and the individual. Also, the importance of understanding cohesion goes well beyond examining its relationship to team performance. There is still much more to understand about cohesion as it relates to sport and physical activity, so more research is needed. In particular, one area that seems to be missing concerns the examination of gender differences. As males and females may have different reasons for joining a team or an exercise group, it is possible that this might translate into differences in perceptions of cohesion. This awaits future research. Despite the need for more research, several points about group cohesion have strong support within the research community. Cohesion was viewed as a unidimensional construct but is now viewed as a multidimensional construct that incorporates at least two dimensions: the individual/group orientation and a task/social distinction. To assess cohesion in the sport setting, the Group Environment Questionnaire is the instrument of choice. The research literature is replete with examples demonstrating that cohesion is related to a number of important environmental, leadership, personal, and team factors. There also is evidence that team-building strategies implemented by exercise leaders or coaches can enhance cohesion in both the exercise and sport setting.

Although it is typically believed by coaches and athletes that cohesion will increase team success, this is not fully supported in the research literature; however, the fact remains that there is some evidence that task and social cohesion contribute to better performance. There is also emerging evidence that cohesion can be used to account for other important relationships. For instance, some research has demonstrated that cohesion is one mechanism to explain why various leadership behaviours may be related to a number of important outcomes, including attendance, intention to return, perceived exertion, and affective states.

 ## COMMON MYTHS ABOUT GROUP COHESION IN SPORT AND EXERCISE REVISITED

MYTH: Team harmony is required for cohesion to develop.
For many coaches, team harmony is synonymous with team cohesion. Conversely, they see slim chances of cohesion developing within a team if there is any form of intrateam conflict. Although this has a nice intuitive feel, research suggests otherwise. As an example, a study by Sullivan and Feltz (2001) with ice hockey teams revealed that negative (destructive) intrateam conflict was associated with lower cohesion, but that positive (constructive) intrateam conflict was associated with higher team cohesion.

MYTH: "There is no 'I' in TEAM."
The standard locker-room fare of "There is no 'I' in TEAM" makes good press, but it does not hold up well in the scientific literature. This statement implies that members of a group are generally less important than the group as a collective; however, there is little scientific evidence to support this contention. It is generally accepted by the scientific community that cohesion is a multidimensional construct that incorporates both group and individual components (Carron et al., 1985). Individuals join and remain in groups for many reasons, and it has been acknowledged that individuals' cognitions about the cohesiveness of their team reflect the overall group as well as the manner in which the group satisfies individual needs (Carron et al., 1998), suggesting that the needs and wants of the individual must be recognized when one examines group cohesion.

MYTH: High cohesion is always a good thing.
There is an old saying that "If a little is good, then more is better." For many people, this saying certainly applies to cohesion since there is a general understanding among lay people that a team and its members glean more benefits as the cohesiveness of the group increases. While it would make life simpler for those who wanted to use the power of group closeness to increase benefits to the team and individuals alike, research suggests that there might be disadvantages to being in a highly cohesive group. In one study examining the consequences of high levels of cohesiveness in sports teams, 56% of the athletes questioned reported possible disadvantages associated with social cohesion, and 31% reported possible disadvantages associated with being on a team high in task cohesion (Hardy et al., 2005).

Review Questions

1. Why is it important to study groups?

2. What is the definition of *group dynamics*?

3. What are three suggestions for improving team communication?

4. What is the definition of *groupthink*? How might groupthink hinder the performance of a group?

5. What are the main differences between the two definitions of cohesion advanced by Bert Carron?

6. Identify the four key characteristics of cohesion.

7. Identify and briefly describe the sport-specific questionnaires that have been used to assess cohesion. Which is the most useful one, and why?

8. Briefly outline the conceptual model of group cohesion.

9. What is the main difference between direct and indirect team-building procedures? Which approach would you use if you were trying to enhance cohesion in a basketball team? Why?

10. Outline the four stages in the team-building model.

11. Identify and briefly explain the relationship between cohesion and the six personal correlates.

12. Identify and describe two relationships in which cohesion has been examined as a mediator.

Suggested Reading

Carron, A. V., & Eys, M. A. (2012). *Group dynamics in sport* (4th ed.). Morgantown, WV: Fitness Information Technology.

Spink, K. (2014). Team building. In R. Eklund, & G. Tenenbaum (Eds.), *Encyclopedia of sport and exercise psychology*. (Vol. 19, pp. 741–744). Thousand Oaks, CA: Sage Publications, Inc.

References

Adler, P. (1981). *Momentum: A theory of social action*. Beverly Hills, CA: Sage.

Ball, J. R., & Carron, A. V. (1976). The influence of team cohesion and participation motivation upon performance success in intercollegiate ice hockey. *Canadian Journal of Applied Sport Sciences, 1*, 271–275.

Bandura, A. (1977). Self-efficacy: Toward a unifying theory of behavioural change. *Psychological Review, 84*, 191–215.

Bass, B. M. (1985). *Leadership and performance beyond expectations*. New York: Free Press.

Beal, D. J., Cohen, R., Burke, M. J., & McLendon, C. L. (2003). Cohesion and performance in groups: A meta-analytic clarification of construct relations. *Journal of Applied Psychology, 88*, 989–1004.

Brawley, L. R., & Paskevich, D. M. (1997). Conducting team building research in the context of sport and exercise. *Journal of Applied Sport Psychology, 9*, 11–40.

Bray, C. D., & Whaley, D. E. (2001). Team cohesion, effort, and objective individual performance of high school basketball players. *The Sport Psychologist, 15*, 260–275.

Brophy, M. (2014). Carey Price most valuable of Olympic goalies. CBC Sochi 2014. Retrieved from http://olympics.cbc.ca/news/article/carey-price-most-valuable-olympic-goalies.html.

Bruner, M., & Spink, K. S. (2010). Evaluating a team-building intervention in a youth exercise setting. *Group Dynamics: Theory, Research, and Practice, 14,* 304–317.

Bruner, M., & Spink, K. S. (2011). Effects of team building on exercise adherence and group task satisfaction in a youth activity setting. *Group Dynamics: Theory, Research, and Practice, 15,* 161–172.

Carron, A. V. (1982). Cohesiveness in sport groups: Interpretations and considerations. *Journal of Sport Psychology, 4,* 123–138.

Carron, A. V., Brawley, L. R., & Widmeyer, W. N. (1998). The measurement of cohesiveness in sport groups. In J. L. Duda (Ed.), *Advancements in sport and exercise psychology measurement* (pp. 213–226). Morgantown, WV: Fitness Information Technology.

Carron, A. V., Colman, M. M., Wheeler, J., & Stevens, D. (2002). Cohesion and performance in sport: A meta-analysis. *Journal of Sport & Exercise Psychology, 24,* 168–188.

Carron, A. V., & Eys, M. A. (2012). *Group dynamics in sport* (4th ed.). Morgantown, WV: Fitness Information Technology.

Carron, A. V., Prapavessis, H., & Grove, J. R. (1994). Group effects and self-handicapping. *Journal of Sport & Exercise Psychology, 16,* 246–258.

Carron, A. V., & Spink, K. S. (1992). Internal consistency of the Group Environment Questionnaire modified for an exercise setting. *Perceptual and Motor Skills, 74,* 1075–1078.

Carron, A. V., & Spink, K. S. (1993). Team building in an exercise setting. *The Sport Psychologist, 7,* 8–18.

Carron, A. V., & Spink, K. S. (1995). The group size–cohesion relationship in exercise groups. *Small Group Research, 26,* 86–105.

Carron, A. V., Widmeyer, W. N., & Brawley, L. R. (1985). The development of an instrument to assess cohesion in sport teams: The Group Environment Questionnaire. *Journal of Sport Psychology, 7,* 244–266.

Carron, A. V., Widmeyer, W. N., & Brawley, L. R. (1988). Group cohesion and individual adherence to physical activity. *Journal of Sport & Exercise Psychology, 10,* 119–126.

Cartwright, D. (1968). The nature of group cohesiveness. In D. Cartwright & A. Zander (Eds.), *Group dynamics: Research and theory* (pp. 91–109). New York: Harper & Row.

Cartwright, D., & Zander, A. (1968). *Group dynamics: Research and theory.* New York: Harper & Row.

Chelladurai, P., & Saleh, S. D. (1980). Dimensions of leadership behaviour in sport: Development of a leadership scale. *Journal of Sport Psychology, 2,* 34–45.

Chin, J. W., & Johnson, J. (2011). Making the team: Threats to health and wellness within sport hazing cultures. *The International Journal of Health, Wellness and Society, 1,* 29–38.

Cota, A. A., Evans, C. R., Dion, K. L., Kilik, L., & Longman, R. S. (1995). The structure of group cohesion. *Personality and Social Psychological Bulletin, 21,* 572–580.

Dawson, K. A., Bray, S. R., & Widmeyer, W. N. (2002). Goal setting by intercollegiate sport teams and athletes. *Avante, 8,* 14–23.

Dunlop, W. L., Falk, C. F., & Beauchamp, M. R. (2013). How dynamic are exercise group dynamics? Examining changes in cohesion within class-based exercise programs. *Health Psychology, 32,* 1240–1243.

Eisler, L., & Spink, K. S. (1998). Effects of scoring configuration and task cohesion on the perception of psychological momentum. *Journal of Sport & Exercise Psychology, 20,* 311–320.

Ellwand, O. (2013, January 8). UNBSJ teams review hazing policy after incident at Dal; sports university created hazing policy last year in response to incidents in the U.S. and Canada. *Telegraph-Journal.* Retrieved from http://search.proquest.com/docview/1266993444?accountid=14739.

Estabrooks, P. A., & Carron, A. V. (1999). Group cohesion in older adult exercisers: Prediction and intervention effects. *Journal of Behavioral Medicine, 22,* 575–588.

Estabrooks, P. A., & Carron, A. V. (2000). The Physical Activity Group Environment Questionnaire: An instrument for the assessment of cohesion in exercise classes. *Group Dynamics, 4*, 230–243.

Eys, M. A., Carron, A. V., Bray, S. R., & Brawley, L. R. (2007). Item wording and internal consistency of a measure of cohesion: The Group Environment Questionnaire. *Journal of Sport & Exercise Psychology, 29*, 395–402.

Eys, M. A., Loughead, T. M., Bray, S. R., & Carron, A. V. (2009). Development of a cohesion questionnaire for youth: The Youth Sport Environment Questionnaire. *Journal of Sport & Exercise Psychology, 31*, 390–408.

Festinger, L. (1950). Informal social communication. *Psychological Review, 57*, 271–282.

Fraser, S., & Spink, K. S. (2002). Examining social support and group cohesion in the compliance behaviour of females in a health-related exercise setting. *Journal of Behavioral Medicine, 25*, 233–249.

Gardner, D. E., Shields, D. L., Bredemeier, B. J., & Bostrom, A. (1996). The relationship between perceived coaching behaviours and team cohesion among baseball and softball players. *The Sport Psychologist, 10*, 367–381.

Granito, V. J., & Rainey, D. W. (1988). Differences in cohesion between high school and college football teams and starters and nonstarters. *Perceptual and Motor Skills, 66*, 471–477.

Harden, S. M., Estabrooks, P. A., Mama, S. K., & Lee, R. E. (2014). Longitudinal analysis of minority women's perceptions of cohesion: The role of cooperation, communication, and competition. *International Journal of Behavioral Nutrition and Physical Activity, 11*, 57–65.

Hardy, J., Eys, M. A., & Carron, A. V. (2005). Exploring the potential disadvantages of high cohesion in sports teams. *Small Group Research, 36*, 166–187.

Hastie, R., & Kameda, T. (2005). The robust beauty of majority rules in group decisions. *Psychological Review, 112*, 494–508.

Hoigaard, R., Safvenbom, R., & Tonnessen, F. E. (2006). The relationship between group cohesion, group norms, and perceived social loafing in soccer teams. *Small Group Research, 37*, 217–232.

Holt, N. L., & Sparkes, A. C. (2001). An ethnographic study of cohesiveness in a college soccer team over a season. *The Sport Psychologist, 15*, 237–259.

Janis, I. (2007). Groupthink. In R. P. Vecchio (Ed.), *Leadership: Understanding the dynamics of power and influence in organizations* (2nd ed., pp. 157–169). Notre Dame, IN: University of Notre Dame Press.

Johnson, J. (2011). Through the liminal: A comparative analysis of communitas and rites of passage in sport hazing and initiations. *Canadian Journal of Sociology, 36*, 199–227.

Jones, E. E., & Berglas, S. (1978). Control of attributions about the self through self-handicapping strategies: The appeal of alcohol and the role of underachievement. *Personality and Social Psychology Bulletin, 4*, 200–206.

Jordan, M. (1994). *I can't accept not trying*. San Francisco: Harper.

Jowett, S., & Chaundy, V. (2004). An investigation into the impact of coach leadership and coach–athlete relationships on group cohesion. *Groups Dynamics, 8*, 302–311.

Karau, S. J., & Williams, K. D. (1993). Social loafing: A meta-analytic review and theoretical integration. *Journal of Personality and Social Psychology, 65*, 681–706.

Latane, B., Williams, K., & Harkins, S. (1979). Many hands make light the work: The causes and consequences of social loafing. *Journal of Personality and Social Psychology, 37*, 822–832.

Lenk, H. (1969). Top performance despite internal conflict: An antithesis to a functional proposition. In J. W. Loy & G. S. Kenyon (Eds.), *Sport, culture and society* (pp. 393–397). New York: Macmillan.

Locke, E. A., & Latham, G. P. (1984). *Goal setting: A motivational technique that works*. Englewood Cliffs, NJ: Prentice Hall.

Lott, A. J., & Lott, B. E. (1965). Group cohesiveness as interpersonal attraction: A review of relationships with antecedent and consequent variables. *Psychological Bulletin, 64*, 259–309.

Loughead, T. M., Colman, M. M., & Carron, A. V. (2001). Investigating the mediational relationship of leadership, class cohesion and adherence in an exercise setting. *Small Group Research, 32*, 558–575.

Marcos, F. M., Miguel, P. A., Oliva, D. S., & Calvo, T. G. (2010). Interactive effects of team cohesion on perceived efficacy in semi-professional sport. *Journal of Sports Science and Medicine, 9*, 320–325.

Martens, R., Landers, D. M., & Loy, J. W. (1972). *Sport cohesiveness questionnaire*. Washington, DC: AAHPERD Publications.

Martin, L. J., Bruner, M. A., Eys, M. A., & Spink, K. S. (2014). The social environment in sport: Selected topics. *International Review of Sport and Exercise Psychology, 7*, 87–105.

Martin, L. J., Carron, A. V., Eys, M. A., & Loughead, T. M. (2012). Development of a cohesion inventory for children's sport teams. *Group Dynamics: Theory, Research, and Practice, 16*, 68–79.

Melnick, M. J., & Chemers, M. (1974). Effects of group social structure on the success of basketball teams. *Research Quarterly, 45*, 1–8.

Mudrack, P. E. (1989). Defining group cohesiveness. A legacy of confusion? *Small Group Behavior, 20*, 37–49.

Mullen, B., & Copper, C. (1994). The relation between group cohesiveness and performance: An integration. *Psychological Bulletin, 115*, 210–227.

Murray, N. P. (2006). The differential effect of team cohesion and leadership behavior in high school sports. *Individual Differences Research, 4*, 216–222.

Newin, J., Bloom, G. A., & Loughead, T. M. (2008). Youth ice hockey coaches' perceptions of a team-building intervention program. *The Sport Psychologist, 22*, 54–72.

Pain, M. A., & Harwood, C. (2007). The performance environment of the England youth soccer teams. *Journal of Sports Sciences, 25*, 1307–1324.

Paradis, K. F., & Loughead, T. M. (2012). Examining the mediating role of cohesion between athlete leadership and athlete satisfaction in youth sport. *International Journal of Sport Psychology, 43*, 117–136.

Paskevich, D. M., Brawley, L. R., Dorsch, L. R., & Widmeyer, W. N. (1999). Relationships between collective efficacy and team measurement factors. *Group Dynamics, 3*, 210–222.

Pease, D. G., & Kozub, S. A. (1994). Perceived coaching behaviours and team cohesion in high school girls' basketball teams. *Journal of Sport & Exercise Psychology, 16*, S93.

Prapavessis, H., & Carron, A. V. (1997a). Cohesion and work output. *Small Group Research, 28*, 294–301.

Prapavessis, H., & Carron, A. V. (1997b). Sacrifice, cohesion, and conformity to norms in sport teams. *Group Dynamics, 1*, 231–240.

Prapavessis, H., Carron, A. V., & Spink, K. S. (1996). Team building in sport. *International Journal of Sport Psychology, 27*, 269–285.

Rosenberg, S., Erlick, D., & Berkowitz, L. (1955). Some effects of varying combinations of group members on group performance measures and leadership behaviors. *Journal of Abnormal and Social Psychology, 51*, 195–203.

Schinke, R. J., Draper, S. P., & Salmela, J. H. (1997). A conceptualization of team building in high performance sport as a season-long process. *Avante, 3*, 57–72.

Senecal, J., Loughead, T. M., & Bloom, G. A. (2008). A season-long team-building intervention: Examining the effect of team goal setting on cohesion. *Journal of Sport & Exercise Psychology, 30*, 186–199.

Shaw, M. E. (1976). *Group dynamics: The psychology of small group behaviour*. New York: McGraw-Hill.

Spink, K. S. (1990a). Collective efficacy in the sport setting. *International Journal of Sport Psychology*, 21, 380–393.

Spink, K. S. (1990b). Group cohesion and collective efficacy in volleyball teams. *Journal of Sport & Exercise Psychology*, 12, 301–311.

Spink, K. S. (1992). Group cohesion and starting status in successful and less successful elite volleyball teams. *Journal of Sports Sciences*, 10, 379–388.

Spink, K. S. (1995). Cohesion and intention to participate of female sport team athletes. *Journal of Sport & Exercise Psychology*, 17, 416–427.

Spink, K. S. (1998). Mediational effects of social cohesion on the leadership–intention to return relationship in sport. *Group Dynamics*, 2, 92–100.

Spink, K. (2014). Team building. In R. Eklund & G. Tenenbaum (Eds.), *Encyclopedia of sport and exercise psychology*. (Vol. 19, pp. 741–744). Thousand Oaks, CA: Sage Publications, Inc.

Spink, K. S., & Carron, A. V. (1992). Group cohesion and adherence in exercise classes. *Journal of Sport & Exercise Psychology*, 14, 78–86.

Spink, K. S., & Carron, A. V. (1993). The effects of team building on the adherence patterns of female exercise participants. *Journal of Sport & Exercise Psychology*, 15, 39–49.

Spink, K. S., & Carron, A. V. (1994). Group cohesion effects in exercise classes. *Small Group Research*, 25, 26–42.

Spink, K. S., Nickel, D., Wilson, K., & Odnokon, P. (2005). Examining the relationship between task cohesion and team task satisfaction in elite ice hockey players: A multilevel approach. *Small Group Research*, 36, 539–554.

Spink, K. S., Ulvick, J. D., Crozier, A. J., & Wilson, K. S., (2014). Group cohesion and adherence in unstructured exercise groups. *Psychology of Sport and Exercise*, 15, 293–298.

Spink, K. S., Wilson, K., & Odnokon, P. (2010). Examining the relationship between cohesion and return to team in elite athletes. *Psychology of Sport and Exercise*, 11, 6–11.

Steers, R., & Rhodes, S. (1978). Major influences of employee attendance: A process model. *Journal of Applied Psychology*, 63, 391–407.

Sullivan, P., & Feltz, D. (2001). The relationship between intrateam conflict and cohesion within hockey teams. *Small Group Research*, 32, 342–355.

Vallerand, R. J., Colavecchio, P. G., & Pelletier, L. G. (1988). Psychological momentum and performance inferences: A preliminary test of the antecedents–consequences psychological momentum model. *Journal of Sport & Exercise Psychology*, 10, 92–108.

Van Raalte, J. L., Cornelius, A. E., Linder, D. E., & Brewer, B. W. (2007). The relationship between hazing and team cohesion. *Journal of Sport Behavior*, 30, 491–507.

Vincer, J. E., & Loughead, T. M. (2010). The relationship among athlete leadership behaviors and cohesion in team sports. *The Sport Psychologist*, 24, 448–467.

Watson, J. D., Martin Ginis, K. A., & Spink, K. S. (2004). Team building in an exercise class for the elderly. *Activities, Adaptation, & Aging*, 28, 35–47.

Westre, K. R., & Weiss, M. R. (1991). The relationship between perceived coaching behaviors and group cohesion in high school football teams. *The Sport Psychologist*, 5, 41–54.

Wherry, A. (2005, October 19). McGill ends season over hazing: *National Post*. Retrieved from http://search.proquest.com/docview/330397252?accountid=14739

Whitton, S., & Fletcher, R. (2014). The Group Environment Questionnaire: A multilevel confirmatory factor analysis. *Small Group Research*, 45, 68–88.

Widmeyer, W. N., Brawley, L. R., & Carron, A. V. (1990). The effects of group size in sport. *Journal of Sport & Exercise Psychology*, 12, 177–190.

Zander, A. (1971). *Motives and goals in groups*. New York: Academic Press.

Chapter 10
Youth Involvement and Positive Development in Sport

Jean Côté   Jessica Fraser-Thomas

Hero Images/Getty Images

Chapter Objectives

After reading this chapter, you should be able to do the following:

1   Define the objectives of youth sport.
2   Describe the positive and negative outcomes that can result from youth sport involvement.
3   Understand the frameworks of positive youth development as applied to youth sport.
4   Discuss youth sport programs and the types of activities likely to lead to positive sport experiences.
5   Discuss how coaches, parents, peers, and siblings can influence positive youth sport involvement.
6   Understand the different pathways and outcomes of youth sport program settings and the developmental model of sport participation.

Support for the writing of this chapter was provided from the Social Sciences and Humanities Research Council of Canada through a Standard Research Grant (SSHRC Grant 410-2011-0472) and a Sport Participation Research Initiative Grant (SSHRC 862-2011-0007).

When aged 7–12, Sebastian and Olivia were neighbours and played on the same local hockey team. In the summer, they played soccer and tennis. They also liked swimming and playing pickup basketball and street hockey in their free time. Their soccer coach, Nick, was a physical education teacher and had many years of experience coaching youth sport. As a coach, Nick taught sport skills sequentially and logically, providing informative, positive, and constructive feedback to his players. Nick believed that sports offered children opportunities to learn important life skills, such as cooperation, responsibility, empathy, respect, and self-control. Accordingly, he modelled these behaviours during practices and games and discussed these life skills with his players. Nick's teams were never the best in the league; however, Nick's goal was to make sure that all his players loved the game and felt good about their sport participation. At age 30, Sebastian and Olivia attribute many of their current successes to the values they learned through their youth sport participation. Sebastian is now an award-winning teacher and a recreational tennis player. Olivia obtained a graduate degree in kinesiology, played university hockey, and is now a member of the women's national hockey team.

Two other children, Madelyn and Rachel, had very different experiences from each other in youth sports. They played hockey year-round when aged 5–12. They were highly involved as early as age 5 in extra hockey training, such as power skating lessons and hockey schools. At age 13, Madelyn dropped out of hockey and did not get involved in any other sports. Now, at age 30, she has a successful career but is not regularly involved in any type of physical activity. She does not have particularly positive memories of her youth sport experiences. Rachel, on the other hand, also 30, is now playing on a line with Olivia on the women's national hockey team. Rachel's life has always revolved around hockey, and she has not yet had a chance to think about what she will do when she retires from hockey.

The final example is Michael: he never had the opportunity to participate in youth sport or other extracurricular activities, such as music or art. He spent much of his youth in unstructured leisure activities, such as watching television or hanging out with friends. At age 30, he has a sedentary lifestyle, is overweight, and is struggling to find a meaningful career.

These scenarios describe a number of different youth sport experiences and outcomes. Sebastian and Olivia were fortunate to experience various sports during their childhood. They had coaches who taught them skills while being caring and understanding. For Sebastian, his youth sport experiences did not lead to elite performance; however, his positive sport experiences helped him to understand the value of regular physical activity and health and gave him assets that helped his personal and professional development. Madelyn and Rachel were intensely involved in one sport from ages 5 to 12 and accordingly developed high-level skills. Rachel persisted with her training and eventually was selected for the national team; on the other hand, Madelyn showed signs of burnout and completely dropped out of hockey and other sports at age 13. Madelyn's intense training at a young age reduced her enjoyment of hockey and eventually led her to an inactive lifestyle. Unfortunately, Michael did not have opportunities to get involved in sports or other extracurricular activities. Spending less time in constructive leisure activities, such as sports, may have limited the number of developmental assets that Michael acquired as a child, which in turn may have led him to a more apathetic lifestyle.

The above scenarios illustrate explicit experiences and outcomes of youth sport that are not always evident. Nevertheless, the scenarios provide examples that raise a number of questions about youth sport involvement. What is the goal of youth sport? What are the best social contexts and training patterns for youth sport participation? How should contexts and training patterns change according to children's age and development? In this chapter, we will provide answers to these and other questions related to youth sport involvement.

 COMMON MYTHS ABOUT YOUTH INVOLVEMENT IN SPORT

MYTH: Involvement in youth sport automatically builds character.

MYTH: Involvement in sport most often leads to negative outcomes, such as violence and aggression.

MYTH: To become elite athletes, children must specialize in their sport by age six or seven.

MYTH: Parents should limit their involvement in their children's sport.

MYTH: Youth sport coaches should be specialists in the sport that they are coaching.

INTRODUCTION

Data from Statistics Canada show that 2 million Canadian children aged 5 to 14 (51%) regularly take part in organized sports (Clark, 2008). The significance of sport involvement for youth is considerable given that most children typically begin their involvement in organized sport when they are in their formative years (Smoll & Smith, 2002). Developmental psychologists have shown, through an emerging research approach called **positive youth development** (PYD), that extracurricular activities, like sport, provide an ideal context to develop thriving youth who will eventually give back to their community. For example, Larson (2000) reviewed the PYD literature and showed that sport activities provide young people with a context that they enjoy, and require sustained concentration. He suggested that these two characteristics of organized activities, such as sport, are critical to the development of initiative and overall positive life skills. Although sport has been shown to be an ideal activity to develop personal assets in youth, there is growing concern around the world that youth sport programs are becoming institutionalized and overorganized, focusing mainly on the development of **sport skills** and performance outcomes often at the cost of **personal development** and continued participation for a large number of young people. Accordingly, an extensive body of research has been conducted in sport to examine the personal factors (e.g., training, confidence, motivation) and social factors (e.g., coaches, parents, peers, and siblings) that are more likely to lead to positive outcomes (Fraser-Thomas et al, 2005). Although sport studies have used different research approaches and theories to examine the positive and negative outcomes that result from sport participation, the PYD research movement that originated from developmental psychology has rapidly gained popularity among youth sport researchers (see Holt, 2008). A PYD approach to youth sport focuses on the personal assets and strengths of all youth to achieve the positive outcomes of sport involvement.

Positive youth development: A strengths-based view of children and adolescents.

Sport skills: Learned abilities related to sport participation and performance.

Personal development: Improvements in self-awareness and initiative.

OBJECTIVES OF YOUTH SPORT

Youth sport has the potential to accomplish three important objectives in children's development. First, sport programs provide youth with opportunities to be physically active, which can lead to improved physical health through sport *participation*. Second, youth sport programs have long been considered important to youth's *personal development*, providing opportunities to learn important life skills such as cooperation, discipline, leadership, and self-control. Third, youth sport programs are critical for the learning and *performance* of motor skills; this *performance* objective constitutes the foundation for future national sport stars and recreational adult sport participants. Youth sport programs are often designed to achieve one of the "three P outcomes" or "3Ps"—*performance, participation*, or *personal development*. Instead of focusing on one outcome, this chapter presents a global picture of youth sport that provides opportunities for all of the 3Ps (Côté & Hancock, 2014).

It is important that youth sport programs focus on all of the 3Ps rather than just one or two at the cost of the others. For example, a youth sport program that focuses solely on performance at the cost of children's physical health and psychosocial development (i.e., participation and personal development) would be inefficient. Similarly, a sole focus on personal development at the cost of developing fundamental sport skills and children's participation would limit the potential influence of sport on children's overall development. Instead, youth sport programs that focus on fun, skill development, and maximum participation encourage people to stay involved and achieve success at all developmental stages of life and at all levels of sport. To promote a culture of sport participation and performance, the roles of physical education, school sports, recreational sports, and performance sports should all be linked because the independent development of these programs is expensive and ineffective. Thus, by focusing on the common building blocks that all young people need, we can reduce costs and increase the benefits associated with youth sport involvement.

REFLECTIONS 10.1

There are three primary objectives of youth sport: to improve children's physical health (e.g., participation), to promote positive psychosocial development (e.g., personal development) among children, and to teach children motor skills (e.g., performance). Think of your experiences in youth sport. How well did sport contribute to each of the above objectives? Describe how children's sport programs can promote the 3Ps objectives.

Clearly, youth sport programs have the potential to contribute to positive youth outcomes, but these positive outcomes do not occur automatically through youth sport involvement. In the next section, we will briefly review the positive and negative physical, psychological, emotional, and social outcomes that have been associated with youth sport involvement. The rest of this chapter will focus on developmental activities and contexts of sport programs that are likely to lead to increased participation, personal development, and performance among youth.

OUTCOMES ASSOCIATED WITH YOUTH SPORT

For the most part, we hear of the positive outcomes associated with youth sport involvement: health benefits, increased self-esteem, friendships, discipline, teamwork, and competence. However, more and more frequently, we are hearing of more negative youth sport experiences: insensitive coaches, pressure from parents, peer victimization, aggression, and decreased self-esteem. Although no studies have empirically shown a cause–effect relationship between youth sport participation and developmental outcomes (due to methodological and ethical difficulties), Table 10.1 outlines the positive and negative outcomes associated with youth sport based on research in the areas of physical health, psychological development, and social development (see Fraser-Thomas et al., 2005, for a review).

As Table 10.1 shows, sport involvement can contribute to physical health and positive psychological and social development; however, there is also evidence of less-desirable relationships between sport involvement and youth development. A key to understanding

Table 10.1 Positive and Negative Outcomes of Youth Sport		
	Positive Outcomes	**Negative Outcomes**
Physical health	• Cardiovascular fitness • Weight control • Muscular strength/endurance • Adult physical activity • Decreased risk of adult heart disease • Decreased risk of diabetes • Decreased risk of osteoporosis • Decreased risk of cancer	• Overuse injuries • Eating disorders
Psychological development	• Fun and enjoyable experiences • Challenging experiences • Increased self-esteem • Decreased stress • Increased life satisfaction • Increased happiness	• Decreased self-perceptions • Decreased confidence/self-esteem • Experience of isolation from teammates • Experience of excessive pressure • Burnout
Social development	• Positive intergroup and peer relationships • Citizenship • Social status and success • Social mobility • Leadership skills • Increased academic performance • Enhanced adult career achievement • Decreased school dropout rate • Decreased delinquent behaviour	• Aggression • Assault • Poor sportspersonship • Decreased moral reasoning • Increased drinking

whether youth sport programs foster positive outcomes is first to identify the processes that occur within them. Youth sport programs provide a platform for positive youth development, and, if structured appropriately, can have direct effects on youth's present and future development and productivity. There is a growing body of literature in developmental psychology recognizing the importance of sports as prosocial activities that can contribute to youth's positive life trajectories and more civil societies (Larson, 2000). Before discussing sport-specific contexts that are likely to lead to positive outcomes in youth, we will discuss major frameworks of positive youth development that could potentially be helpful in promoting participation, performance, and personal development in youth.

REFLECTIONS 10.2

Many sport organizations, programs, and initiatives aim to promote participation, performance, and personal development in youth. Examine the websites below. What are the goals and values of these organizations, programs, and initiatives? What kinds of environments do they aim to create?

Church Athletic League of Kingston: www.calkingston.com
High Five: www.highfive.org
Ontario Soccer Association's Long Term Player Development: http://www.ontariosoccer
.net/Portals/438/Documents/Player/LTPD/How%20Soccer%20Is%20Changing%20
In%20Ontario.pdf
Ottawa Lions Track and Field Club: www.ottawalions.com
Respect in Sport: www.respectinsport.com
Sportball: www.sportball.ca
Stampede City Gymnastic Club: www.stampedecitygym.com
Tao of Peace Martial Arts and Life Skills: http://taoofpeace.com/#!/home
True Sport: www.truesportpur.ca
YMCA Canada: www.ymca.ca

Involvement in sport can foster developmental assets in children and youth.

Tom Merton/Caiaimage/Getty Images

FRAMEWORKS OF POSITIVE YOUTH DEVELOPMENT

Developmental Assets

Developmental assets: Social and psychological "building blocks" for human development; include internal and external assets.

External assets: Positive developmental experiences resulting from the environment or the community.

Internal assets: Positive developmental experiences resulting from internalized skills and competencies.

Benson (1997) has outlined 40 **developmental assets**, commonly termed the "building blocks" for human development. The development of these assets in youth embodies a broad vision of communities and youth interacting in a positive and effective manner. The assets fall into two broad categories: external assets and internal assets. Within each of these two broad categories, four types of assets exist. **External assets** comprise support, empowerment, boundaries and expectations, and constructive use of time. **Internal assets** comprise commitment to learning, positive values, social competencies, and positive identity. Benson and others (Benson, 1997; Scales & Leffert, 1999) found that the more developmental assets an adolescent possesses, the greater is his or her likelihood of developing in a positive and healthy manner. Specifically, the more assets an adolescent possesses, the more likely it is that he or she will "thrive" (e.g., show leadership, volunteer, get good grades) and the less likely it is that he or she will be at risk (e.g., use alcohol or be depressed, suicidal, or violent).

Petitpas and colleagues (Petitpas et al., 2005; Petitpas et al., 2008) offer a framework for planning sport programs that foster psychosocial development, with an emphasis on internal and external developmental assets. We believe that sport programs have the potential to contribute to many developmental assets. For example, involvement in sport programs can foster external assets in the areas of constructive use of time, emotional support from family, empowerment, positive social relationships, and high expectations. Past research also indicates that youth sport programs have the potential to foster numerous internal assets, such as achievement motivation, school engagement, caring, responsibility, social competencies, conflict resolution skills, and a sense of positive identity (Benson, 1997; Scales & Leffert, 1999).

CONSTRUCTIVE ACTIVITIES AND INITIATIVE

Relaxed leisure activities: Activities that are enjoyable but not demanding in terms of effort.

Constructive leisure activities: Activities that require sustained effort toward the achievement of a clear goal.

Initiative: The ability to be motivated from within and to direct attention and effort toward a challenging goal over time.

Researchers have also taken an interest in the types of activities that lead to positive youth development. Children's activities have been classified into two categories: relaxed leisure activities and constructive leisure activities. **Relaxed leisure activities** (e.g., watching television, hanging out) are activities that are enjoyable but not demanding in terms of effort. **Constructive leisure activities** (e.g., sport, music, art) can also be enjoyable but require sustained effort toward the achievement of a clear goal. Larson (2000) argues that constructive leisure activities, rather than relaxed leisure activities, foster initiative development in children. He suggests that **initiative** (the ability to be motivated from within and to direct attention and effort toward a challenging goal over time) is a core quality of positive physical, psychological, and social development in children. As such, activities promoting initiative development must have three essential elements. First, they must be intrinsically motivating. Second, they must involve concerted attention toward specific goals. Third, they must occur over an extended period of time (i.e., regular involvement). Larson argues that constructive leisure activities provide these three elements and thus foster initiative.

When reviewing how youth spend their time around the world, Larson and Verma (1999) found sport participation to be the most popular constructive leisure activity for youth in North America and Europe. In addition, Larson and Kleiber (1993) reported that youth devote more attention to sports and games than to other daily life activities, such as schoolwork or watching television. These findings suggest that for many young people, sport may be more important than any other daily activity in contributing to positive development and the growth of critical adult skills, such as initiative and the capacity for autonomous action. Danish and colleagues (Danish, 2002; Theokas et al., 2008) have done extensive work on teaching life skills in youth sport settings. They have developed a program called SUPER (Sports United to Promote Education and Recreation) to teach life skills to young athletes through a peer-led series of 18 modules taught like sport clinics. SUPER sport programs also provide opportunities for coaches and athletes to demonstrate, model, and practise what they are teaching and learning. Unfortunately, the principles of SUPER programs are not always reproduced within community or school sport systems. Not all community and school sport programs create enjoyable and challenging environments that are able to develop initiative and life skills in youth while sustaining their engagement over time.

The Cs of Positive Youth Development

A final framework of positive youth development is reflected in five desired outcomes of youth, or "5Cs" of positive youth development: *competence, character, connection, confidence,* and *caring* (or *compassion*; Jelicic et al., 2007). This developmental theory of positive youth development suggests that policies must be implemented to allow families and programs to foster and promote positive development. In reviewing the extant sport literature, Côté and colleagues (2010) proposed a collapsed 4Cs framework for studying PYD in a youth sport context. This revised framework integrates caring and compassion with character, due to the similarity and overlap among these constructs within the sport literature. Using the 4Cs framework, Vierimaa and colleagues (2012) have since proposed a measurement approach to assess the 4Cs—competence, confidence, connection, and character. This research represents the realignment of the 5Cs framework to more accurately reflect the unique aspects of the youth sport context. Thus, just as each of the 4Cs is uniquely linked to aspects of sport performance and participation, they jointly facilitate healthy personal development and civic engagement. It becomes apparent that if the 4Cs are the central focus of sport programs, the ultimate outcomes of performance, participation, and personal development (3Ps) are more likely to emerge from sport involvement.

CONSIDERATIONS FOR YOUTH SPORT PROGRAMS

The work of researchers in positive youth development constitutes a solid foundation on which youth sport programs can be based. Developmental assets, initiative, and the 4Cs of positive youth development should be considered when sport programs are being constructed in order to support youth's participation, personal development, and performance. Although it can be assumed that most youth sport programs intend to foster positive youth development, the research behind Table 10.1 indicates that many programs may be failing. This raises a challenging question: How do sport organizations, coaches, peers, siblings, and parents ensure the concerted benefits of increased participation, personal development, and performance through sport involvement? To do this most effectively, it is important first to examine two primary factors contributing to positive and negative experiences in youth sport, as identified in the literature: program activities and social influences.

Youth Sport Program Activities

When coaches develop activities for youth practices and when sport organizations design youth sport programs, they must consider the three objectives of youth sport (3Ps: participation, personal development, and performance). In particular, coaches and programmers must consider the differing implications of deliberate play, deliberate practice, and early specialization.

Deliberate Play, Deliberate Practice, and Early Specialization A common trend among adults involved in regular sport and physical activity is that they were involved in a broad range of organized sports and deliberate play activities during their youth. Côté and colleagues (2007) define **deliberate play** activities in sport as those designed to maximize inherent enjoyment. These activities are regulated by flexible rules adapted from standardized sport rules and are set up and monitored by the children or by an involved adult. Children typically modify rules to find a point where their game most resembles the actual sport but still allows for play at their level. For example, children may change soccer and basketball rules to suit their environment and their needs (e.g., playing in the street, on a playing field, or in someone's backyard). When involved in deliberate play activities, children are less concerned with the outcome of their behaviour than with the behaviour. On the other hand, Ericsson and colleagues (1993) suggest that the most effective learning occurs through involvement in highly structured activities defined as deliberate practice. **Deliberate practice** activities require effort, generate no immediate rewards, and are motivated by the goal of improving performance rather than the goal of enjoyment. Early specialization is often characterized by high amounts of deliberate practice and low amounts of deliberate play. **Early specialization** is defined as limiting participation to one sport that is practised on a year-round basis, usually involving high amounts of deliberate practice and low amounts of deliberate play from a young age.

Deliberate play: Sport activities designed to maximize enjoyment, regulated by flexible rules.

Deliberate practice: Activities that require effort, generate no immediate rewards, and are motivated by the goal of improving performance.

Early specialization: Participation in one sport on a year-round basis, involving high amounts of deliberate practice and low amounts of deliberate play.

Early specialization is one of the most controversial areas in youth sport. Many parents believe that early specialization will enhance their child's prospects for later elite performance.

Peter R.E. Crocker

The two concepts of deliberate play and deliberate practice could be placed at opposite ends of a continuum. Behaviours could be located along the continuum, from those that are primarily motivated by a process-experimentation perspective (deliberate play) to those that are motivated by a goal-directed perspective (deliberate practice). When individuals are involved in deliberate play, they experiment with new or different combinations of behaviours, but not necessarily in the most effective way to improve performance.

In contrast, when individuals are involved in deliberate practice, they exhibit behaviour focused on improving performance by the most effective means available. For example, the backhand skill in tennis could be learned and improved over time by playing matches or by creating fun practice situations. However, players could more effectively improve their backhand performance by practising drills that might be considered less enjoyable. Although the drills used in deliberate practice might not be the most enjoyable, they might be the most relevant to improving performance. When one is considering the optimal amount of deliberate play, deliberate practice, and involvement in other sports that children should have in their early years, one has to consider the three objectives of youth sport: participation, performance, and personal development.

REFLECTIONS 10.3

Looking back on your involvement in sport during childhood, recall all the activities that constituted your sporting experiences. Consider your involvement in deliberate practice, deliberate play, and competition. Now, consider a children's sport program with which you are quite familiar. Does the program focus primarily on deliberate practice or deliberate play? Does the program's focus align with its stated objectives? How is this program different from or similar to your own involvement in sport during childhood? Discuss how involvement during childhood and adolescence in several different sports, deliberate play activities, and deliberate practice activities may contribute to continued sport involvement or dropout.

Early Specialization and Deliberate Practice Considerations From a participation perspective, an overemphasis on deliberate practice at a young age and early specialization can lead to dropout, muscle overuse, injury, and athletes' failure to develop transferable skills (Abernethy et al., 2005; Fraser-Thomas et al., 2008a; Law et al., 2007; Wall & Côté, 2007). Early specialization often has harmful effects on emotional and psychological development. For example, early specialization can lead to decreased enjoyment, disappointment, discouragement, and burnout since youth may experience a sense of failure if they are unable to meet their goals after investing so heavily (Fraser-Thomas et al., 2008b). Early specialization is also a concern for youth's personal development because it can lead to missed social opportunities experienced through early diversification (Wright & Côté, 2003).

From a performance perspective, there is evidence that early specialization and an increased focus on deliberate practice activities during the early years can be effective in producing elite performers (Law et al., 2007); however, as outlined above, there are many costs associated with this pattern of activities. It appears that deliberate play and involvement in various sporting activities may serve as a more cost-effective way for youth to explore their

Table 10.2 Benefits and Costs of Early Specialization in Sport

Dimension of Sport Involvement	Benefits	Costs
Physical	Sport-specific skills learned	Increased injuries and reduced health
Psychosocial	Self-confidence in one sport	Lack of diverse experiences
		Reduced enjoyment
		Parental expectations/pressure
		Coaching expectations/pressure
		Dropout
		Burnout

physical capacities in various contexts and to develop their sport skills. Analyses of elite athletes' early involvement in sports show that deliberate play activities and early diversification in sport activities are important during the first few years of sport participation. For example, Soberlak and Côté (2003) showed that elite ice hockey players spent slightly more time in deliberate play activities than deliberate practice activities before age 20. Although much research suggests that involvement in deliberate practice is a consistent factor that differentiates elite from non-elite athletes (e.g., Helsen et al., 1998), the difference of time invested in deliberate practice activities generally occurs during the adolescent and adult years. Baker and Côté (2006) suggest that reducing the acquisition of sport skills to a single dimension (i.e., deliberate practice) fails to acknowledge important developmental, motivational, and psychosocial aspects of human abilities. However, the peak age in some sports, such as female gymnastics and figure skating, tends to be quite young. Athletes in these sports are sometimes required to specialize early in order to reach the highest levels. In sports such as these, extreme caution should be used. Training programs must always consider children's physical, psychological, social, and cognitive development.

Overall, early specialization and too much emphasis on deliberate practice activities during the early years of sport involvement may lead to health problems or withdrawal. Instead, an emphasis on various sport activities and deliberate play activities during childhood is likely to have immediate developmental and long-term health benefits. Some of the benefits and costs of early specialization are outlined in Table 10.2.

Many youth sport programs are inherently designed to eventually expect specialization as athletes age and mature. Although this is a path that many young athletes choose to follow, it is not a route for all youth. Given that research attributes adolescent sport withdrawal to required time commitment and competitive focus (Rottensteiner et al., 2013), sport programmers during adolescence should aim to offer both specialization and recreational programs so that all adolescents can continue to enjoy and participate in sport.

Youth Sport Social Influences

Many people play significant roles in youth sport and influence young athletes' participation, performance, and personal development. We will consider the roles of coaches, peers and siblings, and parents.

Coaches Coaches are a major adult influence in children's sport participation. They affect children's competence beliefs and play an integral role in shaping youths' performance, participation, and personal development (Smoll & Smith, 2002; Vella et al., 2011). In terms of performance, studies consistently highlight coaches' essential role in helping youth develop the motor skills necessary for athletic success (e.g., Côté et al., 2007). Research also shows that coaches can influence athletes' continued participation by adopting positive interpersonal styles that affect athletes' enjoyment and intrinsic motivation (e.g., Álvarez et al., 2009). Finally, there is an emerging body of research exploring coaches' contributions to youth's personal development (e.g., Côté et al., 2010).

Based on a thorough review of coaching and athlete development literature, Côté and Gilbert (2009) proposed an integrative definition of coaching effectiveness that focuses on coaches' knowledge, the different contexts in which coaches typically work, and athlete outcomes. **Coaching effectiveness** is defined as the consistent application of integrated professional, interpersonal, and intrapersonal knowledge to improve athletes' competence, confidence, connection, and character in specific coaching contexts. In this definition, coach knowledge extends beyond the commonly examined area of professional knowledge (sport-specific knowledge), to include both interpersonal (connection with others) and intrapersonal (openness to continued learning and self-reflection) forms of knowledge. Coaching contexts refer to the varied sport settings in which coaching can take place, such as recreational or competitive, among children, adolescents, or adults. The final component of the integrative definition is athlete personal assets, which are defined as the 4Cs (competence, confidence, connection, and character) framework described earlier. While the nature of the knowledge required by coaches of different sporting contexts is highly variable, the 4Cs remain stable as the ultimate processes that coaches should focus on when trying to develop their athletes' performance, participation, and personal development (Côté & Gilbert, 2009).

Unfortunately, studies observing youth sport coaches indicate that most coaches do not explicitly teach or exhibit behaviours that are associated with enhanced competence, confidence, connection, and character. For example, McCallister and colleagues (2000) explored youth sport coaches' philosophies and values, and while coaches believed they were successful at facilitating a wide range of positive values and life skills, they struggled to articulate exactly how they did so, and their observed behaviours were often inconsistent with their stated values and philosophies. Furthermore, several studies have shown that youth sport coaches' behaviours during games are directed primarily toward winning rather than the development of their players' personal strengths and assets (e.g., 4Cs; Gilbert et al., 1999; Wilcox & Trudel, 1998).

Research indicates that coaches who enhance their athletes' competence, confidence, connection, and character usually include their athletes in decision-making processes, display care and concern for their athletes, evaluate their athletes' performance based on self-improvements and effort, acknowledge their athletes' feelings and input, promote interactive discussions, and behave in a clear and consistent manner (e.g., Erickson et al., 2011; Turnnidge et al., 2014; Turnnidge et al., 2012). Collectively, these studies illustrate the important role that coaches may play in promoting personal assets in youth sport (e.g., 4Cs) and achieving the outcomes of performance, participation, and personal development.

Coaching effectiveness: The consistent application of integrated professional, interpersonal, and intrapersonal knowledge to improve athletes' competence, confidence, connection, and character in specific coaching contexts.

Coaches can promote young athletes' personal assets by engaging them in interactive discussions.

Alistair Berg/Digital Vision/Getty Images

In the realm of youth sport, coaches play a crucial role in enabling young athletes to become competent, self-controlled, constructive members of a team and, ultimately, productive members of society. Unfortunately, for many young athletes, sport settings stimulate a change in social values and moral reasoning patterns, where children tend to believe violent acts are acceptable and would be supported by coaches and parents in game situations. For example, a recent study looking at the introduction of bodychecking in ice hockey found that young boys legitimized the use of bodychecking to hurt, harm, demonstrate control, take out frustrations, and intimidate other players (Fraser-Thomas et al., 2014). Youth sport coaches should not "use language or techniques that might encourage participants to separate their sport experiences from 'real life'" (Bredemeier & Shields, 1996, p. 396). Youth sport should be seen as an activity not different from any other life situation through which personal and social values are respected and learned. Hellison and colleagues (2008) provide a framework for teaching personal and social responsibility through physical activity, and this framework can guide positive youth-development coaching. They highlight the roles of integration, transfer, empowerment, and coach–athlete relationships in leading youth from irresponsibility to respect, participation, self-direction, and caring. They also provide preliminary teaching strategies, including counselling time, awareness talks, group meetings, and reflection time. In a recent review of the literature, Gould and Carson (2008) suggested that coaches' direct and indirect teaching strategies, such as the ones proposed by Hellison and colleagues, are determinants of young athletes' psychosocial development and positive outcomes through sports (i.e., personal development).

The definition of coaching effectiveness presented in this section suggests that effective youth sport coaches require a high level of professional, interpersonal, and intrapersonal knowledge. In other words, effectiveness in coaching resides in one's ability to teach sport specific skills (professional knowledge), create and maintain relationships (interpersonal knowledge), and learn from one's own practice (intrapersonal knowledge). The integration and application of these three types of knowledge—professional, interpersonal, and intrapersonal—toward the goal of developing athletes' 4Cs will result in positive youth sport experiences. The 4Cs provide a concise, yet comprehensive, framework with which to measure performance (competence) and psychosocial outcomes (confidence, connection, and character) that should result from coaching young athletes. Together, these four constructs represent a holistic approach to coaching that incorporates traditional goals of youth sport programs (i.e., performance and participation) with an added emphasis on positive psychosocial development (i.e., personal development).

Peers and Siblings Peers also have a multitude of influences on youths' positive and negative sport experiences (Bruner et al., 2013). From a positive perspective, programs that foster quality peer relationships can facilitate the long-term objectives of enhancing performance, participation, and personal development. Research suggests that when adolescents feel accepted by and affiliated with their peers in their sport contexts, they experience an increased sense of belonging, self-esteem, competence, and intrinsic motivation for continued participation (Allen, 2003; Ullrich-French & Smith, 2009). Sport also offers opportunities for youth to strengthen friendships, which in turn foster youths' enjoyment and commitment to sport (Weiss & Smith, 2002). Further, research has shown that athletes' development of key personal and social skills is facilitated extensively through peer interactions (Holt, Black, et al., 2008).

However, from a negative perspective, studies indicate that peers can also be a source of stress and anxiety (Gould, 1993; Scanlan et al., 1991). As children mature and develop into adolescents, they become more dependent on peers' feedback as a source of information in forming their competence beliefs (Horn, 2004). As such, peers' criticisms and negative feedback may in turn affect the dynamics of peer relationships, whereby interactions may include peers emphasizing athletes' poor performances, engaging in awkward friendly competition, showing off, and demonstrating rivalry (Keegan et al., 2010; Patrick et al., 1999).

Recent work suggests siblings may play unique roles in children's sport development, beyond those of peers and teammates; however, only minimal research has focused in this area, due in part to the multitude of interacting factors influencing these relationships (e.g., birth order, birth spacing, gender, sport interests) (Blazo et al., 2014; Davis & Meyer, 2008). Siblings, like peers, can be the source of positive and negative experiences among youth athletes. For example, sibling-competitors often establish close bonds, and can offer emotional support in the form of cheering, displaying pride, encouraging, and defending in times of need; siblings can also offer youth athletes informational support by providing sport specific advice and assisting with technical, tactical, or mental strategies in their sport. Despite this, sibling rivalries are common. Sometimes younger athletes are living in the shadow of their older siblings, while other times older siblings are struggling to maintain their sport identity as they are outperformed by younger siblings. Siblings often feel constantly compared, resulting in jealousies, and fuelling anger, disappointment, annoyance, anxiety, and frustration. Collectively, these findings speak to the paradoxical nature of siblings' relationships and the need for continued investigation and understanding of sibling relationships in sport.

In order to optimize positive peer and sibling interactions in youth sport, it is important to ensure that the structure of the competitive setting is appropriate and that positive

Children can develop and strengthen friendships through sport, fostering increased sport enjoyment and commitment.

Peter R.E. Crocker

True competition: Competitive situations that serve the interests of all participants and focus their effort and concentration toward a particular goal.

Decompetition: Competitive situations that occur when athletes seek to demonstrate their superiority over opponents.

Under-involved parents: Parents who show lack of involvement.

Moderately involved parents: Parents who show adequate levels of involvement.

Over-involved parents: Parents who show excessive amounts of involvement.

interactions between teammates and among competitors are valued and modelled. Shields and Bredemeier (2009) suggest that different types of competition help to delineate positive and negative peer interactions in youth sport. First, **true competition** is based on a mutual understanding that competitive situations serve the interests of all participants to focus their effort and concentration toward a particular goal. In this case, athletes strive to win the game or race, and defeating an opponent is considered an internal goal of the game that does not affect the particular status of a team or individual. On the other hand, **decompetition** occurs when athletes seek to demonstrate their superiority over opponents—it only serves the interests of winners, as extrinsic rewards or rankings are valued more than the achievement of personal excellence. Decompetitors view competition as a war, and opponents as enemies to be defeated rather than partners in the pursuit of excellence.

Participation in sport should include experiences that exemplify true competition and positive peer interaction, such as teamwork, friendship, trust, loyalty, commitment, and respect. Involvement in sport programs that promote these opportunities has been found to impact young people in a positive way. Youth sport is a microcommunity that offers opportunities to interact with others, learn social skills, and broaden citizenship qualities. Through the integration and reinforcement of positive peer interactions, youth sport can facilitate the development of characteristics and skills that represent ideal citizenship behaviours within sport and in society.

Parents Hellstedt (1987) suggests that parents' involvement in their children's sport involvement can be conceptualized on a continuum from under-involved, to moderately involved, to over-involved. **Under-involved parents** show "a relative lack of emotional, financial, or functional investment" (p. 153). **Moderately involved parents** are characterized by "firm parental direction, but enough flexibility so that the young athlete is allowed significant involvement in decision-making" (p. 153). Finally, **over-involved parents** "have an excessive amount of involvement in the athletic success of their children" (p. 154). Frequent behaviours of over-involved parents include yelling during competitions, disagreeing with coaches about their child's playing time, consistently asking their child to try harder, and coaching their child when unsolicited to do so. Hellstedt suggests that a moderate level of parental involvement promotes the best interests of the child, even if this means that parents must sometimes sacrifice personal interests.

Although a typology of parental involvement in sport (such as the one presented by Hellstedt) is useful, it provides little insight into the specific types of parental behaviours that have the most favourable socialization effects on children in sport. Woolger and Power (1993) identified three dimensions of parent behaviour associated with children's sport socialization, motivation, and behaviour: parental support, expectations, and modelling.

Parental support is an essential element in the development of children's self-esteem, competence, and achievement. Côté and Hay (2002) suggest four categories of psychological needs for young athletes: emotional support, informational support, tangible support, and companionship. **Emotional support** is provided through parents' comforting gestures during times of stress and anxiety. Parents often find it difficult to know how and when to talk to their children in emotionally charged sport environments; however, research has shown the value of parents engaging in intelligent conversations—discussions that are open and honest—which may simply be about the daily issues arising from their sport involvement, or about more challenging or complex issues related to their sport development (e.g., coaching, educational path) (Fraser-Thomas et al., 2008b; Harwood & Knight, 2009). Further, when parents give their child positive feedback on his or her ability or express belief in their child's capabilities, the child believes that he or she is cared for. These supportive efforts and gestures can enhance a child's sense of competence and level of self-esteem (Cutrona & Russell, 1990). Children need to believe that what they do with their time, energy, and talent in sport is meaningful to themselves and others.

Informational support refers to parents' provision of advice or guidance in problematic situations. For example, parents can provide general information on how to choose a suitable sport program or provide specific instructions to a child on how to learn a certain technique. Recently, there has been growing interest in the type of information athletes prefer to receive from their parents, particularly in relation to feedback during training and performances. Research shows that during childhood, athletes generally appreciate extensive positive reinforcement and encouragement, as this increases their competence beliefs, enjoyment, and motivation. However, during later childhood and early adolescence, youth begin to judge their competence to a greater degree from performance outcomes and peer comparison, and as such, are less appreciative of parents' performance-related, technical, or tactical feedback (Knight et al., 2011). One exception to this appears to be when parents have some expertise or background in the sport; however, this remains a problematic issue, as many parents believe themselves to be experts regardless of their actual experience or knowledge of the sport (Holt, Tamminen, et al., 2008).

Recent research also offers understanding of parents' perspective of their provision of informational support, indicating they often stress and struggle to optimally support their child's athletic and personal development (Harwood & Knight, 2009; Knight & Holt,

Parental support:
Involves parents' facilitation of children's self-esteem, competence, and achievement; can include emotional, informational, tangible, and companionship (network) support.

Emotional support:
Comforting gestures during time of stress and anxiety.

Informational support:
Provision of advice or guidance in problematic situations.

2013). For example, parents often feel compelled to help their child–athlete cope with in-sport stressors such as poor coaching, bad referees, poor sportspersonship, transitions to the next level, and educational balance, but parents are unsure how to assist, or feel their involvement is restrained by the sport environment. As such, there is a need for more education, information, and resources to be available to parents of child and adolescent athletes.

Tangible support refers to concrete assistance given to children in stressful situations; parents provide necessary resources to help their children cope with events. Examples of tangible support include providing the financial assistance or the time commitment necessary for lessons, equipment, and travel associated with sport participation. Tangible support is often reflected as "sacrifices" parents make for their children's sport involvement; these can be quite significant, including compromises to parents' social lives, career advancement, and spousal relationships, as well as compromises to family routines and attention to other children (Harwood & Knight, 2009). Overall, tangible support is required for participation in most sport programs, and its lack can certainly become a constraint to a child's sport participation.

Companionship, or "network support," reflects casual relationships that enable an individual to engage in various forms of social and recreational activities (Cutrona & Russell, 1990). Parents can be involved in various kinds of companionship related to their child's participation in sport. For instance, parents can develop special relationships with their children through sport by attending their child's competitive events, collecting sports cards for their child, getting involved in deliberate play with their child, following professional sports with their child, or simply spending time travelling to and from practices with their child (Côté, 1999; Fraser-Thomas & Côté, 2009). Given that parent volunteers are largely responsible for coaching youth sport programs in Canada, parent–child relationships can also be enhanced through parents' coaching roles. Child–athletes may experience additional quality time with their parents, sometimes in a one-on-one setting, and experience enjoyment through a shared interest, while learning skills and values from their parents (Weiss & Fretwell, 2005). Interestingly, despite family sacrifices discussed above, recent research examining families where multiple children are involved in sport provides evidence of network support infiltrating entire families, not only parent–child relationships. Specifically, sport may serve as a backdrop for the development of healthy family dynamics and sibling relationships as a result of extensive quality time spent together, positive mentoring opportunities, the development of strong communication skills, and a shared connection (Davis & Meyer, 2008; Trussell, 2012).

Parental expectations can have a powerful effect on children's emotions and motivation in sport. There is a positive relationship between parental expectations and children's success and enjoyment in sport (Fredericks & Eccles, 2004). On the other hand, parental expectations can also become a source of pressure and stress that interferes with children's participation in sport (Fraser-Thomas et al., 2008b). Parents with inflated expectations can become a source of stress and anxiety for their children. Eccles and Harold (1991) proposed that parental expectations influence children's decisions to engage in particular activities, their intensity of effort expended in these activities, and their actual performance levels.

Tangible support: Provision of concrete assistance and resources to help cope with events.

Companionship: Network of relationships that enable an individual to engage positively in various activities.

Parental expectations: Parents' sets of beliefs regarding their children's behaviours.

Therefore, parents should be sensitive to the positive and negative impacts their expectations can have on their children's involvement in sport.

Parental modelling of physical activity is well recognized for positively influencing children's physical activity, but research on parental modelling of sport has not shown the same clear benefits. For example, one study found that fathers who modelled sport participation had sons who experienced decreased enthusiasm for their sport (Power & Woolger, 1994). Another study indicated that parents who were high-level athletes in their youth were more likely to have their children drop out from sport (Fraser-Thomas et al., 2008a). While more research is needed, these studies suggest that sport-loving families are not a prerequisite for children's motivation and participation in sport.

Parental modelling: Parents serving as a behavioural or moral example to their children.

Nevertheless, the competitive sport environment provides a platform for parents to model and espouse important life skills and personal values such as work ethic, persistence, self-awareness, resilience, positive attitude, respectful behaviour, emotional regulation, and appropriate sportspersonship (Fraser-Thomas & Côté, 2009; Knight et al., 2011). Unfortunately, there is growing evidence that parents may often negatively influence their children's development through overinvolved behaviours discussed above, coupled with poor modelling of communication skills, responsibility, and respect (Gould et al., 2008). Respect in Sport (Respect in Sport, 2014) is an innovative Canadian initiative that has grown extensively since its inception in 2007; the program aims to address these issues and concerns by offering an online parent certification program to empower parents and reinforce their positive roles. Currently, many provincial and national sport organizations are mandating parents' certification through this program, with over 350,000 parents and coaches nationally certified in 2014; however, further empirical research is necessary to determine the program's

Young athletes often experience companionship or network support in sport; parents and siblings often share common sport interests, and can teach young athletes skills and values.

Bruce Ayres/Getty Images

effectiveness in targeted areas (e.g., using guilt on your child, losing perspective, misplaced enthusiasm). Collectively, this research suggests that home environments should offer opportunities for children to witness physically active lifestyles, successful outcomes of sustained efforts, and important life skills and values, and foster positive motivational climates for sport participation. In summary, how children feel about themselves is largely related to how they are seen and treated by others, particularly their parents. Parents need to be constantly aware of their child's desire, motivation, and attitude toward sport so that they can modify and adjust their own behaviours, in turn facilitating optimal outcomes related to participation, personal development, and performance.

CASE STUDY 10.1 — Dufour-Lapointe Sisters, Canadian Freestyle Skiers

Early in the 2014 Olympic Games in Sochi, Russia, a trio of sisters from Montreal captured international attention for their incredible successes—winning gold, winning silver, and finishing twelfth in the women's freestyle skiing moguls event. While these performances were awe-inspiring, it was the family's story as "Canada's first family of emotion" and "platinum winners in family bonding" (MacGregor, 2014) that quickly seized the interest and imagination of audiences worldwide. When and how were they introduced to sport? How did they influence each other growing up? How did their parents support all three of them?

In the flurry of post-Olympic press conferences, the sisters' parents, Yves Lapointe and Johane Dufour, were asked about sacrifices made through the years. Yves first corrected the interviewer, suggesting that the family had made "choices" rather than "sacrifices." Johane explained an early choice they made in their child rearing: "We said, we have to do everything to spend more time with our kids, because tomorrow they will be women. So that's why we made those choices—to watch every single moment that they have success or pain. We want to be there" (Arthur, 2014).

Johane and Yves appeared to be true to their commitment. Johane, with three university degrees, gave up her career to remain at home as the family "rock." Every winter, the family spent weekends on the ski slopes. Maxime (the oldest, twelfth-place-finishing sister) took up moguls. Chloé (the middle, silver-medal-winning sister) followed. Justine (the youngest, gold-medal-winning sister) was enticed with hot chocolate to stick around the hill a bit longer while her older sisters trained. During the off-season, the family spent summers sailing the family boat on Lac Champlain. Then Chloé expressed her goal to go to the Olympics. The family sold the boat, and instead spent summer weekends in Lake Placid, where the sisters trained together by day and camped together by night, sharing homemade meals as a family at the end of each day.

The young women were clearly appreciative of their parents' support. Chloé expressed that "from the time we were very young, they surrounded us with love" (Buffery, 2014). She also spoke of their parents' belief in them as athletes, suggesting that Yves and Johane were their most loyal fans: "They kept telling us we would make it." Yves concurred, commenting, "It was a question of believing in a dream." Yet their parents raised them on key family values—balancing their focus on athletics with school, and having respect for everyone. Johane explained how they never compared their daughters, with each one focusing on her own goals and competing against herself. It is likely their love and respect for each other, coupled with these independent goals, that led them to be so sensitive to each other's successes and challenges, celebrating victories cautiously if their sisters had had more difficult days (Arthur, 2014). As Maxime explained, "We don't have rivalry. We push and support each other to be the best that we can be" (CBC, 2014).

Consider the case of the Dufour-Lapointes in light of family and sibling influences in youth development through sport, as outlined in this chapter. Provide examples of parental support, expectations, and modelling. Consider and comment on the unique dynamics of their sibling relationships within the context of positive youth development in sport.

Table 10.3 Features of Positive Development Settings for Youth
Physical and psychological safety
Appropriate structure
Supportive relationships
Opportunities to belong
Positive social norms
Support for efficacy and mattering
Opportunities for skill building
Integration of family, school, and community efforts

Source: Adapted from National Research Council and Institute of Medicine (NRCIM). (2002). *Community programs to promote youth development.* Washington, DC: National Academy Press.

YOUTH SPORT PROGRAM SETTINGS

The National Research Council and Institute of Medicine (NRCIM, 2002) in the United States outlined eight features of settings that are most likely to foster positive assets in youth. All these features should be considered by policy makers, sport organizations, parents, and coaches when they are designing and implementing youth sport programs. These eight features are shown in Table 10.3.

First, the NRCIM suggest that physical and psychological safety and security are essential to any setting aimed at promoting positive youth development. Although a child's physical safety is often a concern in sport settings, children's psychological and emotional sense of security must not be overlooked. If programs are implemented inappropriately, sport environments can often be intimidating or even frightening to youth. Second, settings must provide clear and consistent (age-appropriate) structure and appropriate adult supervision. All too often in youth sport settings, coaches are volunteers with insufficient knowledge of youths' developmental capabilities. The third and fourth setting features are supportive adult relationships (with parents and coaches) and opportunities to belong. Again, these relationships and opportunities must be worked toward, rather than assumed to occur. The fifth setting feature, positive social norms, is usually assumed to be facilitated by youth sport programs; however, research indicates that many programs may promote exaggerated masculinity, aggression, and competitiveness (Nixon, 1997). For the sixth feature, the NRCIM suggest that settings support youth's efficacy and sense of mattering. More specifically, youth sport programs must be child-centred and promote empowerment, autonomy, and opportunities to experience challenge. The seventh setting feature concerns skill-building opportunities, which are often provided in sport but occur only through developmentally appropriate program designs and coaching. Finally, programs that integrate family, school, and community create optimal environments for positive youth development because this integration creates opportunities for meaningful communication between different settings in youth's lives.

Drawing upon frameworks of children's healthy development such as the NRCIM's (2002) setting features, Ontario Parks and Recreation launched High Five in 2001, an initiative that offers a standard of quality assessment for sport programs across Canada

Sport programs aiming to facilitate PYD should promote positive social norms.

Laurence Mouton/PhotoAlto Agency RF Collections/Getty Images

(High Five, 2014). At the core of the program are five principles of children's health development: (1) a caring adult (i.e., supportive quality relationship), (2) opportunities to play (i.e., fun, creativity, and cooperation), (3) making friends (i.e., inclusion, acceptance, prosocial skills), (4) mastery of skills (i.e., success), and (5) participation (i.e., autonomy, self-expression). To date, there are almost 400 accredited and registered organizations across Canada. Programs such as High Five offer an important first step in assuring quality experiences for youth, while follow-up research ensuring and optimizing effectiveness also plays an important role in the delivery of quality programming.

CASE STUDY 10.2 Bodychecking in Minor Hockey

In recent years, there has been considerable interest in the issue of bodychecking in minor ice hockey in Canada. The skill—which is concisely defined as a defence tactic involving physical extension used to legally separate the puck carrier from the puck (Hockey Canada, 2013)—has typically been introduced in late childhood. Following unequivocal research indicating that bodychecking is associated with higher rates of injury, particularly concussion (e.g., Emery et al., 2010), a landmark decision was made by Hockey Canada in May 2013 to increase the minimum bodychecking age from Pee-Wee (age 11 years) to Bantam (age 13 years). In addition to injury concerns, there is evidence indicating that bodychecking is associated with increased aggression and decreased empathy, and is perceived as a legitimate means by which to harm others (e.g., Fraser-Thomas et al., 2014). At the time of the increase in minimum bodychecking age in 2013, a working group was directed to build an instructional resource program to support the progressive instruction of bodychecking skills.

Consider that you were hired as a consultant by Hockey Canada to ensure that skills are taught through the lens of PYD. Outline your considerations and recommendations, giving particular consideration to the NRCIM's (2002) eight setting features of PYD and High Five's principles of quality experiences.

The Developmental Model of Sport Participation

Although several models of athlete development in sport have been proposed in the literature to explain long-term participation and performance in sport Bruner and colleagues (2010) have found that the developmental model of sport participation (DMSP) is the most prominent conceptualization of athletes' development within the sport literature. The DMSP is a conceptual framework that integrates the developing person in its environment with objective processes and outcomes.

As illustrated in Figure 10.1, the DMSP proposes three possible sport participation trajectories: (1) recreational participation through sampling, (2) elite performance through sampling, and (3) elite performance through early specialization. Two of these trajectories, recreational participation and elite performance through sampling, have the same foundation from ages 6 to 12. After the sampling years, sport participants can choose to either stay involved in sport at a recreational level (recreational years, age 13+) or embark on a path that focuses primarily on performance (specializing years, ages 13–15; investment years, age 16+). These two trajectories have different outcomes in terms of performance but similar psychosocial and physical health benefits. A third possible trajectory consists of elite performance through early specialization (right side of Figure 10.1). Although this trajectory leads to elite performance, it can also result in reduced physical health (i.e., overuse injuries) and enjoyment.

Trajectory 1: Recreational Participation through Sampling During the sampling years (ages 6–12), athletes participate in a variety of sports with the focus being primarily on deliberate play activities. These years are considered essential building blocks for recreational sport participation. The recreational years (age 13+) are usually seen as an extension of the sampling years, with the primary goals being enjoyment and health. Activities can involve deliberate play and deliberate practice, and sport programs are flexible enough to adapt to individual interests and ages. During the sampling and recreational years, coaches are primarily kind, supportive, and encouraging (McCarthy & Jones, 2007). Parents' roles include introducing their children to sports, enrolling their children in diverse activities, and providing their children with necessary resources and equipment.

Trajectory 2: Elite Performance through Sampling For youth interested in a more performance-oriented path, a second trajectory of the DMSP suggests that specialization begins around age 13, after the sampling years (see Case Study 10.3). The specializing years (ages 13–15) are seen as a transitional stage to the investment years (age 16+). During the specializing years, youth engage in fewer activities, which are a mix of deliberate play and deliberate practice activities; during the investment years, youth commit to only one activity and engage primarily in deliberate practice. During both the specializing and the investment years, a more reciprocal coach–athlete respect develops, with coaches' styles becoming more skill oriented and technical. Parents become less involved but provide more financial and emotional support by helping their children through challenges and obstacles. Essentially, parents progress from a leadership role during the sampling years to a following and supporting role during the specializing and investment years (Côté, 1999).

Figure 10.1 Developmental model of sport participation

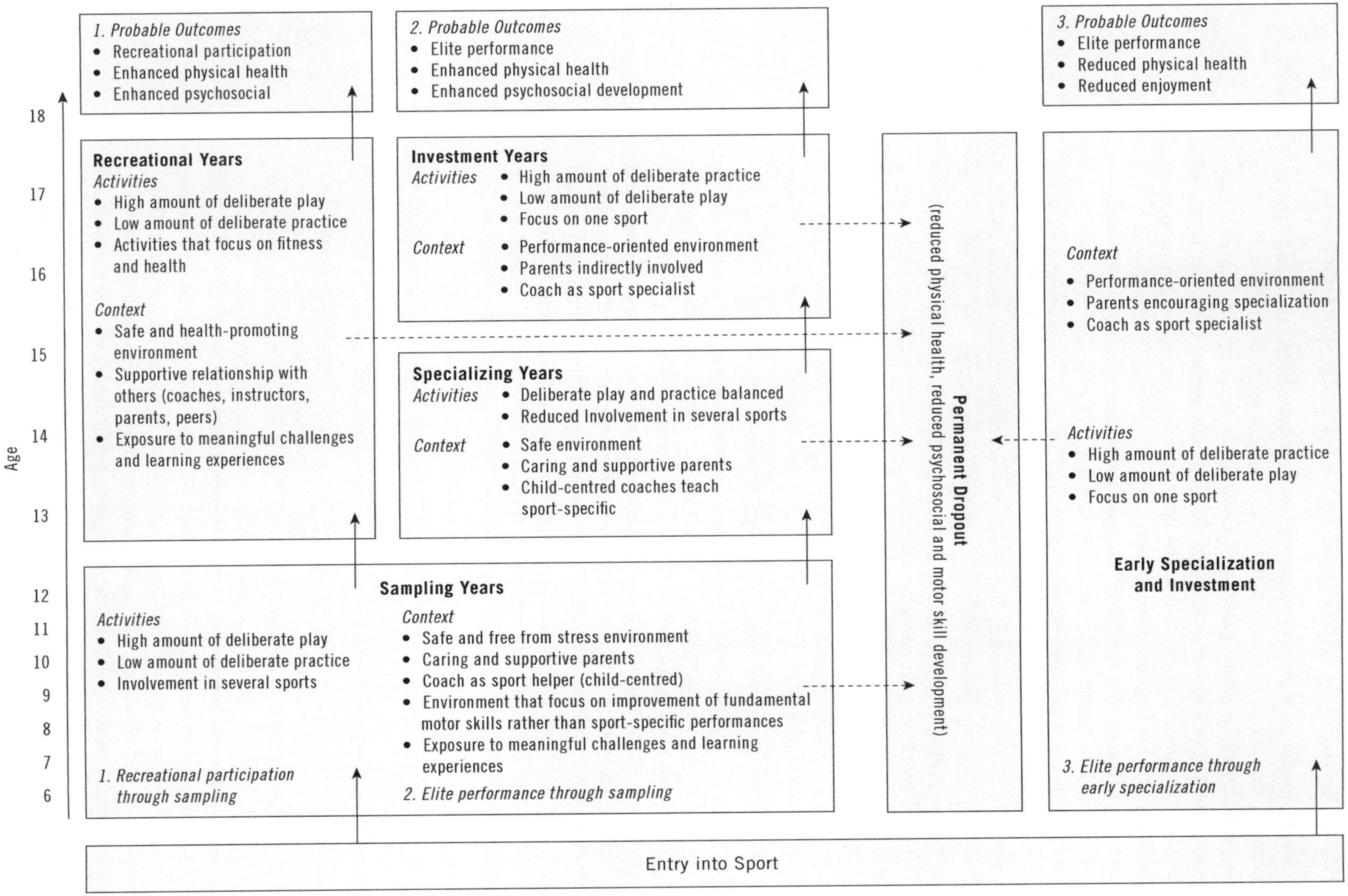

3. Probable Outcomes
- Elite performance
- Reduced physical health
- Reduced enjoyment

Context
- Performance-oriented environment
- Parents encouraging specialization
- Coach as sport specialist

Activities
- High amount of deliberate practice
- Low amount of deliberate play
- Focus on one sport

Early Specialization and Investment

3. *Elite performance through early specialization*

2. Probable Outcomes
- Elite performance
- Enhanced physical health
- Enhanced psychosocial development

Investment Years
Activities
- High amount of deliberate practice
- Low amount of deliberate play
- Focus on one sport

Context
- Performance-oriented environment
- Parents indirectly involved
- Coach as sport specialist

Specializing Years
Activities
- Deliberate play and practice balanced
- Reduced Involvement in several sports

Context
- Safe environment
- Caring and supportive parents
- Child-centred coaches teach sport-specific

Sampling Years
Context
- Safe and free from stress environment
- Caring and supportive parents
- Coach as sport helper (child-centred)
- Environment that focus on improvement of fundamental motor skills rather than sport-specific performances
- Exposure to meaningful challenges and learning experiences

2. *Elite performance through sampling*

Permanent Dropout
(reduced physical health, reduced psychosocial and motor skill development)

1. Probable Outcomes
- Recreational participation
- Enhanced physical health
- Enhanced psychosocial

Recreational Years
Activities
- High amount of deliberate play
- Low amount of deliberate practice
- Activities that focus on fitness and health

Context
- Safe and health-promoting environment
- Supportive relationship with others (coaches, instructors, parents, peers)
- Exposure to meaningful challenges and learning experiences

Activities
- High amount of deliberate play
- Low amount of deliberate practice
- Involvement in several sports

1. *Recreational participation through sampling*

Entry into Sport

Age
18
17
16
15
14
13
12
11
10
9
8
7
6

Source: Handbook of sport psychology. Edited by Gershon Tenenbaum and Robert C. Eklund by Tenenbaum, Gershon; Eklund, Robert C. Reproduced with permission of Wiley in the format Republish in a book via Copyright Clearance Center.

Simon Whitfield, Canadian Triathlete

Simon Whitfield, a native of Kingston, Ontario, was almost unknown to Canadians on September 16, 2000, when he came from behind to win Canada's first gold medal of the 2000 Olympics in Sydney, Australia. Consequently, many immediately took an interest in his path to athletic stardom.

Simon participated in many sports from a very young age. As he suggests, he began playing soccer as soon as he could crawl. His parents played a huge role in his early childhood involvement by enrolling and supporting him in a variety of activities. His older sister was also an avid athlete. As she progressed in her sports, and eventually specialized in rowing, Simon looked up to her as a role model and appreciated her support.

Simon was 11 years old when he was first exposed to triathlons, competing in the local Sharbot Lake Kids of Steel triathlon. He raced on a clunky mountain bike in a pair of boxer shorts and recalls the fun he had hanging out on the beach and enjoying a post-race barbecue.

It was not until age 15 that Simon decided to specialize in triathlon. His training increased in volume, intensity, and focus. Eventually, he relocated to the Pacific National Training Centre in British Columbia and spent a year training in Australia. He worked closely with a variety of coaches, focusing especially on his weakness, the swimming component of the triathlon.

During the weeks and months following Simon's 2000 Olympic victory, Canadians sang his praises and were proud to call him their own. His model citizenship was apparent as he travelled the country visiting schools, reaching out to children, and inspiring adults. A natural public speaker, Simon shared his positive sport experiences and served as a spokesperson for active, healthy living and fun-focused children's sport programs.

Since Simon's victory in 2000, participation in Kids of Steel and adult age-group triathlons has grown exponentially, while the depth of triathlon competition on the international stage has increased substantially. Simon remained a focused and dedicated athlete, as he continued to refine his training regimens, competitive plans, and mental skills, while showing remarkable respect for his competitors and support networks. His persistent popularity among Canadians was evidenced by record viewing rates on Canadian networks as he raced to his Olympic silver medal in the 2008 Beijing Olympics, and his selection as flag bearer in the 2012 London Olympics. Now retired from triathlon, Simon continues to share his contagious passion for sport as a writer, public speaker, creator/designer, and advocate for kids' sport opportunities, claiming that fun is the foundation to any successful youth sport program.

Consider Simon's story in light of the chapter's content. Comment on Simon's sport development path using the models outlined above. Also, using the principles of positive youth development as a guide, comment on Simon's psychosocial development.

Trajectory 3: Elite Performance through Early Specialization In sports where peak performance is achieved before puberty (e.g., women's gymnastics, figure skating), early specialization is often necessary to reach elite performance. Elite performers in these early-specialization sports usually skip the sampling years and, consequently, do not always experience the most positive psychosocial development. In addition, early specializers often experience overuse injuries, as outlined earlier in this chapter. The early specialization path is characterized by high amounts of deliberate practice and low amounts of deliberate play in a context that focuses on performance.

Other Trajectories Opportunities for horizontal movement across stages (e.g., going from investment to recreational) should be provided for participants so that individuals can change their level of participation at any age if they so desire. Unfortunately, in many sports it is difficult for a 16-year-old adolescent to invest in a sport if he or she has not been specializing in that sport since approximately age 13; however, in some sports, such as triathlon, investment in adulthood is possible (Baker et al., 2005).

Finally, at any stage of development, youth may also choose to disengage from sport and physical activity altogether. If this is the case, their youth sport programs clearly failed to achieve the first objective of youth sport programming: the long-term physical health of participants. Unfortunately, many youth sport programs are failing to reach this objective, as evidenced by current adolescent and adult inactivity rates.

Youth Sport Programs: Best Practices

The following is a list of five "best practices" that sport programmers and coaches should integrate into their programs in order to promote children and young adolescents' healthy personal and sport development.

1. *Adopt an inclusive focus as opposed to an exclusive selection policy based on performance.* Sport programs that focus on play and participation for all have been shown to lead to less dropout, more prolonged participation in sport, and greater elite performance in adulthood. On the other hand, youth sport programs that are built upon a rigid skill-based model imply early selection of "talented" children and an increase in resources for a special group of athletes; such programs, consequently, exclude many youth from continuing to participate in sport.

2. *Promote a true competition climate.* People's motivation to stay involved in sport, at either a recreational or an elite level, is largely influenced by their experiences in sport during childhood. Youth sport programs should be designed on motivational principles that are amenable to children and adolescents' needs. A focus on the objectives of true competition and self-improvement as opposed to performance outcomes such as championships is critical to promote participation and personal development in young athletes.

3. *Allow children and young adolescents to take initiative in their learning and development of fundamental motor skills.* One objective of structured training activities in youth sport is for participants to learn fundamental motor skills. However, the main focus of youth sport should be to let participants experiment with various ways of executing sport skills in various contexts through playful activities and fun involvement. A child's number one reason for getting involved in sports is "fun." As such, coaches should be cautious of teaching motor skills through repetitive and boring drills.

4. *Provide opportunities for young athletes to have fun and engage playfully in low-organization games.* Because children's continued motivation for sport is driven largely by their enjoyment and positive experiences in sport, a supportive environment should be created with ample opportunity for children to engage in low-organization games and other sports. Further, because children and young adolescents don't understand competition and sport performances in the same way adults do, coaches should not overorganize competition or overemphasize performance through deliberate practice during childhood.

5. *Promote psychosocial development through sport.* Sport participation can nurture important psychosocial characteristics and life skills. Coaches and parents involved in youth sport programs should use sport experiences as a medium to teach skills that can be applied in all aspects of life. Peer interactions that exemplify teamwork, friendship, trust, loyalty, commitment, and respect should be encouraged and valued.

CHAPTER SUMMARY

In this chapter, we outlined three objectives of youth sport programs: participation, performance, and personal development (i.e., the 3Ps). We reviewed the literature highlighting the positive outcomes (e.g., fitness) and negative outcomes (e.g., overuse injuries) of youth sport and suggested how to foster positive youth sport experiences. Youth sport programs should be conducted in desirable settings, and they should aim to foster developmental assets, initiative, health, performance, and the 4Cs of positive youth development (confidence, competence, character, and connection). To reach these objectives, youth sport programs should promote participation in diverse activities and focus on deliberate play activities at a young age, rather than requiring children to specialize early and focus on deliberate practice activities. Coaches, parents, and peers—through their supportive behaviours and attitudes—have important roles in influencing children's psychological growth, social skills, and motor development.

In the last section of the chapter, we discussed eight features of settings that are most likely to foster positive assets in youth sport and provide the practical example of Canada's High Five initiative. These features should be considered by policy makers, sport organizations, parents, and coaches when they are designing and implementing youth sport programs. The eight setting features reinforce the important roles that sport programs as well as parents and coaches have in building children's competence beliefs, and facilitating environments that lead to positive outcomes. The developmental model of sport participation highlights various factors that lead to continued participation and performance. This model shows that youth sport programmers should not consider participation and performance as separate entities in children's sport (e.g., before age 13). An inclusive focus on diverse youth sport participation and play during the sampling years will maximize retention and decrease dropout. Youth should be encouraged to participate in diverse sports and extracurricular activities that focus on fun, play, excitement, recreation, personal involvement, games, friendships, variety, and choice. Activities and contexts that promote regular participation, enjoyment, and skill acquisition are the building blocks of all effective youth sport programs.

We began this chapter by introducing you to Sebastian, Olivia, Madelyn, Rachel, and Michael, five young adults who had very different sport experiences during their youth, which in turn led them on very different paths. As you read through the chapter, you were introduced to some of the specific factors that caused these individuals to have more-positive or less-positive youth sport experiences. We hope that you will continue to consider these factors as you progress as professionals, coaches, administrators, programmers, and policy makers, in sport, physical activity, health, and other settings.

 ## COMMON MYTHS ABOUT YOUTH INVOLVEMENT IN SPORT REVISITED

MYTH: Involvement in youth sport builds character.
Character-building through sport is not automatic. Sport programs have to be specifically designed to foster positive development in youth. Positive outcomes depend on children's personal experiences, which are heavily influenced by the sport program activities and the coaches and parents who coordinate these activities.

MYTH: Involvement in sport leads to negative outcomes, such as violence and aggression.

Studies indicate some associations between sport and negative outcomes; however, well-designed programs aimed at promoting positive youth development, coupled with appropriate adult support, are less likely to lead to negative outcomes.

MYTH: To become elite athletes, children must specialize in their sport by age six or seven.

There is evidence that early specialization and sport-specific training are effective in producing elite performers; however, evidence also exists that suggests early involvement in a variety of sporting activities can also lead to elite performance in most sports. Current research suggests that there are many physical, psychological, and social benefits to early diversification, while there are many costs associated with early specialization. For this reason, it appears that, in most sports, early diversification is a healthier path to elite performance.

MYTH: Parents should limit their involvement in their children's sport.

Parents are an important source of various forms of support for their children. In addition, parents can influence their children's involvement through their behaviours and expectations. Sport programs must make a greater effort to proactively involve parents in their children's sport development. Parents should be informed about how their sport-related behaviours and beliefs influence their children's behaviours and beliefs.

MYTH: Youth sport coaches should be specialists in the sport that they are coaching.

Past research indicates that coaches play a key role in children's competence beliefs, sport enjoyment, motivation for sport participation, and reasons for sport withdrawal. These responsibilities are as important as teaching sport skills. Thus, coaches play a critical role in children's sport involvement, and they must be trained to understand children's physical, cognitive, social, and psychological development.

Review Questions

1. Describe the three objectives of youth sport.

2. Discuss the positive and negative outcomes of youth sport participation in the areas of health, psychological development, and social development.

3. Differentiate between relaxed leisure activities and constructive leisure activities. Provide examples of each.

4. What are the 4Cs of positive youth development? Provide a sport example of each C.

5. When developing youth programs, sport organizations and coaches should consider the differing implications of two different types of training activities. Name and briefly describe each type of training activity. Outline some of the potential benefits and risks of each approach.

6. Briefly describe coaching behaviours that could be associated with the development of the 4Cs.

7. Peers play an important role in youths' sport experiences. Provide three examples of how peers may positively influence youths' sport experiences or outcomes, as well as three examples of how peers may be a negative influence.

8. What are the three dimensions of parental behaviour that can be associated with children's sport socialization, motivation, and behaviour? Briefly describe how each dimension influences children's sport experiences.

9. Using the eight setting features as a framework, highlight some of the strengths and weaknesses of the youth sport programs you were involved in during childhood.

10. Outline and discuss the key features of the developmental model of sport participation.

Suggested Reading

Côté, J., & Lidor, R. (Eds.) (2013). *Condition of children's talent development in sport*. Morgantown, WV: Fitness Information Technology.

Smoll, F. L., & Smith, R. E. (2002). *Children and youth in sport: A biopsychosocial perspective* (2nd ed.). Dubuque, IA: Kendal Hunt.

References

Abernethy, B., Baker, J., & Côté, J. (2005). Transfer of pattern recall skills as a contributor to the development of sport expertise. *Applied Cognitive Psychology, 19*, 705–718.

Allen, J. B. (2003). Social motivation in youth sport. *Journal of Sport & Exercise Psychology, 25*, 551–567.

Álvarez, M. S., Balaguer, I., Castillo, I., & Duda, J. L. (2009). Coach autonomy support and quality of sport engagement in young soccer players. *Spanish Journal of Psychology, 12*, 138–148. doi: 10.1017/s1138741600001554.

Arthur, B. (2014, February 9). Dufour-Lapointe sisters balance competition and family. Retrieved from http://www.canada.com/olympics/columns/dufour-lapointe-sisters-balance-competition-and-family.

Baker, J., & Côté, J. (2006). Shifting training requirements during athlete development: The relationship among deliberate practice, deliberate play and other sport involvement in the acquisition of sport expertise. In D. Hackfort & G. Tenenbaum (Eds.), *Essential processes for attaining peak performance* (pp. 92–109). Aachen, Germany: Meyer and Meyer.

Baker, J., Côté, J., & Deakin, J. (2005). Expertise in ultra-endurance triathletes: Early sport involvement, training structure, and the theory of deliberate practice. *Journal of Applied Sport Psychology, 17*, 64–78.

Benson, P. L. (1997). *All kids are our kids: What communities must do to raise caring and responsible children and adolescents*. San Francisco: Jossey-Bass.

Blazo, J. A., Carson, S., Czech, D. R., & Dees, W. (2014). A qualitative investigation of the sibling sport achievement. *The Sport Psychologist, 28*, 36–47.

Bredemeier, B. J. L., & Shields, D. L. L. (1996). Moral development and children's sport. In F. L. Smoll & R. E. Smith (Eds.), *Children and youth sport: A biopsychosocial perspective* (pp. 381–404). Chicago: Brown & Benchmark.

Bruner, M. W., Erickson, K., Wilson, B., & Côté, J. (2010). An appraisal of athlete development models through citation network analysis. *Psychology of Sport and Exercise, 11*, 133–139.

Bruner, M. W., Eys, M. A., & Turnnidge, J. (2013). Peer and group influences in youth sport. In J. Côté & R. Lidor (Eds.), *Conditions of children's talent development in sport* (pp. 157–178). Morgantown, WV: Fitness Information Technology.

Buffery, S. (2014, February 9). Dufour-Lapointe sisters offer tear jerking tale. *Toronto Sun*. Retrieved from http://www.torontosun.com/2014/02/09/dufour-lapointe-sisters-offer-tear-jerking-tale.

Canadian Broadcasting Corporation (CBC, 2014, February 9). Dufour-Lapointe family speaks to Ron MacLean. Retrieved from http://olympics.cbc.ca/videos/video/seoname=the-dufour-lapointe-family-interview-olympic-primetime.html.

Clark, W. (2008). Kids' sport. *Canadian Social Trends, 11*, 54–61.

Côté, J. (1999). The influence of the family in the development of talent in sport. *The Sport Psychologist, 13*, 395–417.

Côté, J., Baker, J., & Abernethy, B. (2007). Practice and play in the development of sport expertise. In R. Eklund & G. Tenenbaum (Eds.), *Handbook of sport psychology* (3rd ed., pp. 184–202). Hoboken, NJ: Wiley.

Côté, J., Bruner, M., Strachan, L., Erickson, K., & Fraser-Thomas, J. (2010). Athletes' development and coaching. In J. Lyle & C. Cushion (Eds.), *Sport Coaching: Professionalism and Practice* (pp. 63–83). Oxford, UK: Elsevier.

Côté, J., & Gilbert, W. (2009). An integrative definition of coaching effectiveness and expertise. *International Journal of Sports Science and Coaching, 4*, 307–323.

Côté, J., & Hay, J. (2002). Children's involvement in sport: A developmental perspective. In J. M. Silva III & D. E. Stevens (Eds.), *Psychological foundations of sport* (pp. 484–502). Boston: Allyn & Bacon.

Côté, J., & Hancock, D. (2014). Evidence-based policies for youth sport programs. *International Journal of Sport Policy and Politics*. doi: 10.1080/19406940.2014.919338.

Cutrona, C. E., & Russell, D. W. (1990). Type of social support and specific stress: Toward a theory of optimal matching. In B. R. Sarason, I. G. Sarason, & G. R. Pierce (Eds.), *Social support: An interactional view* (pp. 319–366). New York: Wiley.

Danish, S. (2002). *SUPER (Sports United to Promote Education and Recreation) Program: Leader manual* (3rd ed.). Richmond, VA: Life Skills Centre, Virginia Commonwealth University.

Davis, N. W., & Meyer, B. B. (2008). When sibling becomes competitor: A qualitative investigation of same-sex sibling competition in elite sport. *Journal of Applied Sport Psychology, 20*(2), 220–235.

Eccles, J. S., & Harold, R. D. (1991). Gender differences in sport involvement: Applying the Eccles expectancy-value model. *Journal of Applied Sport Psychology, 3*, 7–35.

Emery, C. A., Hagel, B., Decloe, M., & Carly, M. (2010). Risk factors for injury and severe injury in youth ice hockey: A systematic review of the literature. *Injury Prevention, 16*, 113–118.

Ericsson, K. A., Krampe, R. T., & Tesch-Römer, C. (1993). The role of deliberate practice in the acquisition of expert performance. *Psychological Review, 100*, 363–406.

Erickson, K., Côté, J., Hollenstein, T., & Deakin, J. (2011). Examining coach–athlete interactions using state space grids: An observational analysis in competitive youth sport. *Psychology of Sport and Exercise, 12*, 645–654.

Fraser-Thomas, J., & Côté, J. (2009). Understanding adolescents' positive and negative developmental experiences in sport. *The Sport Psychologist, 23*, 3–23.

Fraser-Thomas, J., Côté, J., & Deakin, J. (2008a). Examining adolescent sport dropout and prolonged engagement from a developmental perspective. *Journal of Applied Sport Psychology, 20*, 318–333.

Fraser-Thomas, J., Côté, J., & Deakin, J. (2008b). Understanding dropout and prolonged engagement in adolescent competitive sport. *Psychology of Sport and Exercise, 9*, 645–662.

Fraser-Thomas, J., Jeffery-Tosoni, S., & Baker, J. (2014). "I like that you can hit a guy and not really get in trouble": Young ice hockey players' experiences with body checking. *International Journal of Sport and Exercise Psychology, 12*, 121–133.

Fraser-Thomas, J. L., Côté, J., & Deakin, J. (2005). Youth sport programs: An avenue to foster positive youth development. *Physical Education and Sport Pedagogy, 10*, 49–70.

Fredericks, J. A., & Eccles, J. S. (2004). Parental influences on youth involvement in sports. In M. R. Weiss (Ed.), *Developmental sport and exercise psychology: A lifespan perspective* (pp. 145–164). Morgantown, WV: Fitness Information Technology.

Gilbert, W. D., Trudel, P., & Haughian, L. P. (1999). Interactive decision making factors considered by coaches of youth ice hockey during games. *Journal of Teaching in Physical Education, 18*, 290–311.

Gould, D. (1993). Intensive sports participation and the prepubescent athlete: Competitive stress and burnout effects. In B. R. Cahill & A. J. Pearl (Eds.), *Intensive training and participation in youth sports* (pp. 19–38). Champaign, IL: Human Kinetics.

Gould, D., & Carson, S. (2008). Life skills development through sport: Current status and future directions. *International Review of Sport and Exercise Psychology, 1*, 58–78.

Gould, D., Lauer, L., Rolo, C., Jannes, C., & Pennisi, N. (2008). The role of parents in tennis success: Focus group interviews with junior coaches. *The Sport Psychologist, 22*, 18–37.

Harwood, C., & Knight, C. (2009). Understanding parental stressors: An investigation of British tennis-parents. *Journal of Sport Sciences, 27*, 339–351.

Hellison, D., Martinek, T., & Walsh, D. (2008). Sport and responsible leadership among youth. In N. Holt (Ed.), *Positive youth development through sport* (pp. 49–60). New York: Routledge.

Hellstedt, J. C. (1987). The coach/parent/athlete relationship. *The Sport Psychologist, 1*, 151–160.

Helsen, W. F., Starkes, J. L., & Hodges, N. J. (1998). Team sports and the theory of deliberate practice. *Journal of Sport & Exercise Psychology, 20*, 12–34.

High Five. (2014). *What Is High Five?* Retrieved from www.highfive.org/what-high-five.

Hockey Canada. (2013). *Player Development*. Retrieved from http://www.hockeycanada.ca/index. php/ci_id/58611/la_id/1.htm.

Holt, N. L. (Ed.) (2008). *Positive youth development through sport*. London: Routledge.

Holt, N. L., Black, D. E., Tamminen, K. A., Fox, K. R., & Mandigo, J. L. (2008). Levels of social complexity and dimensions of peer experiences in youth sport. *Journal of Sport & Exercise Psychology, 30*: 411–431.

Holt, N. L., Tamminen, K. A., Black, D. E., Sehn, Z. L., & Wall, M. P. (2008). Parental involvement in competitive youth sport settings. *Psychology of Sport and Exercise, 9*, 663–685.

Horn, T. S. (2004). Developmental perspectives on self-perceptions in children and adolescents. In M. R. Weiss (Ed.), *Developmental sport and exercise psychology: A lifespan perspective* (pp. 165–196). Morgantown, WV: Fitness Information Technology.

Jelicic, H., Bobek, D. L., Phelps, E., Lerner, R. M., & Lerner, J. V. (2007). Using positive youth development to predict contribution and risk behaviors in early adolescence: Findings from the first two waves of the 4-H study of positive youth development. *International Journal of Behavioral Development, 31*, 263–273.

Keegan, R., Spray, C., Harwood, C., & Lavallee, D. (2010). The motivational atmosphere in youth sport: Coach, parent and peer influences on motivation in specializing sport participants. *Journal of Applied Sport Psychology, 22*, 87–105.

Knight, C. J., & Holt, N. L. (2013). Strategies used and assistance required to facilitate children's involvement in tennis: Parents' perspectives. *The Sport Psychologist, 27*, 281–291.

Knight, C. J., Neely, K. C., & Holt, N. L. (2011). Parental behaviours in team sports: How do female athletes want parents to behave? *Journal of Applied Sport Psychology, 23*, 76–92.

Larson, R. W. (2000). Toward a psychology of positive youth development. *American Psychologist, 55*, 170–183.

Larson, R. W., & Kleiber, D. A. (1993). Structured leisure as a context for the development of attention during adolescence. *Society and Leisure, 16*, 77–98.

Larson, R. W., & Verma, S. (1999). How children and adolescents spend time across the world: Work, play, and developmental opportunities. *Psychological Bulletin, 125*, 701–736.

Law, M. P., Côté, J., & Ericsson, K. A. (2007). Characteristics of expert development in rhythmic gymnastics: A retrospective study. *International Journal of Sport and Exercise Psychology, 5*, 82–103.

MacGregor, R. (2014, February 9). Dufour-Lapointe family bonds over medal wins. *The Globe and Mail*. Retrieved from http://www.theglobeandmail.com/sports/olympics/dufour-lapointe-family-bonds-over-medal-wins/article16772511/#dashboard/follows/.

McCallister, S. G., Blinde, E. M., & Weiss, W. M. (2000). Teaching values and implementing philosophies: Dilemmas of the youth sport coach. *Physical Educator, 57*, 35–46.

McCarthy, P. J., & Jones, M. V. (2007). A qualitative study of sport enjoyment in the sampling years. *The Sport Psychologist, 21*, 400–416.

NRCIM. (2002). Features of positive developmental settings. In NRCIM (Ed.), *Community programs to promote community development* (pp. 86–118). Washington, DC: National Academy Press.

Nixon, H. L. (1997). Gender, sport, and aggressive behavior outside sport. *Journal of Sport and Social Issues, 21*, 379–391.

Patrick, H., Ryan, A. M., Alfeld-Liro, C., Fredricks, J. A., Hruda, L. Z., & Eccles, J. S. (1999). Adolescents' commitment to developing talent: The role of peers in continuing motivation for sports and the arts. *Journal of Youth and Adolescence, 28*, 741–763.

Petitpas, A. J., Cornelius, A. E., Van Raalte, J. L., & Jones, T. (2005). A framework for planning youth sport programs that foster psychosocial development. *The Sport Psychologist, 19*, 63–80.

Petitpas, A. J., Cornelius, A. E., Van Raalte, J. L. (2008). Youth development through sport: It's all about relationships. In N. Holt (Ed.), *Positive youth development through sport* (pp. 61–70). New York: Routledge.

Power, T. G., & Woolger, C. (1994). Parenting practices and age-group swimming: A correlational study. *Research Quarterly for Exercise and Sport, 65*, 59–66.

Respect in Sport (2014). *Parent program*. Retrieved from http://www.respectinsport.com/parent-program/.

Rottensteiner, C., Laakso, L., Tuomo, P., & Konttinen, N. (2013). Personal reasons for withdrawal from team sports and the influence of significant others among youth athletes, *International Journal of Sports Science & Coaching, 8*, 19–32.

Scales, P., & Leffert, N. (1999). *Developmental assets: A synthesis of the scientific research on adolescent development*. Minneapolis, MN: Search Institute.

Scanlan, T. K., Stein, G. L., & Ravizza, K. (1991). An in depth study of former elite figure skaters: III. Sources of stress. *Journal of Sport & Exercise Psychology, 13*, 103–120.

Shields, D. L., & Bredemeier, B. L. (2009). *True competition: A guide to pursuing excellence in sport and society*. Champaign, IL: Human Kinetics.

Smoll, F. L., & Smith, R. E. (2002). Coaching behavior research and intervention in youth sports. In F. L. Smoll & R. E. Smith (Eds.), *Children and youth in sport: A biopsychosocial perspective* (2nd ed., pp. 211–233). Dubuque, IA: Kendal Hunt.

Soberlak, P., & Côté, J. (2003). Developmental activities of elite ice hockey players. *Journal of Applied Sport Psychology, 15*, 41–49.

Theokas, C., Danish, S., Hodge, K, Ihirangi, H., & Forneris, T. (2008). Enhancing life skills through sport for children and youth. In N. Holt (Ed.), *Positive youth development through sport* (pp. 71–82). New York: Routledge.

Trussell, D. E. (2012). Contradictory aspects of organized youth sport: Challenging and fostering sibling relationships and participation experiences. *Youth and Society*, 0044118X12453058.

Turnnidge, J., Côté, J., Hollenstein, T., & Deakin, J. (2014). A direct observation of the dynamic content and structure of coach–athlete interactions in a model sport program. *Journal of Applied Sport Psychology, 26*, 225–240. doi: 10.1080/10413200.2013.821637.

Turnnidge, J., Vierimaa, M., & Côté, J. (2012). An in-depth investigation of a model sport program for athletes with a physical disability. *Psychology, 3*, 1131–1141. doi: 10.4236/psych.2012.312A167.

Ullrich-French, S., & Smith, A. L. (2009). Social and motivational predictors of continued youth sport participation. *Psychology of Sport and Exercise, 10*, 87–95. doi: 10.1016/j.psychsport.2008.06.007.

Vella, S., Oades, L., & Crowe, T. (2011). The role of the coach in facilitating positive youth development: Moving from theory to practice. *Journal of Applied Sport Psychology, 23*, 33–48. doi: 10.1080/10413200.2010.511423.

Vierimaa, M., Erickson, K., Côté, J., & Gilbert, W. (2012). Positive youth development: A measurement framework for sport. *International Journal of Sports Science and Coaching, 7*, 601–614.

Wall, M., & Côté, J. (2007). Developmental activities that lead to drop out and investment in sport. *Physical Education and Sport Pedagogy, 12*, 77–87.

Weiss, M. R., & Fretwell, S. D. (2005). The parent–coach/child–athlete relationship in youth sport. Cordial, contentious, or conundrum? *Research Quarterly for Exercise and Sport, 76*, 286–305.

Weiss, M. R., & Smith, A. L. (2002). Friendship quality in youth sport: Relationship to age, gender, and motivational variables. *Journal of Sport and Exercise Psychology, 24*: 420–437.

Wilcox, S., & Trudel, P. (1998). Constructing the coaching principles and beliefs of a youth ice hockey coach. *Avante, 4*, 39–66.

Woolger, C., & Power, T. G. (1993). Parent and sport socialization: Views from the achievement literature. *Journal of Sport Behavior, 16*, 171–189.

Wright, A. D., & Côté, J. (2003). A retrospective analysis of leadership development through sport. *The Sport Psychologist, 17*, 268–291.

Chapter 11

Coaching Psychology

Gordon A. Bloom

Purestock/Getty Images

Chapter Objectives

After reading this chapter, you should be able to do the following:

1 Describe the coach education structure and process in Canada and abroad.

2 Identify the steps to become an elite coach.

3 Describe the common characteristics and coaching principles of youth sport coaches.

4 Describe the components of Chelladurai's sport leadership model and its relationship to coaching.

5 Define the primary components of the coaching model.

6 Describe effective coaching behaviours.

7 Describe the elements of an effective coach–athlete relationship.

8 Explain the athlete-centred approach adopted by many non-professional Canadian coaches.

9 Explain the model of coaching efficacy.

Coach C, an aspiring third-year coach of an elite women's basketball team, had not been able to sleep for the past week. She had been thinking about her team competing in the upcoming playoffs without her top player and league most valuable player (MVP). With this player, Coach C's team had been ranked as high as first in the province and fifth in the country. They were on a roll, and the playoffs were just around the corner. Coach C wanted to win to establish her reputation as an up-and-coming elite coach.

The loss of this key player was not due to injury, attitude, or academics; rather, it was due to an ethical dilemma that would create the defining moment of this young coach's career. If this athlete played one more game during the season, then she would forfeit a year of eligibility at an NCAA Division 1 university in the United States, for which she was being heavily recruited. Playing at an American Division 1 university would allow this athlete to realize her dream of competing against the best women basketball players in the world and possibly playing basketball for the Canadian national team upon her graduation.

The day before the playoffs began, Coach C received a text message from her athlete indicating her desire to continue playing this year. Would Coach C lessen her chance of coaching a national championship team by not encouraging her star athlete to play in this game? The answer is "yes"; Coach C convinced her league MVP not to play in the game, and the team subsequently lost a close game in the first round of the playoffs. Coach C knew her star athlete's heart was with the team but that deep down she was uncertain and nervous about the consequences of playing and forfeiting a year of NCAA playing eligibility. Coach C believed that the value of a sound education for a student was far more important than adding a notch to her coaching résumé.

This scenario demonstrates how a coach's decision and behaviour affect many people in different ways. Thus, it is not surprising that research on expert performers in domains ranging from the arts and sciences to sport have found that the quality of teaching or coaching is an important factor contributing to an individual's rise to prominence (Bloom, 1985; Salmela & Moraes, 2003). This may also explain the large amount of time, effort, and energy that some parents of gifted children spend searching for the right coach or teacher to help their child realize his or her potential.

Why then is so little respect afforded to many of Canada's greatest coaches by both the media and the general population? Possibly with the exception of professional or national team coaches in ice hockey—where the exploits of Toe Blake, Scotty Bowman, Danièle Sauvageau, and Mike Babcock are lauded—many of our elite-level Canadian coaches have received little acclaim or public adoration. For example, how many people in Canada are aware of the accomplishments of current and former Olympic coaches such as Kathy Shields or Jack Donohue in basketball, Al Morrow in rowing, Julie Sauvé in synchronized swimming, or Paralympic coaches Peter Eriksson in athletics or Tim Frick in wheelchair basketball?

The relative anonymity of these great coaches leads to many interesting questions: Do people value and understand the importance of a good coach? Is there a recipe for coaching development and knowledge acquisition? And, what knowledge is used by coaches to develop successful and well-balanced athletes?

INTRODUCTION

Coaching science: Encompasses research on all aspects of coaching.

Information presented in this chapter falls under the term **coaching science**, which "comprises research on the coaching, learning, and instructional processes as directed by coaches" (Gilbert & Trudel, 2004, p. 389). Gilbert and Trudel compiled and analyzed a database of 611 studies on coaching science published in English-language journals between 1970 and 2001. Among their findings are the following points, which still held true years later (Gilbert & Rangeon, 2012):

- Coaching science research has increased significantly since 1970, now averaging approximately 30 published articles per year.

- There is a relatively small core of authors who have developed a significant line of research in coaching science.

- Research has branched from solely examining coaching behaviours to looking at coaching behaviours in combination with coaching cognition.

- There is no single resource that lists and evaluates the assessment tools created to study coaching practices.

- Coach gender issues are one of the most frequently studied topics in this field; as well, coaching effectiveness (knowledge) and career issues (e.g., burnout) are starting to receive increased attention.

- Coaching science research has seen a continuous increase in qualitative research studies, especially those incorporating an interview technique.

- There is an absence of studies of coaching science that includes athletes, parents, and sport administrators.

- Most coaching scientific studies have focused on team-sport and school-based coaches, and have primarily excluded coaches of professional sports.

- Ninety percent of the studies have not used any criteria of coaching effectiveness.

COACH EDUCATION

Coaching Association of Canada: A not-for-profit organization that governs the coaching profession in Canada.

The path for becoming a coach is not as clearly laid out as it is for other professionals, such as a teacher, lawyer, or nurse. In Canada, coach education and development is governed by the **Coaching Association of Canada** (CAC; www.coach.ca), which was created in 1970 following a task force recommendation on sport in our country. The CAC's mission is to provide the foundation of skills, knowledge, and attitudes needed to ensure effective coaching leadership for Canadian athletes. In 1974, CAC created the **National Coaching Certification Program** (NCCP) to meet the needs of all coaches, from beginner to most experienced. Through a series of workshops, the NCCP trains and certifies coaches in more than 60 sports. Most sources have credited Canada's NCCP as being the first widely adopted national coach education program in the world.

The structure of the NCCP was redeveloped in the mid- to late 2000s. The original model was a knowledge- and course-based program run by the CAC with five levels of certification. The new model is structured around a competency-based approach to coach training and education that places more emphasis on coaches' abilities to meet the needs of their participants. As well, more emphasis is placed on the environment or context (particular level) in which the coach is coaching. In layman's terms, the CAC has moved from a "what a coach should know" approach to a "what a coach should do" approach.

The new NCCP model is divided into three streams (see Figure 11.1):

National Coaching Certification Program: A knowledge- and course-based program run by the Coaching Association of Canada.

Figure 11.1 The new coaching education structure in Canada

Community sport stream	Competition stream	Instruction stream
Initiation CSp-Init **Ongoing participation CSp-Ong**	**Introduction Comp-Int** **Development Comp-Dev** **High performance Comp-HP**	**Beginners Inst-Beg** **Intermediate performers Inst-Imd** **Advanced performers Inst-Adv**
Initiation context Participants of all ages are encouraged to participate in the sport and introduced to sport basics in a fun, safe, and self-esteem building environment regardless of their ability.	**Introduction context** Children and/or adolescents are taught basic sport skills and athletic abilities in a fun and safe environment and are typically prepared for local and/or regional level competitions.	**Beginners context** Participants of all ages, with little or no sport experience, are taught basic sport skills.
Ongoing participation context Participants of all ages are encouraged to continue participating in the sport for fun, fitness, skill development, and social interaction.	**Development context** Adolescents and young adults are coached to refine basic sport skills, to develop more advanced skills and tactics, and are generally prepared for performance at provincial and/or national level competitions.	**Intermediate performers context** Participants, who already have some experience and proficiency in the sport, are taught to refine basic skills and introduced to more complex techniques.
	High performance context Young adults are coached to refine advanced skills and tactics and are typically prepared for performance at national and international level competitions.	**Advanced performers context** Participants who are experienced and already proficient in the sport are taught to refine advanced skills and techniques.

Source: Table from Coaching Association of Canada. Retrieved September 20, 2009, from http://www.coach.ca/files/NCCPModel_en_skin.swf. Used with permission.

1. Community sport stream: This stream focuses on broad-based participation at introductory levels of sport (e.g., house league). Coaches in this stream are instructed to introduce sport for fun, to develop skills, and to foster social interaction and lifelong participation.

2. Competition stream: This stream focuses on skill development for participation in competitive contexts (e.g., high school sport and higher). The coaches are instructed in all areas of athlete training, including physical, technical, tactical, and mental.

3. Instruction stream: This stream focuses on skill proficiency in non-competitive situations (e.g., tennis camp, golf instructor).

Additional coach education and development information in Canada can be acquired through either the education system or the National Coaching Institutes. Regarding the former, some universities in Canada (i.e., Victoria, Alberta, and Laval) offer specialized training in coach education. Perhaps the most well known is the Master of Education in Coaching Studies program at the University of Victoria (http://www.uvic.ca/education/exercise/graduate/med/index.php). This two-year, project-based option caters to those with a particular interest in coaching science and offers both courses and cooperative work terms. It is geared to those with a specific interest in elite coaching. Although not a postgraduate program, Université Laval offers a Baccalauréat en Intervention Sportive (BIS; www.fse.ulaval.ca/reseau-bis) that is also divided into distinct stages that provide both theory (classroom setting) and practical experiences (apprenticeships).

Canada currently has *National Coaching Institutes* (NCIs; www.coach.ca/national-coaching-institutes-p137482), located in seven provinces across the country, whose mission is to enhance the training environment for high-performance coaches (and athletes) through a variety of services. Successful completion of this program grants students a diploma in High Performance Coaching, which attests to expertise in three main areas: (1) planning, designing, and implementing a sport program that fits within their athletes' context, (2) knowledge on practical coaching, and (3) leadership skills and ethical coaching strategies. Overall, the program aims to improve one's critical thinking, communication skills, and overall philosophy on coaching elite athletes.

Similar in many ways to Canada, both Australia and the United Kingdom have coach education systems that were developed in part with government participation and assistance. Created around the same time as Canada's program, Australia's program (www.ausport.gov.au/participating/coaches) ensures that its accredited coaches have received training in coaching principles. The National Coaching Accreditation Scheme (NCAS) is an initiative of the Australian Sports Commission (ASC) and is a progressive coach education program offering courses at various levels, with over 70 sports participating. The ACS has developed an initiative to encourage inexperienced coaches to enter the program and has launched the Beginning Coaching General Principles, a free basic skills course to assist beginner coaches in Australia.

The United Kingdom's coach education program began in 1983 with the National Coaching Foundation, which then changed its name to "sports coach UK" (www.sportscoachuk.org). Its mandate is to guide the education and development of coaches at every level and to promote and establish coaching as a profession. In 2006, sports coach UK was asked to develop the UK Coaching Framework, an initiative that was designed to enhance the quality of coaching at all levels and to be a world leader in coaching development by 2016. One of the developments of this group is the UK Coaching Certificate (UKCC), a coach education program in which more than 30 sports are currently taking part (www.sportscoachuk.org/people-who-develop-coaches/resource-bank/ukcc).

A different approach to coach training and education has taken place in the United States. Unlike the three countries already mentioned, the United States does not have one government-based centralized national coaching organization for training its many volunteer and professional coaches. As a result, several coaching development programs were created around the same time as the NCCP and NCAS. For example, the American Coaching Effectiveness Program, founded in 1976, evolved into the American Sport Education Program (ASEP; see the Human Kinetics Coach Education Center at www.asep.com) and appears to be the most widely used program in the United States. ASEP currently certifies coaches in two streams: volunteer and professional. The National Federation of State High School Associations (NFHS; www.nfhslearn.com) offers an online fundamentals of coaching course that is designed to certify interscholastic teachers/coaches at a number of different levels. Positive Coaching Alliance (PCA) is another American organization that is responsible for educating coaches (www.positivecoach.org). Founded in 1998 at Stanford University, PCA is an independent group that provides research-based training workshops and practical tools for coaches.

The Society of Health and Physical Educators (SHAPE) America has also impacted coach education efforts in the United States. SHAPE America was founded in 1885 and is the largest organization of professionals in the United States that is dedicated to advancing professional practice and promoting research related to health, physical education, physical activity, dance, and sport. One of its accomplishments was the creation of the National Council for the Accreditation of Coach Education. Its goal is to facilitate the development and accreditation of all coaching education/certification programs based on eight domain standards that are set across several levels (http://www.shapeamerica.org/standards/coaching/coachingstandards.cfm). This project has been endorsed by the United States Olympic Committee, several key youth sport organizations, and many universities offering coaching education studies.

The government-funded and -supported coaching education programs in Canada, Australia, and the United Kingdom demonstrate that coaching is becoming recognized as an important profession that can assist the growth and development of today's amateur and professional athletes. Coach education has grown tremendously in the last 40 years since certified programs were introduced. At present, coach education is aided by the International Council for Coaching Excellence (ICCE; www.icce.ws), whose mission is to improve the quality and exposure of coaching at all levels around the world, and to promote sport coaching as an internationally accepted profession. The ICCE is a not-for-profit international organization that has a membership that believes in international collaboration and exchange. To date, progress has been slow in getting countries around the world to restructure their coach education programs. However, it does seem that more people are beginning to understand and value the importance of the coach in the growth and development of athletes and in providing structured training for them. Among its most noteworthy accomplishments, the ICCE established the International Sport Coaching Framework (http://www.humankinetics.com/products/all-products/international-sport-coaching-framework-version-12-ebook-5683626) to

Stanley Cup and Olympic–winning coach Mike Babcock studied physical education at McGill University.

Jay Lapret/Corbis Wire/epa/Corbis

facilitate the development, recognition, and certification of coaches. More specifically, the document outlines the primary roles and responsibilities of the coach in athlete development, the qualifications and competencies required to coach effectively, and the methods by which coaches are educated, developed, and certified. This framework should serve as a landmark document for helping to professionalize and structure the coaching profession.

Coaching education programs offered by national organizations (e.g., NCCP), National Coaching Institutes, and higher education institutions can facilitate coaching effectiveness.

REFLECTIONS 11.1

Canada, the United Kingdom, and Australia have well developed coach education programs that were partly developed with government participation and assistance. What do you think are the advantages of structured coaching education programs? Can you think of any possible drawbacks?

ELITE COACH DEVELOPMENT

Despite the efforts of the ICCE and various coach education programs, there has historically been a lack of scientific research on ways of becoming a successful (Canadian) elite coach. In the last 20 years, a group of researchers have begun identifying common developmental pathways and characteristics that shed light on what it takes to become a top-level coach in Canada (e.g., Carter & Bloom, 2009; Erickson et al., 2007; Gilbert et al., 2006; Rathwell et al., 2014). As athletes, all of the elite Canadian coaches reported living active and successful sporting lives that began with a love of sport that was often fuelled by the encouragement of family members and accessibility to physical resources. They played and excelled in a number of sports as youths (both team and individual) and often had many leadership positions throughout their athletic careers. Not surprisingly, some researchers have found that elite athletic experiences were found to be an important aspect of expert coaches' career development, knowledge, and perhaps even career success. The question that remains unanswered is how much athletic experience is required.

Gilbert and colleagues (2006) found that successful high school and elite sport coaches accumulated several thousand hours of athletic participation, across several sports, for at least 13 years. Erickson and associates (2007) also found that expert coaches had accumulated highly competitive sport experiences. Despite this, neither study was able to identify a minimum standard of athletic excellence required to reach an elite level of coaching, although it was implied that they were "elite" athletes. Carter and Bloom (2009) offered a different viewpoint on the necessity of elite athletic experiences for becoming an expert coach. More specifically, their sample consisted of successful university team-sport coaches who had not competed as athletes at the university level or higher. The coaches in their study demonstrated that, with persistence, it was possible to acquire coaching knowledge without having been an elite athlete. Interestingly, most of their recommendations for acquiring coaching knowledge were similar to other studies on expert coach development (except for the elite athletic experiences), and included:

- Volunteering in the community, particularly at youth sport practices
- Gaining experience as an assistant coach
- Frequently interacting with and forming peer networks with other coaches
- Observing other coaches
- Studying kinesiology and physical education at university
- Attending coaching clinics
- Reading coaching books and acquiring coaching information via the internet

One additional area that may be the most important factor in coaches' growth and development is **mentoring**. There are many professions in which mentoring is a common and expected process. For example, pilots, doctors, and police officers spend years refining their skills with the assistance of experienced and knowledgeable colleagues who ensure that they are allowed to grow and develop in an environment designed to minimize errors and build knowledge and confidence.

An empirical examination of mentoring by researchers Bloom and colleagues (1998) found that all of the 21 expert coaches in their sample were mentored both as athletes and as developing coaches by well-respected individuals. The knowledge they acquired from their mentors helped mould their coaching ideas and philosophies. Interestingly,

Mentoring: The assistance of more experienced and well-respected colleagues who ensure growth and development in an environment that is designed to minimize errors and to build knowledge and confidence.

University of Victoria Vikes

Kathy Shields has influenced many of Canada's athletes and coaches in basketball for more than 30 years.

No discussion about coach and athlete mentoring in Canada would be complete without mentioning Kathy Shields—a former member of our Olympic basketball team, as well as former assistant coach and head coach for our national basketball team. She finished her coaching duties as head coach at the University of Victoria in 2005, where she compiled an astounding 0.865 winning percentage over her 25-year coaching career. Not surprisingly, she has been enshrined in various Halls of Fame throughout our country. Certified as a master coach in 1986 by the CAC, Shields has influenced nearly all of Canada's elite coaches and athletes in women's basketball for the last 35 years. No fewer than eight of her former players and assistant coaches are or have been head coaches of university teams.

these coaches noted that it was important for them not to imitate everything about their mentors; rather, their own beliefs and personalities affected and shaped their coaching style. The importance of mentoring has also been highlighted by researchers in the United States (Gould et al., 1990), the United Kingdom (Jones et al., 2003), Singapore (Koh et al., 2014), and Spain (Jimenez et al., 2009).

Although the NCCP highlights the importance of receiving advice and training from a respected mentor, a question still remains: How much of an impact does good mentoring have on the growth and development of aspiring coaches? The answer to this question may never be known; however, an examination of the pedigree of some of sport's greatest coaches clearly shows the importance of solid mentoring. Former NHL coach Scotty Bowman learned from the greatest predecessor of his time, Toe Blake. Interestingly, many of Bowman's protégés have assumed top leadership roles in hockey, from Jacques Lemaire to Bob Gainey to Ken Dryden. Likewise, Bill Walsh, the successful football coach of the San Francisco 49ers' dynasty of the 1980s, apprenticed under a master coach, Paul Brown. Walsh then mentored a number of successful NFL head coaches, including Mike Holmgren, Dennis Green, and George Seifert.

Despite the efforts of Kathy Shields and other top women coaches in our country, the data on high-level head coaching positions in Canada indicate that women are underrepresented. More specifically, a University of Toronto (2011) study on gender equity found that the number of head coaches in Canadian Interuniversity Sport (CIS) had a proportion of 19% female to 81% male (http://physical.utoronto.ca/docs/csps-pdfs/cis-gender-equity-report—2013.pdf?sfvrsn=2). This data also revealed a clustering effect of coaches in the sports of women's basketball, ice hockey, rugby, and volleyball. While many men were coaching women's teams, only two women (Brenda Willis, volleyball, at Queen's University; and Olga Hrycak, basketball, at the Université du Québec à Montréal) had been head coaches of men's CIS programs. At the Olympic level, women are also dramatically underrepresented. In the most recent Winter Olympics (Sochi, 2014), women took only 10% of the coaching roles.

In sum, effective coach development in Canada seems to involve a combination of educating coaches through programs such as the NCCP, forming peer networks with other coaches, observing other coaches, and mentoring. Evidence for this can be seen in Wilson and colleagues' (2010) investigation of the career progression of Canadian high school coaches. Their results indicated that formal coach education provides coaches with an essential knowledge base. However, they also found that this needs to be supplemented with informal learning opportunities such as working with more experienced coaches.

YOUTH SPORT COACHING

Up to this point in the discussion, most information has been slanted toward coaches of elite sport. The context of youth sport has many interesting nuances that distinguish it from other levels of coaching. More specifically, the role of the coach in youth sport may have more important global implications than it does for elite sport. For example, physical inactivity usually begins at a young age; the medical and economic impact of physical inactivity accounts for over $5 billion in Canadian healthcare costs (Katzmarzyk & Janssen, 2004). One way to increase physical activity is to focus on factors that increase motives for youth sport participation, specifically the nature of the environment surrounding the learning and implementation of physical skills (see Chapter 12 for more details). The person who is responsible for creating this positive youth sport environment is the coach.

Characteristics of Youth Coaches

Trudel and Gilbert (2006) outlined a number of characteristics of youth sport coaches:

- Most are male.
- Most are in their mid-30s.
- As few as 10% of these coaches continue coaching for 10 years or more.
- Almost all of these coaches competed in sport, and most were above-average athletes.
- Most of these coaches acquired athletic experience for five years or more in the sport they now coach.
- Love of the sport, wanting to remain associated with the sport, a desire to help young people develop skills, and a desire to serve as a leader and supervisor for young people were the main reasons for coaching.
- Most coaches had a child of their own on the team they coached.
- Just over half of the coaches were university educated.

Research at the University of Ottawa has examined the acquisition and sharing of knowledge of youth sport coaches (e.g., Lemyre et al., 2007; Werthner & Trudel, 2006). Interestingly, this research found that many youth sport coaches were reluctant to share coaching knowledge with their peers for fear of giving away their secrets. On the other hand, many youth sport coaches have complained that they operate in isolation and that there are few opportunities to meet and engage with other coaches at their level of competition. These findings support Lemyre and colleagues' suggestion that more empirical attention be given to the factors affecting youth sport coaches—in particular, ways to acquire and share knowledge.

Ideal Behaviours of Youth Coaches

Ideal behaviours for youth sport coaches have been studied extensively by Smith and Smoll (2002a, 2002b; http://y-e-sports.com/index.html). These researchers believed in the importance of training youth sport coaches to ensure young athletes had fun, enjoyed being a part of a team, learned skills, and developed and increased their self-esteem. Their research over the past 40 years can be divided into two phases. The first phase involved the development of the mediational model of leadership and the coaching behaviour assessment system (CBAS) to categorize coaching behaviours (Smith et al., 1977). Findings from their research using the CBAS demonstrated that coaching behaviours influenced children's self-perceptions, anxiety, and adherence levels. In addition, Smith, Smoll, and colleagues noted that coaching behaviours could be modified through structured coach training and education programs.

These findings influenced the second phase of their research, which involved the implementation of an intervention program called coach effectiveness training (CET), and the subsequent testing of the program in the youth sport setting. Applied research using the CET has demonstrated that children playing for trained coaches, as opposed to untrained volunteers, had significant increases in self-esteem, had decreases in anxiety levels, enjoyed their sporting experience more, and evaluated their coach and teammates more favourably, regardless of the win–loss record (Smith & Smoll, 2002a). Results also indicated that children who played for trained coaches were also more likely to return the following season (Smith & Smoll, 2002a). Table 11.1 summarizes the researchers' key recommended coaching behaviours.

Table 11.1 Effective Practices for Coaching Youth Sport

Reinforce effort as much as results.

Give encouragement after a mistake but in positive and encouraging ways.

Establish clear expectations, involve athletes in behavioural guidelines, and work to build team unity in achieving them.

Set a good example of behaviour, encourage athletes to be supportive of each other, and reinforce them when they do so.

Always give instructions positively and do so in a clear, concise manner.

Foster two-way communication, and respond to the needs of individual players appropriately.

Source: From Smith, R. E., & Smoll, F. L. (2002). *Way to go coach!: A scientifically-proven approach to youth sports coaching effectiveness* (2nd ed., pp. 31–48). Palo Alto, CA: Warde Publishers.

Coaches can be trained so that their behaviours improve the psychosocial development of their athletes.

Lasting approximately three hours, a CET workshop followed five coaching principles (Smith & Smoll, 2002a; Smoll & Smith, 2002). The first principle was to create a healthy climate that was enjoyable and was focused on mastering skills instead of trying to beat an opponent. As well, coaches must understand that their success or failure was not dependent on the outcome of the game or the win–loss record, but rather on their ability to get their athletes to give maximum effort. The second principle was to utilize a positive approach to coaching that involved positive reinforcement, encouragement, and appropriate instruction. Punitive behaviours were highly discouraged. The third principle was to establish norms that emphasize athletes' obligations to help and support one another, thereby increasing cohesion and personal commitment to the team. Coaches must also model and support these behaviours. The fourth principle was to include athletes in decision-making roles regarding team rules and compliance. The fifth principle was to engage in self-monitoring and assessment in order to focus on positive coaching behaviours.

Smith and colleagues (2007) modified the CET program and renamed it the *Mastery Approach to Coaching* (MAC). The philosophy of the program remains the same, which is the promotion of team cohesion and a positive coach–athlete interaction that creates an atmosphere that allows for skill development and reduces the fear of failure. As well, the goal of both programs is to increase intrinsic motivation in young athletes. Among the key changes, the five principles in the CET were reduced to two themes: emphasizing reinforcement in positive ways and measuring success based on maximum effort. Other differences include the length (75 minutes compared to 180 minutes) and the method used to deliver material (lecture-based rather than discussion-based).

In summary, many of today's successful high-profile coaches have gone through common developmental patterns that began during their athletic careers and continued as they moved through the coaching ranks. While they were athletes, most of these experts acquired leadership skills and knowledge from their coaches. As well, most acquired information through the NCCP and supplemented this information with a developmental pattern that included exposure to positive role models (mentors). Their initiation into coaching, combined with the encouragement of their own coaches and their burning desire for sport, helped them excel as elite coaches. Although research on youth sport coaching is comparatively lacking, some common characteristics and ideal coaching principles have been forwarded by experts in this field. For example, coaches' behaviours strongly influenced athletes' attitudes toward the coach, themselves, and the sport. Moreover, athletes of trained coaches perceived their coaches to use more positive behaviours, liked their coaches and teammates more, and had more fun than players of untrained coaches. This provides strong evidence that coaches can be taught to promote some developmental outcomes such as self-esteem, self-worth, and motivation. As the importance of the youth sport coach becomes more apparent in the overall physical activity level of adults, one can expect more research on this sector of coaching.

COACHING KNOWLEDGE

This section will focus on the knowledge of coaches, including their goals, roles, relationships, and responsibilities, as well as the extent to which they can affect the learning and performance of their athletes. In order to present this information, five bodies of literature in coaching psychology will be examined: (1) Chelladurai's sport leadership model, (2) Feltz and colleagues' coaching efficacy model, (3) Jowett and colleagues' 3 + 1 Cs model, (4) athlete-centred coaching, and (5) Côté and colleagues' coaching model.

Sport Leadership

Given its apparent practical appeal, it is not surprising that leadership has been one of the most studied areas in industrial and organizational psychology. In spite of the rich background of research on leadership, this concept is one of the least understood phenomena because almost every finding about leadership (e.g., personality characteristics, gender differences) can be contradicted by other results (Klenke, 1993). In sport, effective leadership has been cited by athletes and coaches as a vital component of achievement (Bucci et al., 2012; Dupuis et al., 2006) and athlete satisfaction (Riemer & Chelladurai, 1995; Chelladurai & Riemer, 1998). At present, most sport leadership research has focused on coaching effectiveness by identifying personality traits, behavioural attributes, and situational determinants.

Several models of sport leadership have been advanced, the most noteworthy being Chelladurai's (1993) **multidimensional model of leadership** (MML), a linear model comprising antecedents, leader behaviours, and consequences (see Figure 11.2). Created specifically for sport situations, Chelladurai's MML conceptualizes leadership as an interactional process, and thus it allows researchers to evaluate leadership effectiveness through team member satisfaction and performance of athletes (consequences). These consequences are directly affected by the degree of congruence among the three states of leader behaviours, called required, preferred, and actual. Required leader behaviours are those that are expected of a coach. For example, coaches are not allowed to make physical contact with their athletes. Preferred leader behaviours are how a coach acts and are generally based on the athletes' preferences. For example, most professional coaches

Multidimensional model of leadership: A linear model comprising antecedents, leader behaviours, and consequences.

Figure 11.2 Multidimensional model of leadership

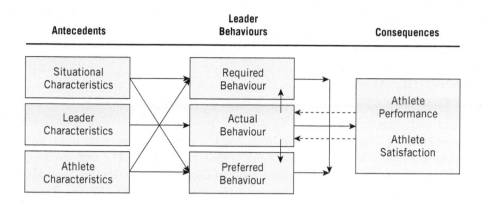

Source: From Singer. HANDBK RES SPORT PSYHOL, 1E. © 1993 Gale, a part of Cengage Learning, Inc. Reproduced by permission. www.cengage.com/permissions.

do not socialize with their players after games. Finally, actual leader behaviours are the behaviours that a coach exhibits, regardless of team standards. These leader behaviours are influenced by antecedent factors, which can be classified into situational (e.g., team goals, norms), leader (e.g., leader's experience or personality), and team-member characteristics (e.g., gender, ability). To date, the majority of research using this model has been for individuals rather than teams.

Chelladurai's model benefited coaching research because it attributed coaches' success to more than great leadership skills. It stressed that success was a function of coaches' capacity to display actual leadership behaviours that responded to a combination of demands from the environment, the players, and the coaches themselves. Furthermore, successful coaches were able to adjust to these demands by incorporating the required and preferred behaviours into their actual behaviours. The majority of research using the MML has primarily focused on the leadership behaviours of adult coaches of elite sports.

REFLECTIONS 11.2

Who was your favourite coach? What were his or her actual leader behaviours? Did all players prefer these behaviours? Does the multidimensional model of leadership help explain your own experiences with this coach?

Outside of sport psychology, research in leadership has begun to focus on the nature and effects of transformational leadership in organizations. Bass and Avolio (Avolio & Bass, 1991; Bass, 1999; Bass & Avolio, 1994) suggest that transformational leaders were, among other things, inspirational motivators who were able to elevate the interest of their followers. Transformational leadership utilizes four leader behaviours that have been shown to influence followers' values, needs, awareness, and performance (Bass & Riggio,

2006). Research in sport shows improved athlete functioning in areas such as intrinsic motivation, commitment, and satisfaction, as well as improved team performance and cohesion, for those who were coached by transformational leaders. The area of transformational leadership is discussed in greater detail in Chapter 8.

Coaching Efficacy

Sport psychology practitioners generally believe that athletes' confidence levels can be changed and improved over time. Thus, the experts would argue that stars—such as Wayne Gretzky, Clara Hughes, Steve Nash, and Christine Sinclair—were not born with exceptionally higher levels of confidence than their competitors. The same analogy can be made with elite coaches. In fact, the topic of confidence has recently been applied to the coaching psychology literature under the title of **coaching efficacy**. This term is defined as "the extent to which coaches believe they have the capacity to affect the learning and performance of their athletes" (Feltz et al., 1999, p. 765). The authors have identified four key dimensions at the core of their model:

1. Game strategy: This refers to the degree to which coaches believe they can effectively coach (i.e., devise strategies) during competitions.

2. Motivation: This refers to the degree to which coaches believe they can effectively affect their athletes' psychological attributes.

3. Technique: This refers to the degree to which coaches believe they can teach the effective skills and techniques of their sport and recognize talent.

4. Character building: This refers to the degree to which coaches believe they can instill a sense of respect or fair play in their athletes.

Those coaches who scored high in each of these four areas were said to have teams that performed better with higher winning percentages, were more committed to their profession, used more praise and encouragement, and had more satisfied athletes who had higher levels of confidence. Furthermore, a coach's level of efficacy was affected by four sources: previous experiences and preparation, previous level of success, perceived skill of the athletes, and the level of community support (see Figure 11.3). The most important of these sources was prior success; coaches who had experienced success as either coaches or athletes felt more confident, especially in devising strategy and motivating athletes.

Since the creation of the conceptual model of coaching efficacy, a group of researchers have begun investigating the effects of coach education courses on a coach's level of efficacy (e.g., Malete & Feltz, 2000; Sullivan & Gee, 2008; Sullivan et al., 2012). Among their conclusions, it was found that coaches who completed a coach education course showed an increase in all four dimensions of coaching efficacy. These findings demonstrate how an important coaching dimension (efficacy) can be learned and improved through coach education programs.

3 + 1 Cs Model

Jowett and colleagues created the 3 + 1 Cs model for studying the relationship between a coach and an athlete's emotions, behaviours, and cognitions (Jowett, 2003; Jowett &

Coaching efficacy: The belief of a coach that he or she can effectively perform various coaching duties.

Figure 11.3 Model of coaching efficacy

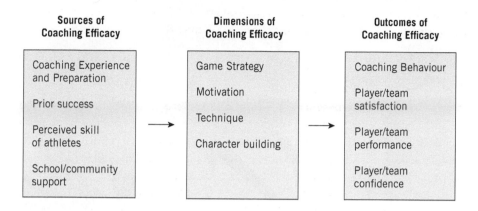

Sources of Coaching Efficacy	Dimensions of Coaching Efficacy	Outcomes of Coaching Efficacy
Coaching Experience and Preparation Prior success Perceived skill of athletes School/community support	Game Strategy Motivation Technique Character building	Coaching Behaviour Player/team satisfaction Player/team performance Player/team confidence

Source: From Sullivan, P. J., & Feltz, D. L. (2002). The psychological effect of Canada's national coaching education program (final grant report). Ottawa, ON: Social Sciences and Humanities Research Council of Canada.

Lavallee, 2007). They suggested that a successful working relationship between the coach and athlete was interdependent and required closeness, commitment, and complementarity.

Closeness is the emotional element of the coach–athlete relationship and occurs when coaches and athletes have a mutual feeling of trust, respect, and liking for one another. **Commitment** represents the cognitive element of the coach–athlete relationship, and involves the coaches' and athletes' thoughts of attachment to one another and the intentions of maintaining their relationship. **Complementarity** encompasses the behavioural element of the coach–athlete dyad, and involves the cooperative interactions between player and coach during training or competition. Finally, **co-orientation** involves the degree of symbiosis in the coach–athlete relationship as far as sharing similar interests, goals, and knowledge in the other three constructs. An example of this relationship would be an athlete saying that he is committed to the coach and the coach responding that she feels and thinks that the athlete is committed to her in the same way.

Research investigating the 3 + 1 Cs model has examined players' and coaches' perceptions of their relationship (Jowett & Clark-Carter, 2006), their beliefs about how their relationship worked (Jowett, 2003; Philippe & Seiler, 2006), and how it affected team cohesion (Jowett & Chaundry, 2004) and motivational climate (Olympiou et al., 2008). For example, Jowett and Chaundry studied 111 university team sport athletes and found that athletes who believed they had stronger relationships with their coaches perceived their team as more cohesive and in sync with their teams' collective tasks. Like team cohesion, coaches' motivational climate was correlated with team sport athletes' relationships with their coaches. Olympiou and colleagues (2008) had athletes of all levels of competition (e.g., recreational to international athletes) fill out questionnaires regarding their perceived motivational climate and their relationship with their coach. Among their findings, athletes who perceived their coaches created a climate that emphasized cooperation, learning, and effort (i.e., task involving climate) felt closer, felt more committed, and believed their relationship with their coach was more complementary than

Closeness: Aspect of the coach–athlete relationship that deals with affective elements such as trust and respect.

Commitment: Aspect of the coach–athlete relationship that deals with intention to maintain an athletic relationship.

Complementarity: Aspect of the coach–athlete relationship that deals with cooperative interactions between them.

Co-orientation: Aspect of the coach–athlete relationship that deals with the degree of common ground in their relationship.

Coach–athlete relationships are an important part of athlete satisfaction.

players who perceived that their coaches stressed winning and competition among the team members (i.e., ego involving climate). Where the two aforementioned studies focused on athletes' individual feelings about their relationship with their coach, Jowett and Clark-Carter looked at 121 independent sport coach–athlete dyads and evaluated their abilities to predict each other's feelings of closeness, commitment, and complementarity. They discovered that athletes were more accurate at describing their coaches' feelings concerning their relationship, which they said was a result of their less powerful position and a need to feel more comfortable and in control.

Other researchers have examined the 3 + 1 Cs model through the subjective experiences of coaches and athletes (Jowett, 2003; Jowett & Meek, 2000; Philippe & Seiler, 2006). For example, Jowett conducted a case study on one Olympic level coach–athlete dyad whose relationship had deteriorated. In her study, the dyad stressed the importance of trust and respect and indicated the need to establish a level of closeness. However, both noted that there could be negative consequences if the athlete and coach become too close to each other, suggesting a coach needs to establish a balance between being nice and being demanding. Furthermore, the coach noted that during training he needed to be closer, but when the competitive season began he had to pull away to allow his athlete to develop her autonomy. Similar results were found in Philippe and Seiler's study of Swiss national swimmers. Each athlete mentioned that feelings of respect, admiration, esteem, appreciation, and regard were requirements for an ideal working relationship. The swimmers also spoke about the importance of good communication with their coach and how a closer relationship made it easier for athletes to communicate openly about a variety of topics with their coach. Finally, athletes addressed the importance of respecting the role of their coach. Taken together, these results indicate that having a close, committed, and complementary coach–athlete relationship will lead to the maximization of athlete potential in training and competition.

In conclusion, researchers have investigated the importance of the 3 + 1 Cs model in the coach–athlete relationship. Athletes and coaches believed that having a strong coach–athlete relationship was vital to the success and performance of athletes, while a lack of closeness, commitment, complementarity, and co-orientation was associated with interpersonal conflicts in their relationships. Findings also indicated that athletes' performance and perceptions of team cohesion and motivational climate were positively influenced by having a close, respectful relationship with their coach, where they worked together toward a collective goal. Finally, researchers found that athletes were more accurate at evaluating their relationship with their coach than coaches were.

Athlete-Centred Coaching

Developing a mutually respectful coach–athlete relationship is also part of **athlete-centred coaching**. While there is no direct theoretical framework for this coaching approach, it does involve the holistic growth and development of both the athlete and the person, a finding which has appeared in numerous coaching publications (e.g., Cassidy, 2013; Duchesne et al., 2011; Vallée & Bloom, 2005). Moreover, some experts have suggested that an athlete-centred approach (ACA) to coaching can lead to increased sport engagement, communication, competence, and motivation (see Lyle, 2010; Mallett & Rynne, 2010). The role of the coach in an ACA to coaching promotes autonomy by using strategies that empower athletes to make choices inside and outside the sporting environment that help players establish an environment in which they share responsibility for individual and team performance (de Souza & Oslin, 2008). Given this information, Coach C, who was introduced at the beginning of this chapter, would be an example of someone who has adopted an ACA to coaching.

Athlete development has been described as the "most obvious task of the coach . . . from youth participants to Olympic athletes" (Côté, Salmela, Trudel, et al., 1995, p. 9). Legendary American university basketball coach John Wooden was famous for teaching both basketball and life skills to his athletes (Gilbert, 2010). He believed that the fundamental principles of teaching were the same in the classroom and on the playing field and he often spoke about the personal relationships he developed with his athletes outside of the basketball court (Nater & Gallimore, 2010). Wooden also believed strongly in team spirit, loyalty, enthusiasm, and determination and felt that his athletes should work with him rather than for him (Wooden & Jamison, 2010). In the same vein, John Wooden (1988) wrote, "I often told my players that, next to my own flesh and blood, they were the closest to me. They were my children. I got wrapped up in them, their lives, and their problems" (p. 62). Wooden's philosophy is even more impressive, considering the on-court success of his UCLA basketball teams: they set all-time records with four perfect 30–0 seasons, 88 consecutive victories, 38 straight NCAA tournament victories, and 10 national championships, including seven in a row.

Wooden's secret to success undoubtedly lies in his pyramid of success (www. coachwooden.com), which explains the necessary steps to achieve success in basketball

Athlete-centred coaching: A recently developed and still understudied coaching strategy that is designed to enhance youth growth and development by building trusting relationships with athletes and using positive reinforcement and open communication.

and in life. Wooden once explained that no building is better than its structural foundation, and no man is better than his mental foundation. Two foundations at the bottom of the pyramid are industriousness and enthusiasm, which stress the value of each player's consistent hard work in games and practices. These two mental components are linked with teamwork principles, such as loyalty, friendship, and cooperation. Wooden's pyramid also highlights the value of establishing clear and realistic goals. As well, it shows that poise and confidence will be achieved only after hours of conditioning and drills in practice and a commitment to proper behaviour off the court. At the top of the pyramid is success, which is defined as knowing you did your best to become the best that you are capable of becoming. In other words, each block constitutes specific principles that must be in place in order to move up the pyramid.

Pat Summitt, former head coach of the University of Tennessee Lady Vols, is perhaps the most widely recognized women's head coach in North America. Coach Summitt won more U.S. national basketball championships (eight) than any other coach, man or woman, since John Wooden. Further to this, she is the all-time winningest coach in American university basketball history of either a men's or women's team in any division, with a win–loss record of 1098–208 (www.coachsummitt.com). Interestingly, she has attributed her coaching success to a change of coaching philosophy that involved adopting a more athlete-centred approach, about 10 years into her coaching career. She recounts,

> Then, in 1987, we won our first title. And four more in the next ten years. What changed? For one thing, me. Over the years, I matured and learned from my experiences. I was forced out from behind my desk to deal with drugs, alcohol, injury, broken hearts, and emotional breakdowns of every other description. I was confronted by unwanted pregnancies, drinking problems, a player in a near-fatal car wreck, and countless instances of love gone wrong. . . . I was learning that a coach is far more than a strategist or a disciplinarian. You are a peculiar form of crisis counselor and interim substitute parent (Summitt & Jenkins, 1998, pp. 67–68).

In Canada, there is also a body of empirical research of successful university team sport coaches who focused on promoting athlete growth and development (e.g., Davies et al., 2005; Rathwell et al., 2014; Vallée & Bloom, 2005), in addition to their many administrative responsibilities including recruiting, fund raising, budgeting, community involvement, publicity, and interactions with the school's athletic director. Vallée and Bloom analyzed coach behaviour in the team sport setting to investigate common elements among expert coaches to determine how they built successful programs. It was found that effective coach leadership behaviour was imperative to ensuring positive athlete development and that coaches possessed a personal desire to foster individual growth among their athletes. The coaches were concerned about instilling life skills into their athletes; one coach said, ". . . when the players finish their final year, I hope their toolbox will be full and that it will help them to succeed in life" (Vallée & Bloom, 2005, p. 187). These coaches established a safe environment where the skills and values taught for their sport were promoted and encouraged both in and out of the sporting environment. This study illustrated the importance of a balanced coaching philosophy and how values the coaches instilled in their athletes proved to create successful teams on the court and equally successful individuals off the court.

In sum, the use of an ACA to coaching is still rudimentary in the field of sport coaching. Cassidy (2010) suggested that an ACA is still hindered by an unclear understanding of what it is and how it can be applied to coaching. Nonetheless, coaches' roles and responsibilities in North American university sport extend beyond practice and competition, and include the adoption of an ACA with their athletes.

Coaching Model

Côté, Salmela, Trudel, and colleagues (1995) created a coaching model that allows for connections to be established between the accumulated knowledge of how and why coaches perform as they do (see Figure 11.4). The **coaching model** implies that coaches begin their job by developing a mental model of the potential of their athletes or teams. This mental model is influenced by three peripheral components (coach's personal characteristics, athletes' personal characteristics, and contextual factors) that are integrated into their operational strategies to determine which of the three primary components of organization, training, and competition must be used to maximize the development of the athlete and the team. The primary components of the coaching model are what distinguish it from other more specific models of coaching, including the MML. Moreover, the

> **Coaching model:** Provides a systematic view of coaching by broadly capturing the most influential factors and emphasizing the relationships among these factors.

Figure 11.4 Coaching model

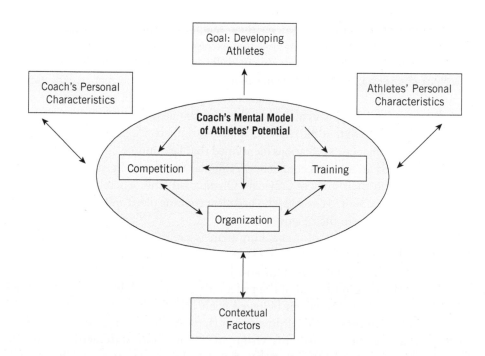

Source: Reprinted, by permission, from Côté, J., Salmela, J., Trudel, P., Baria, A., & Russell, S. (1995). The coaching model: A grounded assessment of expert gymnastic coaches' knowledge. *Journal of Sport & Exercise Psychology, 17*(1):1-17.

coaching model proposes that success includes more than a specific set of personality traits, organizational behaviours, or interpersonal skills of the coach. Overall, coaching success appears to be related to various interpersonal, cognitive, and operational aspects of leadership and thus it is not surprising that this model has served as a theoretical framework for much research on expert Canadian coaching.

Primary Components of the Coaching Model

Organization Côté and Salmela (1996) stipulated that organization for individual sport coaches involves the use of their knowledge in arranging the ideal plans for the team to train and compete, while considering other responsibilities such as working with staff members and the athletes' families, as well as dealing with athletes' personal concerns. Desjardins (1996) alluded to the multitude of organizational tasks of team-sport coaches. These included the following seven tasks: creating a vision, establishing a seasonal plan, selecting a team, setting goals, developing team cohesion, working with support staff, and attending to administrative matters. Whether in individual or team sports, organizational tasks are present before, during, and after the season and represent the foundation of the coaches' knowledge base. Moreover, a coach's ability to organize the season and to deal with organizational issues reveals much about his or her coaching and management skills. If a coach is organized, there will be a solid foundation from which to build a championship team. This should lead to more effective training sessions that, in turn, might improve the team's success at competitions.

Support for the value and importance of a coach's organizational skills can be found in two interview-based studies led by Dan Gould and his colleagues (e.g., Gould et al., 1999; Greenleaf et al., 2001). Based on their sample of American Olympic coaches and their athletes, they found teams that met/exceeded performance expectations had coaches who had excellent time management skills and a detailed plan for performance that was not changed. Coaches from teams that failed to meet performance expectations attributed this to a lack of planning or failure to follow the plans. In some cases the plans were implemented too late, which suggests the importance of having a vision from the beginning of the season so that the team has time to assimilate the plan. Other teams that failed to meet performance expectations mentioned that last-minute changes made by the coach likely affected an athlete's confidence. A similar finding emerged from Orlick and Partington (1988) in their study of Canadian Olympic athletes, whereby athletes attributed performance successes to coaches who had clear training plans and who did not make any last-minute changes to their plans.

Coaching vision: Coaches' long-term goals for their programs.

A fundamental element of a coaching plan is creating and selling a **coaching vision**. Desjardins (1996) found that expert coaches began coaching their teams with a vision of where they could go and how they could get there. This vision involved both the long-term goal of the program's growth and development and the short-term goal of what the coach believed each athlete or the entire team could achieve in any given season. Desjardins stated that once the vision was established, the expert coaches transformed this vision into a **mission statement**, a tangible written statement that gave the team direction for the upcoming year. The mission statement then influenced the seasonal plan, daily practices, training regimens,

Mission statement: A written statement that gives a team direction for the upcoming year.

Establishing optimal conditions for training and competition will help athletes attain performance and personal goals.

team selection, and goal setting. Desjardins also mentioned that expert coaches drew up a complete plan for the upcoming season, taking into consideration the mental, physical, tactical, and technical aspects of training. In other words, a mission statement was not merely a target to aim for—it was the team's absolute reason for being.

Further evidence about the need for a solid vision can be found in a Canadian study on expert university basketball and volleyball coaches (Vallée & Bloom, 2005). The participants in this study all took over losing programs, and, in a short time, turned the teams into perennial contenders with excellent reputations on and off the court. These authors found that it was important for the coaches to possess strong organizational and interpersonal skills, including a vision for the team (highlighting personal growth and development). Early on in their appointments, coaches worked at changing past philosophies, setting higher standards and goals, and leading the team in a new direction. Coaches also emphasized the importance of the athletes buying into the vision for the team to achieve success.

REFLECTIONS 11.3

As a newly hired physical education teacher who must also coach, you have been assigned the varsity girls' volleyball team. Should you develop a vision for this team? Why or why not? If so, what factors would you need to consider in developing this vision?

Training Training encompasses the knowledge coaches utilize to maximize their athletes' ability to acquire and perform various skills during practice. Training has been found to include coaches' application of technical training, physical training, mental training, tactical training, and intervention style (Côté, Salmela, Trudel, et al., 1995; Durand-Bush, 1996).

Tharp and Gallimore (1976) performed a classic study on the technical skills of expert coaches by observing and analyzing coaching great John Wooden during basketball practice sessions over the course of one season. Results revealed that the majority of Wooden's cues were technical. He was focusing on the basic fundamentals of playing basketball, which in a recent re-analysis accounted for his apparent lack of positive praise (Gallimore & Tharp, 2004). This seemingly successful approach led to a new way of seeing coaching success. According to Tharp and Gallimore, Wooden was successful because of the quality of his teaching, interventions, and instructions. Additionally, research revealed that technical instructions were the most common form of instruction, and coaches stressed the importance of sound technical training to ensure their athletes were prepared for games and practices (Côté et al., 1995; Durand-Bush, 1996).

Physical training focuses on the athletes' physical strength, endurance, and conditioning. With regard to physical training, expert coaches have commented on the uniqueness of each athlete and how they often created individualized training programs to meet their athletes' needs (Durand-Bush, 1996). Many of these coaches have utilized strength and conditioning specialists to work with their teams. Research has also shown that many expert coaches spend a large portion of practice time on tactical training—offensive and defensive strategies—as well as on creatively inventing drills to improve tactical difficulties (Bloom et al., 1999; Durand-Bush, 1996). According to Durand-Bush, elite coaches are knowledgeable about their sport and are able to adjust each practice to fit the current needs of their athletes.

Over the years, there have been mixed messages, both anecdotally and empirically, about the use and importance of mental training by high-level coaches. Some elite coaches have given mental training less attention than physical and technical training (Durand-Bush, 1996). On the other hand, some expert coaches felt it was beneficial to use a sport psychology specialist to work with their team on the more specific aspects of mental training, such as motivation, visualization, and controlling anxiety (Côté et al., 1995). Thus, it appears that expert coaches are beginning to realize that in order to get the best out of their athletes, they must incorporate mental training, and perhaps the best way to do so is by utilizing the assistance of a person trained in sport psychology. This issue was discussed previously in Chapter 1.

Research has revealed that an authoritative intervention style was not present among top-level Canadian gymnastics coaches (Côté et al., 1995). However, two European studies presented very different perspectives from that of Canadian coaches. For example, d'Arrippe-Longueville and colleagues (1998) reported that French judo coaches were not only authoritarian with their large number of world and Olympic champions, but they also used sarcasm and divisive training strategies to increase rivalry, and they created hostility among players; however, this was associated with great international success. In another European study, Chantal and associates (1996) found that elite Bulgarian athletes, while being self-determined, were not motivated by needs of inner fulfillment and ownership, but rather by external rewards and medals. In Brazil, especially in soccer, the primary goal is winning; for coaches, the consequence for losing is immediate dismissal (Salmela & Moraes, 2003). Thus, while more research is needed to reach any global conclusions, it appears that Canadian Olympic and university coaches use a different coaching style than some of their European and Brazilian counterparts. As well, there are likely differences based on the sport itself.

Competition This primary component relates to the coaching knowledge applied throughout the day of competition and the tasks performed. Researchers have reported that elite coaches developed pre-match routines for both themselves and their athletes, mastered the contingencies that they could control during a match (e.g., time-outs, rapport with officials), and dealt with emotions following the match to better deal with their athletes' performances (Bloom, 1996; Bloom et al., 1997; Côté et al., 1995). This section on competition will focus on team-sport coaches because of their active role on game day, compared with a more passive approach for individual and combat sport (martial arts) coaches.

Pre-competition tasks involve coaches' activities leading up to their arrival on site. Research has indicated that these expert coaches are very meticulous in their plans for both themselves and their athletes on game day (Bloom, 1996; Bloom et al., 1997). With respect to themselves, coaches need time alone to mentally prepare and rehearse for the game, often by taking a game-day jog. With respect to their athletes, coaches wanted them to have set routines so that they were not wasting energy thinking about what to eat or how to get to the competition site. As well, coaches preferred that their athletes spend time together as a way of improving team cohesion.

An interesting finding from the research on expert Canadian coaches focused on the **pre-game pep talk** (Bloom, 1996; Bloom et al., 1997). Likely because of Hollywood's preoccupation with sensationalizing the pre-game talk (e.g., Knute Rockne's "Win one for The Gipper" speech), many outsiders expect coaches to fire up the team prior to every competition. Nothing could be further from the truth, according to the expert Canadian coaches. These coaches preferred a calm, even-tempered pre-game pep talk. The coaches' final words were process-centred and reviewed three or four of the most important points stressed in the previous week's preparation.

Bloom's (1996) research revealed a number of important factors for expert team-sport coaches once competition began. Their coaching required attention to detail, an even-tempered demeanour, and an ability to out-think the opposing coach. This was accomplished in many ways: through strategically using time-outs and substitutions, relaying two or three important points of information during intermissions, developing productive relationships with officials, and providing athletes with appropriate playing time. The coaches' understanding of sport went beyond the basic textbook strategies. Some have compared expert team-sport coaches with chess grandmasters because both have to think many steps ahead of the opposition. For example, while watching the game, these coaches put their players in the right position to maximize their strengths and minimize their opponents' strengths, and they regularly monitored their own behaviours, all with the goal of helping their team achieve success.

Post-competition activities of expert team-sport coaches dealt with four areas: how the coaches handled the outcome, how they coped with their own emotions, what they did and said in the locker room, and what their post-game evaluation was (Bloom et al., 1997). The content and focus of the post-competition meeting depended on both the

Pre-game pep talk: Words used to fire up a team prior to competition.

outcome and the coaches' perceptions of whether the team played well or poorly. Most coaches gave their teams a few pointers, saving the in-depth analysis for the next practice or team meeting. Winning was the easiest outcome to handle. When the team played well and won, coaches emphasized effort and performance, not just outcome. When the team played poorly but won, coaches stressed areas needing improvement and acknowledged those individuals who gave a solid effort. The coaches did not want to spoil the thrill of victory, no matter how poorly they thought the team had played.

Losses were more demanding on the coaches. Most importantly, they had to decide if their players performed up to their capabilities. For example, when the team played well but lost, the expert team-sport coaches said that it was important to remain encouraging, focusing on the positive aspects of their performance. However, when the team played poorly and lost, most of these coaches felt that it was best to say little to their players because the emotional climate for themselves and their athletes was very high, and they worried about saying something they would later regret.

After any competition, the expert team-sport coaches also had to deal with their own emotions before entering the locker room. Many chose to take some time for themselves in order to "wind down." Most coaches said very little because they realized that both they and their athletes were still very emotional. They were especially aware that they should not single out any individual player. One reason for not analyzing the game in the locker room was that the coaches wanted to complete a thorough post-game evaluation, something that took place within 24 hours of the match. They wanted to consult a number of resources, such as videos, statistics, and assistant coaches, before finalizing their post-game evaluation. Regardless of the outcome, the coaches used every game as a learning experience to help prepare for future contests.

Successful coaches are able to adapt to a number of unanticipated factors during a game without disrupting the climate of the team or the performance of each athlete.

Monkey Business/Fotolia

CHAPTER SUMMARY

Coaching science is one of the newest areas of sport psychology research. As such, there is opportunity for empirical research at all levels of coaching, from the grassroots to the highest levels. The chapter began with a discussion of coach education, with particular emphasis on the NCCP program in Canada. Every year, more than 60,000 coaches take the NCCP, and more than 1 million have passed through this program.

The chapter presented information pertaining to the knowledge and leadership skills of coaches, as well as how to become a coach. More specifically, a summary of research from a small group of Canadian researchers reported various pathways to becoming an expert coach, including the importance of mentoring and working with top professionals in the sport of interest. Information on youth sport coaching highlighted the characteristics and ideal behaviours of these coaches.

The attributes of expert coaches were also discussed. One of the most important findings to emerge from research is that coaching is an art that requires years of hard work and practice; it also requires an ability to integrate and translate knowledge effectively to the specific sport environment. Moreover, many of Canada's top Olympic and university coaches were shown to focus on both the athletic and personal growth and development of their athletes. This was partly accomplished by adopting a mutually respectful coach–athlete relationship that is also part of an athlete-centred approach to coaching.

 COMMON MYTHS ABOUT COACHING PSYCHOLOGY REVISITED

MYTH: Outstanding athletes have an advantage in becoming excellent coaches.
Although many people believe that elite athletes can more easily become elite coaches than less-skilled athletes, the scientific evidence suggests otherwise. Although most expert coaches played at a high level in their sport, few were exceptional performers. Moreover, there are very few Hall of Fame athletes who reach the same level of success as coaches. Finally, some recent research found that it is possible to become an expert coach without any elite sporting background.

MYTH: Aspiring coaches must emulate the most successful coaches in their sport, regardless of their own personality, beliefs, or philosophy.
Studies have found that individuals should create their own coaching style based on their traits, beliefs, and philosophy, rather than emulate someone who has achieved success in their sport.

MYTH: All elite-level coaches are focused on winning at the expense of athlete growth and development.
Research on elite Canadian coaches at the university and Olympic levels has found these coaches to be just as concerned about the personal growth and development of their athletes as they are with their athletic growth and development. Similar findings have also emerged with some elite American coaches at similar levels of competition.

> **MYTH:** Coaching confidence is determined solely by one's innate personality. Coaching confidence can be improved over time with positive performances, coach education seminars, community support, and perceived team ability.

Review Questions

1. Outline some of the methods of knowledge acquisition for becoming an elite coach.
2. Summarize the role of the NCCP in Canada.
3. How is mentoring important in the career progression of an elite coach?
4. An effective practice for coaching youth sport is to give encouragement after a mistake in a positive way. Provide an example of a real-life situation to illustrate this recommendation.
5. List some effective practices for coaching youth sport.
6. Explain how coaching leadership is an interactional process.
7. Explain the factors that contribute to a strong coach–athlete relationship.
8. What are the four key dimensions of coaching efficacy?
9. What can a coach do to improve the mental component of athlete development?
10. Describe the coaching philosophy and style that made John Wooden such a unique and popular coach.

Suggested Readings

Potrac, P., Gilbert, W., & Denison, J. (Eds.) (2013). *Routledge handbook of sports coaching.* New York: Routledge.

Smith, R. E., & Smoll, F. L. (2002). *Way to go coach!: A scientifically-proven approach to youth sports coaching effectiveness* (2nd ed.). Palo Alto, CA: Warde Publishers.

References

Avolio, B. J., & Bass, B. M. (1991). *The full range of leadership development: Basic and advanced manuals.* Birmingham, NY: Bass, Avolio, & Associates.

Bass, B. M. (1999). Two decades of research and development in transformational leadership. *European Journal of Work and Organizational Psychology, 8,* 9–32. doi: 10.1080/135943299398410.

Bass, B. M., & Avolio, B. J. (1994). *Improving organizational effectiveness through transformational leadership.* Thousand Oaks, CA: Sage.

Bass, B. M., & Riggio, R. E. (2006). *Transformational leadership* (2nd ed.). Mahwah, NJ: Lawrence Erlbaum.

Bloom, B. S. (1985). *Developing talent in young people.* New York: Ballantine.

Bloom, G. A. (1996). Competition: Preparing for and operating in competition. In J. H. Salmela (Ed.), *Great job coach! Getting the edge from proven winners* (pp. 138–179). Ottawa, ON: Potentium.

Bloom, G. A., Crumpton, R., & Anderson, J. E. (1999). A systematic observation study of the teaching behaviors of an expert basketball coach. *The Sport Psychologist, 13,* 157–170.

Bloom, G. A., Durand-Bush, N., & Salmela, J. H. (1997). Pre- and postcompetition routines of expert coaches of team sports. *The Sport Psychologist, 11,* 127–141.

Bloom, G. A., Durand-Bush, N., Schinke, R. J., & Salmela, J. H. (1998). The importance of mentoring in the development of coaches and athletes. *International Journal of Sport Psychology, 29,* 267–281.

Bucci, J., Bloom, G. A., Loughead, T. M., & Caron, J. G. (2012). Ice hockey coaches' perceptions of athlete leadership. *Journal of Applied Sport Psychology, 24,* 243–259.

Carter, A. D., & Bloom, G. A. (2009). Coaching knowledge and success: Going beyond athletic experiences. *Journal of Sport Behavior, 32,* 419–437.

Cassidy, T. (2010). Holism in sports coaching: Beyond humanistic psychology. *International Journal of Sport Science & Coaching, 5,* 439–443. doi: 10.1260/1747-9541.5.4.439.

Cassidy, T. (2013). Holistic sports coaching: A critical essay. In P. Potrac, W. Gilbert, & J. Denison (Eds.), *Routledge handbook of sports coaching* (pp. 172–183). New York: Routledge.

Chantal, Y., Guay, F., Dobreva-Martinova, T., & Vallerand, R. J. (1996). Motivation and elite performance: An exploratory investigation with Bulgarian athletes. *International Journal of Sport Psychology, 27,* 173–182.

Chelladurai, P. (1993). Leadership. In R. N. Singer, M. Murphey, & L. K. Tennant (Eds.), *Handbook of research on sport psychology* (pp. 647–671). New York: Macmillan.

Chelladurai, P., & Riemer, H. A. (1998). Measurement of leadership in sport. In J. L. Duda (Ed.), *Advances in sport and exercise psychology measurement* (pp. 227–253). Morgantown, WV: Fitness Information Technology.

Côté, J., & Salmela, J. H. (1996). The organizational tasks of high-performance gymnastic coaches. *The Sport Psychologist, 10,* 247–260.

Côté, J., Salmela, J. H., & Russell, S. J. (1995). The knowledge of high-performance gymnastic coaches: Competition and training considerations. *The Sport Psychologist, 9,* 76–95.

Côté, J., Salmela, J. H., Trudel, P., Baria, A., & Russell, S. J. (1995). The coaching model: A grounded assessment of expert gymnastic coaches' knowledge. *Journal of Sport & Exercise Psychology, 17,* 1–17.

d'Arripe-Longueville, F., Fournier, J. F., & Dubois, A. (1998). The perceived effectiveness of interactions between expert French judo coaches and their athletes. *The Sport Psychologist, 12,* 317–332.

Davies, M. J., Bloom, G. A., & Salmela, J. H. (2005). Job satisfaction of accomplished male university basketball coaches: The Canadian context. *International Journal of Sport Psychology, 36,* 173–192.

Desjardins, G., Jr. (1996). The mission. In J. H. Salmela (Ed.), *Great job coach! Getting the edge from proven winners* (pp. 1–35). Ottawa, ON: Potentium.

de Souza, A., & Oslin, J. (2008). A player-centered approach to coaching. *Journal of Physical Education, Recreation & Dance, 79,* 24–30. doi: 10.1080/07303084.2008.10598195.

Duchesne, C., Bloom, G. A., & Sabiston, C. M. (2011). Intercollegiate coaches' experiences with elite international athletes in an American sport context. *International Journal of Coaching Science, 5,* 49–68.

Dupuis, M., Bloom, G. A., & Loughead, T. M. (2006). Team captains' perceptions of athlete leadership. *Journal of Sport Behavior, 29,* 60–78.

Durand-Bush, N. (1996). Training: Blood, sweat, and tears. In J. H. Salmela (Ed.), *Great job coach! Getting the edge from proven winners* (pp. 103–139). Ottawa, ON: Potentium.

Erickson, K., Côté, J., & Fraser-Thomas, J. (2007). The sport experiences, milestones, and educational activities associated with the development of high-performance coaches. *The Sport Psychologist, 21,* 302–316.

Feltz, D. L., Chase, M. A., Moritz, S. E., & Sullivan, P. J. (1999). A conceptual model of coaching efficacy: Preliminary investigation and instrument development. *Journal of Educational Psychology, 91,* 765–776. doi: 10.1037/0022-0663.91.4.765.

Gallimore, R., & Tharp, R. (2004). What a coach can teach a teacher, 1975–2004: Reflections and reanalysis of John Wooden's teaching practices. *The Sport Psychologist, 18,* 119–137.

Gilbert, W. D. (2010). The passing of a legend: Coach John Wooden. *International Journal of Sport Science & Coaching, 5,* 339–342. doi:10.1260/1747-9541.5.3.339.

Gilbert, W. D., Côté, J., & Mallett, C. (2006). Developmental pathways and activities of successful sport coaches. *International Journal of Sport Science and Coaching, 1,* 69–76.

Gilbert, W. D., & Rangeon, S. (2012). Current directions in coaching research. *Revista de Iberoamericana de Psicologia del Ejercicio Y el Deporte*, 6, 217–236.

Gilbert, W. D., & Trudel, P. (2004). Analysis of coaching science research published from 1970–2001. *Research Quarterly for Exercise and Sport*, 75, 388–399. doi: 10.1080/02701367.2004.10609172.

Gould, D., Giannini, J., Krane, V., & Hodge, K. (1990). Educational needs of elite U.S. national team, Pan American, and Olympic coaches. *Journal of Teaching in Physical Education*, 9, 332–344.

Gould, D., Guinan, D., Greenleaf, C., Medbery, R., & Peterson, K. (1999). Factors affecting Olympic performance: Perceptions of athletes and coaches from more and less successful teams. *The Sport Psychologist*, 13, 371–394.

Greenleaf, C., Gould, D., & Dieffenbach, K. (2001). Factors influencing Olympic performance: Interviews with Atlanta and Nagano US Olympians. *Journal of Applied Sport Psychology*, 13, 154–184. doi: 10.1080/104132001753149874 *International Sport Coaching Framework*, Version 1.2 (2013). Champaign, IL: Human Kinetics.

Jimenez, S., Lorenzo, A., & Ibanez, S. (2009). Development of expertise in Spanish elite basketball coaches. *International Journal of Sport Science*, 17, 19–32. doi: 10.5232/ricyde2009.017.02.

Jones, R. L., Armour, K. M., & Potrac, P. (2003). Constructing expert knowledge: A case study of a top-level professional soccer coach. *Sport, Education and Society*, 8, 213–229. doi: 10.1080/13573320309254.

Jowett, S. (2003). When the "honeymoon" is over: A case study of a coach–athlete dyad in crisis. *The Sport Psychologist*, 17, 444–460.

Jowett, S., & Chaundry, V. (2004). An investigation into the impact of coach leadership and coach–athlete relationship on group cohesion. *Group Dynamic Theory and Practice*, 8, 302–311.

Jowett, S., & Clark-Carter, D. (2006). Perceptions of empathetic accuracy and assumed similarity in the coach–athlete relationship. *British Journal of Social Psychology*, 45, 617–637. doi: 10.1348/014466605X58609.

Jowett, S., & Lavallee, D. (2007). *Social psychology in sport*. Windsor, ON: Human Kinetics.

Jowett, S., & Meek, G. A. (2000). The coach–athlete relationship in married couples: An exploratory content analysis. *The Sport Psychologist*, 14, 157–175.

Katzmarzyk, P. T., & Janssen, I. (2004). The economic costs associated with physical inactivity and obesity in Canada: An update. *Canadian Journal of Applied Physiology*, 1, 90–115. doi: 10.1139/h04-008.

Klenke, K. (1993). Meta-analytic studies of leadership: Added insights or added paradoxes? *Current Psychology: Developmental, Learning, Personality, Social*, 12, 326–343. doi: 10.1007/BF02686813.

Koh, K. T., Bloom, G. A., Fairhurst, K. E., Paiement, D. M., & Kee, Y. H. (2014). An investigation of a formalized mentoring program for novice basketball coaches. *International Journal of Sport Psychology*, 45, 11–32. doi: 10.7352/IJSP2014.45.011.

Lemyre, F., Trudel, P., & Durand-Bush, N. (2007). How youth-sport coaches learn to coach. *The Sport Psychologist*, 21, 191–209.

Lyle, J. (2010). Holism in sports coaching: Beyond humanistic psychology: A commentary. *International Journal of Sport Science & Coaching*, 5, 449–452. doi: 10.1260/1747-9541.5.4.449.

Malete, L., & Feltz, D. (2000). The effect of a coaching education program on coaching efficacy. *The Sport Psychologist*, 14, 410–417.

Mallett, C. J., & Rynne, S. B. (2010). Holism in sports coaching: Beyond humanistic psychology: A commentary. *International Journal of Sport Science & Coaching*, 5, 453–457. doi: 10.1260/1747-9541.5.4.439.

Nater, S., & Gallimore, R. (2010). *You haven't taught until they have learned; John Wooden's teaching principles and practices*. Morgantown, WV: Fitness Information Technology.

Olympiou, A., Jowett, S., & Duda, J. L. (2008). The psychological interface between the coach-created motivational climate and the coach–athlete relationship in team sports. *The Sport Psychologist*, 22, 423–438.

Orlick, T., & Partington, J. (1988). Mental links to excellence. *The Sport Psychologist, 2,* 105–130.

Philippe, R. A., & Seiler, R. (2006). Closeness, co-orientation and complementarity in coach–athlete relationships: What male swimmers say about their male coaches. *Psychology of Sport and Exercise, 7,* 159–171. doi: 10.1016/j.psychsport.2005.08.004.

Rathwell, S., Bloom, G. A., & Loughead, T. M. (2014). Head coaches' perceptions on the roles, selection, and development of the assistant coach. *International Sport Coaching Journal, 1,* 5–16. doi: 10.1123/iscj.2013-0008.

Riemer, H. A., & Chelladurai, P. (1995). Leadership and satisfaction in athletics. *Journal of Sport & Exercise Psychology, 17,* 276–293.

Salmela, J. H., & Moraes, L. C. (2003). Development of expertise: The role of coaching, families and cultural contexts. In J. L. Starkes & K. A. Ericsson (Eds.), *Expert performance in sports: Advances in research on sport expertise* (pp. 275–296). Champaign, IL: Human Kinetics.

Smith, R. E., & Smoll, F. L. (2002a). Youth sport as a behavioral setting for psychosocial interventions. In J. L. Van Raalte, & B. W. Brewers (Eds.), *Exploring sport and exercise psychology* (pp. 341–371). Washington, DC: American Psychological Association.

Smith, R. E, & Smoll, F. L. (2002b). *Way to go coach!: A scientifically-proven approach to youth sports coaching effectiveness* (2nd ed.). Palo Alto, CA: Warde Publishers.

Smith, R. E., Smoll, F. L., & Cumming, S. P. (2007). Effects of a motivational climate intervention for coaches on young athletes' sport performance anxiety. *Journal of Sport & Exercise Psychology, 29,* 39–59.

Smith, R. E., Smoll, F. L., & Hunt, E. (1977). A system for the behavioral assessment of athletic coaches. *Research Quarterly, 48,* 401–407.

Smoll, F. L., & Smith, R. E. (2002). *Children and youth in sport* (2nd ed.). Dubuque, IA: Kendall/Hunt.

Sullivan, P. J., & Feltz, D. L. (2002). *The psychological effect of Canada's national coaching education program* (Final Grant Report). Ottawa, ON: Social Sciences and Humanities Research Council of Canada.

Sullivan, P., & Gee, C. (2008). The effect of different coaching education content on the efficacy of coaches. *International Journal of Coaching Science, 2,* 1–8.

Sullivan, P., Paquette, K. J., Holt, N. L., & Bloom, G. A. (2012). The relation of coaching context and coach education to coaching efficacy and perceived leadership behaviors in youth sport. *The Sport Psychologist, 26,* 122–134.

Summitt, P., & Jenkins, S. (1998). *Raise the roof.* New York: Broadway.

Tharp, R. G., & Gallimore, R. (1976). What a coach can teach a teacher. *Psychology Today, 9,* 75–78.

Trudel, P., & Gilbert, W. D. (2006). Coaching and coach education. In D. Kirk, M. O'Sullivan, & D. McDonald (Eds.), *Handbook of research in physical education* (pp. 516–539). London, UK: Sage.

University of Toronto (2011). *Gender equity in Canadian interuniversity sport: A biannual report.* University of Toronto, Faculty of Physical Education & Health.

Vallée, C. N., & Bloom, G. A. (2005). Building a successful university sport program: Key and common elements of expert coaches. *Journal of Applied Sport Psychology, 17,* 179–196. doi: 10.1080/10413200591010021.

Werthner, P., & Trudel, P. (2006). A new theoretical perspective for understanding how coaches learn to coach. *The Sport Psychologist, 20,* 198–212.

Wilson, L. M., Bloom, G. A., & Harvey, W. J. (2010). Sources of knowledge acquisition: Perspectives of the high school teacher/coach. *Physical Education and Sport Pedagogy, 15,* 383–399. doi: 10.1080/17408980903273154.

Wooden, J. (1988). *They call me coach.* Chicago, IL: Contemporary Books.

Wooden, J. R., & Jamison, S. (2010). *The wisdom of Wooden: My century on and off the court.* New York: McGraw-Hill.

Chapter 12

Aging and Involvement in Sport and Physical Activity

Joseph Baker   Sean Horton

Lisa F. Young/Fotolia

Chapter Objectives

After reading this chapter, you should be able to do the following:

1   Present a profile of physical activity and sport involvement in older persons.

2   Understand the consequences of low levels of physical activity in this group.

3   Discuss and differentiate between models of skill maintenance.

4   Discuss the factors influencing sport and physical activity involvement in this group.

5   Consider the impact of societal perceptions of aging on physical and cognitive performance.

6   Identify strategies for increasing sport and physical activity involvement in older populations.

7   Discuss whether the Masters athlete is an effective model of successful aging.

Support for this chapter was provided by a standard research grant from the Social Sciences and Humanities Research Council of Canada (grant # 435-2013-0647).

Ed spent his childhood and adolescence playing a range of school sports. As an adult, he moved from his hometown to a small city to start a family of his own. Recently, Ed found out that he was at increased risk of having a heart attack because he has high blood pressure. His doctor advised him to add some physical activity to his daily routine. This negative bill of health surprised Ed since he'd always been active as a child and adolescent. After decades of working at a sedentary job and low amounts of leisure time physical activity, Ed finds it difficult to make changes to his routine. He tries joining a local fitness club but finds that he has little in common with the club's other members. He inquires about the aerobic and stretching programs available at the club, but the club's personal trainer informs him that their programs are likely too advanced for someone of his age and fitness level.

Ed finally has some success when he begins a walking routine with his friend Ruth. This activity is well suited to their neighbourhood since it has wide sidewalks and minimal traffic. After a few months, Ruth moves to live with her daughter's family, and Ed quickly becomes discouraged walking by himself. At his checkup one year later, Ed still hasn't made any consistent changes to his physical activity habits and remains at increased risk of having a heart attack.

In the above scenario, Ed has difficulty making the necessary changes to add a greater amount of physical activity to his lifestyle. Unfortunately, this situation is commonplace among older adults in Canadian society. In this chapter, we look at the factors influencing physical activity involvement in aging populations to determine the most effective courses of action for optimal health and performance in this group. Further, it will examine whether the effects of physical activity involvement are always positive in later life.

 COMMON MYTHS ABOUT AGING AND INVOLVEMENT IN SPORT AND PHYSICAL ACTIVITY

MYTH: Getting older involves the inevitable loss of the ability to function in society.

MYTH: Stereotypes about "old people" are generally accurate.

MYTH: Participating in competitive sports is too strenuous for older persons.

MYTH: In older people, exercise is just as likely to damage health as it is to improve it.

INTRODUCTION

In 2012, the first wave of the Canadian baby boomer generation reached retirement age (i.e., 65 years). Persons over 85 years are the fastest-growing segment of the population, and even very conservative estimates predict a tenfold increase in the number of people over 100 years of age by 2050. Clearly, this is a section of the population that is of considerable importance in Canadian society.

In the past 160 years, our average life expectancy has increased at a rate of about three months per year. Back in 1840, the average lifespan was approximately 40 years. Some lucky people still lived to an advanced age, but many died young. As medical technology and health care have improved over the years, fewer people die at an early age, and the elderly are living even longer. In fact, the relationship between increasing life expectancy and the passage of time is so consistent that some researchers have considered it to be "the most remarkable regularity of mass endeavor ever observed" (Oeppen & Vaupel, 2002, p. 1029). Although this is an exciting finding since it suggests that we have a longer life to look forward to, an increased lifespan does not necessarily mean a better **quality of life** (overall well-being). In fact, many Canadians run the risk of spending a significant portion of their senior years in states of **morbidity** (being unhealthful) or in complete dependence. A significant factor contributing to this decreased quality of life is physical inactivity.

Quality of life: A multidimensional construct referring to an overall sense of well-being with a strong relation to a person's health perceptions and ability to function; includes aspects of physical and mental health and functioning, and social support.

Morbidity: The quality or state of being morbid or unhealthful.

PHYSICAL ACTIVITY IN OLDER PERSONS

Data from the Canadian Health Measures Survey (CHMS; Statistics Canada, 2013) support a robust and rather unsettling trend in physical activity research—physical activity levels decrease as we get older. These data indicate that among older adults aged 60–79 years, only 11% meet Canada's Physical Activity Guidelines and that this is lower in females (9.5%) than males (13.3%). Furthermore, both male and female older adults spent approximately 10 hours each day sedentary (not including sleep), which has been shown to be an independent predictor of ill health. Collectively, these data support the conclusion that the majority of older men and women are not active enough for optimal health.

The most common physical activities for adults over 65 are outlined in Table 12.1. Walking, gardening, and exercising at home have the greatest rates of participation in older adults. These forms of physical activity are excellent avenues for staying active. However, because they are low in aerobic intensity, older adults need to be mindful of

Table 12.1 Most Popular Physical Activities among Canadian Adults over 65 Years

Activity	Participation (%)
Walking	66
Gardening	40
Home exercise	23
Swimming	9
Social dancing	9
Bicycling	7
Golf	6
Bowling	4
Fishing	4
Exercise classes	3
Weight training	1

Source: Data from Statistics Canada, *Canadian Community Health Survey, Cycle 3.1* (2005), Public Use Microdata File.

performing enough activity to meet their physical activity requirements. (The Canadian Fitness and Lifestyle Research Institute monitors physical activity involvement in various age groups across Canada; see its website at www.cflri.ca.)

REFLECTIONS 12.1

Compare the activities you typically see youth participating in with the activities of older adults. What implications do you think these differences have for targeting physical activity interventions for older adults?

Data indicate that involvement in aerobic exercise is not enough. To reduce the loss of muscle mass (**sarcopenia**) that typically occurs with age, older adults must also regularly participate in exercise that taxes their muscle strength (e.g., weight training). *Canada's Physical Activity Guide to Healthy Active Living for Older Adults* recommends up to 60 minutes of moderate to vigorous physical activity on most days, including a variety of endurance, flexibility, strength, and balance activities. There is overwhelming support that habitual involvement in these forms of physical activity is related to increased physical and mental health, as well as increased functional autonomy in aging populations

Sarcopenia: A deficiency in the amount of skeletal muscle tissue.

(see Table 12.2). Physical activity guidelines for older adults (as well as for other age groups) are available on Health Canada's website (http://www.phac-aspc. gc.ca/hp-ps/hl-mvs/pa-ap/index-eng.php).

Weight training is essential to prevent sarcopenia.

One of the reasons for this relates to the barriers older adults face when trying to incorporate physical activity and exercise into their lives. In the sections below, we examine the evidence for the benefits of physical activity and exercise in older adults and discuss how physical and cognitive function declines over time. We also examine the specific and general barriers that older adults have to overcome in order to become physically active. Finally, we examine the concept of "successful aging" and whether Masters athletes represent ideal role models for aging adults.

aletia2011/Fotolia

Table 12.2 Benefits of Exercise in Older Adults

Increase in cardiovascular function

Decrease in cardiovascular disease risk factors

Increased muscle mass and strength

Improved bone health and decreased risk of osteoporosis

Improved balance and postural stability

Improved flexibility

Improved psychological health

Source: Adapted from American College of Sports Medicine. (2009). Exercise and Physical Activity for Older Adults (position stand), Salem, George J.; Skinner, James S.; Chodzko-Zajko, Wojtek J.; Proctor, David N.; Fiatarone Singh, Maria A.; Minson, Christopher T.; Nigg, Claudio R. *Medicine & Science in Sports & Exercise.* 41(7):1510–1530, July 2009.

COGNITIVE AND PHYSICAL DECLINE WITH ADVANCING AGE

Examinations of cognitive and physical performance across time indicate that these capacities decline as we get older. Some researchers believe that 0.5% per year is a general rate of decline for *all* skills and capacities after we have reached peak performance. For example, performance in many aerobic sports such as running, swimming, and rowing appears to decline at this rate (see Bortz & Bortz, 1996). Although there is consistent evidence indicating that physical and cognitive abilities decline as we age, there is conflicting evidence as to whether this is actually due to age. Some researchers have suggested that many of the physical and cognitive declines associated with aging are in fact the result of a "long-standing sedentary lifestyle or disuse" (Maharam et al., 1999, p. 274). As mentioned earlier, involvement in physical activities also declines as we age. Current thinking is that these two factors—declining involvement and declining ability—are inextricably linked.

Studies of cognitive and motor skills suggest that performance can be maintained at high levels in spite of advancing age provided that there is continued involvement in the activity. For instance, studies of golfers (Baker et al., 2006) and handball goalkeepers (Schorer & Baker, 2009) have shown that high levels of performance could be maintained as the performers got older. The maintenance of skilled performance over time has been explained primarily using one of two models, the compensation model (e.g., Salthouse, 1984; 2012) or the selective maintenance model (Krampe & Ericsson, 1996).

MODELS OF SKILL MAINTENANCE

The Compensation Model

Compensation theory: A theory of aging based on the notion that age-related losses in one area can be offset by improvements in another area.

The basis of **compensation theory** is that although individual components of a skill may decline with age, it is possible for overall performance to remain the same because of an increased reliance on other aspects of performance (see Figure 12.1). Put more simply, the theory suggests that skilled performers strategically compensate for a decline in one skill area by developing or improving in another. Two excellent examples of this research come from studies examining chess players and typists. Charness (1981) found

Figure 12.1 The compensation model of aging.

Although components of performance may decline (A), increases in a compensatory skill (B) allow for stability of performance over time (C).

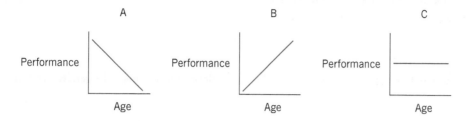

that skilled, older chess players could perform at the same level as younger skilled players despite age-related deficiencies in memory ability. Charness explained these results by suggesting that older players compensate for their declining memory by using more efficient information processing; they perform a more systematic search of the problem space and make a better global evaluation of chess positions. In addition, studies have found little decline in expert typing skill with advancing age (Bosman, 1993; Salthouse, 1984). The evidence indicates that expert typists suffer a decline in reaction time, but they compensate by scanning farther ahead in the text, which allows them to begin keystroke preparation earlier. As a result of this advanced planning, aging typists can offset a deficiency in one area by their improved performance in another.

The Selective Maintenance Model

Ericsson and Krampe (Ericsson, 2000; Krampe & Ericsson, 1996) advocate that expert performance in skilled domains is maintained in very specific capacities. In their **selective maintenance model**, this is possible through appropriate attention to deliberate practice (see Chapter 10 for more on deliberate practice). Through extensive focus on this type of practice, experts are able to develop domain-specific mechanisms that allow them to circumvent general age-related limitations, and these mechanisms are more resistant to degradation over time, as long as training persists.

To test this hypothesis, Krampe and Ericsson (1996) compared older and younger pianists on a range of performance-related measures. In addition, they compared performers at the expert and amateur levels (i.e., older expert, older amateur, younger expert, and younger amateur). They found that older performers, both amateur and expert, showed the same pattern of age-related decline on general measures of performance, such as reaction time; however, domain-specific measures of performance, such as finger-tapping speed and quality of performance, were maintained

Selective maintenance model: A model of aging emphasizing the role of high quality training and practice in acquiring and maintaining the domain-specific characteristics required for high levels of skill.

Research indicates that golf skill is resistant to degradation over time.

to a greater extent in older experts. In most cases, differences in domain-specific measures of performance between younger and older experts were explained by differences in the amount of training and practice rather than age. Based on these results, the authors concluded that persistent regular involvement in a domain over time would allow aging performers to maintain their skills.

Maintenance of Athletic Performance

Researchers have also examined the decline of athletic skill with age. In general, cognitive and motor skills appear to be more resistant to age-related decline than physiological factors, such as aerobic capacity. For example, data from running, rowing, and swimming events indicate a decline in performance in the range of 0.35% to 0.5% from peak performance per year (Bortz & Bortz, 1996; Starkes et al., 2003). However, examinations of cognitive and motor skills reveal that these skills are more resistant to the aging process. In their investigation of performance in PGA golfers, Baker and colleagues (2006) found that although performance among elite golfers consistently declined with age, this rate of decline was much less than we see in sports that are more physiological in nature. Figure 12.2 shows their data on scoring average over time; the scoring average is the number of strokes required to play the entire course. Until age 50, players competed primarily on the PGA Tour. After 50, players are

Figure 12.2 Performance decline data from Baker et al.'s (2006) study of elite PGA golfers

Until age 50 players competed primarily on the PGA Tour while after 50 players are eligible to play on the slightly easier Champions Tour, which accounts for the considerable decrease in scoring average from 49 to 51 years of age.

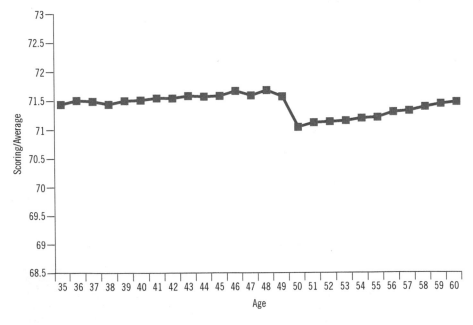

Source: Adapted from Baker, J., Horton, S., Pearce, W., & Deakin, J. (2006). A longitudinal examination of performance decline in champion golfers. *High Ability Studies, 16:2* 179–185, Figure 1, p. 181. Copyright © 2006 Routledge. (Taylor & Francis Group, www.tandfonline.com)

eligible to play on the slightly easier Champions Tour, which accounts for the considerable decrease in scoring average from 49 to 51 years of age.

They also found that the rate of decline accelerated as the golfers got older (after 50 years of age), which matches previous examinations of athletic performance over time (e.g., Sterken, 2003; Stones & Kozma, 1984). This may not have been entirely due to age, however. Examinations of the training profiles of **Masters athletes** (e.g., Weir et al., 2002) report significant differences in training volume and content compared with younger athletes, which may account for much of the decline. Just as more effective training leads to performance improvements (e.g., Ericsson et al., 1993), decreased training intensity or duration leads to diminished performance. Collectively, these research studies indicate that, with proper attention to physical activity, the aging process can be much more positive than previously assumed. The logical question, therefore, is, "Why are more older adults not physically active?"

Masters athletes: Athletes who are aged 30 years or older competing at the Masters level of competition.

BARRIERS TO EXERCISE FOR OLDER ADULTS

The idea that physical activity is useful for preventing premature morbidity and **mortality** (i.e., death) is not new, and most of us are aware that involvement in physical activity leads to health benefits and a higher quality of life. However, for older persons, physical and psychological barriers can impede the adoption of a physically active lifestyle. In one study, Cohen-Mansfield and colleagues (2003) found that the most common barrier to physical activity involvement in older adults was an existing health problem or pain. In fact, nearly 60% of inactive older adults in the study reported this as a barrier to their physical activity and sport involvement. Other factors are listed in Figure 12.3. As you can see, there is a combination of general and older adult-specific barriers. Effective intervention programs to promote physical activity involvement in older populations should consider the diverse nature of these barriers.

Mortality: Frequency of number of deaths in proportion to a population.

Figure 12.3 Barriers to exercise in older adults

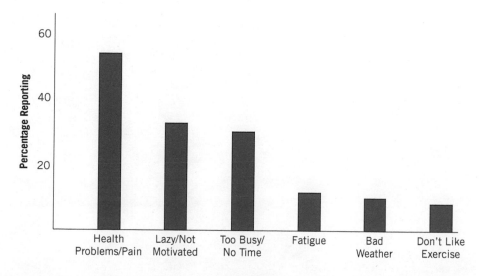

Source: From Cohen-Mansfield, J., Marx, M. S., & Guralnik, J. M. (2003). Motivators and barriers to exercise in an older community-dwelling population. *Journal of Aging and Physical Activity, 11*, 242–253.

NEGATIVE STEREOTYPES: A UNIQUE BARRIER FOR OLDER ADULTS

The majority of the factors outlined in the sections above are significant barriers to physical activity for adults in general. In addition to these factors, older adults must contend with a barrier that is exclusive to their group—ageism. In his seminal essay, Butler (1969, p. 243) defined ageism as "prejudice by one age group toward other age groups." Studies have shown that attitudes toward aging in North America, held by the young and old alike, are predominantly negative (Horton et al., 2007). Such widespread agreement about a group can lead to the development of **stereotypes** (i.e., popularly held beliefs), which in turn can lead to expectations about performance (Wheeler & Petty, 2001). These negative expectations can have considerable effect on the behaviour of members of the stereotyped group.

Stereotypes: Popularly held beliefs (which do not take into account individual differences) about a type of person or a group of people.

Societal beliefs about aging have also been shown to influence physical activity behaviour in older adults. For instance, O'Brien Cousins (2003) revealed that often "seniors say the darndest things" about physical activity and exercise. For example, when confronted with the question, "Why are some older people less active?" many older adults respond with the equivalent of, "Why bother?" despite awareness of the benefits of physical activity. This may be due to several factors, including inaccurate perceptions about the risks associated with physical activity in older adults. Older adults often report that they are physically unable to participate in physical activity because "their heart couldn't take it." Although chronic periods of sedentary behaviour increase the risk of various medical conditions, many older adults perceive exercise itself as high-risk behaviour. Contradictory messages may come from several sources, including significant others and society in general (Chogahara et al., 1998).

Social support is an important component of older adults' exercise programs.

Monalyn Gracia/Fancy/AGE Fotostock

Becca Levy (2000, 2009), a psychologist from Yale University, has done extensive work on the ways in which stereotypes of aging can influence older adults' performance on cognitive and physical tasks. Her experimental research has examined how exposure to a negative or positive stereotype about aging can influence performance in older adults. Levy used **implicit priming** to activate either a positive or a negative stereotype in older adults. She did this by having a computer flash either positive words (e.g., *wise, sage*) or negative words (e.g., *old, decrepit*) related to aging while participants were engaged in a computer game. The words were flashed so quickly, however, that they could not be detected by the participants; thus, the words did not interrupt the game they were playing. While the participants had no conscious awareness of the words being flashed, they were picked up at a subconscious level.

Levy found that priming older adults with a positive stereotype improved performance on cognitive measures, such as memory, as well as on physical measures, such as walking speed and handwriting (Hausdorff et al., 1999; Levy, 2000). Her research also indicated that priming older adults with negative stereotypes of aging had marginal effects on performance. Arguably, this is due to the fact that negative stereotypes of aging are continually reinforced in our society. Older adults are continually exposed to negative stereotypes about aging (and therefore, about themselves) through media and social interactions and, as a result, live in an environment that perpetually emphasizes a negative view of aging.

Unfortunately, seniors tend to buy into these negative characterizations. Montepare and Zebrowitz (2002) noted that older adults view members of their own age group as "lower in status, less likeable, unhappier, more dependent, and less goal oriented than younger adults" (p. 90). One of the unique characteristics of the elderly as a social group is that eventually we all become members of that group. If we are lucky enough to live a long life, we inevitably become members of a group that we have most likely stigmatized from an early age. As Levy (2009) noted, by the time younger individuals become elderly, they have spent upward of 50 years expressing and internalizing negative stereotypes of aging. Perhaps it is not surprising that the stereotypes elderly individuals have of their own social group are not dramatically different from those the rest of society holds.

Although most studies have examined short-term performance effects of negative stereotypes, some researchers have speculated that the most damaging effects may be long-term, such as feelings of dissatisfaction and, ultimately, disengagement (see Major et al., 1998). Steele (1997) postulated that under chronic situations of stereotype exposure, individuals become pressured to "disidentify" with the domain to preserve feelings of self-worth. **Disidentification** involves reconceptualizing one's self-image to remove the value associated with a domain, thereby reducing the impact of negative performance. Although useful for maintaining self-image, disidentification often results in serious performance decline because it undermines the motivation required for long-term involvement in an activity.

For example, some women disidentify with the domains of math and science due to societal stereotypes that these are "male" subjects dominated by men. This can result in some women avoiding these subjects or avoiding careers that require them. In the same manner, negative stereotypes about the elderly and athletic performance can lead older people to give up sports sooner than they otherwise might. Society expects older adults to slow down and take it easy as they age, and many comply, even though they may still have the ability and desire to continue in high-level athletics.

Implicit priming: A technique used to activate or reinforce a belief without conscious awareness.

Disidentification: Reconceptualizing your self-image to remove the value associated with a domain, thereby reducing the impact of negative performance.

As detailed in Chapter 3, sustained motivation is often dependent on feelings of achievement and accomplishment. Older adults who believe that physical and cognitive decline is an inevitable part of growing older may disengage from activities that challenge these abilities in order to preserve their self-image. As discussed earlier, this can have important ramifications because the lack of physical and cognitive activity is believed to be the principal cause of the functional decline in aging populations (Maharam et al., 1999). Stereotypes have tremendous influence on behaviour. Older adults may be limiting their involvement in physical activity because they internalize negative stereotypes about their group. Indeed, examinations of older adults' beliefs about physical activity confirm that negative stereotypes about the aging process have a significant effect on involvement (O'Brien Cousins, 2003).

Furthermore, the belief that old age is inevitably associated with the gradual loss of physical and cognitive functionality may promote a disengagement from other positive health behaviours. Meisner and colleagues (Meisner & Baker, 2013; Meisner et al., 2013) examined how older adults' expectations for aging affected their health behaviours. Their results revealed that older adults who had more positive expectations of aging were more likely to practise preventive health behaviours such as physical activity and regular physical examinations. Although these results point to a strong influence of age-related beliefs in determining physical activity involvement, the issue is complex. Research reviews suggest that exercise can have significant positive effects on measures of emotional and psychological health (Biddle & Mutrie, 2008; Walsh, 2011). Thus, there may be a dynamic, reciprocal relationship between physical activity and age beliefs, such that positive age beliefs promote physical activity and physical activity promotes positive age beliefs.

REFLECTIONS 12.2

When you think of a 70-year-old, what words or images come to mind? Are they predominantly negative or positive? Consider ways in which your day-to-day experiences may reinforce negative stereotypes of aging.

DETERMINANTS OF PHYSICAL ACTIVITY AND SPORT INVOLVEMENT IN OLDER ADULTS

Generally, the factors influencing participation in physical activity and sport fall into five categories, each of which is explored below. They are demographic and biological factors, behavioural attributes, social and cultural factors, physical environment factors, and psychological, cognitive, and emotional factors.

Demographic and Biological Factors

Among Canadian adults, age and gender are the most consistent predictors of physical activity involvement, with rates of participation declining as age increases and males being consistently more active than females (Statistics Canada, 2013). As a matter of fact, gender is a fundamentally important variable in understanding exercise behaviour among older adults. This variable is particularly relevant given the social realities of later life, namely, that women tend to outlive men, resulting in a greater proportion of older women than older men in North America. In addition, other demographic factors also play significant roles. For instance, **socioeconomic status** (i.e., social position) and educational level are two factors that are commonly linked with lifelong physical activity involvement (Shankar et al., 2010). Older adults with higher socioeconomic status and a higher level of education are more likely to be involved in physical activity than those with lower socioeconomic status and a lower level of education. Research has also linked marital status and occupation with physical activity as an older adult (e.g., Dergance et al., 2003), although more research is necessary to determine precisely how these factors affect participation levels.

Socioeconomic status: The relative position of a family on a societal hierarchy based on access to, or control over, wealth, prestige, and power.

Behavioural Attributes

Patterns of behaviour throughout the lifespan have been good predictors of physical activity involvement. However, some variables we might expect to be strongly related to adult physical activity level are not; one example is the amount of physical activity performed as a child or adolescent. Researchers involved in tracking studies have found that childhood and adolescent physical activity habits are only weakly correlated with physical activity as an adult (Seefeldt et al., 2002; Trudeau et al., 2004). There is also research that suggests that the strength of the relationship between childhood/adolescent physical activity levels and adult physical activity levels decreases as individuals age (Malina, 2001). For example, childhood physical activity may be a good predictor of involvement for a young adult, but it is not as effective at predicting physical activity for an older adult.

Perhaps surprisingly, some studies have shown that alcohol consumption is negatively related to physical activity involvement in older adults; that is, more activity generally means less alcohol use (Smith & Storandt, 1997); however, other research (Westerterp et al., 2004) has shown a positive relationship between habitual physical activity and alcohol use. This suggests that the relationships between physical activity and other preventive health behaviours (e.g., alcohol consumption) are more complex than they might seem on the surface.

Social and Cultural Factors

Although individual barriers are often the focus of research and interventions, social and cultural barriers also play an important role. For instance, studies have reported that adequate levels of social support are critical to physical activity involvement (Kouvonen et al., 2012). Researchers have found a variety of sources of support that can affect how much older adults exercise. For instance, endorsement of physical activity by their spouse (Pettee et al., 2006), by peers (O'Brien Cousins, 1998), or by physicians (King, 2001) can positively affect the likelihood that older adults will initiate and maintain physical activity involvement.

The dynamic interaction among members of an exercise group can also influence physical activity levels. A study by Estabrooks and Carron (2000) used a team-building task to foster group cohesion. Their results showed that groups with greater cohesion had better rates of attendance and better adherence than control groups. Often, the dynamics of the group are influenced by the behaviour of the group's leader. Research examining the role of an exercise leader or class instructor has found that these individuals can have considerable influence on the quality of their participants' experience (McAuley & Jacobson, 1991).

Some expectations about behaviour are rooted in cultural beliefs, and these expectations can significantly impede an older individual's involvement in physical activity and exercise. A group that is particularly disadvantaged by cultural barriers is aging women. As mentioned earlier, women have typically been less physically active than men, and this trend persists as women age. Characterizations of female older adults as fragile or delicate reinforce the notion that physical activity for them is risky, and often these perceptions are reinforced by healthcare practitioners (Horton et al., 2007; Vertinsky, 1995).

Physical Environment Factors

Factors related to the physical activity environment can also impede exercise involvement in older adults. An investigation by O'Neill and Reid (1991) examined barriers to physical activity in Canadian older adults, and reported that between 5% and 15% felt that environmental factors negatively affected their participation. More specifically, the respondents indicated that difficulties getting to the facility, excessive costs of programs, unappealing activities, and inconvenient activity times were significant barriers to involvement. These factors may be less powerful predictors of physical activity participation than others (e.g., gender and age), but they are relatively easy to remedy. Simple changes to the way in which a program is administered can correct many environmental factors impeding physical activity involvement in older adults.

Psychological, Cognitive, and Emotional Factors

This final category of determinants is perhaps most applicable and salient to our discussion of the psychology of the older athlete. Several variables have been identified as important correlates of physical activity in adults, for example, locus of control, expected benefits, knowledge of health and exercise, perceived health or fitness, personality variables, body image, and perceived value of exercise outcomes (Trost et al., 2002). Despite the fact that more research is necessary to determine their relevance in predicting physical activity in older adults, several factors have been identified as central to understanding such activity. The two most common are enjoyment and perceived health and fitness.

Enjoyment Researchers examining the factors that determine involvement in physical activity at any age have found that enjoyment is usually the best predictor (e.g., Lewis et al., 2002; Salmon et al., 2003). Evidence indicates that this variable is an important predictor of physical activity involvement in older adults (Dergance et al., 2003; McAuley et al., 2003).

Perceived Health and Fitness A powerful barrier to physical activity involvement in older persons is a low perception of their current level of health and fitness. Many older adults believe that they are unable to participate in any type of exercise because of functional limitations (Cohen-Mansfield et al., 2003). Although in many cases these limitations are perceived rather than actual, they still limit older adults' inclination toward physical activities.

It is important to note that there is considerable interaction among the barriers outlined above. For instance, demographic barriers, such as socioeconomic status, affect physical environment barriers (e.g., proximity to exercise facilities) as well as psychological and emotional barriers (e.g., enjoyment and perceived health). These relationships reinforce the view that involvement in physical activity across the lifespan is an enormously complex issue and that successful physical activity programs and interventions should recognize this complexity.

SELF-EFFICACY AND OLDER ADULTS

A criticism of the majority of research available on older adults' motives for participating in sport and physical activity is that the research has been descriptive and atheoretical (Biddle & Nigg, 2000; Standage & Duda, 2004); this means that it is not driven by a theory or hypothesis. Although descriptive studies are enormously important in the initial stages of behavioural research, they are limited in that they do little to explain the motivational processes underlying behaviour.

One theory of motivation that has been considered in aging populations is Bandura's theory of self-efficacy (Bandura, 1997), as outlined in Chapter 3. **Self-efficacy** refers to feelings of self-confidence in a given situation and has been found to be a central factor in explaining individuals' enthusiasm for different activities. A significant body of research has been amassed on the power of self-efficacy in predicting physical activity behaviour in youth, and research has confirmed its utility in older adults as well (McAuley et al., 2003).

Bandura's theory is based on the notion that individuals with high feelings of self-efficacy about physical activity are more likely to initiate and continue participation. Researchers examining this assumption in older adults have confirmed the importance of self-efficacy in predicting program initiation (McAuley, 1993) and adherence (McAuley et al., 1993). What is perhaps more interesting is that when older individuals participate in physical activity, their feelings of self-efficacy go up (Li et al., 2001); however, these levels decline when regular participation stops (McAuley et al., 1999). This finding suggests that feelings of self-efficacy and participation have a reciprocal relationship—feelings of self-efficacy promote participation, which promotes increases in self-efficacy.

A positive finding from this research is that feelings of self-efficacy are readily modifiable. This has important implications for program design and interventions intended to promote physical activity in older populations. By focusing on increasing feelings of self-efficacy regarding physical activity, program administrators can support older individuals' exercise involvement in a powerful way.

Self-efficacy: A person's belief about his or her capacity to produce a designated level of performance.

REFLECTIONS 12.3

Although other theories of motivation have not been examined in aging populations, such theories may still explain the factors that influence older persons' participation in sport and physical activity. Recall one of the other theories discussed in Chapter 3 and consider how it might apply to motivation in older adults.

CANADIAN PROFILE   Ed Whitlock, Rewriting the Record Books

In 1896, the Olympic marathon was won in a time of two hours and 56 minutes. In 2003, Ed Whitlock, a Canadian marathoner, ran just a few minutes slower than this in the Toronto marathon.

What is remarkable about this feat is that Whitlock was 72 years old when he achieved this performance and became the first person over 70 years of age to break three hours for the marathon distance (two hours, 59 minutes).

Throughout his running career, Whitlock has established numerous age-group records, and he continues to train and compete at the highest levels of competition, regularly representing Canada at international events. As remarkable as Whitlock is, he is not as rare as you might expect. With each passing year, aging athletes are rewriting the sports record books as they demolish previous standards of performance. This aging vanguard forces us to re-evaluate our perspective of what it means to grow older.

Ed Whitlock, marathon runner.

SUCCESSFUL AGING

In the fields of gerontology and geriatrics, evidence supporting the maintenance of high levels of functioning into advanced age has motivated many researchers to examine the antecedents of optimal or "successful" aging. Currently, the most popular model of successful aging is the one developed by Rowe and Kahn (1987). Their model suggests that successful aging is the balance of three components: (1) absence of chronic disease, (2) maintenance of cognitive and physical functioning, and (3) active engagement with life. The Rowe and Kahn model, like most models of successful aging, is based on the notion that positive behaviour choices throughout life (e.g., eating a balanced diet, attending regular doctor visits) influence one's likelihood of aging well. Baker and colleagues (2009) considered the extent to which involvement in physical activity predicted whether an older person aged successfully. They found a strong **dose–response relationship**, whereby greater involvement in physical activity promoted a greater likelihood of aging successfully.

The notion of successful aging seems to be a very positive perspective from which to view health and function in older adults; however, some researchers have been critical of this notion on the basis that dividing older adults in binary categories (i.e., successful vs. unsuccessful) does not reflect the nuances of health and functioning during later stages of life. For instance, it would be easy to be critical of Rowe and Kahn's model because it designates older adults with any form of chronic disease as "unsuccessfully" aging regardless of whether this disease is managed well with little effect on function (e.g., mild forms of asthma or arthritis). Moreover, it has a definite focus on biomedical health and functioning without considering variables such as life satisfaction or quality of life.

Despite these criticisms, the notion that older adults can have lives full of health and high function, and that these outcomes are affected by behavioural choices (e.g., involvement in sport and physical activity), is important. In the section below, we consider whether Masters athletes, who are highly involved in competitive sport, are good models of aging well.

Dose–response relationship: In simple terms, refers to the change in an outcome caused by differing doses of a stressor. With respect to exercise, it refers to the strong positive relationship between doses of exercise and positive health effects.

THE MASTERS ATHLETE: A MODEL OF SUCCESSFUL AGING?

The increasing popularity of Masters-level competition is evident in such events as the World Masters Games and the Senior Olympic Games in the United States. The age at which one qualifies for Masters-level competition varies significantly across sports, but generally these athletes are 30 years of age and older. These highly competitive events continue to grow with each passing year, providing older athletes with the opportunity to participate in sport at a highly competitive level against the best athletes in the world at their age. Canada has played an important role in the development of Masters sport. The first World Masters Games were held in Toronto in 1985, and, in 2005, the sixth World Masters Games were held in Edmonton. Recent games have seen more than 20,000 athletes compete in 27 sports, making the games the largest multi-sport event in the world. (The World Masters Games are governed by the International Masters Games Association, www.imga.ch.)

Because of their ability to maintain high levels of physical and cognitive competency, Masters athletes represent a unique population that defies the stereotypical views of aging we hold in North America. For instance, Masters athletes consistently report high levels of physical (Wroblewski et al., 2011) and cognitive functioning (e.g., Tseng et al., 2013).

One criticism of research on Masters athletes and the application of that research to models of general aging is that the Masters data represent individuals who are often at extraordinarily high levels of performance. Masters athletes may not accurately reflect the age-related decline of the average individual. Although this is a valid criticism, this population is still extremely valuable for age-related research, primarily because it reflects a group of individuals who have maintained involvement in physical activity and exercise for extended periods of time. Data from Masters athletes represent the performance levels possible for adults who perform large amounts of physical activity throughout their lifespan. In general, research on Masters athletes indicates that maintaining a high level of involvement in physical activity as we age allows us to maintain above average levels of ability. As a result, Masters athletes appear to provide an important model of successful aging.

Masters athletes may also serve as role models (e.g., as stereotype busters) for society as a whole. Individuals who attempt amazing athletic feats at late ages are often profiled in the popular press and force us to re-evaluate our notions of what is possible for older people to accomplish. While there are anecdotal examples of how these athletes affect society's perceptions of aging, there has been little in the way of systematic research in this area. This is an intriguing field of inquiry for future researchers.

There has been some investigation into the effect that elite Masters athletes have on those in their peer group. Some researchers have suggested that older elite athletes are more likely to intimidate their peers rather than inspire them to be more active in their own lives (Ory et al., 2003). The authors noted that most older adults would have trouble relating to individuals with such an extreme level of fitness. They suggested that it is likely more effective to portray average older people doing average things—out walking with friends, for example. A study by Horton and colleagues (2008) has added some complexity to this argument, however. The findings suggested that, while some older adults will indeed find elite Masters athletes intimidating, others will find inspiration in their example. This may be tied to current physical activity levels—older adults

Older Athletes: Role Models or Anomalies?

Anna is a lifelong runner who continues to compete in distance running events as she approaches 80 years of age. Although she has noticed a decline in her running performance as she has moved through each decade of life, she still enjoys competing against other runners. She also takes a lot pride in the fact that she is still active while most of her peers spend their days watching television or in other forms of sedentary behaviour.

As she gets older, Anna gets increasing attention from the popular media about her ability to "break the aging barrier" by continuing to compete in sports; however, most of her peers don't identify with the kind of high functioning Anna demonstrates. As a result, rather than being a role model for her older peers, she is written off as an anomaly. Moreover, most of the popular media reports about Anna emphasize how different she is rather than challenging popular perceptions of what older people are capable of achieving.

This case study highlights the dynamics of individual and societal perceptions about older people. Recall from Chapter 3 that motivation and self-efficacy are influenced by a range of individual and social factors. On the one hand, Anna should have a very high level of self-efficacy and confidence built upon decades of performance as an athlete, while on the other hand, the lack of social endorsement of her performance may undermine her self-efficacy beliefs. From a different perspective, we can see how difficult it will be to deconstruct negative conceptions about aging when those who challenge these conceptions are rare and dismissed as anomalies.

who are already somewhat active in their own lives may be more likely to find Masters athletes to be appropriate role models. Once again, however, this research is in its very early stages.

Questions remain with respect to how positive role models of aging can best be used to motivate older adults to engage in physical activity. Considering how negative stereotypes can discourage older adults from engaging in exercise, it is important to discover ways of challenging those stereotypes. Positive role models, whether they are Masters athletes or older adults performing at high levels in other areas, have the potential to challenge and change the most negative stereotypes of aging.

Although Masters-level competition has been around for quite some time, we actually know very little about those who compete at this level compared with performers at younger levels of competition. However, some general conclusions can be made from research conducted to date.

Participant Motives and Perceived Benefits of Masters Sport

Participant motives of Masters athletes range from improving general health and dealing with weight concerns, to gaining additional meaning in their lives and being affiliated with other runners (Ogles & Masters, 2000). Moreover, researchers have found that motives of younger and older runners for participating are often appreciably different. Older runners are more often motivated by physical and social benefits of participation, while younger athletes are more often motivated by personal goal achievement (e.g., running a personal best, improving overall running speed).

Similarly, athletes see a host of different benefits from participation in Masters sport. A recent study by Rylee Dionigi and her colleagues (2011) found that athletes see Masters sport as the ideal context for testing their capabilities and gaining satisfaction from knowing "they can still do it". In addition, their study showed that many older athletes enjoyed the companionship and opportunities to travel provided by Masters sport.

Master-Level Competitors versus Non-Competitor Older Athletes Masters runners have higher self-esteem, lower consumption of alcohol, better sleep patterns, and fewer physical problems than their non-active contemporaries (Morgan & Costill, 1996). In addition, Masters athletes view their participation as an effective means of dealing with stress and improving mood (Smith & Storandt, 1997).

Early Sport Involvement An investigation of competitors, non-competitors (i.e., physically active but not competitive older athletes), and non-exercisers found that there was no difference among the groups with regard to activity levels during childhood and adolescence (Smith & Storandt, 1997). However, a critical time for Masters athletes seems to be their 20s, when many adults are focusing on establishing families and careers. Masters athletes were more likely to maintain involvement in sport and physical activity during this period, while non-competitors and non-exercisers were less likely to.

There are many psychological and physical benefits from participation in Masters sport.

Leland Bobbe/Getty Images

Mood and Personality In the past, researchers have examined the relationships between performance and personality in elite athletes. Similar investigations have been undertaken with Masters athletes. Ungerleider et al. (1989) found that, similar to other athletes examined, Masters track-and-field athletes demonstrated an iceberg profile: lower scores on tension, depression, fatigue, and confusion and higher scores on vigour than normative samples. Of interest, the Masters athletes' profile was lower in depression and anger than reported by other athletes. A single study examining measures of personality (Smith & Storandt, 1997) found little difference between Masters-level competitors and non-competitors.

General Recommendations for Working with Masters Athletes

Although many of the sport psychology concepts are equally applicable to Masters-level performers (e.g., goal setting and imagery), some concepts require an approach specifically designed with older athletes in mind. First, the specific needs of this population should be recognized. The psychological needs of Masters athletes are unique; therefore, training programs and interventions must be designed to address and meet those needs. Second, the athlete's experience and knowledge should be acknowledged. In the majority of cases, Masters athletes will have an enormous depth of experience in their sport, in many cases superior to the knowledge of the sport psychologist working with them. Rather than attempting to learn as much as or more than the athlete they are working with, sport psychologists should consider ways in which they can access and incorporate the athlete's knowledge. This will reduce the amount of background reading needed and improve the rapport between the sport psychologist and the Masters athlete. Third, attitudes toward older adults should be assessed for stereotypes. North American society reinforces a predominantly negative perspective of the aging process, and, as a result, this may be entrenched in personal outlooks about aging. Changing a negative outlook to something more positive (and more accurate) is, unfortunately, not done overnight. Being aware of any preconceived beliefs will assist practitioners in dealing with older athletes.

CHAPTER SUMMARY

The focus of this chapter has been on physical activity and sport involvement in older persons. Unfortunately, there is a continuing trend among Canadians toward a decreasing level of physical activity as we age. There is, however, growing support for the notion that much of the cognitive and physical decline seen in aging populations is a result of disuse, rather than aging per se. The variables influencing involvement in physical activity in older adults include demographic and biological factors, behavioural attributes, social and cultural factors, physical environment factors, and psychological, cognitive, and emotional factors. In addition, negative cultural stereotypes about aging are unique barriers for older adults in our society.

One group of older adults seems to defy the typical profile of aging—Master athletes. This group has been able to maintain high levels of ability in the face of advancing age. Researchers examining these athletes have indicated that they are unique, different from sedentary older adults and younger athletes in several areas (e.g., mood, self-esteem, and motives). Further research is clearly required to describe the factors influencing sport involvement and competitive performance in this group.

COMMON MYTHS ABOUT AGING AND INVOLVEMENT IN SPORT AND PHYSICAL ACTIVITY REVISITED

MYTH: Getting older involves the inevitable loss of the ability to function in society.
Although a certain degree of ability loss appears to be inevitable with age, most of this loss is due to decreased participation in cognitively and physically stimulating activities. With continued involvement in challenging activities, older adults can maintain (and even increase) physical and cognitive abilities.

MYTH: Stereotypes about "old people" are generally accurate.
The stereotype commonly endorsed in North America is that older adults have diminished capacities, almost as though they are reverting to childlike levels of development. In fact, the majority of stereotypes about older adults promoted in our society have no basis in scientific evidence.

MYTH: Participating in competitive sports is too strenuous for older persons.
The field of competitive sports for aging populations is rapidly growing. Masters-level

competition is now possible in a wide range of organized sports throughout the world, and competitors regularly participate at the regional, national, and international levels.

MYTH: In older people, exercise is just as likely to damage health as it is to improve it.

Although there are concerns when beginning an exercise program, particularly in older adults with some form of chronic disease, there is an overwhelming evidence base indicating that regular involvement in physical activity and exercise improves the health and functioning of older persons.

Review Questions

1. Compare and contrast the compensation model and the selective maintenance model of skill maintenance.
2. Describe four characteristics of Masters-level performers.
3. Briefly explain the influence that negative cultural stereotypes of aging may have on older adults.
4. Define *sarcopenia* and explain why older adults should be aware of this condition.
5. Describe the typical profile of physical activity involvement in older adults.
6. Provide a list of barriers to physical activity involvement in older adults and provide a possible strategy to address these barriers.

Suggested Reading

Baker, J., Horton, S., & Weir, P. (2010). *Masters athletes: Understanding the role of exercise in optimizing aging.* London, UK: Routledge.

O'Brien Cousins, S. (1998). *Exercise, aging, and health: Overcoming barriers to an active old age.* Philadelphia: Taylor and Francis.

Poon, L., Chodzko-Zajko, W., & Tomporowski, P. (2006). *Active living, cognitive functioning, and aging.* Champaign, IL: Human Kinetics.

References

Baker, J., Horton, S., Pearce, W., & Deakin, J. (2006). A longitudinal examination of performance decline in champion golfers. *High Ability Studies, 16,* 179–185.

Baker, J., Meisner, B., Logan, J., Kungl, A. M., & Weir, P. (2009). Physical activity and successful aging in Canadian seniors. *Journal of Aging and Physical Activity, 17,* 223–235.

Bandura, A. (1997). *Self-efficacy: The exercise of control.* New York: Freeman.

Biddle, S., & Mutrie, N. (2008). *Psychology of physical activity: Determinants, well-being, and interventions* (2nd edition). Oxford, UK: Routledge.

Biddle, S. J. H., & Nigg, C. R. (2000). Theories of exercise behavior. *International Journal of Sports Psychology, 31,* 290–304.

Bortz IV, W. M., & Bortz II, W. M. (1996). How fast do we age? Exercise performance over time as a biomarker. *Journal of Gerontology: Medical Sciences, 51,* 223–225.

Bosman, E. A. (1993). Age-related differences in the motoric aspects of transcription typing skill. *Psychology and Aging, 8,* 87–102.

Butler, R. N. (1969). Age-ism: Another form of bigotry. *The Gerontologist, 9,* 243–246.

Charness, N. (1981). Search in chess: Age and skill differences. *Journal of Experimental Psychology: Human Perception and Performance, 7,* 467–476.

Chogahara, M., O'Brien Cousins, S., & Wankel, L. M. (1998). Positive and negative social influences on the physical activity of older adults. *Journal of Aging and Physical Activity, 6,* 1–17.

Cohen-Mansfield, J., Marx, M. S., & Guralnik, J. M. (2003). Motivators and barriers to exercise in an older community-dwelling population. *Journal of Aging and Physical Activity, 11,* 242–253.

Dergance, J. M., Calmbach, W. L., Dhanda, R., Miles, T. P., Hazuda, H. P., & Mouton, C. P. (2003). Barriers to and benefits of leisure time physical activity in the elderly: Differences across cultures. *Journal of the American Geriatrics Society, 51,* 863–868.

Dionigi, R. A., Baker, J., & Horton, S. (2011). Older athletes' perceived benefits of competition. *International Journal of Sport and Society, 2,* 17–28.

Ericsson, K. A. (2000). How experts attain and maintain superior performance: Implications for the enhancement of skilled performance in older individuals. *Journal of Aging and Physical Activity, 8,* 346–352.

Ericsson, K. A., Krampe, R. T., & Tesch-Römer, C. (1993). The role of deliberate practice in the acquisition of expert performance. *Psychological Review, 100,* 363–406.

Estabrooks, P. A., & Carron, A. V. (2000). Predicting scheduling self-efficacy in older adult exercisers: The role of task cohesion. *Journal of Aging and Physical Activity, 8,* 41–50.

Hausdorff, J. M., Levy, B. R., & Wei, J. Y. (1999). The power of ageism on physical function of older persons: Reversibility of age-related gait changes. *Journal of the American Geriatric Society, 47,* 1346–1349.

Horton, S., Baker, J., & Deakin, J. (2007). Stereotypes of aging: Their effects on the health of seniors in North American society. *Educational Gerontology, 33,* 1–15.

Horton, S., Baker, J., Côté, J., & Deakin, J. M. (2008). Understanding seniors' perceptions and stereotypes of aging. *Educational Gerontology, 34,* 997–1017.

King, A. C. (2001). Interventions to promote physical activity in older adults. *Journal of Gerontology, Series A: 56,* 36–46.

Kouvonen, A., De Vogli, R., Stafford, M., Shipley, M. J., Marmot, M. G., Cox, T., et al. (2012). Social support and the likelihood of maintaining and improving levels of physical activity: The Whitehall II Study. *European Journal of Public Health, 22,* 514–518.

Krampe, R. T., & Ericsson, K. A. (1996). Maintaining excellence: Deliberate practice and elite performance in young and older pianists. *Journal of Experimental Psychology: General, 125,* 331–359.

Levy, B. R. (2000). Handwriting as a reflection of aging self-stereotypes. *Journal of Geriatric Psychiatry: A Multidisciplinary Journal of Mental Health, 33,* 81–94.

Levy, B. R. (2009). Stereotype embodiment: A psychosocial approach to aging. *Current Directions in Psychological Science, 18,* 332–336.

Lewis, B. A., Marcus, B. H., Pate, R. R., & Dunn, A. L. (2002). Psychosocial mediators of physical activity behavior among adults and children. *American Journal of Preventive Medicine, 23,* 26–35.

Li, F., Harmer, P., McAuley, E., Fisher, K. J., Duncan, T. E., & Duncan, S. C. (2001). Tai chi, self-efficacy and physical function in the elderly. *Prevention Science, 2,* 229–239.

Maharam, L. G., Bauman, P. A., Kalman, D., Skolnik, H., & Perle, S. M. (1999). Masters athletes: Factors affecting performance. *Sports Medicine, 28,* 273–285.

Major, B., Spencer, S., Schmader, T., Wolfe, C., & Crocker, J. (1998). Coping with negative stereotypes about intellectual performance: The role of psychological disengagement. *Personality and Social Psychology Bulletin, 24,* 34–50.

Malina, R. M. (2001). Adherence to physical activity from childhood to adulthood: A perspective from tracking studies. *Quest, 53,* 346–355.

McAuley, E. (1993). Self-efficacy and the maintenance of exercise participation in older adults. *Journal of Behavioral Medicine, 16,* 103–113.

McAuley, E., & Jacobson, L. (1991). Self-efficacy and exercise participation in sedentary adult females. *American Journal of Health Promotion, 5,* 185–191.

McAuley, E., Jerome, G. J., Elavsky, S., Marquez, D. X., & Ramsey, S. N. (2003). Predicting long-term maintenance of physical activity in older adults. *Preventive Medicine, 37,* 110–118.

McAuley, E., Katula, J., Mihalko, S. L., Blissmer, B., Duncan, T., Pena, M., et al. (1999). Mode of physical activity and self-efficacy in older adults: A latent growth curve analysis. *Journal of Gerontology: Psychological Sciences, 54B,* 283–292.

McAuley, E., Lox, C. L., & Duncan, T. (1993). Long-term maintenance of exercise, self-efficacy, and physiological change in older adults. *Journal of Gerontology, 48,* 218–223.

Meisner, B., & Baker, J. (2013). An exploratory analysis of aging expectations and health care behavior among aging adults. *Psychology and Aging, 28,* 99–104.

Meisner, B., Weir, P., & Baker, J. (2013). The relationship between aging expectations and various modes of physical activity among aging adults. *Psychology of Sport and Exercise, 14,* 569–576.

Montepare, J. M., & Zebrowitz, L. A. (2002). A social–developmental view of ageism. In T. D. Nelson (Ed.), *Ageism: Stereotyping and prejudice against older persons* (pp. 77–125). Cambridge, MA: MIT Press.

Morgan, W. P., & Costill, D. L. (1996). Selected psychological characteristics and health behaviors of aging marathon runners: A longitudinal study. *International Journal of Sports Medicine, 17,* 305–312.

O'Brien Cousins, S. (1998). *Exercise, aging and health: Overcoming barriers to an active old age.* Philadelphia: Taylor and Francis.

O'Brien Cousins, S. (2003). Seniors say the "darndest" things about exercise: Quotable quotes that stimulate applied gerontology. *The Journal of Applied Gerontology, 22,* 359–378.

Oeppen, J., & Vaupel, J. W. (2002). Broken limits to life expectancy. *Science, 296,* 1029–1031.

Ogles, B. M., & Masters, K. S. (2000). Older vs. younger adult male marathon runners: Participant motives and training habits. *Journal of Sport Behavior, 23,* 130–143.

O'Neill, K., & Reid, G. (1991). Perceived barriers to physical activity by older adults. *Canadian Journal of Public Health, 82,* 392–396.

Ory, M., Hoffman, M. K., Hawkins, M., Sanner, B., & Mockenhaupt, R. (2003). Challenging aging stereotypes: Strategies for creating a more active society. *American Journal of Preventive Medicine, 25,* 164–171.

Pettee, K. K., Brach, J. S., Kriska, A. M., Boudreau, R., Richardson, C. R., Colbert, L. H., et al. (2006). Influence of marital status on physical activity levels among older adults. *Medicine and Science in Sports and Exercise, 38,* 541–546.

Rowe, J. W., & Kahn, R. L. (1987). Human aging: Usual and successful. *Science, 237,* 143–149.

Salmon, J., Owen, N., Crawford, D., Bauman, A., & Sallis, J. F. (2003). Physical activity and sedentary behavior: A population-based study of barriers, enjoyment, and preference. *Health Psychology, 22,* 178–188.

Salthouse, T. A. (1984). Effects of age and skill in typing. *Journal of Experimental Psychology: General, 113,* 345–371.

Salthouse, T. A. (2012). Consequences of age-related cognitive decline. *Annual Review of Psychology, 63,* 201–226.

Schorer, J., & Baker, J. (2009). An exploratory study of aging and perceptual–motor expertise in handball goalkeepers. *Experimental Aging Research, 35,* 1–19.

Seefeldt, V., Malina, R. M., & Clark, M. A. (2002). Factors affecting levels of physical activity in adults. *Sports Medicine, 32,* 143–168.

Shankar, A., McMunn, A., & Steptoe, A. (2010). Health-related behaviors in older adults: Relationships with socioeconomic status. *American Journal of Preventive Medicine, 38,* 39–46.

Smith, C. L., & Storandt, M. (1997). Physical activity participation in older adults: A comparison of competitors, noncompetitors, and nonexercisers. *Journal of Aging and Physical Activity, 5,* 98–110.

Standage, M., & Duda, J. L. (2004). Motivational processes among older adults in sport and exercise settings. In M. R. Weiss (Ed.), *Developmental sport and exercise psychology: A lifespan perspective* (pp. 357–381). Morgantown, WV: Fitness Information Technology.

Starkes, J. L., Weir, P. L., & Young, B. W. (2003). What does it take for older athletes to continue to excel? In J. L. Starkes & K. A. Ericsson (Eds.), *Expert performance in sports: Advances in research on sport expertise* (pp. 251–272). Champaign, IL: Human Kinetics.

Statistics Canada. (2005). *Canadian Community Health Survey, 2000/01*. Ottawa, ON: Statistics Canada.

Statistics Canada. (2013). *Directly measured physical activity of Canadian adults, 2007–2011*. Retrieved June 29, 2014, from http://www.statcan.gc.ca/pub/82-625-x/2013001/article/11807-eng.htm.

Steele, C. M. (1997). A threat in the air: How stereotypes shape intellectual identity and performance. *American Psychologist, 52*, 613–629.

Sterken, E. (2003). From the cradle to the grave: How fast can we run? *Journal of Sports Sciences, 21*, 479–491.

Stones, M. J., & Kozma, A. (1984). Longitudinal trends in track and field performances. *Experimental Aging Research, 10*, 107–110.

Trost, S. G., Owen, N., Bauman, A. E., Sallis, J. F., & Brown, W. (2002). Correlates of adults' participation in physical activity: Review and update. *Medicine and Science in Sports and Exercise, 34*, 1996–2001.

Trudeau, F., Laurencelle, L., & Shephard, R. J. (2004). Tracking of physical activity from childhood to adulthood. *Medicine and Science in Sports and Exercise, 36*, 1937–1943.

Tseng, B. Y., Uh, J., Rossetti, H. C., Cullum, C. M., Diaz-Arrastia, R. F., Levine, B. D., et al. (2013). *Journal of Magnetic Resonance Imaging, 38*, 1169–1176.

Ungerleider, S., Golding, J. M., & Porter, K. (1989). Mood profiles of masters track and field athletes. *Perceptual and Motor Skills, 68*, 607–617.

Vertinsky, P. (1995). Stereotypes of aging women and exercise: A historical perspective. *Journal of Aging and Physical Activity, 3*, 223–237.

Walsh, R. (2011). Lifestyle and mental health. *American Psychologist, 66*, 579–592.

Weir, P. L., Kerr, T., Hodges, N. J., McKay, S. M., & Starkes, J. L. (2002). Master swimmers: How are they different from younger elite swimmers? An examination of practice and performance patterns. *Journal of Aging and Physical Activity, 10*, 41–63.

Westerterp, K. R., Meijer, E. P., Goris, A. H., & Kester, A. D. (2004). Alcohol energy intake and habitual physical activity in older adults. *British Journal of Nutrition, 91*, 149–152.

Wheeler, S. C., & Petty, R. E. (2001). The effects of stereotype activation on behavior: A review of possible mechanisms. *Psychological Bulletin, 127*, 797–826.

Wroblewski, A. P., Amati, F., Smiley, M. A., Goodpaster, B., & Wright, V. (2011). Chronic exercise preserves lean muscle mass in Masters athletes. *The Physician and Sportsmedicine, 39*, 172–178.

Chapter 13

Physical Activity and Mental Health

Guy E. Faulkner   Linda Trinh   Kelly Arbour-Nicitopoulos

Les and Dave Jacobs/Getty Images

Chapter Objectives

After reading this chapter, you should be able to do the following:

1 Differentiate between mental health and mental illness.

2 Provide an overview of the prevalence of mental illness in Canada.

3 Describe the four functions of physical activity in enhancing mental health.

4 Explain some of the different mechanisms that could explain the relationship between physical activity, exercise, and mental health.

5 Distinguish between sedentary behaviour and physical activity, and describe the relationship between sedentary behaviour and mental health.

6 Provide guidelines for using exercise to improve mental health in both non-clinical and clinical settings.

Over the last several months, Danna's mood seemed to be gradually deteriorating. She felt stressed out and depressed for no apparent reason and had trouble sleeping. Although she didn't feel that her problems were serious enough to see a doctor, she did notice that they were affecting the way she felt during most of the day. The feelings were made worse by her lack of sleep. She didn't have her usual level of energy and worried that this would have a noticeable effect on her university studies. In addition, her worsening mood was starting to undermine her self-confidence. At one point, Danna considered trying some over-the-counter sleeping pills to see if they might help, but she didn't feel totally comfortable with that idea. One day after class, a close friend told her about a book that outlined a program of exercise to improve overall mood and overall psychological well-being. Although this seemed like a somewhat unusual idea, she decided to give it a try. Besides, since coming to university a little over a year ago, her level of physical activity had declined drastically because of her change in lifestyle. She had been telling herself for months to get more physically active, so the news of the exercise and mental health book was just the prompt she needed to start exercising again. In no time, Danna was glad she had. She noticed improvements with her very first exercise session and, better yet, her feelings continued to improve over the first several weeks of regular exercise. Danna still feels down from time to time, but overall, her mood has been greatly improved by a simple exercise program.

The above vignette highlights that regular exercise may have a positive effect on elements of mental health. The last 10 years have seen increasing interest in the relationship between physical activity and mental health. A new journal is dedicated to this topic (http://www.journals.elsevier.com/mental-health-and-physical-activity), and several textbooks examine the relationship (e.g., Carless & Douglas, 2010; Clow & Edmunds, 2013; Faulkner & Taylor, 2005), including the most comprehensive edited collection to date (see Ekkekakis, 2013). The result of this developing research is that we now have a convincing evidence base that supports the existence of a relationship between physical activity and a number of dimensions of mental health. This relationship may be critical. Mental health outcomes are important in their own right but they may also be critical in motivating people to stay physically active. Without regular participation, mental and physical benefits will not accumulate.

The scenario with Danna also raises a number of questions when we consider using exercise to improve mental health. What aspects of mental health have been shown to benefit from a regular exercise program? What mechanisms explain the relationship between exercise and mental health? What types of exercise work best? How often, how hard, and how long must someone exercise to experience the most benefit? How soon after starting an exercise program can positive results be expected? Can exercise serve as a preventive intervention as well as a treatment intervention? How do prolonged bouts of sitting relate to mental health? In this chapter, we will address these and several other questions related to the physical activity and mental health relationship.

COMMON MYTHS ABOUT PHYSICAL ACTIVITY AND MENTAL HEALTH

MYTH: Mental health problems are not that common in the general population.

MYTH: Exercise is more effective for treating mental problems in clinical populations than it is for improving or preventing them in non-clinical populations or in asymptomatic participants.

MYTH: In order for exercise to improve mental health, the participant must experience fitness gains by engaging in vigorous physical activity.

MYTH: Meeting recommended levels of physical activity has a protective effect for physical and mental health outcomes regardless of the time spent in sedentary pursuits.

MENTAL ILLNESS AND MENTAL HEALTH: A TWO CONTINUA MODEL

It is important to distinguish between mental health and mental illness. **Mental health** has been defined as a state of well-being in which the individual realizes personal potential, can cope with the normal stresses of life, can work productively and fruitfully, and is able to make a contribution to the community (World Health Organization, 2001). A **mental illness** is any health condition that is characterized by alterations in thinking, mood, or behaviour (or some combination thereof) associated with distress and/or impaired functioning (United States Department of Health and Human Services, 1999). Common examples include depression, anxiety, and substance misuse disorders. The two continua model of mental illness and mental health holds that both are related but distinct dimensions: one continuum indicates the presence or absence of mental health, the other the presence or absence of mental illness (Westerhof & Keyes, 2010). This has several implications. First, it allows the possibility of having a diagnosis of mental illness but still striving to achieve positive mental health. As such it justifies promoting mental health to individuals with a mental illness rather than just considering treatment or prevention. Second, mental health problems, such as subclinical levels of depression or anxiety, can affect us all without necessarily becoming a clinical, diagnosed condition. Consequently, mental health promotion has the capacity to improve the quality of life of clinical and non-clinical populations alike.

Mental health: A state of well-being in which the individual realizes personal potential, can cope with the normal stresses of life, can work productively and fruitfully, and is able to make a contribution to the community.

Mental illness: Any health condition characterized by alterations in thinking, mood, or behaviour (or some combination thereof) associated with distress and/or impaired functioning.

MENTAL ILLNESS IN CANADA

No one is immune to mental illness or less than optimal mental health. In any given year, one in five people in Canada experience a mental health problem or illness, with a cost to the economy of well in excess of $50 billion (Smetanin et al., 2011). This is a global concern. In a review of 155 international studies (Steel et al., 2014), approximately one in five respondents were identified as meeting common criteria for a common mental illness and nearly 30% of respondents were identified as having a common mental illness at some time during their lifetimes. There was also a consistent gender effect in that women had higher rates of mood and anxiety disorders than men, while men had higher rates of substance use disorders. The Ontario Burden of Mental Illness and Addictions Report (2013) is the most thorough evaluation of the impact of mental illness and addictions in the Canadian context. The burden of mental illness and addiction in Ontario is more than 1.5 times the burden of all cancers, and seven times the burden of all infectious diseases (Ratnasingham et al., 2012). Poor mental health is not a trivial issue. Strategies are required to promote mental health across the lifespan in homes, schools, and workplaces, and prevent mental illness and suicide wherever possible (Mental Health Commission of Canada, 2012) (see Case Study 13.1).

CASE STUDY 13.1	Clara Hughes: Successful Athlete and Mental Illness Activist

AFP/Getty Images

Many people may not seek mental health treatment because of the stigma associated with mental illness, while others experience discrimination because of a mental illness. Clara Hughes is one of the most successful athletes in Canadian history: She is a six-time Olympic medallist in cycling and speed skating, and the only athlete in history to win multiple medals in both the Summer and Winter Olympic Games. She has also struggled with depression throughout her life. As part of Bell's Let's Talk initiative (http://letstalk.bell.ca/en/), Clara Hughes completed a 110-day national bicycle tour across Canada supporting local mental health initiatives by community groups, schools, and other local organizations. Clara's Big Ride visited every province and territory between March 14, 2014, and July 1, 2014, to increase awareness and action in mental health and help end the stigma around mental illness.

PHYSICAL ACTIVITY AS MENTAL HEALTH PROMOTION

Physical activity: Any movement of the body that results in energy expenditure above that of resting level.

Exercise: A subset of physical activity in which the activity is structured, often supervised and undertaken with the aim of maintaining or improving physical fitness or health.

We use **physical activity** (PA) to refer to any movement of the body that results in energy expenditure above that of resting level (Caspersen et al., 1985). **Exercise** refers to a subset of physical activity in which the activity is structured, often supervised, and undertaken with the aim of maintaining or improving physical fitness or health. Examples of exercise include working out at a gym, jogging, taking an aerobics class, or taking part in recreational sport for fitness. A focus of much research into mental health has considered the effects of well-controlled exercise sessions. More recently, given the ability to accurately measure physical activity in daily life (through accelerometry for example), researchers have been able to explore the links between other dimensions of physical activity and mental health.

What is the rationale for considering physical activity and/or exercise as a mental health promotion strategy? First, complementary means of treating and preventing poor mental health are clearly needed. For example, Canadian guidelines recommend pharmacological and psychological interventions, alone or in combination, in the treatment of moderate to severe depression (Parikh et al., 2009). Although there is scientific merit in both techniques, they are far from perfect. Whilst antidepressants offer benefits in both the short and long term for some individuals, important problems remain, such as delayed therapeutic onset, limited efficacy in milder depression, and the existence of treatment-resistant depression (Penn & Tracy, 2012). Additionally, adherence remains very low, in part because of patients' concerns about side-effects and possible dependency (Hunot et al., 2007). Yet non-drug treatments, such as cognitive behavioural therapy, can be costly and difficult to access. Also, accessing effective treatment may take time.

If physical activity "works," then it has a number of positive attributes. First, it could be a cost-effective alternative for those who prefer not to use medication or who cannot access therapy. It can be self-sustaining in that it can potentially be maintained, unlike pharmacological and psychotherapeutic treatments which usually have a specified endpoint. Second, physical activity is associated with negligible deleterious side-effects. Third, physical activity is an effective method for improving important aspects of physical health (see Lee et al., 2012); thus, the promotion of physical activity for mental health can be seen as a "win–win" situation with both mental and physical health benefits accruing (Mutrie & Faulkner, 2003). Fourth, given the scope of the burden of poor mental health, we need to develop population-based promotion, prevention, and treatment strategies. Physical activity is already being promoted at a population level, for example, through social marketing campaigns developed by agencies such as ParticipACTION, and through development and dissemination of physical activity guidelines (see Chapter 15 for more details). Such efforts can also be framed as mental health promotion given the weight of the evidence we will review. Arguably, physical activity is a population-level intervention for promoting mental health unlike pharmacotherapy and counselling.

REFLECTIONS 13.1

Do you know anyone who has experienced a mental health problem? How did it affect their lives?

Physical Activity and Mental Health

We will provide an overview of existing evidence in terms of four main functions of physical activity for impacting mental health. First, physical activity may prevent mental illness. Second, exercise has been examined as a treatment or therapy for existing mental illness. Third, physical activity may improve the quality of life for people with chronic physical and/or mental health problems. Fourth, physical activity may improve the mental health of the general public. In addition to promoting physical activity, reducing sedentary behaviour may also complement improvements in mental health and this will be highlighted at the end of the chapter. To a large extent, we will focus on systematic reviews and meta-analyses as they provide useful overviews of a particular research focus.

Meta-analyses are particularly useful because they commonly report a common metric, known as the effect size, that aggregates findings from lots of different studies. For example, in an exercise intervention for depression, we might compare two groups over a 12-week period: one group exercises and one group takes antidepressant medication. We could measure depression before and after the intervention using a recognized scale, such as the Beck Depression Inventory (BDI; Beck et al., 1996). The effect size is typically calculated by taking the difference in means between two groups and dividing that number by their combined (pooled) standard deviation. This then tells us how many standard deviations' difference there is between the means on the depression scale of the intervention (i.e., individuals doing an exercise program) and the comparison condition (i.e., individuals taking medication). An effect size of 0.25 indicates that the treatment group was better than the comparison group by a quarter of a standard deviation. Cohen (1992) proposed guidelines for interpreting effect sizes: a "small" effect size is 0.20, a "medium" effect size is 0.50, and a "large" effect size is 0.80. Meta-analyses can then aggregate findings from lots of studies using this effect size formula. Meta-analyses are also very useful because they allow researchers to examine potential moderators of any relationship—for example, whether effects are stronger for aerobic exercise or strength training, for men or for women.

1. The Preventive Function In terms of preventing poor mental health, the strongest evidence supporting the role of physical activity comes in the area of depression. In a recent systematic review, Mammen and Faulkner (2013) reviewed studies with a longitudinal design examining relationships between physical activity and depression over at least two time intervals. A total of 25 of the 30 studies found a significant, inverse relationship between baseline physical activity and follow-up depression, suggesting that physical activity is preventive in the onset of depression. Given the different ways physical activity was measured in the reviewed studies, a clear dose–response relationship between physical activity and reduced depression was not apparent. However, there was evidence that any level of physical activity, including low levels, can prevent future depression.

Such studies involve large numbers of people and measure physical activity status prior to the incidence of depression. In one of the most well cited examples, Camacho and colleagues (1991) found an association between inactivity and incidence of depression in a large population from Alameda County in California who provided baseline data in 1965 and were followed up in 1974 and 1983. Physical activity was categorized as low, medium, or high. Researchers used an odds ratio (OR) to represent the odds that an outcome (in this case, depression) will occur given a particular exposure (in this case, low physical activity), compared to the odds of the outcome occurring in the absence of that exposure. In the first wave of follow-up (1974), the ORs of developing depression were significantly greater for both men and women who were low active in 1965 (OR 1.8 for men, 1.7 for women), compared to those who were high active. These ORs suggest individuals were nearly twice as likely to report depression if they reported low levels of physical activity at baseline.

Although these findings are consistent, they cannot rule out the potential for self-selection. It is possible that individuals who are more physically active represent a selection of people who happened to have greater education, be of higher socioeconomic status, or have strong social support networks that made them less likely to develop depression, irre-

Meta-analyses: The use of statistical methods to aggregate results of individual studies.

spective of their participation in physical activity. However, even when these studies take account of a wide range of possible confounding factors in the statistical modelling (e.g., disability, body mass index, smoking, alcohol, and socioeconomic status), the relationship between physical activity and a decreased risk of depression remains. Despite consistency in the literature regarding a protective function of physical activity, some caution is required given that there may be a number of other factors, such as genetic variations (De Moor et al., 2008), that predict both physical activity and depression and these may not have been fully accounted for in the reviewed studies (Mammen & Faulkner, 2013).

How might physical activity prevent mental health problems? A Canadian study (Cairney et al., 2009) explored whether changes in physical activity were associated with changes in psychological distress, defined as a psychological construct incorporating symptoms of depression and anxiety, in adults 65 years or older over a six-year period using the longitudinal National Population Health Survey (NPHS). They also examined whether this association was mediated by changes in global self-esteem, mastery, and physical health status. Individuals who had a reduction in physical activity after six years showed a dramatic increase in psychological distress. Conversely, those with increases in physical activity showed a decrease in distress over time. It appears that even late-life improvements in physical activity may reduce psychological distress among older adults.

The key finding of this study, however, concerns the other potential mediators in the relationship between physical activity and distress among older adults. The results demonstrated that a substantial part of the association between physical activity and distress (39%) was influenced by changes in self-esteem (see the later section on mechanisms). That is, higher levels of activity were associated with greater self-esteem, as well as lower levels of psychological distress. Framing the promotion of physical activity and structuring physical activity interventions for older adults in ways that target mastery or enhance perceptions of self-worth may better facilitate the alleviation of distress than interventions with a narrow focus on fitness or endurance improvements.

The evidence for a preventative role for physical activity in other mental illnesses is less convincing at this point. This may be because large-scale epidemiological studies do not often assess other mental health conditions and the incidence of other mental illnesses is often small. However, one longitudinal study in Germany demonstrated that participants participating in regular physical activity had a lower incidence rate of anxiety disorders compared to those who were inactive (Strohle et al., 2007).

Canada's population is aging. Due to a number of factors, such as increasing life expectancy and low fertility rates, older adults are representing more of the total Canadian population. The number of seniors (>65 years) in Canada is projected to increase from 4.2 million to 9.8 million between 2005 and 2036, and their share of the population is expected to almost double, increasing from 13.2% to 24.5% (Turcotte & Schellenberg, 2007). One outcome of this shift will be an increased prevalence in diseases such as dementia. Strategies that may delay the onset of dementia are of great interest in terms of both preserving quality of life and reducing healthcare costs. Mainly affecting older adults, dementia is a syndrome in which there is deterioration in memory, thinking, behaviour, and the ability to perform everyday activities. Alzheimer's disease is the most common type of dementia. One review examined the association between physical activity and all-cause dementia and Alzheimer's disease (Hamer & Chida, 2009). Combined results from 16 studies demonstrated that individuals in the highest physical activity group in the analyses had a 28% lower risk of developing dementia and a 45% lower risk of developing Alzheimer's disease when compared to individuals in the lower physical activity group.

Overall, this evidence supports the notion that physical activity promotion at a population level might also be considered a strategy for promoting mental health in terms of lowering the risk of mental health problems such as depression, anxiety, and dementia.

2. The Treatment Function We will examine the evidence for using exercise to treat depression and anxiety disorders.

Depression In terms of using exercise to treat mental illness, we see the most convincing evidence in the area of clinical depression. This likely reflects that because **depression** is the most common mental illness, there may be more opportunities to intervene with this population. Depressive episodes are characterized by a depressed/sad mood, loss of interest, reduced or excessive sleep, loss of energy, anhedonia (inability to experience pleasure), impaired concentration, slowed thoughts and motor activity, low motivation and suicidal thoughts. The most recent review on the topic of exercise as a treatment for depression was conducted by Cooney and colleagues (2013), who found 39 studies that met their inclusion criteria. Studies used the **randomized controlled trial** (RCT), which is typically understood as being the strongest research design. The key distinguishing feature of an RCT is that study participants are randomly allocated to receive either the intervention or some comparison. This is done to reduce allocation bias. The meta-analysis of these RCTs showed a moderate effect size (–0.62 (95% confidence interval (CI) –0.81 to –0.42), for exercise versus no treatment control conditions. This is a medium effect size. For the six trials considered to be at low risk of bias that may influence the results, a further analysis showed a small clinical effect in favour of exercise which did not reach statistical significance—or showed no effect. Finally, the authors compared the exercise effects to those of cognitive behavioural therapy for the seven trials that had these comparisons and found no significant difference. Similarly, four trials compared exercise with antidepressant medication and no significant difference was found.

This research suggests that exercise has a similar effect size to other recognized therapies for depression including medication. James Blumenthal at Duke University has conducted some of the strongest exercise and depression intervention research in the United States. In the first groundbreaking study, the effects of aerobic exercise were compared to sertraline (Zoloft) treatment among 156 older adults with depression (Blumenthal et al., 1999). Participants were randomized to either aerobic exercise (three times per week at 70–85% of their heart rate reserve), sertraline (an antidepressant), or combined sertraline and exercise for 16 weeks. After 16 weeks of treatment, patients in all three groups exhibited significant reductions in depressive symptoms. Notably patients responded more quickly in the medication group. After 10 months, remitted participants (those who no longer met diagnostic criteria for depression) in the exercise group had significantly *lower relapse rates* than participants in the medication group (Babyak et al., 2000).

One limitation of the first study is that participants were exercising in groups under the supervision of an exercise physiologist. In a second study, participants exercised at home without supervision (Blumenthal et al., 2007). Participants were randomized to either home-based or supervised aerobic exercise, sertraline, or placebo pill for 14 weeks. Again, results revealed that participants in either the exercise or sertraline groups tended to show greater improvement in comparison with placebo participants. Participants

Depression: A mood disorder characterized by a depressed/sad mood, loss of interest, reduced or excessive sleep, loss of energy, anhedonia, impaired concentration, slowed thoughts and motor activity, low motivation, and suicidal thoughts over an extended period of time.

Randomized controlled trial: The most rigorous study of determining whether a cause–effect relation exists between treatment and outcome. Participants are randomly assigned to separate groups that compare different treatments.

engaged in regular exercise regardless of initial group assignment were less likely to be depressed one year after completing their initial treatment (Hoffman et al., 2011).

An important lesson from these studies is that exercise is not necessarily better than psychological or pharmacological therapies in terms of treatment effect in alleviating depression. Rather, consistent evidence is accumulating that it may be another *evidence-based option* for individuals to consider—one with a host of positive side-effects!

Discussing the advantages and disadvantages of different treatment strategies is an important part of the therapeutic alliance. Exercise might be an option if patients are concerned by possible medication side-effects. For example, sexual dysfunction is highly prevalent in patients with clinical depression that is further exacerbated by common anti-depressant medication. In a secondary analysis of their 2007 trial, Hoffman et al. (2009) found that exercisers reported improvements in sexual functioning that were better compared to participants taking a placebo pill. The beneficial effects of exercise were generally comparable to sertraline, with a trend toward better sexual functioning, particularly among participants who were 50 years old and older. Alternatively, some patients may be concerned about the speed of response and that physical activity may take longer to help than taking medication.

There are many unanswered questions about depression and physical activity, such as the exact dosage and mode of activity that might work best. One reason for this is the variability in the dosage that researchers examine. A recent review (Stanton & Reaburn, 2014) examined the dose characteristics of five RCTs reporting a significant treatment effect of exercise in the treatment of depression. They concluded that the exercise dose should likely use supervised aerobic exercise, and occur three times weekly at moderate intensity for a minimum of nine weeks in the treatment of depression.

CASE STUDY 13.2 Exercise Prescription for Depression

Consider a scenario in which a certified kinesiologist is advising a client who has been experiencing problems with depression. The individual tells the consultant that he has heard about the potential of exercise to improve depression, if used correctly. He asks the consultant for advice and, after discussing the details, the consultant prescribes a walking program to be performed two times per week at a moderate intensity for 20 to 30 minutes per session.

The exercise prescription was based, in part, on the fact that the client has been relatively physically inactive over the years. During the next scheduled appointment three weeks later, the client reports no noticeable improvement. Consider this scenario in light of what you have learned in this chapter. What might the consultant say to this individual during the second meeting? What questions should the consultant ask? What change in treatment should the consultant suggest, if any, and why?

sturti/Getty Images

Anxiety Disorders The current evidence concerning exercise and anxiety disorders is less convincing. **Anxiety disorders** are a broad umbrella for a range of disorders, such as panic disorder, social phobia, generalized anxiety disorder, obsessive–compulsive disorder, and post-traumatic stress disorder. The most recent meta-analysis (Bartley et al., 2013) examined seven RCTs (compared to 39 in the most recent exercise and depression meta-analysis). All studies were relatively small in nature (<85 participants in each study), and covered a range of diagnoses including generalized social anxiety disorder, generalized anxiety disorder, and panic disorder. In addition, a challenge of comparing studies was that all studies had different control conditions ranging from mindfulness-based stress reduction, to medication, to strength training. This *heterogeneity*, or variability in some key methodological components, will make comparisons more difficult within a relatively immature evidence base. Overall, aerobic exercise did not demonstrate a significant effect for the treatment of anxiety disorders (Standardized Mean Difference [SMD] = 0.02).

Meta-analyses convey a sense of objectivity but, as with any type of report results, are open to interpretation. For example, in the two studies examining the efficacy of aerobic exercise compared to pharmacotherapy (Broocks et al., 1998; Wedekind et al., 2010), there was a non-significant difference. That is, exercise was as effective as medication in terms of treatment effect. In the one study comparing exercise to group based cognitive behavioural therapy (CBT) (Hovland et al., 2013), *both* group CBT and exercise were found to be effective for the treatment of panic disorder. Indeed, exercise was associated with large and significant effects on the majority of measures at both post-treatment and the follow-up assessments (12 months). However, the effects were greater and more consistent for CBT. The authors of the meta-analysis concluded that "current evidence does not support the use of aerobic exercise as an effective primary treatment for anxiety disorder" (p. 38). An alternative conclusion might be that there is promising, although limited, evidence that the effects of exercise may be comparable to medication and, while still effective, those effects appear less than those seen with CBT. Again, for those concerned with anxiety medication or unable to access CBT, exercise might be worth a try with appropriate support.

Science is always incomplete and in many areas, such as the treatment of anxiety disorders, further research is clearly required. Studies employing consistent exercise dosages are needed, as are further trials with adequate sample sizes to detect clinically meaningful differences. The selection of an appropriate control group is particularly critical, while better efforts might be made to blind raters to experimentation design. A more important problem is how to reliably get individuals with mental illness to initiate and sustain participation in physical activity.

3. The Quality of Life Function for People with Chronic Physical and Mental Health Problems
For people with chronic mental and/or physical health problems, improvement in quality of life tends to enhance an individual's ability to cope with and manage their disorder or illness. Two examples include a serious mental illness like **schizophrenia** or **physical disabilities** like spinal cord injury.

Physical Disabilities Depression is a common secondary health concern for those individuals who have a physical disability such as a spinal cord injury, multiple sclerosis, or arthritis (Murphy et al., 2012; Patten et al., 2003; Rosenberg et al., 2013). However, there is accumulating evidence to support exercise as a preferred and effective treatment for reducing depressive symptoms among individuals with physical disabilities (e.g., Fann et al., 2013; Bombardier et al., 2013).

Hicks and colleagues (2003) conducted a RCT to examine the effects of a nine-month, twice weekly, aerobic and resistance-training intervention on depressive symptomatology in males and females (aged 19–65 years) with traumatic spinal cord injury. Results showed that the participants in the exercise condition reported significantly less depression in comparison to those assigned to the wait-list control condition. Indeed, those individuals who were participating in a regular exercise regime had experienced fewer depressive symptoms than the individuals who were waiting to participate in the exercise intervention. Three months following the study, psychological well-being (i.e., stress, pain, quality of life) and exercise adherence were significantly lower among a subsample of the participants in the exercise condition in comparison to their values reported at the end of the nine-month exercise trial (Ditor et al., 2003). This research demonstrates the important role exercise plays for improving depressive symptoms among individuals with a physical disability like spinal cord injury, and the need for continued exercise participation in order to maintain these psychological health benefits.

Serious Mental Illness Depression is also of concern among individuals diagnosed with a serious mental illness such as schizophrenia or bipolar disorder. Exercise has been shown to be a preferred and, often, effective adjunctive treatment for coping with the comorbid depressive symptoms and, in some cases, the core psychiatric symptoms among individuals diagnosed with a serious mental illness (Gorczynski & Faulkner, 2010). Exercise is not going to "cure" illnesses such as schizophrenia, but it may help individuals cope with their illness.

In one of the RCTs on exercise within the schizophrenia population, Scheewe and colleagues (2013) compared the effects of a six-month exercise therapy program with an active "wait-list" control condition (in this case, occupational therapy) on measures of depressive and psychiatric symptoms in a sample of patients with schizophrenia. In the exercise condition, participants engaged in an hour of moderate to vigorous-intensity cardiovascular and muscular exercises twice weekly, such as brisk walking and weight-training. Meanwhile, those participants assigned to the occupational therapy condition engaged in a maximum of 60 minutes per week of creative and recreational activities such as painting and reading. At the end of the six months, the researchers found that depression scores were significantly better for patients who were compliant to the exercise therapy—that is, they engaged in at least one day per week of the exercise regime—than those assigned to the occupational therapy condition. The core psychiatric symptoms of schizophrenia (like delusions, social withdrawal, and blunted affect) and cardiovascular fitness also showed greater improvements for those individuals who participated in the exercise therapy compared to those individuals who took part in the occupational therapy. Based on these findings, regular engagement (i.e., one to two hours per week) in moderate to vigorous-intensity exercise can provide benefits to individuals with severe mental illness like schizophrenia for coping with depressive and psychiatric symptoms.

4. The "Feel Good" Function In this function of physical activity, we are primarily interested in its role in promoting emotional well-being—feelings of happiness, satisfaction, and interest in life (Keyes, 2007). Researchers have studied many different domains that could be incorporated under this umbrella term of well-being. We will briefly review research looking at two of these: (1) affect, and (2) self-esteem and physical self-perceptions. The study of affect is receiving increasing attention because of its potential impact on longer-term adherence to physical activity. Self-esteem has been considered by some to be the single most important indicator of psychological well-being, so any improvements in this area through physical activity may be particularly significant.

Affect Feeling good during and/or after physical activity is motivational, serves as an important health outcome in itself, and contributes to well-being. The acute effects of physical activity have received increasing attention given its presumed motivational properties. It is certainly now established that moderate levels of exercise intensity below the ventilatory threshold (the point at which relatively more carbon dioxide is produced than the oxygen that is consumed) is associated with "feeling better" (see Ekkekakis et al., 2011). At this level of activity you can easily talk to someone beside you. Beyond the ventilatory threshold it becomes more difficult to do so.

Positive activated affect:
A subjective mental state of positive energy and engagement.

Positive activated affect is described as a subjective mental state of positive energy and engagement. In two well-cited meta-analyses, both acute (Reed & Ones, 2006) and regular aerobic physical activity (Reed & Buck, 2009) are associated with a moderate increase in self-reported positive activated affect. Simply, exercise can help people "feel good" in the right circumstances.

Interesting research can be done exploring what those circumstances might be in terms of potential moderators of the relationship between a bout of physical activity and affective response. This is usually done by manipulating the exercise dosage in some way in terms of the duration and intensity of exercise, the type of exercise, and even where the exercise takes place (Thompson et al., 2011). We may also be interested in demographic factors such as age, gender, or weight; medical characteristics such as comorbid conditions; or other psychosocial characteristics of the participant that may be of interest. This work is important in identifying the circumstances in which exercise is most likely to be perceived as "pleasant" by an individual.

REFLECTIONS 13.2

Dave Long/E+Getty Images

Think back on your own exercise history. How does a bout of exercise affect how you feel? How long does the effect last for you? Were there specific types of exercise that had more or less benefits?

Self-Esteem and Physical Self-Perceptions **Self-esteem** has been described as a "personal judgment of worthiness" (Coopersmith, 1967, p. 5). High self-esteem is associated with a number of important life adjustment qualities, whereas low self-esteem is associated with poor health behaviour decisions and is characteristic of many mental disorders such as depression (Fox, 1997).

A common approach to examining self-esteem and other self-perceptions is through considering a self-system that is multidimensional and hierarchical in nature. An example of a hierarchical model of the self, including the physical self, is presented in Figure 13.1. At the apex is global self-esteem but this is then made up of different domains such as the academic and non-academic (Shavelson et al., 1976). Each domain can then be further subdivided into subdomains. For example, the work of Ken Fox (Fox & Corbin, 1989) proposed that physical self-worth can be divided into various subdomains, such as sport competence, physical conditioning, body attractiveness, and physical strength. Competence, for example, could then be broken down into further subdomains of specific sports, and then specific skills in those sports.

Sport and exercise psychology researchers have asserted that physical activity should have a greater impact on physical self domains compared to other domains (e.g., academic) or the higher-order domains like global self-esteem (Fox, 2000). This is supported in one meta-analysis examining the effects of exercise (Spence et al., 2005). The authors reviewed 113 empirical research studies and concluded that exercise results in small but significant improvements in global self-esteem (average weighted effect size was d = 0.23). In addition, this meta-analysis suggests that increases in physical fitness are required to produce this improvement in self-esteem. Although systematic reviews are rare in

> **Self-esteem:** A personal judgment of worthiness that reflects the degree to which an individual feels positive about him- or herself.

Figure 13.1 Hierarchical structure of self-concept

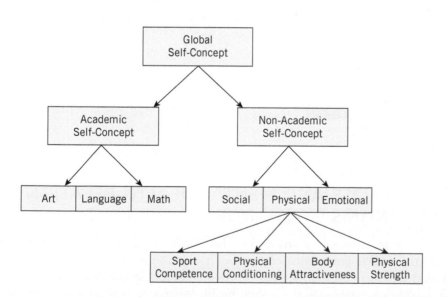

Source: Adapted from "Advances in the Measurement of the Physical Self," by K. R. Fox, 1998. In J. L. Duda (Ed.), *Advances in Sport and Exercise Psychology Measurement* (pp. 295–310). Reprinted by permission from FiT Publishing.

this domain, reviews tend to conclude that physical activity interventions consistently improve perceptions of the physical self (Crocker et al., 2013). Significant improvements have been reported following participation in activities that include running, walking, cycling, weight-training, cardiopulmonary training, step dance, and golfing (Leith, 2010). It therefore appears that many types and doses of exercise have a positive benefit on physical self-perceptions. That is, physical activity consistently makes people feel better about themselves physically.

Direct links have been found between physical self-worth and mental health independent of the effects of global self-esteem (Sonstroem & Potts, 1996). This may be due to the centrality of the physical self—it is very much the public self of who we are. This is even more pronounced in physical activity settings where our appearance and performance are open to public evaluation. Performing well can make us feel great and confident, while performing badly may be embarrassing and make us feel incompetent. Over time, repeated experiences like this may shape our choices and performances in different physical activity contexts, and this may have consequences for our global self-esteem.

CASE STUDY 13.3	Exercise and Self-Esteem

Hero Images/Getty Images

As a kinesiologist, you spend much time working with individuals who are inactive and may have had negative experiences of physical activity and sport in the past. Often, your clients are uncertain about what to do and are worried that they will look silly starting exercise for the first time in many years. What strategies can you adopt to help these clients experience positive self-esteem and self-perceptions as they get going?

Regular exercise can produce significant improvements in how you feel about yourself physically.

THE EXERCISE AND MENTAL HEALTH RELATIONSHIP: MECHANISMS OF CHANGE

The ability to explain how and under what conditions mental health changes occur allows the reliable prescription of exercise. It may also serve to legitimize the case for physical activity in different settings. There is considerable agreement that the underlying mechanisms explaining the mental health benefits of exercise are not definitively known. Notably, nor does anyone know with certainty how antidepressant medication works! Mental health is a complex phenomenon. "The causes of most mental disorders lie in some combination of genetic and environmental factors, which may be biological or psychosocial" (US DHHS, 1999, pp. 16–17).

In accepting that both biological and psychosocial factors cause mental disorders, it is also necessary to acknowledge that both biological and psychosocial changes might alleviate a disorder (Faulkner & Carless, 2006). For example, if a person's depression is caused by a combination of biochemical, social, and environmental factors, then it is likely that improvements in any combination of these factors could explain remission. The difficulty in identifying a single mechanism to explain the mental health benefits of physical activity is likely explained by the complex, individual causes of mental illness.

Several neurobiological and psychosocial hypotheses have been advanced to explain the mental health benefits of physical activity, although different mechanisms may be more relevant for acute versus chronic benefits of physical activity. This section will provide a brief overview of some of the mechanisms that might explain this relationship.

Endorphin Hypothesis

Despite the absence of compelling scientific evidence, the endorphin hypothesis represents the most popular explanation of the psychological benefits of exercise. When endorphins were discovered (Hughes et al., 1975), they were termed the "brain's own morphine" because of their ability to ease pain, and, in some cases, produce a feeling of euphoria. This latter effect has been referred to as the "runner's high" in the popular literature. This overall euphoria produced by endorphins is believed to be responsible for reducing levels of anxiety, depression, confusion, and a host of other negative mood states.

Endorphin is a general classification label for beta-endorphin. This important body chemical is a peptide and mimics the chemical structure of morphine. It is particularly important in regulating emotion and perceiving pain. Although science is routinely able to measure the activity of beta-endorphin in the brains of rats through examining brain tissue, we obviously cannot examine beta-endorphin receptor site occupancy in humans. Research on the effects of exercise on beta-endorphin levels in humans has been restricted to measuring levels of beta-endorphin and its metabolites in peripheral blood (the blood outside the blood–brain barrier).

Although early research (e.g., Riggs, 1981) provided reason for guarded optimism that endorphins may be responsible for the positive benefits of exercise on mental health, several later studies reported opposite findings. Studies performed on humans (e.g., Kraemer et al., 1990) have failed to support a role for endorphins in the exercise and mood relationship. In fact, the Kraemer and colleagues (1990) study actually demonstrated a decrease in blood plasma endorphins in association with an increase in positive mood. These and other similar findings have led others (Hoffman, 1997) to conclude that, while endorphin release into the bloodstream may have an effect on mood changes, there are several other transmitter systems involved that may be responsible for the enhanced mood effects following exercise (see Dishman & O'Connor, 2009).

Endorphin: A general classification label for beta-endorphin. This important body chemical is a peptide and mimics the chemical structure of morphine.

Neurotrophin Hypothesis

Brain derived neurotrophic factor (BDNF): A chemical that plays an important role in various aspects of developmental and adult brain plasticity.

One of the most popular and often studied hypotheses concerns the effect that both acute and chronic physical activity has on neurotrophins, like the **brain derived neurotrophic factor (BDNF)**. BDNF plays an important role in various aspects of developmental and adult brain plasticity. In his popular book, John Ratey describes BDNF acting as a fertilizer of the brain's neurons, making them grow more quickly and develop stronger connections—making it the "Miracle-Gro" of the brain (Ratey, 2009). Increasing research suggests low levels of BDNF are implicated in the pathophysiology of mental disorders such as depression (Hashimoto, 2010). For example, Shimizu and colleagues (2003) examined serum BDNF in antidepressant-naïve patients with major depression, antidepressant-treated patients with depression, and otherwise healthy control participants. Serum BDNF was significantly lower in the antidepressant-naïve group than in the treated or in the control group. There was a significant negative correlation between serum BDNF and depression scores in all patients. Most critically, the reduced BDNF values of three drug-naïve patients recovered to basal levels after antidepressant treatment.

Could exercise provoke a similar effect? In a systematic review (Huang et al., 2014), 14 of 15 studies demonstrated that peripheral BDNF concentrations were elevated significantly in response to acute aerobic exercise, although the effects were not long lasting. Five of seven studies failed to show a significant change in BDNF in response to a single bout of strength training. Finally, four of six RCTs demonstrated that resting BDNF levels were increased to some extent after a period of endurance training. This emerging body of evidence suggests that this may be a plausible mechanism through which exercise might act as an antidepressant and also improve cognitive functioning.

Monoamine Hypothesis

Monoamines: Neurotransmitters believed to be involved in the pathogenesis of several mental disorders and include dopamine, norepinephrine, and serotonin.

The monoamine hypothesis suggests the improved affect associated with exercise can be explained by changes in one or more of the brain **monoamines** (Chaouloff, 1989). Monoamines are neurotransmitters such as dopamine, norepinephrine, and serotonin. Until recently, the relationship between our behaviour and brain neurochemistry had remained a mystery. Modern technology has now allowed neurochemists to begin exploring the biological aspects of psychology. It has now been established that certain areas of the brain, and particular neural pathways, form systems that are associated with mental processes such as anxiety, depression, pleasure, pain, and even organized thought. Each system utilizes particular neurotransmitters (chemical messengers) that transmit signals across synapses (gaps) between neurons making up the system. Messages travel along the neural pathways in the form of electrical energy. When this electrical energy terminates at the end of a presynaptic neuron, it releases neurotransmitters. These neurotransmitters travel across the synaptic gap and bind to specific receptor sites (much as a specific key fits a specific lock) on the postsynaptic neuron. If enough neurotransmitters bind to receptor sites, the message is transmitted. If a sufficient number of neurotransmitters are not present, the message is not transmitted. Of special interest to us is the finding that the number of neurotransmitters available

A number of potential mechanisms might explain why exercise produces benefits in mental health. These mechanisms include endorphins, brain mono-amines, thermogenic changes, and psychological distraction, as well as other psychological variables.

at synapses along each neural pathway is related to our mood, which in turn is affected by such things as drugs and exercise.

Research on the effects of exercise on monoamine activity in humans has been restricted mostly to assessing levels of the urinary metabolite of epinephrine (namely, 3-methoxy-4-hydroxyphenolglycol, or MHPG). Because brain norepinephrine is unable to cross the blood–brain barrier, research has been restricted to the metabolites of nor-epinephrine found in cerebrospinal fluid, blood, or urine. Although cerebrospinal fluid measures provide the most direct indication of brain levels of norepinephrine, blood and urine samples are safer and easier to obtain. Because the technology required to detect MHPG in blood plasma is relatively recent, most research has utilized the urinary source of MHPG.

Pioneering research revealed that regular exercise alters both plasma and urinary levels of MHPG (Doctor & Sharkey, 1971; Pierce, Kupprat, & Harry, 1976). In fact, blood plasma and urinary levels of MHPG have been shown to increase 200% to 600% above normal levels during bouts of acute exercise (Howley, 1981). Another early study on endurance athletes reported that experienced runners competing in a mara-thon experience norepinephrine and dopamine plasma levels that are 300% above normal (Appenzeller & Schade, 1979). This elevated level is maintained until the 42-kilometre race ends, then peaks to 600% above normal levels before dropping back to normal levels in about one hour. A study examining the effect of short-term bicycle work at mild, moderate, and heavy workloads also suggests that exercise intensity may be an important variable (Hartley et al., 1972). In this study, mild exercise was found to have little effect on the plasma MHPG, while moderate and heavy workouts resulted in significant elevations. However, as in the case of endorphins, we still do not know what happens to monoamine levels in human brains and there has been a lack of convincing evidence for both functional changes in monoamine transmission and a causal relationship between changes in monoamine metabolism and changes in affect after exercise (Chaouloff et al., 2013).

All these mechanisms remain plausible and animal model research will play an important initial role in their further investigation. Speculatively, they are likely to be operating at more intense or greater volumes of physical activity. Certainly, evidence suggests that the magnitude of increase in BDNF might be exercise intensity dependent (Huang et al., 2014). We also see antidepressant effects through walking interventions that are likely well below the ventilatory threshold for participants (Robertson et al., 2012). This suggests that neurobiological mechanisms are perhaps not necessary for mental health benefit but could be operating for more seasoned exercisers.

Distraction Hypothesis

In contrast to the previous three explanations, which use physiological mechanisms to explain the exercise and mental health relationship, Bahrke and Morgan's (1978) distraction hypothesis proposes a psychological mechanism. This explanation maintains that being distracted from stressful stimuli, or taking "time out" from daily routine activities, is responsible for the improvements in mental health associated with exercise. Research can compare the effects of exercise with other forms of activities that might be considered distracting, such as reading, watching TV, resting quietly, meditating, or using a variety of relaxation techniques. An example of this type of study was conducted by Daniel and colleagues (2006). There is evidence that a short bout of physical activity can alleviate cigarette cravings among abstaining smokers (Haasova et al., 2014). In exploring the mechanisms of this effect, Daniel and colleagues (2006) had 40 participants complete either 10 minutes of moderate-intensity exercise on a stationary bicycle ergometer or 10 minutes of a cognitive distraction task (paced visual serial addition task) after 11–15 hours of smoking abstinence. There was a reduction in cravings during and immediately following exercise that was not observed in the cognitive distraction condition. In this case, the authors concluded that distraction was not a mechanism although the role of distraction will be difficult to rule out completely in most contexts.

Self-Efficacy

Several additional psychological variables have also been suggested as potential explanations for the exercise and mental health relationship. Self-efficacy, or the strength of belief that one can successfully execute a behaviour, is one such viewpoint (Bandura, 1997). According to Bandura, a person's perception of his or her ability to perform in a demanding situation, such as exercise, affects that person's emotions. Self-efficacy can be improved by past performance accomplishments, vicarious experience, verbal persuasion, or level of arousal. The basic tenet of self-efficacy theory is that as a person engages in exercise and experiences fitness gains or bodily changes, self-efficacy improves. This results in the person feeling better about him- or herself and may partially explain the positive benefits of exercise on mental health. When this person ultimately succeeds in becoming a regular exerciser, he or she will experience a feeling of accomplishment and self-efficacy. This, in turn, may break the negative downward spiral of negative affect, such as depression, anxiety, and other negative mood states.

A Process Approach

In acknowledging the huge diversity of potential triggers (such as exercise type, environment, and social context) and individual circumstances (such as state of mental health, needs, preferences, and personal background), Fox (1999) suggests that several mechanisms are most likely operating in concert, with the precise combination being highly individual-specific. Studying the process of mental health change as a result of physical activity participation must therefore allow for the diverse range of factors that influence an individual's sense of psychological well-being (Faulkner & Carless, 2006). The isolation of a specific mechanism cannot realistically address the large number of potential influences that may be experienced through physical activity. Faulkner and Carless (2006) have advocated for a process-oriented approach to allow for the broad range of potential influences on mental health.

A self-determination perspective is one example of such a process-oriented approach. Deci and Ryan (2000) have proposed that the basic needs for competence, autonomy, and relatedness must be satisfied across the life span for an individual to experience an ongoing sense of integrity and well-being. These three basic needs, which were described in more detail in the chapter on motivation, are commonly reported outcomes of physical activity interventions. Existing research suggests that physical competence and self-perceptions can be improved through physical activity, and that this can have a positive mental health effect (Phillips et al., 2013). Exercise self-efficacy can be increased through interventions and is associated with positive exercise emotion (Biddle & Mutrie, 2008). Autonomy, or perceptions of personal control, is frequently reported to be lacking among people with depression, where feelings of powerlessness and helplessness are common (Seligman, 1975). Physical activity offers a potential avenue where meaningful control can be gradually taken, as the individual assumes responsibility for the organization of the exercise schedule, or feels in control of how his or her body looks or performs (Faulkner & Carless, 2006). Finally, the provision of physical activity in a supportive group environment represents one approach to providing opportunity for positive social interaction that may be valuable (Faulkner & Biddle, 2004).

Structuring the physical activity experience to support feelings of autonomy, competence, and social relatedness is a good basis for promoting adherence to exercise and enhancing mental health.

REFLECTIONS 13.3

How important do you think it is to identify the mechanisms through which physical activity improves mental health? If physical activity does improve mental health, does it really matter?

SEDENTARY BEHAVIOUR AS A NEW AND EMERGING HEALTH RISK

Considerable research on sedentary behaviour has demonstrated unique adverse health outcomes associated with "too much sitting" independent of moderate-to-vigorous physical activity (Bauman et al., 2013). To express the intensity of different physical activities for comparison purposes, researchers use the **metabolic equivalent (MET)**, the ratio of an individual's working metabolic rate relative to their baseline metabolic rate. **Sedentary behaviour** is defined as any waking behaviour characterized by an energy expenditure of ≤1.5 metabolic equivalents (METs) while in a sitting or reclining posture (Barnes et al., 2012). It is important to distinguish that sedentary behaviour is not synonymous with physical inactivity or exercising too little, as there are separate and distinct deleterious health effects for chronic diseases. In contrast, **physical inactivity** refers to not achieving physical activity guidelines. For example, an individual can be sufficiently active according to the physical activity guidelines, but can still spend the majority of their day engaged in prolonged sitting (see Figure 13.2) (Saunders et al., 2014). Sedentary behaviour is ubiquitous to activities of modern living and accumulates each day while watching television, using a computer, driving a car, and sitting at work. Prolonged sitting time, together with reduced physical activity levels, has increased significantly over the past decade especially due to economic, social, environmental, and technological changes such as increased prevalence of sedentary occupations and use of screen-based entertainment (Owen et al., 2014). In fact, data from the Canadian Health Measures Survey has shown that Canadian adults spend approximately 69% of their waking time (i.e., 9.5 hours) in sedentary behaviours (Colley et al., 2011). Screen time activities (i.e., TV, computer) generally represent the largest type of sedentary behaviour in both adults (Bauman et al., 2013) and adolescents (Stamatakis et al., 2013).

Metabolic equivalent (MET): The ratio of an individual's working metabolic rate relative to their baseline metabolic rate, used to express the intensity of different physical activities.

Sedentary behaviour: Any waking behavior characterized by an energy expenditure of ≤1.5 METs while in a sitting or reclining posture.

Physical inactivity: Not achieving physical activity guidelines (i.e., 150 minutes of physical activity per week and/or 75 minutes of vigorous physical activity per week according to the Canadian Physical Activity Guidelines).

Sedentary Behaviour and Mental Health

Emerging evidence demonstrates an inverse association between sedentary behaviour and mental health. In a review of 11 studies examining the possible link between sedentary behaviour and depression, seven studies (six observational and one intervention) found a positive association between sedentary behaviours and risk of depression

Figure 13.2 Sedentary behaviour and physical activity as distinct constructs

Source: Based on Saunders, T. J., Chaput, J. P., & Tremblay, M. S. (2014). Sedentary behaviour as an emerging risk factor for cardiometabolic diseases in children and youth. *Canadian Journal of Diabetes, 38,* 53-61.

(Teychenne et al., 2010). An updated systematic review on adult sedentary behaviour found television viewing time showing positive associations with depressive symptoms in four out of the six studies, with no effect identified for computer use (Rhodes et al., 2012). In terms of quality of life, seven studies that measured life satisfaction/well-being/happiness showed television viewing to be associated with lower satisfaction and higher viewing among four studies, and suggests that high television viewing is related to lower psychological well-being (Rhodes et al., 2012). Although there have been some reported associations between sedentary behaviour and mental health, methodological limitations were present where 70% of studies in these reviews were cross-sectional, making causal inferences difficult to determine. The majority of the studies also used self-reported measures of sitting time.

One of the few longitudinal cohort studies examined 6359 adults from the English Longitudinal Study of Ageing to explore the association between several types of common sedentary behaviours (i.e., television viewing, reading, and internet use) and mental health over a two-year period (Hamer & Stamatakis, 2014). Findings demonstrated that television viewing time was associated with higher depressive symptoms and poorer global cognitive function. In contrast, internet use was associated with lower depressive symptoms and higher global cognitive function. These findings were only present at baseline and, given the lack of evidence for longitudinal findings, reverse causation cannot be ruled out. For example, it may be that adults with poorer mental health engage in more sedentary pursuits and vice versa. Overall, this study demonstrates that prolonged passive sedentary behaviour is associated with depressive symptoms and reduced cognitive function, whereas sedentary behaviour that is cognitively stimulating is potentially related to improved mental health.

The mechanisms through which sedentary behaviours impact mental health can only be speculated on at this point. Passive sedentary activities, such as television viewing, might promote social isolation and limit the development of social networks (Hamer & Stamatakis, 2014). Additionally, it may not be the total time spent in sedentary behaviour that is important. Rather, specific sedentary behaviours may contribute to mental health in different ways (Faulkner & Biddle, 2013). For example, exposure to different sedentary behaviours, such as talking to friends or playing violent video games, might promote mental health positively or negatively in undetermined ways. Additionally, the relationship with mental health might be influenced partly through the same mechanisms that affect cardiometabolic health. For example, potential mechanistic outcomes, such as neurogenesis and synaptic plasticity, regional fat deposits including visceral fat and pericardial fat, disrupted glucose metabolism, and/or inflammation, are pathways in which sedentary behaviour may influence cognition and brain health (Voss et al., 2014).

There are important public health implications if sedentary behaviour is detrimental to mental health. Given the challenges in engaging people in regular moderate to vigorous physical activity, targeting reductions in sedentary behaviour may be a feasible and attractive alternative for many people. Further prospective research is warranted in looking at the temporal relationships between sedentary behaviour and mental health outcomes. Intervention research should examine the mental health benefits (e.g., improvements in concentration) of interrupting extended bouts of sitting with light activity during the day.

PRACTICAL IMPLICATIONS

A framework for understanding physical activity, sedentary behaviour, and mental health relationships has recently been proposed, with a focus on translating research findings into practice (Taylor & Faulkner, 2014). Physical activity and inactivity are going to be influenced by support for behavioural change and psychosocial mediators (e.g., beliefs, attitudes, perceptions of competence and control). Links between physical activity and mental health are meditated by biological and psychosocial factors as well as the actual physical activity dosage. Questions of physical activity dosage are tied into what we believe the mechanisms explaining benefit to be for a specific mental health outcome. Certainly, identifying a dose–response relationship between physical activity and mental health is still not possible. Effects are likely to be highly individualized and depend on preferences, experiences, and setting conditions, and vary in terms of the dimensions of well-being of interest and whether we are interested in the acute or chronic effects of physical activity. For example, does a brisk 10-minute walk reduce cigarette cravings in individuals trying to quit smoking (acute)? Or does a 12-week exercise program designed to assist with weight loss help female smokers quit smoking (chronic)? In the absence of a single definitive dosage for mental health, standard adult physical activity guidelines of accumulating 150 minutes of moderate to vigorous physical activity each week should apply equally to mental health promotion. The most effective dose is likely the one that individuals enjoy and can sustain. Critically, a range of exercise modes and intensities should be recommended based on the participant's previous exercise experiences, personal preferences, and goals.

However, the critical challenge remains in helping people get active and stay active. Interventions need to be developed that are acceptable to patients, clinicians, and health service providers. Relatively little is known about whether existing behaviour change theories (see Chapter 3) are appropriate for people with different mental illnesses. Furthermore, little is known about how much and what type of support is needed, and by whom, to facilitate changes in physical activity of sufficient amount to improve mental health. Instead of targeting activities that only account for 2% of our day (i.e., moderate-to-vigorous physical activity), we may also need to consider the contributions of light-intensity physical activity that can potentially displace high levels of sedentary time and may be beneficial for mental health. Answering these questions should be the primary focus of future research in advancing the field of physical activity, sedentary behaviour, and mental health.

CHAPTER SUMMARY

This chapter started by making the distinction between mental health and mental illness. The prevalence of mental health problems was presented, along with some evidence for why physical activity might be an effective mental health promotion strategy. A convincing evidence base supports the existence of a consistent relationship between physical activity and a number of dimensions of mental health. Existing evidence suggests that physical activity may perform a preventive function, a treatment function, and a clear function for emotional well-being among healthy populations and those with existing mental or chronic illness. Reducing sedentary behaviour, especially screen-based activities, may also contribute to lower levels of depressive symptoms and improved mental health. The literature indicates that a number of different doses of exercise are effective in various populations for a wide range of mental health indicators. Therefore, the actual dosage of exercise (frequency, intensity, and duration) required to produce beneficial results is not clear. Similarly, dose–response relationships are lacking in terms of sedentary behaviour and mental health. However, the most effective dose of physical activity is likely the one that individuals enjoy and find pleasant. Several mechanisms have been proposed to underlie the changes in mental health. However, the exact mechanism for specific mental health benefits is still not clear. A process approach in exploring a range of potential mechanisms that may be operating simultaneously is recommended in examining the psychological benefits of physical activity. While methodological quality does vary in different foci of research, we would contend that the potential of psychological benefits accruing through exercise far outweighs the potential risk that no effect will occur. In hand with its inherent physical benefits, increasing physical activity and reducing sedentary behaviour is a "win–win" strategy for promoting mental health (Mutrie & Faulkner, 2003).

 ## COMMON MYTHS ABOUT PHYSICAL ACTIVITY AND MENTAL HEALTH REVISITED

MYTH: Mental health problems are not that common in the general population.
Mental health problems are actually widespread in modern society. For example, one out of three Canadians in hospital beds at any given moment are there for mental health reasons. One out of every five Canadians will experience a mental health problem over the course of their lifetime. So, in actual fact, mental health problems are very common in the general population.

MYTH: Exercise is more effective for treating mental problems in clinical populations than it is for improving or preventing them in non-clinical populations or in asymptomatic participants.
Although this was the original view, the empirical literature shows that exercise is equally effective for treating mental health problems in individuals who are considered asymptomatic. This is probably because everyone experiences problems with mood, depression, anxiety, and self-concept from time to time. Extensive research has shown exercise to be every bit as effective for reducing these problems in the general population.

MYTH: In order for exercise to improve mental health, the participant must experience fitness gains by engaging in vigorous physical activity.
In the early literature, it was assumed that this was true, but the assumption was not based on solid empirical evidence. A relatively substantial number of empirical studies that have measured fitness gains and another significant number of studies that did not even document this information have shown that we cannot conclude that

fitness is a prerequisite for improved mental health. There is evidence that fitness is related to changes in global self-esteem, but not to other mental health indicators such as anxiety, depression, and mood.

MYTH: Meeting recommended levels of physical activity has a protective effect for physical and mental health outcomes regardless of the time spent in sedentary pursuits.

In recent years, emerging research has shown that greater sedentary time is significantly associated with an increased risk of diabetes, and cardiovascular disease and death. The reported associations were largely independent of the protective effects of physical activity, further adding to the concept that sedentary behaviour is a distinct behaviour contributing to health risks. Not only are prolonged bouts of sitting detrimental for cardiometabolic risk, obesity, and all-cause mortality, but a growing body of literature has started to show an inverse association between sedentary behaviour and mental health. Higher amounts of sedentary time—especially screen-time behaviours—are associated with depressive symptoms and lower psychological well-being. The protective effects of physical activity for health seem to be reduced with high levels of sedentary behaviour.

Review Questions

1. Why are mental health problems so prevalent in today's society? Could you draw the conclusion that this is due to low levels of physical activity? Why or why not?

2. In terms of depression, who do you feel would benefit more from an exercise program: clinical or non-clinical populations? Explain your answer.

3. Do you think that certain types of exercise have more potential to improve aspects of affect? Explain your answer.

4. How can exercise change global and physical self-esteem? Do you think that specific types of exercise are more effective in changing particular aspects of physical self-concept? How might individual differences in the importance attached to specific dimensions of the physical self (fitness, muscularity/strength, or body appearance) impact self-esteem?

5. Compare and contrast three mechanisms that are believed to be responsible for the positive effect of exercise on mental health. How might each of these be associated with specific changes in depression, anxiety, or affect?

6. Do you think health professionals and practitioners should target physical activity, sedentary behaviour, or both for health promotion? Explain your answer.

Suggested Reading

Ekkekakis, P. (2013). *Routledge handbook of physical activity and mental health.* Abingdon, Oxford: Routledge.

Mental Health Commission of Canada. (2012). *Changing directions, changing lives: The mental health strategy for Canada.* Calgary, AB: Author.

Mental Health and Physical Activity is an international forum for scholarly reports on any aspect of relevance to advancing our understanding of the relationship between mental health and physical activity. See http://www.journals.elsevier.com/mental-health-and-physical-activity.

References

Appenzeller, O., & Schade, D. R. (1979). Neurology of endurance training III: Sympathetic activity during a marathon run. *Neurology, 29,* 542.

Babyak, M., Blumenthal, J. A., Herman, S., Khatri, P., Doraiswamy, M., Moore, K., Craighead, E., Baldewicz, T. T., & Krishnan, K. R. (2000). Exercise treatment for major depression: Maintenance of therapeutic benefit at 10 months. *Psychosomatic Medicine, 62,* 633–638.

Bahrke, M. S., & Morgan, W. P. (1978). Anxiety reduction following exercise and meditation. *Cognitive Therapy and Research, 2,* 323–333.

Bandura, A. (1997). *Self-efficacy: The exercise of control.* New York, NY: Freeman.

Barnes, J., Behrens, T. K., Benden, M. E., Biddle, S., Bond, D., Brassard, P., & Wilson, J. (2012). Letter to the Editor: Standardized use of the terms 'sedentary' and 'sedentary behaviours.' *Applied Physiology, Nutrition, and Metabolism, 37,* 540–542.

Bartley, C. A., Hay, M., & Bloch, M. H. (2013). Meta-analysis: aerobic exercise for the treatment of anxiety disorders. *Progress in Neuro-Psychopharmacology & Biological Psychiatry, 45,* 34–39.

Bauman, A. E., Chau, J. Y., Ding, D., & Bennie, J. (2013). Too much sitting and cardio-metabolic risk: An update of epidemiological evidence. *Current Cardiovascular Risk Reports, 7,* 293–298.

Beck, A. T., Steer, R. A., & Brown, G. K. (1996). *Manual for the Beck Depression Inventory-II.* San Antonio, TX: Psychological Corporation.

Biddle, S. J. H., & Mutrie, N. (2008). *Psychology of physical activity: Determinants, well-being, and interventions* (2nd ed.). London, UK: Routledge.

Blumenthal, J. A., Babyak, M. A., Doraiswamy, P. M., Watkins, L., Hoffman, B. M., Barbour, K. A., & Sherwood, A. (2007). Exercise and pharmacotherapy in the treatment of major depressive disorder. *Psychosomatic Medicine, 69,* 587–596.

Blumenthal, J. A., Babyak, M. A., Moore, K. A., Craighead, E., Herman, S., Khatri, P., & Krishnan, K. R. (1999). Effects of exercise training on older patients with major depression. *Archives of Internal Medicine, 159,* 2349–2356.

Bombardier, C. H., Ehde, D. M., Gibbons, L. E., Wadhwani, R., Sullivan, M. D., Rosenberg, D. E., & Kraft, G. H. (2013). Telephone-based physical activity counseling for major depression in people with multiple sclerosis. *Journal of Consulting and Clinical Psychology, 81,* 89–99.

Broocks, A., Bandelow, B., Pekrun, G., George, A., Meyer, T., Bartmann, U., Hillmer-Vogel, U., & Ruther, E. (1998). Comparison of aerobic exercise, clomipramine, and placebo in the treatment of panic disorder. *American Journal of Psychiatry, 155,* 603–609.

Cairney, J., Faulkner, G., Veldhuizen, S., & Wade, T. J. (2009). Changes over time in physical activity and psychological distress among older adults. *Canadian Journal of Psychiatry, 54,* 160–169.

Camacho, T. C., Roberts, R. E., Lazarus, N. B., Kaplan, G. A., & Cohen, R. D. (1991). Physical activity and depression: Evidence from the Alameda county study. *American Journal of Epidemiology, 134,* 220–231.

Carless, D., & Douglas, K. (2010). *Sport and physical activity for mental health.* Oxford, UK: Wiley-Blackwell.

Caspersen, C. J., Powell, K. E., & Christenson, G. M. (1985). Physical activity, exercise and physical fitness: Definitions and distinctions for health-related research. *Public Health Reports, 100,* 126–131.

Chaouloff, F. (1989). Physical exercise and brain monoamines: A review. *Acta Physiologica Scandinavica, 137,* 1–13.

Chaouloff, F., Dubreucq, S., Matias, I., & Marsicano, G. (2013). Physical activity feel-good effect: The role of endocannabinoids. In P. Ekkekakis (Ed.), *Routledge Handbook of Physical Activity and Mental Health* (pp. 71–87). Oxford, UK: Routledge.

Clow, A., & Edmunds, S. (Eds.). (2013). *Physical activity and mental health*. Champaign, IL: Human Kinetics.

Cohen, J. (1992). A power primer. *Psychological Bulletin, 112*, 155–159.

Colley, R. C., Garriguet, D., Janssen, I., Craig, C. L., Clarke, J., & Tremblay, M. S. (2011). *Physical activity of Canadian adults: Accelerometer results from the 2007 to 2009 Canadian Health Measures Survey* (pp. 7–14). Ottawa, ON: Statistics Canada.

Cooney, G. M., Dwan, K., Greig, C. A., Lawlor, D. A., Rimer, J., Waugh, F. R., & Mead, G. E. (2013). *Exercise for depression. Cochrane Database of Systematic Reviews*, article number: CD004366.

Coopersmith, S. (1967). *The antecedents of self-esteem*. San Francisco, CA: Freeman.

Crocker, P. R. E., McEwen, C. E., & Mosewich, A. D. (2013). Physical activity and self-perceptions among adults. In P. Ekkekakis (Ed.), *Routledge Handbook of Physical Activity and Mental Health* (pp. 200–211). Oxford, UK: Routledge.

Daniel, J. Z., Cropley, M., & Fife-Schaw, C. (2006). The effect of exercise in reducing desire to smoke and cigarette withdrawal symptoms is not caused by distraction. *Addiction, 101*, 1187–1192.

Deci, E. L., & Ryan, R. M. (1985). *Intrinsic motivation and self-determination in human behavior*. New York, NY: Plenum Press.

De Moor, M. M., Boomsma, D. I., Stubbe, J. H., Willemsen, G., & De Geus, E. C. (2008). Testing causality in the association between regular exercise and symptoms of anxiety and depression. *Archives of General Psychiatry, 65*, 897–905.

Dishman, R. K., & O'Connor, P. J. (2009). Lessons in exercise neurobiology: The case of endorphins. *Mental Health & Physical Activity, 2*, 4–9.

Ditor, D. S., Latimer, A. E., Ginis, K. M., Arbour, K. P., McCartney, N., & Hicks, A. L. (2003). Maintenance of exercise participation in individuals with spinal cord injury: Effects on quality of life, stress and pain. *Spinal Cord, 41*, 446–450.

Doctor, R., & Sharkey, B. J. (1971). Note on some physiological and subjective reactions to exercise and training. *Perceptual and Motor Skills, 32*, 233–237.

Ekkekakis, P. (2013). *Routledge handbook of physical activity and mental health*. Oxford, UK: Routledge.

Ekkekakis, P., Parfitt, G., & Petruzzello, S. J. (2011). The pleasure and displeasure people feel when they exercise at different intensities: Decennial update and progress towards a tripartite rationale for exercise intensity prescription. *Sports Medicine, 41*, 641–671.

Fann, J. R., Crane, D. A., Graves, D. E., Kalpakjian, C. Z., Tate, D. G., & Bombardier, C. H. (2013). Depression treatment preferences after acute traumatic spinal cord injury. *Archives of Physical Medicine and Rehabilitation, 94*, 2389–2395.

Faulkner, G., & Biddle, S. J. H. (2004). Physical activity and depression: Considering contextuality and variability. *Journal of Sport and Exercise Psychology, 26*, 3–18.

Faulkner, G., & Biddle, S. J. H. (2013). Standing on top of the world: Is sedentary behavior associated with mental health? *Mental Health and Physical Activity, 6*, 1–2.

Faulkner, G., & Carless, D. (2006). Physical activity and the process of psychiatric rehabilitation: Theoretical and methodological issues. *Psychiatric Rehabilitation Journal, 29*, 258–266.

Faulkner, G., & Taylor, A. (Eds.). (2005). *Exercise, health and mental health: Emerging relationships between physical activity and psychological well-being*. London, UK: Routledge.

Fox, K. (1997). *The physical self: From motivation to well-being*. Champaign, IL: Human Kinetics.

Fox, K. (1998). Advances in the measure of the physical self. In J. L. Duda (Ed.), *Advances in sport and exercise psychology measurement* (pp. 295–310). Morgantown, WV: Fitness Information Technology, Inc.

Fox, K. R. (1999). The influence of physical activity on mental well-being. *Public Health Nutrition, 2*, 411–418.

Fox, K. (2000). The effects of exercise on self-perceptions and self-esteem. In S. J. H. Biddle, K. Fox, & S. Boutcher (Eds.), *Physical activity and psychological well-being* (pp. 88–117). London, UK: Routledge.

Fox, K. R., & Corbin, C. B. (1989). The physical self-perception profile: Development and preliminary validation. *Journal of Sport and Exercise Psychology, 11*, 408–430.

Gorczynski, P., & Faulkner, G. (2010). Exercise therapy for schizophrenia. *Cochrane Database of Systematic Reviews, 2010*, article number: CD004412.

Haasova, M., Warren, F. C., Ussher, M., Janse Van Rensburg, K., Faulkner, G., Cropley, M., & Taylor, A.H. (2014). The acute effects of physical activity on cigarette cravings: Exploration of potential moderators, mediators and physical activity attributes using individual participant data (IPD) meta-analyses. *Psychopharmacology, 231*, 1267–75.

Hamer, M., & Chida, Y. (2009). Physical activity and risk of neurodegenerative disease: A systematic review of prospective evidence. *Psychological Medicine, 39*, 3–11.

Hamer, M., & Stamatakis, E. (2014). Prospective study of sedentary behavior, risk of depression, and cognitive impairment. *Medicine and Science in Sports and Exercise, 46*, 718–723.

Hartley, L. H., Mason, J. W., Hogan, R. P., Jones, L. G., Kotchen, T. A., Mougey, E. H., & Ricketts, P. T. (1972). Multiple hormonal responses to graded exercise in relation to physical training. *Journal of Applied Physiology, 33*, 602–606.

Hashimoto, K. (2010). Brain-derived neurotrophic factor as a biomarker for mood disorders: An historical overview and future directions. *Psychiatry and Clinical Neurosciences, 64*, 341–357.

Hicks, A. L., Martin, K. A., Ditor, D. S., Latimer, A. E., Craven, C., Bugaresti, J., & McCartney, N. (2003). Long-term exercise training in persons with spinal cord injury: Effects on strength, arm ergometry performance and psychological well-being. *Spinal Cord, 41*, 34–43.

Hoffman, B. M., Babyak, M. A., Sherwood, A., Hill, E. E., Patidar, S. M., Doraiswamy, P. M., & Blumenthal, J. A. (2009). Effects of aerobic exercise on sexual functioning in depressed adults. *Mental Health and Physical Activity, 2*, 23–28.

Hoffman, B. M., Babyak, M. A., Craighead, W. E., Sherwood, A., Doraiswamy, P. M., Coons, M. J., & Blumenthal, J. A. (2011). Exercise and pharmacotherapy in patients with major depression: One-year follow-up of the SMILE study. *Psychosomatic Medicine, 73*, 127–133.

Hoffman, P. (1997). The endorphin hypothesis. In W. P. Morgan (Ed.), *Physical activity and mental health* (pp. 163–177). Washington, DC: Taylor & Francis Publisher.

Hovland, A., Nordhus, I. H., Sjobo, T., Gjestad, B. A., Birknes, B., Martinsen, E. W., & Pallesen, S. (2013). Comparing physical exercise in groups to group cognitive behaviour therapy for the treatment of panic disorder in a randomized controlled trial. *Behavioural and Cognitive Psychotherapy, 41*, 408–432.

Howley, E. T. (1981). The excretion of catecholamines as an index of exercise stress. In F. J. Nagel, & H. J. Montoye (Eds.), *Exercise in health and disease* (pp. 22–31). Springfield, IL: Charles C. Thomas.

Huang, T., Larsen, K. T., Ried-Larsen, M., Moller, N. C., & Andersen, L. B. (2014). The effects of physical activity and exercise on brain-derived neurotrophic factor in healthy humans: A review. *Scandinavian Journal of Medicine and Science in Sports, 24*, 1–10.

Hughes, J., Smith, T. W., Kosterlitz, H. W., Fothergill, L. A., Morgan, B. A., & Morris, H. R. (1975). Identification of two related pentapeptides from the brain with potent opiate agonist activity. *Nature, 258*, 577–579.

Hunot, V. M., Horne, R., Leese, M. N., & Churchill, R. C. (2007). A cohort study of adherence to antidepressants in primary care: The influence of antidepressant concerns and treatment preferences. *Primary Care Companion to the Journal of Clinical Psychiatry, 9*, 91–99.

Keyes, C. L. M. (2007). Promoting and protecting mental health as flourishing: A complementary strategy for improving national mental health. *American Psychologist, 62*, 95–108.

Kraemer, R. R., Dzewaltowski, D. A., Blair, M. S., Rinehardt, K. F., & Castracane, V. D. (1990). Mood alteration from treadmill running and its relationship to beta-endorphin, coricotrophin, and growth hormone. *The Journal of Sports Medicine and Physical Fitness, 30,* 241–246.

Lee, I. M., Shiroma, E. J., Lobelo, F., Puska, P., Blair, S. N., Katzmarzyk, P. T., & Lancet Physical Activity Series Working Group. (2012). Effect of physical inactivity on major non-communicable diseases worldwide: An analysis of burden of disease and life expectancy. *Lancet, 380,* 219–229.

Leith, L. (2010). *Foundations of exercise and mental health.* Morgantown, WV: Fitness Information Technology.

Mammen, G., & Faulkner, G. (2013). Physical activity and the prevention of depression: A systematic review of prospective studies. *American Journal of Preventive Medicine, 45,* 649–657.

Mental Health Commission of Canada. (2012). *Changing directions, changing lives: The mental health strategy for Canada.* Calgary, AB: Author.

Murphy, L. B., Sacks, J. J., Brady, T. J., Hootman, J. M., & Chapman, D. P. (2012). Anxiety and depression among US adults with arthritis: prevalence and correlates. *Arthritis Care & Research, 64,* 968–976.

Mutrie, N., & Faulkner, G. (2003). Physical activity and mental health. In T. Everett, M. Donaghy, & S. Fever (Eds.), *Physiotherapy and occupational therapy in mental health: An evidence based approach* (pp. 82–97). Oxford, UK: Butterworth Heinemann.

Owen, N., Salmon, J., Koohsari, M. J., Turrell, G., & Giles-Corti, B. (2014). Sedentary behaviour and health: Mapping environmental and social contexts to underpin chronic disease prevention. *British Journal of Sports Medicine, 48,* 174–177.

Parikh, S. V., Segal, Z. V., Grigoriadis, S., Ravindran, A. V., Kennedy, S. H., Lam, R. W., & Patten, S. B. (2009). Canadian Network for Mood and Anxiety Treatments (CANMAT) clinical guidelines for the management of major depressive disorder in adults. II. Psychotherapy alone or in combination with antidepressant medication. *Journal of Affective Disorders, 117,* S15–S25.

Patten, S. B., Beck, C. A., Williams, J. V., Barbui, C., & Metz, L. M. (2003). Major depression in multiple sclerosis: A population-based perspective. *Neurology, 61,* 1524–1527.

Penn, E., & Tracy, D. (2012). The drugs don't work? Antidepressants and the current and future pharmacological management of depression. *Therapeutic Advances in Psychopharmacology, 2,* 179–188.

Phillips, S. M., Wójcicki, T. R., & McAuley, E. (2013). Physical activity and quality of life in older adults: An 18-month panel analysis. *Quality of Life Research, 22,* 1647–1654.

Pierce, D., Kupprat, I., & Harry, D. (1976). Urinary epinephrine and norepinephrine levels in women athletes' training and competition. *European Journal of Applied Physiology, 36,* 1–6.

Ratey, J. (2009). *Spark: The revolutionary new science of exercise and the brain.* New York, NY: Little, Brown, & Company.

Ratnasingham, S., Cairney, J., Rehm, J., Manson, H., & Kurdyak, P. A. (2012). *Opening eyes, opening minds: The Ontario burden of mental illness and addictions report.* An ICES/PHO Report. Toronto, ON: Institute for Clinical Evaluative Sciences and Public Health Ontario.

Reed, J., & Buck, S. (2009). The effect of regular aerobic exercise on positive activated affect: A meta-analysis. *Psychology of Sport and Exercise, 10,* 581–594.

Reed, J., & Ones, D. (2006). The effect of acute aerobic exercise on positive activated affect: A meta-analysis. *Psychology of Sport and Exercise, 7,* 477–514.

Rhodes, R. E., Mark, R., & Temmel, C. (2012). Adult sedentary behaviour: A systematic review. *American Journal of Preventive Medicine, 42,* e3–28.

Riggs, C. E. (1981). Endorphins, neurotransmitters and/or neuromodulators and exercise. In M. H. Sacks, & M. L. Sachs (Eds.), *Psychology of running* (pp. 224–230). Champaign, IL: Human Kinetics.

Robertson, R., Robertson, A., Jepson, R. & Maxwell, M. (2012). Walking for depression or depressive symptoms: A systematic review and meta-analysis. *Mental Health and Physical Activity, 5*, 66–75.

Rosenberg, D. E., Bombardier, C. H., Artherholt, S., Jensen, M. P., & Motl, R. W. (2013). Self-reported depression and physical activity in adults with mobility impairments. *Archives of Physical Medicine and Rehabilitation, 94*, 731–736.

Saunders, T. J., Chaput, J. P., & Tremblay, M. S. (2014). Sedentary behaviour as an emerging risk factor for cardiometabolic diseases in children and youth. *Canadian Journal of Diabetes, 38*, 53–61.

Scheewe, T. W., Backx, F. J. G., Takken, T., Jörg, F., Strater, A. V., Kroes, A. G., & Cahn, W. (2013). Exercise therapy improves mental and physical health in schizophrenia: A randomised controlled trial. *Acta Psychiatrica Scandinavica, 127*, 464–473.

Seligman, M. E. P. (1975). *Helplessness: On depression, development, and death*. New York, NY: W.H. Freeman.

Shavelson, R. J., Hubner, J. J., & Stanton, G. C. (1976). Self-concept: Validation of construct interpretations. *Review of Educational Research, 46*, 407–441.

Shimizu, E., Hashimoto, K., Okamura, N., Koike, K., Komatsu, N., Kumakiri, C., & Iyo, M. (2003). Alterations of serum levels of brain-derived neurotrophic factor (BDNF) in depressed patients with or without antidepressants. *Biological Psychiatry, 54*, 70–75.

Smetanin, P., Stiff, D., Briante, C., Adair, C., Ahmad, S., & Khan, M. (2011). *The life and economic impact of major mental illnesses in Canada*. Mental Health Commission of Canada. Toronto, ON: Risk Analytica.

Sonstroem, R. J., & Potts, S. A. (1996). Life adjustment correlates of physical self-concepts. *Medicine and Science in Sports and Exercise, 28*, 619–25.

Spence, J. C., McGannon, K. R., & Poon, P. (2005). The effect of exercise on global self-esteem: A quantitative review. *Journal of Sport & Exercise Psychology, 27*, 311–334.

Stamatakis, E., Coombs, N., Jago, R., Gama, A., Mourão, I., Nogueira, H., & Padez, C. (2013). Type-specific screen time associations with cardiovascular risk markers in children. *American Journal of Preventive Medicine, 44*, 481–488.

Stanton, R., & Reaburn, P. (2014). Exercise and the treatment of depression: A review of the exercise program variables. *Journal of Science & Medicine in Sport, 17*, 177–182.

Steel, Z., Marnane, C., Iranpour, C., Chey, T., Jackson, J. W., Patel, V., & Silove, D. (2014). The global prevalence of common mental disorders: A systematic review and meta-analysis 1980-2013. *International Journal of Epidemiology, 43*, 476–493.

Strohle, A., Hofler, M., Pfister, H., Muller, A., Hoyer, J., Wittchen, H., & Lieb, R. (2007). Physical activity and prevalence and incidence of mental disorders in adolescents and young adults. *Psychological Medicine, 37*, 1657–1666.

Taylor, A. H., & Faulkner, G. (2014). Evidence and theory into practice in different health care contexts: A call for more translational science. *Mental Health and Physical Activity, 7*, 1–5.

Teychenne, M., Ball, K., & Salmon, J. (2010). Sedentary behavior and depression among adults: A review. *International Journal of Behavioral Medicine, 17*, 246–254.

Thompson, C. J., Boddy, K., Stein, K., Whear, R., Barton, J., & Depledge, M. H. (2011). Does participating in physical activity in outdoor natural environments have a greater effect on physical and mental wellbeing than physical activity indoors? A systematic review. *Environmental Science & Technology, 45*, 1761–1772.

Turcotte, M., & Schellenberg, G. (2007). *A portrait of seniors in Canada*. Ottawa, ON: Statistics Canada.

United States Department of Health and Human Services (US DHHS) (1999). *Mental health: A report of the surgeon general*. Rockville, MD: U.S. Department of Health and Human Services,

Substance Abuse and Mental Health Services Administration, Center for Mental Health Services, National Institutes of Health, National Institute of Mental Health.

Voss, M. W., Carr, L. J., Clark, R., & Weng, T. (2014). Revenge of the "sit" II: Does lifestyle impact neuronal and cognitive health through distinct mechanisms associated with sedentary behavior and physical activity? *Mental Health and Physical Activity, 7*, 9–24.

Wedekind, D., Broocks, A., Weiss, N., Engel, K., Neubert, K., & Bandelow, B. (2010). A randomized, controlled trial of aerobic exercise in combination with paroxetine in the treatment of panic disorder. *World Journal of Biological Psychiatry, 11*, 904–913.

Westerhof, G. J., & Keyes, C. L. M. (2010). Mental illness and mental health: The two continua model across the lifespan. *Journal of Adult Development, 17*, 110–119.

World Health Organization (2001). *Mental health: A call for action by world health ministers.* Retrieved from http://www.who.int/mental_health/media/en/249.pdf.

Chapter 14

Body Image in Sport and Exercise

Catherine Sabiston   Jennifer Brunet

Jonathan Storey/Photodisc/Getty Images

Chapter Objectives

After reading this chapter, you should be able to:

1   Define body image and distinguish between the different body image dimensions.
2   Provide examples of ways that each body image dimension can be measured.
3   Identify the main theories related to body image and physical activity.
4   Identify factors that may influence the development and maintenance of body image.
5   Understand how physical activity can influence body image.
6   Summarize the key findings related to body image and physical activity to guide your practice.

Lexi constantly tells her friends that she is fat and ugly and she is always looking for ways to improve her weight and appearance. She just wants to be as skinny as most of her friends on Facebook. She also wants to have a toned body like the models in the pop-up advertisements. Her friends are always telling her that she is beautiful and there is no need for her to lose weight, but she just can't seem to appreciate her body. She looks at herself in the mirror every day, constantly weighs herself, and is always pulling at the small amount of fat on her waistline and wishing it wasn't there. Lexi is always late for school because she spends so much time getting ready, and every day she feels bad about eating junk food and not exercising enough. While sitting in class, her thoughts often drift to her appearance. She asks herself: "I wonder if the person behind me can see my muffin top?" . . . "I hope none of the guys have to lift me during gymastics class" . . . "I wish I'd worn a long-sleeved sweater today so no one could see my big arms." She hates physical education class because she has to wear shorts and a T-shirt, which means her body is exposed to others. She thinks about the changerooms long before class since there is only one bathroom stall, which will be taken if she doesn't get there first, and then she will have to change out in the open with all her female classmates. She often fakes being sick or injured to avoid participating in physical education so she doesn't have to change. Sometimes, she even skips classes, especially when she knows the teacher will test her on a skill in front of all the other students. During the basketball unit, she had to do lay-ups and free throws, and all she thought about was whether her shirt might come up enough to reveal her stomach to others. Lexi can't wait until next year when she can opt out of physical education. She has already convinced her parents to stop sending her to swimming lessons. Soon she won't have to do any physical activity unless she chooses to do it at home and alone.

Maddox is in many of Lexi's classes at school. He is a class clown and always tries to be the centre of attention. In fact, he is one of the students Lexi worries will try to pick her up or grab the fat on the back of her arms. In spite of his outward antics, Maddox struggles with his physique—he sees himself as being too thin even though he isn't. In some ways, he is always joking around as a cover for his negative thoughts and feelings about his thin body. He would be so embarassed if his friends knew how he really felt—it's certainly not something guys talk about. If any of his friends on the football team saw him admiring their larger muscles, he would likely be made fun of to the point of being ostracized from the team. Maddox keeps his disdain to himself, which is often heightened in the locker room at school when he gets ready for football practice. One senior player, Jake, is particularly ruthless in his comments about his teammates' body shapes and sizes. Jake walks around the locker room in his underwear, saying that he is bigger and tougher than everyone else. Maddox is frustrated because he wants nothing more than to gain weight and he often takes protein shakes and tries to eat a lot of calories to bulk up. He sometimes goes to the gym twice a day to try to build muscle but isn't seeing many results. When his friends ask him to go out to social events, he often makes excuses so that he can work out without anyone else knowing. When he can't manage to go to the gym, he feels really guilty and overcompensates during his next workout. He has started to think about taking steroids to bulk up faster, and wishes there was an easy way to get access to these drugs. He is afraid to ask around at the gym because he is intimitated on the inside and would be super embarrassed if a classmate saw him buying steroids. After all, he has to maintain the persona of the outgoing, confident, carefree athlete that he is thought to be, rather than the "real" Maddox who feels badly about his physique and wishes he could change his body size more than anything.

In the above scenario, Lexi and Maddox struggle with the images they have of their bodies. They both have negative thoughts and inaccurate perceptions, express many negative emotions, and spend a lot of time monitoring their respective body shapes, sizes, and appearances. As will be discussed in the chapter, these are common attributes associated with body image. Lexi and Maddox also worry very much about how they are perceived by others, and fear being evaluated negatively. Defined in the chapter as social physique anxiety, this is a commonly studied body image emotion. Common influences on body image are pervasive in these scenarios. Lexi is a female adolescent who compares herself to others on Facebook and to models in advertisements. Media-presented images are often discussed as sources of negative body image. Maddox is a male adolescent who compares himself to athletic peers who are more muscular than he is. Social comparisons among peers, in particular during adolescence, are also highly predictive of negative body image. Also, Lexi clearly avoids physical activity when she can, which is a behavioural outcome associated with negative body image. Conversely, Maddox is dependent on physical activity and engages in other muscle-building behaviours such as consuming protein products. He is also contemplating using steroids. These avoidance and remedial actions are behavioural outcomes associated with negative body image. Since adolescence is a time when physical activity levels drop significantly, it may be important to address people's body image experiences through education, training, and practice.

 COMMON MYTHS ABOUT BODY IMAGE IN SPORT AND EXERCISE

MYTH: Negative body image is the opposite of positive body image.

MYTH: A person with a negative body image is also said to have an eating disorder.

MYTH: Males don't have body image issues.

MYTH: People with negative body image will always avoid physical activity, whereas people with positive body image will engage in physical activity.

INTRODUCTION

It is estimated that a majority of children, adolescents, and adults in modern Western cultures report disatisfaction with some aspect of their body shapes, sizes, weights, and appearances. This prevalence of body-related concerns or dissatisfaction has been described as a **normative discontent** because of how widespread it is. Even so, most people can also identify physical attributes that they appraise as positive, and may report some acceptance toward their bodies in spite of also experiencing some discontent. Both negative and positive body image have been associated with various psychological, physical, and social outcomes, as well as with behavioural outcomes such as physical activity.

Normative discontent: Concept that most women experience weight and appearance dissatisfaction.

While different types of physical activities can promote positive body image, many situations related to sport and exercise participation, and physical education, naturally involve interpersonal comparisons, physical evaluations and judgments from others, and may also promote negative body image.

In the current chapter, the historical roots of body image are presented and definitions of body image are provided to show that it is more complex than simply "I like or dislike my body." Important body image-related concepts, such as physical self-concept and self-perceptions, are presented, and the links between body image-related concepts and physical activity are identified. The chapter ends by providing strategies that can be used in practice—whether by kinesiologists, physical educators, coaches, clinicians, or other specialists—to help decrease negative body image and increase positive feelings, attitudes and thoughts about the body.

THE HISTORICAL ROOTS OF BODY IMAGE SCIENCE

Body schema: A representation of the position and configuration of the body.

Body image has been studied since the early 1900s when neurologists were attempting to explain unusual body perceptions and experiences reported by patients with brain injuries (e.g., phantom limb pain, whereby amputees experience sensation in the amputated limb). The early neurological construct was coined by Sir Henry Head and labelled **body schema**. He explained it as a representation of the position and configuration of the body. Paul F. Schilder (1935) argued for a biopsychosocial approach to body image to include the neurological aspects as well as psychological and socialcultural aspects. This was among the first multidimensional conceptualizations of body image, and his 1935 book *The Image and Appearance of the Human Body* prompted a shift in the way researchers thought about body image. In the 1950s and 1960s, Seymour Fisher introduced it as a psychodynamic concept in which **body image boundaries** were identified and described as an individual's perception of meaning of specific body parts, general body awareness, and distortions in body perception. In the late 1960s, Franklin Shontz articulated cognitive and perceptual dimensions of body image since his findings showed that people's perceptions of their body shapes, sizes, and weights are often discrepant from their actual measurements.

Body image boundaries: An individual's perception of meaning attributed to specific body parts, overall body awareness, and distortions in body perception.

Body cathexis: People's subjective evaluations outlined by a degree of satisfaction or dissatisfaction with their bodies.

Another term emanating from a psychological perspective was **body cathexis**. Presented by Paul Secord and Sidney Jourard in the early 1950s, it corresponds to people's subjective evaluations by capturing the degree of their satisfaction or dissatisfaction with their bodies. At that time, body cathexis was tied to self-concept since it had been observed that people's evaluation of body and self were virtually one in the same. As such, cognition and affect were both highly tied to body image. In the early 1980s, Stephen Fanzoi and Stephanie Shields conceptualized body image within a self-esteem framework and used the term **body esteem** to reflect self-evaluations of one's body and/or appearance. As such, body esteem shared similiarities with the concept of body cathexis.

Body esteem: Self-evaluations of one's body and/or appearance.

In the 1990s, Thomas Cash and Thomas Pruzinsky wrote several papers stressing the importance of considering body image as a multidimensional concept. They pioneered body image theory, research, and practice in areas such as disability and rehabilitation. Thomas Cash is the editor of the first journal dedicated to the topic (*Body Image: An International Journal*), and has recently edited what is arguably the biggest collection of work in this area (*Encyclopedia of Body Image and Human Appearance*). J. Kevin

Thompson contributed to the clinical manifestations and associations between body image, eating disorders, and obesity while highlighting advances in the assessment and treatment of body image disorders. This era was marked by specific cognitive–behavioural treatment approaches for body image problems that are still favoured today. Another shift in thinking about body image came at the turn of the century, when Harrison Pope and colleagues published a book highlighting the body concerns of boys and men (*The Adonis Complex: The Secret Crisis of Male Body Obsession*). Since that time, there has been a slow but gradual increase in understanding male body image concerns. Finally, one of the biggest contributions of more recent theory, research, and practice is the shift away from pathology-focused approaches (i.e., a focus on the negative, or body image problems) to the focus on **positive psychological perspectives** of body image (Tylka, 2011).

Over the more recent decades, Canadian academics have played a role amid the developments of body image theory, research, and practice. Kathleen Martin Ginis has led a number of experimental research studies linking body image to physical activity. Donald McCreary has pioneered work on body image among men, with a specific focus on drive for muscularity. Kent Kowalski, Peter Crocker, and Diane Mack have all advanced research on body image emotions during adolescence with a particular focus on social physique anxiety. Catherine Sabiston has advanced the affective body image literature by highlighting a range of self-conscious emotions associated with the body and calling for a positive psychology focus on body-related emotions. Caroline Davis has been instrumental in examining body image pathologies (e.g., eating disorders) among athletes. Jennifer Brunet has focused on body image perspectives among individuals across the lifespan. And Kimberly Gammage has examined the effects of exercise on body image and self-presentational concerns. Many other Canadian sport and exercise psychology reserchers have also studied body image in various contexts and their work is highlighted throughout this chapter.

BODY IMAGE DIMENSIONS AND THEIR MEASUREMENT

As alluded to in the historical accounts of the term, there are various definitions for body image. However, there is a growing consensus that **body image** is a multidimensional construct that reflects a person's feelings, perceptions, thoughts, cognitions, and behaviours related to his/her body appearance and function. These different dimensions of body image are discussed in the next few paragraphs.

The **affective dimension of body image** is defined as body-related feelings and emotions that an individual experiences. Commonly assessed feelings and emotions that stem from thinking about one's body size, shape, and function include anxiety, shame, guilt, pride, embarrassment, and envy. **Social physique anxiety**, arguably the most studied affective body image construct, is defined as the anxiety a person experiences as a result of perceived or actual judgments from others (Hart et al., 1989). For example, in the opening scenario, Lexi is worried about performing in physical tasks since she feels that her classmates might judge her. She also expresses concern that people are judging her body shape while she is sitting in class. These are examples of experiences of social physique anxiety. **Body-related shame** is defined as a negative emotion that is focused on the self (e.g., "I *am* an ugly person"), whereas **body-related guilt** is a negative emotion attributed to a failure to complete an action or behaviour (e.g, "I *didn't exercise* for two weeks") that often involves tension and regret. Maddox displays

Positive psychological perspectives: Health promotion framework suggesting that removing negative/maladaptive characteristics but not teaching positive/adaptive characteristics will lead to mental health characterized by a lack of pathology but also absence of vitality.

Body image: A multidimensional construct that reflects a person's feelings, perceptions, thoughts, cognitions, and behaviours related to his/her body appearance and function.

Affective dimension of body image: Body image dimension defined as body-related feelings and emotions that an individual experiences.

Social physique anxiety: The anxiety a person experiences as a result of perceived or actual judgments from others.

Body-related shame: A negative emotion that is focused on the self.

Body-related guilt: A negative emotion attributed to a failure of completing an action or behaviour.

Body-related pride: A positive emotion that results from an individual feeling satisfied with his/her body-related behaviour or physical attributes.

Authentic pride: A type of pride focused on achievement and behaviour.

Hubristic pride: A type of pride focused on grandiose attributes of the self.

Perceptual dimension of body image: Body image dimension defined by the mental representation and/or reflections that an individual has of his/her body appearance and function.

Cognitive dimension of body image: Body image dimension reflecting an individual's thoughts, beliefs, and evaluations of his/her body appearance and function.

feelings of guilt when he doesn't get to the gym. **Body-related pride** is defined as a positive emotion that results from an individual feeling satisfied with behaviour (such as exercising) or with physical attributes (such as appearance). There are two types of pride, which are distinguished by the focus being on the behaviours and outcomes (**authentic pride**) or on the self attributes (**hubristic pride**). Hubristic pride often involves an inflated sense of satisfaction of the self and feelings of superiority over others (e.g., "I am better looking than everyone on this beach"). In this sense, hubristic pride is associated with being egotistical or conceited. In the opening vignette, Jake demonstrates hubristic pride by walking around and showing off. Authentic pride comes from feeling a sense of satisfaction from having fulfilled one's intentions (e.g., "I feel proud because I have been working out and achieved my weight loss goal").

The **perceptual dimension of body image** refers to the mental representation and/or reflections that an individual has of body appearance and function. It relates to the level of accuracy between a person's perceived characteristics and actual characteristics, either in relation to specific body parts or to the body as a whole. In a seminal study of body image perception, Traub and Orbach (1964) designed an adjustable mirror that could distort a person's body or provide an actual reflection of the body (i.e., undistorted). Individuals were asked to adjust the mirror until the reflection represented their actual body shapes, and the researchers were able to detect differences in what the individuals perceived to be their actual body shapes and the "true" undistorted reflection. This work inspired the development of various tools that are now commonly used to measure the perceptual dimension of body image. Some of these include having respondents manipulate the size of a body on a computer screen to fit their body shape and size, using a compass-like device with which people indicate how wide they perceive their body to be, asking individuals to open a door as wide as is needed for them to fit through, or having people illustrate their perceived body shapes and sizes on a figure drawing. All of these measurement techniques highlight that a person's subjective self-perception can be quite different from the actual self. You could imagine giving one of these tasks to Lexi, the young woman in the scenario at the beginning of this chapter. Based on her friends' perceptions, Lexi is not "big," although she perceives herself to be. As such, she is likely to open the compass much wider than she would need to match her actual body width, or to open a door wider than needed for her to fit through. Alternatively, Maddox would likely open the door very little given that he perceives himself to be thinner than he actually is.

The **cognitive dimension of body image** reflects an individual's thoughts, beliefs, and evaluations of his/her body appearance and function. This dimension is often assessed using measures in which respondents are asked to describe their level of satisfaction (or dissatisfaction) with their body shape, size, weight, and functions. There are a multitude of cognitive body image measures in circulation that explicitly ask respondents to indicate the degree of (dis)satisfaction with different body parts (e.g., chest, arms, face), attributes (e.g., thinness, weight, appearance, muscularity), or physical function (e.g., strength, endurance). Also, a common method of indirectly assessing body satisfaction or dissatisfaction is to present respondents with two identical sets of gendered specific drawings or photos that represent a series of possible body shapes and sizes ranging from very thin to very overweight (or more recently from very thin to very muscular). For the first set, a person is asked to identify the body that most resembles their actual body. For the second set, they are asked to identify the body that most resembles their ideal body (i.e., the one they would like to look like). A difference score between the two sets (i.e., actual and ideal) is then used as an index of body dissatisfaction, with higher scores generally presumed to reflect more dissatisfaction. Finally, there are also measures that assess favourable thoughts about the body regardless of actual appearance (e.g., Body Appreciation Scale; Avalos et al., 2005). The cognitive body image dimension has received the most clinical and research attention.

The **behavioural dimension of body image** relates to the choices and actions people take based on the perceptions, feelings, thoughts, and cognitions they have about their body size, shape, weight, and functions. These may include avoiding situations or events, diverting attention away from the body by wearing loose-fitting clothing, and engaging in behaviours such as physical activity, dieting, steroid use, cosmetic surgery, and body checking (e.g., weight monitoring, measuring areas of one's body, pinching oneself as a measure of fatness). In focus group discussions among teenage girls, Sabiston and colleagues (2007) reported that common behavioural strategies used to reduce experiences of social physique anxiety included exercising, limiting calories or the consumption of certain foods, using drugs, and employing appearance management efforts such as wearing certain clothing or make-up. The behavioural dimension of body image is often assessed using self-report questionnaires measuring frequency and intensity of behaviours, likelihood of taking action, or body checking frequency.

Maddox engages in different behavioural strategies when he consumes protein shakes, eats extra calories, goes to the gym multiple times a week, and considers using steroids. Lexi also engages in behavioural strategies when she checks what fat she has around her waistline. She also takes a long time to get ready for school so she can use make-up and clothing to manage her appearance. But in contrast to Maddox, Lexi avoids physical activity. Thus, negative body image can lead people to avoid or engage in both health and risk behaviours, which can impact their physical and mental health.

Behavioural dimension of body image: Body image dimension related to the choices and actions people take based on the perceptions, feelings, thoughts, and cognitions they have about their body sizes, shapes, weights, and functions.

There are multiple dimensions to body image.

Sandro Di Carlo Darsa/PhotoAlto/Brand X Pictures/Getty Images

Is Body Image Positive or Negative?

The short answer to this question is, "Both." Each of the body image dimensions—affective, cognitive, perceptual, and behavioural—can be either positive or negative. Positively valenced body image in any dimension may imply accurate perceptions, positive thoughts and feelings about the body, and predominantly adaptive actions or health-promoting behaviours. Negative body image refers to unfavourable perceptions, predominantly negative thoughts and feelings, and maladaptive actions or health-risk behaviours driven by body-related self-evaluations. Thus, positive and negative perspectives are essential to consider in research and practice focused on each body image dimension.

It is important to understand, however, that low negative body image does not reflect positive body image. Many researchers have erroneously suggested that low body dissatisfaction scores or absence of negative affect suggests people are satisfied and happy with their bodies. Accordingly, few researchers have included measures of positive body image. Thus, while we have gained a better understanding of negative body-related emotional experiences, it has been at the expense of understanding experiences of positive body image. Considering that positive and negative body image have different predictors and outcomes, and can be simultaneously endorsed and reported, focusing on positive body image will help advance body image theory, research, and practice.

Body Image Investment

Body image is highly influenced by the positive and/or negative evaluation of one's body. However, it is also tied to how important the body is to the individual. This **body image investment** dictates the overall impact of body image on related perceptions, emotions, cognitions, and behaviours. Specifically, body image investment takes into account an individual's beliefs or assumptions about the importance, meaning, and influence of appearance in his or her life. For example, Sam is a university student–athlete who has a generally negative evaluation of her body, but she doesn't really care about her body as much as about her success at school and her role on the field hockey team. Sam would say, "I don't like my body, but whatever—I don't have the time to do anything about it!" Ryan is on the university hockey team. He thinks his body looks great (positive body image) and it is really important to him. In fact, Ryan is quite worried that next year, when he has graduated from university and is no longer competing on the university hockey team, he will lose his toned physique. Sam displays low body image investment, whereas Ryan depicts someone with high body image investment.

Focused on helping overweight women improve body image, Carraça and colleagues (2011) had women in their intervention examine their body reflections in a mirror, develop realistic weight and body change goals, and develop realistic ideal body types based on genetics and familial history. These strategies helped to improve body image evaluation. The body image investment component of the sessions included a focus on decreasing the preoccupation with appearance by helping women understand body image, explore the triggers of negative body image, keep a diary of negative self-talk and related feelings, and examine stereotypes and weight prejudice. The researchers also helped to illustrate the idea that there is no one particular ideal body. Overall, the strategies helped to improve body image and highlight the value of focusing on both body image evaluation and investment.

Body image investment: An individual's certain beliefs or assumptions about the importance, meaning, and influence of appearance in his or her life.

Think about how you feel about your body. Do you have a tendency to evaluate your body as generally positive or negative? Does it matter to you? How valuable is your appearance and weight to you? Now think about times in your life when this evaluation and investment might change. Consider life transitions such as when you leave university, when you start a new job or go back for a professional degree, when you have a family, and when you age.

Is Body Image Only Relevant to Women?

In the opening scenario, it is clear that Lexi and Maddox express body image concerns that are rooted in the gendered notion of what the body should look like for women and men, respectively. Historically, body image has been considered a "women's issue" and many researchers have focused their attention exclusively on women. However, emerging research over the last two decades has highlighted prominent body image challenges among men. While the bulk of research evidence demonstrates that women report more negative body image than men, these findings may be misleading because researchers have often used measures that do not adequately capture men's body image issues (i.e., few questions pertain to desires to gain weight or become more muscular). As such, there are many debates about the nature of these differences. As was clearly evident in the opening vignette, females and males pursue different body sizes and shapes; men in Western societies tend to desire a more muscular physique and women desire a thinner physique (Smolak & Murnen, 2008). For instance, Lexi wants to be thinner and Maddox wants to be more muscular. If Maddox were to complete a typical body image questionnaire focused on thinness and appearance, he would likely respond that he does not want to be thinner or lose weight. These responses would be interpreted as him having little negative body image. However, if he were to complete a body image questionnaire that captured attitudes and behaviours relating to muscularity, Maddox's responses would likely illustrate his dislike for his current physique. These responses, in contrast, would be interpreted as his having negative body image concerns.

Recognizing these different body ideals, there is much speculation about how these differences for particular body shapes and sizes emerge. It is likely that socialization processes play a role in perpetuating gendered body ideals. Parents may foster the media-idealized body types (i.e., thin for females, muscular for males) in their homes by allowing their children to watch television and movies that portray these ideals. They may also do this by providing their children with toys that support the thin and beautiful ideal for girls and muscular and athletic ideal for boys. For instance, Barbie, Bratz, and Princess dolls (common toys among young girls) have become taller, thinner, and more attractive over time, whereas action figures that are often found in young boys' toy boxes (i.e., GI Joe, Superman, Batman, and Spiderman) have big chests, muscular arms and legs, and a "six-pack" of sculpted abdominal muscles. While these types of fictional characters have unrealistic anatomies that are almost impossible for most people to attain, many girls and boys grow up wanting to look like these respective body types (Murnen, 2011). Accordingly, body image is not merely a women's issue and it is important to recognize and address body image concerns in both genders. With a better understanding of body image among the likes of Lexi and Maddox, we can help to ensure that gender-specific interventions are developed to assist both women and men in establishing and maintaining a positive body image.

Body Image Pathologies

Body dysmorphia: Overexaggerated and inaccurate perceptions of flaws related to body parts and characteristics.

Body dysmorphic disorder: A recognized disorder reflecting a preoccupation with an imagined defect in appearance.

Muscle dysmorphia: A specified condition within body dysmorphic disorder represented by a chronic preoccupation with insufficient muscularity and inadequate muscle mass.

While the majority of individuals would like to change something about their body size, shape, weight, or functions, this normative discontent is not usually indicative of a serious body image issue. However, an individual may be extremely preoccupied with an aspect of their appearance that is perceived to be flawed. As a result, they have negative thoughts about their appearance and may experience clinically significant levels of distress that impairs functioning. **Body dysmorphia** is used to describe overexaggerated and inaccurate perceptions of flaws related to body parts and characteristics. Recognized as a disorder in the Diagnostic and Statistical Manual of Mental Disorders (DSM-5), **body dysmorphic disorder** is described as a preoccupation with an imagined defect in appearance, which causes severe distress and impairment in daily functioning. In sport and exercise settings, symptoms may manifest as withdrawal from others, constant need for reassurance from coaches or exercise staff, or extreme body checking and monitoring. **Muscle dysmorphia**, a specified condition within body dysmorphic disorder, is a chronic preoccupation with insufficient muscularity and inadequate muscle mass. Individuals presenting with muscle dysmorphia perceive themselves as much thinner than they actually are, and experience pressure to increase muscle mass and strength, despite possessing high muscle mass. In the opening vignette, Maddox displays muscle dysmorphia tendencies. This condition involves excessive attention to muscularity, distress over presenting the body to others, extreme

Some people have a chronic preoccupation with insufficient muscularity and inadequate muscle mass.

Iulianvalentin/Fotolia

weight training, and focus on diet. Impaired function in daily life is also an outcome of these compulsive behaviours, along with a high risk of abusing physique-enhancing supplements and performance-enhancing drugs. Whereas males and females are generally equally likely to present with body dysmorphia, males are more likely to experience muscle dysmorphia.

Many people suffering from body dysmorphic disorder are also diagnosed with an eating disorder. **Eating disorders**, which are recognized mental disorders in the DSM-5, are defined as abnormal eating habits that result in insufficient or excessive consumption of food. Commonly recognized eating disorders include **bulimia nervosa** (characterized by recurrent binge eating and purging through self-induced vomiting, laxative/diuretic use, and/or excessive exercise), **anorexia nervosa** (defined by considerable food restriction brought about by a refusal to maintain a healthy body weight, heightened fear of gaining weight, and unrealistic perception of current body weight), and **binge eating disorder** (compulsive and excessive overeating without purging). Many people diagnosed with an eating disorder often also suffer from body dysmorphic disorder.

THEORIES LINKING BODY IMAGE AND PHYSICAL ACTIVITY

Body image begins as early as preschool through socialization processes, awareness of attractiveness, social comparison, and exposure to body-related prompts such as dolls and figurines, images, movies, and television shows. Several researchers have developed theories to offer new insights into the development and maintenance of body image.

Sociocultural Theories of Body Image

Sociocultural theories are useful in understanding factors associated with body image. The importance of societal ideals and perceived pressures to conform to these ideals are highlighted as potential sources for the development and maintenance of body image. Specifically, social agents serve to convey social ideals, norms, and standards through direct and interect interactions. The **tripartite influence model of body image** (Thompson et al., 1999) is a popular theory found throughout the body image literature. It integrates sociocultural factors by proposing that media, parents, and peers influence body image.

Repeated exposure to idealized and attractive images presented in the mass media (i.e., television, movies, magazines, newpapers) can promote criticism of oneself rather than criticism of the models, which often leads to negative affective and cognitive body image. For example, Dittmar and Howard (2004) showed women a series of images that emphasized societal ideals of thinness and attractiveness or neutral stimuli not related to appearance. They found that women felt worse about their bodies after viewing the images depicting thinness and attractiveness than after viewing the neutral images. Similarly, Sabiston and Munroe-Chandler (2010) demonstrated that women who were exposed to model-focused fitness advertising reported higher social physique anxiety than those exposed to product-focused images (i.e., athletic shoes) or neutral images. Additionally, exposure to television and viewing of related media such as music videos impacts body image. It is also likely that, as observed in the opening scenario, social media such as Facebook and Instagram are emerging media outlets that support both negative and positive body image.

Eating disorders: Recognized mental disorders that are defined as abnormal eating habits that result in insufficient or excessive consumption of food.

Bulimia nervosa: Mental disorder characterized by recurrent binge eating and purging through self-induced vomiting, laxative/diuretic use, and/or excessive exercise.

Anorexia nervosa: Mental disorder defined by considerable food restriction brought about by a refusal to maintain a healthy body weight, heightened fear of gaining weight, and unrealistic perception of current body weight.

Binge eating disorder: Compulsive and excessive overeating without purging.

Tripartite influence model of body image: Theory suggesting that media, parents, and peers are key socializing agents in the development of body image.

Think about how you use social media. Why do you use it? Do you use it to look at other people's pictures and profiles? Do you find yourself scrutinizing their pictures? How do you portray yourself on your online profiles? What types of photos do you post? How often do you change your profile picture? Now think about *why* you post what you do. Write down your answers to these questions and then think about how your body image is reflected in your use of social media.

Body-related envy: A negative emotion that occurs when a person feels they lack another person's superior quality and either desires to have it or wishes the other(s) lacked it.

With the introduction of Facebook over a decade ago, and related social media outlets such as Twitter and Instagram, came a very easy and mainstream way for people to offer real-time status updates, send emoticons (i.e., pictorial representations of their facial expression) to communicate their feelings, and post photos. Given people's inherent desire to present favourably (which is called self-presentation motivation and will be discussed later in the chapter), most have a tendency to use Facebook, or other similar forums, to either self-loathe or self-promote by selecting to post only favourable pictures. Some self-presentation strategies include posting the newest diet or indulgence, revealing a weight loss struggle or achievement of the day, and clocking the longest run to present oneself as someone who is healthy and involved in healthy eating and exercise. Also, posting photos is usually a highly reflective act in which the humorous and attractive images prevail. This prevalence of attractive, beautiful, "everyone at their best" photos can lead those who view the photos to experience feelings of **body-related envy** and shame. Envy is a negative emotion that occurs when a person feels they lack another person's superior quality and they either desire to have it or wish that the other(s) lacked it. In the opening story, Lexi demonstrates some emotion of envy by wanting to look more like her Facebook friends. This is an example of body-related envy. Maddox also displays envy in the context of his comparisons to other teammates—especially Jake, who is not shy about flaunting his six-pack abdominals, V-shaped chest, and general muscle bulk.

More recently, "selfies" (i.e., the act of posting photos of oneself, taken by oneself) have drawn a lot of media attention. There is some evidence that people who consistently post selfies are at risk of negative body image. Moreover, this act can cause alienation from others and thus negatively affect one's social relationships. Also, some people who are preoccupied with selfies and capturing the "perfect self picture"—the right light, angle, and distance from the lens—may experience body dymorphia that can negatively impact their mental health. Research on social media and the effects on body image is in its infancy, but the evidence is starting to show that people need to take caution in what they share online. This type of media may have similar effects on body image compared to the more traditional outlets, such as print and digital images in magazines and on television.

In addition to exposure to idealized images in the mass media, peers and parents can influence people's cognitive, affective, and behavioural dimensions of body image. Parents can play a key role in the development of negative body image through rejection,

Figure 14.1 Percentage of older adolescent females and males reporting that their mothers, fathers, siblings, and peers give them negative comments and encouragement to change their weight

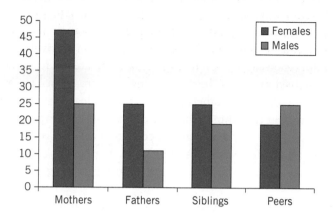

Source: Based on Pinsonnault-Bilodeau, G., & Sabiston, C. M. (2012). Weight-related social pressures related to perceptions of the physical self. Abstract presented at the Canadian Society for Psychomotor Learning and Sport Psychology conference, Halifax, NS.

setting appearance norms and modelling behaviour, encouragement to control weight and shape, and unsupportive behaviours such as teasing and negative verbal commentary. Peers can also affect body image through social disapproval/rejection, teasing, and giving body-related feedback (e.g., making comments about weight and body shape, encouraging weight or body shape changes). For example, over 250 older adolescent girls and boys aged 16 to 19 years reported on the type of weight-related pressures that they perceived from their social networks (Pinsonnault-Bilodeau & Sabiston, 2012). As presented in Figure 14.1, 25–45% of girls and 10–25% of boys reported receiving negative comments and encouragement to change their weight from significant others. When looking at the sources of weight-related pressures, mothers were the most prominent source of weight-related commentary for girls, and fathers were more likely to offer negative comments to girls than to boys. Interestingly, peers were cited as more frequently offering negative comments to boys than to girls. In physical activity settings, coaches, exercise staff, teammates, other exercisers, physical educators, and spectators can all act as agents of influence on body image.

Self-Presentation

As briefly alluded to in the sections above, people tend to feel pressured to present an image that is consistent with social norms. This can result in a desire to regulate the impressions that others may have, and attempts to construct desirable images based on obtaining the approval from others. For example, Brady is in an undergraduate kinesiology program and thinks that being athletic is important and socially desirable. Every day, he dresses as an athlete to "look the part"—even if he has no intention to work out on any particular day. He engages in conversations with his classmates that always involve

Self-presentation: Motivation and attempts to control how one appears to the group; also called impression management.

Impression motivation: How motivated individuals are to control how they are perceived by others.

Impression construction: Creating an image that one wishes to convey to others along with the particular strategies individuals use to create this impression.

Self-presentation efficacy: Reflects the perceived probability of successfully conveying one's desired impressions to others. Driven by self-efficacy beliefs: self-presentational efficacy expectancy, self-presentational outcome expectancy, and self-presentational outcome value.

Self-presentational efficacy expectancy: The belief that one is capable of conveying a desired impression or performing the desired behaviour.

Self-presentational outcome expectancy: The belief that the conveyed impression and behaviours will lead to the desired outcome.

Self-presentational outcome value: Importance placed on the outcome involving self-presentation.

Downward social comparison: Comparing oneself to individuals who are worse off on attributes of value.

Upward social comparison: Comparing oneself to others who are better off on some attributes that are valued.

physical activity, and he often exaggerates the amount of time he spends in athletics. He certainly only shares his really long run times on Facebook, with comments such as "another great run of the week," in spite of only doing the run once. Brady's motivation and attempts to control how he appears to the group reflect the processes of impression management or **self-presentation**.

According to Leary and Kowalski (1990), self-presentation is a goal-directed process that involves two discrete sets of processes: impression motivation and impression construction. **Impression motivation** refers to how motivated individuals are to control how they are perceived by others. In the opening vignette, both Lexi and Maddox are highly motivated to control how others perceive and evaluate them. They are preoccupied by the opinions that they think others may have of them. **Impression construction** involves creating an image that one wishes to convey to others along with the particular strategies individuals use to create this impression. Impression construction strategies can include behaviours such as wearing athletic clothing, putting on makeup, and using self-tanning lotions.

Since the development of this two-component model, self-presentation has been used to explore participation in physical activity yet there is no clear story. Self-presentation can discourage individuals from participating in physical activity if they are concerned about their ability to convey an attractive image in front of others (Hausenblas et al., 2004), or can motivate physical activity participation as a way of achieving the desired image and perpetuating a more positive impression from others.

Based on work advanced by Gammage and colleagues (2004), it is also important to understand people's confidence in their ability to convey a desired image, the likelihood that behaviours might lead to the desired impression, and the importance of the impression. **Self-presentation efficacy** reflects the perceived probability of successfully conveying one's desired impressions to others. There are three related self-efficacy beliefs: **self-presentational efficacy expectancy** (i.e., the belief that one is capable of conveying a desired impression or performing the desired behaviour), **self-presentational outcome expectancy** (i.e., the belief that the conveyed impression and behaviours will lead to the desired outcome), and **self-presentational outcome value** (i.e., importance placed on the outcome).

Social Comparison Theory

According to social psychologist Leon Festinger (1954), people have a need to evaluate their abilities by comparing them to those of other people. People may engage in **downward social comparison** in which they compare themselves to those who are worse off than they are on attributes of value (e.g., appearance, body shape, physical skill). An example of downward social comparison would be a star soccer player comparing her technique or skill to that of a junior player, or a muscular and toned avid exerciser comparing himself to a thin man at the gym. In the opening vignette, Jake displays evidence of downward social comparison by comparing his superior muscular physique to his football teammates' in the locker room. On the other hand, people may engage in **upward social comparison** by comparing themselves to others who are better off than they are on some attributes that are valued. Lexi and Maddox both engage in these types of social comparisons. Whereas downward social comparisons often lead to positive feelings, thoughts, and behaviours, there may be two possible outcomes in response to upward social comparisons. On the one hand, this type of comparison can lead to positive outcomes whereby people react by engaging in actions to reduce the discrepancy between themselves and their comparison candidate. For example, Ben is a 75-year-old Master-level athlete who finished in eighth place in a race and can't help but compare himself to Mark, who is a more toned and muscular 80-year-old who just won the race. Ben may use this comparison to fuel longer and harder workouts to win the next competition. On the other hand, the comparison may lead to negative body image. If Ben doubted that he'd ever be able to measure up to Mark, he'd perhaps be inclined to feel bad about his physical ability and not make changes to his training regimen or give up altogether. Based on social comparison theory, men and women with a higher tendency to make upward comparisons on body appearance and function attributes are more likely to experience body-related envy (Pila et al., 2014). Moreover, people who have a high tendency to compare themselves to others report greater body image dissatisfaction regardless of the direction of comparison.

Self-Discrepancy Theory

Based on Higgins' self-discrepancy theory (1987), people compare themselves to internalized standards called self-guides (i.e., internalized social standards that people strive to obtain). There are two types of self-guides: **ideal self** (which reflects hopes and aspirations of what people want to be) and **ought self** (which reflects what people think they should be). Accordingly, there are two types of self-discrepancies, namely an **actual:ideal discrepancy** which occurs when people perceive that their current state is discrepant from their ideal state (e.g., "I am fat but I would ideally like to be thin" or "I am weak but I would like to be strong"), and an **actual:ought discrepancy**, which occurs when individuals perceive that their current state is discrepant from the state they feel they should be in (e.g., "I am fat but I should be thin" or "I am weak but I should be strong"). The degree and direction of discrepancy between people's self-views and their self-guides result in specific affective and motivational states that, in turn, may trigger behaviours such as physical activity aimed at decreasing the discrepancy between the self-states and self-guides.

In the context of body image, the degree of actual:ideal and actual:ought discrepancies is believed to reflect the degree of body image dissatisfaction. Generally, greater body weight and shape discrepancies have been linked to cognitive and affective outcomes, such as greater body dissatisfaction and body-related shame, and behavioural outcomes, such as higher eating disorder rates and lower levels of physical activity. For example, Sabiston and colleagues (2005) found that women who identified an actual body shape that was larger than their ideal body shape, based on figure drawings, reported more negative body image.

The notion of self-discrepancies is likely more complicated among athletes. For example, women involved in many sports are likely to be more muscular than what is typically portrayed (and expected) for women's bodies. For men, the role that they play on a team may necessitate lean physiques and their sport performance may be hindered by muscle bulk. Thus the struggle to achieve an "ideal" or "ought" body shape and size in the context of sport may perpetuate negative body image through heightened actual:ideal and actual:ought self-discrepancies.

Ideal self: A self-reflection characterized by one's hopes and aspirations of what people want to be.

Ought self: A self-reflection characterized by one's hopes and aspirations of what people think they should be.

Actual:ideal discrepancy: Occurs when people perceive that their current states are discrepant from their ideal states.

Actual:ought discrepancy: Occurs when individuals perceive that their current states are discrepant from the states they feel they should be.

FACTORS ASSOCIATED WITH THE DEVELOPMENT OF NEGATIVE BODY IMAGE

We will look at several factors that are associated with the development of negative body image, including gender, age, weight status, culture, illness, sport involvement and type, social and physical environmental factors,

Gender

As was mentioned earlier in this chapter, it is commonly accepted that men and women experience body image differently. For instance, women may experience greater levels of body-related shame and guilt, body-related envy, social physique anxiety, and higher drive for thinness compared to men. While there are various potential reasons for this, the stronger societal emphasis placed on women to be thin and slender likely contributes to women's body image experiences (Thompson et al., 1999). Women's life experiences—such as puberty, pregnancy, and transition into menopause—can contribute to weight gain and increased adiposity, which can make their bodies more unlike what society dictates as attractive and increase their likelihood experiencing negative body image.

Much more is known about body image in women, and to better understand body image among men it is important to study boys' and men's appearance and physical functioning concerns. One concept that may help advance research and practice on body image among males is the **drive for muscularity** (McCreary & Sasse, 2000). It reflects the pursuit of cultural and gender-explicit muscular body shape ideals for men. The rising interest in this construct likely reflects the increasing societal pressures for men to be muscular, the greater imporance placed on appearance by men, and the widespread depiction of muscular men in the media. Consistently, men have reported higher drive for muscularity scores compared to women. As such, both women and men can experience negative body image. There is evidence that people's desire to become more muscular may influence their attitudes and feelings toward their bodies, as well as their behaviours in order to become more muscular. For example, people experiencing more drive for muscularity report more social physique anxiety and lower self-esteem (Brunet et al., 2010). They are also at greater risk for excessive exercising, dieting, bingeing, and using performance-enhancing substance and nutritional supplements.

Drive for muscularity: Reflects the pursuit of cultural and sex explicit muscular body shape ideals.

Age

Body image experiences may differ across the lifespan as a result of changing physiques, values, goals, and health circumstances, or because external factors change. For example, adolescents and young adults may experience more negative body image because of the increased pressure for them to look good and gain social approval. However, older adults are not immune to negative body image. In data collected from adults across the lifespan (see Figure 14.2), body-related shame and social physique anxiety were highest among adults 25 to 44 years of age, followed by adults over 45 years old. Those under 25 reported the lowest levels. Body-related guilt was also highest among adults aged 25 to 44 years. Body-related pride was lowest among adults aged 25 to 44 years. Finally, body dissatisfac-

Figure 14.2 Age differences for emotions related to affective body image

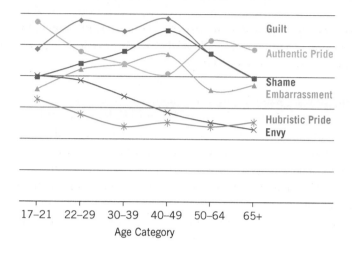

Source: Based on Pila, E., Brunet, J., Crocker, P. R. E., Kowalski, K. C., & Sabiston, C. M. (2013). Intrapersonal characteristics of body-related self-conscious emotion experiences. Abstract presented at the Canadian Society for Psychomotor Learning and Sport Psychology conference, Kelowna, British Columbia, October.

tion, assessed as actual:ideal weight discrepancy, was highest among adults over 45 years of age (Pila et al., 2013). Nonetheless, several studies have also shown that affective, cognitive, and behavioural body image factors do not differ between young and older age groups, and that body image is fairly stable. These data demonstrate that the influence of age on body image is complex and non-linear.

Weight Status

Little is known about the timing of an association between weight and body image. Does weight change precede body image concerns, or does negative body image lead to avoidance behaviours that lead to unfavourable weight change? Both of these scenarios are possible, as is the general idea that weight and body image are independent factors. Nonetheless, consistent evidence shows that individuals who are overweight report more body image dissatisfaction (Latner & Wilson, 2011; Neumark-Sztainer, 2011). For example, males and females across the lifespan who have higher body mass index (BMI), body fat percentage, skinfold measurements, and fat mass assessed by dual-energy X-ray absorptiometry (DEXA) report heightened body image concerns.

Culture

In most Westernized cultures—such as in Canada, the United States, Australia, and the United Kingdom—people are often rewarded for being beautiful and youthful. Thus, many people will engage in behaviours to enhance their appearance. People often feel like others will approve of them if they conform to societal norms of attractiveness, yet these norms are unattainable for upwards of 90% of the population. Based on this perspective, one would think that negative body image is most prevalent in Westernized cultures. However, many researchers have challenged this notion by showing that body dissatisfaction is also an issue in non-Western populations. For instance, McCabe and colleagues (2012) reported similar levels of body dissatisfaction across adolescents from eight countries including Australia, Fiji, Malaysia, Tonga, Tongans in New Zealand, China, Chile, and Greece. Moreover, there can be considerable variations within cultures, due at least partially to the "Westernization phenomenon" (i.e., the extent to which people within non-Westernized cultures adopt the Western ideals of body appearance and function). In multicultural Canada, this phenomenon is often discussed as people try to conform to two standards—the Western ideals of thin or muscular that are perceived to be endorsed for women and men in Canada, which may not align with the person's native cultural standards that may have very different definitions of attractiveness. In Sabiston and colleagues' (2007) report on interviews with adolescents, some of the young women discussed feeling the need to "straddle" two sets of body-related expectations. The young women described trying to conform to the body ideals supported by their social surroundings in Canada but then being criticized by friends and family for being too thin or too muscular when travelling to their parent countries. This straddling meant that they had a hard time attaining one particular body standard. This idea of not fitting in was also discussed by Canadian rural Aboriginal young women (Fleming & Kowalski, 2009). These young women discussed having different body shapes and characteristics than any of their peers in the community and feeling that they were constantly being evaluated. In these case studies, the Aboriginal young women also discussed the lack of culturally appropriate role models presented in the media.

Illness

Major life events can bring changes to people's physical characteristics, which can influence their body-related thoughts, feelings, actions, and interactions with others. Physical illness, such as a heart attack, cancer diagnosis, or serious physical injury, can amplify existing body image concerns or elicit new ones. The illness itself can cause debilitating symptoms, physical changes, and a loss of control over one's body which can have a negative impact on body image. As well, the physical changes resulting from surgeries and treatments can act as a catalyst to influence body image, especially if they are visible (e.g., scars, paralysis, amputation, or hair loss). People with a chronic illness tend to report greater body dissatisfaction than people without chronic illnesses. However, the pattern of change in body image throughout an illness (i.e., from diagnosis through treatment) is not well understood. In spite of the negative consequences, it is also possible that a chronic illness diagnosis encourages people to reevaluate their lives such that the importance of body image decreases as they come to value health and well-being more than appearance. This was evident in interviews with breast cancer survivors. Brunet and colleagues (2013) found that cancer allowed some women to value non-appearance aspects of their bodies and develop self-acceptance and self-realization. Even so, they noted that women continued to experience dissatisfaction with their bodies and negative emotions. In light of these findings, it is important that body image concerns be addressed early on in the illness trajectory, as this may help protect people from negative body image experiences.

Sport Involvement and Type

There is a general trend that individuals involved in physical activity tend to report lower negative affective and cognitive body image compared to inactive individuals. Athletes, for example, are at heightened risk for developing eating disorders and engaging in risky behaviours to control their weight. This is likely because they face additional weight-related pressures from coaches and teammates. Moreover, they may compare themselves with teammates (as Maddox does in the vignette), may have to meet a certain weight requirement, and may be judged on their appearance. Boone and Leadbeater (2006) reported that lower body dissatisfaction was associated with team sport participation among adolescent boys and girls. There also appear to be differences when looking across types of sports. Athletes participating in aesthetic and subjectively rated sports (such as figure skating, gymnastics, cheerleading, and some martial arts) commonly report higher negative body-related emotions compared to athletes participating in non-aesthetic sports (Thompson et al., 1999). This difference in body image between types of sports is likely due to the high importance placed on aesthetics, lean body types, and evaluative judging components in certain sports (Smolak et al., 2000). Nonetheless, Haase and Prapavessis (2001) found no significant differences in social physique anxiety (an affective measure of body image) experiences among female athletes involved in physique salient sport, weight restricted sport, and non-physique salient sports, and non-athletes. There may also be differences in the types of weight-control behaviours athletes engage in. Sports that promote leanness may lead athletes to engage in self-induced vomiting, use of laxatives, fasting, or diuretics to control their weight, whereas sports that promote strength may promote bingeing and steroid use. It is clear that in both cases, these behaviours can lead to serious health problems, and should therefore be monitored.

Social and Physical Environmental Factors

Physical evaluations and judgments, whether real or perceived, can influence body image. Unfortunately, many physical activity environments are prone to being evaluative in nature—"spotlighting" athletes on the court or playing field, exercisers working out at the gym, and students in physical education class having to do drills in front of their peers for grades. Body image experiences have been compared across a variety of social and environmental contexts. For example, Carron and Prapavessis (1997) reported that social physique anxiety was lowest when undergraduate students reported being around their best friends or a group of friends compared to being alone. While in this case friends had a positive influence, the opposite has been observed. Brunet and Sabiston (2011) found that adolescents reported higher social physique anxiety when around their peers compared to their parents. This might be because of the perceived pressure peers put on each other to alter appearance (Mack et al., 2007). Influential features of the exercise environment also extend beyond social factors. It appears that exercising in front of a mirror (Lamarche, Gammage, & Strong, 2009; Martin Ginis, Jung, & Gauvin, 2003) or being exposed to videos which depict physique salient instructors (Martin Ginis et al., 2008) can heighten experiences of social physique anxiety. This highlights the importance of the social and physical environment in regards to body image; however, most of the findings are focused on the affective dimension of body image.

CASE STUDY 14.1	Environmental Design Considerations for Reducing Negative Body Image

You are a kinesiologist who has been contracted to help design a new local fitness centre targeting university students and young professionals. How could you design a fitness centre that attempts to avoid body-related evaluations and focuses on physical and mental health promotion? Consider the infrastructure as well as the rules and regulations of the fitness centre. Draft a list of the possible benefits and drawbacks of the design you have proposed.

BODY IMAGE OUTCOMES

Body image can have far-ranging effects on health and well-being, influencing physical activity, health-compromising behaviours, mental health, and cardiometabolic risk factors.

Physical Activity

It is thought that body image can serve two functions: (1) motivate self-protection and avoidance/withdrawal from physical activity behaviour, or (2) motivate physical activity behaviour as a means of self-enhancement. Consequently, many Canadian researchers have adopted motivational theories to understand the relationship between negative body image and physical activity. These developments have shown that negative affective (e.g., social physique anxiety, envy, shame, guilt) and cognitive (e.g., actual:ideal discrepancies) body image factors are related to controlling forms of physical activity motivation, which are associated with lower levels of physical activity behaviour (Brunet et al., 2012; Pila et al., 2014). Together, these efforts have advanced conceptual frameworks linking the body image and physical activity behaviour.

Historically, the emphasis has been on understanding negative body image and the relationship to health behaviours such as physical activity. However, there is evidence that positive body image is also tied to physical activity. Specifically, body-related pride has been linked to more self-determined forms of motivation and higher levels of physical activity behaviour (Castonguay et al., 2013; Sabiston et al., 2010). However, narratives (i.e., stories related to personal experiences) written by men and women

Body image may motivate some individuals to engage in exercise.

reveal that hubristic pride may also reduce the likelihood of participating in physical activity because individuals with these grandiose feelings of their bodies feel there is "no need" to exercise (Castonguay et al., 2013). Nonetheless, the narratives also presented evidence that authentic pride was associated with engagement and persistence in physical activity. These findings show the importance of distinguishing between types of body-related pride.

In addition, there has been some research taking a stress and coping perspective to understanding the association between body image and physical activity. Findings generally support the notion that negative body image affect (predominantly studied as social physique anxiety) can motivate engagement in or avoidance of physical activity among adolescents. For example, Kowalski and colleagues (2006) reported that the most frequently used coping strategy to manage social physique anxiety was behavioural avoidance (i.e., keeping away from a stressor such as physical activity environments). Other common coping strategies included appearance management (e.g., make-up, clothing), social support (e.g., seeking support from friends and family), cognitive avoidance (e.g., trying to avoid thoughts related to social physique anxiety), and acceptance (i.e., accepting the situation).

Health-Compromising Behaviours

In addition to the increased likelihood of eating disorders among individuals with high negative body image, a range of other health-compromising behaviours may occur. For example, individuals with high negative body image tend to want and get more cosmetic surgery (Magee, 2012; Sarwer & Spitzer, 2012). These individuals may take up smoking cigarettes or start abusing substances like alcohol and drugs if they believe this will help them manage their weight. Sexual function is commonly studied among people with negative body image. There are some reports of earlier sexual encounters for youth with negative body image, or avoidance of sexual behaviours. Individuals across the lifespan also report greater sexual problems and sexual dissatisfaction associated with negative body image (Wiederman, 2011). Furthermore, it is likely not surprising that individuals with high negative body image are also more likely to diet and follow unhealthy eating regimes (Grogan, 2008). While many will avoid physical activity, some engage in excessive exercise—a maladaptive strategy people use to try to improve their body shape, weight, and function. Additionally, males (more so than females) with more negative body images are likely to have higher levels of binge drinking and to use drugs such as steroids (Grogan, 2008; Yager & O'Dea, 2014). This list is not exhaustive but illustrates the dangers that may be involved with negative body image.

Mental Health

Negative body image has been associated with mental health factors such as higher levels of depressive symptoms. For example, McCreary and Sasse (2000) found that higher drive for muscularity was associated with higher depression in adolescent boys and girls. Social physique anxiety has also been positively associated with depression symptoms (Martin Ginis et al., 2012). Among adolescent girls in Quebec, Chaiton et al. (2009) documented that weight was indirectly associated with depressive symptoms through its influence on pressure to be thin and body dissatisfaction. Moreover, the authors reported that body dissatisfaction was associated with depressive symptoms for boys. These studies conducted by Canadian researchers provide evidence for the potential detrimental mental health effects of negative body image. Given that depression is a significant public health burden that is increasing at alarming rates, the importance of promoting positive body image and decreasing negative body image cannot be overstated.

Cardiometabolic Risk Factors

Cortisol: A stress hormone.

Body image may affect one's physical health by working in a similar manner to a stress response. For example, heightened chronic stress is related to increased **cortisol** and immune markers in the body, which have been linked to poor health outcomes such as cardiovascular disease, weight problems, and depression. If we look back to Lexi, the young woman in the vignette, we can see that her negative body image likely creates considerable stress. This stress may be manifested as heightened cortisol, and over time this may affect her physical health. Martin Ginis and colleagues (2012) looked at whether physique evaluative threat, akin to negative body image affect, is related to biological stress (measured as a cortisol response in saliva). Women who were asked to try on highly revealing attire while also being told that someone was judging them (i.e., high physique threat) demonstrated an activated cortisol response. Furthermore, Sabiston and colleagues (2009) found that body dissatisfaction was related to a heightened immune marker (measured as C-reactive protein) in adolescents. These studies are early evidence of a possible link between body image, stress, and physical health.

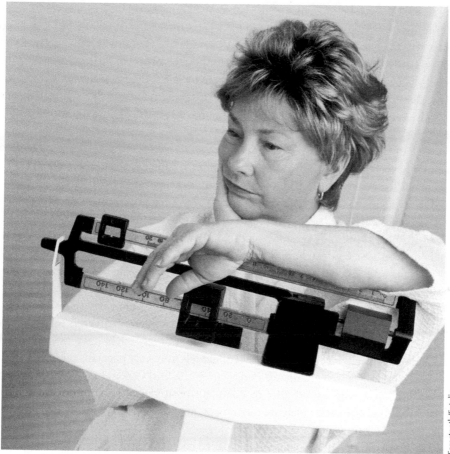

Negative body image is associated with a number of mental and physical health symptoms.

Forestpath/Fotolia

PRACTICAL CONSIDERATIONS FOR HEALTH PROFESSIONALS, COACHES, AND PHYSICAL EDUCATORS

Shifting the focus away from body appearance and function is not always feasible in sport, exercise, and physical education settings. Nonetheless, creating supportive environments that limit judgments and evaluations of the body can help reduce negative body image. Furthermore, creating situations that allow for the appreciation of one's unique body and feelings of pride can help enhance positive body image.

The adverse consequences of negative body image discussed in this chapter underscore the importance of enhancing people's body image across the lifespan. Intervention strategies aimed at increasing people's skills for effectively managing appearance-related social pressures may help reduce negative body image. Moreover, developing interventions that involve parents and peers might help to promote positive body image social norms. Given the consistent connection between mass media (e.g., television, movies, children's books, magazines) and body image, intervention strategies centred on dispelling the body ideals for men and women are needed. This could involve teaching people to limit their exposure to idealized images, and increasing awareness of the processing that occurs on a model photo. In the last few years, many worldwide initiatives have focused on transparency around airbrushing of models portrayed in the media. Israel is among the first countries to adopt a "Photoshop Law" mandating that any modifications to a photo must be disclosed. Researchers and practitioners in other countries are also calling for similar mandates to be endorsed as a way of reducing body image dissatisfaction. A quick Google search will show you how important this topic is for today's society. There are also hundreds of YouTube videos demonstrating the "benefits" of digital photo manipulation and the extent of modifications that can be done to a male or female model.

There is some evidence of body image programs being used in secondary schools among primarily younger adolescent girls. In a review of 16 universal, classroom-based body image programs focused on media literacy and peer influences, Yager and colleagues (2013) found that body image improved in some ways but no program was effective at targeting body image equally among boys and girls. The programs were also most beneficial to younger adolescents aged 12 and 13 years. The pressures that students face to achieve and maintain a certain type of body type are considerable, and more efforts are needed to create positive environments.

In an untested but emerging strategy, some summer camps have adopted "no body talk" rules. At some camps, reminders are posted around the social areas that comments about one's physical appearance are to be replaced with comments on one's general spirit or well-being. At other camps, the mirrors are completely covered up to avoid body checking behaviours altogether. Other general strategies that have been implemented include setting a lower limit to the BMI of models in beauty pageants and in media. There is also a "Love Yourself Challenge Badge" from the Girl Guides organization offering girls aged 5–18 years the opportunity to complete positive body image tasks (e.g., creating crafts that highlight and celebrate differences, posting body thoughts on forums, developing art, and writing letters) to earn the badge.

Cognitive dissonance training: A program involving arguing against body ideals in a way that is incongruent with their personal beliefs.

Another intervention perspective is called **cognitive dissonance training** and involves individuals arguing against the body ideals in a way that is incongruent with their personal beliefs. For example, programs might involve individuals voluntarily speaking and writing critiques against the "ideal" even if they themselves internalize the ideal. The activities are thought to produce discomfort that motivates paticipants to reduce their own pursuit of the ideal, which subsequently decreases negative body image. The benefit of cognitive dissonance training is that that it does not require delivery by a trained psychologist. As such, coaches and teachers could use this approach to helping to reduce negative body image.

CASE STUDY 14.2 — Body Image Interventions for Sport and Physical Education

Aiden was just hired as a grade 7 boys' physical education teacher at a school in southwestern Ontario. He is also the coach of the school's girls volleyball team. Growing up, Aiden watched many of his friends enjoy sport early on and then drop out when they all reached high school. Now that he has gone through school himself, he knows that the dropout happened around the time puberty hit and negative body images became prevalent. Since he feels that he works with kids at a critical developmental time, he wants to address body image with his physical education students and his sports team. Given what you have read about interventions throughout this chapter, what key strategies do you think Aiden should include in sessions on body image? Are the strategies different when he is targeting his boys in physical education class compared to his girls in volleyball?

Furthermore, **cognitive–behavioural therapy** (CBT) has demonstrated the most effectiveness at reducing negative body image. Specifically, cognitive–behavioural therapy is a problem-based and action oriented approach used to address dysfunctional emotions and maladaptive behaviours and cognitions. Strategies, which are delivered by trained therapists, can include psychoeducation, biofeedback, desensitization, and cognitive dissonance. Given the nature of CBT, it is less practical to implement in sport and physical education settings.

Final considerations for interventions may be to alter the social and physical environment in physical activity settings. Changing the environment may help reduce the frequency of negative body-related experiences given that the attire generally worn (e.g., uniforms in physical education class or on sports teams), opportunities for attractiveness comparisons and seeing own reflections in mirrors, pressure to show competency, and presence of opposite sex peers are common factors linked to negative body image. It is important to attend to the contextual factors that may increase negative body image experiences and implement strategies to help diminish the possibility of these experiences on the court, in the field, or in the gym.

> **Cognitive–behavioural therapy:** Problem-based and action oriented approach used to address dysfunctional emotions, and maladaptive behaviours and cognitions.

COMMON MYTHS ABOUT BODY IMAGE IN SPORT AND EXERCISE REVISITED

MYTH: Negative body image is the opposite of positive body image.

As illustrated in this chapter, you cannot say that an individual reporting low on negative body image will automatically report high levels of positive body image. Positive body image has been studied far less frequently, and is measured differently, than negative body image. For example, positive body image is assessed as body appreciation, pride, and engaging in healthy behaviours, whereas negative body image is often assessed as body dissatisfaction, discrepancies, and emotions such as social physique anxiety, shame, and guilt.

MYTH: A person with a negative body image is also said to have an eating disorder.

A person with negative body image characterized by dissatisfaction, high discrepancy between actual and ideal selves, low physical self-worth, and/or negative emotions such as shame and guilt may be at higher risk for an eating disorder, but the two terms are not synonymous. Upwards of 80–90% of youth and adults report some degree of negative body image, whereas 10–15% of these individuals may suffer from an eating disorder.

MYTH: Males don't have body image issues.

Based on the research evidence to date, negative body image has been found among women more so than men. However, with the advances in body image measurement appropriate for males, it is clear that males are also likely to experience negative body image. Most of the body image concerns among women stem from desires to be thinner and more attractive, whereas the concerns for men are focused on desires for more muscularity and strength. Regardless of the underlying reasons, women and men are likely to report both positive and negative body image.

MYTH: People with negative body image will always avoid physical activity, whereas people with positive body image will engage in physical activity.

As discussed throughout this chapter, body image is related to physical activity in a number of ways. Negative body image may lead to reduced physical activity levels because people may avoid social environments where the body can be judged and evaluated, and situations in which they do not feel competent. Alternatively, negative body image may motivate individuals to engage in physical activity in an attempt to change their current circumstance (e.g., lose weight, gain muscle, etc.). Although preliminary, there is also evidence that positive affective body image, such as pride, may also enhance or reduce the likelihood of physical activity participation.

CHAPTER SUMMARY

In this chapter, the historical foundations of body image have been presented. Several of the body image dimensions were evident over 100 years ago but have only recently been defined and studied. The multidimensional nature of body image has been identified, along with examples of measures used to capture each of the affective, cognitive, perceptual, and behavioural dimensions. Common theories used to understand the development of body image, as well as outcomes related to body image, are discussed. Overall, reseachers have used several approaches (e.g., motivation, stress, and coping) to study the association between body image and physical activity outcomes. Prominent factors studied in the development of negative body image include gender, age, weight status, culture, illness, sport type, and social and environmental factors. Also, the association between body image, mental health, and cardiometabolic outcomes such as stress and immune function biomarkers have been shown in preliminary studies. Finally, there are many practical strategies that could be used to help reduce negative body image and/or enhance positive body image in sport and exercise settings. With these strategies in practice, individuals like Lexi and Maddox might be able to change their perspectives on their bodies and enhance their respective well-being.

Review Questions

1. What are the four dimensions of body image described in this chapter? Give one example of how you would measure each dimension.

2. Describe the theories of body image that have been used in research linking body image and physical activity.

3. What are some of the factors that can influence the development of body image?

Additional Readings

Cash, T. F. (2012). *Encyclopedia of body image and human appearance*. London, UK: Elsevier.

Crombie, P.-A., Brunet, J., & Sabiston, C. M. (2011). Stop staring! Proposed strategies to reduce body image concerns in physical education. *Journal of Physical Education, Recreation and Dance*, *82*, 39–43.

Edwards, C., Tod, D., & Molnar, G. (2014). A systematic review of the drive for muscularity research area. *International Review of Sport and Exercise Psychology, 7*, 18–41.

Sabiston, C. M., Pila, E., Pinsonnault-Bilodeau, G., & Cox, A. (2014). Social physique anxiety experiences in sport and exercise: An integrative review. *International Review of Sport and Exercise Psychology, 7*, 158–183.

References

Avalos, L., Tylka, T. L., & Wood-Barcalow, N. (2005). The Body Appreciation Scale: Development and psychometric evaluation. *Body Image, 2*, 285–297.

Boone, E. M., & Leadbeater, B. J. (2006). Game on: Reducing risks for depressive symptoms in early adolescence through positive involvement in team sports. *Journal of Research on Adolescence, 16*, 79–90.

Brunet, J., Burke, S., & Sabiston, C. M. (2013). Surviving breast cancer: Women's experiences with their bodies. *Body Image, 10*, 344–351.

Brunet, J., & Sabiston, C. M. (2011). In the company we keep: Do experiences of social physique anxiety differ around parents and peers? *Journal of Health Psychology, 16*, 42–49.

Brunet, J., Sabiston, C. M., Castonguay, A., Ferguson, L., & Bessette, N. (2012). The association between physical self-discrepancies and women's physical activity: The mediating role of motivation. *Journal of Sport & Exercise Psychology, 34*, 102–134.

Brunet, J., Sabiston, C. M., Dorsch, K. D., & McCreary, D. R. (2010). Exploring a model linking social physique anxiety, drive for muscularity, drive for thinness and self-esteem among adolescent boys and girls. *Body Image, 7*, 137–142.

Carraça, E. V., Silva, M. N., Markland, D., Vieira, P. N., Minderico, C. S., Sardinha, L. B., & Teixeira, P. J. (2011). Body image change and improved eating self-regulation in a weight management intervention in women. *International Journal of Behavioral Nutrition and Physical Activity, 18*(18), 75.

Carron, A. V., & Prapavessis, H. (1997). Self-presentation and group influence. *Small Group Research, 28*, 500–516.

Castonguay, A., Gilchrist, J., Mack, D. E., & Sabiston, C. M. (2013). Body-related pride in young adults: An exploration of the triggers, contexts, outcomes, and attributions. *Body Image: An International Journal, 9*, 335–343.

Chaiton, M., Sabiston, C. M., O'Loughlin, J., McGrath, J., Maximova, K., & Lambert, M. (2009). A structural equation model relating adiposity, psychosocial indicators of body image, and depressive symptoms among adolescents. *International Journal of Obesity, 33*, 588–596.

Dittmar, H., & Howard, S. (2004) Thin-ideal internalization and social comparison tendency as moderators of media models' impact on women's body-focused anxiety. *Journal of Social and Clinical Psychology, 23*, 768–791.

Festinger, L. (1954). A theory of social comparison processes. *Human Relations, 7*, 117–140.

Fleming, T.-L., & Kowalski, K. C. (2009). Body-related experiences of rural Aboriginal women. *Journal of Aboriginal Health, 4*, 44–51.

Gammage, K. L., Hall, C. R., & Martin Ginis, K. A. (2004). Self-presentation in exercise contexts: Differences between high and low frequency exercisers. *Journal of Applied Social Psychology, 34*, 1638–1651.

Grogan, S. (2008). *Body image: Understanding body dissatisfaction in men, women and children.* New York: Routledge.

Haase, A., & Prapavessis, H. (2001). Social physique anxiety and eating attitudes in female athletic and non-athletic groups. *Journal of Medicine and Science in Sport, 4*, 396–405.

Hart, E. A., Leary, M. R., & Rejeski, W. J. (1989). The measurement of social physique anxiety. *Journal of Sport & Exercise Psychology, 11*, 94–104.

Hausenblas, H., Brewer, B., & Van Raalte, J. L. (2004). Self-presentation and exercise. *Journal of Applied Sport Psychology, 16,* 3–18.

Higgins, E. T. (1987). Self-discrepancy: A theory relating self and affect. *Psychological Review, 94,* 319–340.

Kowalski, K. C., Mack, D. E., Crocker, P. R. E., Niefer, C. B., & Fleming, T.-L. (2006). Coping with social physique anxiety in adolescence. *Journal of Adolescent Health, 39,* 275–279.

Lamarche, L., Gammage, K. L., & Strong, H. A. (2009). The effect of mirrored environments on self-presentational efficacy and social anxiety in women in a step aerobics class. *Psychology of Sport and Exercise, 10,* 67–71.

Latner, J. D., & Wilson, R. E. (2011). Obesity and body image in adulthood. In T. Cash & L. Smolak (Eds.), *Body image: A handbook of science, practice, and prevention* (pp. 189–197). New York: Guilford.

Leary, M. R., & Kowalski, R. M. (1990). Impression management: A literature review and two-component model. *Psychological Bulletin, 107,* 34–47.

Mack, D. E., Strong, H. A., Kowalski, K. C., & Crocker, P. R. E. (2007). Does friendship matter? An examination of social physique anxiety in adolescence. *Journal of Applied Social Psychology, 37,* 1248–1264.

Magee, L. (2012). Cosmetic surgical and non-surgical procedures for the face. In Thomas Cash (Ed.), *Encyclopedia of body image and human appearance* (pp. 350–359). London, UK: Academic.

Martin Ginis, K. A., Jung, M. E., & Gauvin, L. (2003). To see or not to see: Effects of exercising in mirrored environments on sedentary women's feeling states and self-efficacy. *Health Psychology, 22,* 354–361.

Martin Ginis, K. A., Prapavessis, H., & Haase, A. M. (2008). The effects of physique-salient and physique non-salient exercise videos on women's body image, self-presentational concerns, and exercise motivation. *Body Image, 5,* 164–172.

Martin Ginis, K. A., Strong, H. A., Arent, S. M., & Bray, S. R. (2012). The effects of threatened social evaluation of the physique on cortisol activity. *Psychology and Health, 27,* 990–1007.

McCabe, M. P., Fuller-Tyszkiewicz, M., Mellor, D., Ricciardelli, L., Skouteris, H., & Mussap, A. (2012). Body satisfaction among adolescents in eight different countries. *Journal of Health Psychology, 17,* 693–701.

McCreary, D. R., & Sasse, D. K. (2000). An exploration of the drive for muscularity in adolescent boys and girls. *Journal of American College Health, 48*(6), 297–304.

Murnen, S. K. (2011). Gender and body images. In T. Cash & L. Smolak (Eds.) *Body image: A handbook of science, practice, and prevention,* pp. 173–179. New York: Guilford.

Neumark-Sztainer, D. (2011). Obesity and body image in youth. In T. Cash & L. Smolak (Eds.), *Body image: A handbook of science, practice, and prevention* (pp. 180–188). New York: Guilford.

Pila, E., Brunet, J., Crocker, P. R. E., Kowalski, K. C., & Sabiston, C. M. (2013). Intrapersonal characteristics of body-related self-conscious emotion experiences. Abstract presented at the Canadian Society for Psychomotor Learning and Sport Psychology conference, Kelowna, British Columbia, October.

Pila, E., Castonguay, A., Stamiris, A., & Sabiston, C. M. (2014). Body-related envy in sport and exercise. *Journal of Sport & Exercise Psychology. 36,* 93–106.

Pinsonnault-Bilodeau, G., & Sabiston, C. M. (2012). Weight-related social pressures related to perceptions of the physical self. Abstract presented at the Canadian Society for Psychomotor Learning and Sport Psychology conference, Halifax, NS.

Sabiston, C. M., Brunet, J., Kowalski, K. C., Wilson, P., Mack, D. E. & Crocker, P. R. E. (2010). The role of body-related self-conscious emotions in motivating women's physical activity. *Journal of Sport & Exercise Psychology,32,* 417–437.

Sabiston, C. M., Castonguay, A., Barnett, T., O'Loughlin, J., & Lambert, M. (2009). Body image and C-reactive protein in adolescents. *International Journal of Obesity, 33,* 597–600. PMID: 19204727.

Sabiston, C. M., & Munroe-Chandler, K. J. (2010). Effects of fitness advertising on weight and body shape satisfaction, social physique anxiety, and exercise motives. *Journal of Applied Biobehavioral Research, 14,* 165–180.

Sabiston, C. M., Munroe-Chandler, K. J., & Crocker, P. R. E. (2005). Examining current–ideal discrepancies and reasons for exercise as predictors of social physique anxiety. *Journal of Sport Behavior, 28,* 1–18.

Sabiston, C. M., Sedgwick, W. A., Crocker, P. R. E., Kowalski, K. C., & Stevens, D. (2007). Social physique anxiety in adolescents: an examination of influences, coping strategies and health behaviours. *Journal of Adolescent Research. 22,* 78–101.

Sarwer, D. B., & Spitzer, J. C. (2012). Cosmetic surgical procedures for the body. In Thomas Cash (Ed.) *Encyclopedia of body image and human appearance,* pp. 360–365. London, UK: Academic.

Schilder, P. (1935). *The image and appearance of the human body.* Oxford, England.

Smolak, L., & Murnen, S. K. (2008). Drive for leanness: Assessment and relationship to gender, gender role and objectification. *Body Image, 5,* 251–260.

Smolak, L., Murnen, S. K., & Ruble, A. E. (2000). Female athletes and eating problems: A meta-analysis. *International Journal of Eating Disorders, 27,* 371–380.

Thompson, K., Heinberg, L., Altabe, M, & Tantleff-Dunn, S. (1999). *Exacting beauty: Theory, assessment, method, and treatment of body image disturbance.* Washington, DC: APA.

Traub, A. C., and Orbach, J. (1964). Psychophysical studies of body-image I. The adjustable body-distorting mirror. *Archives of General Psychiatry, 11,* 53–66.

Tylka, T. (2011). Positive psychology pespectives on body image. In T. Cash & L. Smolak (Eds.) *Body image. A handbook of science, practice, and prevention* (pp. 56–66). New York, NY: Guilford.

Wiederman, M. W. (2011). Body image and sexual functioning. In T. Cash & L. Smolak (Eds.), *Body image: A handbook of science, practice, and prevention* (pp. 271–278). New York: Guilford.

Yager, Z., Diedrichs, P. C., Ricciardelli, L. A., & Halliwell, E. (2013). What works in secondary schools? A systematic review of classroom-based body image programs. *Body Image, 10,* 271–281.

Yager, Z., & O'Dea, J. (2014). Relationships between body image, nutritional supplement use, and attitudes towards doping in sport among adolescent boys: Implications for prevention programs. *Journal of the International Society of Sports Nutrition, 11:* doi: 10.1186/1550-2783-11-13.

Chapter 15

Physical Activity Interventions

Kimberley A. Dawson   Jennifer Robertson-Wilson

Deklofenak/Shutterstock

Chapter Learning Objectives

After reading this chapter, you should be able to do the following:

1. Explain how physical activity can be both an outcome variable and an intervention variable in exercise intervention research.

2. Describe how the theory of planned behaviour, social cognitive theory, the transtheoretical model, self-determination theory, and the health action process approach have contributed to intervention research.

3. Understand how technology has influenced physical activity interventions.

4. Comprehend how decisions regarding community design by urban planners influence the activity levels of people living in their neighbourhoods.

5. Outline the eight key components that increase the probability of successful physical activity interventions.

6. Identify the ways in which physical activity interventions improve the lives of people living with chronic diseases.

Sue and John Brown live in Toronto, Ontario. They have a 16-year-old daughter named Kerri and a 12-year-old son named Carter. John works shifts at the Cadbury Chocolate Company while Sue works part time at St. Joseph's Hospital in the laundry department. They earn enough money to meet their living expenses but do not have any extra money left over for anything else. They do not own a car. John and Sue just had their annual physicals, where they were informed by their doctor that Sue is 30 pounds overweight with high blood pressure and that John has high cholesterol levels. Neither participates in physical activity of any kind and both take public transportation to work. Their doctor has recommended that they both start a regular exercise program to combat their medical problems.

Kerri is in grade 10. Because her family has never had a lot of extra cash, she has relied on school sports to keep her active. With school budget cuts, the after-school sports she enjoyed previously are no longer available. She is currently selecting her courses for grade 11 and is thinking that she won't have room in her schedule for physical education because she should be taking more mathematics and computer courses in preparation for university. Her best friend, Anita, just got her driver's licence and a new car from her parents so they can now drive to school. As a result, Kerri has become more sedentary than ever.

Carter is in grade 6. His favourite thing to do is to play on his friend's Xbox. He delivers papers to make spare cash and spends most of it at the corner store on candy and pop. He has gained about 40 pounds in the last two years. With the gained weight, he has become more self-conscious about his body and stopped swimming at the community pools with his friends. He has also decided that he does not really need to participate in gym class in order to obtain a good mark; he's happy just to stand around and pass the course.

The Brown family is typical of many families living in Canada. In order to help families like the Browns, researchers have to address political situations (school board cutbacks), motivational issues (choosing to play video games *about* skateboarding rather than to go skateboarding), economic factors (not making a lot of money for extras such as gym memberships), work obstacles (working shift work), and peer issues (friends are inactive). Successful strategies or interventions are based on manipulating the specific factors that affect exercise behaviour. All effective behaviour change is based on understanding the commonalities among people while appreciating the differences that exist between individuals.

Interventions: Modifications of the specific factors that affect physical activity based on an understanding of the commonalities in human behaviour with an appreciation of the differences that exist between individuals.

COMMON MYTHS ABOUT PHYSICAL ACTIVITY INTERVENTIONS

MYTH: It is easy to get people to become or stay physically active.

MYTH: If you have a positive attitude toward physical activity, you will always exercise.

MYTH: Individuals with chronic illnesses do not want to exercise because they have other things to worry about.

MYTH: An individual's physical activity level is determined by his or her motivation. It is not dependent upon other key factors such as public health policies or environmental barriers.

Table 15.1 Occupational Situations That Involve Physical Activity Interventions

Occupation	Situation	Behavioural Recommendation
Medical doctor	Patient has high blood pressure	Do cardiovascular exercise three times per week by joining a community exercise program
Physical education teacher	Student has diabetes	Sign up for a recreational basketball league
Coach	Player wants to become a stronger rebounder	Supplement playing with resistance training
Physiotherapist	Client has a knee injury	Ride a bicycle three times per week in the clinic
Personal trainer	Client wants to lose weight	Participate in a variety of cardiovascular group fitness classes

INTRODUCTION

Many individuals have specific physical activity needs. You may have come across some of them already in your work, sport, or volunteer experiences. In many cases, people who need to change their exercise behaviour will require the help of trained professionals who understand how to help them successfully fit physical activity into their lives. You have chosen to study kinesiology, physical education, exercise science, or sport and exercise psychology for your own reasons. But if you choose to follow this path, and become a teacher, doctor, personal trainer, physiotherapist, or other health and education professional, you can be certain that you will be dealing with people and their relationship with physical activity (see Table 15.1). Therefore, it is important that you understand how to utilize physical activity and exercise behaviour research to help people maintain a healthy lifestyle. Prescribing exercise is the first part of the equation; helping people to comply with the recommendation is the second.

The overall objective of this chapter is to help you understand what interventions have been successful for increasing physical activity, as well as to discuss how physical activity has been used to help individuals with special needs or chronic illnesses. Recommendations that you may find useful in your future pursuits are provided to increase the probability of successfully modifying behaviour in a physical activity context.

THE IMPORTANCE OF MAINTAINING A PHYSICALLY ACTIVE LIFESTYLE

The benefits of an active lifestyle are becoming increasingly well known. You need only watch a nightly news program or read your local paper to learn about the latest research proclaiming the benefits of exercise. There are well-established benefits of decreasing the risk of diabetes, cancer, osteoporosis, obesity, and cardiovascular disease—as well as improving mental health—and these have been highlighted at various points throughout this book.

In order to accrue these health benefits, however, individuals have to exercise with a high degree of regularity. Unfortunately, in 2008 only 48% of all Canadians older than 20 years were classified as at least moderately active (which is defined as walking a total of half an hour per day) (Canadian Fitness and Lifestyle Research Institute, 2010). That leaves 52% of Canadians to be classified as inactive or sedentary. Similar to what has been found in previous national surveys reported by the Canadian Fitness and Lifestyle Research Institute, men tend to be more active than women, activity level increases with increasing education and household income, and activity decreases with increasing age.

This is troublesome for two reasons. First, despite the abundant information documenting the benefits of an active lifestyle, 85% of adults and 93% of young people are not meeting the recommended amount of daily physical activity outlined in the Canadian Physical Activity Guidelines (Colley, et al., 2011a; 2011b). Unfortunately, Canadians at any age remain largely sedentary. Second, from a public health perspective, Canadians are living longer (Statistics Canada, 2006) and this increased life expectancy will place an increased strain on our healthcare system. Katzmarzyk and colleagues (2000) documented that physical inactivity among Canadians is a very costly issue. An active lifestyle will help to diminish this burden by keeping more people healthier, longer. This is not a uniquely Canadian problem, either: All industrialized countries are experiencing a decline in physical activity and health. The World Health Organization identified physical inactivity as the fourth leading cause of death worldwide and has launched a Global Action Plan for 2013–20 designed to reduce physical inactivity by 10% by 2025 internationally (www.who.int). It is their intention that, by 2025, only 20% of the world's population will be inactive.

Clearly, there is a need to intervene and help people become more active. Recognizing this priority, Active Canada (20/20) A Physical Activity Strategy and Change Agenda for Canada (www.activecanada2020.ca) was established in 2010 by stakeholders, such as politicians, researchers, sport bodies, and individuals like you, who have a vested interest in the physical inactivity problem that currently exists in Canada. Active Canada (20/20) has a lofty goal of increasing the physical activity level of every person in Canada, and the organization plans to make this happen by addressing Canadian policy, education, programming, and individual communities. Clearly, a multifaceted intervention approach will be necessary to instill physical activity changes in our Canadian culture.

Government initiatives are impressive and timely in their attempts to address the issue of Canada's inactivity problem. However, the heart of the problem—*why* Canadians remain inactive and *how* we can get them to exercise with the frequency, intensity, and duration necessary to accrue some of the aforementioned health benefits—remains an issue. In the end, political strategies like the one above must be based on the success of researchers addressing these very questions. Fortunately, in the past 20 years there has been a plethora of researchers evaluating physical activity and behaviour change! Clearly, this is currently a hot topic and is likely to remain so in future.

DETERMINANT AND INTERVENTION RESEARCH

This chapter is primarily dedicated to discussing intervention research, but what exactly do we mean by "intervention-based research"? There is often confusion regarding what exactly defines an exercise intervention study, usually revolving around two distinct, yet related fields of research: determinant and intervention research.

Determinant research is dedicated to evaluating factors that affect exercise behaviour (Sallis & Owen, 1999). These **determinants** are generally based on five factors: genetic, psychological, social, program, and physical features of the environment. A genetic factor resides within the person. Individuals generally exercise less frequently as they age. More men than women also tend to be physically active. Psychological factors address what the individual thinks or traits that they may possess. For example, self-efficacy is regularly found to be related to maintaining an exercise program. Social factors involve aspects within the social setting or human interactions. Social support is a strong predictor of exercise adherence for most individuals. Program factors are based on the program context. Programs that are accessible, convenient, and economically feasible lead to greater participation. Physical features of the environment may include weather, feeling safe in one's neighbourhood, lighting, and sidewalks. Such features can either inhibit or promote regular activity.

Intervention research, on the other hand, does not directly alter exercise behaviour, but rather seeks to manipulate the different factors that affect exercise behaviour (Sallis & Owen, 1999). For example, determinant research established that Canadian mothers with young children are the least likely population to exercise (Verthoef, Love, & Rose, 1992). One possible explanation for this sedentary behaviour is the increased barriers associated with becoming a parent. In corresponding intervention research, Canadians Cramp and Brawley (2006) designed a successful physical activity intervention to help new mothers develop skills to overcome postnatal specific barriers. Putting the research into action, Mothers in Motion (http://www.caaws-mothersinmotion.ca/e/) was developed for mothers who want to maintain a physically active lifestyle, and includes on its website information on how to overcome child-related barriers to physical activity.

It is a great accomplishment when research comes full circle. First, factors determining physical activity patterns are established; second, a successful intervention based on these determinants is completed; and third, the information is passed to the public. However, there are major challenges in completing this desirable cycle. One current problem is that there is an abundance of evidence-based exercise intervention research but only a fraction has been translated into practical settings (Glasgow et al., 2006).

The average Canadian family presented in the vignette demonstrates many of the factors that have been found to determine whether or not an individual is likely to exercise. John and Sue represent middle aged, sedentary individuals with dual careers and health issues. Working shifts is a strong barrier to regular activity. Kerri and Carter demonstrate a reliance on passive transportation and a preference for sedentary activities such as video games. Carter also has low self-esteem and body issues. All of these factors have been found to influence exercise behaviour. Therefore, the challenge for professionals dealing with people like the Brown family is to develop successful programs that address and attempt to manipulate as many of these factors as possible, thereby, increasing the probability of the Browns becoming active in the future.

Researchers are working hard to understand the determinants of exercise behaviour, as well as how to build successful interventions that influence these determinants.

INTERVENTION RESEARCH INVOLVING PHYSICAL ACTIVITY

Kahn and colleagues (2002) evaluated the effectiveness of interventions established through well-known factors. Changes in physical activity and aerobic capacity post-intervention were used as measures of intervention effectiveness. Their comprehensive systematic review of a multitude of studies found only five studies dealing with how to modify exercise behaviour effectively. This demonstrates the complexity involved in developing effective activity interventions.

Individuals reviewing intervention research have tried to classify their studies according to a number of systems intended to make sense of the vast amount of material. To help you better understand the literature, we have chosen to classify research according to the role that physical activity plays within the intervention study.

Research into the role of physical activity can be of two types. The first type of research, and the one that we will examine in the first section, evaluates physical activity as an **outcome variable** (see Figure 15.1). The focus of **outcome based exercise research** is to develop an intervention and test whether or not it positively affects exercise behaviour. It could be as simple as placing a sign beside an elevator encouraging individuals to

Outcome variable: A response that occurs as a consequence of being involved in physical activity.

Outcome based exercise research: Research that develops interventions and tests whether or not they positively affect exercise behaviour.

Figure 15.1 Physical activity as the outcome variable

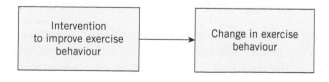

Figure 15.2 Physical activity as the treatment variable

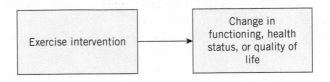

take the stairs, or as complex as increasing an individual's confidence to exercise regularly through educational programs. While the intervention strategies are distinct, the goal is the same: to increase physical activity patterns.

The second type of research uses physical activity as the **treatment variable** (see Figure 15.2). The intent of **treatment-based exercise research** is to modify an individual's life experience in some way through the use of physical activity. For example, an exercise program could be used to help a cancer patient cope better with their disease or the side-effects of their treatment. With treatment exercise research, the population may change, as may the outcome variables of interest, but the treatment stays the same: physical activity.

PHYSICAL ACTIVITY AS AN OUTCOME IN INTERVENTION RESEARCH

A great number of Canadian researchers have contributed to the physical activity intervention research, however, there are subject areas that lack Canadian content. It is important to keep in mind that not all research based on Canadian participants will apply to other countries with different populations, ethnicities, healthcare systems, and climate. Nor will research that is conducted elsewhere in the world necessarily apply to Canada. Remember this fact when you are reading the research in this area. A lot of intervention research is conducted in California, and this begs a question—does it apply to people living in the Maritimes in January?

Numerous approaches have been used to increase physical activity. Intervention research at one level can be theory-based or non-theory–based in nature (Sallis & Owen, 1999). **Theory-based research** evaluates relationships among constructs that are proposed by theories or models of behaviour change. Painter et al. (2008) sorted the use of theory in health research into four categories according to whether the goal was to (1) test a theory by exploring relationships between the theoretical constructs, (2) apply a theory to develop an intervention, (3) develop a brand new theory, or (4) inform a study using a theory that was listed but not explained. **Non-theory–based research** can include interventions informed by theory without any evaluation of construct relationships or research that has absolutely no mention or consideration of theoretical constructs.

Intervention Research Based on Theoretical Constructs

We will be describing interventions based on constructs identified in prominent theories of behaviour change. We highlight the models that have been given the most attention and show the most promise in leading to effective interventions to change

Treatment variable: A variable that is presented to an individual to see its effect on an outcome variable.

Treatment-based exercise research: Research that modifies an individual's life experiences through the use of physical activity. Physical activity is presented to the individual to influence life outcomes and other relevant factors.

Theory-based research: Interventions based on theoretically proposed relationships among constructs.

Non-theory–based research: Interventions that are not based on theoretically proposed relationships.

exercise behaviour: the theory of planned behaviour, social cognitive theory, the transtheoretical model, and self-determination theory. Because all of these theories were described in Chapter 3, we provide a limited review of the theories and focus on exercise interventions based on key theoretical concepts contained within each theory. We conclude our discussion of theoretical constructs with the health action process approach (HAPA) (Schwarzer, 2008), which attempts to combine key elements of key theoretical constructs contained within health research. We also discuss some of the popular intervention strategies that have been used recently to influence exercise behaviour, such as computer technology, reality television, and school initiatives. We finish the section by providing specific recommendations based on key components of successful interventions.

Theory of Planned Behaviour Recall from Chapter 3 that the theory of planned behaviour (TPB) (Ajzen, 1985) postulates that attitudes and social norms will directly influence behavioural intentions, and intentions will then directly affect behaviour. Perceived behavioural control is proposed to affect both the intentions to engage in the behaviour and the behaviour itself. Symons Downs and Hausenblas (2005) completed a statistical review of the theory of planned behaviour applied to exercise, and concluded that intention and perceived behavioural control were most strongly associated with exercise, and attitude was most strongly associated with intention. These authors suggested that intentions and perceived behavioural control would be useful for designing exercise intervention studies. Maddux and Dawson (2014) identified that information about the benefits of exercise can easily lead to changes in intention; however, most people find it difficult to translate intentions into actual changes in exercise behaviour.

Interventions based on TPB should focus on four key aspects: (1) changing attitudes toward physical activity (Sallis & Owen, 1999), (2) evaluating social influences, (3) bridging the intention–behaviour gap (e.g., Maddux & Dawson, 2014), and (4) promoting perceptions of personal control or self-regulation of the physical activity. **Persuasive communication** is one way to provoke **attitude change** and is based on providing specific information regarding beliefs about physical activity (Bright et al., 1993). One area of research that helps to bridge the intention–behaviour gap addresses **implementation intentions**. Gollwitzer (1999) describes implementation intentions as those strong mental associations that form between a situational cue and a specific behaviour (e.g., "When I get in the car, I will drive to the gym"). Whereas the intention construct captured by the TPB specifies people's general behavioural goals (e.g., "I intend to exercise three times per week"), implementation intentions specify when, where, and how that general goal intention will be translated into action. Nevertheless, expanding our view of intentions may help to further bridge the gap between intentions and action.

Research by Chatzisarantis and Hagger (2005) evaluated the effectiveness of two persuasive communication conditions designed to promote positive physical activity attitudes, increase intentions, and change behaviour in teenagers. One message was relevant to the participants and discussed things meaningful to this cohort: "Physical activity helps you get fit, have fun, and avoid injuries." The second message targeted the benefits of exercise that were previously found not to be meaningful to youth: "Physical activity helps you relax, feel better mentally, and forget about your cares." Results demonstrated

Persuasive communication: A strategy of behavioural change that provides specific belief-targeted messages.

Attitude change: Specific techniques geared at changing the beliefs that an individual holds toward physical activity.

Implementation intentions: Mental associations between a situational cue and a specific behaviour.

that the relevant persuasive message resulted in more positive attitudes and stronger intentions to be physically active. However, neither group actually increased its physical activity participation.

Arbour and Martin Ginis (2008) evaluated whether implementation intentions could help sedentary women increase the number of steps they walked each week. Women in the implementation intentions condition were required to choose three days each week over the course of the study, and to specify the time, place, and number of minutes they intended to walk on each of those days. Women in a control condition did not formulate implementation intentions. All study participants were given a pedometer and were asked to keep track of the number of steps they walked each day for 11 weeks. Participants in the implementation intention condition walked more steps over the course of the study than the control condition.

Promoting perceptions of control or **self-regulation** is a key construct in many successful exercise interventions. One way of increasing perceptions of control is to provide the individual with **behavioural strategies** that increase self-regulation. Three behavioural strategies used to change physical activity are goal setting, behaviour monitoring, and signing a physical activity contract (Lox, et al., 2006).

In order to be effective, **goal setting** must include two crucial steps. In the first step, the individual must identify what they would like to achieve through their physical activity participation. Many individuals erroneously stop at this first step. Goals are not magical! Just setting a goal will not automatically translate into success. The second step is the most important element of goal setting. An individual must be able to identify specific and doable **action plans** that are necessary to achieve their goal. Successful behavioural change strategies are the only means by which change will occur. For example, a goal of losing five pounds will not come to fruition for an individual unless they can identify what they must do to lose five pounds. If they do not identify and commit to decreasing their caloric intake while increasing their energy expenditure through exercise, the goal will not be met. Effective goal setting requires both planning (the goal) and action (the behaviour change) to be successful.

Another strategy to facilitate physical activity behaviour change is **behaviour monitoring**, or keeping track of physical activity behaviour (Baumeister & Heatherton, 1996). Monitoring can be achieved by keeping a physical activity diary, chart, or calendar and recording daily or weekly physical activity. Any pertinent details related to physical activity can also be included, such as the duration of the activity and how the person felt while completing it. Advancements in modern technology have increased the ways in which physical activity can be monitored. One popular technology that is cost effective and easily utilized is the pedometer. Bravata and colleagues (2007) examined the utility of pedometers in increasing physical activity and found that physical activity (steps) was higher among those using a pedometer and setting goals for their steps attained. Fitbit One is a new lightweight, portable activity monitor that records multiple measures of physical activity including step count and distance travelled. Information can be uploaded wirelessly to a website for individual record keeping. It is exciting to think how evolving technology can improve adherence to physical activity!

Signing a **physical activity contract** is another self-regulation strategy used to promote physical activity. Contracts are thought to enhance an individual's commitment

Self-regulation: Controlling one's own behaviour by navigating around obstacles or barriers.

Behavioural strategies: Actions that an individual can do that increase their probability of engaging in physical activity.

Goal setting: Identifying what an individual would like to work toward in terms of their physical activity participation. The goal is specific in terms of the frequency, type, and duration of physical activity identified.

Action plans: Effective behavioural strategies (e.g., limiting food intake or exercising in the morning before work) that have been identified as necessary to fulfill a goal.

Behaviour monitoring: Keeping track of exercise behaviour in a physical activity diary, chart, or calendar and recording physical activity and related details each day or each week.

Physical activity contract: A written document specifying the physical activity behaviour to be achieved.

AntonioDiaz/Fotolia

Exercise behaviour can be enhanced by changing attitudes and developing effective implementation strategies.

and motivation to attain the physical activity goal. Cress and colleagues (2005) list contracts as one of several "best-practice" strategies to foster physical activity among older adults. A physical activity contract specifies in writing the physical activity behaviour to be achieved. In addition to identifying the physical activity goal a person agrees to, physical activity contracts may include other details like rewards (e.g., a dinner out) to be received for fulfilling the contract.

Clearly, the TPB has the potential to help guide exercise interventions by focusing on ways to manipulate attitudes, social influences, perceptions of control, and intentions so that individuals are more likely to exercise. Maddux and Dawson (2014) suggested that one important aspect of translating intention into behaviour is developing a manageable action plan. According to these authors, individuals intent on exercising must develop an action plan that includes a breakdown of long-term goals into manageable short-term goals, the identification of what behaviours need to be performed and when they need to be completed, realistic time-management estimations, and development of effective Plans A, B, and C.

Social Cognitive Theory Social cognitive theory (SCT) (Bandura, 1997) is an all-encompassing theory used to describe human behaviour in a number of situations, including exercise. As described in Chapter 3, the model comprises a number of constructs and proposed relationships. Of key importance in this theory is the concept of **self-efficacy**, an individual's belief in their ability to produce desired outcomes, which has been found to be an important determinant of physical activity (Bauman et al., 2012) As self-efficacy increases, so too does desirable behaviour. In response to positive behaviour changes, self-efficacy rises, and so continues the cycle. Perceptions of self-efficacy are a large part of the self-regulation identified previously.

Self-efficacy: An individual's belief in their ability to produce desired outcomes.

Targeting and improving self-efficacy will be a large part of any successful intervention. Regardless of the type of intervention, the goal remains the same: to improve individual perceptions of ability. Once an individual feels competent, they are more likely to change the targeted behaviour. Many types of self-efficacy can be influenced in the exercise setting, including **barrier self-efficacy** (confidence in one's ability to overcome barriers that may arise when participating in exercise); **scheduling self-efficacy** (confidence in one's ability to plan and organize exercise in one's life); **task self-efficacy** (confidence in one's ability to complete the exercise task); and **exercise self-efficacy** (confidence in one's ability to engage in physical activity). Some researchers have combined multiple forms of behaviours into one general **self-regulatory efficacy** for exercise (Dowd et al., 2014).

Self-efficacy can be raised in many ways in an exercise context. General ways of manipulating self-efficacy identified by Bandura (1997) are to focus on mastery or performance accomplishments, watch similar others complete the same behaviours successfully, listen to significant others who are evaluating an individual's ability, and monitor changes that are occurring within the body as one becomes increasingly fit. Specific ways of raising self-efficacy that have been targeted in intervention research are through goal setting, encouraging social support, and providing information or educational programs. Recall that Cramp and Brawley (2006) improved barrier self-efficacy perceptions of postnatal women by having group-based sessions geared toward helping new moms develop skills to manage specific postnatal barriers. Dawson and colleagues (2008) also raised barrier and exercise self-efficacy through educational programs.

Another way of increasing an individual's self-efficacy to exercise is through the aid of a **physical activity counsellor**. Blanchard and colleagues (2007) compared the effects of a physical activity intervention delivered by a primary healthcare provider (control group) with physical activity counselling provided by a trained member of the healthcare team who used behaviour modification techniques that included helping

Canadians face many environmental barriers to regular physical activity. Enhancing self-efficacy to overcome such barriers is a key to increasing physical activity for all Canadians.

Teo Barker/Moment/Getty Images

individuals overcome barriers to exercise. They attempted to modify the task and barrier self-efficacy of sedentary individuals midway through an exercise program to see the effect on subsequent physical activity. Results demonstrated that task and barrier self-efficacy evaluated midway through the program significantly predicted later physical activity.

One key component of any intervention geared toward changing exercise behaviour will be finding ways to increase perceptions of self-efficacy. Whatever the means (e.g., educational programs, counselling), it is important to raise people's evaluation of their capabilities regarding barriers, scheduling, and the task in order to see effects on behaviour. However, while targeting self-efficacy was a successful means of increasing physical activity in a multitude of studies, some interventions may increase self-efficacy while still failing to improve actual physical activity rates (Williams & French, 2011).

Transtheoretical Model Recall from Chapter 3 that the transtheoretical model (TTM) (Prochaska et al., 1992) suggests that an individual passes through distinct stages when attempting to change behaviours: precontemplation (no intention to make changes), contemplation (intending to make changes within six months), preparation (intending to make changes in the next month), action (starting a new behaviour), maintenance (sustaining the behaviour), and termination (removing relapse potential).

Stage-targeted activity promotion interventions are more likely to induce changes in motivation than approaches that do not consider changes (Brug & Kremers, 2005). This implies that individuals think and behave differently in each stage, and different processes motivate them. **Stage-matching interventions** are sensitive to strategies that are different and tailored to the specific needs of the individual. This means that individuals are first evaluated for their current stage on the exercise continuum and then provided with relevant information for that specific stage. The information is usually based on constructs from TPB (e.g., attitudes, intentions) and SCT (e.g., self-efficacy).

Dawson and colleagues (2008) used a stage-matched approach in their comparison of a traditional group-based intervention with an internet-based physical activity intervention in an Ontario workplace. Both interventions were based on SCT integrated with TTM. All participants completed a stage of change questionnaire each week, with the resulting information being used to determine the stage relevant information that was provided for the participants. Thus, for each week of the 10-week intervention, information was provided that was relevant to their unique motivational and behavioural processes. Results demonstrated that although the internet-based intervention attracted more participants, the group-based intervention cohort showed significant increases in exercise and barrier self-efficacy. With respect to stages, more than a statistically expected number of participants in the preparation stage were found in both intervention groups. Also, more individuals in the preparation and maintenance stage of exercise chose the internet-based intervention over the group-based intervention. This study demonstrates how individuals in different stages might be unique in their preferences for intervention delivery mode and psychological and behavioural factors.

It is clear that individuals will follow unique paths in their own exercise journeys, and therefore interventions need to be tailored to the specific stage that each

Stage-matching interventions: Specific intervention strategies that are sensitive to the specific needs of the individuals within different stages of change according to the transtheoretical model.

individual is currently in. The TTM does a good job of describing these stages and keeping researchers aware that successful interventions will need to be stage-matched in some way.

REFLECTIONS 15.1

What stage describes your exercise behaviour? Think of interventions that would be effective to change your physical activity. Now think of how you could help someone in the contemplation stage.

Self-Determination Theory Self-determination theory (SDT) (Deci & Ryan, 2000) is a general theory of human motivation that applies to a number of achievement oriented domains including exercise. SDT is the only theory that identifies autonomy as a human need that when fulfilled facilitates increases in self-regulation (Ng et al., 2012). What does it mean to be autonomous? In most basic terms, individuals are **autonomous** when they determine their own behaviour and are not controlled by outside or external sources. You can see how important this would be in the domain of people selecting and adhering to their own self-selected exercise regime. The main tenet of SDT is that individuals will engage in successful self-regulation of exercise behaviour when they are intrinsically motivated to participate in physical activity based on their personal interests and values. Gunnell and colleagues (2014) concluded that psychological need fulfillment during physical activity may facilitate increased exercise behaviour in the future. Similarly, Ng and colleagues (2012) found that SDT constructs, such as autonomy supportive climates and satisfaction of basic needs, were important components of physical health.

Autonomous: When individuals determine their own behaviour and are not influenced by outside sources.

SDT is currently one of the trending research paradigms for advancements in exercise behaviour. Fortier and colleagues (2012) reviewed three large exercise intervention trials in three different countries based on SDT, including the Canadian PAC trial (Fortier et al., 2007), and concluded that interventions that influence psychological needs through need-supporting environments will promote more autonomous motivation within individuals and subsequently promote positive physical activity.

REFLECTIONS 15.2

Pact (www.gym-pact.com) is an interesting new app for mobile devices that uses money to punish or reinforce the regulation of exercise behaviours. Individuals make a weekly pact about how much they would like to exercise and then they set what their price will be if they don't meet their weekly goals. Whether or not people have met their targeted goals is determined through GPS tracking of phones and other surveillance techniques. If you meet your weekly goals, you earn money from members who didn't reach their goals for that week. Would you like to be part of Pact? Would it help you meet your physical activity goals? Do you think that people would be honest about their activities?

Figure 15.3 The health action process approach

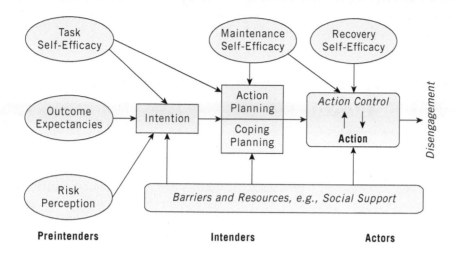

Source: "Modeling health behavior change: How to predict and modify the adoption and maintenance of health behaviors", by Ralf Schwarzer, *Applied Psychology: An International Review*, 2008, pg 6, Figure 1. © Wiley. Downloaded with permission from Schwarzer http://userpage.fu-berlin.de/health/hapa.htm

Health Action Process Approach By now, you should have recognized that a key aspect of all of the previous theories is the emphasis placed on self-regulation. What if all of the important concepts derived from each theory were collected and placed in one theory designed to predict exercise behaviour? This idea is exactly what is behind the super build health action process approach (HAPA) model proposed by Schwarzer (2008). Figure 15.3 demonstrates how variables that you are familiar with relate to behavioural control in the proposed HAPA model.

HAPA is concerned with translating intention into action, and suggests that there is a difference between (a) motivation processes that lead to behavioural intentions, and (b) motivational processes that lead to a change in actual behaviour (Schwarzer, 2008). Parschau and colleagues (2012) utilized the HAPA model to evaluate changes in key social cognitive variables that are associated with stage transitions in physical activity. The authors concluded that exercise promotion should focus on increasing self-efficacy for individuals who are in the non-intending, intending, and acting stages of behaviour change, and that more focus must be placed on planning interventions for intending individuals. Once again, interventions will be more effective if they are stage-relevant. The HAPA model recognizes the dynamic journey that exercise can be for an individual.

Research by Parschau and colleagues (2014) evaluated the ability of HAPA to improve the physical activity patterns of 484 obese men and women. HAPA-specific variables that were evaluated were motivational self-efficacy, outcome expectancies, risk perception, intention, maintenance self-efficacy, action planning, coping planning, recovery self-efficacy, and social support. Self-reported physical activity was evaluated as average days per week an individual exercised and the duration of their activity on those days. While not all relationships proposed in HAPA were confirmed, enough positive associations among variables were found (e.g. motivational self-efficacy, outcome expectancies, and social support were related to intention) to have the authors conclude that HAPA is an important model for developing successful interventions geared toward increasing physical activity.

| CASE STUDY 15.1 | The Case of Sue Brown |

Recall that Sue Brown is a middle-aged mother of two who works part-time at a hospital. She does not have additional money to spend on herself after all mandatory expenses are completed. She is 30 pounds overweight and has just been diagnosed with high blood pressure. How would the HAPA model predict Sue's success at integrating physical activity into her life?

The model predicts that if Sue can find an exercise that she feels capable of succeeding at, perceives some risk for further consequences from her high blood pressure or weight status, and expects a favourable outcome from the behaviour, she is more likely to form an intention to exercise. Once ready, Sue could start with something under her personal control that is not limited by the obstacle of shift work. Walking is an ideal exercise for Sue. She can productively schedule it into her life and can manage the task effectively. Sue must translate the intention into action by developing a plan as to how she will incorporate walking into her daily life (an action plan), as well as developing strategies to overcome potential obstacles such as fatigue and family schedules. Her successful walking behaviours will increase her appraisals of self-efficacy, which will lead to future successful behaviours. Adding a friend for social support would be an ideal resource. Ongoing evaluation and planning will effectively guide Sue through the intention to action control stage.

Current and Topical Intervention Research

We stated earlier that some interventions are based on constructs derived from theory, while others are not. If we reviewed only theory-based research, a large part of the intervention picture would be missing, as some effective interventions do not include constructs proposed by the theories that we discussed previously. However, some of these unique intervention approaches are as helpful and effective as the ones based on theoretical constructs.

Interventions Based on Motivational Interviewing Another approach that has gained interest in promoting behaviours such as physical activity is **motivational interviewing** (MI). At its most basic level, Miller and Rollnick (2013) described MI as a way of communicating with the goal being "to strengthen a person's own motivation and commitment to change" (p. 12) their behaviour in some way. MI attempts to get those people attempting to change an individual's exercise behaviour to think about what they say, how to say it, how much to say, and when to say it to the individual. Not all communication styles and approaches will be effective. By using MI as a focused guiding framework for behaviour modification communications, the probability of the person actually being motivated to change their physical activity behaviour may in some way be increased.

MI utilizes four general processes to motivate people to change: (1) actively working with the individual to establish a trusting relationship and connection,

Motivational interviewing: A focused method of communication used to help facilitate behaviour change by helping the person to consider their own reasons for wanting to engage in a new behaviour.

(2) discussing with the individual what it is they want to discuss or change, (3) assisting the person in thinking and talking about the behaviour change they have agreed to discuss, and (4) helping the individual plan the practical steps for how to implement change in their lives. Although key skills used during these processes include reflective listening and asking open ended questions, there is no set script to follow; the conversation must unfold based on the needs of the individual using the skills as appropriate (Miller & Rollnick, 2013).

Some have suggested that MI could be examined alongside SDT (Miller and Rollnick, 2012), since the three human needs emphasized in SDT (autonomy, relatedness, and competence) are all directly related to successful behaviour change through MI. Martens and colleagues (2012) found that participants receiving MI engaged in more vigorous physical activity than a control group that did not receive MI.

CASE STUDY 15.2 — Motivational Interviewing in Action

Let's focus specifically on how a personal trainer would begin to utilize MI principles effectively with a client. Imagine Rashid arrives at a personal training session at a gym.

A personal trainer who has no MI background may hit the ground running with fitness assessments and exercise program development because he assumes that Rashid signed himself up at the gym (wants to be there) and likely wants to get into shape. Why would he be there otherwise?

However, Rashid's personal trainer (Aimée) is familiar with MI. She welcomes Rashid, introduces herself, and asks Rashid to tell her a little bit about himself. Rashid shares that he is retired, has some back pain, and likes to be outdoors working with his hands. Rashid seems open to talking, so Aimée asks him if he would share why he signed up for personal training. This is where she learns that it was actually Rashid's grown children who got him

the personal training sessions as a 68th birthday gift, and that he is a little nervous about being in a "gym for all those fit people" as he doesn't really know if working out is for him. The non-MI trainer may use this time to tell Rashid how wonderful gyms are, how great he will feel in six months, not to worry about his back pain, and how he is lucky someone else paid for the cost. Aimée instead reflects back Rashid's concerns about being anxious and feeling like he might be out of his comfort zone given that it was not his idea to be here. Aimée then asks Rashid what made him attend the session with her, despite his concerns.

Only by continuing this conversation guided by MI can Aimée and Rashid begin to consider why he is really there, what he might want to get out of the personal training sessions, and how ready for a change he actually is. As you can see, there is a lot to MI!

Interventions Based on Dog Walking Hoerster and colleagues (2011) found that dog walking was associated with individuals meeting the American guidelines for physical activity. Similarly, Brown and Rhodes (2006) found that individuals in Victoria, British Columbia, who owned dogs were much more likely to walk regularly than those without dogs. More recently, Rhodes and his colleagues (2012) found that a group of dog owners who were given information related to the importance of walking for the health of their dog walked more steps than a non-information group. A recent review (Christensen et al., 2012) supported the idea of increased walking among those who have a dog. These authors called for additional studies to be completed on the effectiveness of dog walking for increasing physical activity. Not a bad idea!

There are many ways to get regular health-promoting physical activity that do not involve formal exercise settings.

Computer Technology Interventions We have spent a lot of time discussing the content of the intervention, but the method of information delivery is also an important aspect of the intervention strategy. When determining the most compatible intervention format for the targeted audience, practitioners might consider some new and interesting ways of utilizing computer technology through computer websites, social media, and exergaming.

Website Technology Designing exercise interventions that use website or internet technology has become so popular that a new term—"eHealth"—has been coined (Eng, 2001). The content included on most physical activity websites usually involves educational information about exercise and techniques to help individuals manage their own activity. Websites attempt to be dynamic and interactive, allowing for new information to be updated and for users to log in and track their own unique behaviours, emotions, and thoughts.

Two highly interactive Canadian websites attempting to influence people's physical activity choices are ParticipACTION (www.participaction.com) and the Heart and Stroke Foundation (www.heartandstroke .on.ca). ParticipACTION seeks to engage individuals of all ages by including a Twitter feed, incorporating blogs, and providing apps for mobile phones that include fun and active games for kids. The Heart and Stroke Foundation employs a number of etools designed to help individuals assess their risk of heart attack and stroke and plan programs for maintaining a healthy weight and managing blood pressure. The website also includes tips to raise healthy kids and has a section for heart healthy recipes.

A number of internet sites geared toward children's health also exist. The Childhood Obesity Foundation (www.childhoodobesityfoundation.ca) is a website designed to provide facts about obesity and solutions for families, schools, and communities about how to address the obesity issue in children and engage in healthier lifestyles. Active Healthy Kids Canada (www.activehealthykids.ca) is an organization based on a membership of stakeholders in the promotion of children's physical activity in Canada. The website provides suggestions about how to get kids to exercise more regularly and identifies where changes need to take place. Active Healthy Kids Canada has been distributing a report card on the status of youth physical activity across a variety of settings since 2005, and the 2013 report card (Active Healthy Kids Canada, 2013) identified that the increase in driving children to school has contributed to the lack of physical activity in our nation's children.

Research by Davies and colleagues (2012) evaluated 34 computer and internet delivered interventions between 1990 and 2011. The authors concluded that the ability of these interventions to produce positive changes in long-term physical activity remains unclear. While computer technology may inspire short-term changes in physical activity, it may be less effective in the long run. Vandelanotte and colleagues' (2007) review of web-based physical intervention studies found that effects were short lived and there was limited evidence of maintenance behaviours.

Social Media Many people today have a Facebook account, post pictures on Instagram, watch videos on YouTube, tweet their activities over Twitter, and do not go a day without texting! All of these activities fall under the social media umbrella of *social networking* (which includes Facebook) and *microblogs* (such as Twitter). The question for researchers is how social media can be used to promote physical activity. While social media may have certain appeal (e.g., they could send specific messages to individuals or groups), their utility is necessarily limited as not everyone uses social media. According to Statistics Canada (2013), such sites are used by 67% of Canadians, but by the end of 2012, only eight studies had used social networking in a physical activity intervention (Maher et al., 2014). Clearly we have more work to do in this area.

Cavallo and colleagues (2012) developed a social support intervention for exercise with female US college students. The women in the main intervention group used a website with information and tools (e.g., tracking of activity), communicated via email with a study moderator, and joined a Facebook group with a study moderator. A second group used a modified website (without all the tools or information), were emailed specific information only, and did not have access to the Facebook group. At the end of the study, the groups showed no differences in social support or physical activity, possibly because both the control and experimental groups had a high frequency of contact through social media, even without the control group having a specific assigned Facebook physical activity group.

Texting may be another way to get people moving. In general, cellphones may use various functions (or apps) that can help users to track or assess their physical activity. When considering texting, Weber Buchholz and colleagues (2013) found that common features of the text messaging interventions including using texts to send out information or prompts, motivate users, or gather information from users. This review found a notable degree of difference between users in texting groups compared to non-texting groups.

Exergaming A final trend worthy of discussion is active gaming or **exergaming**. In recent years, active games have appeared on the commercial market that involve more than just using your fingers and thumbs; popular examples include DanceDance Revolution and the WiiFit (e.g., boxing, tennis). The question for researchers is whether or not active games can be used successfully to promote activity.

Exergaming: Physically active games that are played on home gaming systems.

The research on exergaming is typically split into two populations: children/youth and older adults. Overall, research suggests that active games provide light to moderate levels of activity, and cautions that exergaming is not a valid substitute for real physical activity in children (LeBlanc et al., 2013). This is one of the reasons why Active Healthy Kids Canada developed a position statement against using active gaming among this population (www.activehealthykids.ca). Unlike with youth, there may be more support for the use of active gaming among older adults. Verheijden

Klompstra and colleagues (2013) found that active gaming resulted in light to moderate activity, increased energy expenditure, and promoted better cognitive functioning in seniors. The authors conclude that exergaming is a safe way to engage older adults in physical activity.

Computer technology is an exciting and interesting tool in physical activity interventions. The main advantage of this technology is that it is highly interactive, and researchers are able to give and receive information quickly and directly. Educational information can be delivered to the individual through a website, smartphone app, email, or text message, and the participants can respond and track their progress in return. This is a very cost effective and comprehensive approach to modifying behaviour as large numbers of people can be serviced with minimal cost. The main disadvantage of computer technology is the lack of face time and accountability it provides. The more anonymity a person has, quite often, the less they feel supported or responsible for their individual behaviours.

However, it is an exciting time in intervention research when exercise participants can be contacted individually and immediately to receive or obtain relevant information. However, when designing successful physical activity interventions, it is important to remember that a large component of behaviour change is based on supportive and positive environments. Oftentimes, computer technology does not provide this component.

Mass Media Interventions **Mass media campaigns** are interventions that attempt to reach large numbers of individuals simultaneously through public forums. Types of mass media are internet, video, television, radio, and print. These techniques reach a potentially greater audience than interventions based on personal contact. "Bring Play Back" is a provocative mass media campaign utilizing television, print, and the internet by ParticipACTION (www.participaction.ca), implying that kids are currently not playing enough to be healthy. "We All Play for Canada" is an initiative of Canadian Tire (www.weallplayforcanada.ca), attempting to get kids outside to play and to expand their skills to include a variety of sports. Both television campaigns utilized the 2014 Winter Olympics to relay their message to Canadian television viewers.

> Mass media campaigns: Interventions that attempt to reach large numbers of individuals simultaneously through public forums.

One criticism of mass media campaigns is that, although they lead to increased population awareness, it has been difficult to show their effects on behaviour change. For example, Bauman and colleagues (2004) noted that although Canadians had high awareness of ParticipACTION, they could not attribute physical activity patterns to the campaign. Similarly, Abioye and colleagues (2013) found a significant effect for walking only in their evaluation of multiple mass media campaigns. It appears that while media campaigns increase our awareness, future intervention research is necessary to evaluate the long-term effectiveness of this awareness in terms of changes in physical activity.

Environmental Approaches Dr. Mark Tremblay, a leading Canadian expert in the causes of childhood obesity, stated on CBC television in 2014 that we have systematically engineered physical activity out of our everyday lives over the past 30 years. He was alluding to the fact that we find efficient ways to avoid moving (e.g., we use remote controls to change television channels, or drive to work and school) and that our choice of free time activity involves large amounts of sedentary screen time. His solution for Canadians is to find ways to re-engineer physical activity back into our lives and our environments.

Dr. Tremblay is alluding to the **built environment** of our Canadian cities—the elements that are built or designed by people (Saelens & Handy, 2008). The built environment promotes physical activity by offering accessibility to activities that are appealing and safe. City and urban planners are in control of many aspects of the community environment that can influence physical activity patterns. City bylaws on sidewalk placement will affect who walks to work. Distance of community schools from homes will determine children's ability to walk to school, while the placement of street lights, stop signs, bike lanes, and crosswalks will all influence who will elect to use active transportation. Aarts and colleagues (2012) found that modifiable factors, such as presence of sidewalks and traffic safety measures, were associated with increased outdoor play in children in the Netherlands.

A systematic review found that outdoor activity led to greater feelings of revitalization and positive engagement than indoor physical activity (Thompson et al., 2011). Outdoor natural environments can provide some of the best overall health benefits by increasing physical activity, improving stress reduction, decreasing mental fatigue, and improving mood (Gladwell et al., 2013). Installing fitness parks or outdoor fitness equipment within green spaces or park settings was found to be a cost-effective way to increase the energy expenditure of the individuals within the park for the short term (Cohen et al., 2012). Roult et al. (2014) evaluated the impact that the addition of a free outdoor skating rink had on a community in North Montreal, and found that three clear trends emerged. First, the ice rink was found to be a place to discover and rediscover sport for the community. Second, it became a new meeting place for individuals within the community. And third, not surprisingly, individuals who elected to use the ice rink were already individuals with an active lifestyle. Long-term sustainable changes in physical activity patterns in response to environmental manipulations remain to be examined.

Built environment: Any element in a community that is designed or constructed by people.

REFLECTIONS 15.3

How could you change your environment at school or at home to increase your probability of becoming more physically active? Is your school community more conducive to activity than your home environment? How could active transportation be developed in this community?

Reality Television Reality TV is currently a television and internet presence, and a number of these shows are dedicated to helping individuals lose weight and live a healthier lifestyle. The very popular weight loss show *The Biggest Loser* has contestants compete to lose the most weight for the season and win a monetary prize. Each week, participants are sent home if they are the person who lost the least amount of weight.

You may have wondered whether these shows help to motivate and inspire people to make healthy behavioural changes in their own lives, or if they are sensationalizing real health issues in a willing group of participants for entertainment purposes. Advantages of the shows are that they highlight the need for individuals to be accountable for their weight loss and promote the reality of hard work. The major problem associated with *The Biggest Loser* and its counterparts is that the environment in which contestants lose weight (with personal trainers, nutritionists, and the like) has no application to the real world, and the weight loss that occurs on the show promotes unrealistic weight loss expectations in viewers.

Berry and colleagues (2013) examined whether watching an episode of *The Biggest Loser* resulted in exercise-related attitudes different from those shown by participants in a control condition who were not primed with the TV show prior to their evaluations. Results demonstrated that the participants who watched *The Biggest Loser* had more negative attitudes toward physical activity than the control group did. Perhaps, seeing individuals engage in exercise that was so intense for the participant and so inappropriate for the audience negatively affected the viewers' attitude toward exercise. This demonstrates that reality shows depicting extreme weight loss regimens may not be just neutral to the viewer, but rather, potentially negative. Inducing a negative emotional reaction to exercise decreases the probability of exercise engagement for the viewer.

School-Based Physical Activity Interventions Childhood obesity is an ongoing concern in Canada, and there have been numerous attempts at interventions to get children to become more active in order to stop gaining weight. Interventions have largely targeted schools, the family, or both. All approaches can be highly successful. In 2005, a comprehensive school health (CSH) program for improving diets, activity levels, and body weights of children was initiated in Alberta as part of the "Alberta Project Promoting active Living and healthy Eating" (APPLE) (www.appleschools .ca). Fung and colleagues (2012) compared students from 10 APPLE schools with non-APPLE schools. They found that children in APPLE schools were eating more fruits and vegetables, were consuming fewer calories, and were more physically active and less obese. These findings demonstrate the effectiveness of utilizing a CSH program in Canadian schools.

REFLECTIONS 15.4

School-based body mass index (BMI) report cards that are sent to parents when their children's BMI is higher than recommended are being implemented by schools in the United States and Europe but not in Canada. Some obesity experts fear that BMI report cards will increase the stigma against overweight children. What are the advantages of letting parents and children know when their BMI is too high? What are the disadvantages? Do you think that Canada should adopt this policy?

Participant Age Considerations in Interventions Most exercise studies that we have reviewed in this section were based on adult participants (aged 20–55).

Table 15.2 Interventions That Work Best for Children and Older Adults

Children	Older Adults
Provide opportunities that are fun and enjoyable.	Highlight the health benefits associated with physical activity.
Target task self-efficacy.	Take into consideration individual differences in health status (e.g., an individual with heart disease will need a different exercise program than someone with osteoporosis).
Provide social support from family and friends.	Exercise activities should be conveniently located in safe environments.
Environments to complete interventions are physical education classes, sport teams and physical activities.	Older adults prefer lower intensity and less structured activities, such as walking.
Use tangible behavioural and environmental strategies, such as providing more parks, increasing lighting, and adding more physical activity time into the school curriculum.	Provide lots of social support from peers and health professionals.
Target the entire family in the behavioural change.	Educational programs should increase understanding of physical activity benefits.
Provide qualified supervision of activities.	Programs should build self-efficacy for exercise and activities of daily living.
Make sure that all kids are moving as much as possible in structured activities.	Group exercise classes should be specific to older adults.
Provide physical activity that is outdoors whenever possible.	Activities in exercise programs should be geared toward balance and keeping individuals more functionally well and independent.

Have you worked with children in a physical activity capacity as a coach or camp counsellor? Have you found it difficult to get kids to be active? What techniques did you use to motivate them to be active?

Children and seniors require special consideration as their needs may change as a function of their age. Children's physical activity is largely determined by outside sources such as parents, schools, communities, and sport organizations. They may require interventions that are based on behavioural and environmental manipulations. Seniors may need physical training programs that allow for the functional decline associated with aging, and overcoming the considerable barriers to exercise faced by seniors is a continuous challenge. Table 15.2 highlights some of the research findings pertaining to children and older adults.

Beau Lark/Corbis

CONCLUSION ABOUT INTERVENTIONS USED TO INCREASE PHYSICAL ACTIVITY

The most successful interventions will be based on many of the key components discussed throughout this chapter. What are most likely to be effective are structured, multi-component interventions that utilize a variety of strategies (Maddux & Dawson; in press). When attempting to change individuals' exercise behaviour, increase the probability of your intervention becoming successful by implementing these recommendations:

1. Base your intervention on trying to change an individual's attitude toward exercise. In order to change an individual's attitude, you will need to use specific information that is based on their unique beliefs about physical activity.

2. Have individuals identify a specific implementation intention. By attaching an activity-related behaviour with a situational cue that is relevant in their life, individuals are more likely to bridge the intention–behaviour gap.

3. Use creative ways to increase individuals' perceptions of their ability to take part in physical activity and to overcome specific barriers that are unique to their situation.

4. Be sensitive to the exercise stage that an individual is currently in. Use strategies that are helpful at each stage. For example, if someone has not exercised previously, provide them with information highlighting the benefits of exercise. Conversely, if someone has been exercising regularly, discuss strategies to avoid pitfalls.

5. If you are implementing an educational program, consider carefully how you will deliver the information. Recognize the advantages and disadvantages of all delivery styles, as well as their relevance to your target population. For example, you would not want to use the internet for seniors who may not be technically savvy and are looking for social companionship through exercise.

6. Use behavioural strategies that motivate the individual to be involved in regulating their own exercise program, such as setting goals or monitoring their progress in some way

7. Develop a plan of action. Make sure you are planning for best case scenarios when exercising is easy for the individual, as well as for circumstances when mental barriers (such as lack of motivation) or physical obstacles (such as lack of time) may impede ability to exercise.

8. Be sensitive to the age of the individual whom you are trying to help become more physically active. Use information delivery modes that are desirable for different age groups.

PHYSICAL ACTIVITY AS A TREATMENT FOR UNHEALTHY INDIVIDUALS

In the previous section, we discussed interventions that may influence adherence to physical activity in healthy individuals. Chronic disease or disabilities impose many disruptions to people's lives and have a great impact on individuals' psychological functioning. The role of physical activity changes when an individual becomes unhealthy or inhibited

Cancer survivors can gain many psychological, social, and physical benefits from regular physical activity. However, they may face unique barriers.

Steve Debenport/E+/Getty Images

for a long period of time. In these cases, researchers are no longer concerned with how specific interventions affect adherence rates, but rather with a much more practical question: "What can physical activity do to help individuals manage the many challenges that occur with a long-term illness or disability?"

The last 30 years have produced empirical validation of the importance of physical activity in managing and coping with various illnesses, physical limitations, diseases, and mental impairments. It is beyond the scope of the present chapter to review interventions addressing all of these health issues. However, it is important to note that many Canadian researchers have adapted a research program that evaluates how physical activity can affect outcomes associated with various illnesses or disability or physical limitations. People facing health and wellness issues will benefit from many of the outcomes associated with regular exercise.

Depression is often a side-effect of cancer and its treatment. Craft and colleagues (2011) conducted a systematic review of 15 random control trials to examine if exercise affects depression symptoms in individuals dealing with cancer. The authors concluded that exercise during cancer treatment can reduce pain and fatigue, and lead to improvements in quality of life. Exercise was found to have a modest positive effect on symptoms of depression. The best effects were found for supervised exercise programs that were not conducted at home and lasted at least 30 minutes or more.

Physical activity interventions have been used to target a variety of populations and illnesses. While each group is unique, one thing is true for all: Physical activity is beneficial! However, the same challenges that affect asymptomatic populations with respect to exercise adherence also affect individuals with special needs. Therefore, it is imperative to understand how to address the specific challenges and barriers faced by people who are dealing with chronic illnesses, disabilities, diseases, and mental health issues. An intervention approach to physical activity promotion that recognizes factors similar across all populations (e.g., attitudes, self-efficacy), while addressing the unique concerns or barriers that different populations might also experience, will lead to the most successful changes in exercise behaviour. Many of these issues were discussed in the chapters on motivation (Chapter 3), mental health (Chapter 13), and body image (Chapter 14).

CHAPTER SUMMARY

Facilitating physical activity behaviour change is a complex process that will require a number of considerations. We began this chapter by introducing the idea of intervention research. Intervention differs from determinant research in that interventions manipulate determinants believed to influence physical activity behaviour. In intervention research, physical activity can be either an outcome of the intervention or the intervention itself to attain another health outcome. Interventions where physical activity is an outcome can be based on theoretical constructs (e.g., HAPA) or concerned with understanding the effectiveness of non-theory–based approaches (e.g., computer technology, mass media, and reality TV). In order for interventions to be effective, they need to be specifically designed to effectively target adults, children, or seniors. Multifaceted interventions based on the recommendations that we provided previously are needed to optimize physical activity behaviour change.

As an intervention itself, physical activity has been used to help individuals deal with chronic diseases, disabilities, illnesses, and mental health issues. Continued work is needed to find optimal strategies for improving physical activity patterns among diseased populations.

From a public health perspective, it is necessary to continue to develop and evaluate the long-term effects of interventions geared toward increasing the activity levels and quality of life of all Canadians, healthy or diseased. While individuals will readily adopt an exercise program, it is difficult for them to maintain it. Practitioners in this area believe that doing something to try to change physical inactivity is better than doing nothing at all. All interventions are successful if they help even one person to maintain a healthier lifestyle!

 COMMON MYTHS ABOUT PHYSICAL ACTIVITY INTERVENTIONS REVISITED

MYTH: It is easy to get people to become or stay physically active.
The Canada Fitness and Lifestyle Research Institute documented that only 48% of the Canadian adult population is at least moderately physically active, and that activity level is dependent upon geographic location. Overall, 52% of Canadians are inactive.

MYTH: If you have a positive attitude toward physical activity, you will always exercise.
Symons Downs and Hausenblas (2005), in a review of exercise research based on the theory of planned behaviour, concluded that successful exercise behaviour is most

strongly associated with intention and perceived behavioural control. Attitudes can affect our intentions, however, which is why having a positive attitude toward exercise may not always translate into successful behavioural change. A positive attitude will generate a favourable intention, but only intentions that are specific in terms of context, time, and action will evoke actual activity change.

MYTH: Individuals with chronic illnesses do not want to exercise because they have other things to worry about.

Individuals with chronic conditions, such as cancer or cardiovascular disease, are strongly motivated to utilize physical activity to help improve survival rates, physiological functioning, psychological health, and emotional health.

MYTH: An individual's physical activity level is determined by his or her motivation. It is not dependent upon other key factors such as public health policies or environmental barriers.

Physical activity patterns are determined by individual factors (such as motivation or confidence); demographic factors (such as ethnicity, geography, or culture); community factors (such as the availability of resources or neighbourhood safety); political factors (such as tax incentives or health strategies); and environmental factors (such as climate and season changes).

Review Questions

1. What is the difference between determinant and intervention research?
2. Explain how physical activity can be an intervention outcome and an intervention itself.
3. What is the best way to change attitudes?
4. What four types of self-efficacy are important in exercise settings?
5. Why should you consider the exercise stage that an individual is currently in when designing an intervention?
6. What physical activity interventions are most successful for youths and seniors?
7. Are findings based on research undertaken in other countries applicable to Canada? Why or why not?
8. Design an intervention to help a busy working mom become more physically active.
9. Identify the barriers to regular exercise that typical university students face. Develop a mass media campaign to target these barriers.
10. What is the difference between theory-based and non-theory–based interventions?

Suggested Readings

Alberga, A. S., Medd, E. R., Adamo, K. B., Goldfield, G. S., Prudhomme, D., Kenny, G. P., & Sigal, R. J. (2013). Top 10 practical lessons learned from physical activity interventions in overweight and obese children and adolescents. *Applied Physiology and Nutrition Metabolism, 38,* 249–258. Dx.doi.org/10.1139/apnm- 2012-0227.

Kahn, E. B., Ramsey, T. L., Brownson, R. C., Heath, G. W., Howze, E. H., Powell, K. E., Stone, E. J., Rajab, M. W., Corso, P., & Task Force on Community Preventive Services. (2002).

The effectiveness of interventions to increase physical activity: A systematic review. *American Journal of Preventive Medicine, 22(4S),* 73–107.

Maddux, J. E., & Dawson, K. A. (2014). Predicting and changing exercise behavior: Bridging the information–intention–behavior gap. In A. R. Gomes, R. Resende, & A. Albuquerque (Eds.) (Volume 2), *Functioning from a multidimensional perspective: Promoting healthy lifestyles* (pp. 97–120). NY: Nova Science Publishing.

References

Aarts, M. J., DeVries, S. I., van Oers, H. A., & Schult, A. J. (2012). Outdoor play among children in relation to neighborhood characteristics: A cross-sectional neighborhood observation study. *International Journal of Behavioral Nutrition and Physical Activity, 9,* 98.

Abioye, A. I., Hajifathalian, K., & Danaei, G. (2013). Do mass media campaigns improve physical activity? A systematic review and meta-analysis. *Archives of Public Health, 71,* 20. http://www.archpublichealth.com/content/71/1/20.

Active Healthy Kids Canada. (2013). Are we driving our kids to unhealthy habits? 2013 Active Health Kids Canada Report Card on physical activity for children and youth. Retrieved from http://www.activehealthykids.ca/2013ReportCard/en/.

Ajzen, I. (1985). From intentions to actions: A theory of planned behaviour. In J. Kuhl & J. Beckman (Eds.), *Action control: From cognition to behaviour* (pp. 11–30). New York: Springer-Verlag.

Arbour, K. P., & Martin Ginis, K. A. (2008). A randomised controlled trial of the effects of implementation intentions on women's walking behaviour. *Psychology and Health. Epub ahead of print:* doi: 10.1080/08870440801930312.

Bandura, A. (1997). *Self-efficacy: The exercise of control.* New York: W. H. Freeman.

Bauman, A., Madill, J., Craig. C. L., & Salmon, A. (2004). ParticipACTION: This mouse roared but did it get the cheese? *Canadian Journal of Public Health, 95,* S14–24.

Bauman, A. E., Reis, R. S., Sallis, J. F., Wells, J. C., Loos, R. J. F., & Martin, B. W. (2012). Correlates of physical activity: Why are some people physically active and others not? *Lancet, 380,* 258–271.

Baumeister, R. F., & Heatherton, T. F. (1996). Self-regulation failure: An overview. *Psychological Inquiry, 7,* 1–15.

Berry, T., McLeod, N. C., Pankratow, M., & Walker, J. (2013). Effects of *biggest loser* exercise depictions on exercise-related attitudes. *American Journal of Health Behavior, 37(1):*96–103. doi: http://dx.doi.org/10.5993/AJHB.37.1.11.

Blanchard, C. M., Fortier, M., Sweet, S., O'Sullivan, T., Hogg, W., Reid, R. D., & Sigal, R. J. (2007). Explaining physical activity levels from a self-efficacy perspective: The physical activity counselling trial. *Annals of Behavioral Medicine, 34(3),* 323–328.

Bravata, D. M., Smith-Spangler, C., Sundaram, V., Gienger, A. L., Lin, N., Lewis, R., et al. (2007). Using pedometers to increase physical activity and improve health: A systematic review. *Journal of the American Medical Association, 298,* 2296–2304.

Bright, A., Manfredo, M., Fishbein, M., & Bath, A. (1993). Application of the theory of reasoned action to the National Park Services controlled burn policy. *Leisure Research, 25,* 263–280.

Brown, S., & Rhodes, R. (2006). Relationships among dog ownership and leisure-time walking in Western Canadian adults. *American Journal of Preventive Medicine, 30(2),* 121–136.

Brug, J., & Kremers, S. (2005). The transtheoretical model and stages of change: A critique. *Health Education Research 20(2),* 244–258.

Buckworth, J., & Dishman, R. K. (2002). *Exercise psychology.* Champaign, IL: Human Kinetics.

Canadian Fitness and Lifestyle Research Institute. (2010). Bulletin 02: Physical activity levels of Canadians. Retrieved from http://www.cflri.ca/document/bulletin-02-physical-activity-levels-canadians.

Cavallo, D. N., Tate, D. F., Ries, A. V., Brown, J. D., DeVellis, R. F., & Ammerman, A. S. (2012). A social media-based physical activity intervention. *American Journal of Preventative Medicine, 43*(5), 527–532. http://dx/doi/org/10.1016/j.amepre.2012.07.019.

Christensen, H. E., Westgarth, C., Bauman, A., Richards, E. A., Rhodes, R. E., Evenson, K., & Thorpe, R. J. (2012). Dog ownership and physical activity: A review of the evidence. *Journal of Physical Activity and Health, 10,* 750–759.

Chatzisarantis, N. L. D., & Hagger, M. S. (2005). Effects of a brief intervention based on the Theory of Planned Behavior on leisure-time physical activity participation. *Journal of Sport & Exercise Psychology, 27,* 470–487.

Cohen, D., Marsh, T., Williamson, S., Golinelli, D., & McKenzie, T. L. (2012). Impact and cost-effectiveness of family fitness zones: A natural environment in urban public parks. *Health Place, 18(1):* 39–45.

Colley, R. C., Garriguet, D., Janssen, I., Craig, C. L., Clarke, J., & Tremblay, M. S. (2011a). Physical activity of Canadian adults: Accelerometer results from the 2007 to 2009 Canadian Health Measures Survey. *Statistic Canada Health Reports, 22,* 1–8. Retrieved from http://www .statcan.gc.ca/pub/82-003-x/2011001/article/11396-eng.pdf.

Colley, R. C., Garriguet, D., Janssen, I., Craig, C. L., Clarke, J., & Tremblay, M. S. (2011b). Physical activity of Canadian children and youth: Accelerometer results from the 2007 to 2009 Canadian Health Measures Survey. *Statistic Canada Health Reports, 22,* 1–8. Retrieved from http://www.statcan.gc.ca/pub/82-003-x/2011001/article/11397-eng.pdf.

Craft, L. L., Vaniterson, E. H., Helenowski, I. B., Rademaker, A. W., & Courneya, K. S. (2011). Exercise effects on depressive symptoms in cancer survivors: A systematic review and meta-analysis. *Cancer, Epidemiology, Biomarkers, and Prevention, 21,* 3–19. doi: 10.1158/1055-9965.EPI-11-0634.

Cramp, A. G., & Brawley, L. R. (2006). Moms in motion: A group-mediated cognitive–behavioral physical activity intervention. *International Journal of Behavioral Nutrition and Physical Activity, 3(23),* 1–9.

Cress, M. E., Buchner, D. M., Prochaska, T., Rimmer, J., Brown, M., Macera, C., et al. (2005). Best practices for physical activity programs and behavior counseling in older adult populations. *Journal of Aging and Physical Activity, 13,* 61–74.

Davies, C. A., Spence, J. C., Vandelanotte, C., Caperchione, C. M., & Mummery, W. K. (2012), Meta-analysis of internet-delivered interventions to increase physical activity levels. *International Journal of Behavioral Nutrition and Physical Activity, 9,* 52.

Dawson, K. A., Tracey, J., & Berry, T. (2008). Evaluation of work place group and internet based physical activity interventions on psychological variables associated with exercise behaviour change. *Journal of Sports Science and Medicine, 7,* 537–543.

Deci, E. L., & Ryan, R. M. (2000). The "what" and "why" of goal pursuits: Human needs and the self-determination of behavior. *Psychological Inquiry, 11,* 227–268. doi: 10.1207/SI5327965PLI1104_01.

Dowd, A. J., Schmader, T., Sylvester, B. D., Jung, M. E., Zumbo, B. D., Martin, L. J., & Beauchamp, M. R. (2014). Effects of social belonging and task framing on exercise cognitions and behavior. *Journal of Sport & Exercise Psychology, 36,* 80–92.

Eng, T. R. (2001). The eHealth landscape: A terrain map of emerging information and communication technologies in health and health care. Princeton, NJ: Robert Wood Johnson Foundation.

Fortier, M. S., Duda, J. L., Guerin, E., & Teixeira, P. J. (2012). Promoting physical activity: Development and testing of self-determination theory-based interventions. *International Journal of Behavioral Nutrition and Physical Activity 9,* 20.

Fortier, M. S., Hogg, W., O'Sullivan, T. L., Blanchard, C., Reid, R. D., Sigal, R. J., Boulay, P., Doucet, E., Sweet, S. N., Bisson, E., & Beaulac, J. (2007). The Physical Activity Counselling (PAC) Randomized Trial: rationale, methods, and interventions. *Applied Physiology and Nutrition Metabolism, 32,* 1170–1185.

Fung, C., Kuhle, S., Lu, C., Purcell, M., Schwartz, M., Storey, K., & Veugelers, P. J. (2012). From "best practice" to "next practice": The effectiveness of school-based health promotion in improving healthy eating and physical activity and preventing childhood obesity. *International Journal of Behavioral Nutrition and Physical Activity, 9,* 27.

Gladwell, V. F., Brown, D. K., Wood, C., Sandercock, G. R., & Barton, J. L. (2013). The great outdoors: How a green exercise environment can benefit all. *Extreme Physiology and Medicine, 2,* 3.

Glasgow, R. E., Davidson, K. W., Dobkin, P. L., Ockene, J., & Spring, B. (2006). Practical behavioural trials to advance evidence-based behavioural medicine. *Annals of Behavioral Medicine, 31*(1), 5–13.

Gollwitzer, P. M. (1999). Implementation intentions: Strong effects of simple plans. *American Psychologist, 54,* 493–503.

Gunnell, K. E., Crocker, P. E., Mack, D. E., Wilson, P. M., & Zumbo, B. D. (2014). Goal contents, motivation, psychological need satisfaction, well-being and physical activity: A test of self-determination theory over 6 months. *Psychology of Sport and Exercise, 15,* 19–29.

Hoerster, K. D., Mayer, J. A., Sallis, J. F., Pizzi, N., Talley, S., Pichon, L. C., & Butler, D. A. (2011). Dog walking: Its association with physical activity guidelines adherence and its correlates. *Preventive Medicine, 52,* 33–38.

Kahn, E. B., Ramsey, L. T., Brownson, R. C., Heath, G. W., Howze, E. H., Powell, K. E., Stone, E. J., Rajab, M. W., Corso, P. C., & Task Force on Community Preventive Services. (2002). The effectiveness of interventions to increase physical activity: A systematic review. *American Journal of Preventive Medicine, 22*(4S), 73–107.

Katzmarzyk, P. T., Gledhill, N., & Shepard, R. J. (2000). The economic burden of physical inactivity in Canada. *Canadian Medical Association Journal, 163,* 1435–1440.

LeBlanc, A. G., Chaput, J.-P., McFarlane, A., Colley, R. C., Thivel, D., Biddle, S. J. H., & Tremblay, M. S. (2013). Active video games and health indicators in children and youth: A systematic review. *PLOS One, 8,* E65351.

Lox, C. L., Martin Ginis, K. A., & Petruzello, S. J. (2006). *The psychology of exercise: Integrating theory and practice* (2nd ed.). Scottsdale, AZ: Holcomb Hathaway Publishers.

Maddux, J. E., & Dawson, K. A. (2014). Predicting and changing exercise behavior: Bridging the information–intention–behavior gap. In A. R. Gomes, R. Resende, & A. Albuquerque (Eds.) (Volume 2), *Functioning from a multidimensional perspective: Promoting healthy lifestyles* (pp. 97–120). NY: Nova Science Publishing.

Maddux, J. E., & Dawson, K. A. (in press). Promoting physical fitness in adulthood: A focus on exercise. To appear in M. Bloom & T. Gullotta (Eds.), *Encyclopedia of primary prevention and health promotion* (2nd ed.). New York: Springer.

Maher, C. A., Lewis, L. K., Ferrer, K., Marshall, S., Bourdeauhuij, I. D., & Vandelanotte, C. (2014). Are health behaviour change interventions that use online social networks effective? A systemic review. *Journal of Medical Internet Research, 16*(2). doi: 10.2196/jmir.2952.

Martens, M. P., Buscemi, J., Smith, A. E., & Murphy, J. G. (2012). The short-term efficacy of a brief motivational intervention designed to increase physical activity among college students. *Journal of Physical Activity and Health, 9,* 525–532.

Miller, W. R., & Rollnick, S. (2012). Meeting in the middle: Motivational interviewing and self-determination theory. *International Journal of Behavioral Nutrition and Physical Activity, 9,* 25. doi: 10.1186/1479-5868-9-25.

Miller, W. R., & Rollnick, S. (2013). *Motivational interviewing: Helping people change* (3rd ed). New York: Guilford Press.

Ng, J. Y. Y., Ntoumanis, N., Thogersen-Ntoumani, C., Deci, E. L., Ryan, R. M., Duda, J. L., & Williams, G. C. (2012). Self-determination theory applied to health contexts: A meta-analysis. *Perspectives on Psychological Science, 7:* 325. doi: 10.1177/1745691612447309.

Painter, J. E., Borba, C. P. C., Hynes, M., Mays, D., & Glanz, K. (2008). The use of theory in health behavior research from 2000–2005: A systematic review. *Annals of Behavioral Medicine, 35*, 358–362. doi: 10.1007/s12160-008-9042-y.

Parschau, L., Barz, M., Richert, J., Knoll, N., & Lippke, S. (2014). Physical activity among adults with obesity: Testing the health action process approach. *Rehabilitation Psychology, 59*(1), 42–49.

Parschau, L., Richert, J., Koring, M., Ernsting, A., Lippke, S., & Schwarzer, R. (2012). Changes in social–cognitive variables are associated with stage transitions in physical activity. *Health Education Research, 27*(1), 129–140.

Prochaska, J. O., DiClemente, C. C., & Norcross, J. C. (1992). In search of how people change: Applications to addictive behaviours. *American Psychologist, 47*, 1102–1114.

Rhodes, R. E., Murray, H., Temple, V., Tuokko, H., & Warf Higgins, J. (2012). Pilot study of a dog walking randomized intervention: Effects of a focus on canine exercise. *Preventive Medicine, 54*, 309–312. doi: 10.1016/j.ypmed2012.02.014.

Roult, R., Adjizian, J. M., Lefebvre, S., & Lapierre, L. (2014). The mobilizing effects and health benefits of proximity sport facilities: Urban and environmental analysis of the Bleu, Blanc, Bouge project and Montreal North's outdoor rink. *Sport in Society, 17*(1), 68–88. doi.org/10.10 80/1730437.2013.828698.

Saelens, B. E., & Handy, S. L. (2008). Built environment correlates of walking: A review. *Medicine and Science and Sports and Exercise, 40*(7Suppl); S550–S566. doi: 10.1249/MSS.0b013e31817c67a4.

Sallis, J. F., & Owen, N. (1999). *Physical activity & behavioural medicine*. Thousand Oaks, CA: Sage Publications.

Schwarzer, R. (2008). Modeling health behavior change: How to predict and modify the adoption and maintenance of health behaviors. *Applied Psychology: An international review, 57*(1), 1–29. doi: 10.1111/j.1464-0597.2007.00325.x.

Statistics Canada. (2006). Deaths. Catalogue No. 84F0211X. Ottawa, Canada: Ministry of Industry. Retrieved from http://www5.statcan.gc.ca/olc-cel/olc.action?objId=84F0211X&objType=2& lang=en&limit=0.

Statistics Canada (2013, Oct. 28). Individual internet use and e-commerce, 2012. Retrieved from http://www.statcan.gc.ca/daily-quotidien/131028/dq131028a-eng.htm.

Symons Downs, D., & Hausenblas, H. A. (2005). The theories of reasoned action and planned behaviour applied to exercise: A meta-analytic update. *Journal of Physical Activity and Health, 2*, 76–97.

Thompson, C. J., Boddy, K., Stein, K., Whear, R., Barton, J., & Depledge, M. H. (2011). Does participating in physical activity in outdoor natural environments have a greater effect on physical and mental wellbeing than physical activity indoors? A systematic review. *Environmental Science & Technology, 45*(5), 1761–1772.

Vandelanotte, C., Spathonis, K. M., Eakin, E. G., & Owen, N. (2007). Website-delivered physical activity interventions: A review of the literature. *American Journal of Preventive Medicine, 33*(1), 54–64.

Verthoef, M., Love, E., & Rose, M. (1992). Women's social roles and their exercise participation. *Women's Health, 19*, 15–29.

Verheijden Klompstra, L., Jaarsoma, T., & Strömberg, A. (2013). Exergaming in older adults: A scoping review and implementation potential for patients with heart failure. *European Journal of Cardiovascular Nursing*. doi: 10.1177/1474515113512203.

Weber Buchholz, S., Wilbur, J., Ingram, D, & Fogg, L. (2013). Physical activity text messaging interventions in adults: A systematic review. *Worldviews on Evidence-Based Nursing, 10*, 163–173.

Williams, S. L., & French, D. P. (2011). What are the most effective intervention techniques for changing physical activity self-efficacy and physical activity behaviour—and are they the same? *Health Education Research, 26*(2), 308–322.

Glossary

Chapter 1: Introducing Sport and Exercise Psychology

Dependent variable (DV): A non-manipulated variable (outcome) that is expected to change as a result of manipulating the independent variable.

Emic focus: Captures the participant's viewpoint in a particular setting.

Ethics: Concerned with matters of right and wrong as they relate to human behaviour.

Independent variable (IV): The manipulated variable (cause) that produces a change in the dependent variable.

Positive psychology: An area of psychology concerned primarily with understanding the processes that enable people and groups to thrive.

Psychologist: A term that is defined and regulated by provincial and territorial boards in Canada.

Qualitative inquiry: Often assumes that reality is constructed by the person in a particular situation or context.

Quantitative inquiry: Focuses on quantifying or counting the amount of a particular variable or set of variables.

Research hypotheses: Educated guesses about the nature of the relationships among scientific constructs given specific conditions.

Scientific constructs: Specifically defined terms that have been created for a scientific purpose.

Sport and exercise psychology: An interdisciplinary scientific and applied field that embraces the integration of sport science and psychological knowledge.

Theory: Specifies relationships across a number of scientific constructs and attempts to explain phenomena across a number of different times, contexts, and people.

Variable: A scientific construct that can be assigned a specific value to be counted.

Chapter 2: Personality in Sport and Exercise

Activity: Trait involving a general tendency for a fast lifestyle, high energy, fast talking, and keeping busy.

Agreeableness: Trait involving general compliance and positive approach toward others.

Competitiveness: Desire to engage in and strive for success.

Conscientiousness: Trait comprising striving for achievement and self-discipline.

Disposition: Broad, pervasive, encompassing ways of relating to particular types of people or situations.

Ethical principles: Guidelines that shape professional judgment and behaviour.

Evaluative concerns perfectionism: Reflects aspects of the negative social evaluation including excessive self-criticism, concerns over mistakes, and doubts about actions.

Extraversion: Trait involving level of assertiveness and energetic approach to the world.

Harmonious passion: Engaging in an activity as part of one's identity and for the pleasure of the activity.

Humanistic psychology: Psychological approach that focuses on personal responsibility, human growth, personal striving, and individual dignity.

Industriousness–ambition: Trait comprising aspects of achievement–striving and self-discipline.

Interactionist approach: Interplay between a person and the environment that determines specific behaviours of the individual.

Mental toughness: Personal characteristics that allow individuals to cope with stress and anxiety while remaining focused on competition demands.

Neuroticism: Trait comprising feelings of tension and nervousness.

Observational learning (modelling): Learning through observing others' behaviours.

Obsessive passion: Involves a more rigid and uncontrolled urge to engage in activities because of external control or feelings of guilt.

Openness to experience: Trait including level of curiosity, the opposite of being closed-minded.

Personal standards perfectionism: Refers to establishing high personal performance standards and self-oriented achievement striving.

Personality: The overall organization of psychological characteristics—thinking, feeling, and behaving—that differentiates us from others and leads us to act consistently across time and situations.

Psychological states: Momentary feelings and thoughts that change depending on the situation and time.

Risk taking: Narrowing of the margin of safety, both physically and psychologically.

Self-actualization: An individual's attempt to be the best he or she can be or a desire to fulfill one's potential.

Self-efficacy: Belief in one's capacities to achieve a specific goal or outcome.

Sensation (stimulus) seeking: Seeking of varied, novel, complex, and intense sensations and experiences, and the willingness to take multiple risks for the sake of such experiences.

Social learning theory: Theory that suggests people are active agents in shaping their behaviours, influenced by their inner drives and environments.

Trait: A relatively stable characteristic or quality that may represent a portion of one's personality; a quality used to explain an individual's behaviour across time and situations.

Type A personality: Blend of ambition, low patience, competitiveness, high organization, and hostility with agitated behaviour patterns.

Chapter 3: Motivation and Behavioural Change

Achievement goal orientation: A theory of motivation that focuses on differences in how individuals evaluate competence and define success and failure.

Action: A stage of change in which individuals have begun exercising in the past six months.

Amotivation: The absence of motivation.

Approach goals: An individual is focused on approaching a positive outcome (e.g., success).

Attitude: Positive or negative evaluations of engaging in a behaviour.

Autonomy: The feeling that one has choice and is in control of one's behaviour.

Autonomy support: An interpersonal style associated with the provision of choices and options.

Avoidance goals: An individual is focused on avoiding a negative outcome (e.g., failure).

Behavioural approach: An approach to understanding motivated behaviour that focuses on conditioning, or learning from the environment.

Behavioural beliefs: Consideration of the consequences of engaging in a behaviour and evaluation of these consequences.

Behavioural capacity: Behaviour is dependent on the individual's knowledge and skills.

Cognitive approach: An approach to understanding motivated behaviour that emphasizes the role of thought patterns and cognitive habits.

Cognitive–behavioural approaches: Approaches to understanding motivated behaviour that outline the reciprocal influence between cognitions and behaviour.

Competence: Feeling effective and capable when undertaking challenging tasks.

Contemplation: A stage of change in which individuals are considering exercising in the next six months.

Control beliefs: Perceived barriers and facilitators of engaging in a behaviour.

Decisional balance: Advantages and disadvantages of behavioural change.

Ego goal orientation: Performance evaluations are based on comparisons with others as the determinant of competence.

External regulation: Activities are performed to fulfill an external demand, achieve a reward, or avoid punishment.

Goals: Ambitions that direct people's behaviour.

Identified regulation: Physical activity participation is linked to important and valued goals.

Integrated regulation: Physical activity participation is consistent with a person's identity.

Intention: A person's readiness to perform a behaviour.

Intrinsic regulation: Activity is undertaken because it is enjoyable, interesting, stimulating, or self-rewarding.

Introjected regulation: Activity is engaged in to avoid negative emotions.

Involvement: An interpersonal style whereby individuals feel others are invested in their health and well-being.

Maintenance: A stage of change in which individuals exercise and have done so for more than six months.

Mastery experience: Past performance success and failure for similar behaviours influence self-efficacy.

Motivation: The internal processes such as your needs, thoughts, and emotions that give your behaviour energy and direction.

Normative beliefs: Perceptions of the values and importance that significant others place on behavioural engagement.

Observational learning: Behaviour is learned and acquired by watching the actions and outcomes of others' behaviours.

Outcome expectancies: Expectations that a valuable outcome will follow a given behaviour.

Outcome expectations: Behaviour is a function of its expected positive and negative consequences.

Perceived behavioural control: The extent to which behaviour is volitional.

Physiological and affective states: Physical and emotional cues associated with performance and behaviour.

Precontemplation: A stage of change in which individuals do not consider exercising in the next six months.

Preparation: A stage of change in which individuals have taken small steps toward becoming more physically active.

Processes of change: Strategies that individuals use to progress through the stages of change.

Reciprocal determinism: Three sets of influences—person, environment, and behaviour—all interact to influence one another.

Relatedness: Feeling meaningful connections with others in environments such as exercise.

Self-determination theory: A global theory of human motivation and development.

Self-efficacy: Beliefs in one's capabilities to organize and execute the course of action required to produce given attainments.

Self-regulation: Behaviour is self-directed and is initiated, monitored, and evaluated by the individual in a way that is consistent with accomplishing personal goals.

Social cognitive theory: The personal, behavioural, and environmental factors that affect and determine behaviour.

Social persuasion: Verbal and nonverbal feedback from significant knowledgeable others.

Structure: An interpersonal style associated with the provision of feedback and the clarification of expectations.

Subjective norms: Perceived social pressures to perform a behaviour from personal and/or environmental sources.

Task goal orientation: Focuses on past performance or knowledge as the origin of perceptions of competence.

Theory of planned behaviour: Personal and social factors influencing intention to engage in a behaviour.

Vicarious experience: Modelled behaviours are associated with the development and change in self-efficacy.

Chapter 4: Stress, Emotion, and Coping in Sport and Exercise

Acute stressors: Stressors that occur within a short period of time, and their onset is much more sudden.

Avoidance coping: Coping efforts in which athletes attempt to remove themselves from the stressful situation.

Bad news coping: Coping attempts that are rigid, disorganized, and destructive.

Challenge appraisal: An appraisal that although there are obstacles in the way, they can be overcome.

Chronic stressors: Stressors that occur over a long period of time.

Competitive stressors: Stressors that are experienced prior to, during, or immediately following competition.

Coping: Cognitive and behavioural efforts to manage specific external or internal demands (and conflicts between them) that are appraised as taxing or exceeding the resources of the person.

Coping effectiveness: A decision about whether or not a coping strategy helped to deal with the problem and/or to deal with any distress associated with the problem.

Disengagement-oriented coping: Coping strategies to disengage from the process of trying to make progress on a personal goal.

Distraction-oriented coping: Coping strategies to focus on internal and external stimuli that are unrelated to the stressful situation.

Emotion regulation: The processes by which individuals influence which emotions they have, when they have them, and how they experience and express these emotions.

Emotion-focused coping: Coping efforts to change the way a situation is attended to or interpreted, to deal with the emotions that arise during the situation.

Expected stressors: Stressors that an athlete plans or prepares for.

Good news coping: Coping attempts that are organized, flexible, and constructive.

Harm/loss appraisal: An evaluation of a situation in which psychological damage has already been done and the loss is irrevocable.

Management skills: Behaviours that are routine but that still help the individual to avoid problems and help prevent stress from happening in the first place.

Non-competitive stressors: Stressors that are related to sport but are not directly part of an actual competition performance.

Organizational stressors: Environmental demands associated primarily and directly with the organization within which an individual is operating.

Primary appraisal: An evaluation of what is at stake for a person in a situation.

Problem-focused coping: Coping efforts that help people change the actual situation.

Secondary appraisal: An evaluation of what can be done in the situation, which depends on an individual's available resources, level of perceived control, and expectations regarding what is likely to occur in the future.

Self-compassion: The desire to be moved by one's own suffering, as well as a desire to alleviate that suffering. It involves three components: self-kindness, common humanity, and mindfulness.

Self-presentation: The process by which individuals attempt to control the impressions others form of them (also referred to as impression management).

Stress: An experience that is produced through a person–situation relationship that is perceived as taxing or exceeding the person's resources.

Stress response: Physiological, cognitive, affective, and behavioural reactions when we are faced with heavy demands.

Stressors: External events, forces, and situations that have the potential to be interpreted as stressful.

Task-oriented coping: Coping strategies aimed at dealing directly with the source of stress and its resulting thoughts and emotions.

Threat appraisal: An appraisal of a situation where an individual anticipates harm might occur or is likely to occur.

Unexpected stressors: Stressors that are not anticipated and cannot be prepared for.

Chapter 5: Anxiety in Sport and Exercise

Anxiety: A negative emotion that is elicited following an appraisal of a situation or event.

Arousal: Physiological and psychological activation that varies on a continuum from deep sleep to peak activation (or frenzy).

Choking: An acute, significant decrement in performance that occurs in situations of high pressure or anxiety.

Cognitive anxiety: Mental component of anxiety referring to worries and concerns.

Competitive anxiety: A sub-type of social anxiety that occurs in competitive sport situations, and results from worry about their body, performance, or skills being evaluated negatively by others.

Competitive trait anxiety: The tendency for athletes to experience anxiety during competitive sport situations.

Reinvesting: Consciously controlling physical movements, even for well-learned tasks, rather than performing them automatically.

Self-handicapping: Behaviours that are used in performance settings such as sport or exercise, in order to excuse any failures that may occur in advance.

Self-presentation: The process by which people attempt to monitor and control the impressions that other people form of them.

Self-presentational efficacy: Confidence in one's ability to successfully present a desired image to others.

Social anxiety: A specific sub-type of anxiety that occurs when people believe they will receive a negative evaluation from others.

Social physique anxiety: A specific sub-type of social anxiety that occurs when people are worried about receiving a negative evaluation about their body from others.

Somatic anxiety: Physical component of anxiety referring to perceptions of body states, such as a racing heart or butterflies in the stomach.

State anxiety: Anxiety that is experienced at a particular moment in time, and can change from moment to moment.

Trait anxiety: A general predisposition to perceive a variety of situations as threatening.

Chapter 6: Aggression and Moral Behaviour in Sport

Aggression: Any overt verbal or physical act that is intended to injure another living organism either psychologically or physically.

Antisocial behaviour: A behaviour that is intended to harm or disadvantage another individual or team.

Assertive behaviour: Actions that are forceful, vigorous, and legitimate, performed by an individual who does not intend to harm another living being.

Bullying: Imbalance of power between peers where the one who is more powerful repeatedly attacks the less powerful with the intention to harm.

Catharsis: To purge or cleanse the self of aggressive feelings; typically, venting of aggressive tendencies through socially acceptable means.

Collective efficacy for aggression: A team's perception of their ability to use aggressive behaviour as a tactic or strategy.

Deindividuation: The process occurring when an individual feels less identifiable by others.

Fan identification: Extent to which fans feel psychologically connected to a team.

Hazing: Any potentially humiliating, degrading, abusive, or dangerous activity expected of an individual to belong to a group, regardless of their willingness to participate.

Hostile aggression: Aggressive acts undertaken for the purpose of harming or injuring the victim.

Instrumental aggression: Aggressive acts serving as a means to a particular goal—such as winning, money, or prestige—in which injury to the opponent is involved. This type of injury is impersonal and designed to limit the effectiveness of the opponent.

Moral behaviour: The carrying out of an action that is deemed right or wrong.

Moral development: The process in which an individual develops the capacity to reason morally.

Prosocial behaviour: A behaviour that is intended to assist or benefit another individual or team.

Self-presentation: The way individuals present themselves (i.e., behave, dress) in social situations.

Team norms: Standards for the behaviour that is expected of members of the group.

Violent behaviour: An extreme act of physical aggression that bears no direct relationship to the competitive goals of sport, and relates to incidents of uncontrolled aggression outside the rules of sport.

Chapter 7: Sport Psychology Interventions

Association: Turning focus inward and toward bodily sensation (e.g., breathing, muscle soreness).

Attention: A multidimensional construct having at least two components (limited resources and selectivity).

Attention simulation training: Training in which athletes replicate the kinds of attention-demanding situations they find themselves in during competition.

Attentional cues: Words and actions that direct the athlete's attention.

Autogenic training: Training that focuses on feelings associated with limbs and muscles of the body.

Cognitive general imagery: Images of strategies, game plans, or routines.

Cognitive specific imagery: Images of specific sport skills.

Dissociation: Focusing outward and away from the body (e.g., a favourite song, a relaxing setting).

Event occlusion: The process of examining which characteristics of the performance people use to make a correct response.

Goal: A target or objective that people strive to attain.

Goal setting: The practice of establishing desirable objectives for one's actions.

Imagery: An experience that mimics real experience. It differs from dreams in that we are awake and conscious when we form an image.

Instructional self-talk: The overt or covert speech that individuals use for skill development, skill execution, strategy development, and general performance improvement.

Meditation: A relaxation technique that allows for deep relaxation of the mind which, in turn, relaxes the body.

Motivational general imagery: Images relating to physiological arousal levels and emotions.

Motivational general–arousal: Imagery associated with arousal and stress.

Motivational general–mastery: Imagery associated with the notion of being mentally tough, in control, and self-confident.

Motivational self-talk: The overt or covert speech that individuals use for mastery, arousal control, and drive.

Motivational specific imagery: Images related to an individual's goals.

Outcome goals: Goals that focus on social comparison and competitive results.

Performance goals: Goals that focus on improvement and attainment of personal performance standards.

Performance profiling: A flexible assessment tool that allows for the identification of athletes' performance related strengths and weaknesses.

Performance routines: A set sequence of thoughts and actions before the performance of key skills.

Process goals: Goals that focus on specific behaviours in which athletes must engage throughout a performance.

Progressive relaxation: The systematic tensing and relaxing of specific muscles in a predetermined order.

Psyching up strategies: Strategies used to increase arousal levels.

Psychological skill training: A program or intervention that entails a structured and consistent practice of psychological skills and generally has three distinct phases (education, acquisition, and practice).

Self-talk: Verbalizations or statements that are addressed to the self, are multidimensional in nature and dynamic, have interpretive elements associated with the content of the self-statements employed, and serve at least two functions, instructional and motivational.

Temporal occlusion: The process of examining the amount of time people take to select the information they need in order to respond.

Chapter 8: Leadership in Sport and Exercise

Athlete leader: A team member, acting in a formal or informal capacity, who guides and influences other team members toward a common objective.

Contingency model: A model of leadership which suggests that the effectiveness of specific leadership styles depends (is contingent) upon how much control the leader has over that situation (i.e., situational control).

Followership: The way in which followers interact with and respond to a leader.

Full range model of leadership: A leadership model that includes a spectrum of leadership behaviours ranging from ineffective to highly effective.

Laissez-faire leadership: A style of leadership that is characterized by indifference, absence, and a hesitancy to make any substantive decisions.

Leadership scale for sports (LSS): A scale designed to assess five leadership behaviours/dimensions.

Meta-analysis: A powerful statistical technique that involves combining the results of multiple studies to examine the overall effect of a variable (or intervention) in relation to an outcome of interest to the researcher.

Multidimensional model of leadership (MML): A complex model of leadership that was specifically designed to examine leadership behaviours in the context of sport, and their effects in relation to athlete satisfaction and team performance.

Path–goal theory: A model of leadership which suggests that effective leadership is dependent on the match between the situation and the behaviours utilized by a leader in that situation.

Relationship-oriented leadership: A leadership style concerned with maximizing the quality of relationships among those being led.

Task-oriented leadership: A leadership style that involves the pursuit of goal and performance attainment.

Transactional leadership: A leadership style that is characterized by exchanges between the leader and the person being led whereby the leader looks to make use of rewards and recognition as well as compliance-maximizing behaviours to get that other person to accede to the leader's requests.

Transformational leadership: A leadership style that involves going beyond one's own self-interests with the purpose of empowering, inspiring, and giving those being led the confidence to achieve a higher level of functioning.

Chapter 9: Group Cohesion in Sport and Exercise

Assembly effect: Variations in group behaviour that are a result of the particular combinations of individuals in the group.

Autocratic style: A decision style that involves independent decision-making and stresses personal authority on the part of the leader.

Collective efficacy: A group's shared perception of the group's capabilities to succeed at a given task.

Decision style: The degree to which a leader allows participation by subordinates in decision-making.

Democratic style: A decision style that allows participation by team members in joint decision-making with the leader.

Group dynamics: The study of the nature of groups and their development, and the interrelationships of groups with individuals, other groups, and larger institutions.

Groupthink: A mode of thinking that people engage in when the members of a cohesive group so strongly desire a unanimous decision that this overrides their motivation to realistically evaluate other possible options.

Hazing: Using harassment, abuse, or humiliation as a way of initiating new members to a group.

Majority rule: A rule of decision-making in groups based on the principles of equal participation and equal power for all members.

Mediators: Mechanisms that account for the effect of one variable on another variable.

Positive feedback: Behaviours by a coach that reinforce an athlete by recognizing and rewarding strong performance.

Psychological momentum: A perception on the part of team members that the team is progressing toward its goal.

Self-handicapping: Using strategies that protect one's self-esteem by providing excuses for forthcoming events.

Social loafing: The reduction in individual effort when individuals work collectively compared to when they work alone.

Social support: Leader behaviours that are characterized by a concern for the welfare of the individual athletes, the fostering of a positive group atmosphere, and warm relationships with team members.

Sociograms: Diagrams of the relationships among group members.

Sociometry: Research technique that graphs and mathematically summarizes patterns of intermember relationships.

Team building: Programs promoting an increased sense of unity and cohesiveness within a team.

Training and instruction: Behaviours by the coach that are geared to improving team members' performance.

Transformational leadership: A method of leadership where the leader builds relationships with followers through inspirational exchanges that serve to increase the motivation, confidence, and satisfaction of followers beyond normal expectations.

Chapter 10: Youth Involvement and Positive Development in Sport

Coaching effectiveness: The consistent application of integrated professional, interpersonal, and intrapersonal knowledge to improve athletes' competence, confidence, connection, and character in specific coaching contexts.

Companionship: Network of relationships that enable an individual to engage positively in various activities.

Constructive leisure activities: Activities that require sustained effort toward the achievement of a clear goal.

Decompetition: Competitive situations that occur when athletes seek to demonstrate their superiority over opponents.

Deliberate play: Sport activities designed to maximize enjoyment, regulated by flexible rules.

Deliberate practice: Activities that require effort, generate no immediate rewards, and are motivated by the goal of improving performance.

Developmental assets: Social and psychological "building blocks" for human development; include internal and external assets.

Early specialization: Participation in one sport on a year-round basis, involving high amounts of deliberate practice and low amounts of deliberate play.

Emotional support: Comforting gestures during time of stress and anxiety.

External assets: Positive developmental experiences resulting from the environment or the community.

Informational support: Provision of advice or guidance in problematic situations.

Initiative: The ability to be motivated from within and to direct attention and effort toward a challenging goal over time.

Internal assets: Positive developmental experiences resulting from internalized skills and competencies.

Moderately involved parents: Parents who show adequate levels of involvement.

Over-involved parents: Parents who show excessive amounts of involvement.

Parental expectations: Parents' sets of beliefs regarding their children's behaviours.

Parental modelling: Parents serving as a behavioural or moral example to their children.

Parental support: Involves parents' facilitation of children's self-esteem, competence, and achievement; can include emotional, informational, tangible, and companionship (network) support.

Personal development: Improvements in self-awareness and identity.

Positive youth development: A strengths-based view of children and adolescents.

Relaxed leisure activities: Activities that are enjoyable but not demanding in terms of effort.

Sport skills: Learned abilities related to sport participation and performance.

Tangible support: Provision of concrete assistance and resources to help cope with events.

True competition: Competitive situations that serve the interests of all participants and focus their effort and concentration towards a particular goal.

Under-involved parents: Parents who show lack of involvement.

Chapter 11: Coaching Psychology

Athlete-centred coaching: A recently developed and still understudied coaching strategy that is designed to enhance youth growth and development by building trusting relationships with athletes and using positive reinforcement and open communication.

Closeness: Aspect of the coach–athlete relationship that deals with affective elements such as trust and respect.

Coaching Association of Canada: A not-for-profit organization that governs the coaching profession in Canada.

Coaching efficacy: The belief of a coach that he/she can effectively perform various coaching duties.

Coaching model: Provides a systematic view of coaching by broadly capturing the most influential factors and emphasizing the relationships among these factors.

Coaching science: Encompasses research on all aspects of coaching.

Coaching vision: Coaches' long-term goals for their programs.

Commitment: Aspect of the coach–athlete relationship that deals with intention to maintain an athletic relationship.

Complementarity: Aspect of the coach–athlete relationship that deals with cooperative interactions between them.

Co-orientation: Aspect of the coach–athlete relationship that deals with the degree of common ground in their relationship.

Mentoring: The assistance of more experienced and well-respected colleagues who ensure growth and development in an environment that is designed to minimize errors and to build knowledge and confidence.

Mission statement: A written statement that gives a team direction for the upcoming year.

Multidimensional model of leadership: A linear model comprising antecedents, leader behaviours, and consequences.

National Coaching Certification Program: A knowledge- and course-based program run by the Coaching Association of Canada.

Pre-game pep talk: Words used to fire up a team prior to competition.

Chapter 12: Aging and Involvement in Sport and Physical Activity

Compensation theory: A theory of aging based on the notion that age-related losses in one area can be offset by improvements in another area.

Disidentification: Recon-ceptualizing your self-image to remove the value associated with a domain, thereby reducing the impact of negative performance.

Dose–response relationship: In simple terms, refers to the change in an outcome caused by differing doses of a stressor. With respect to exercise, it refers to the strong positive relationship between doses of exercise and positive health effects.

Implicit priming: A technique used to activate or reinforce a belief without conscious awareness.

Masters athletes: Athletes who are aged 30 years or older competing at the Masters level of competition.

Morbidity: The quality or state of being morbid or unhealthful.

Mortality: Frequency of number of deaths in proportion to a population.

Quality of life: A multidimensional construct referring to an overall sense of well-being with a strong relation to a person's health perceptions and ability to function; includes aspects of physical and mental health and functioning, and social support.

Sarcopenia: A deficiency in the amount of skeletal muscle tissue.

Selective maintenance model: A model of aging emphasizing the role of high quality training and practice in acquiring and maintaining the domain-specific characteristics required for high levels of skill.

Self-efficacy: A person's belief about his or her capacity to produce a designated level of performance.

Socioeconomic status: The relative position of a family on a societal hierarchy based on access to, or control over, wealth, prestige, and power.

Stereotypes: Popularly held beliefs (which do not take into account individual differences) about a type of person or a group of people.

Chapter 13: Physical Activity and Mental Health

Anxiety disorders: A broad umbrella for a range of disorders such as panic disorder, generalized anxiety disorder, obsessive-compulsive disorder, and post-traumatic stress disorder.

Brain derived neurotrophic factor (BDNF): A chemical that plays an important role in various aspects of developmental and adult brain plasticity.

Depression: A mood disorder characterized by a depressed/sad mood, loss of interest, reduced or excessive sleep, loss of energy, anhedonia, impaired concentration, slowed thoughts and motor activity, low motivation, and suicidal thoughts over an extended period of time.

Endorphin: A general classification label for beta-endorphin. This important body chemical is a peptide and mimics the chemical structure of morphine.

Exercise: A subset of physical activity in which the activity is structured, often supervised and undertaken with the aim of maintaining or improving physical fitness or health.

Mental health: A state of well-being in which the individual realizes personal potential, can cope with the normal stresses of life, can work productively and fruitfully, and is able to make a contribution to the community.

Mental illness: Any health condition characterized by alterations in thinking, mood, or behaviour (or some combination thereof) associated with distress and/or impaired functioning.

Meta-analyses: The use of statistical methods to aggregate results of individual studies.

Metabolic equivalent (MET): The ratio of an individual's working metabolic rate relative to their baseline metabolic rate, used to express the intensity of different physical activities.

Monoamines: Neurotransmitters believed to be involved in the pathogenesis of several mental disorders and include dopamine, norepinephrine, and serotonin.

Physical activity: Any movement of the body that results in energy expenditure above that of resting level.

Physical disabilities: Disabilities is an umbrella term encompassing impairments, activity limitations, and participation restrictions.

Physical inactivity: Not achieving physical activity guidelines (i.e., 150 minutes of physical activity per week and/or 75 minutes of vigorous physical activity per week according to the Canadian Physical Activity Guidelines).

Positive activated affect: A subjective mental state of positive energy and engagement.

Randomized controlled trial: The most rigorous study of determining whether a cause–effect relation exists between treatment and outcome. Participants are randomly assigned to separate groups that compare different treatments.

Schizophrenia: A serious mental illness in which individuals are affected by delusions (fixed false beliefs), hallucinations (sensory experiences, such as hearing voices talking about them when there is no one there), social withdrawal, and disturbed thinking.

Sedentary behaviour: Any waking behaviour characterized by an energy expenditure of ≤1.5 METs while in a sitting or reclining posture.

Self-esteem: A personal judgment of worthiness that reflects the degree to which an individual feels positive about him- or herself.

Chapter 14: Body Image in Sport and Exercise

Actual:ideal discrepancy: Occurs when people perceive that their current states are discrepant from their ideal states.

Actual:ought discrepancy: Occurs when individuals perceive that their current states are discrepant from the states they feel they should be.

Affective dimension of body image: Body image dimension defined as body-related feelings and emotions that an individual experiences.

Anorexia nervosa: Mental disorder defined by considerable food restriction brought about by a refusal to maintain a healthy body weight, heightened fear of gaining weight, and unrealistic perception of current body weight.

Authentic pride: A type of pride focused on achievement and behaviour.

Behavioural dimension of body image: Body image dimension related to the choices and actions people take based on the perceptions, feelings, thoughts, and cognitions they have about their body sizes, shapes, weights, and functions.

Binge eating disorder: Compulsive and excessive overeating without purging.

Body cathexis: People's subjective evaluations outlined by a degree of satisfaction or dissatisfaction with their bodies.

Body dysmorphia: Overexaggerated and inaccurate perceptions of flaws related to body parts and characteristics.

Body dysmorphic disorder: A recognized disorder reflecting a preoccupation with an imagined defect in appearance.

Body esteem: Self-evaluations of one's body and/or appearance.

Body image: A multidimensional construct that reflects a person's feelings, perceptions, thoughts, cognitions, and behaviours related to his/her body appearance and function.

Body image boundaries: An individual's perception of meaning attributed to specific body parts, overall body awareness, and distortions in body perception.

Body image investment: An individual's certain beliefs or assumptions about the importance, meaning, and influence of appearance in his or her life.

Body schema: A representation of the position and configuration of the body.

Body-related envy: A negative emotion that occurs when a person feels they lack another person's superior quality and either desires to have it or wishes the other(s) lacked it.

Body-related guilt: A negative emotion attributed to a failure of completing an action or behaviour.

Body-related pride: A positive emotion that results from an individual feeling satisfied with his/her body-related behaviour or physical attributes.

Body-related shame: A negative emotion that is focused on the self.

Bulimia nervosa: Mental disorder characterized by recurrent binge eating and purging through self-induced vomiting, laxative/diuretic use, and/or excessive exercise.

Cognitive dimension of body image: Body image dimension reflecting an individual's thoughts, beliefs, and evaluations of his/her body appearance and function.

Cognitive dissonance training: A program involving arguing against body ideals in a way that is incongruent with their personal beliefs.

Cognitive–behavioural therapy: Problem-based and action oriented approach used to address dysfunctional emotions, and maladaptive behaviours and cognitions.

Cortisol: A stress hormone.

Downward social comparison: Comparing oneself to individuals who are worse off on attributes of value.

Drive for muscularity: Reflects the pursuit of cultural and sex explicit muscular body shape ideals.

Eating disorders: Recognized mental disorders that are defined as abnormal eating habits that result in insufficient or excessive consumption of food.

Hubristic pride: A type of pride focused on grandiose attributes of the self.

Ideal self: A self-reflection characterized by one's hopes and aspirations of what people what to be.

Impression construction: Creating an image that one wishes to convey to others along with the particular strategies individuals use to create this impression.

Impression motivation: How motivated individuals are to control how they are perceived by others.

Muscle dysmorphia: A specified condition within body dysmorphic disorder represented by a chronic preoccupation with insufficient muscularity and inadequate muscle mass.

Normative discontent: Concept that most women experience weight and appearance dissatisfaction.

Ought self: A self-reflection characterized by one's hopes and aspirations of what people think they should be.

Perceptual dimension of body image: Body image dimension defined by the mental representation and/or reflections that an individual has of his/her body appearance and function.

Positive psychological perspectives: Health promotion framework suggesting that removing negative/maladaptive characteristics but not teaching positive/adaptive characteristics will lead to mental health characterized by a lack of pathology but also absence of vitality.

Self-presentation efficacy: Reflects the perceived probability of successfully conveying one's desired impressions to others. Driven by self-efficacy beliefs: self-presentational efficacy expectancy, self-presentational outcome expectancy, and self-presentational outcome value.

Self-presentation: Motivation and attempts to control how one appears to the group; also called impression management.

Self-presentational efficacy expectancy: The belief that one is capable of conveying a desired impression or performing the desired behaviour.

Self-presentational outcome expectancy: The belief that the conveyed impression and behaviours will lead to the desired outcome.

Self-presentational outcome value: Importance placed on the outcome involving self-presentation.

Social physique anxiety: The anxiety a person experiences as a result of perceived or actual judgments from others.

Tripartite influence model of body image: Theory suggesting that media, parents, and peers are key socializing agents in the development of body image.

Upward social comparison: Comparing oneself to others who are better off on some attributes that are valued.

Chapter 15: Physical Activity Interventions

Action plans: Effective behavioural strategies (e.g., limiting food intake or exercising in the morning before work) that have been identified as necessary to fulfill a goal.

Attitude change: Specific techniques geared at changing the beliefs that an individual holds toward physical activity.

Autonomous: When individuals determine their own behaviour and are not influenced by outside sources.

Barrier self-efficacy: Confidence in one's ability to overcome barriers that may arise when participating in exercise.

Behaviour monitoring: Keeping track of exercise behaviour in a physical activity diary, chart, or calendar and recording physical activity and related details each day or each week.

Behavioural strategies: Actions that an individual can do that increase their probability of engaging in physical activity.

Built environment: Any element in a community that is designed or constructed by people.

Determinant research: Examines the factors that affect exercise behaviour.

Determinants: Factors that predict exercise behaviour.

Exercise self-efficacy: Confidence in one's ability to engage in physical activity.

Exergaming: Physically active games that are played on home gaming systems.

Goal setting: Identifying what an individual would like to work toward in terms of their physical activity participation. The goal is specific in terms of the frequency, type, and duration of physical activity identified.

Implementation intentions: Mental associations between a situational cue and a specific behaviour.

Intervention research: Research that evaluates how manipulating important factors identified through determinant research affects exercise behaviour.

Interventions: Modifications of the specific factors that affect physical activity based on an understanding of the commonalities in human behaviour with an appreciation of the differences that exist between individuals.

Mass media campaigns: Interventions that attempt to reach large numbers of individuals simultaneously through public forums.

Motivational interviewing: A focused method of communication used to help facilitate behaviour change by helping the person to consider their own reasons for wanting to engage in a new behaviour.

Non-theory–based research: Interventions that are not based on theoretically proposed relationships.

Outcome-based exercise research: Research that develops interventions and tests whether or not they positively affect exercise behaviour.

Outcome variable: A response that occurs as a consequence of being involved in physical activity.

Persuasive communication: A strategy of behavioural change that provides specific belief-targeted messages.

Physical activity contract: A written document specifying the physical activity behaviour to be achieved.

Physical activity counsellor: A primary health team member who has skills to assist patients in making sustainable physical activity changes.

Scheduling self-efficacy: Confidence in one's ability to plan and organize exercise in one's life.

Self-efficacy: An individual's belief in their ability to produce desired outcomes.

Self-regulation: Controlling one's own behaviour by navigating around obstacles or barriers.

Self-regulatory efficacy: A multifaceted form of self-efficacy that involves personal control over the task, scheduling regular activity, and planning for and overcoming barriers.

Stage-matching interventions: Specific intervention strategies that are sensitive to the specific needs of the individuals within different stages of change according to the trans-theoretical model.

Task self-efficacy: Confidence in one's ability to complete the exercise task.

Theory-based research: Interventions based on theoretically proposed relationships among constructs.

Treatment-based exercise research: Research that modifies an individual's life experiences through the use of physical activity. Physical activity is presented to the individual to influence life outcomes and other relevant factors.

Treatment variable: A variable that is presented to an individual to see its effect on an outcome variable.

Index

Barling, J., 211, 218
basic psychological needs theory (BPNT), 67–68, 69
Bass, B. M., 301
Bass, Bernard, 208–211, 216, 218
Batty, Emily, 39
Bauman, A., 418
Beal, D. J., 246
Beauchamp, Mark. R., 208
Beck, Aaron, 55
Beck Depression Inventory (BDI), 346
behaviour monitoring, 408
behavioural beliefs, 60
    aging and barrier to physical activity, 329
behavioural capacity, 64
behavioural dimension of body image, 377
behavioural strategies, 408
behaviourism, 33–34
    motivation and, 55
behaviours, 31
    achievement-oriented, 206
    directive path–goal clarifying, 205
    participative leader, 206
    supportive, 205–206
Beller, J. M., 142
Bengoechea, E. G., 76
Benson, P. L., 262
Berglas, S., 245
Berkowitz, L., 149
Bernstein, D. A., 186
Berry, T., 420
Bertuzzi, Todd, 140, 143, 146
Bessette, N., 158
Biddle, S. J. H., 58, 72
Bilodeau, Alex, 30
binge eating disorder, 381
biofeedback, 187
Bird, A. M., 205
Blake, Toe, 289, 296
blame attribution, 152
Blanchard, C. M., 411
Blanchard, Ken, 211
Blondin, J. P., 93, 111
Bloom, Gordon A., 154, 295, 306, 311
Blumenthal, James, 348
body cathexis, 374
body dysmorphia, 380
body dysmorphic disorder, 380
body esteem, 374
body image, 375
    age as factor in, 386–387
    cardiometabolic risk factors, 392
    culture and, 387–388

    dimensions and their measurement, 375–381
    factors associated with development of negative, 386–390
    gender as factor in, 386
    health-compromising behaviours, 391–392
    historical roots of, 374–375
    illness and, 388
    investment, 378
    mental health and, 392
    myths, 373, 395–396
    outcomes, 390–392
    pathologies, 380–381
    and physical activity, 381–385, 390–391
    positive or negative, 378
    practical considerations for health professionals, coaches and physical educators, 393–395
    self-discrepancy theory, 385
    self-presentation, 383–384
    social and physical environment factors, 389–390
    social comparison theory, 384–385
    sociocultural theories of, 381–383
    sport involvement and type, 389
    weight status, 387
Body Image: An International Journal, 374
body image boundaries, 374
body schema, 374
bodychecking, 276
body-related envy, 382
body-related guilt, 375
body-related pride, 376
body-related shame, 375
Boone, E. M., 389
Bortoli, L., 91
Botterill, Cal, 14
Bowman, Scotty, 289, 296
brain derived neurotrophic factor (BDNF), 356
Brawley, Dr. Larry, 14, 231, 233, 239, 404, 408, 411
Bray, S. R., 218
breathing,
    to increase arousal, 188
    to reduce overarousal, 185–186
Bredemeier, B. L., 270
Brice, J. G., 155, 156
Bring Play Back, 418
British Association of Sport and Exercise Sciences (BASES), 16
Brown, Paul, 296
Brown, S., 415
Bruner, M. W., 277
Brunet, Jennifer, 375, 388, 390
Bryant, J., 161
Buchholz, Weber, 417

built environment, 419
bulimia nervosa, 381
Bull, S., 179
bulletin boards, 188
bullying behaviours, 148
burnout, 97
Butler, R. N., 326

C

Cahoon, M. A., 159
Callow, N., 178, 216
Camacho, T. C., 346
Camiré, Martin, 142
Canada,
    coaching education in, 292
    history of sport psychology in, 12–15
    sport psychology consultants in, 8
    trends in sport psychology in, 22–24, 23, 24
Canada's Physical Activity Guide to Healthy Active
    Living, 66
Canadian Fitness and Lifestyle Research Institute
    (CFLRI), 403, 424
Canadian Health Measures Survey (CHMS), 320
Canadian Interuniversity Sports (CIS), 296
Canadian PAC trial, 412
Canadian Psychological Association (CPA), 4, 21
    Canadian Code of Ethics for Psychologists, 11, 12, 13t
    standards, 11
Canadian Society for Psychomotor Learning and Sport
    Psychology/Société Canadienne D'Apprentissage
    Psychomoteur et de Psychologie du Sport
    (SCAPPS), 7, 14
Canadian Sport Psychology Association (CSPA), 7
    Code of ethics, 11
    criteria for membership of, 11t
    standards, 11
cancer, 403
cardiovascular disease, 403
Carless, D., 359
Carlson, C. R., 186
Carpenter, B. N., 85
Carraça, E. V., 378
Carroll, D., 99
Carron, Dr. Albert, 12, 13, 14, 230, 231, 232, 233, 234, 239,
    241, 242, 244, 246, 247, 329, 389
Carson, S., 268
Carter, A. D., 295
Carter, Vince, 188
Cartwright, D., 229
Cash, Thomas, 374
Cassidy, T., 307
catastrophe, 129

catharsis, 149
Cattell, R. B., 32
Cattell's trait personality model, 32
causality orientation theory (COT), 67, 70
Causgrove Dunn, J. L., 40
Cavallo, D. N., 417
Chantal, Y., 311
Charness, N., 322–323
Chatzisarantis, N. L. D., 407
Chaundry, V., 303
Chelladurai, P., 207, 211, 218, 237, 300, 301
Chiellini, Giorgio, 36, 140
child constructive leisure activities, 262
child relaxed leisure activities, 262
choking, 131–132, 190
Chow, G. M., 144
Clark, T. P., 131
Clark-Carter, D., 304
clinical and counselling psychologists,
    training, 11
clinical psychology, 11
closeness, 303
Clough, P. J., 42
coach education, 290–294
coach effectiveness training (CET), 298–299
coaches' roles, 267–269
coaching,
    development, 295–297
    mentoring, 295
    myths, 290, 313–314
    pyramid of success model, 305–306
    training component, 311–311
    women in, 296
    youth, 297–300
Coaching Association of Canada (CAC), 290
coaching behaviour assessment systems (CBAS), 298
coaching effectiveness, 267
coaching efficacy, 302
    dimensions, 302
    models of, 303f
coaching knowledge, 300–312
coaching model, 307–312, 307f
    competition component, 311–312
    components, 308–312
coaching science, 290
coaching vision, 308
cognition,
    aging and, 322
    motivation and, 55
cognitive anxiety, 115
cognitive appraisal, 87–88, 90
cognitive dimension of body image, 376–377

European Federation of Sport Psychology/Fédération
      Européenne de Psychologie des Sports et des Activités
      Corporelles (FEPSAC), 7, 16
evaluative concerns perfectionism (ECP), 40–41
event occlusion, 190
evidence-based practice, 21–22
exercise, 344
exergaming, 417–418
expectancy theory, 57
expressive writing, 114
external regulation, 68
extraversion, 32, 44
      sport activities and, 46
extrinsic motivation, 68
Eys, M. A., 230, 232, 235

F

Fallon, E. A., 125
fan identification, 159
fan violence, 159–160
Fanzoi, Stephen, 374
Faulkner, G., 346, 359
Felicien, Perdita, 129
Feltz, D., 250
Festinger, Leon, 231, 384
Fiedler, F. E., 204–205
Fisher, Seymour, 374
Fitbit One, 408
Fletcher, D., 89
Focht, B. C., 123
Folkesson, P., 156
followership, 217
Fortier, M. S., 412
4C model of mental toughness, 42–43
Fox, K. R., 353, 359
Fox, Terry, 33
Freud, S., 149
Frick, Tim, 289
Friedrichs, W. D., 208
frustration-aggression theory, 149
full range model of leadership, 208, 209f
Fung, C., 420

G

Gainey, Bob, 296
Gallimore, R., 311
Gammage, Kimberly L., 375, 384
Garber, C. E., 58
García Bengoechea, E., 20
Gaudreau, Patrick, 40, 41, 93, 96, 111
gender,
      aggression and, 154

anxiety and, 118–119
      competitiveness and, 39
      coping with stress and, 110
gender socialization hypothesis, 110
geriatrics, 332
gerontology, 332
Gifford, S. M., 89
Gilbert, W. D., 267, 290, 295, 297
Gill, D. L., 39
Ginis, Kathleen Martin, 375, 392, 408
Global Action Plan, 403
goal contents theory (GCT), 68
goal orientation, 144–145
goal profiling, 72
goal setting, 170–175, 408
      assessment, 171–172
      conclusions about, 175
      effectiveness, 171
      guidelines, 173t
      problems, 174–175, 174t
      recommendations for, 172–174
      specificity, measurability, adjustability, realism,
            and timeliness (SMART) principles and, 172, 173t,
            174, 175
      weakness correction using, 175
goals, 64
      outcome, 170
      performance, 170
      process, 170
      types of, 170–171
Godin, G., 61
Goldberg, A. S., 42
Gollwitzer, P. M., 407
Gomes, Naide, 116
good news coping, 95
Gorczynski, P., 58
Gould, Dan, 39, 268, 308
Graham, T. R., 92
Granito, V. J., 236, 247
Great Britain,
      sport psychology in, 16
Green, Dennis, 296
Gretzky, Wayne, 302
Gross, James, 94
group cohesion,
      affective relationships in, 232–233
      aggression and, 158
      athlete's starting status as correlate for, 247
      characteristics of, 232
      coach as a correlate of, 236–237
      collective efficacy for, 246–247
      conceptual model of, 233–234, 234f

Stephens, D. E., 145
stereotyping, 326–328
    master athletes and, 336
Stoll, S. K., 142
stress,
    challenge, 87
    cognitive appraisal process of, 87–88
    definitions of, 85
    emotion and, 86–87
    harm/loss, 87
    kinds of, 85–86
    mental toughness and, 44
    myths, 85, 116–117
    neurophysiological effects, 90–91
    reduction, 113
    specific sports effect, 89–90
    threat, 87
stress response, 85
stressors, 20–21, 85
    acute, 88
    chronic, 88
    competitive, 89, 90
    expected, 88–89
    non-competitive, 89
    organizational, 89
    types of, 88–90
    unexpected, 88–89
structural-development theory, 142
structure, 70, 71t
Stuart, M. E., 144
Suárez, Luis, 36, 140
subjective norms, 60
Sullivan, P., 250
Summitt, Pat, 306
supportive behaviour, 205–206
Swain, A. B. J., 122
Symons-Downs, D., 407, 424

T

Tamminen, A. Katherine, 112
Tamres, L. K., 110
tangible support (by parents), 272
task goal orientation, 72
    characteristics, 73t
task-oriented leadership, 203
teaching career, 7
team building, 238
    approaches to, 238
    conceptual framework for, 239–240, 239f
    definition of, 238
    distinctiveness as factor in, 239
    four-stage model for, 238–243

principles of, 240t
    see also group cohesion
team effectiveness,
    decision making for, 230
    group cohesion and, 230
team norms, 144, 158
temporal occlusion, 190
Tenenbaum, G., 161, 191
Test of Attentional and Interpersonal Style
    (TAIS), 191
testosterone, 150
Tharp, R. G., 311
The Childhood Obesity Foundation, 416
The Ontario Burden of Mental Illness and Addictions
    Report, 344
theoretical models, 18
theory, 18
theory of planned behaviour (TPB), 59–62, 60f, 407–409
    antecedents, 59–60
    applications, 62
    physical exercise and, 407–409
    research, 60–62
theory-based research, 406
Thompson, A., 40
Thompson, J. Kelvin, 374–375
threat appraisal, 87, 90
3 + 1 Cs model, 302–305
3-methoxy-4-hydroxyphenolglycol (MHPG), 357
Tod, D., 184
Toews, Jonathan, 200
traits (personality), 31–32
    models, 32
transactional leadership, 208–209
transformational leadership, 209, 211–212, 238, 301–302
    in physical education, 213–215, 214t
transformational parenting, 212–213
transformational teaching, 213–215, 214t
transtheoretical model (TM) of motivation, 57–59, 411–412
    action stage, 57
    applications, 58
    concepts, 59t
    contemplation stage, 57
    factors influencing stage progression, 57–58
    maintenance stage, 57
    physical activity and, 411–412
    pre-contemplation stage, 57
    preparation stage, 57
    research, 58
    stages, 57
Traub, A. C., 376
treatment research, 406
    physical activity, 406f

Tremblay, Dr. Mark, 418–419
tripartite influence model of body image, 381
Trudel, Pierre, 142, 290, 297, 307
true competition, 270
Tucholsky, Sara, 141
Tucker, S., 212
Turner, E. E., 218

U

UK Coaching Certificate (UKCC), 293
UK Coaching Framework, 292
under-involved parents, 270
Ungerleider, S., 335
United States,
 coaching education in, 293
 history of sport psychology in, 12–15
United States Olympic Committee, 293
Université de Montréal, 14
universities,
 growth in sport psychology, 12–16, 22–23
 post-World War II, 12
 research and teaching opportunities, 22–23
 see also individual universities
 sport psychology and, 12–14
 training demands, 23
University of Alberta, 13, 14, 40, 420
University of California, Berkeley, 12, 14
University of Ottawa, 14, 33, 39, 40, 298
University of Saskatchewan, 14
University of Tennessee, 306
University of Toronto, 14
University of Waterloo, 56
University of Western Ontario, 14, 181
 School of Kinesiology, 14
University of Winnipeg, 14
Uphill, M., 131
upward social comparison, 384–385

V

valence (of self-talk), 182
Vallance, Jeffrey, 61
Vallée, C. N., 306
Vallerand, Robert J., 41, 42, 156, 247
Vandelanotte, C., 417
variable, 17
Vealey, Robin, 4
verbal cues, 188
Verheijden Klompstra, L., 417–418
Verma, S., 262
vicarious conditioning, 56
vicarious experience, 65
Vierimaa, M., 263

Vierling, Leigh, 39
violent behaviours, 145–146
Virtue, Tessa, 185
Visek, A. J., 154, 157
visualization, 174, 176
 see also imagery
Vividness of Movement Imagery Questionnaire-2
 (VMIQ-2), 179

W

Wallace, Liz, 141
Walsh, Bill, 296
Wankel, Len, 14
Wanlin, C. M., 171, 174
Wann, D. L., 156, 160
Watson, Brad, 159
Watson, John, 55, 154
We All Play for Canada, 418
Weber, Shea, 200
website technology, 416
Weinberg, R. S., 183
Weir, Mike, 113, 175, 191
Weiss, M. R., 208
Wenger, Arsene, 204
White, A., 176
Whitfield, Simon, 92, 245, 279
Whitlock, Ed, 332
Why, Y. P., 46
Wickenheiser, Hayley, 215
Widmeyer, Dr. Neil, 14, 156, 157, 231, 233
Wilberg. Dr. Robert, 14
Williams, K. D., 244
Wilson, L. M., 297
Wilson, P. M., 20, 76
Wooden, John, 305–306, 311
Woolger, C., 271
World Congress of Sport Psychology (Rome 1965),
 16

Y

Yager, Z., 394
Yale University, 327
youth coaching, 297–300
 characteristics, 297–298
 coach effectiveness training and, 298–299
 developmental patterns, 299–300
 effectiveness of, 298, 298t
 leadership and, 300–302
 Mastery Approach to Coaching (MAC), 299
 multidimensional model of leadership (MML),
  300–301, 301f
 principles, 299